Modern Artisan

French Edition

Editorial Director: *Julie Rouart*
Administration Manager: *Delphine Montagne*
Editor: *Marion Doublet*, assisted by *Claire Francillon*
Picture Research: *Marie-Catherine Audet*
Design Concept: *Sarah Martinon*
Graphic Design: *Marie-Lou Étienne*

English Edition

Editorial Director: *Kate Mascaro*
Editor: *Helen Adedotun*
Translation from the French: *Kate Robinson*
Copyediting: *Lindsay Porter*
Typesetting: *Marie-Lou Étienne*
Proofreading: *Sarah Kane*

Production: *Élodie Conjat*
Color Separation: *Hyphen, Bergamo, Italy*
Printed in Slovenia by *Florjancic*

This book is typeset in Bellini Original and Jjannon.

Simultaneously published in French as *Atlas mondial de l'artisanat d'art*

Éditions Flammarion
82 Rue Saint-Lazare
75009 Paris
France
editions.flammarion.com
@flammarioninternational

23 24 25   3 2 1
ISBN: 978-2-08-028095-4
Legal Deposit: 11/2023

This book is published with the support of the Michelangelo Foundation for Creativity and Craftsmanship and the Homo Faber Guide.
michelangelofoundation.org
homofaber.com

MICHELANGELO FOUNDATION
FOR CREATIVITY AND CRAFTSMANSHIP

Isabelle Dupuy Chavanat

Modern Artisan

A World of Craft Tradition and Innovation

Flammarion

Contents

"And first I must ask you to extend the word art beyond those matters which are consciously works of art, to take in not only painting and sculpture, and architecture, but the shapes and colours of all household goods, nay, even the arrangement of the fields for tillage and pasture, the management of towns and of our highways of all kinds; in a word, to extend it to the aspect of the externals of our life. . . .

How does it fare therefore with our external surroundings in these days? What kind of an account shall we be able to give to those who come after us of our dealings with the earth, which our forefathers handed down to us still beautiful, in spite of all the thousands of years of strife and carelessness and selfishness? . . . How have we of these latter days treated the beauty of the earth, or that which we call art?"

—William Morris, "Art Under Plutocracy," 1883,
reprinted in *Collected Works of William Morris (1910–1915)*, vol. 23,
Signs of Change: Lectures on Socialism, ed. May Morris
(London: Longmans, Green & Co., 1915)

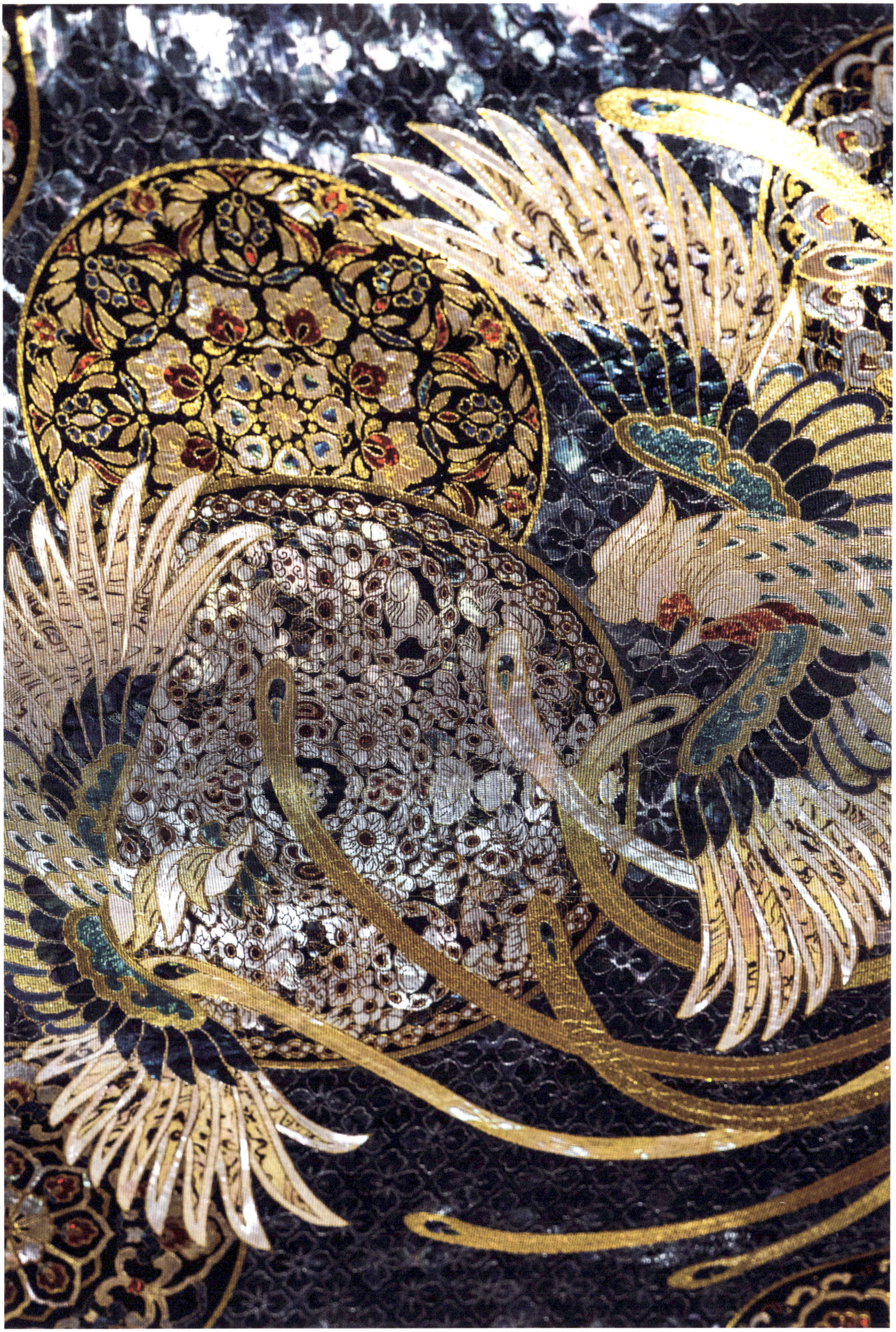

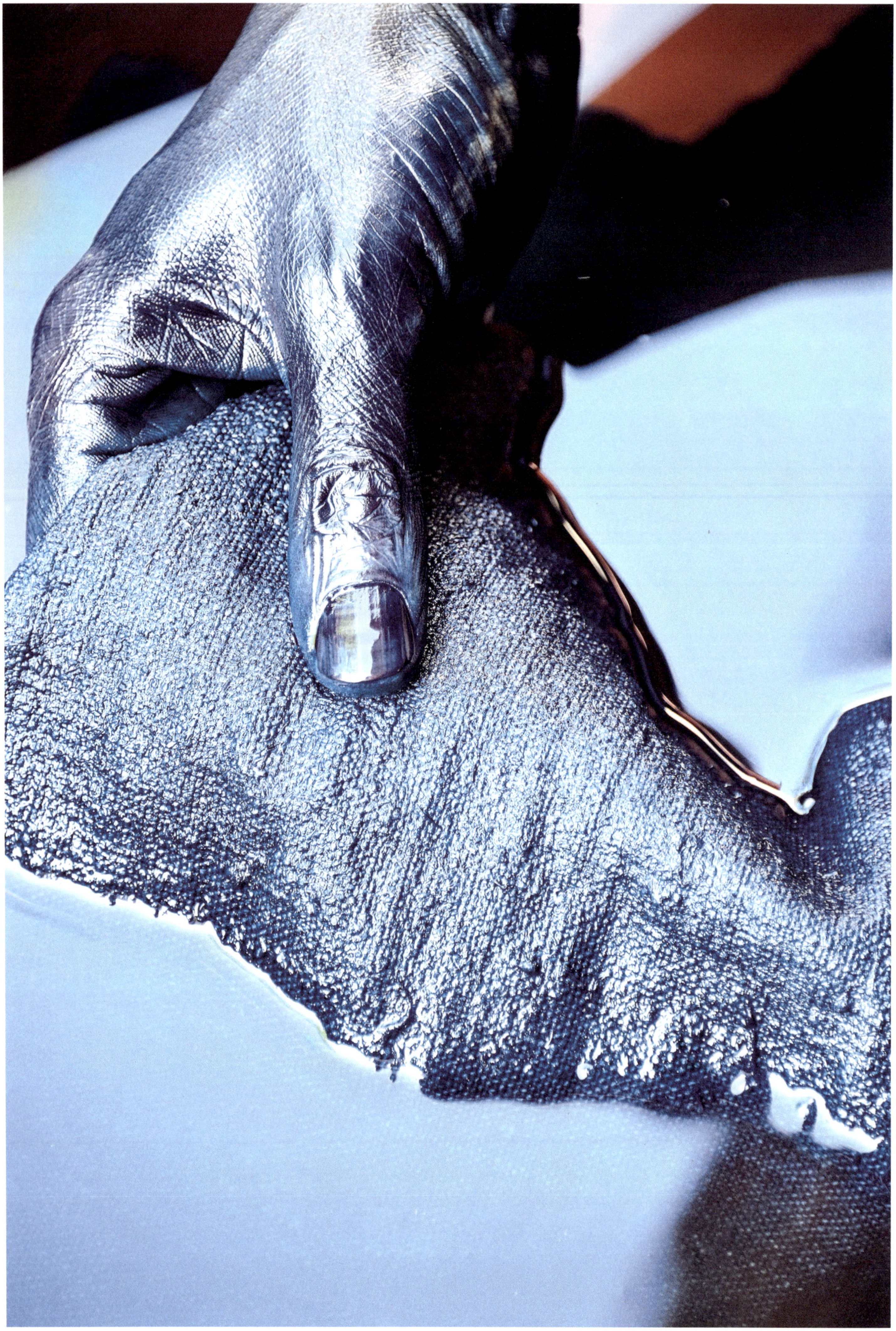

Introduction: Committed Artisans

For centuries, humanity has demonstrated a steadfast faith in progress, leading to technical and technological development that now exceeds the common good. The worldwide pandemic and the climate emergency have forced us to ask ourselves a crucial question: How can we continue to live on our planet? How should we respond to this ecological, health, and social crisis? This situation has brought to light the fact that we have lost our intimate relationship to the earth, yet this relationship is essential for the well-being of our species.

Can we reestablish our connection with nature and reconstruct our relationship with the living world? We are poised at the beginning of a new era in which humanity must, at all costs, rethink its place within nature.

No matter the age, nationality, or technique of the artisans featured in this volume, each one displays remarkable vitality, enthusiasm, and commitment. They work to highlight the incredible wealth of the natural world and the urgent need to protect it. This book offers portraits of the artisans, men and women, who have been selected because their work provides a glimpse of the world's abundant craft traditions. They have all developed a powerful connection with their materials, which are also the focus of this book. Clay, glass, leather, fiber, among others—each one helps us to understand the relationship that an artisan develops with their practice, how they address it and approach it within the specific context of their own culture. Starting with the material and each craftsperson's perception of it, I wanted to initiate a conversation between the diversity of the crafts and the skills from different continents. The crafts resonate with one another and the skills respond to each other, but each one remains distinct.

These artisans live in Taiwan, the United Kingdom, Argentina, Mexico, Mali, France, India, Japan, the United States, and elsewhere around the world. Some of them have inherited ancestral knowledge; others—younger and self-taught—have mastered their craft alone, resorting at times to online learning tools or internet tutorials. These women and men are shaping a brave new world.

How did I make the selection? First of all, I was captivated by the beauty and simplicity of line of each piece: these objects conveyed a combination of restraint and a mastery of gesture that revealed the soul of the craftsperson, of the artist. Then I discovered each individual's engagement or their use of new materials, which also guided my choice. Artisans spend their life endeavoring, by way of making an object, to surpass themselves. The aim is not only to create a vase, a basket, or a rug of the highest quality, but also to convey the spirit of the creator through the object itself—it becomes a means by which these men and women share their inner selves. The interviews that I conducted reveal their backgrounds, their experience, how they came to work with their specific material and their impressions of it, their solutions for overcoming difficulties; more than mere investigations into technical skill, these interviews have allowed me to present veritable life stories. I wanted to focus on the poetry of their narratives and their vision of the world today. These artisans are deeply rooted in our contemporary societies: they do not live in the nostalgic hope of a return to the past, nor do they isolate themselves in idealistic visions of a more craft-focused future.

The system founded by artisans—that of transforming a material into an object by hand, guided by the heart—is fragile, because it exists in a world where every second seems to grow shorter and shorter. If the frenetic pace of this intensive production continues, what will happen to the very essence of artisanal work: the indispensable focus on materials, the precise gestures, the significant time and attention spent on each object? The pandemic we experienced clearly revealed the dangers of excessive overconsumption and of our disdain for the ecosystems that surround us. The values upheld for decades by artisans should be seen as models for others to adopt: the use of environmentally sound materials; the visceral need to reconnect with the essential things in life; or the decision to consume locally produced, sustainable, high-quality products.

I see these artisans as forming a community of women and men who are engaged by their driving passions. From east to west and from north to south, they contribute to our world heritage with objects that are imbued with their talent, their unique practice, and their geographic identities. They are connected by an intrinsic understanding of the act of making. Each of them speaks with a singular and distinct voice, from the four corners of the earth, yet they all share a universal message. This volume seeks an equal level of engagement and attempts to give substance to this collective fight for the recognition and protection of craft skills, for the upholding of culture through craftsmanship, and for the education of future generations so that they may cultivate understanding and respect for artisanal expertise.

These artisans are powering a new worldwide movement whose spirit guides their hands to fashion objects that resonate with us. Through their stories, the way in which they use their raw materials, and the beauty of the pieces they create, their art (and craft) becomes a political act.

They have all chosen an alternative lifestyle that places quality at the forefront. They are the leaders of a new form of craftsmanship: committed craftsmanship.

—Isabelle Dupuy Chavanat

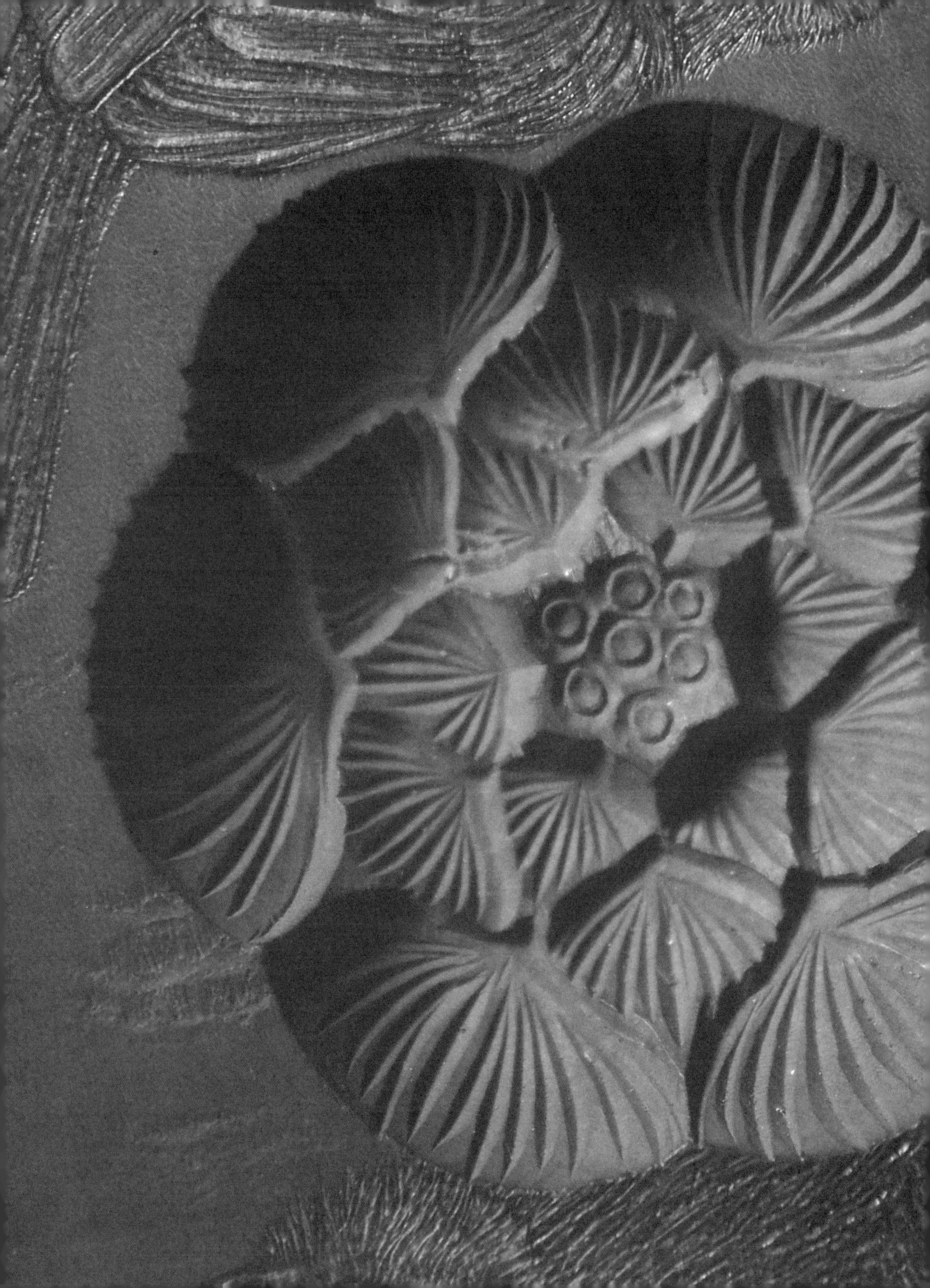

Wood

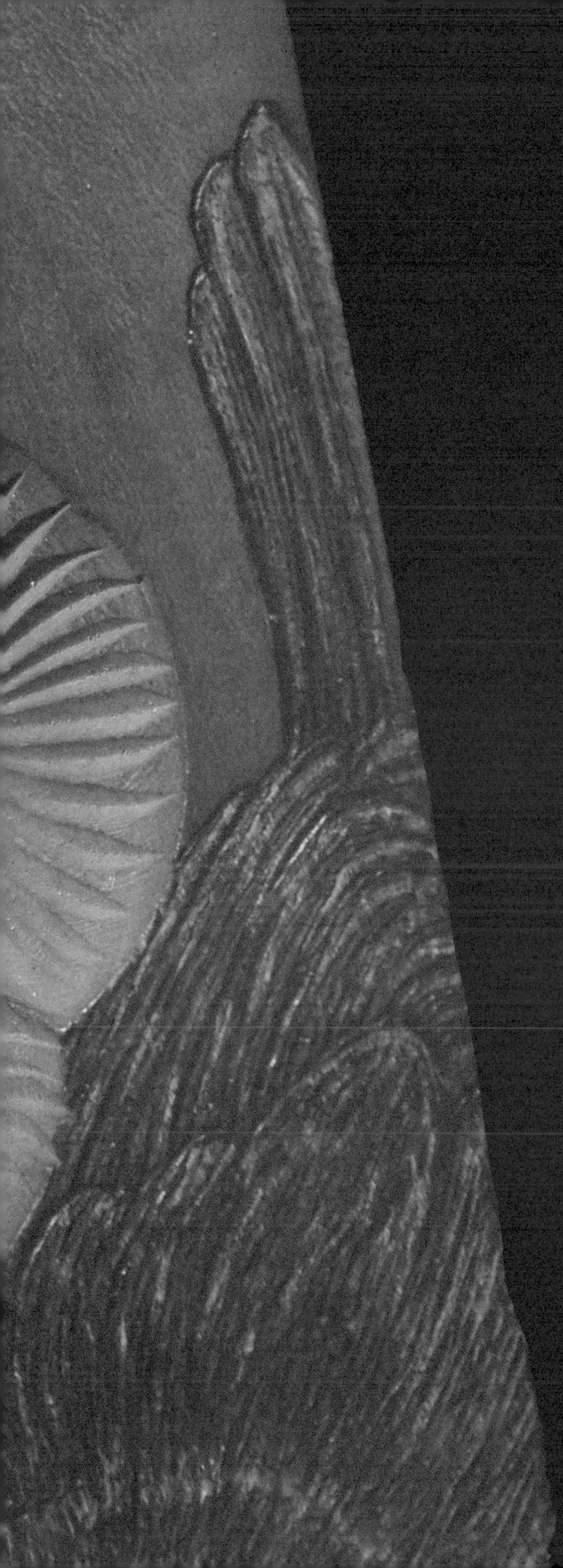

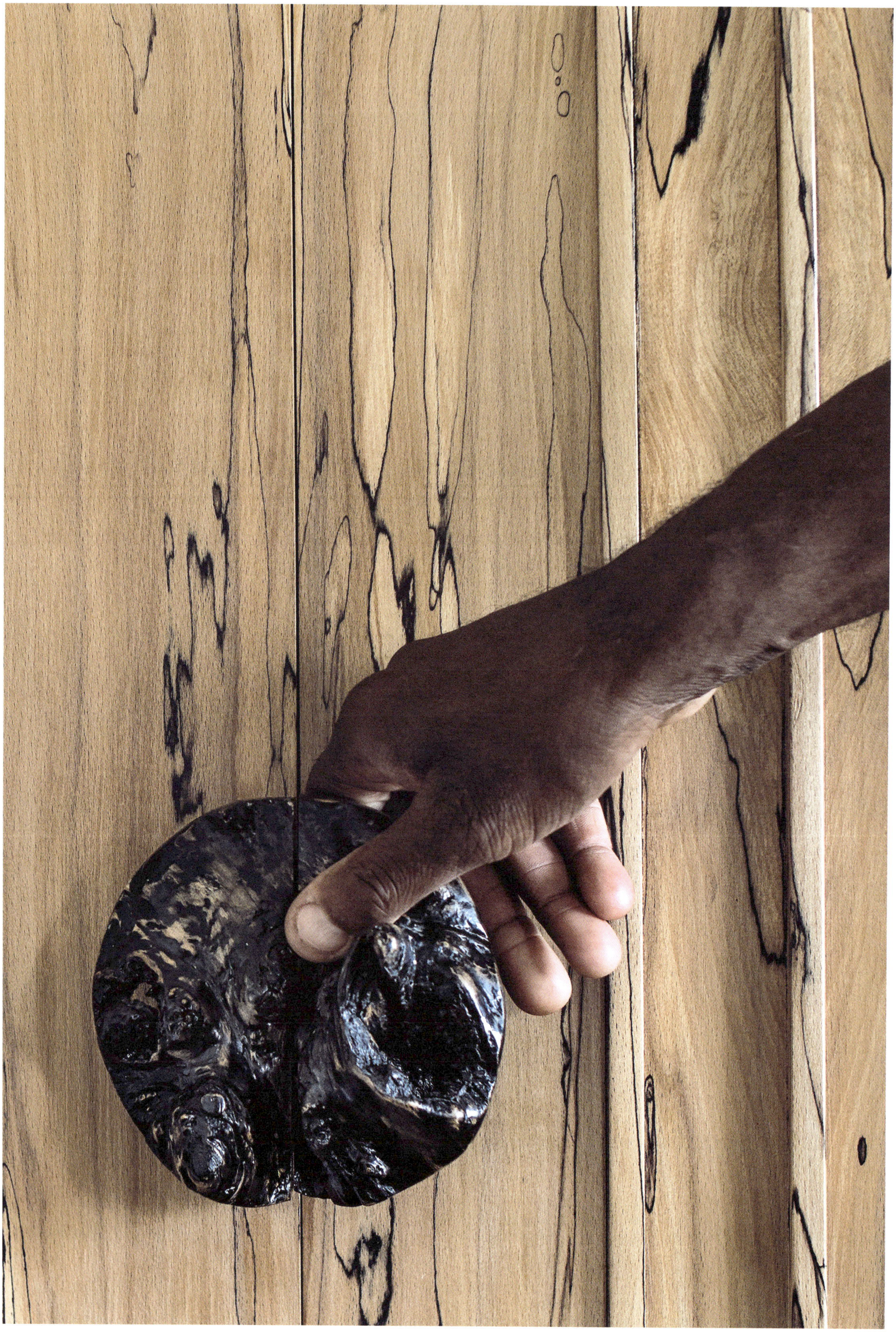

John Alfredo Harris

Woodworker and furniture designer

Hertfordshire,
United Kingdom

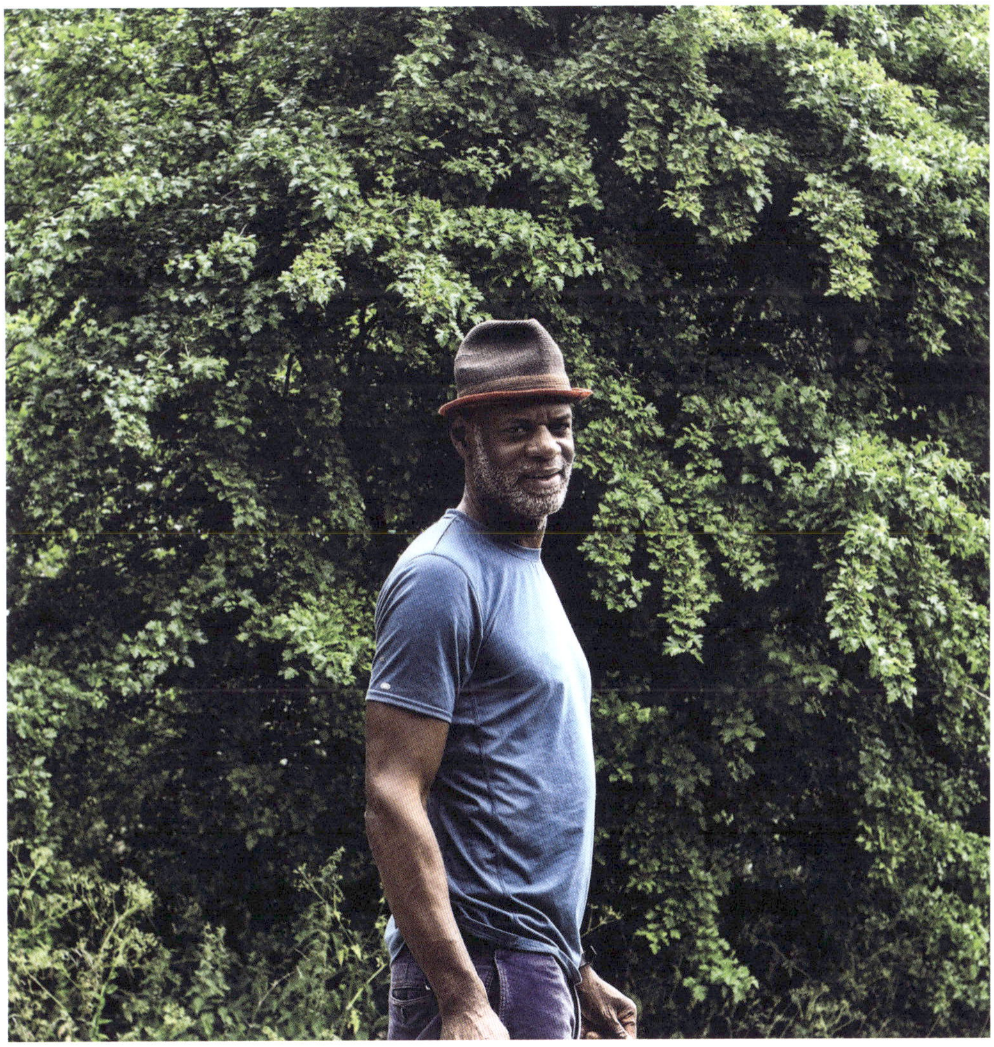

Craftsmanship begins in the mind and then moves to the hands.

My name is John Alfredo Harris. I'm a carpenter, but I also sculpt and turn wood. I have a very diverse background. First, I studied horticulture and worked as a gardener and landscape designer; then I worked in fashion, before picking up carpentry when my son was born. At the time, I lived in an old farm cottage in the middle of the woods in Wiltshire. There was an old barn next to the house where elm and oak timber was stored. We needed a coffee table, so I decided to make one out of some wood from the barn. The result was a bit crude, but I loved the process of making it, the physical sensations, and the end product. You could say wood "found" me.

Working with this material presents a challenge, but it has brought me peace, harmony, and unity, with no room for ego. I discovered its qualities, its strength and adaptability—although it can be capricious. When wood turning you have to stay alert; you never know what hidden surprise the wood might have in store.

When I'm working with wood, I feel the same closeness as I would with a friend, but unlike most human beings, this friend isn't bigoted and has no prejudices. I have a close relationship with wood; we share an infinite history and understanding. We don't need words to communicate. Maybe it comes from an inner harmony with the wood, some kind of cosmic link with nature and the tools it takes to reshape form with respect. My ideas come from what I observe around me. I'm inspired by the past, present, and future.

I had no formal training; I taught myself. I started out with a small lathe and gradually, over the years, I gained experience. Using that knowledge, I continued to experiment and upgrade my machines and tools, improving my skills, technique, and understanding of the process. I'm still learning, which is why it is so exciting.

When turning wood, I've learnt over the years to let the material dictate the pace. The wood decides what it wants to become.

For a long time, I loved my workshop; it provided me with the perfect environment in which to express myself, and I didn't think any other place on earth could replace it. But with age comes reason, and today I realize that I don't have to be bound to any one place in order to be creative. The world is a workshop.

Today, in England, it is becoming increasingly difficult to live as a craftsman. I feel that most people do not appreciate or understand what it takes to create any kind of well-made, handcrafted object of beauty. I think that craftsmanship could be a model for our society, but for that to happen, there has to be a real global revolution of the mind.

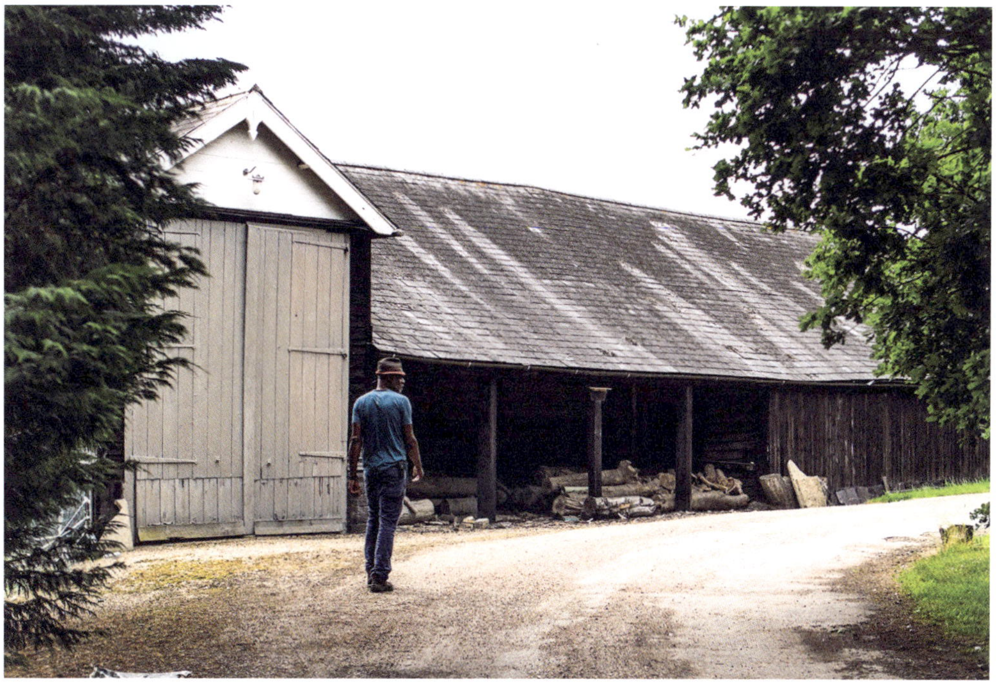

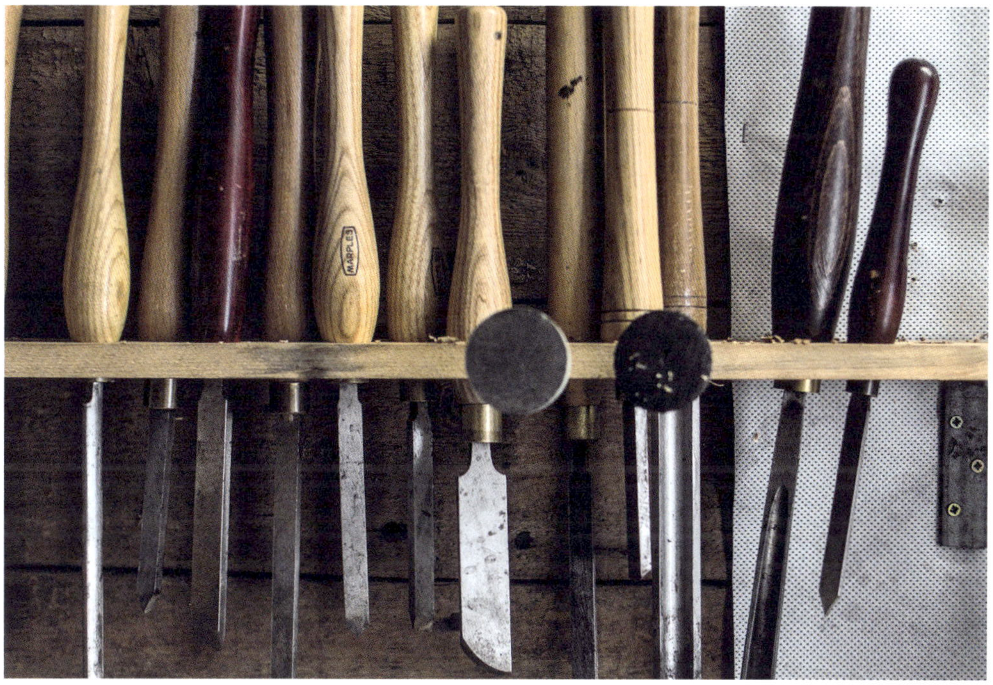
MARPLES

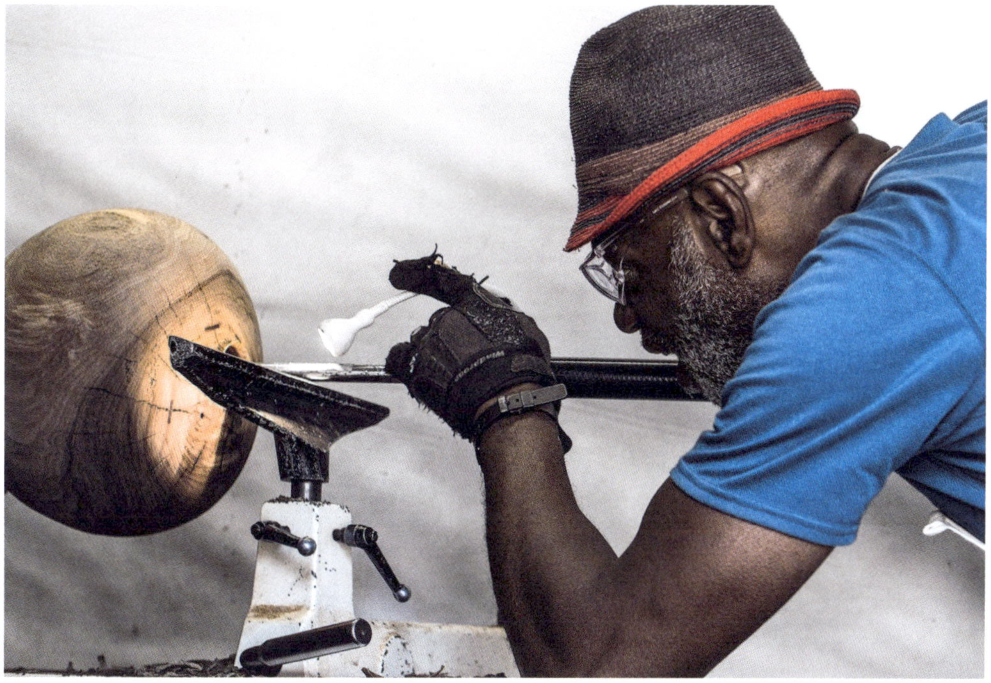

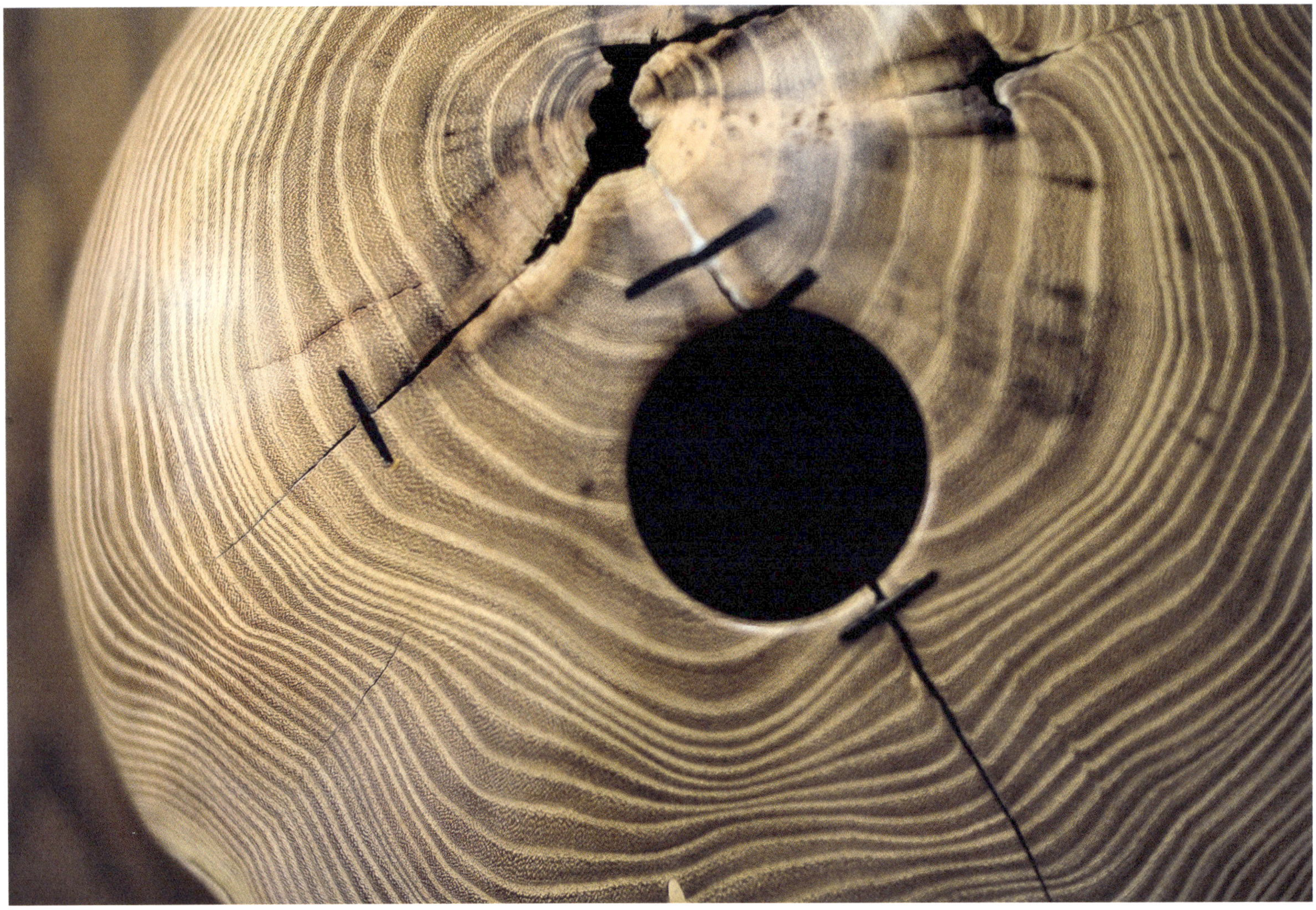

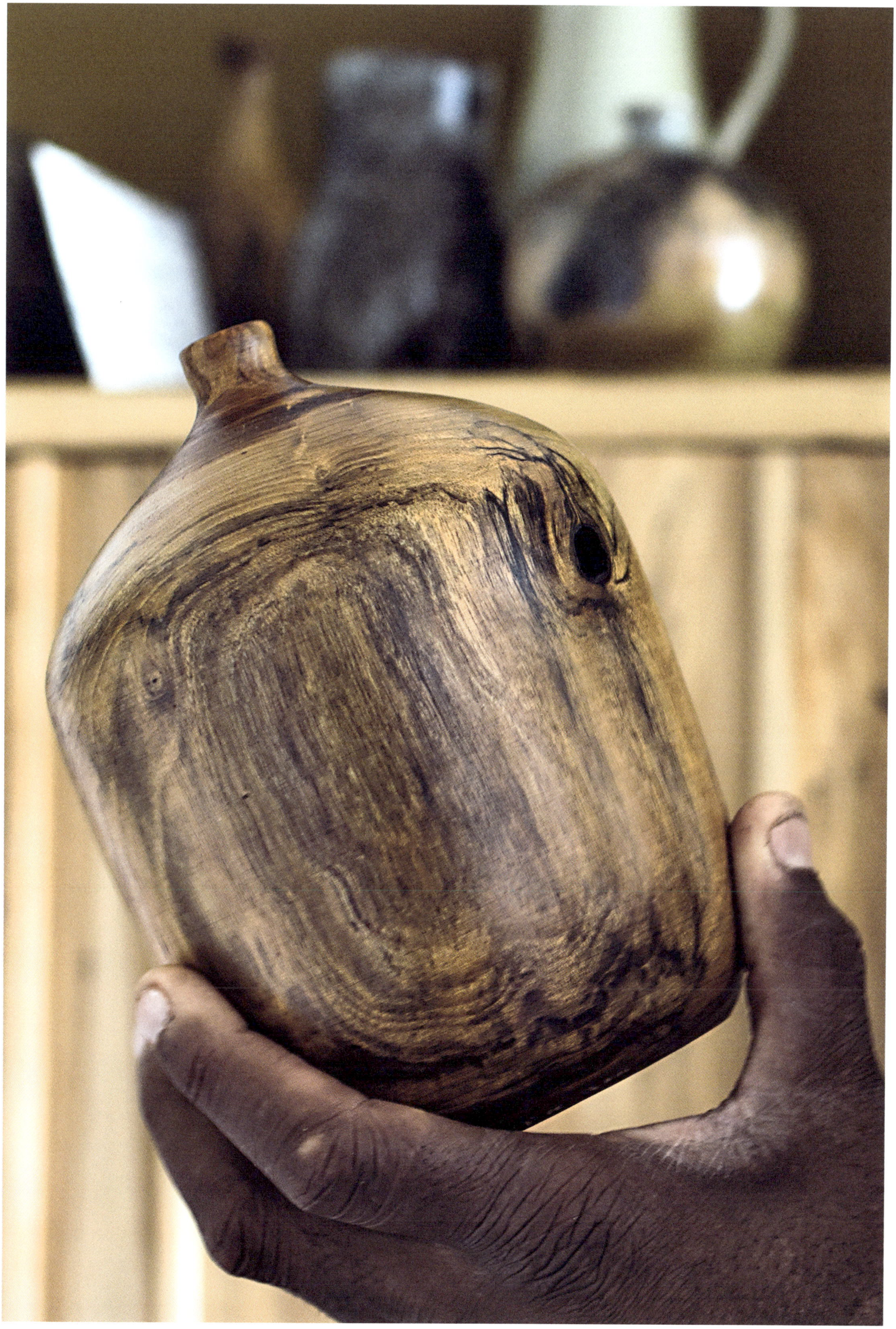

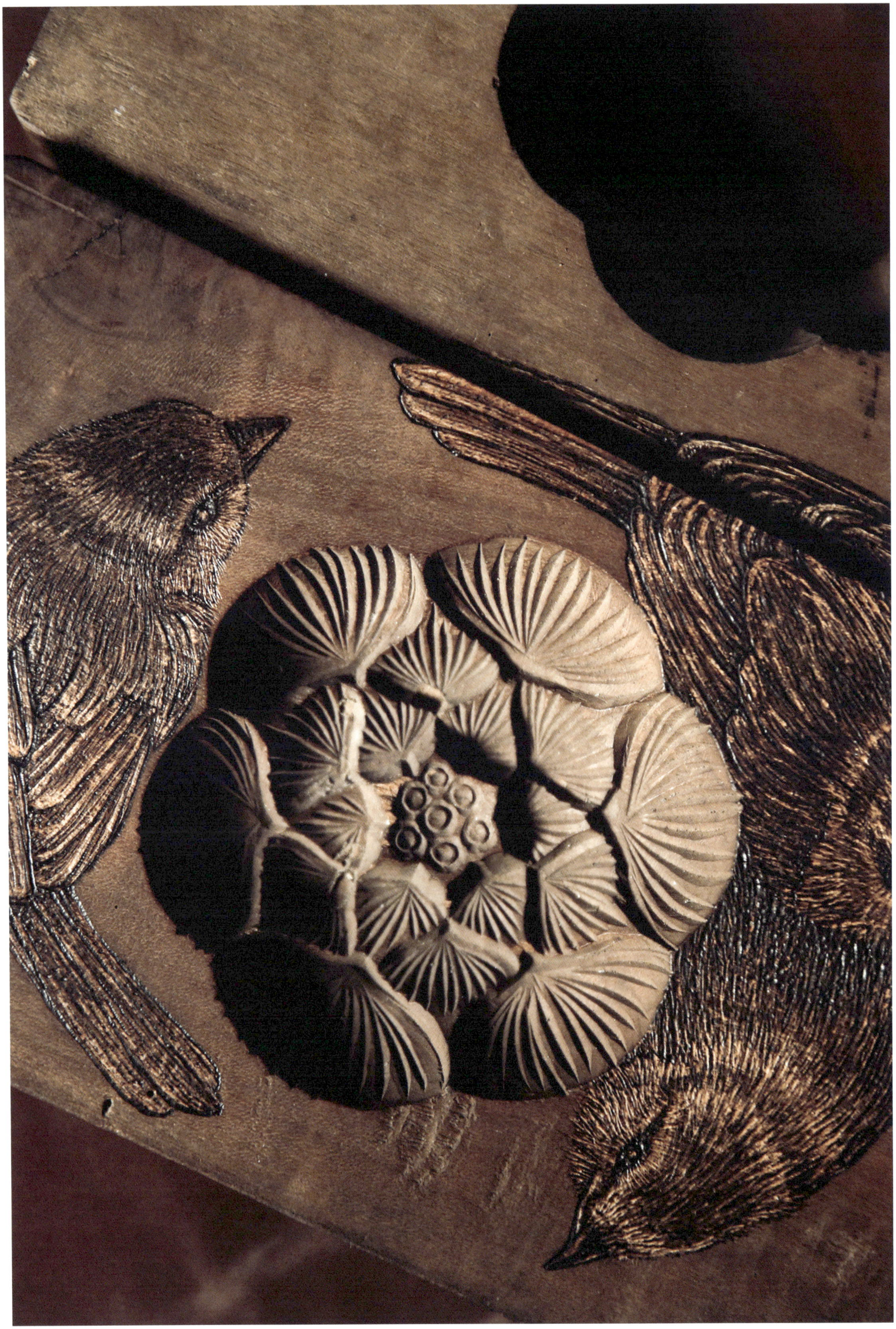

Yen-An Chen

Pyrographer and designer

Taipei, Taiwan

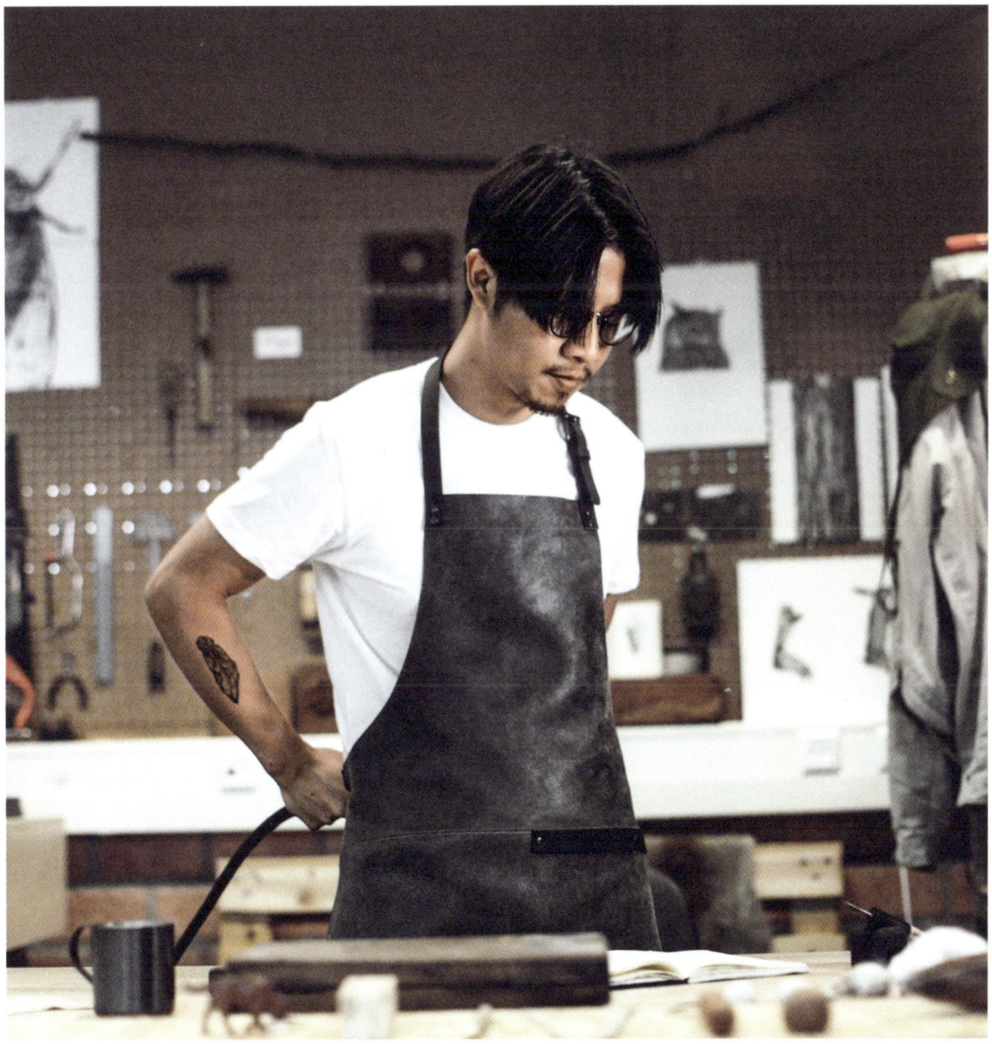

My name is Yen-An Chen, and I work with wood. My greatest source of inspiration was my grandfather, although he was a musician, not a craftsman. I always liked going to his studio when we visited him. He had an answer for each of my questions, and he taught me the value of the objects he cherished. In his studio, I began to work with my hands to execute my ideas, although I wouldn't say it was craftsmanship as such yet.

When I was young, I sometimes stayed with my grandparents, who lived in an old Japanese-style apartment on the university campus. I can still remember the texture of the wood furniture and the smell of the wood floors. I admired how the sunlight created shadows in the space. When I close my eyes, even though the apartment is now gone, I can still see myself standing there, engulfed in the scent of wood. This is my most treasured childhood memory.

Wood, more than any other material, has often brought me comfort. As a child, I enjoyed observing the cracks and knots in wood, and I was always trying to create a story or character from these patterns.

I remember my first encounter with this material. It was in Taiwan, at a market, where I noticed several pieces of camphor tree wood. They were crudely cut, and I began to see animals hiding in the tree rings.

I bring this invisible world to life through pyrography: a technique that uses a heated metal pen to burn decorative patterns into wood and other materials. I began practicing pyrography in 2011. I used leather until I discovered the pieces of camphor wood in the market. I work with antique items, so I start by studying their function and history. I observe them attentively. I like to reveal the purpose the item once served and revive the historical memories, or simply allow people to cherish these abandoned objects and learn to really see them again, giving them a second life. I want to highlight their existence once again.

When I first moved to England in 2012, I realized how popular flea markets are and, most importantly, that people are willing to sell or give away their old items. This discovery fired my imagination. I pictured myself growing up in a different context, surrounded by Taiwanese antiques, and wondered if I would have acquired a greater understanding of my own culture through these objects. Since then, whenever I travel to countries in Europe, I take the time to visit flea markets and observe the differences between each country.

As a Taiwanese artist, I feel that the young people of my generation are facing a serious threat to their identity. The substitution of modern objects in our environment has erased our understanding of our own culture. To be honest, it's not that easy to find antiques in my country. It is sad to see our society put efficiency and modernity before cultural preservation.

These objects tell the story of our lives and represent a period of time in our culture. They bear witness to our history, and now it's my turn to speak up for them—by reminding people that what we leave behind is essential to building our future.

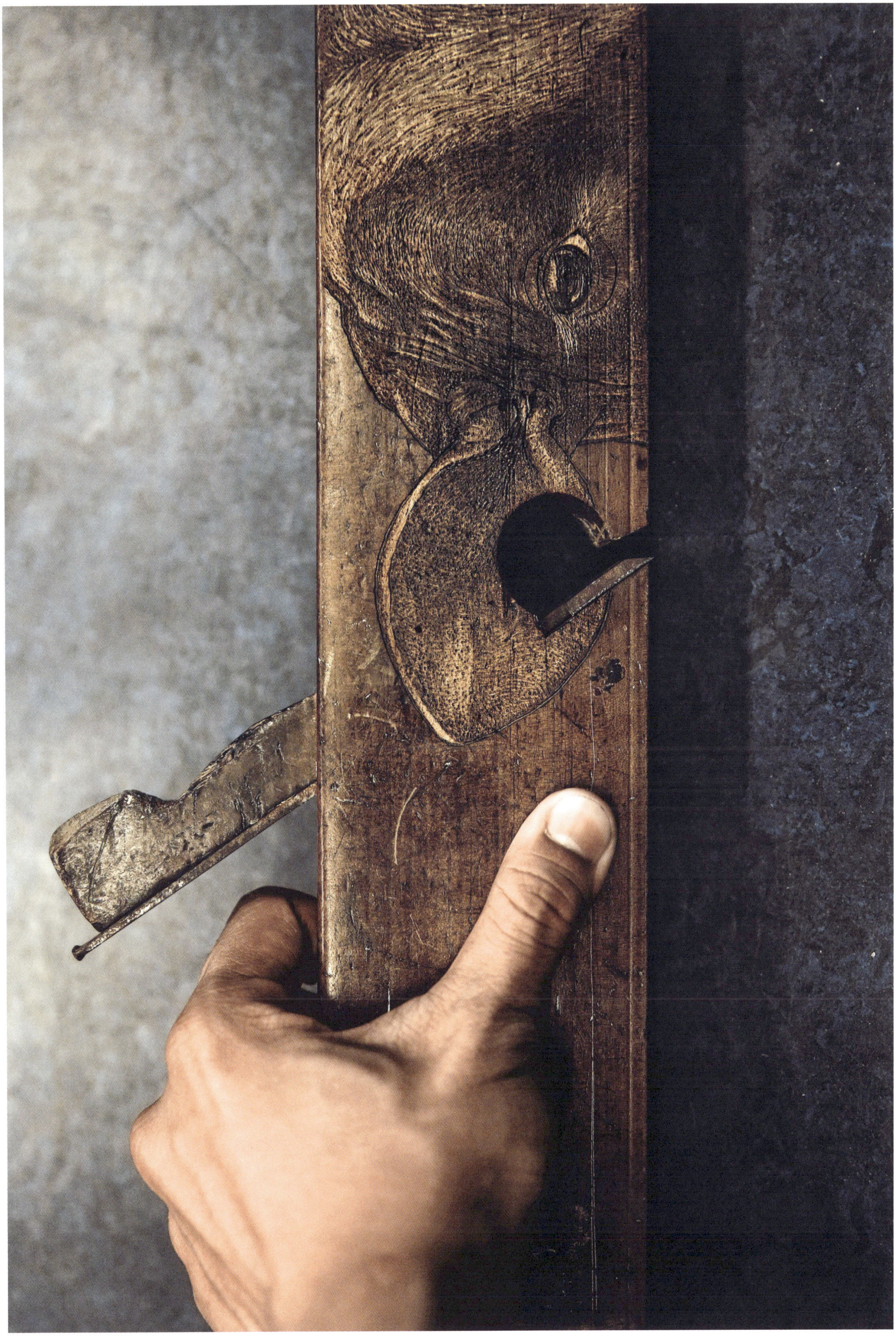

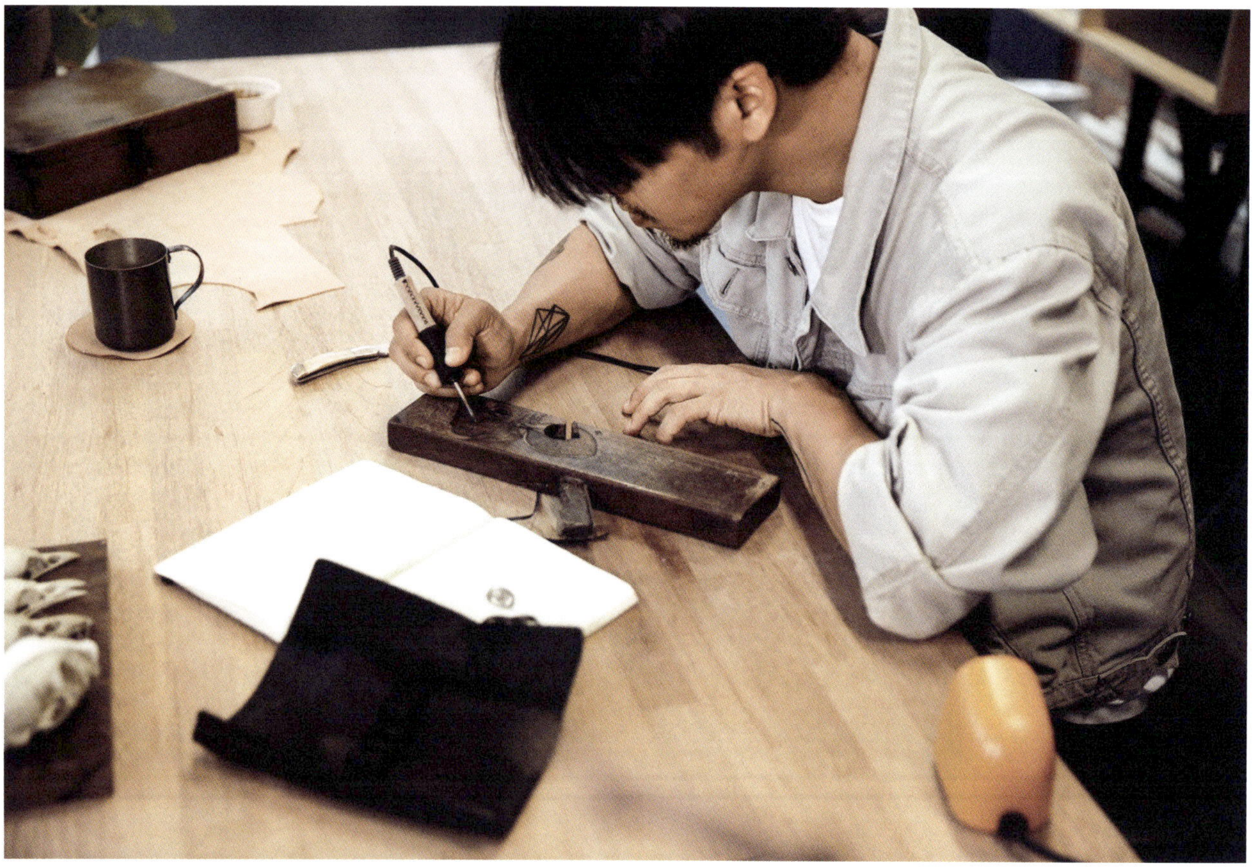

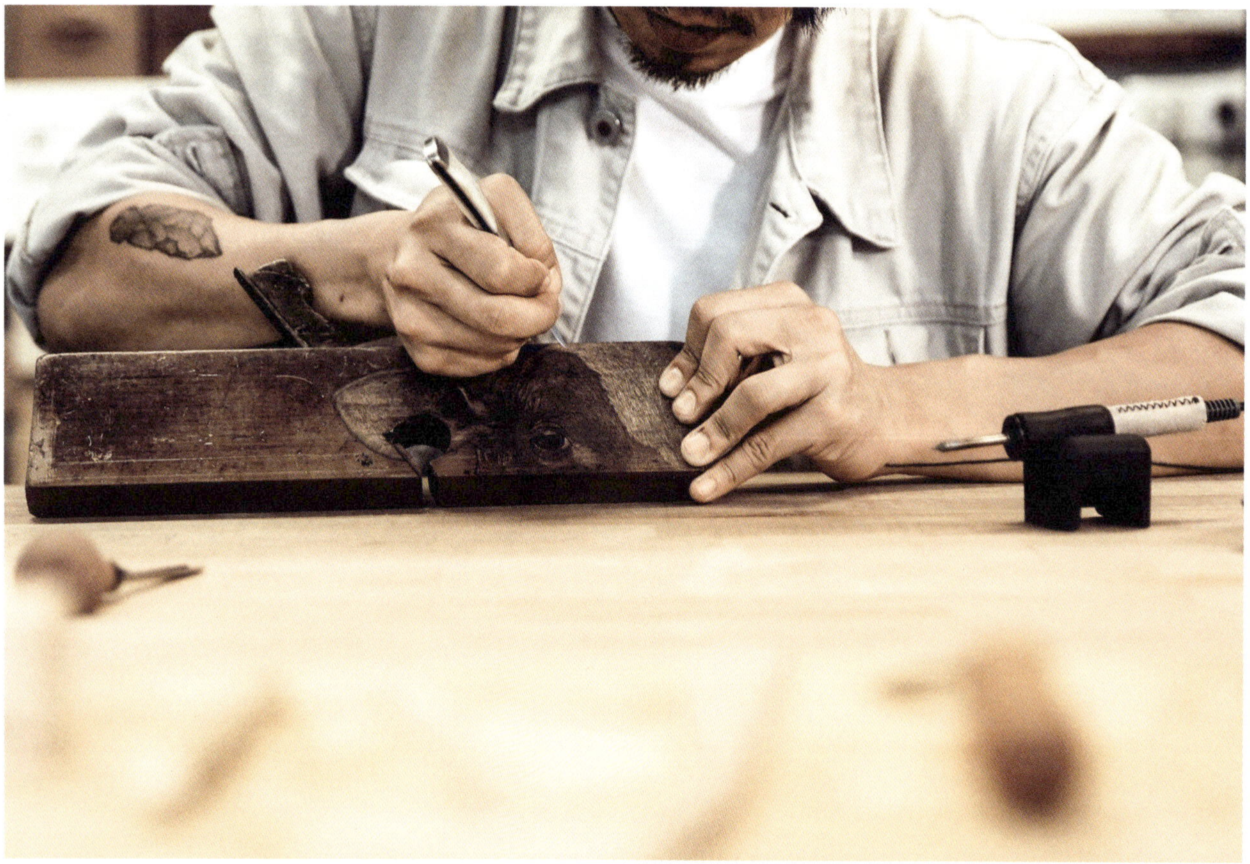

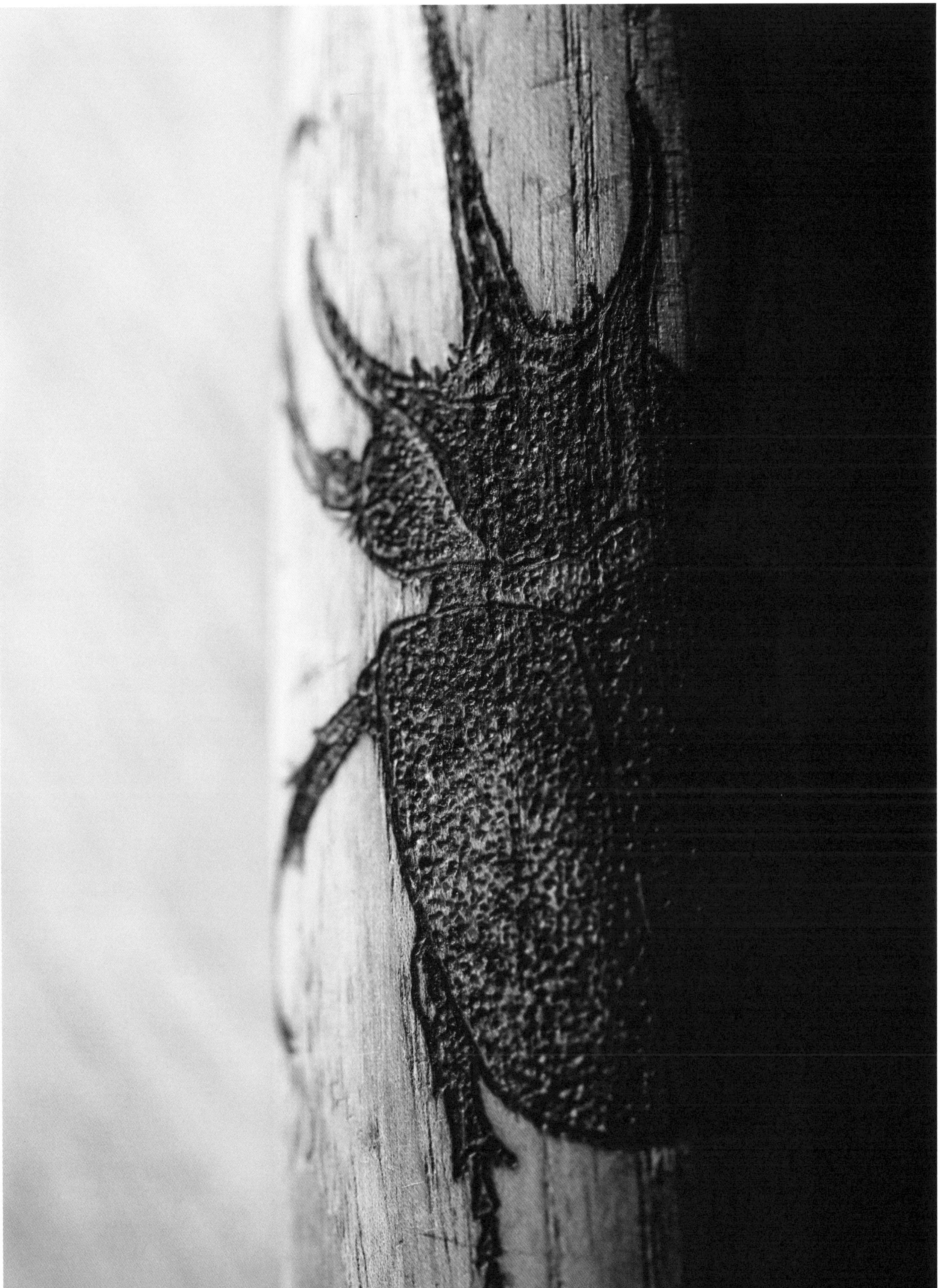

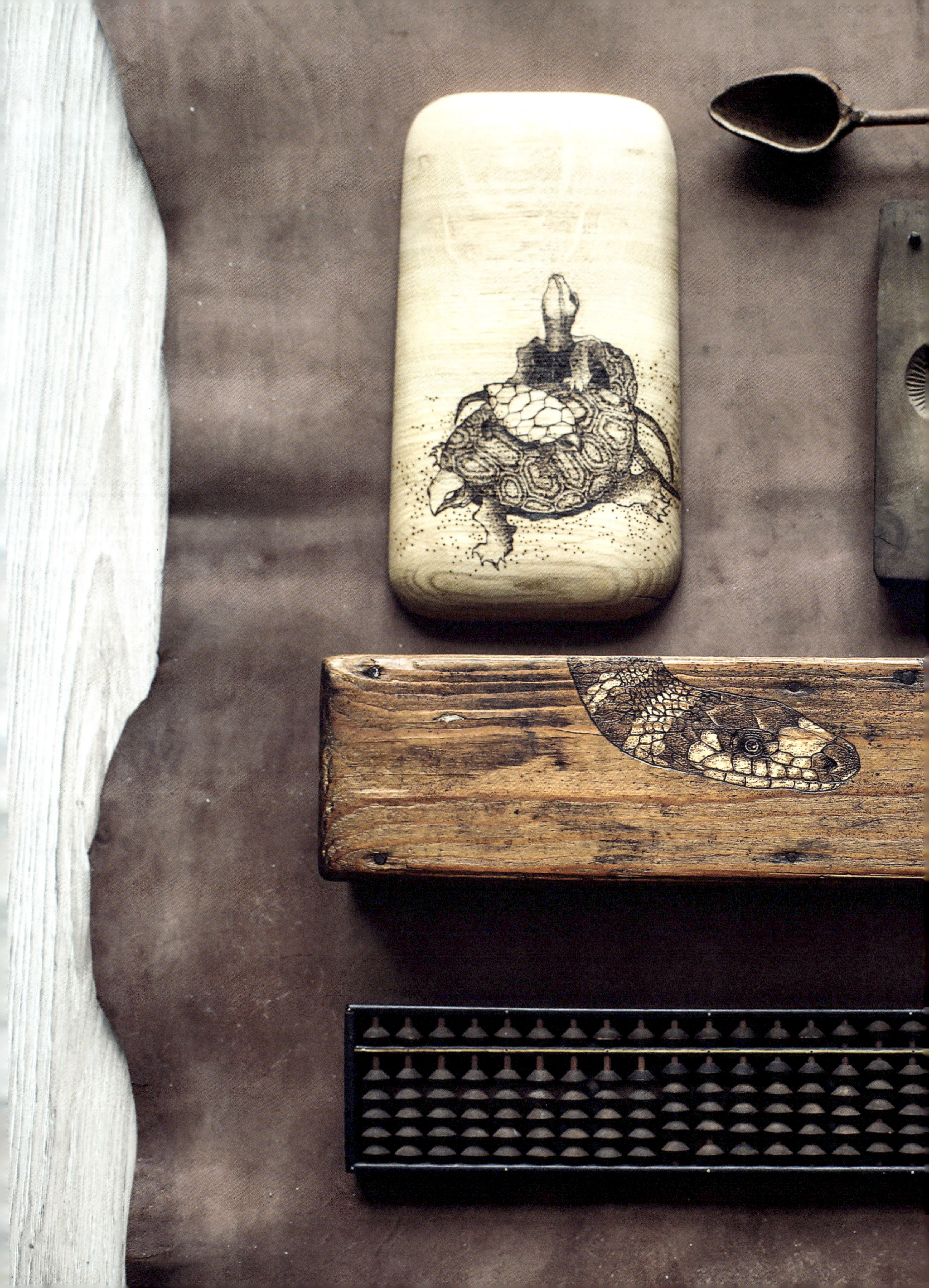

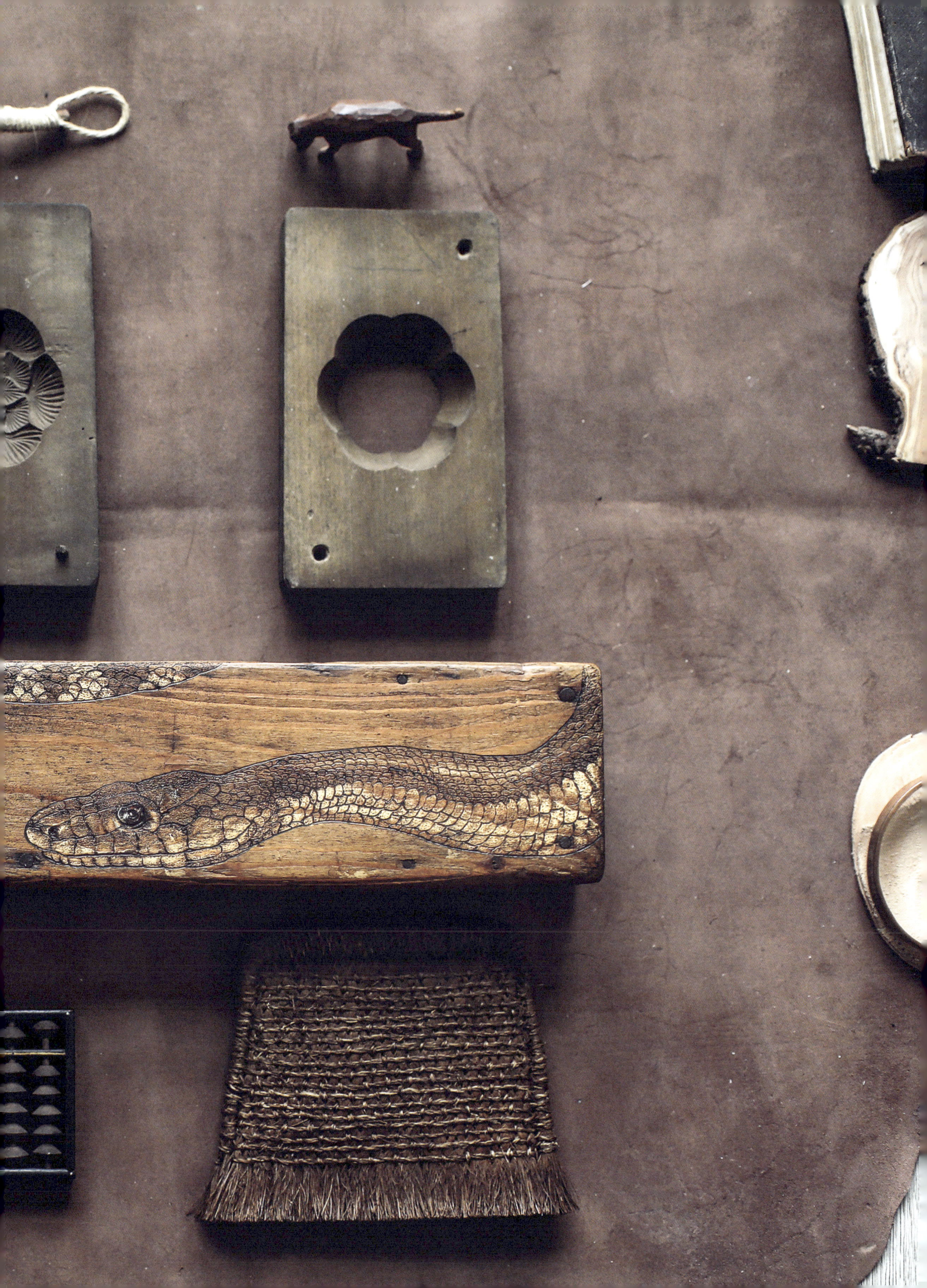

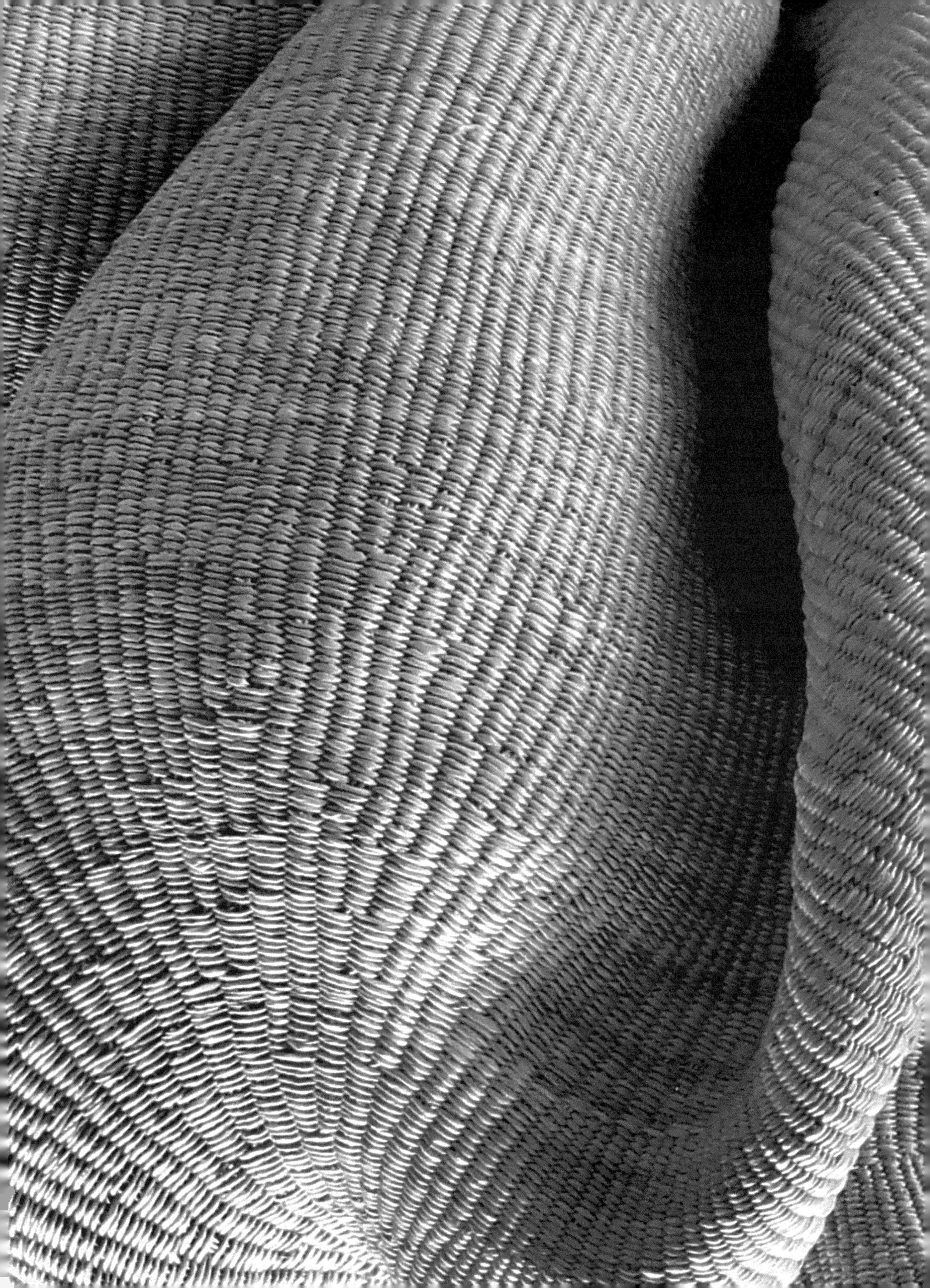

Fiber

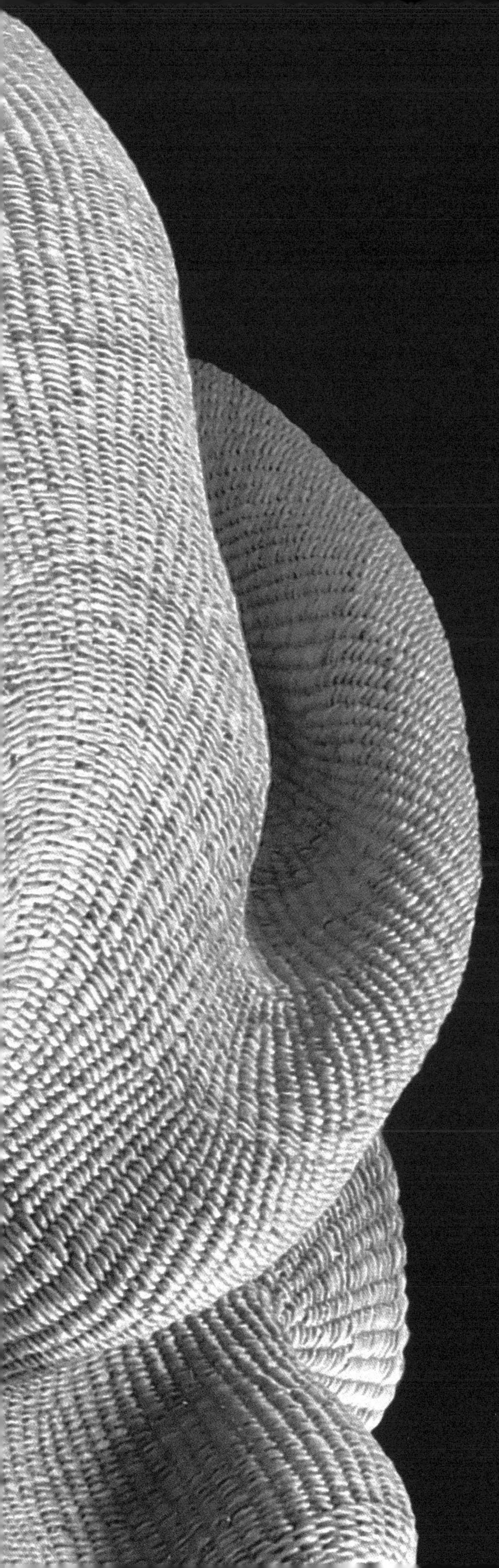

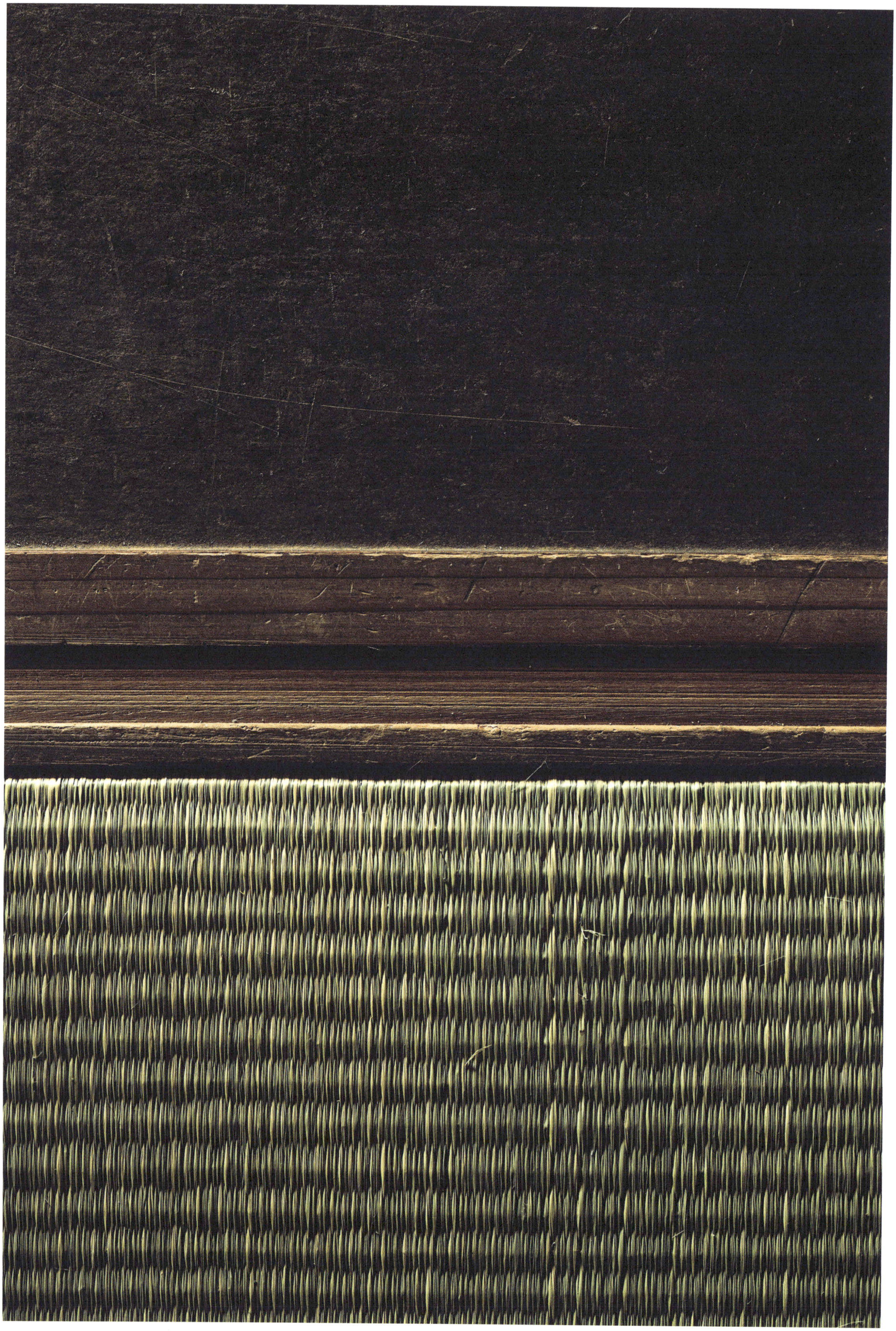

Mitsuru Yokoyama

Tatami maker

Kyoto, Japan

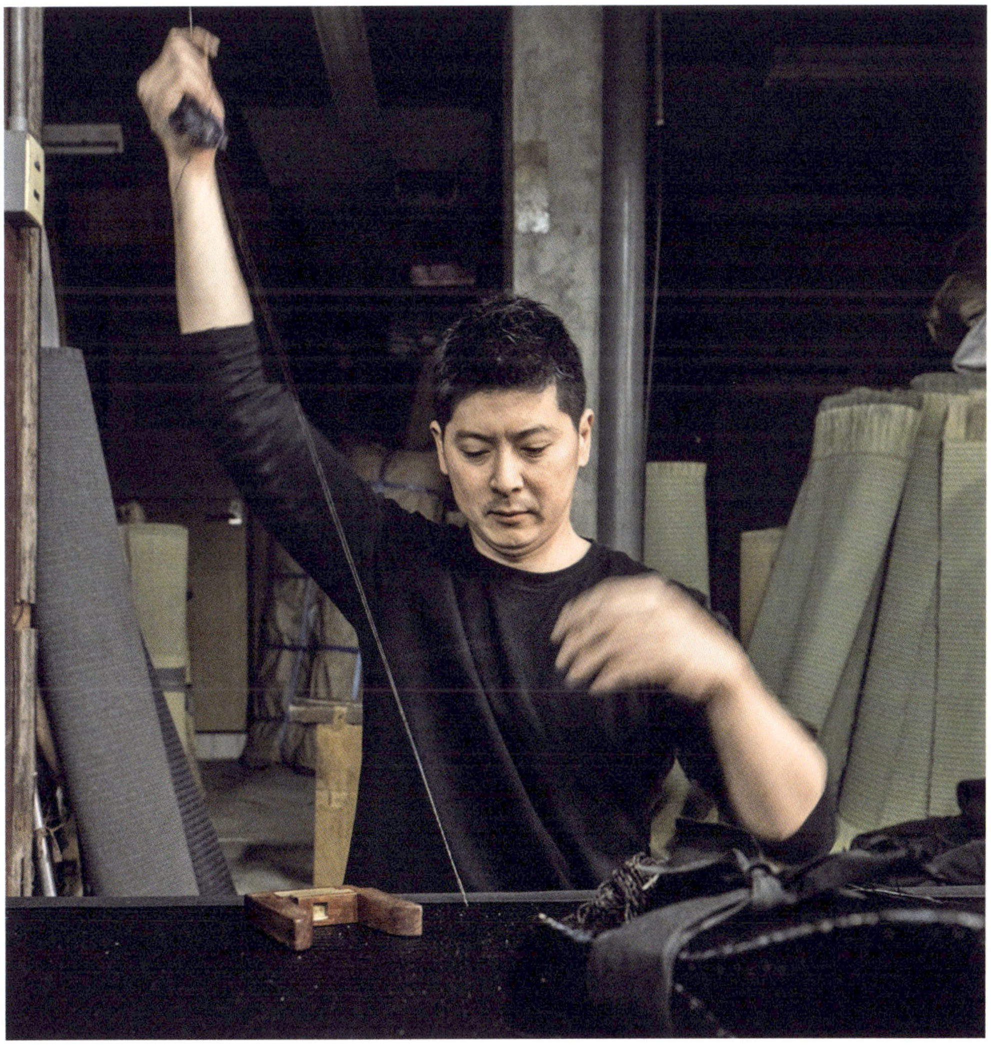

My name is Mitsuru Yokoyama, and I make tatami mats. The tatami is a centerpiece of Japanese homes. It can follow a person throughout their entire life: Japanese people begin and end their lives on tatami mats. They are central to our way of life and we treat them with respect. They also serve as our unit of measure. An essential part of home life, they are used for sleep, meals, meditation, worship, and entertainment. Due to their ability to gather experiences, I see tatami as more of a "space" than an object.

I was born in Tokyo in 1978. Years later, I headed to Australia, where I built luxury yachts and catamarans. Then, one day, I felt a powerful desire to pass on my culture to others: I wanted people outside of Japan to be able to engage deeply with it. I wanted to do this as much for myself as for others; after living abroad for so long, I felt that I had missed out on certain aspects of Japanese life.

Traditionally, the craft of tatami making is passed down from generation to generation. But today, few young people are interested in learning it. So I decided to move to Kyoto with my wife, Lauren, who is Australian, and learn to make tatamis so I could become a skilled craftsman.

The core of the tatami is made of rice straw. But not just any rice straw—we use a variety grown on farms that respect very strict growing criteria. This is one reason why Japanese materials are more expensive and look different from their Chinese equivalents.

My work consists of assembling the *omote*, or the top covering of the tatami, and the base. We buy the woven *omote*, which is made of *igusa* (a variety of rush), then I dye it and sew it by hand to a natural (straw) base. For the *omote*, I prefer the more rustic *ryukyu* weaving technique from Okinawa.

The fabrication process of tatamis hasn't really evolved over the years; what has changed is our approach. I often work in collaboration with my wife, designers, architects, and other craftspeople. My ideas don't always work out, but it's good to try and to adapt, while staying attuned to the material and the craft technique. The color black is a defining feature of my work; I have carried out many tests to make this black unique.

Once the tatami is in place, it's difficult to evaluate the quality. To do so, you have to turn it over and examine details like the stitches on the *heri* (edges). A new tatami mat has a wonderful odor—it's like being outdoors in nature. The mat absorbs carbon dioxide and regulates the temperature in the house by absorbing humidity in the air.

Tatamis have changed, largely because of demand. Some Japanese people prefer more Western-style homes, while others opt for low-cost imitation tatamis. New architectural styles and interior decoration trends from abroad have also brought about exciting changes. Tastes may change, but the basic product and my trade remain the same; I'm very proud of my craft. Certain people endeavor to transform the tatami (and I'm one of them), but it always returns to its original form, even if it features slight variations.

A good tatami maker is attentive to detail, and must be strong, prudent, and open to new ideas. For the tatami to survive and capture the interest of my daughter's generation, it must appeal to young people and foreigners. And that is the goal I'm pursuing today.

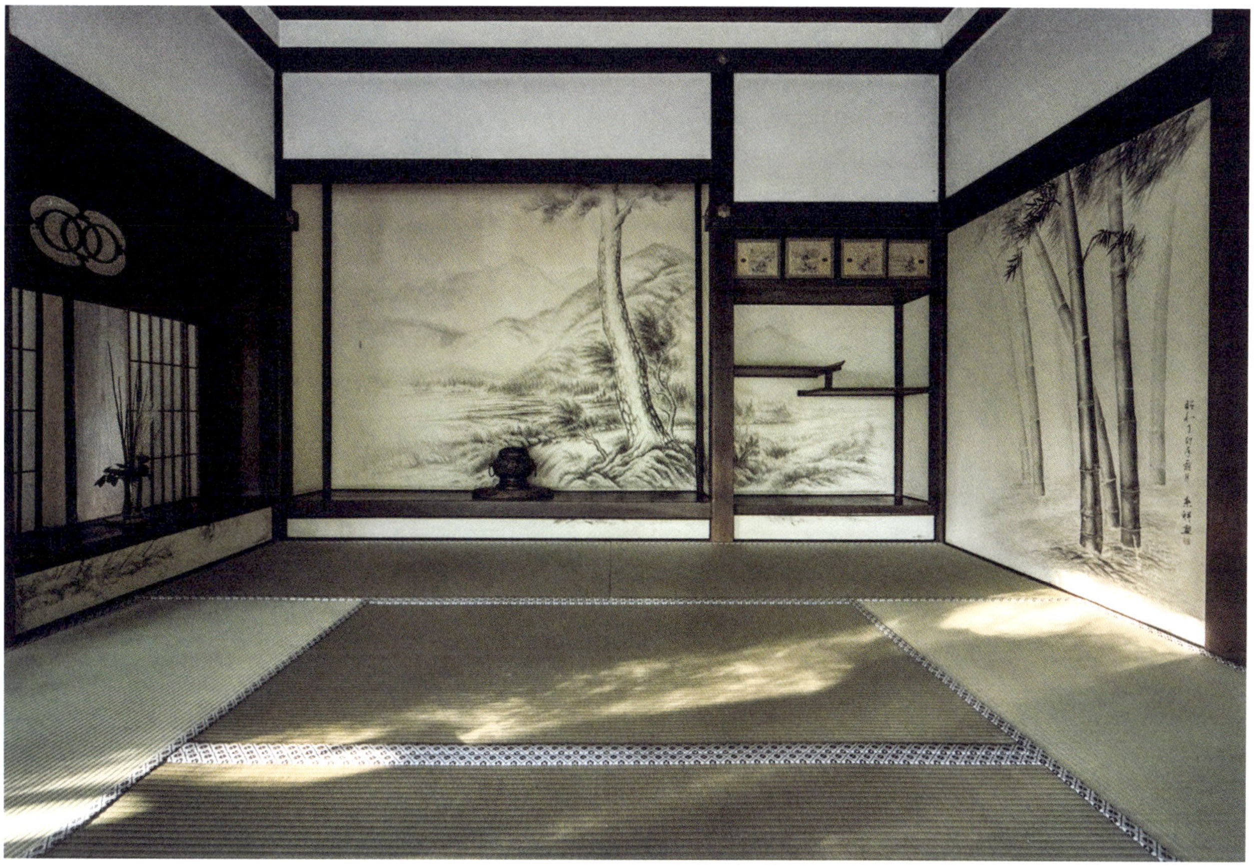

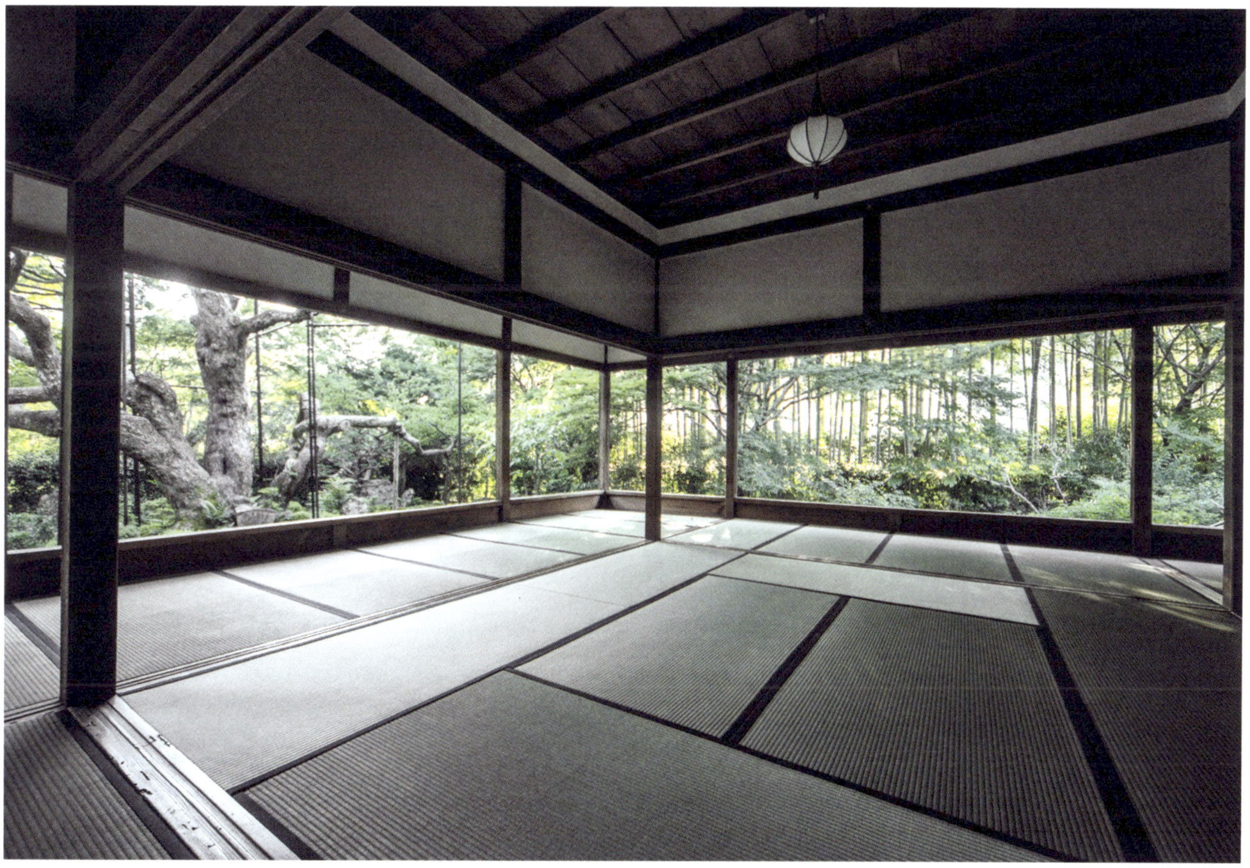

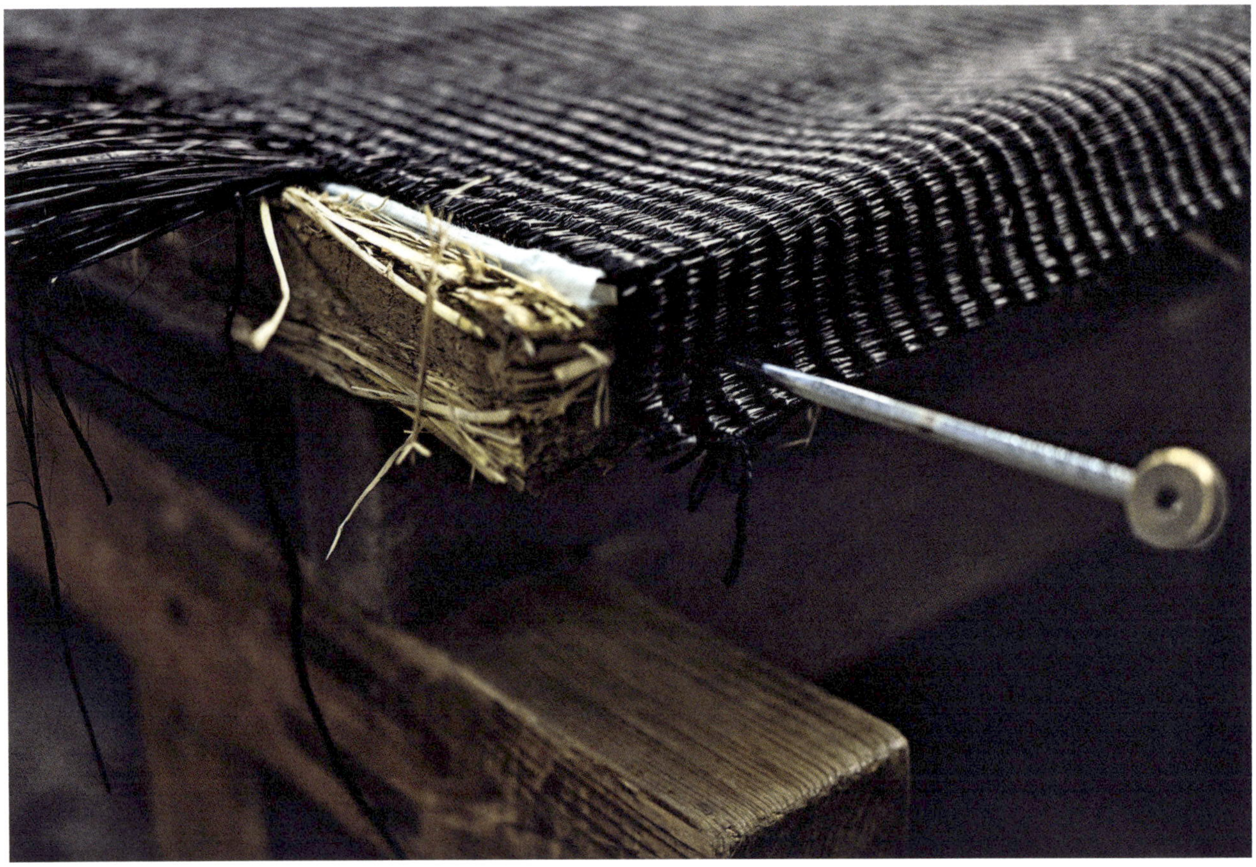

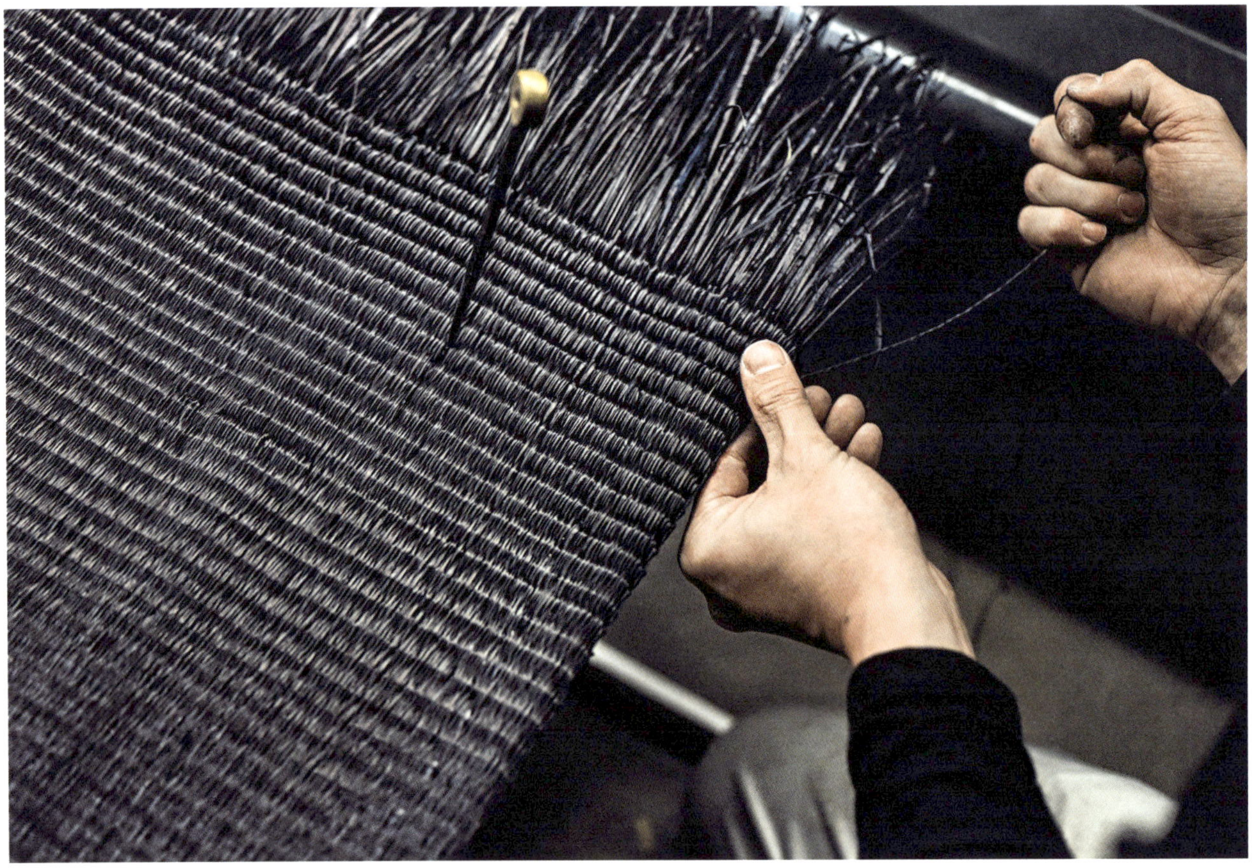

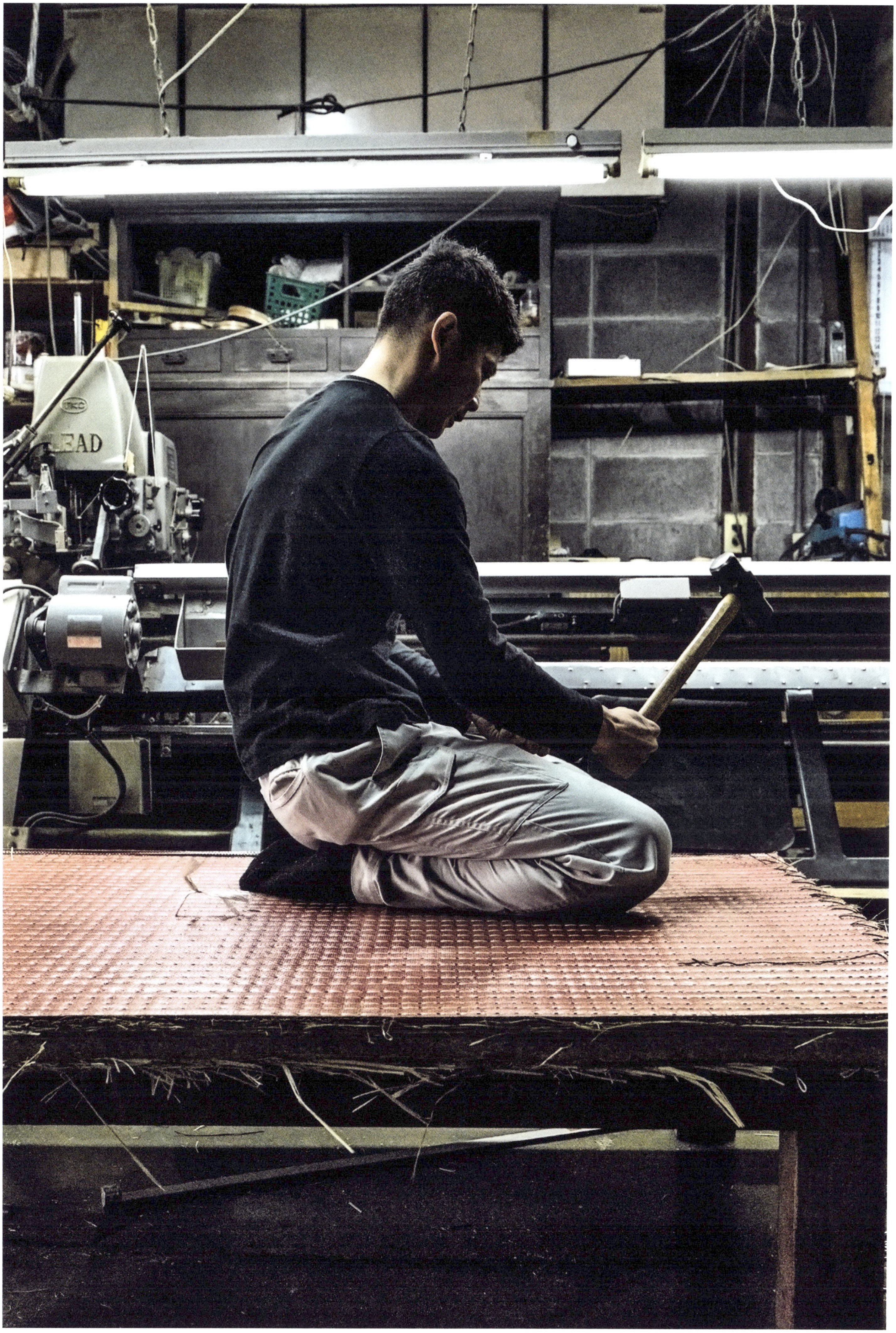
LEAD

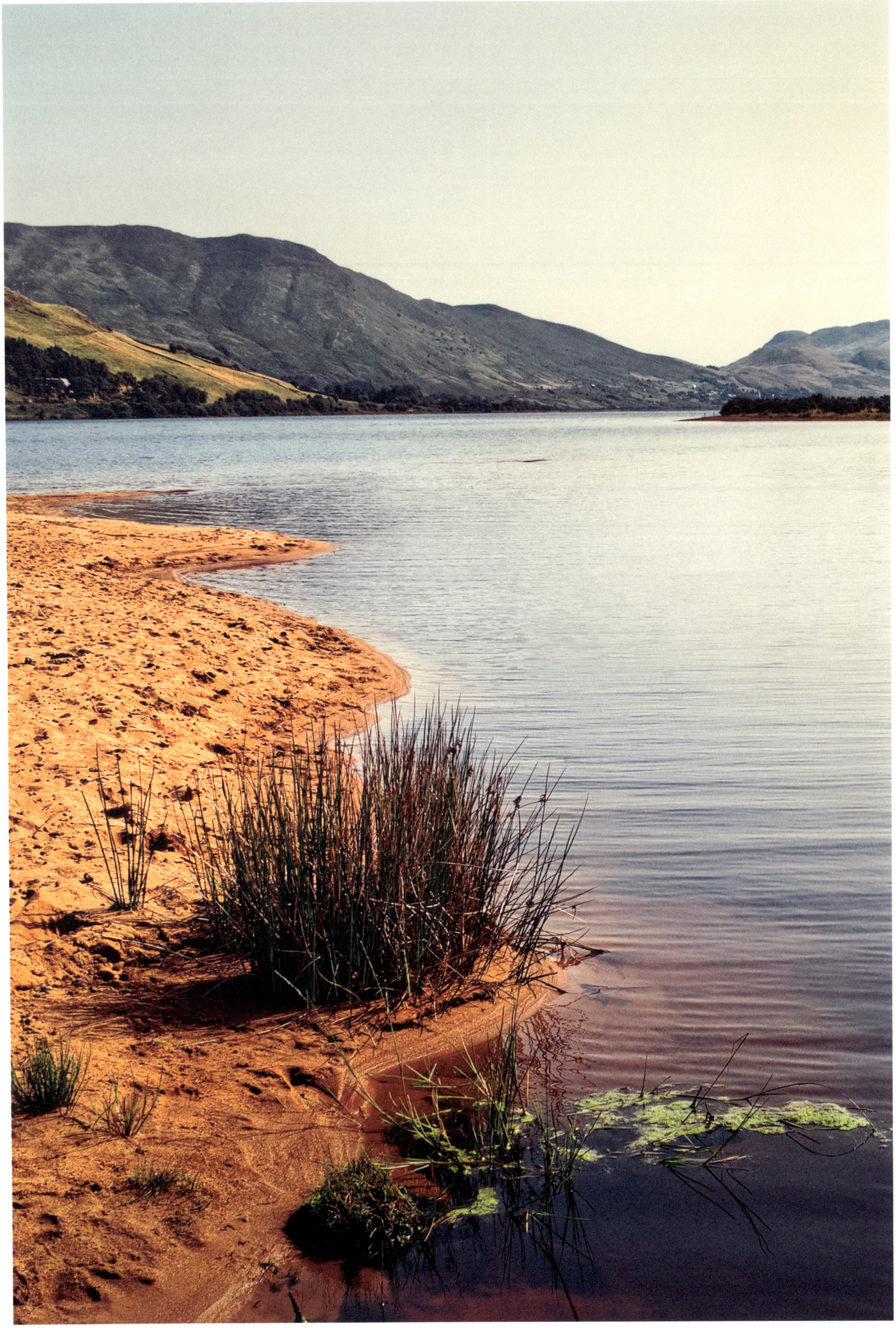

Joe Hogan

Basket maker

Loch Na Fooey,
Ireland

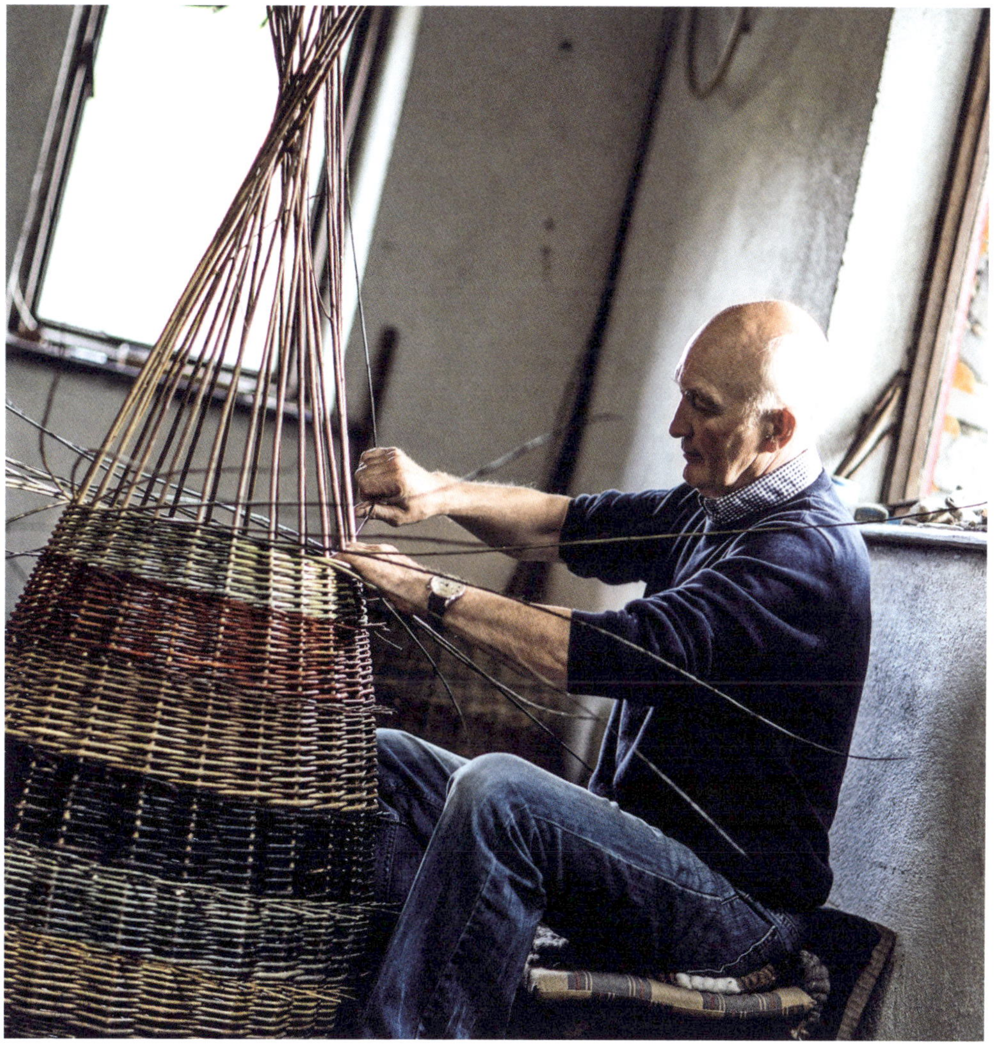

My name is Joe Hogan, and I am a basket maker. A basket can tell us a lot about the landscape: the type of material used in a basket speaks volumes about the region where it was made. This is particularly true if the materials were grown locally, as was always the case in the past.

In the warm regions of Spain, baskets are made of esparto grass. Farther north, in the Pyrenees, baskets are produced from split sweet chestnut, and to the east, in the Catalan region, river cane is most often used. Heading north into France, willow becomes the dominant material, especially in the more fertile regions. Thus baskets from a particular place provide a wonderful response to the materials that nature has made available to us.

In the mid-1970s, my wife Dolores and I traveled through the Connemara region of Ireland. We found the wild beauty of the landscapes so incredible that we decided to settle there. I had originally studied philosophy, and initially I saw craft work merely as a means of earning a living. At the time, I was more interested in farming and gardening. When we moved to Loch Na Fooey, I knew it was possible to grow willow from cuttings, and this is what attracted me to basketmaking rather than to any other craft.

During our first spring on the loch, we planted willows on a plot of land that hadn't been properly prepared—we had a bad harvest. The following year, we planted them in one of our most fertile fields, and the harvest was much better. In the region, some people continued to make baskets for their own use, so I began creating baskets using my willow trees.

I embarked on the craft of basketmaking without any formal training; instead, I repeated the same gestures and techniques over and over again to improve my skills. I learned through trial and error and from my many mistakes. Then I heard about the Quinlan brothers from County Waterford and they were a great help. They explained techniques and helped me understand the importance of passing on knowledge and giving encouragement. I believe it is my duty to be as helpful as I can to those who wish to learn the craft trades, to keep these skills alive.

I have been a basket maker for over forty years, and baskets have become a way for me to express my ideas. Almost all of the techniques I use come from traditional basketmaking. The idea for artistic baskets with collars made of driftwood I had found was inspired by the Irish donkey creel, or pannier. It was simply a question of following my inspiration. There's a nice insight by John O'Donohue in his poem "For the Artist at the Start of Day," and it is one I aspire to:

"May this be...
A morning when you become a pure vessel
For what wants to ascend from silence."

(from *To Bless the Space Between Us: A Book of Blessings* [Doubleday, 2008])

Craftsmanship is a minority pursuit today in Ireland, but I think Irish people are interested in crafts and are supportive of the survival of craft skills. As artisans, we must strive to do the best work possible, even if it is never perfect.

I feel very privileged to be able to live in this region. The landscape here gives sustenance to the soul.

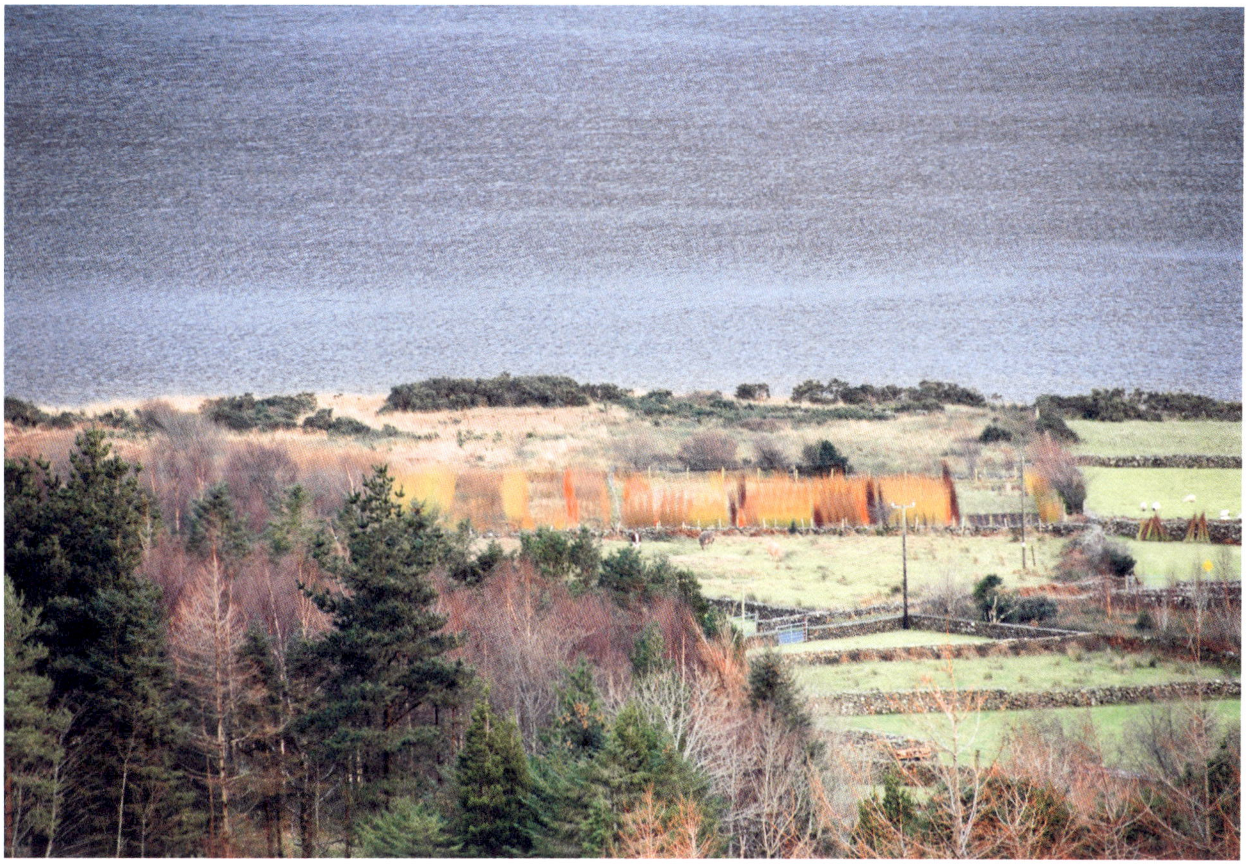

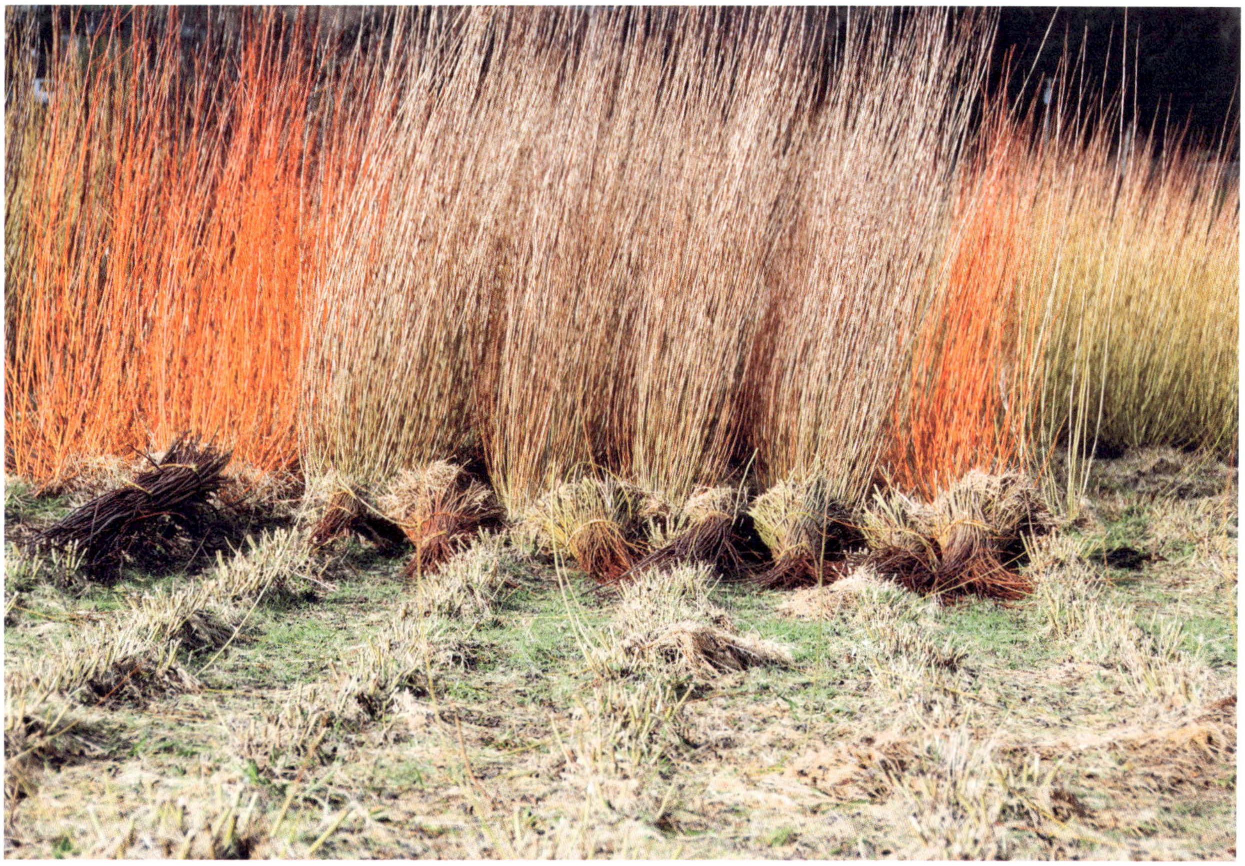

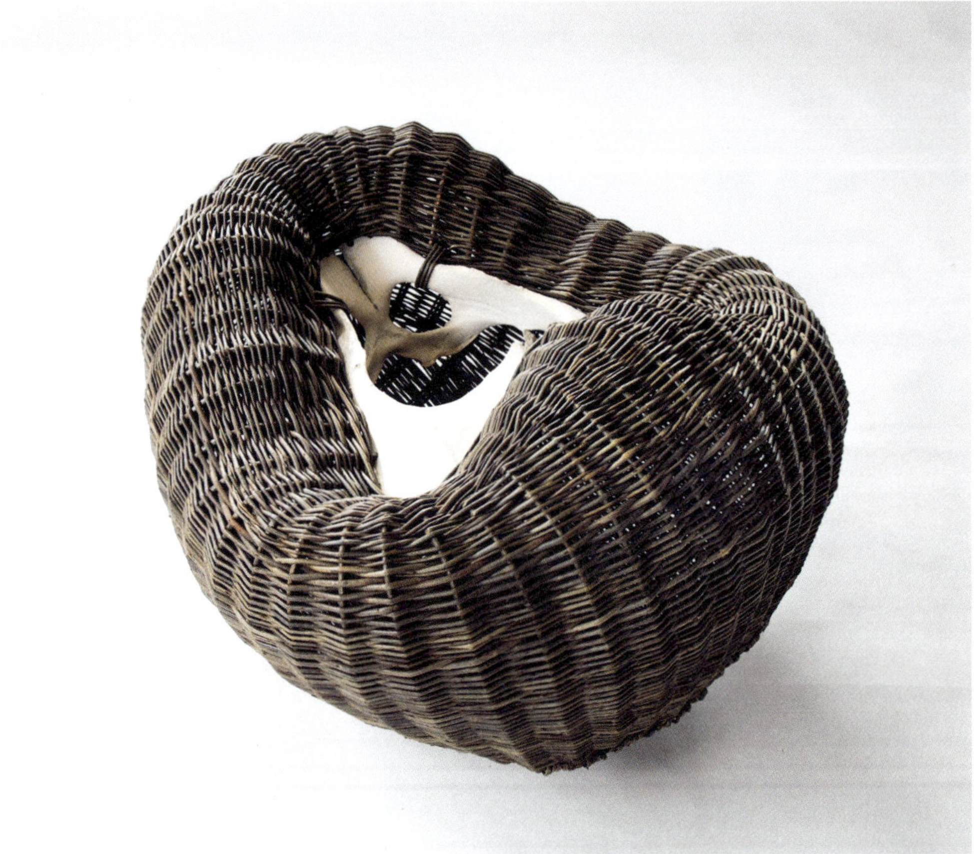

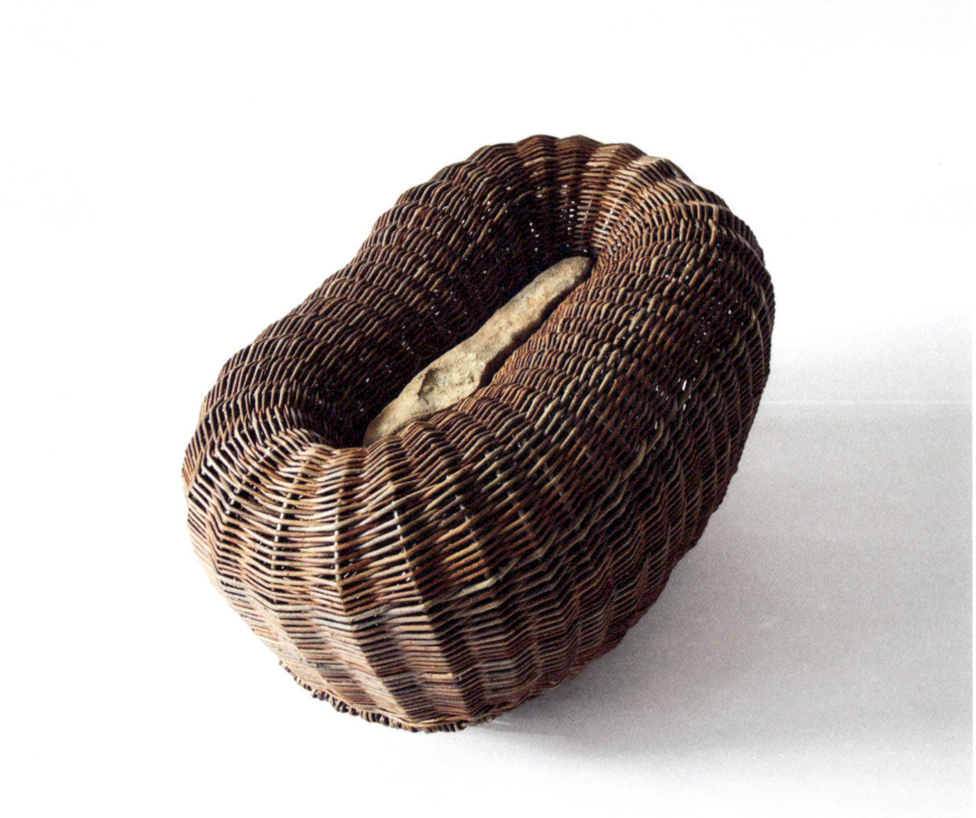

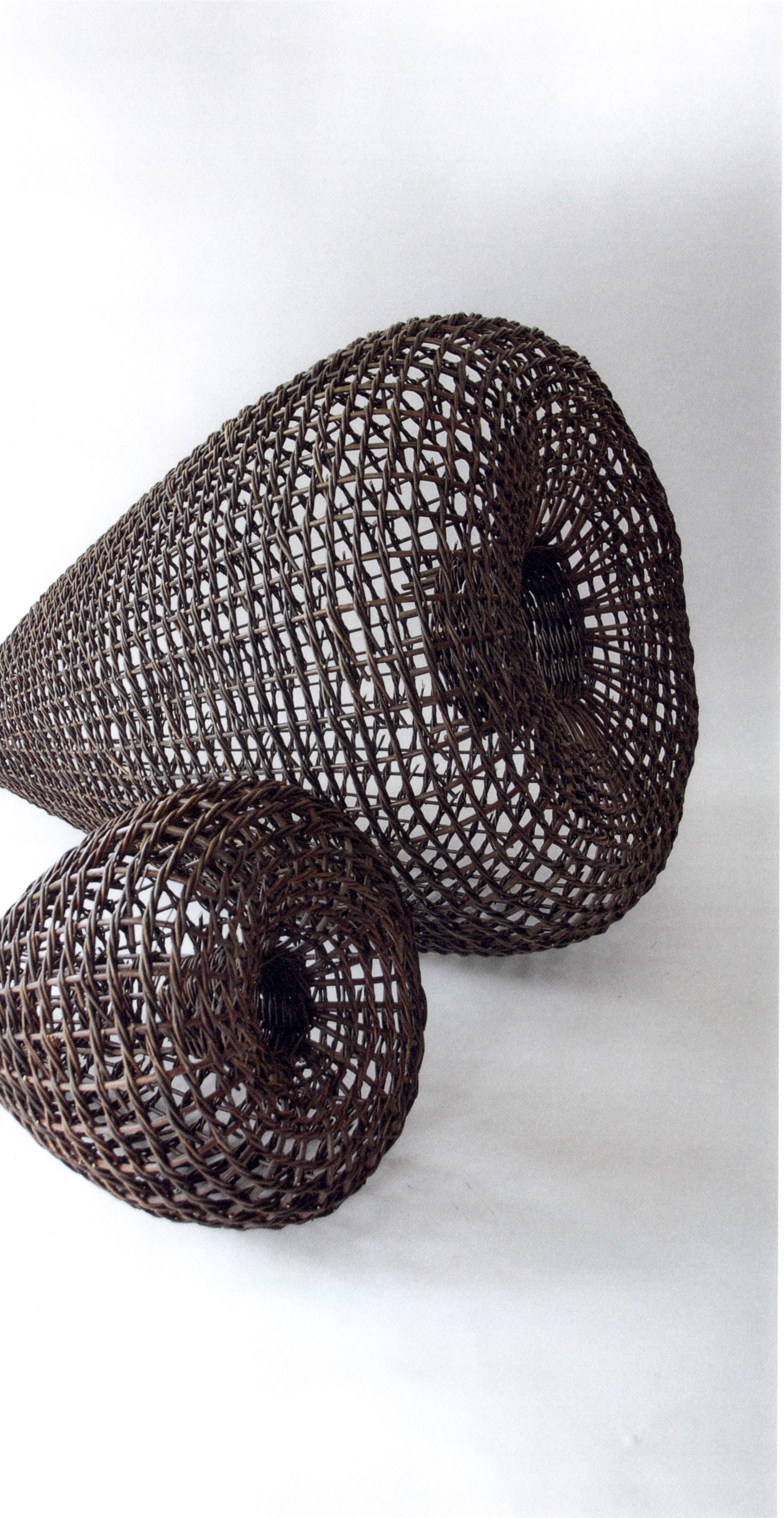

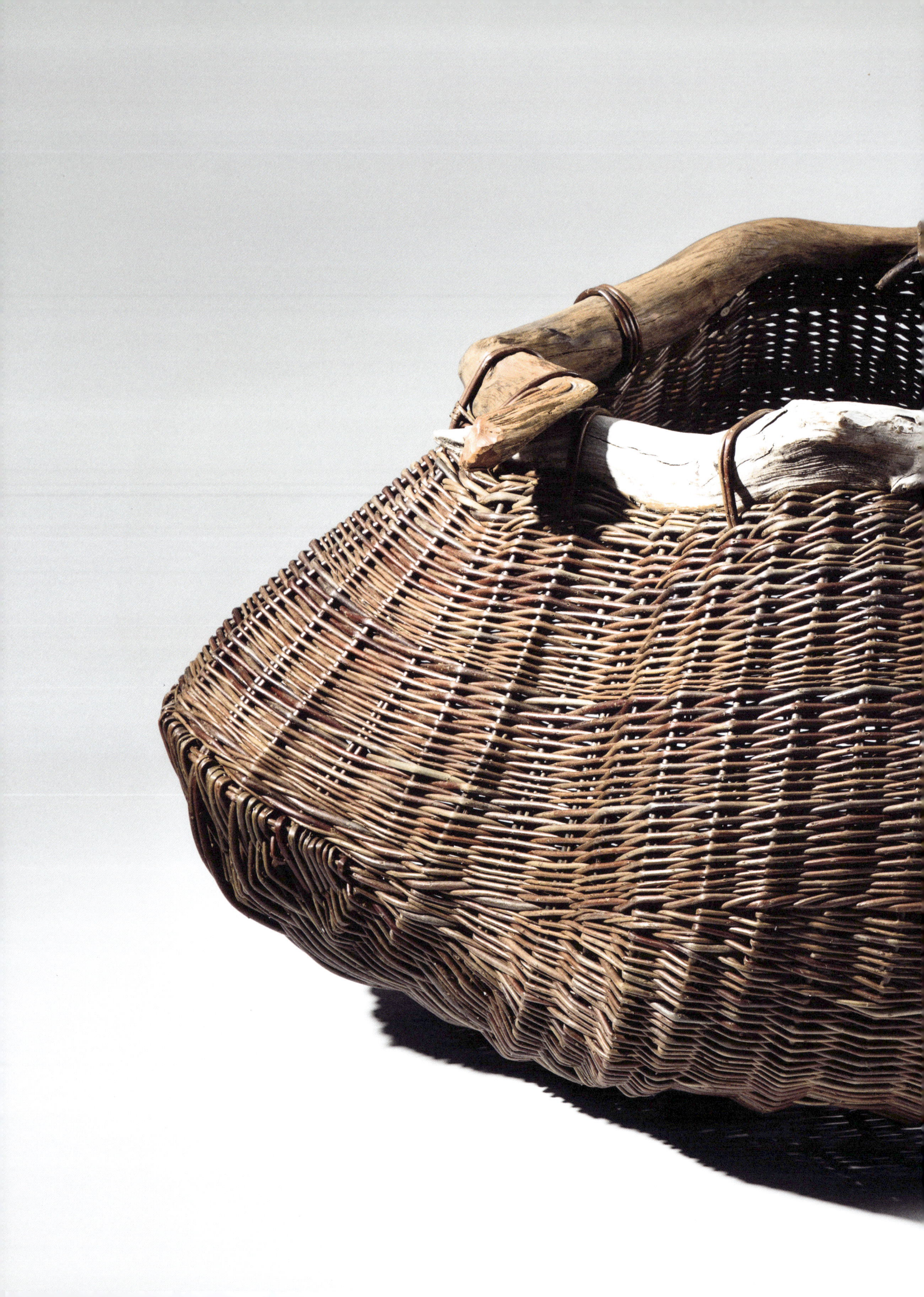

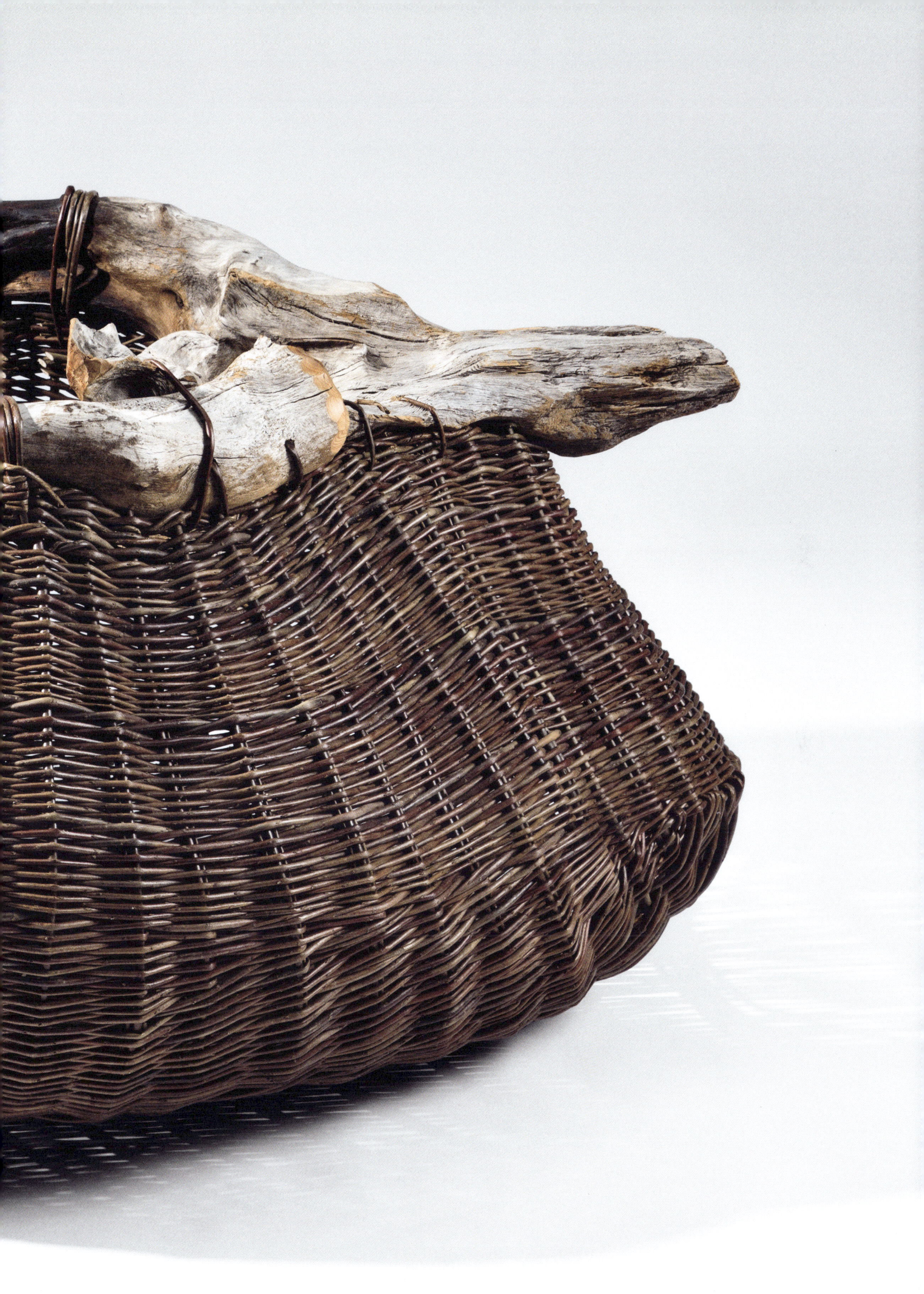

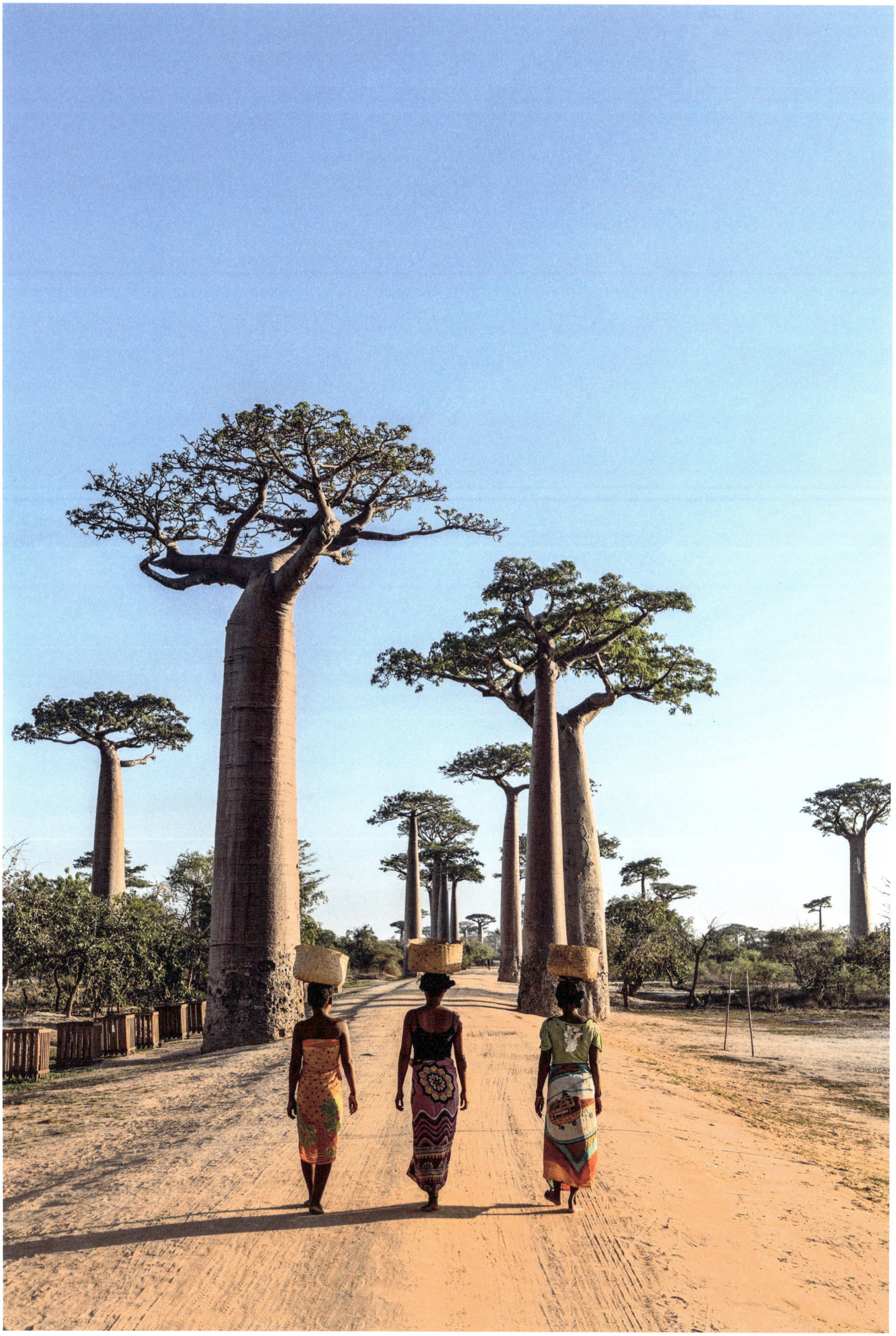

Akabare Abentara

Baba Tree Basket Company

Basket weaver

Bolgatanga, Ghana

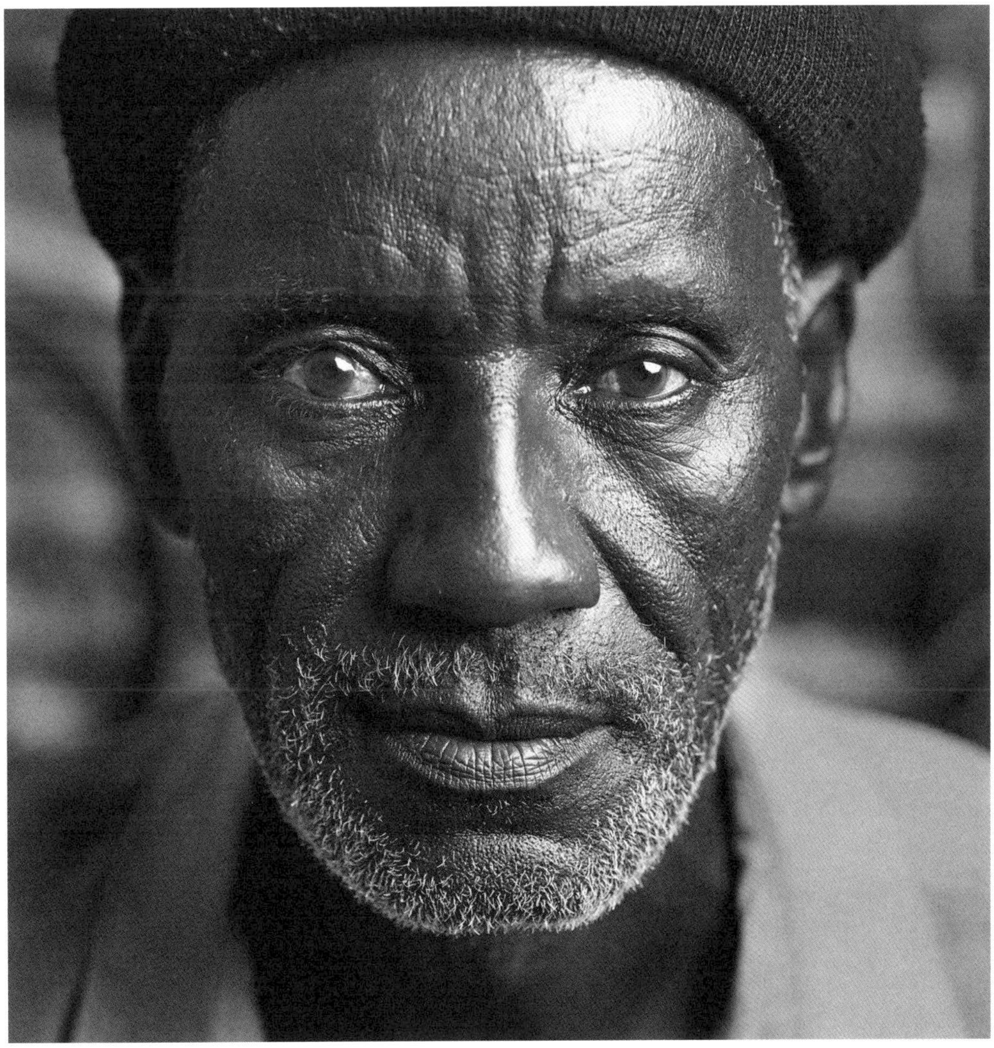

My name is Akabare Abentara, and I am a basket weaver. I grew up on a farm where my parents taught me to work the earth and where I tended cows in the fields. On our land, there was a grass called *kinkanhe*—straw or elephant grass—that we harvested during the rainy season, then split with our teeth and used to weave hats to protect ourselves from the sun when we were farming. We would also weave small baskets from this straw to strain *pito*, a beer we make from millet.

Relatives from Kumasi—a city located in southern Ghana, the most humid part of the country—came to our village and saw us weaving with the local straw. They told us about a better kind that grew in Kumasi. When they returned home, they harvested some and sent it to us to try. We observed that the southern straw was much sturdier than ours.

I typically start weaving in the morning if I'm feeling well. I buy my straw, which I split and then roll in preparation for weaving. If I'm making a basket, I first arrange the straw together in the form of a cross, then I start weaving in the particular way that the Gurunsi people weave.

I often have an idea of what I want to make before I dye the straw. Once it has been dyed, I place the bundles of straw in a row to see how the colors work together. Then I start making smaller rows with a few colors and I pick out the best combinations. Sometimes new ideas come to me while I'm weaving and I change color associations as I go along.

I met Gregory McCarthy when he came to buy baskets in Bolgatanga. At the market, a skillfully woven basket caught his eye and he asked who had made it. No one could tell him. So he cycled to the village of Dulugu and asked again. The weaver wasn't from there either. Further on, in my village, Gambibgo, he inquired at several groups of weavers. Eventually, one of them gave him my address. Ayinedollah [Gregory's Gurunsi name] got back on his bicycle and continued to my family compound, where he found a group of us weaving high-quality baskets.

So, we began working with him. At first, we would take our finished baskets to his house. Then he asked us to come and weave at his home. Now that we are organized and have grown enough, we can afford to have cold water—we have acquired a *ko'ohmahasika*, the Gurunsi word for refrigerator. We also have more storage space in the form of two metal shipping containers. A roof was constructed between the two containers, providing us with an additional work area. We now have Motokings and Candoos [basic vehicles from China and India] that we sometimes use to get home if we can't cross the river during the rainy season. We even have lights in our new structure so that we can work later if we want.

Some of us would like to use the baskets that we weave, but we put so much time and money into making them that we can't use them ourselves. If we didn't weave baskets, it would be difficult for us to take care of our families.

Today, I have hope for the future and I don't feel burdened. When I'm sitting with people who all respect one another, sharing ideas and working together toward a common goal, I think, "Now this is beauty." People believe that beauty resides in the face, but that's not true—beauty comes from the heart.

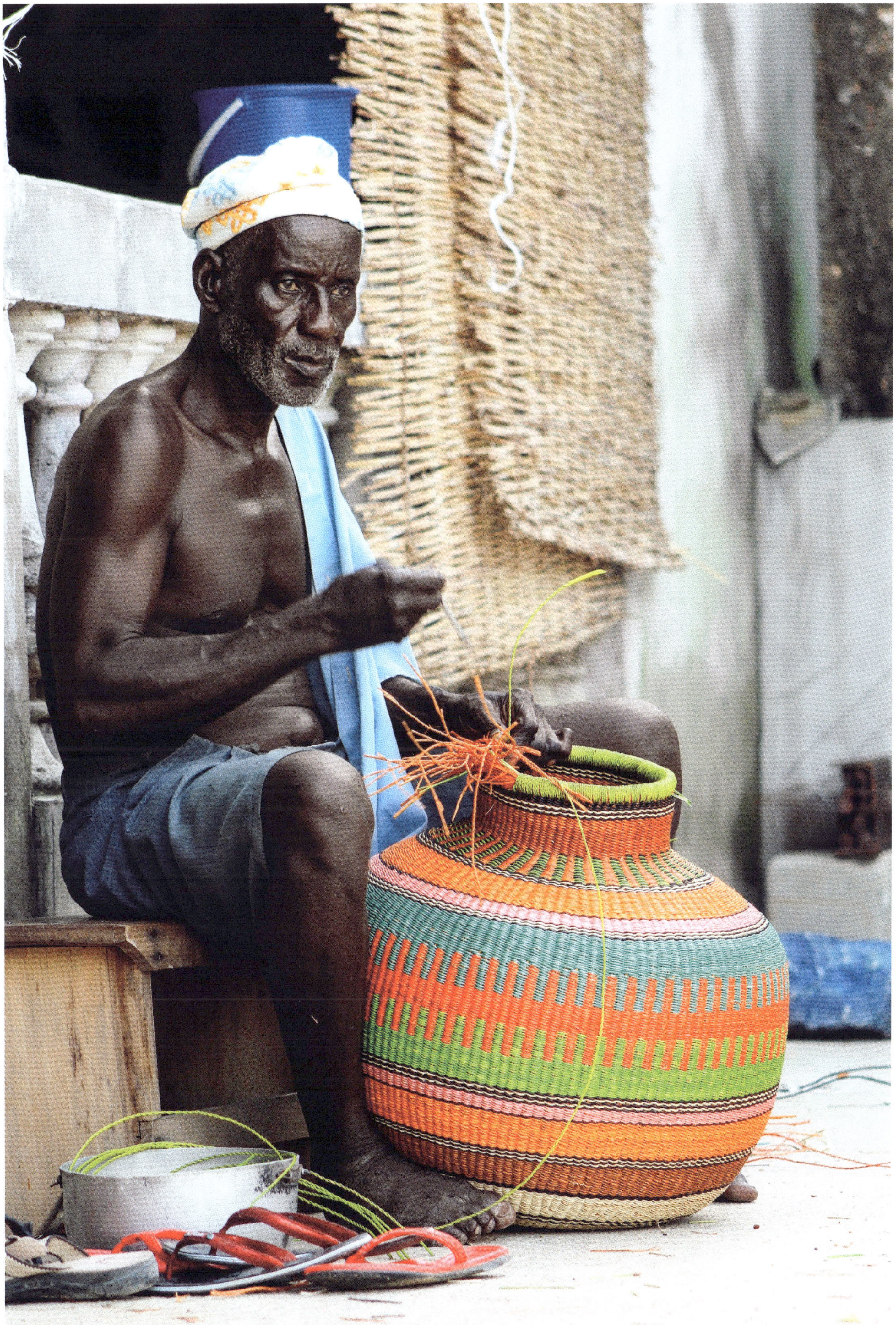

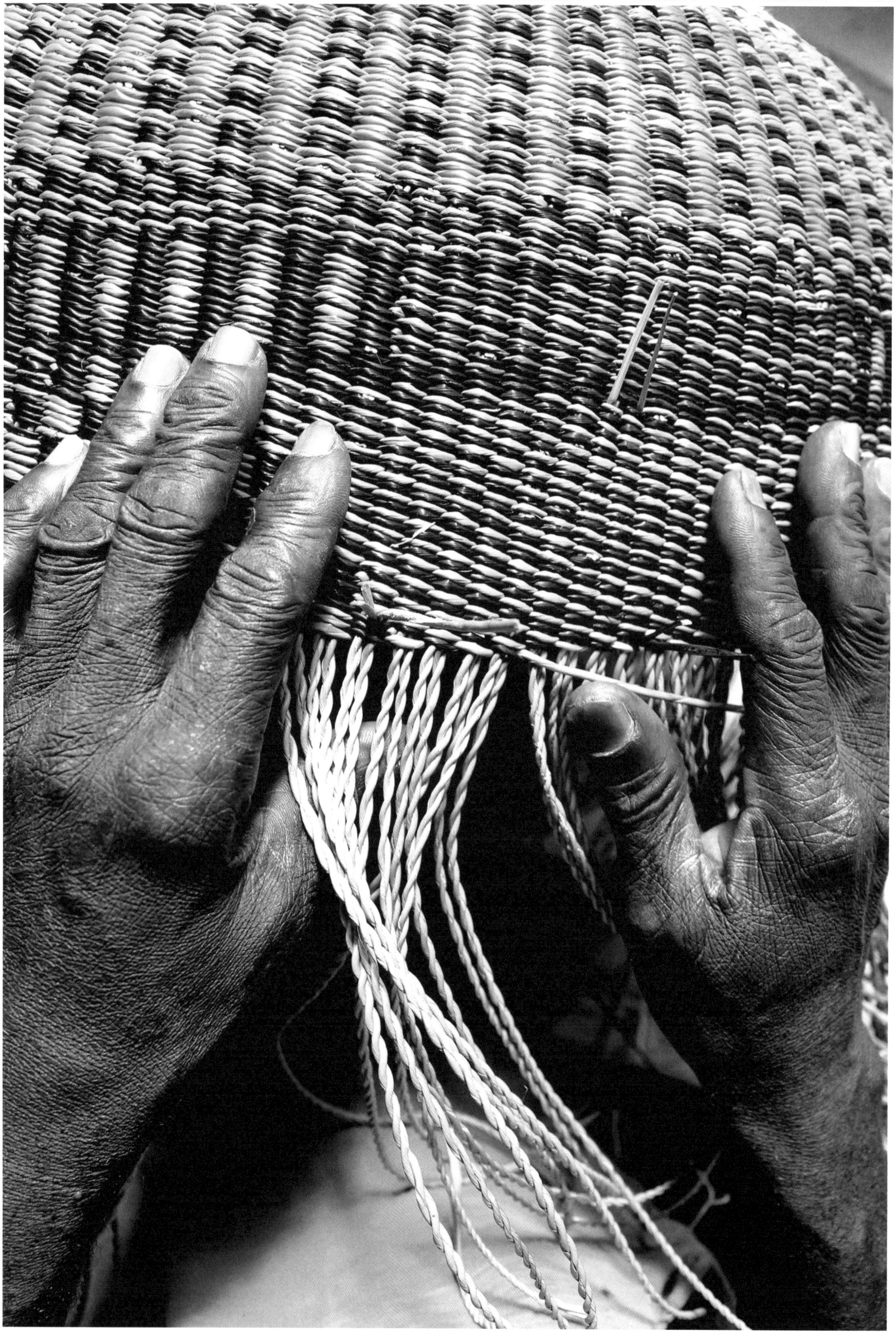

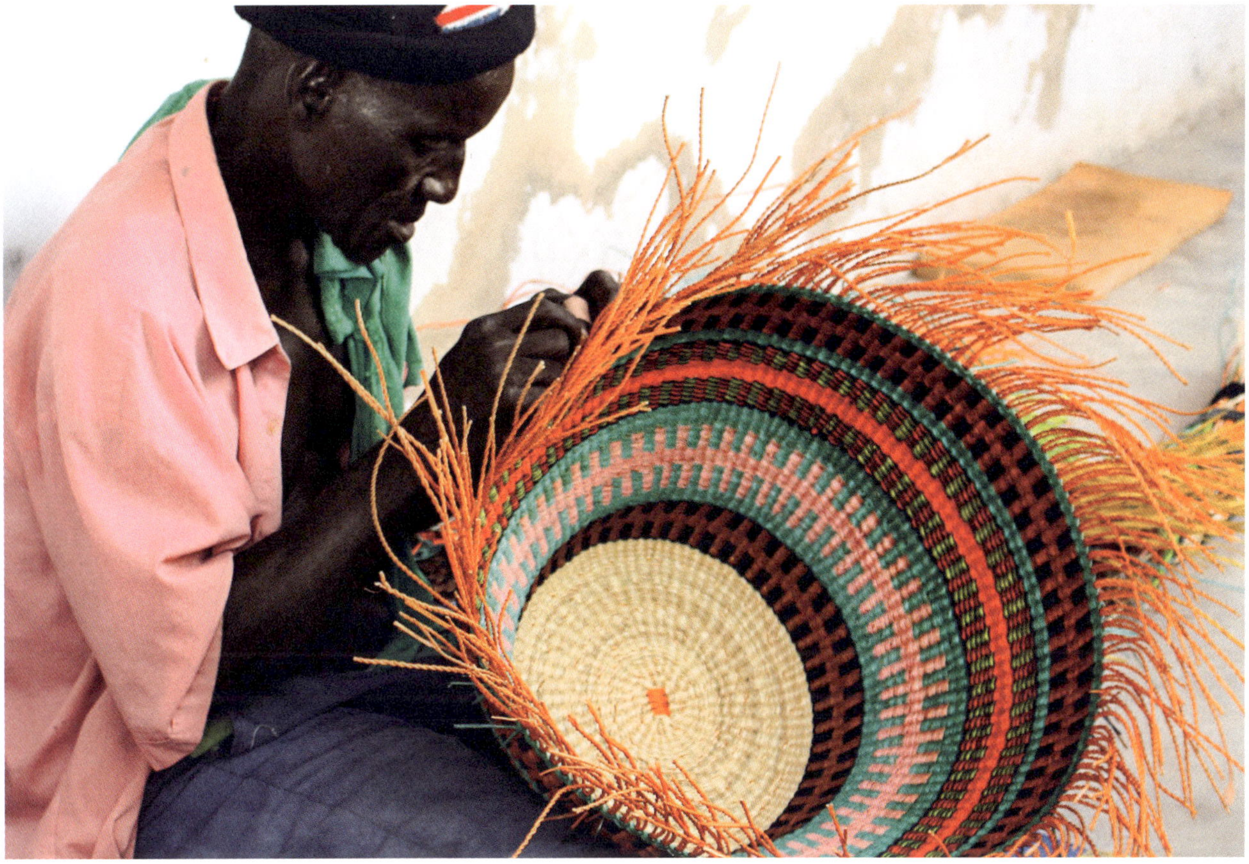

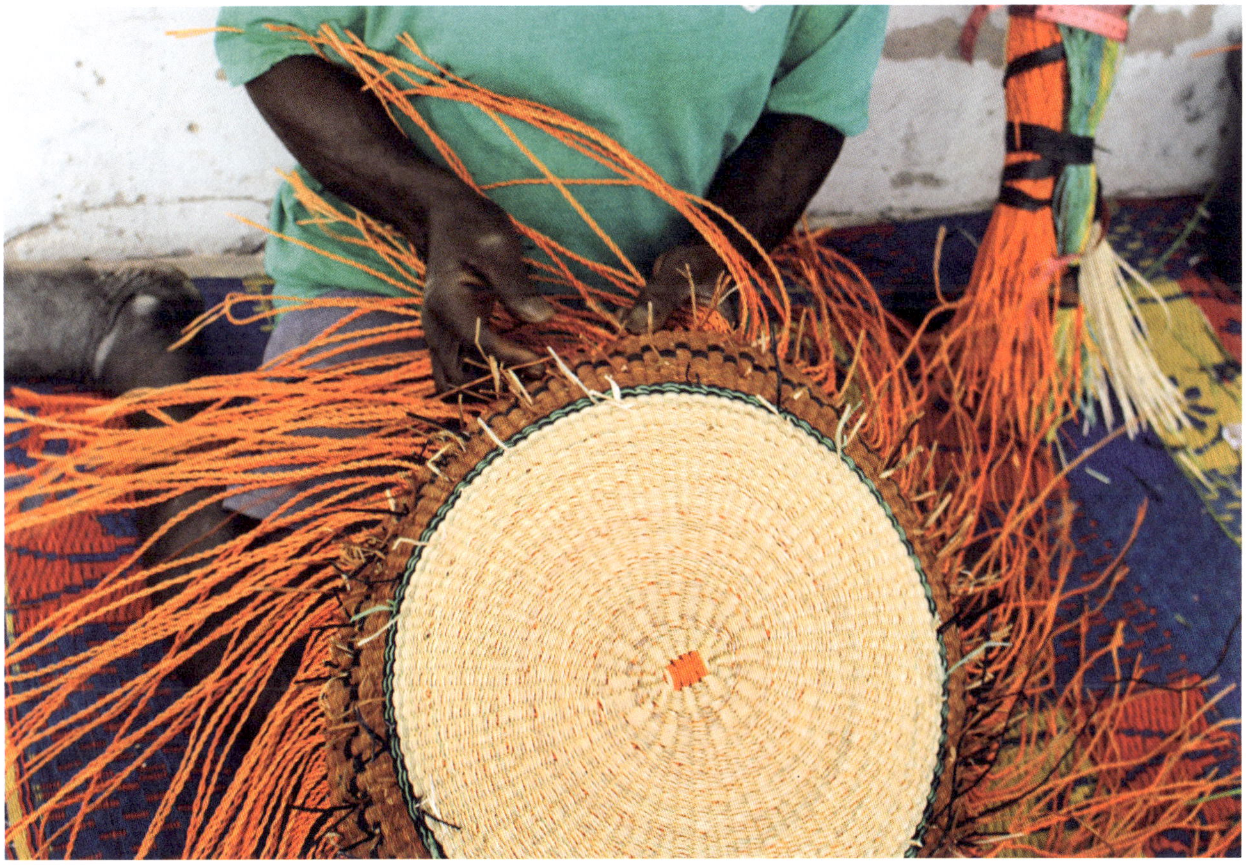

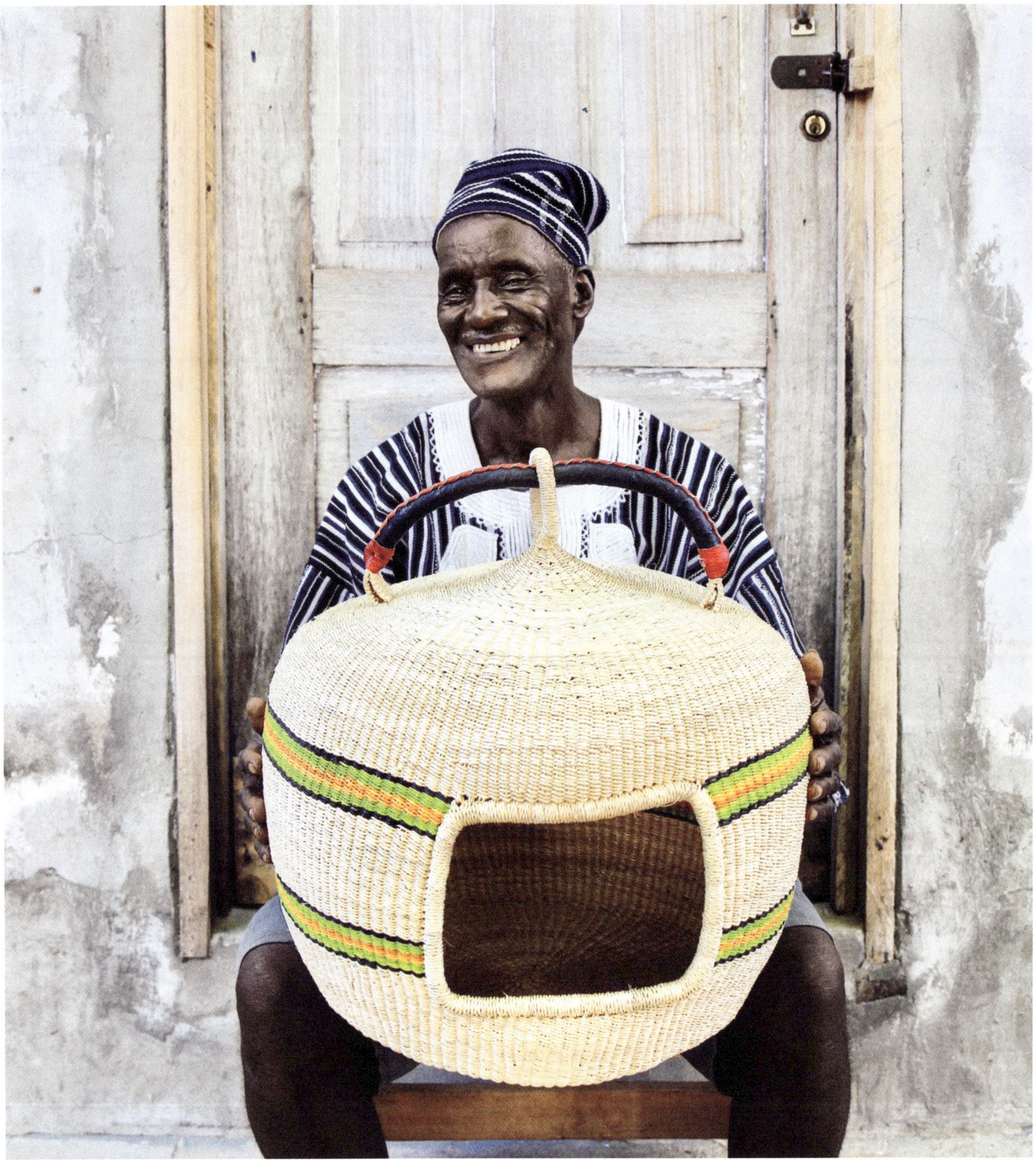

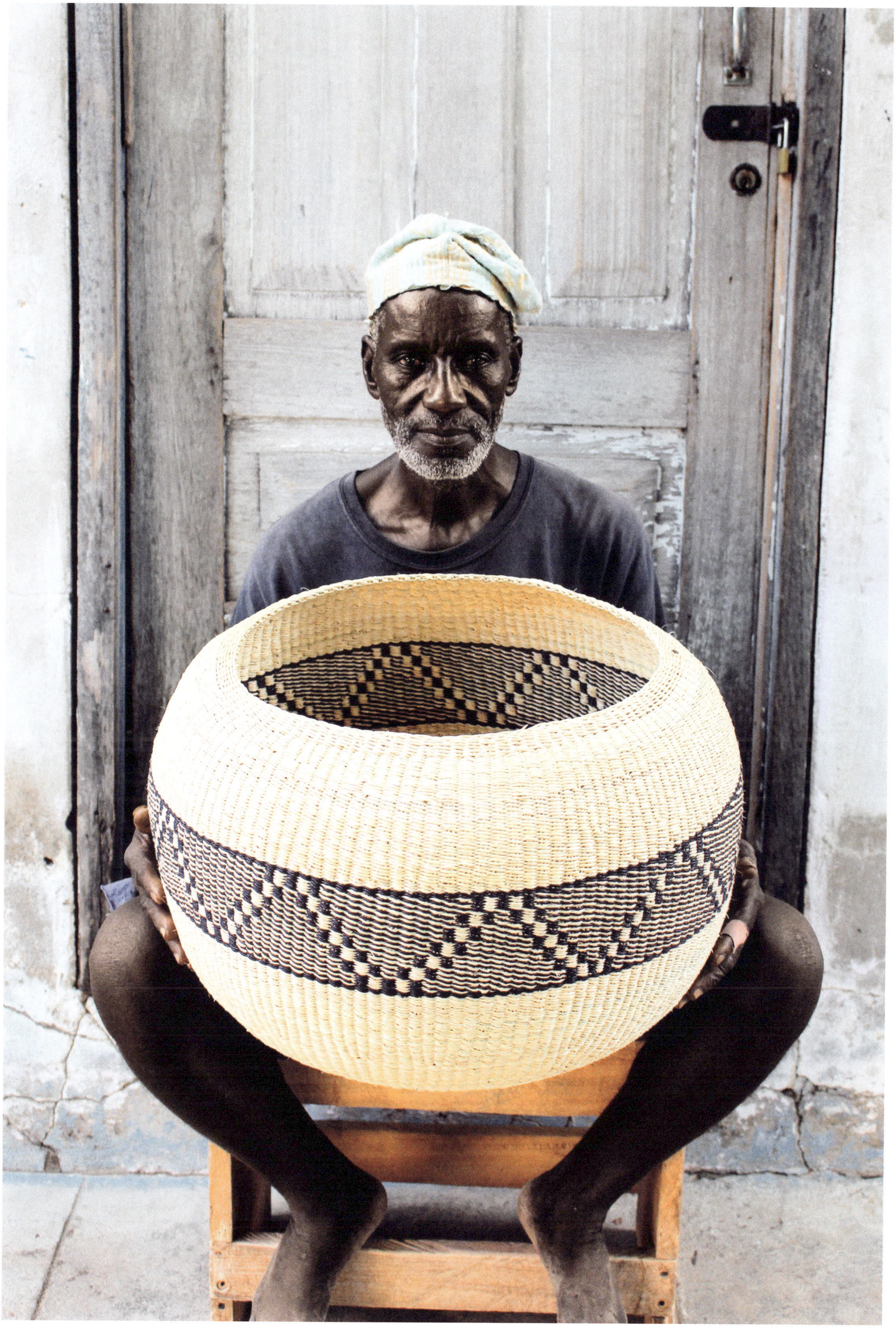

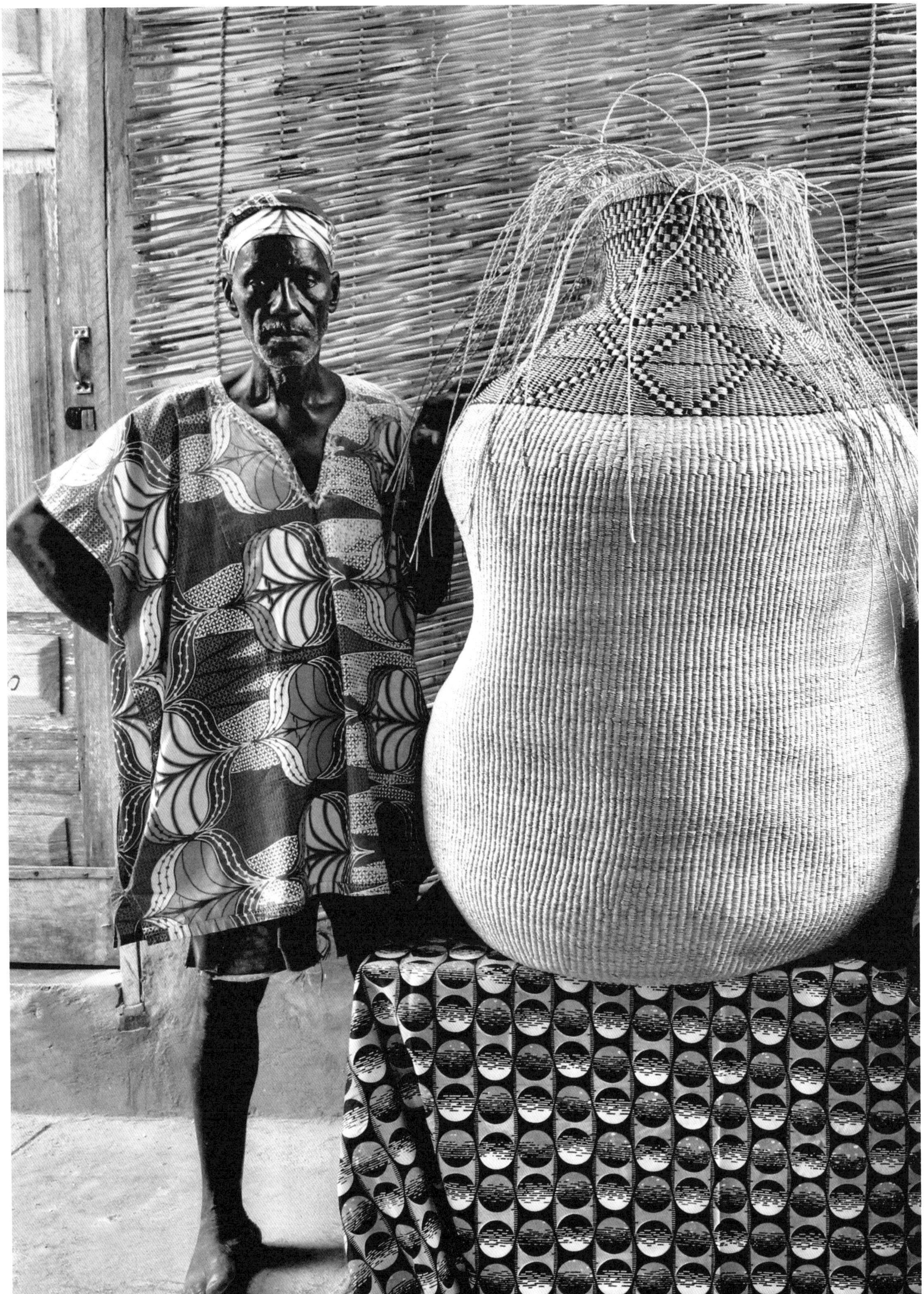

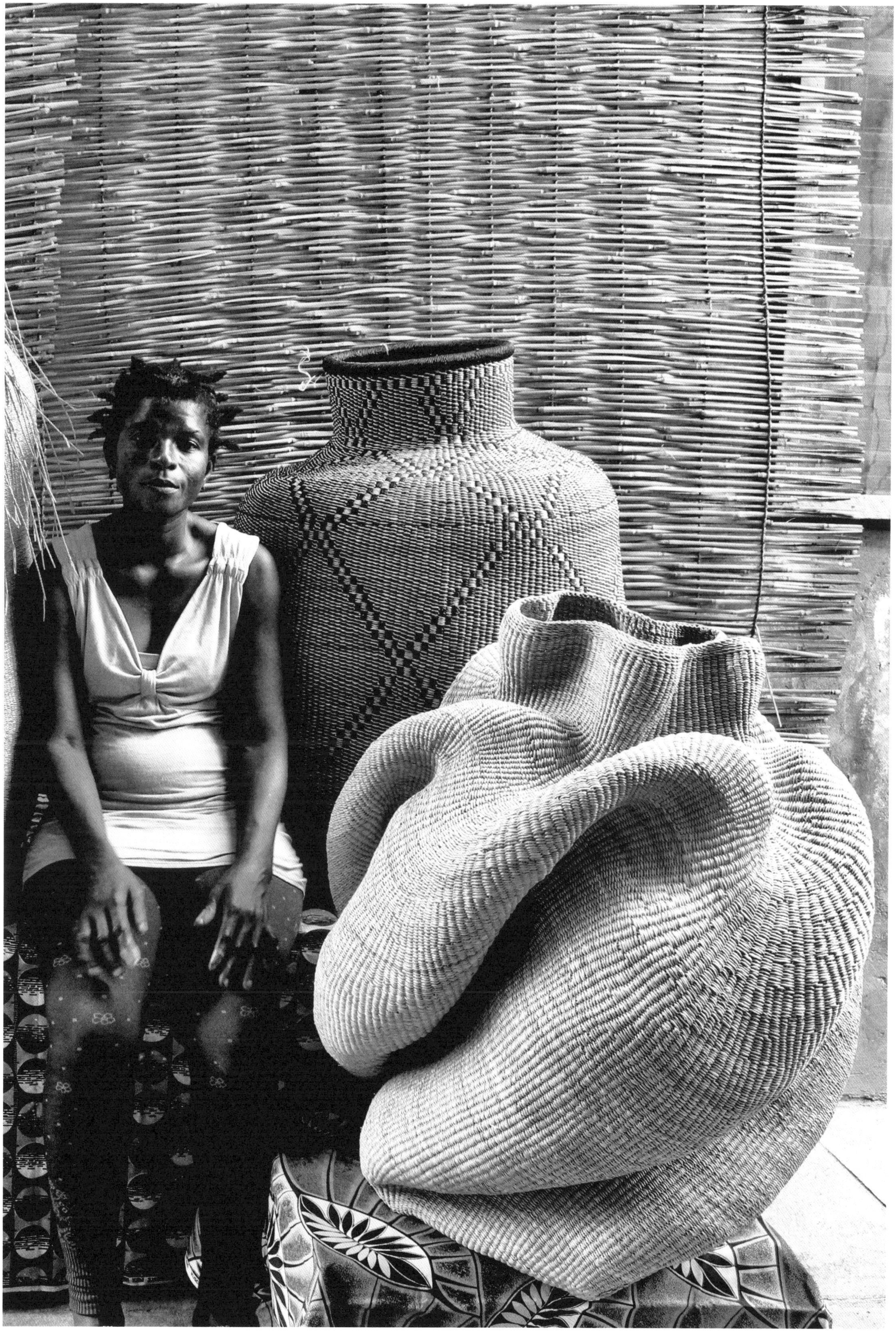

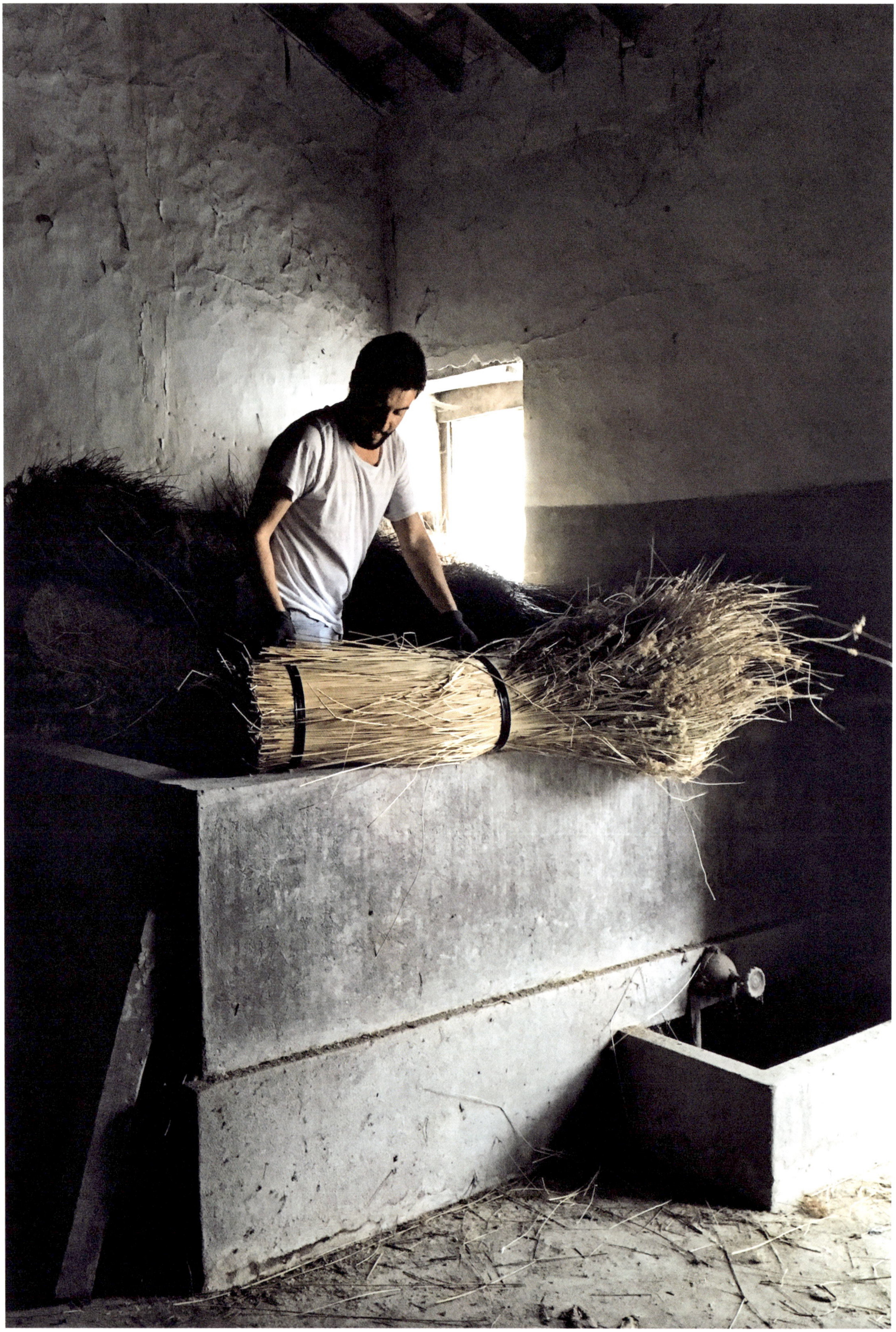

Nuno Henriques

Basket maker

Castanheira,
Portugal

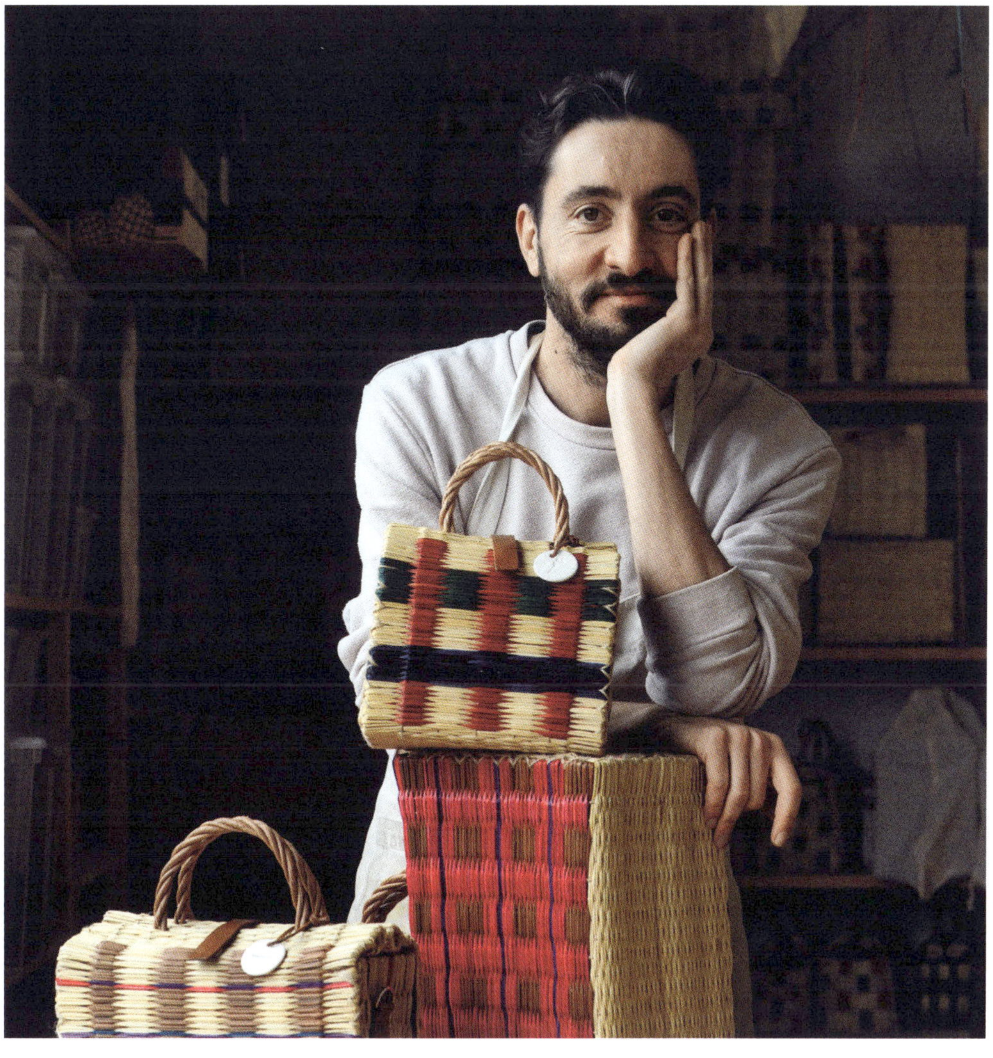

My name is Nuno Henriques, and I work with young, talented craftspeople to perpetuate the tradition of basketmaking.

I studied painting at the faculty of fine arts in Lisbon before moving to Berlin in 2008. There, I met like-minded people who aspired to a society founded on trust and respect—something that was very different from what I had learned in Portugal. In Berlin, I could truly be myself.

In 2010, while still living in Germany, I created the brand Toino Abel, which I named after my grandfather, whom I adored. I wanted to understand the hidden story that lay behind these baskets, to learn more about their origins and the people who make them. I knew that basketmaking was becoming a dying trade and that it was only a question of time before it vanished entirely. The last generation of artisan basket makers was going to die out and with them their history, their skills, and the many basket designs they had created.

So I decided to radically change my life: I left Berlin, the city I loved, for Castanheira, where people have been handcrafting baskets for generations. I joined the "old ladies' club," sitting with them around two or three rudimentary looms in their courtyards, listening to their stories, their pain, and their silence.

When I arrived, many of the basket makers were approaching retirement and were extremely resistant to change. I was reserved at first, then I started to wonder why these baskets were made as they were, and rarely found an answer. So I put together a team and we worked with the residents to guide, support, and advise them. Over a period of five years, we increased basket makers' income by 120 percent. Since 2019, we have carried out each step in the basketmaking process ourselves: preparing the reeds, dyeing, weaving, sewing, and creating handles. Rather than negotiating a simple business deal with local craftspeople, we reached out to them and gained much from their skills. In the process, we have become artisans ourselves.

Today in Castanheira we use *Juncus effusus*: a reed that we harvest from the wild, free of treatments and pesticides. Resistant to insects and disease, reeds are very hardy plants that grow in wetlands around the world. Seasonal workers harvest them for us about sixty miles (100 km) away, south of the Tagus River. But when they retire, we may find ourselves facing a material shortage. In a bid to avoid this, we created an experimental plantation and, decades after they had last been seen, we reintroduced reeds into our village, where the baskets are made. With a little luck, we'll be able to enjoy guaranteed harvests and accessible raw materials to support a simple, convivial, local economy.

In light of the pandemic, I fear that industrial manufacturers will not meet their environmental objectives, on the pretext that they have suffered significant economic losses. I've seen manufacturers use climate change to their advantage in their marketing strategies and engage in greenwashing. Our lifestyle is a threat to our future. We must consume less and favor small, independent firms, quality, and sustainability. In this way, craftsmanship and small-scale local production could truly be a model for our society.

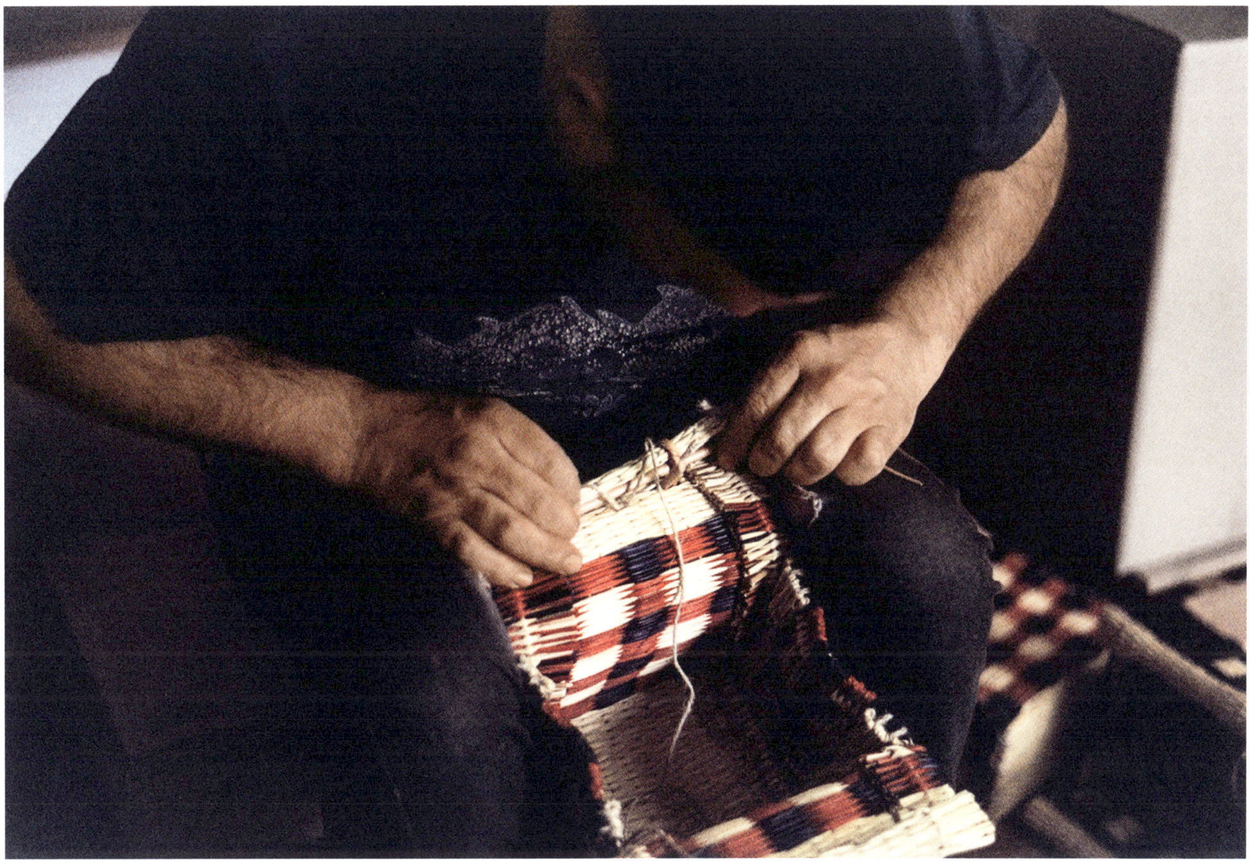

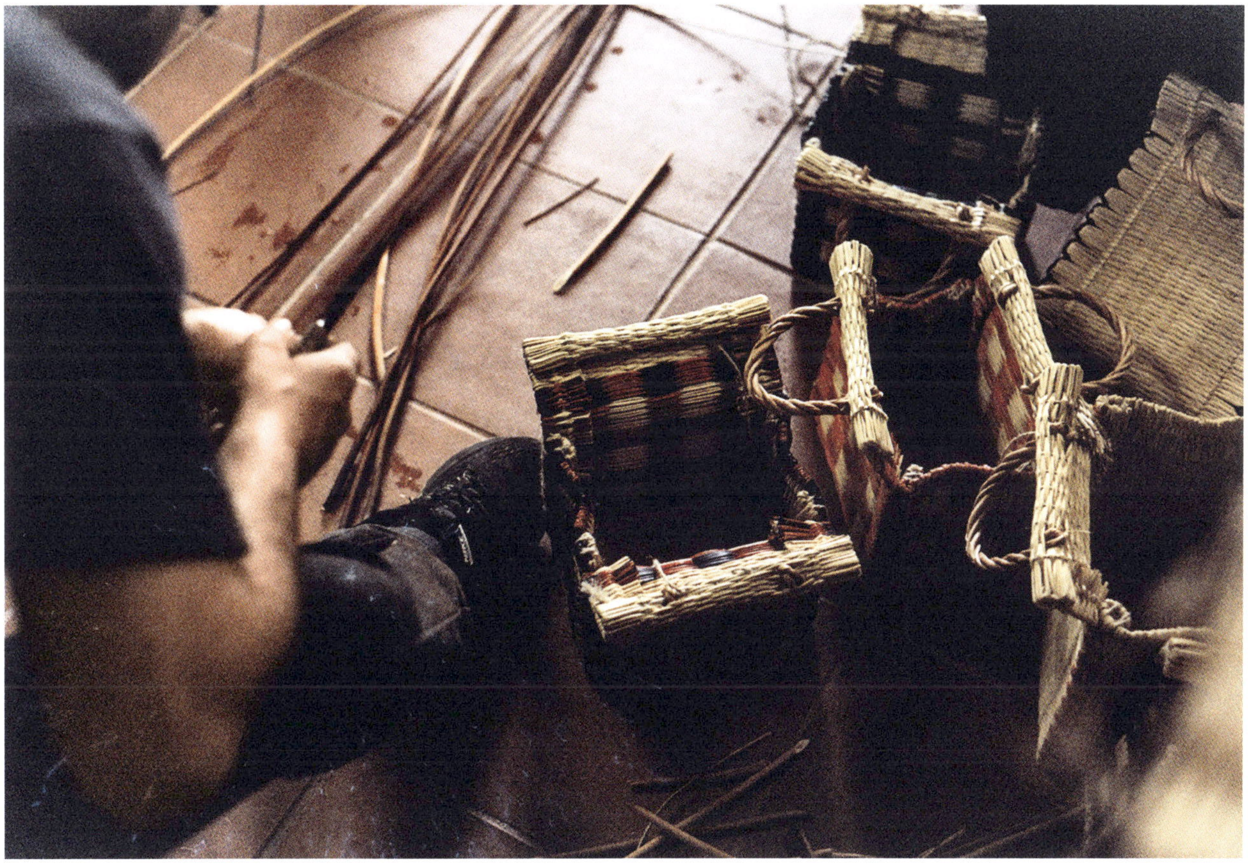

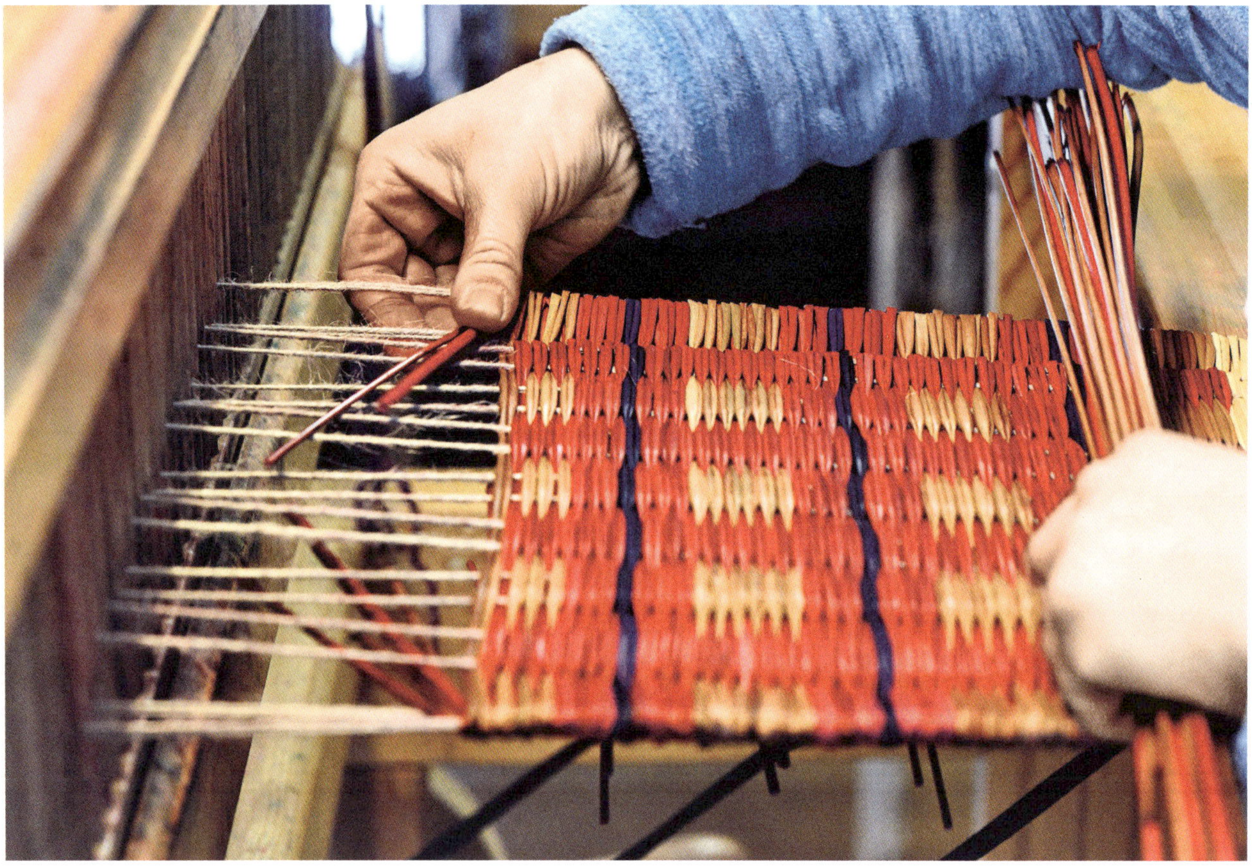

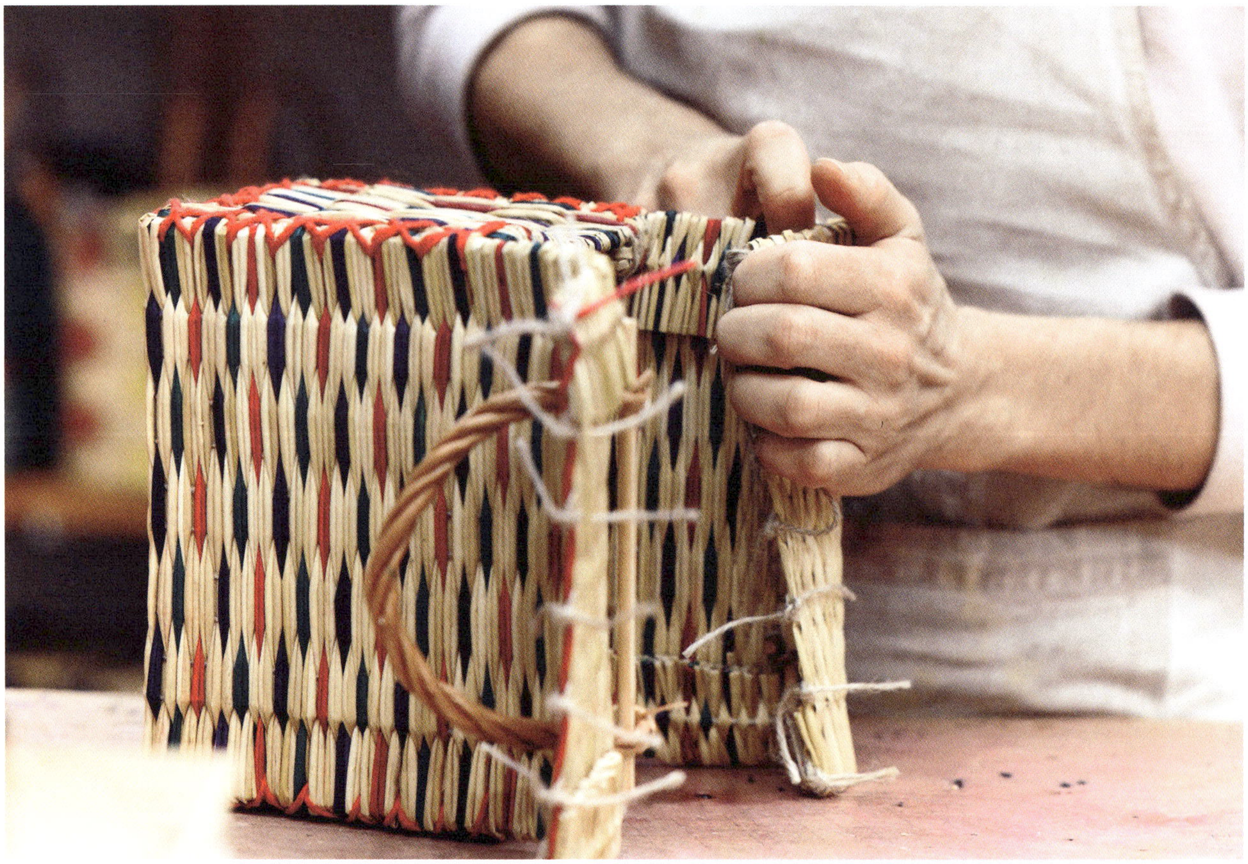

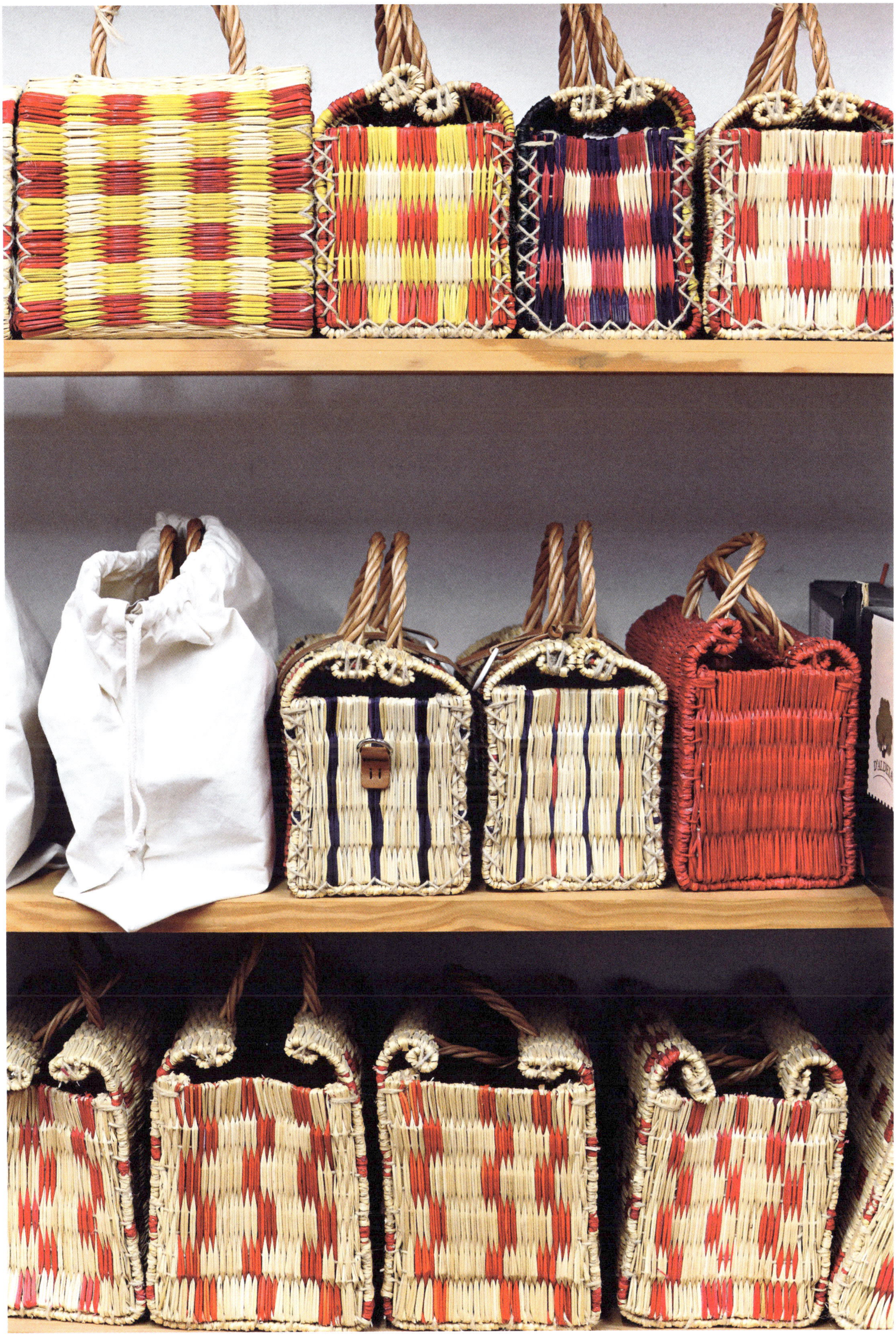
D'ALDEIA

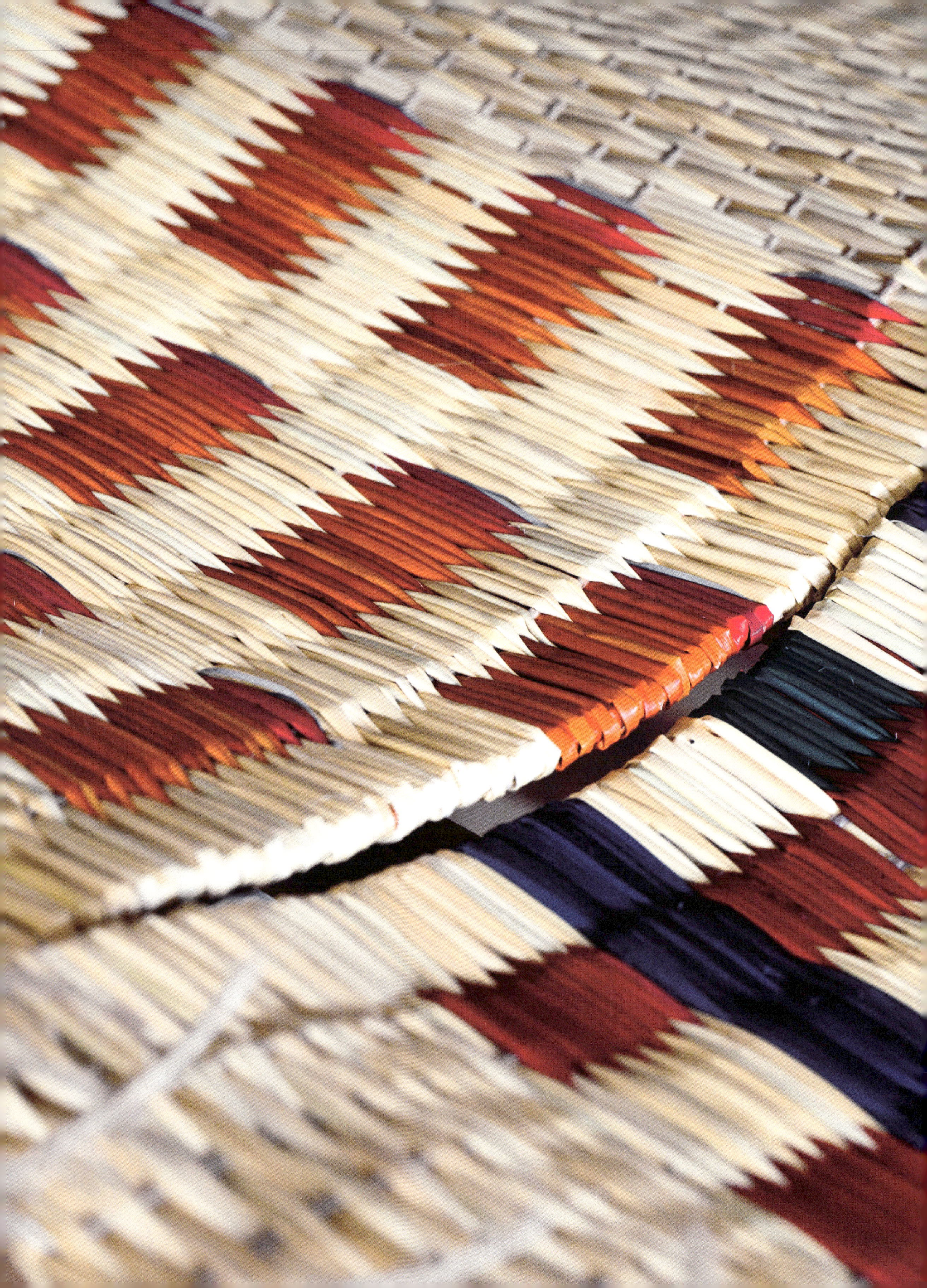

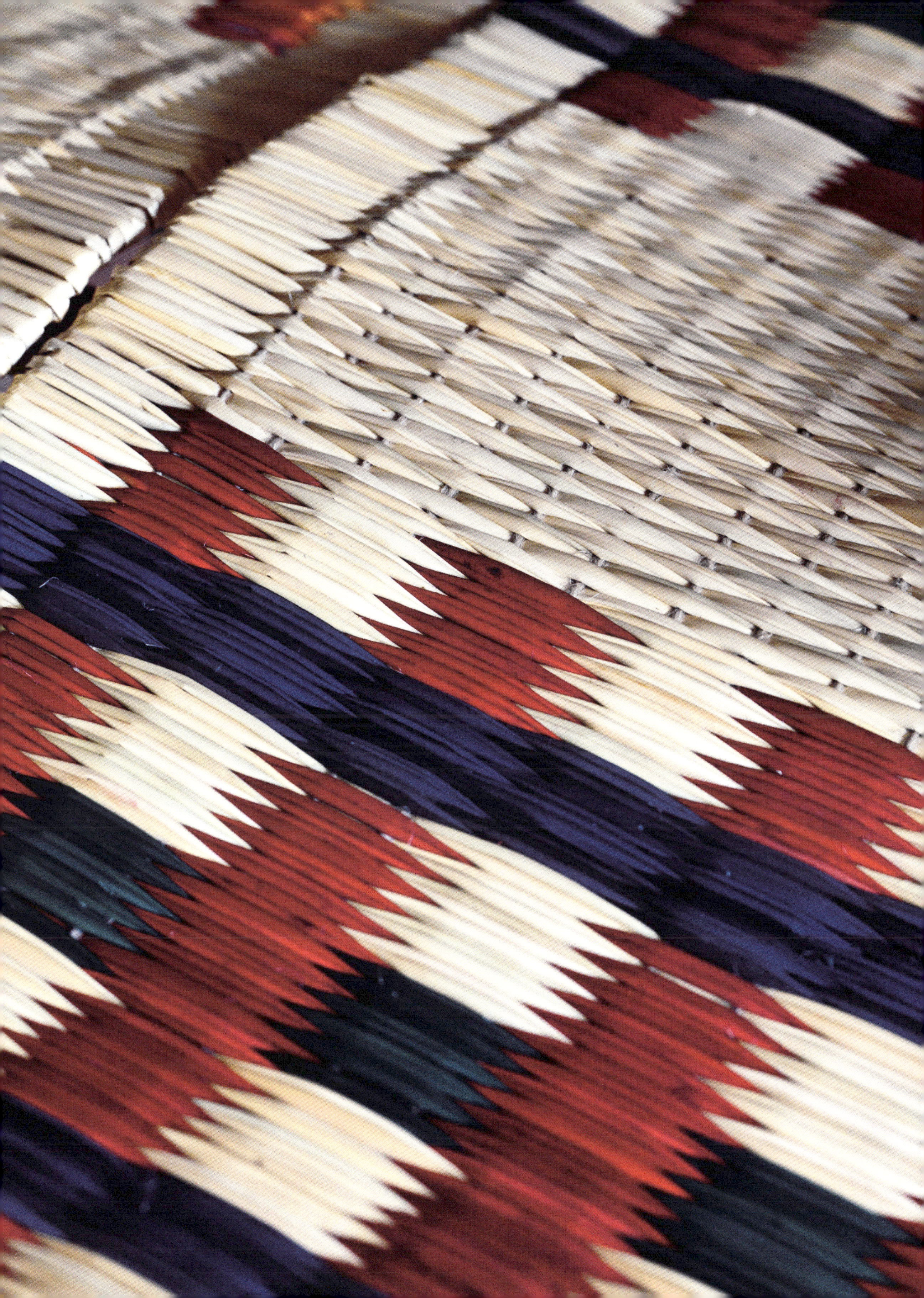

Paper

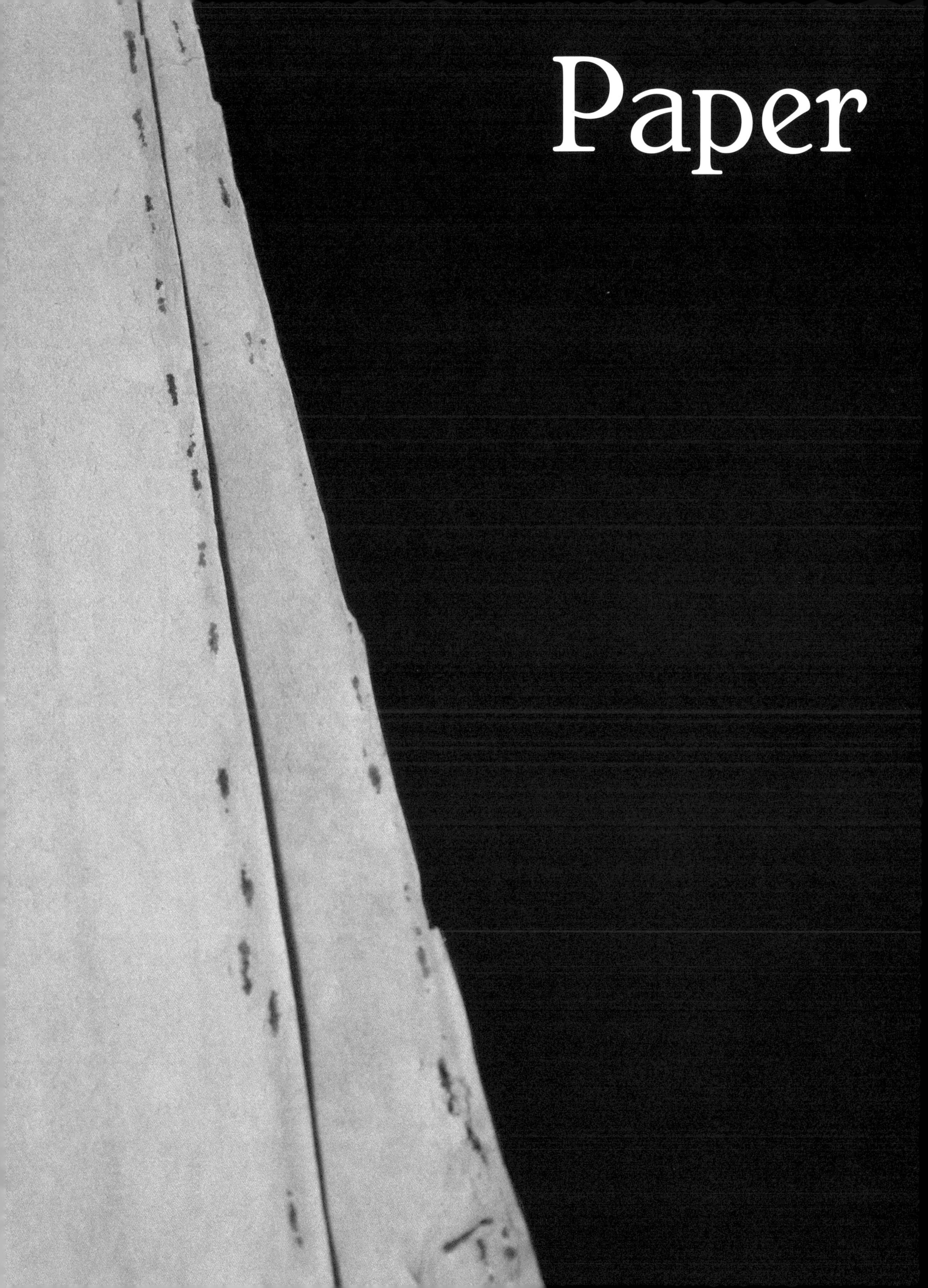

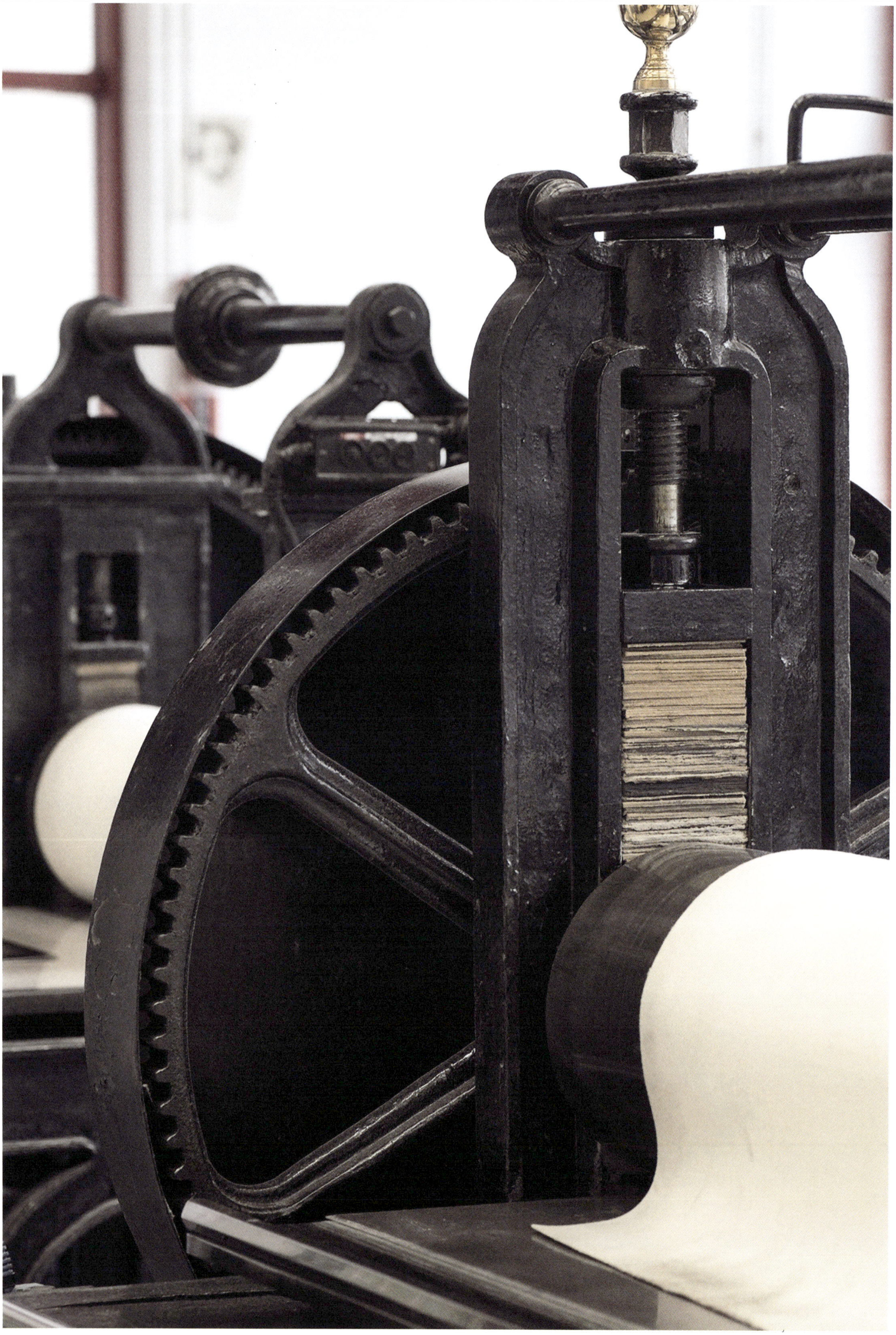

Lucile Vanstaevel

Printmaker and engraver

La Plaine Saint-Denis, France

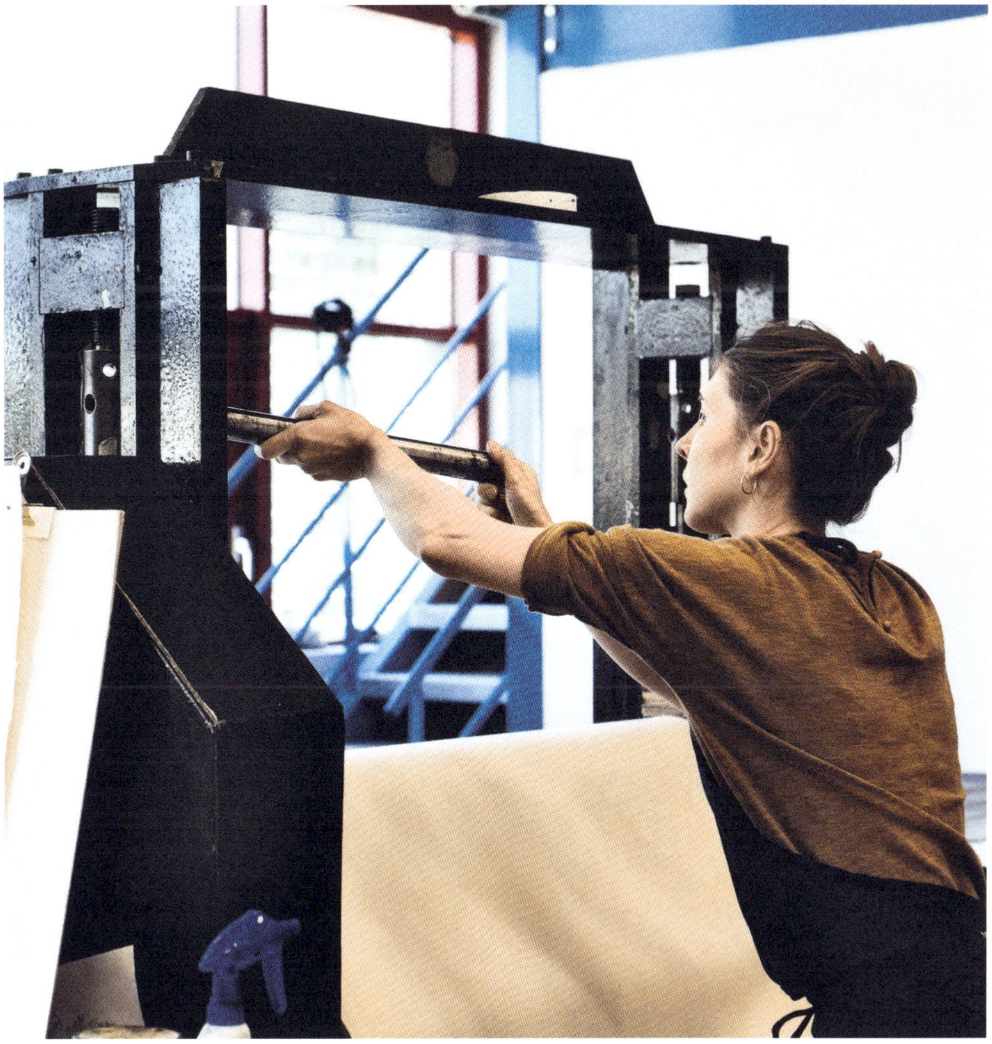

My name is Lucile Vanstaevel. I'm a printmaker specialized in intaglio: a very old technique developed in the seventeenth century that uses an engraved metal plate to reproduce an image.

After studying applied arts in high school and training in the embroidery atelier at the École Duperré in Paris, I enrolled at the École Estienne to study the printed image, a field that held a strong attraction for me. I studied under the painter and engraver Bo Halbirk, who taught me about the subtleties of inking techniques and working with color, which can make printing a creative process.

I continued my training in the Louvre's chalcography [the art of engraving on copper or brass] workshop, which holds more than fourteen thousand engraved copper plates. That was nine years ago, and I'm still working there today. Until recently, the printmaking profession was predominately male. I was very surprised to learn that I was the first woman at the Louvre to print using chalcography techniques.

Printing consists of a set of endlessly repeated actions that require intense concentration: they must be thought out, evaluated, and selected according to the plate that is being used to print. The first step is to cover the surface of the engraved copper with a generous layer of ink to fill in each of the various incisions. The excess ink is removed with a soft muslin cloth, then with the palm of the hand. Finally, a sheet of damp paper is placed over the inked plate and both are passed through a press: the ink is transferred to the paper, creating a printed, reproducible image also known as an etching. A print run should be consistent, but each individual print will be unique in some way.

The paper designed for intaglio is "rag paper" or "vellum paper," composed primarily of cotton fibers. It is manufactured according to different processes and produced in a variety of weights, and the choice of paper depends on the size and thickness of the plate. Paper is crucial in the process of reproducing images. It has to be thick enough to withstand the printing plate, but supple enough to be forced into the deepest engraved lines and to pick up ink from the smallest incisions. This is why the paper is immersed in water before printing, toincrease its flexibility. I particularly enjoy this step because the paper gradually changes in appearance: the fibers swell, and the paper sways and floats on the surface. It comes to life in a way, and becomes an extremely malleable organic material.

We often work alone from historic plates, commemorating the work of past engravers, so collaborating with a living artist provides an opportunity for stimulating exchanges enriched by fascinating background research. Artists—whether painters, visual artists, textile designers, photographers, or sculptors—are often unfamiliar with engraving techniques. We work with emerging talents such as Rosanna Lefeuvre, as well as internationally recognized artists, including Hervé Di Rosa, Eva Jospin, Jean-Michel Othoniel, JR, and Annette Messager. They bring me a drawing, an idea, or a photograph, which allows me to understand their expectations, and we discuss them together so that I can suggest the most suitable technique for their project. Then we begin engraving, and I help them transfer the drawing to the copper plate. In rare cases, when an artist entrusts me with engraving the plate based on their drawing, I take a more interpretive approach.

Like many artisanal crafts, printing requires much care and delicacy, and close attention to detail.

In a constantly changing technical environment, the artisan approaches their profession according to a different relationship with time: one that is longer and more patient—out of time, in a way. It's this unique relationship with time that I believe connects the "know" and the "how" in know-how—an irreducible time made of detours, errors, and exchanges. In short, time that is living and human.

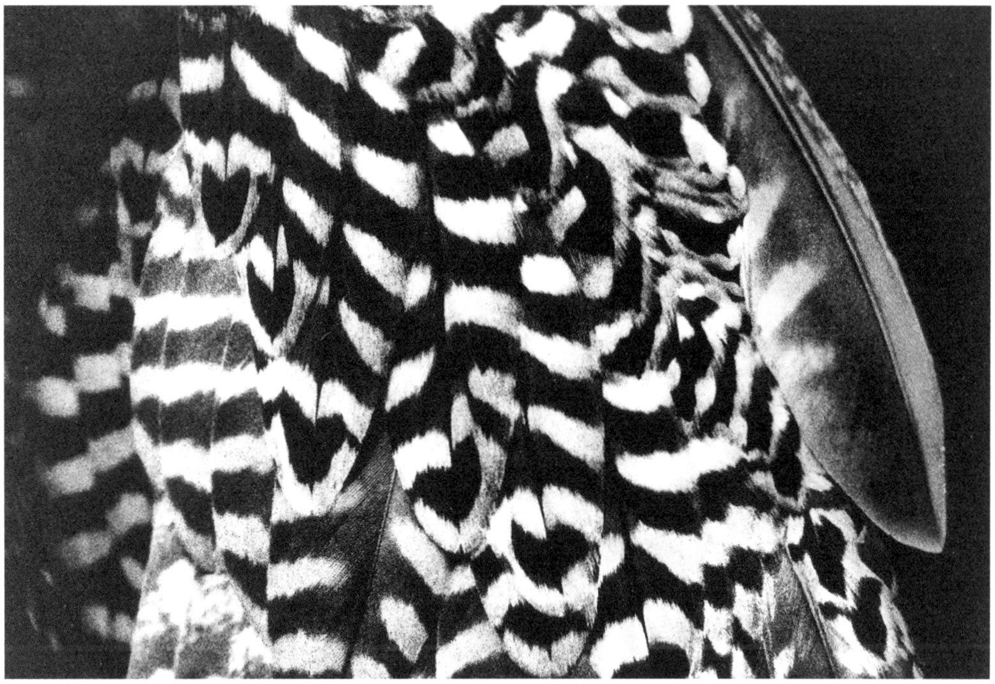

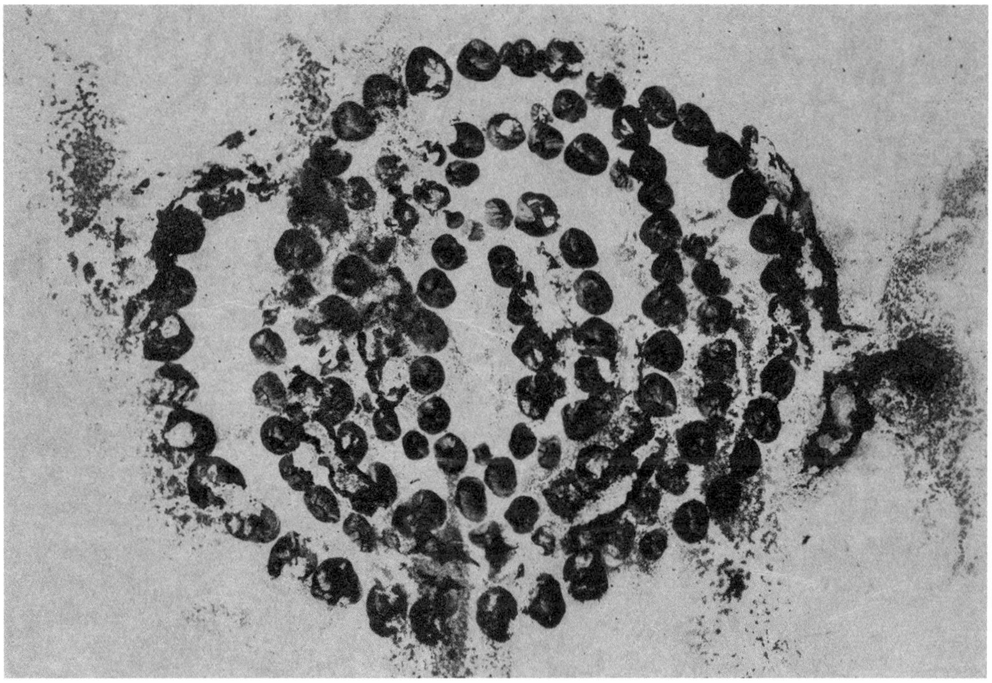

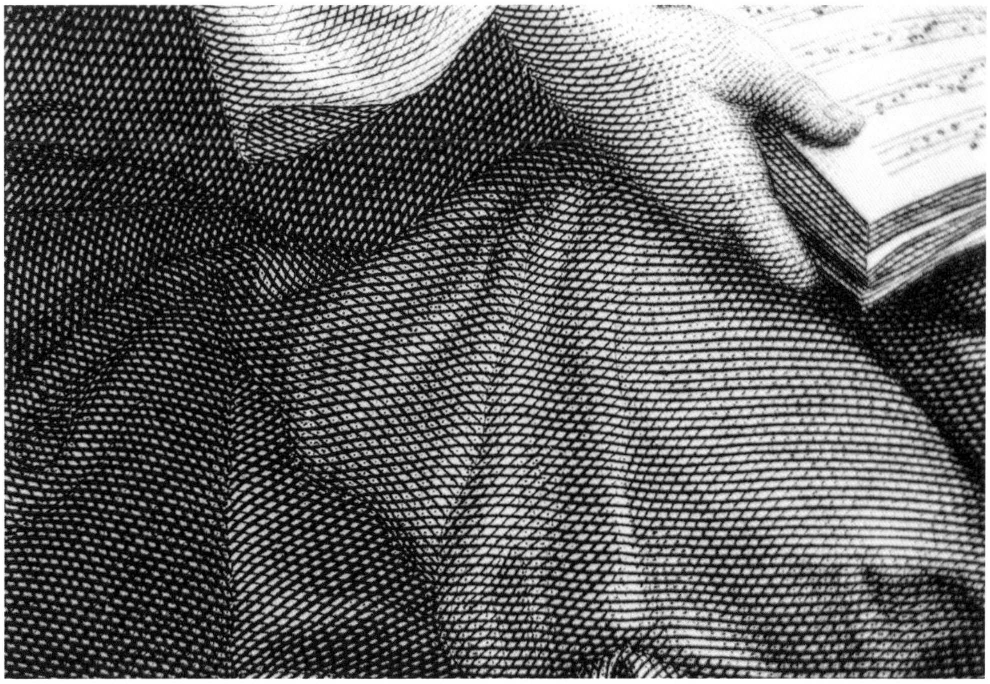

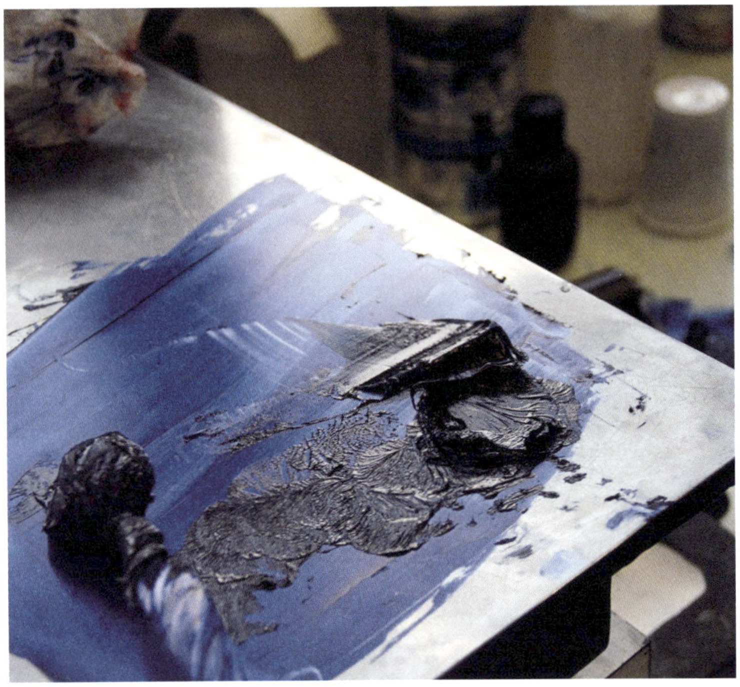

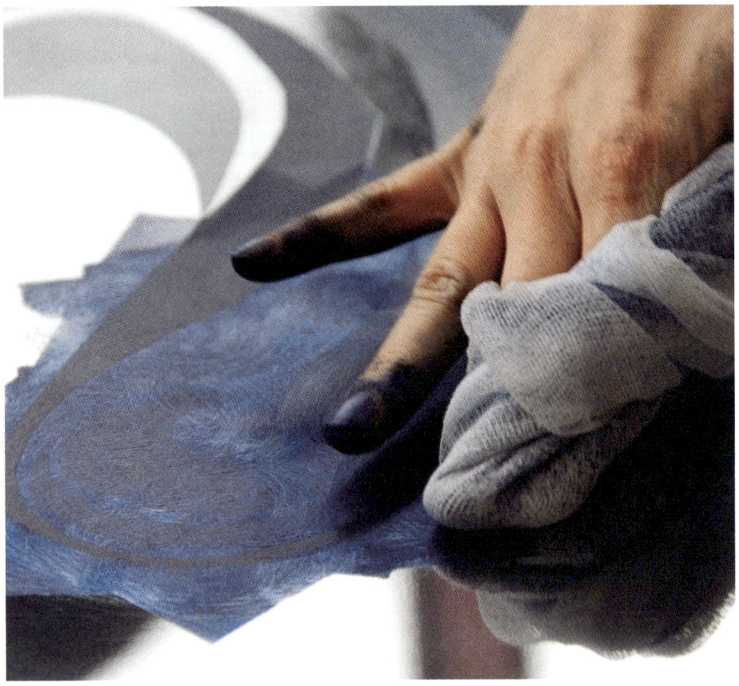

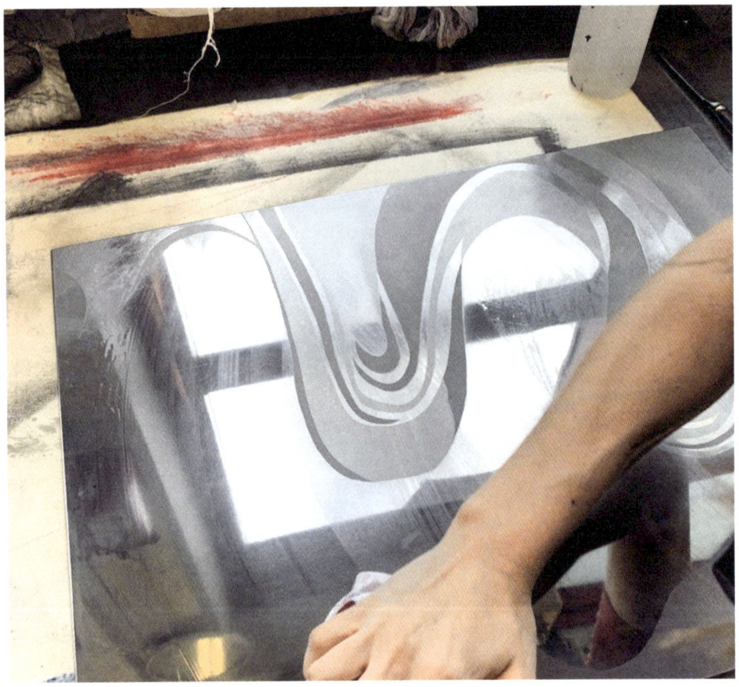

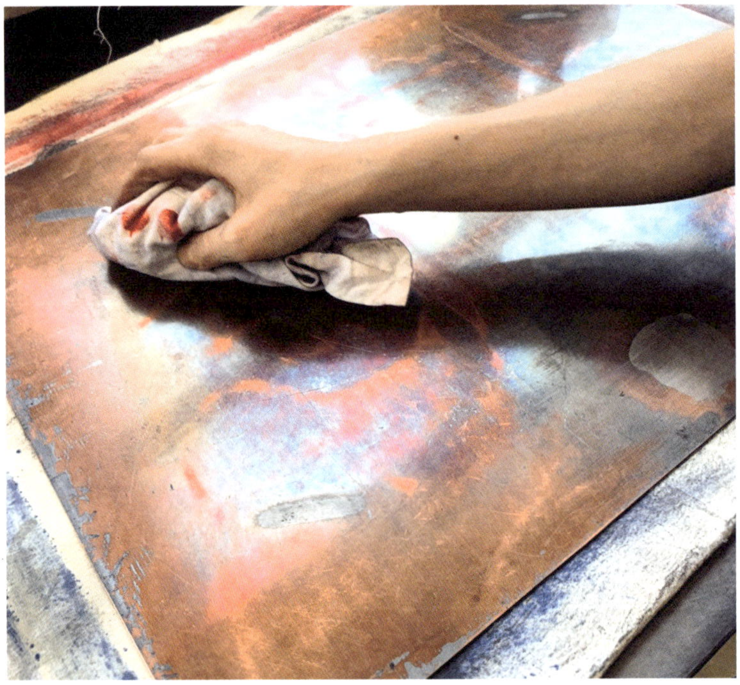

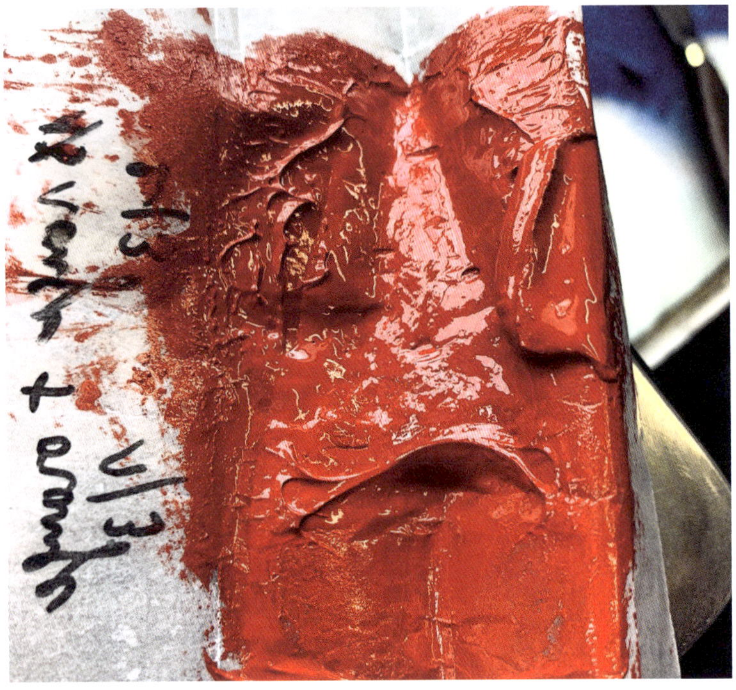

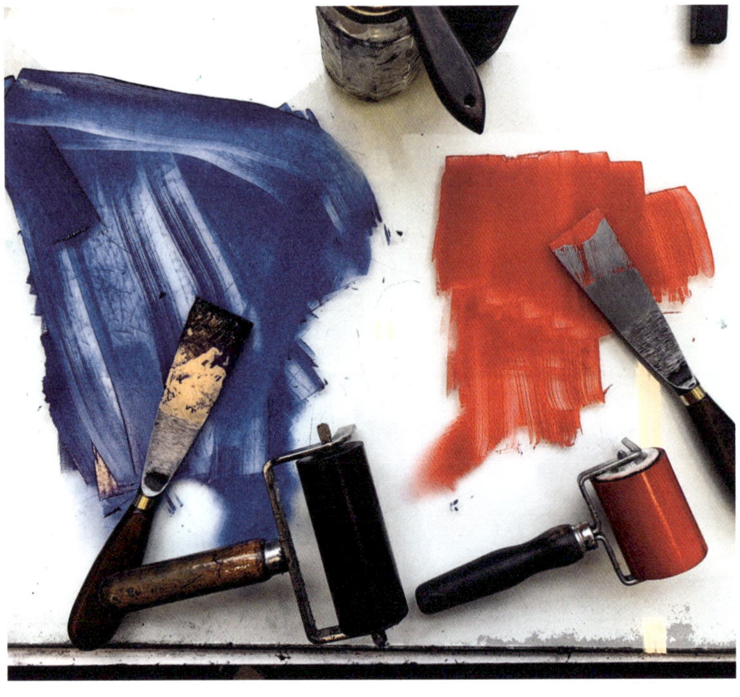

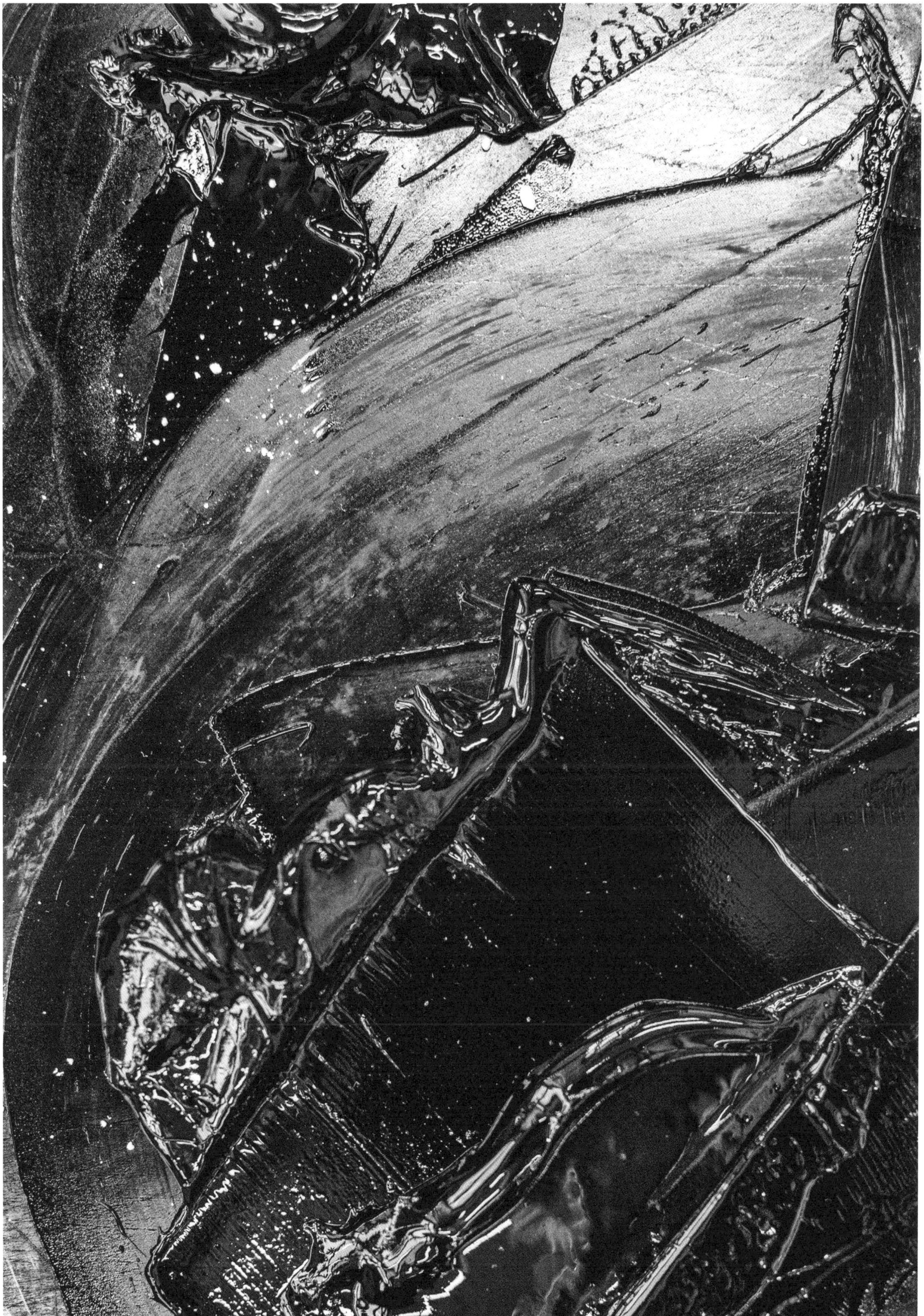

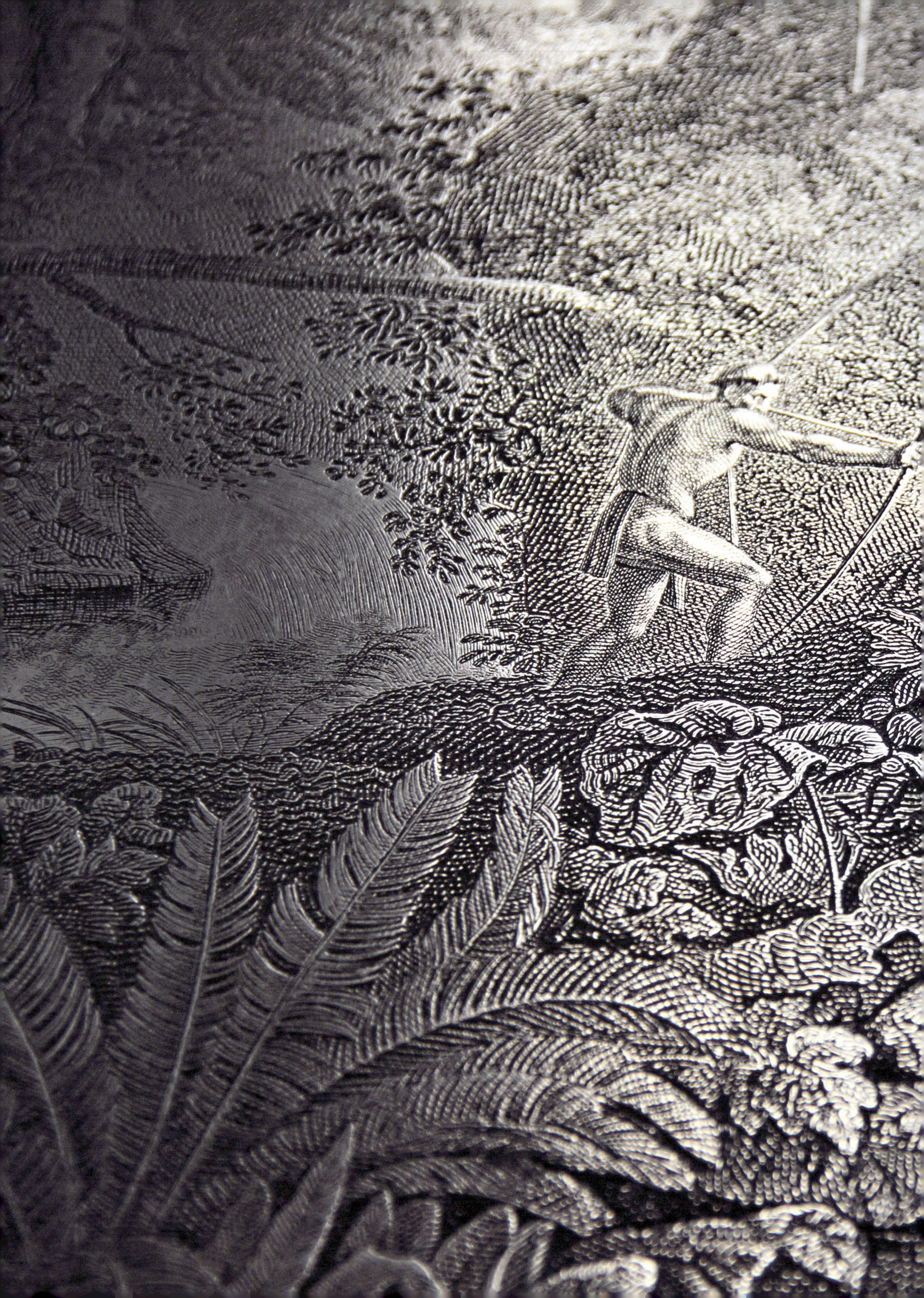

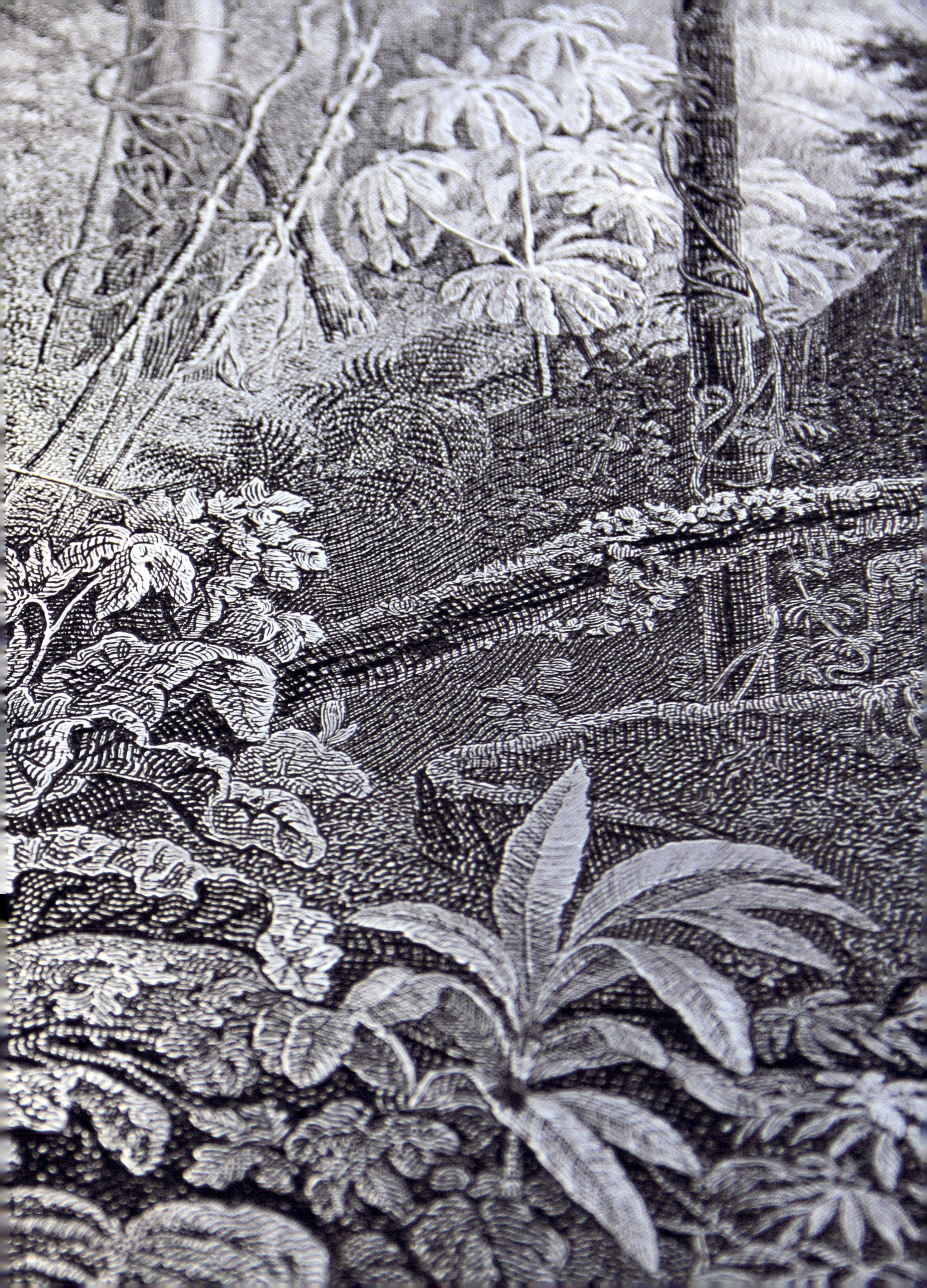

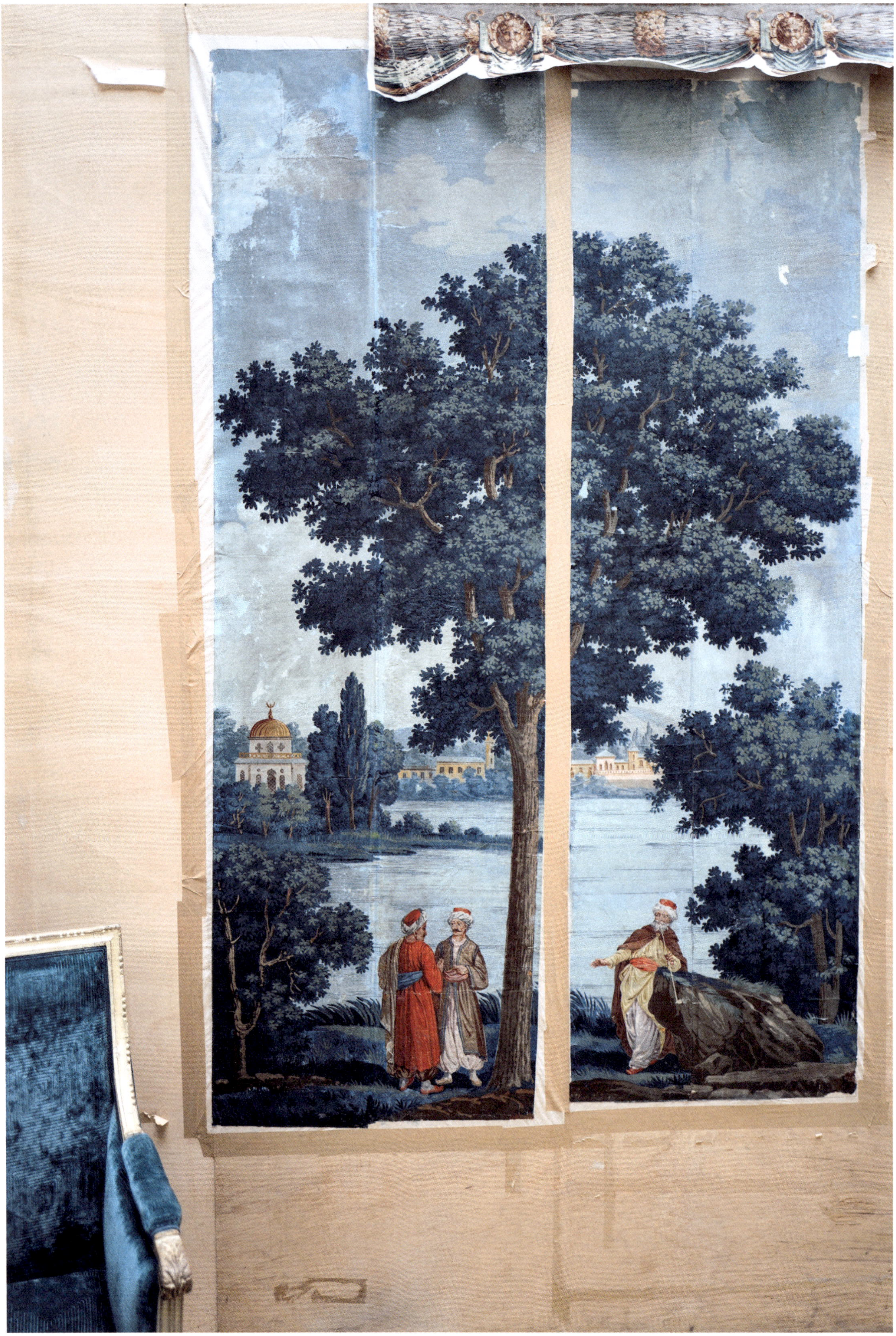

Béatrice Racine

Wallpaper restorer

Paris, France

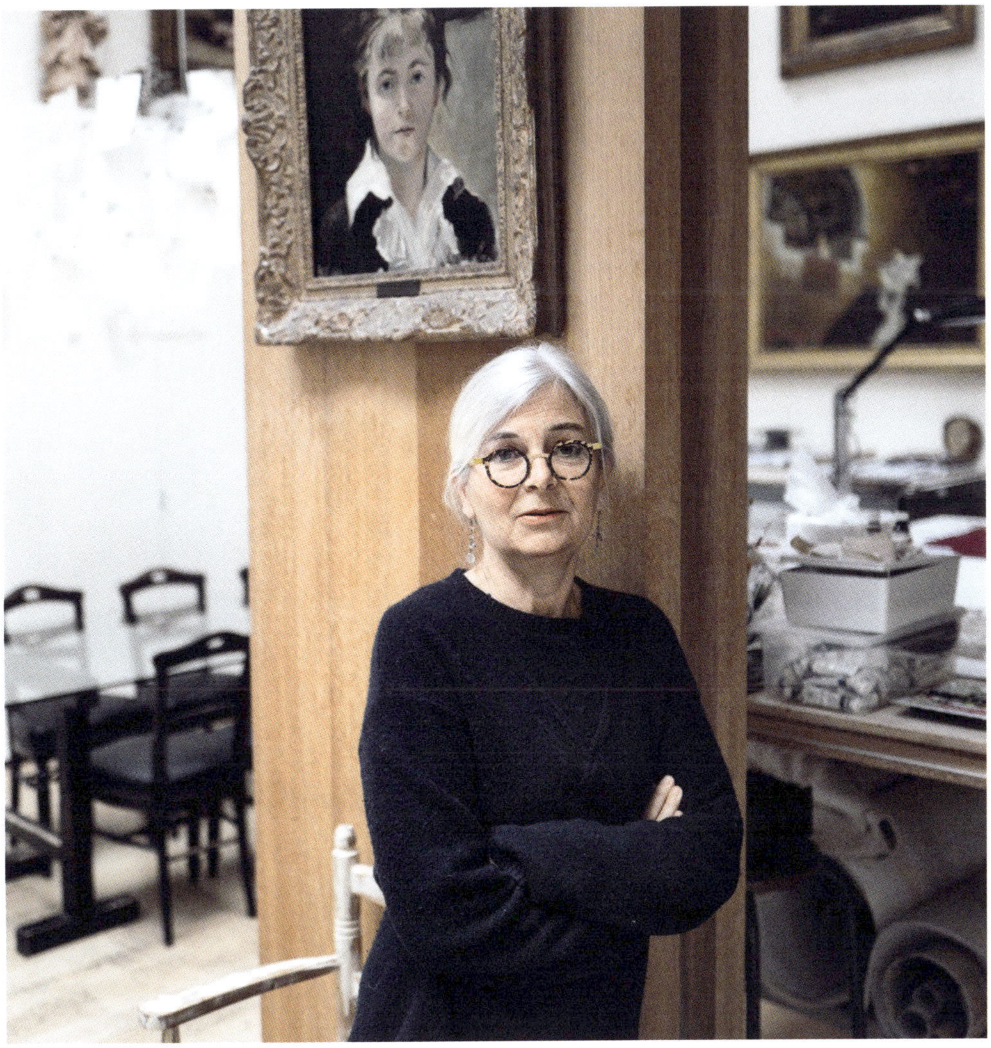

Wallpaper holds the memories of a house; it always has a story to tell about the residence or its inhabitants.

My name is Béatrice Racine. I conserve and restore artworks on paper, particularly nineteenth-century panoramic wall coverings, which were the pride of major French manufacturers and exported throughout the world. I also restore drawings and pastels on paper.

I grew up in Paris, in a large family that maintained strong ties to the land. I was not predisposed to study art; a magnificent wall covering in the dining room of our family home is what ultimately inspired my calling. I had been studying for an undergraduate degree in classical literature at the Sorbonne University when my grandmother decided she wanted to restore the wallpaper in her country home. It was a remarkable set of panels called *Les Chasses de Compiègne*, produced in 1815 and designed by the painter Carle Vernet. On the advice of Odile Nouvel, a wallpaper curator at the Musée des Arts Décoratifs, she entrusted it to a restorer in Paris. I often visited him in his workshop, and, perhaps in an attempt to get rid of me, he offered to teach me the trade. He worked the old-fashioned way, using only traditional paste and paints. In addition to the knowledge he had accumulated over time, his strength lay in his intimate understanding of materials. Then, together with one of my sisters, I bought the press and plates from a historic Parisian wallpaper manufacturer, Hans & Fils: the project was short-lived, but I learned a lot. At the same time, I was pursuing work as a restorer, but I quickly realized that the profession had begun to evolve and demanded more scientific knowledge, which spurred me to enroll in various training programs. The goal of restoration was no longer to make a work look shiny and new, which is how my first teacher viewed the craft, but rather to respect the integrity of the original as much as possible. Clarity should be restored to the work, but the aim is not to erase the traces of time, which, in fact, contribute to its charm.

I carried out my first large project over thirty years ago in Corsica. It involved a color copy of *Les Voyages du Capitaine Cook*, produced in 1804, that had enthralled Napoleon Bonaparte, who was first consul of France at the time. The wallpaper was complete, which is incredibly rare, and had lined the living-room walls of a beautiful home in Ajaccio for nearly two hundred years. I was tasked with removing and restoring it because the owners were selling their home and wanted to take the wallpaper with them.

The first step in the restoration process is to conduct a preliminary evaluation of the paper and the underlying walls. There's no point, for example, in restoring wallpaper on a wall with an untreated humidity issue. Wallpapers still in situ are usually pasted directly to the wall, so their restoration and long-term preservation begins with their removal. This delicate process often requires moistening the paper, which, when possible, is then plunged into a bath of pure water to remove all dirt and mold. Any residual paste is then meticulously scraped away from the back. If the wallpaper was pasted onto paper or fabric backing, this, too, must be removed. This step often reveals interesting information, such as inscriptions on the back of the paper, or newspaper pages that can be dated. Sometimes I find several layers of paper pasted on the same wall, which allows me to discover the history of tastes and trends as if reading a book.

The wallpaper is then dried and lined, panel by panel, with fine, sturdy Japanese paper. Once the wall covering has been stretched out on my workshop wall, restoration of the pictorial layer begins. For this, I use watercolor or pastel to fill in unsightly gaps or to reduce the intensity of stains that could not be removed with cleaning. Thanks to my initial training, and my previous experience with printing wallpapers, I am perfectly able to reproduce colors using techniques from the eighteenth and nineteenth centuries. But more importantly, this knowledge helps me to understand how an older wallpaper has changed over time. Finally, depending on its ultimate destination, the wallpaper is mounted on canvas so it can be hung on a wall with the least possible risk and moved, if necessary.

Older paper made from cotton rags, as opposed to wood-based industrial paper, is an extraordinary material. It is both extremely resistant—in the right conditions, it can last for centuries—and vulnerable: humidity, light, wear and tear, smoke, insects, and mold, not to mention human intervention, can cause serious damage. For this reason, most cotton-based wallpapers have now been lost.

Each paper has its own unique consistency and odor; each one is different and you can never be certain how an older paper will react to restoration. It all depends on its history. In this field, experience is crucial. With each project, I feel the same apprehension, followed by the same sense of relief, as I did when I first started out. In any case, it gives me immense pleasure to know that a carefully restored wallpaper will withstand the centuries and delight all those who look at it.

Today, French public collections of wall coverings are very rich, particularly the one at the Musée des Arts Décoratifs in Paris. But since works on paper should not be exposed to light for long periods of time, they are largely unknown to the general public. The Bibliothèque Nationale—the French national library—had the wonderful idea of digitizing its collection, amassed through legal deposit, and making it accessible online via Gallica, its digital library: the collection illustrates how bold and innovative nineteenth-century French wallpaper designers were, but twentieth-century and contemporary creators have proved equally inventive.

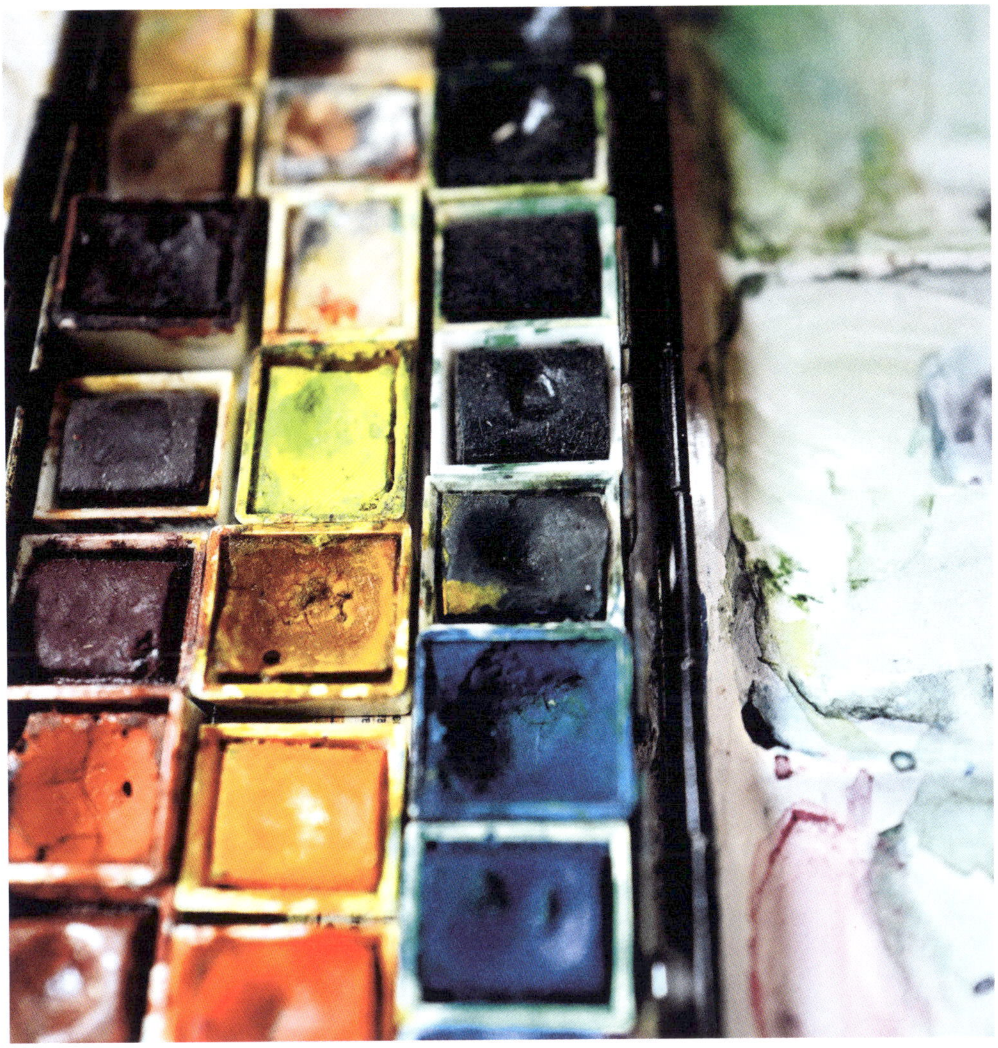

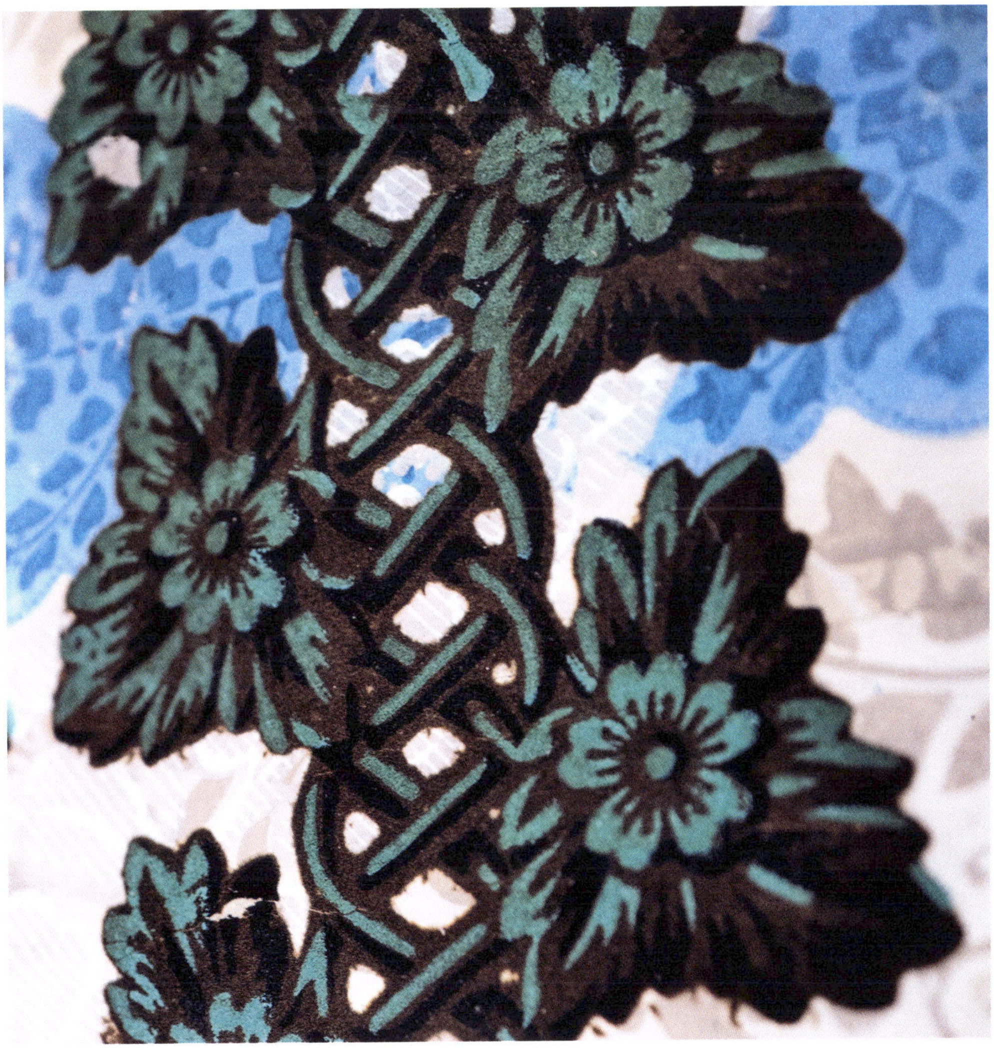

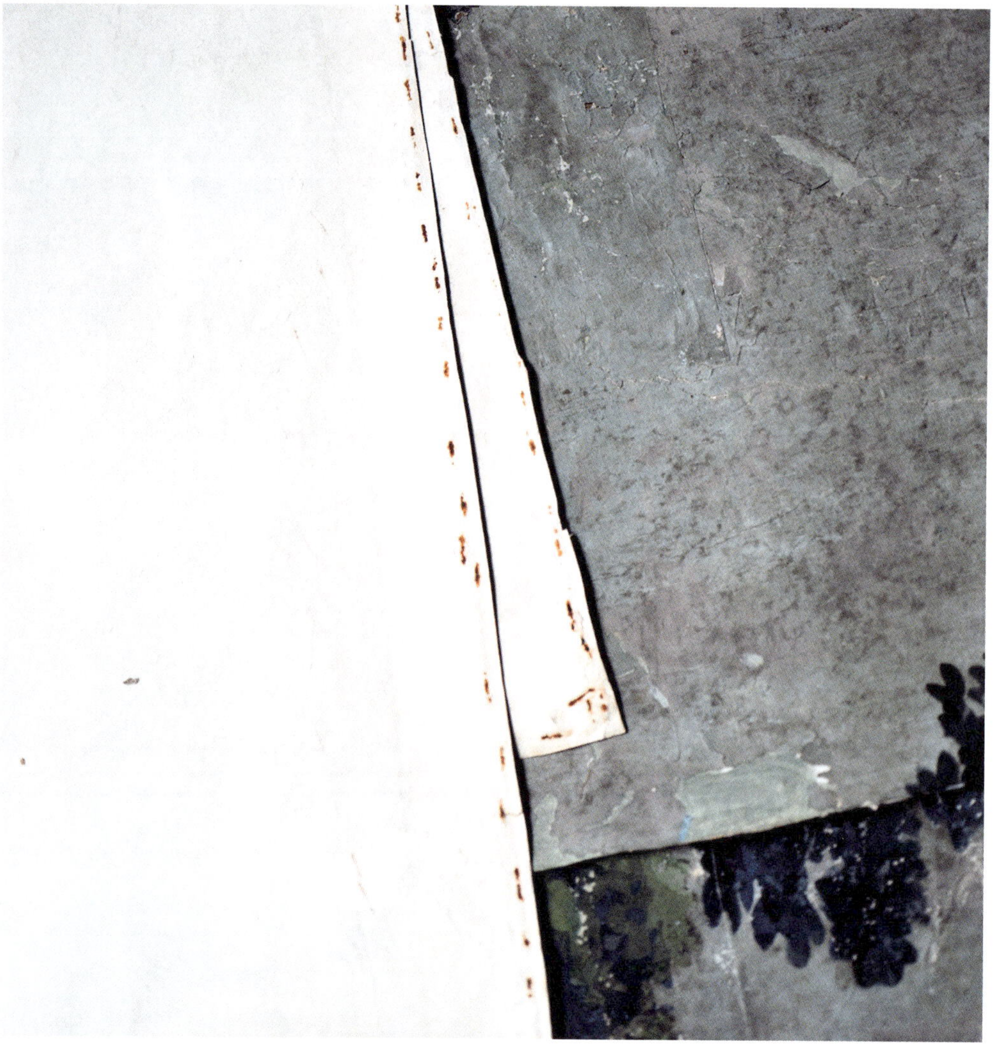

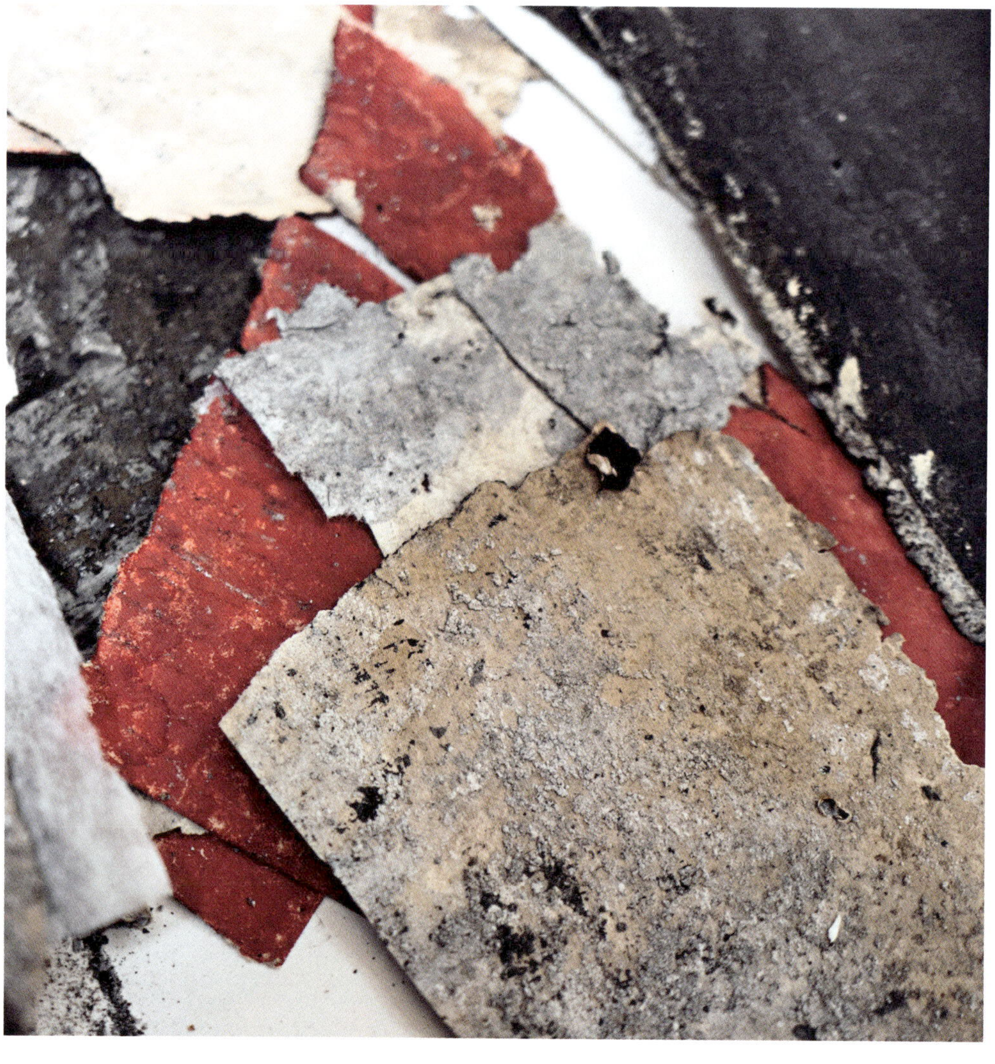

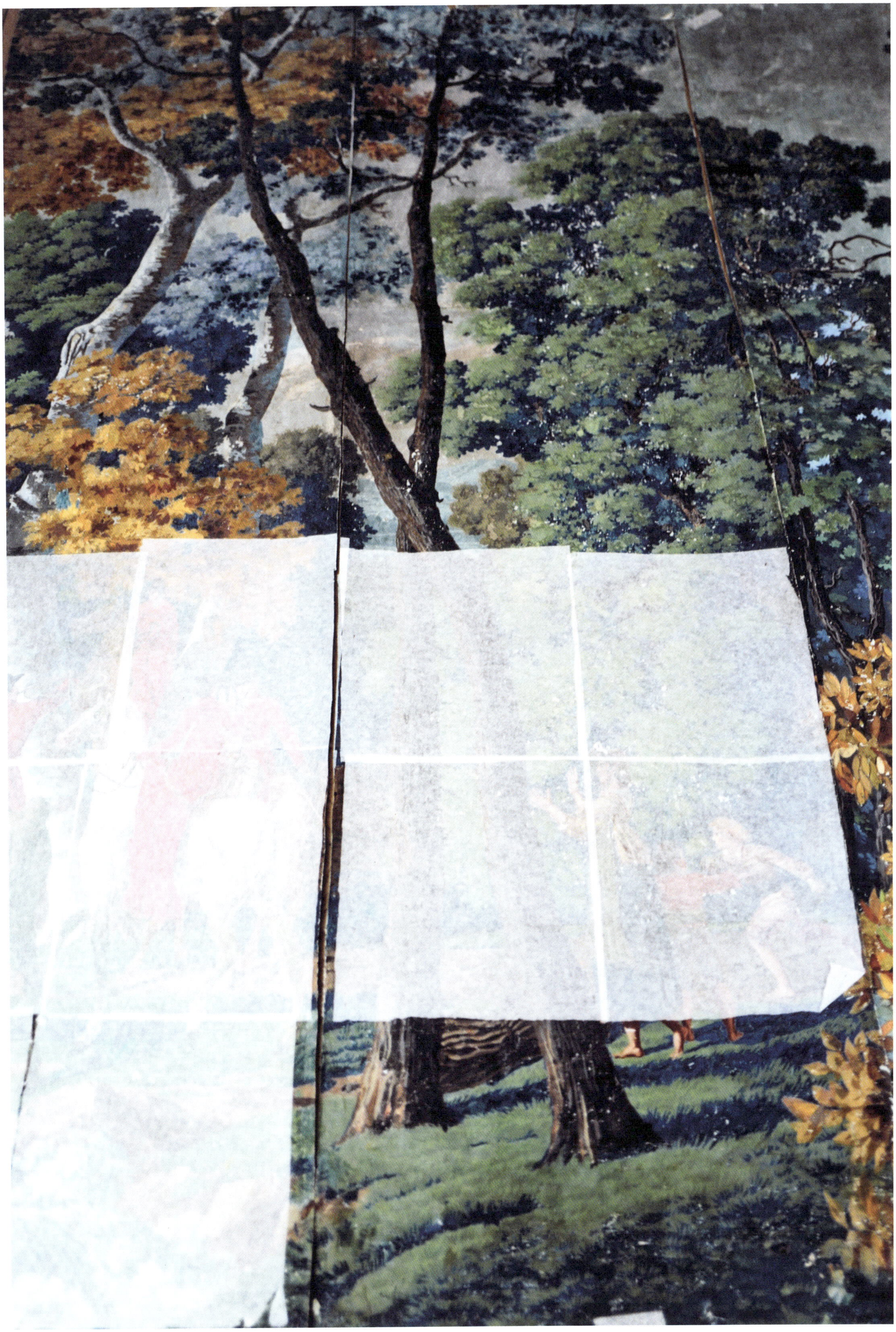

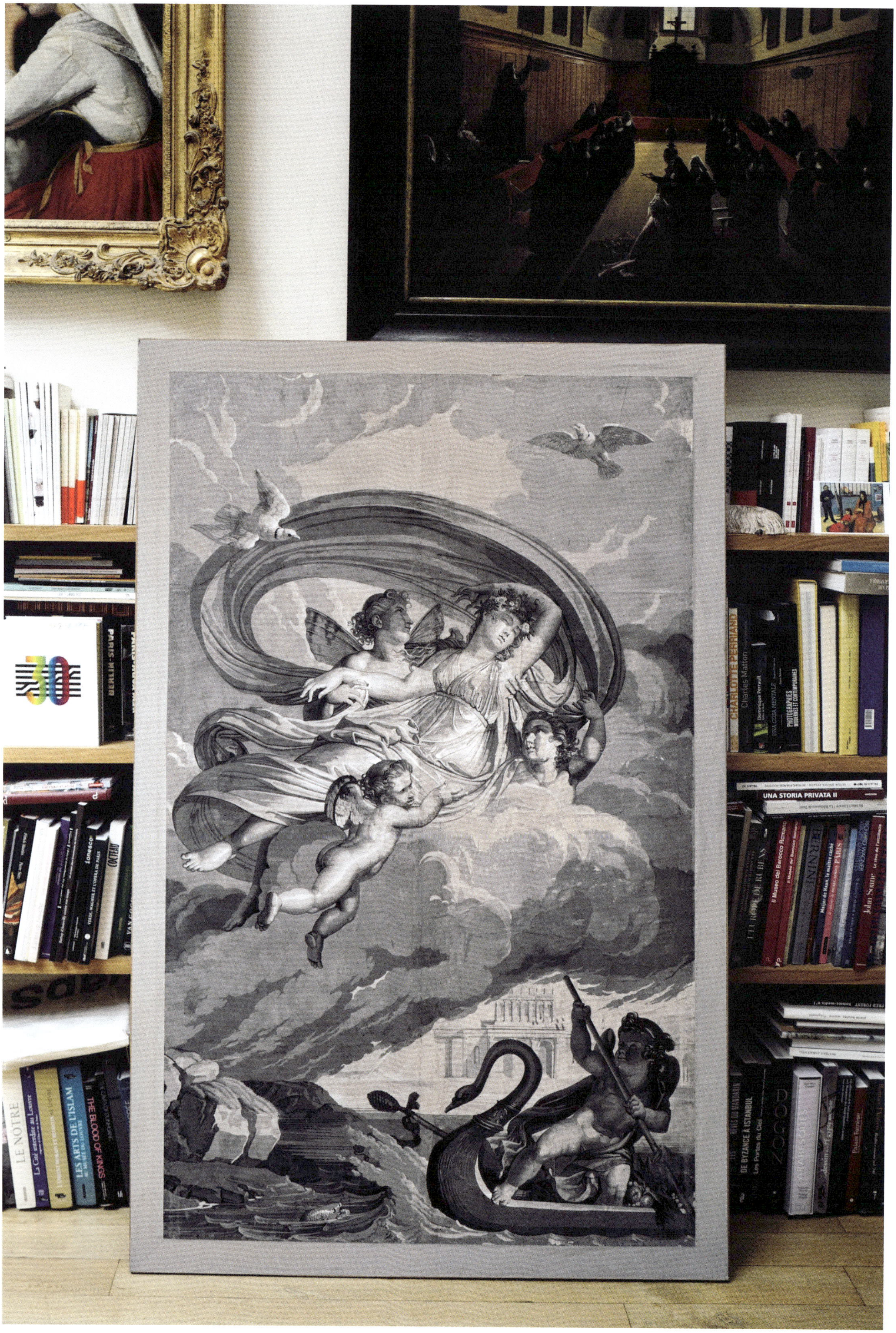
UNA STORIA PRIVATA II
CHARLOTTE PERRIAND
Charles Matton
PARIS-BERLIN
BERNINI
LE NOTRE
LES ARTS DE L'ISLAM
THE BLOOD OF KINGS
DE BYZANCE À ISTANBUL
DOGON
ARABESQUES

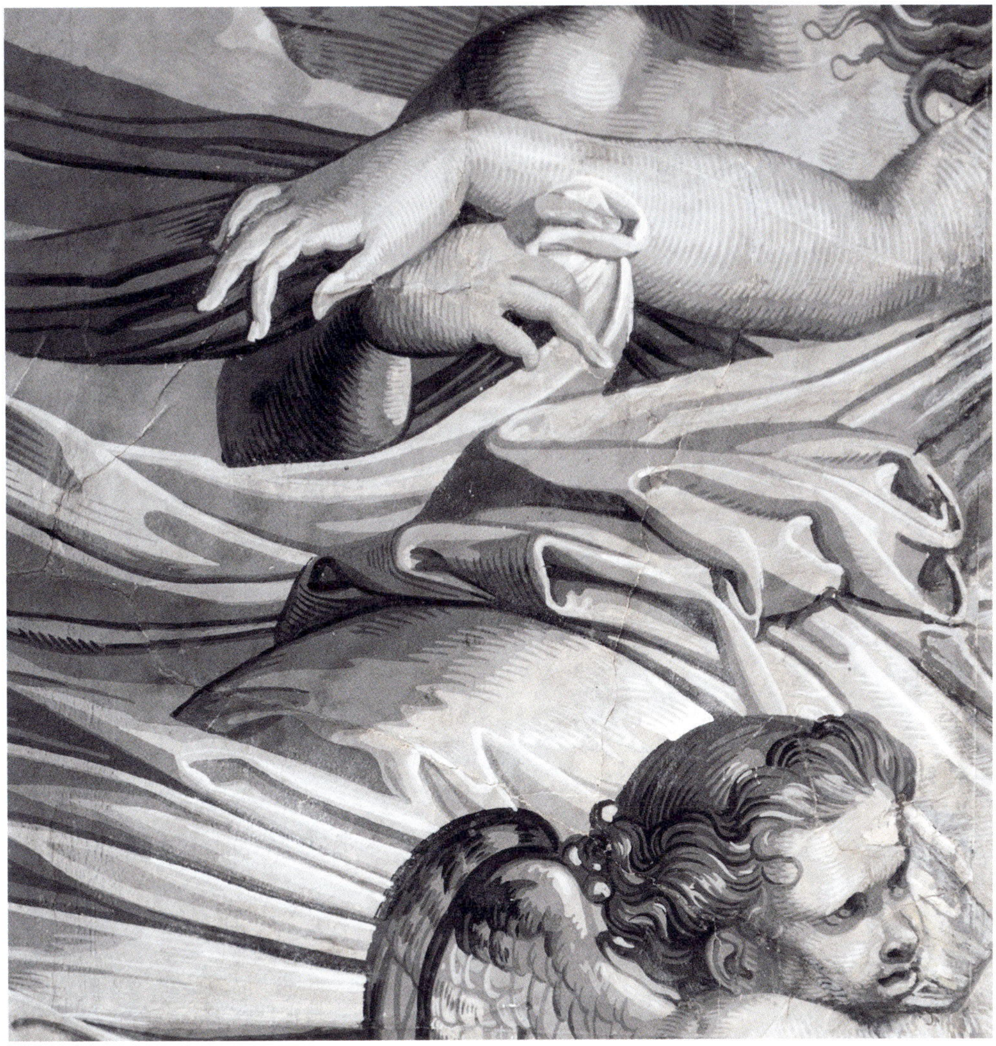

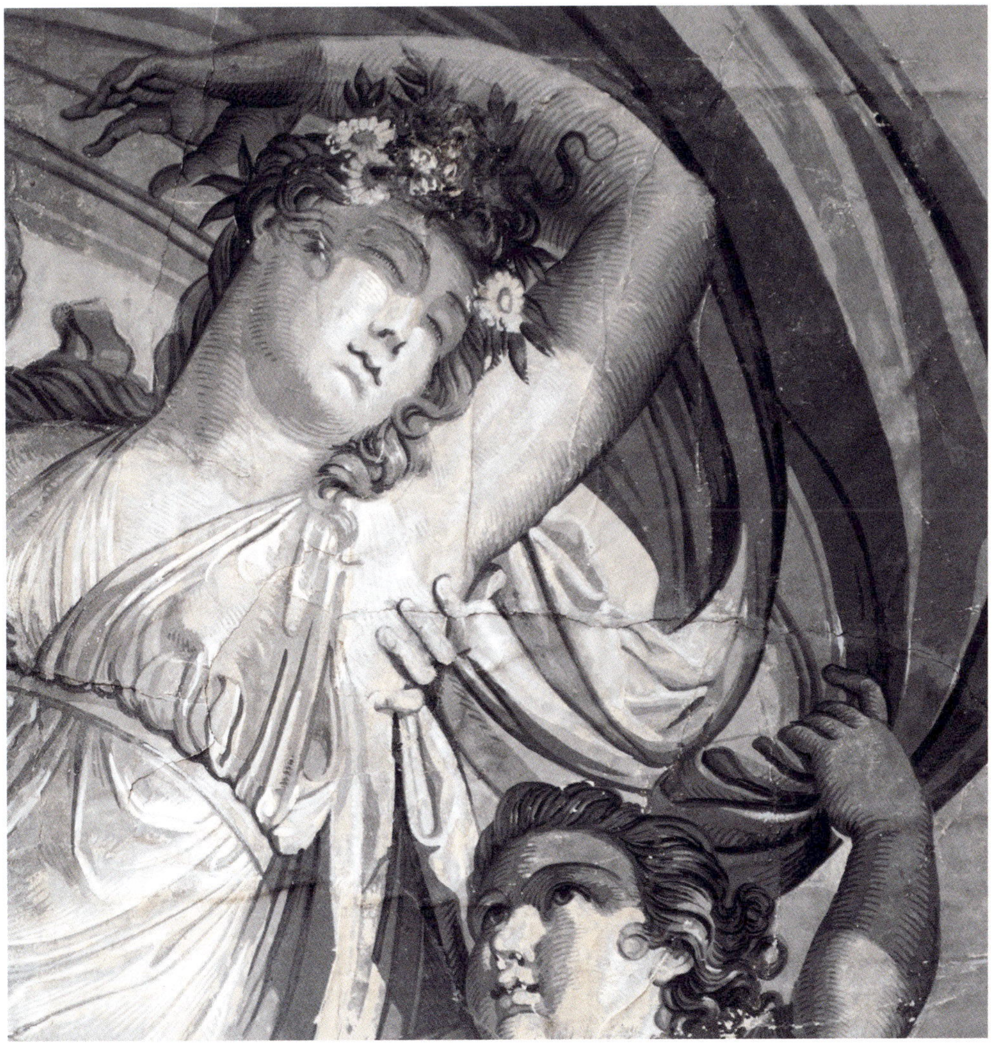

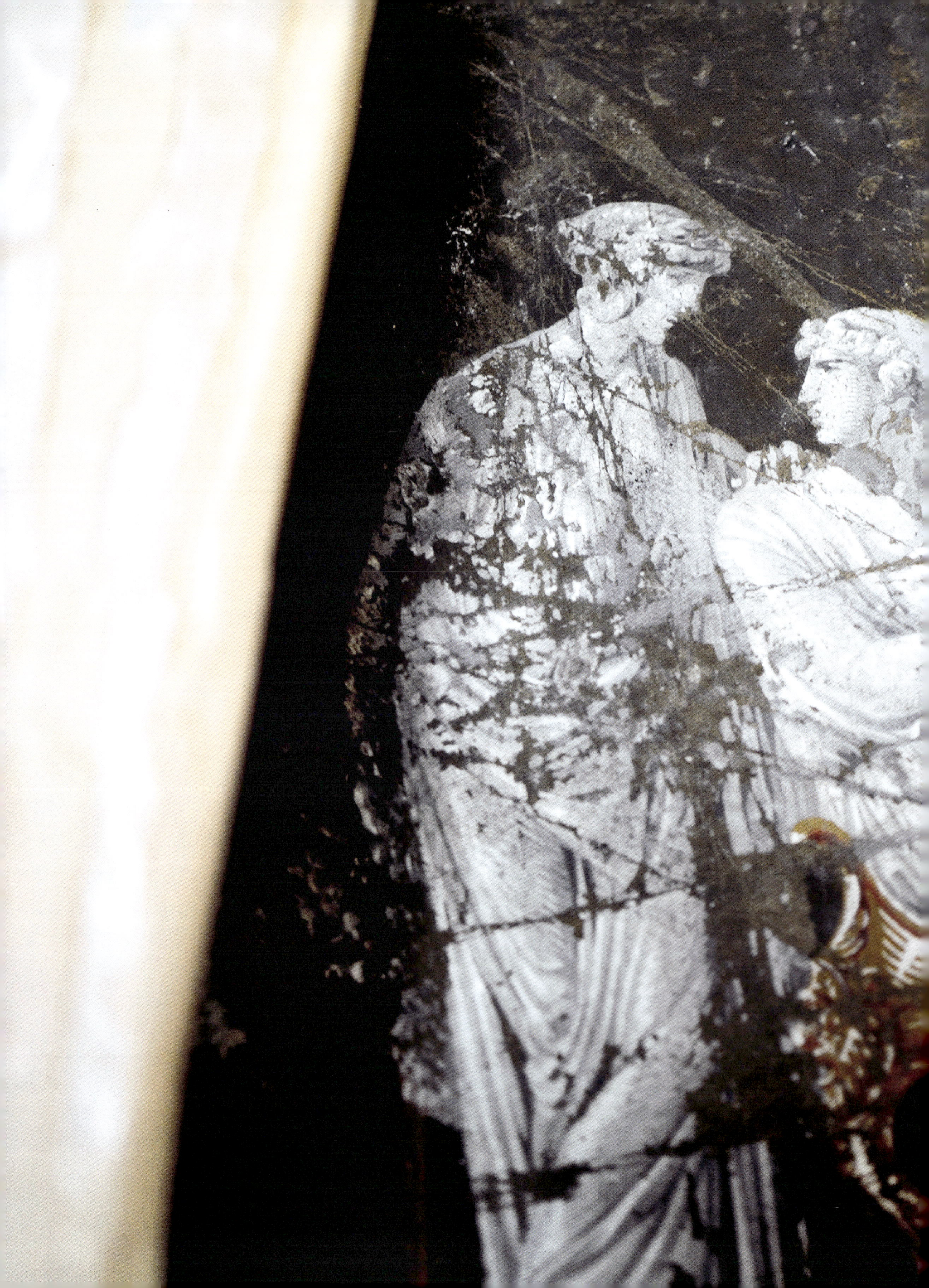

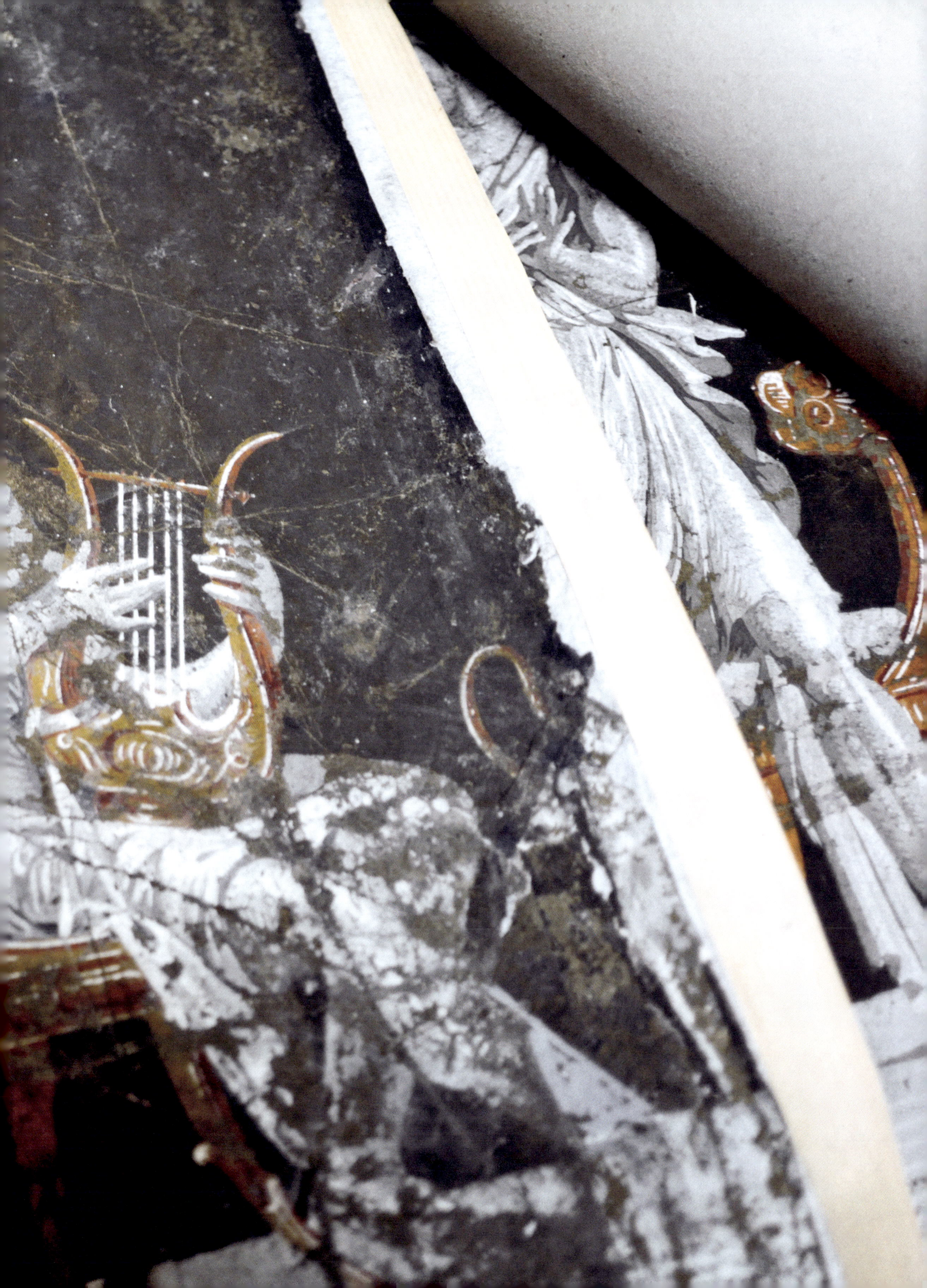

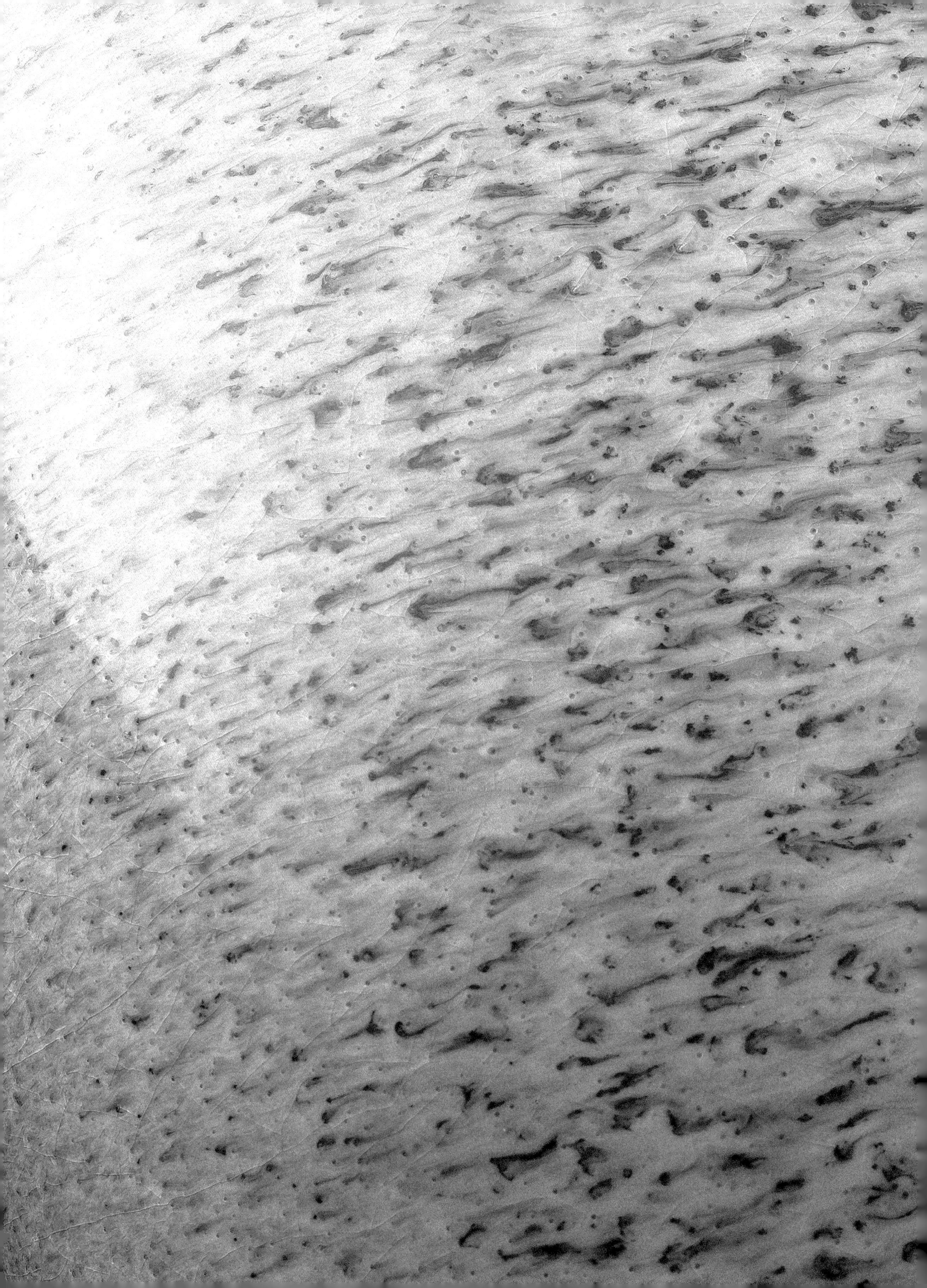

Clay

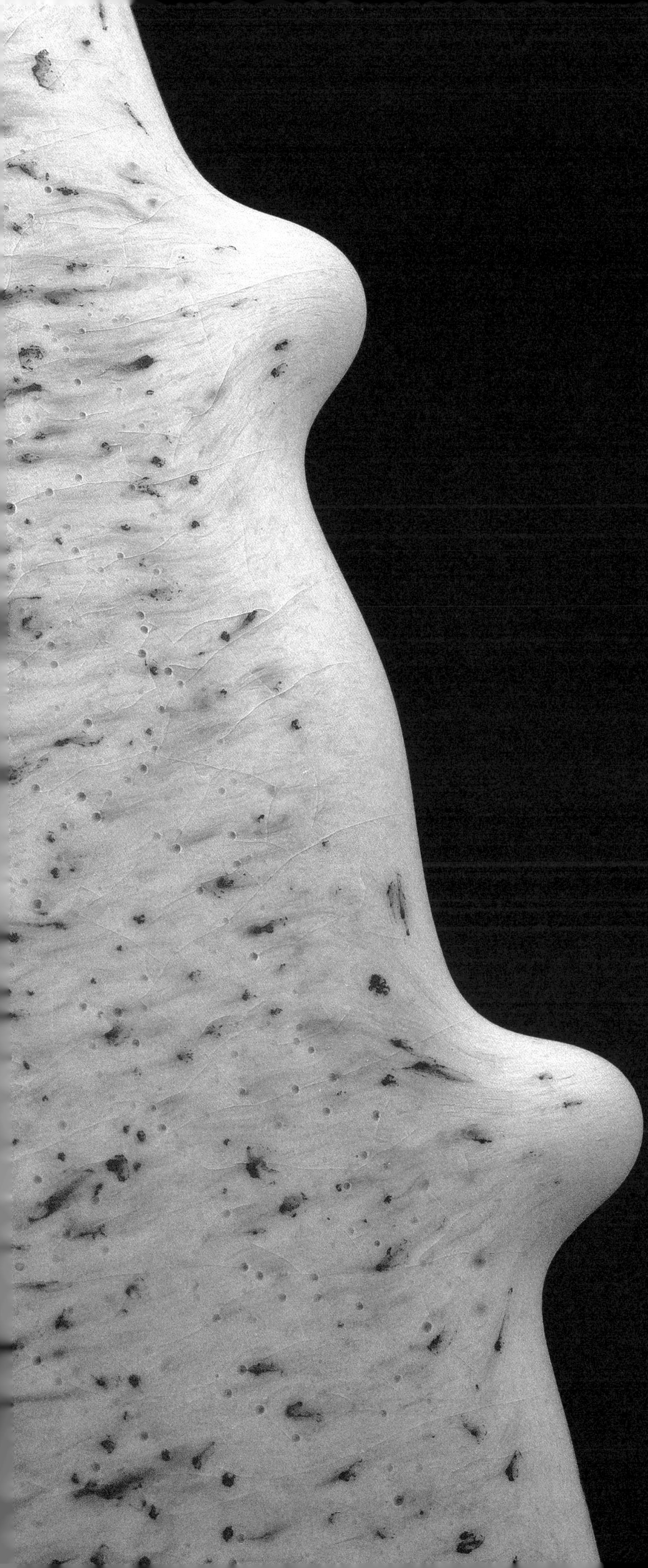

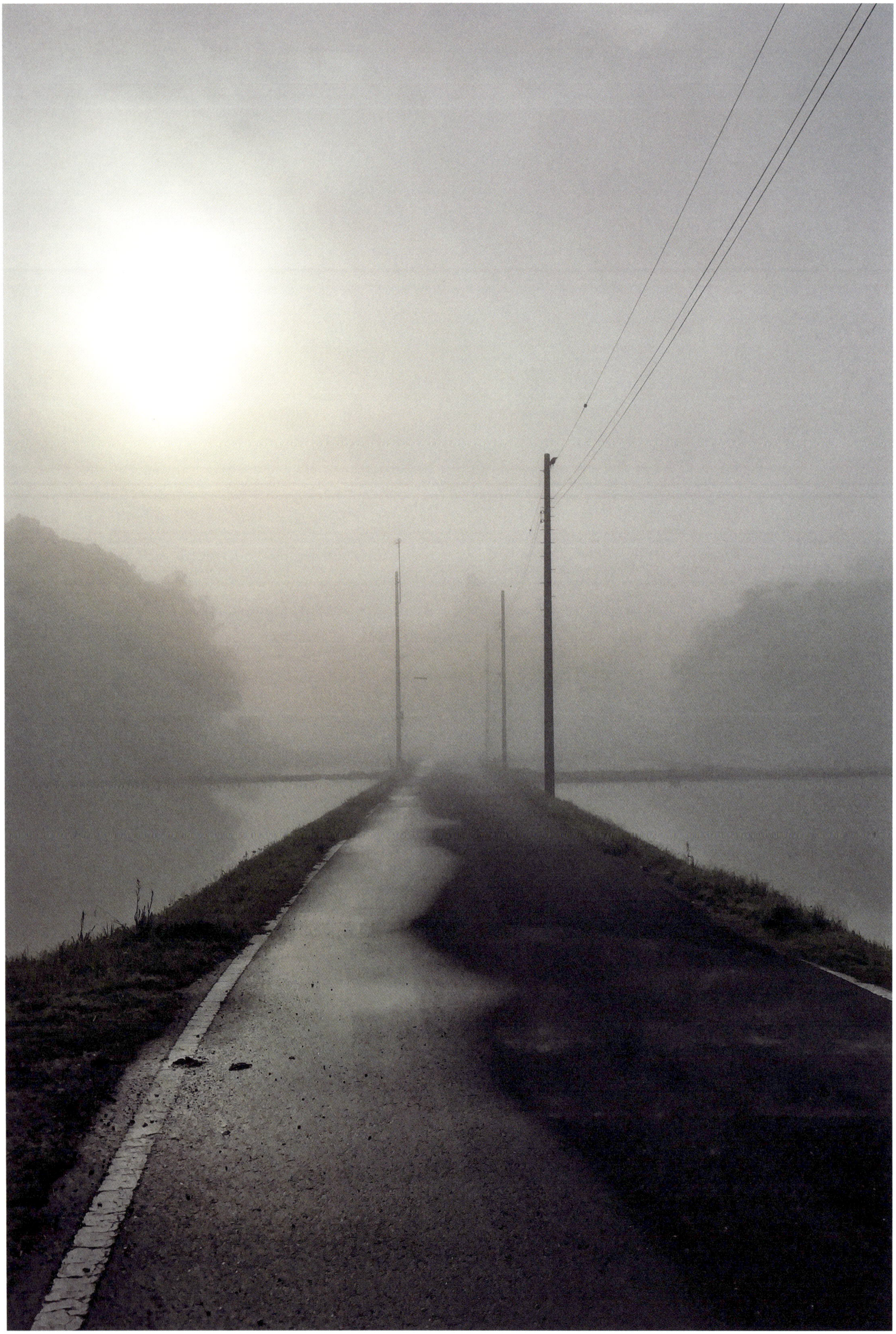

Kazunori Hamana

Ceramist

Isumi, Japan

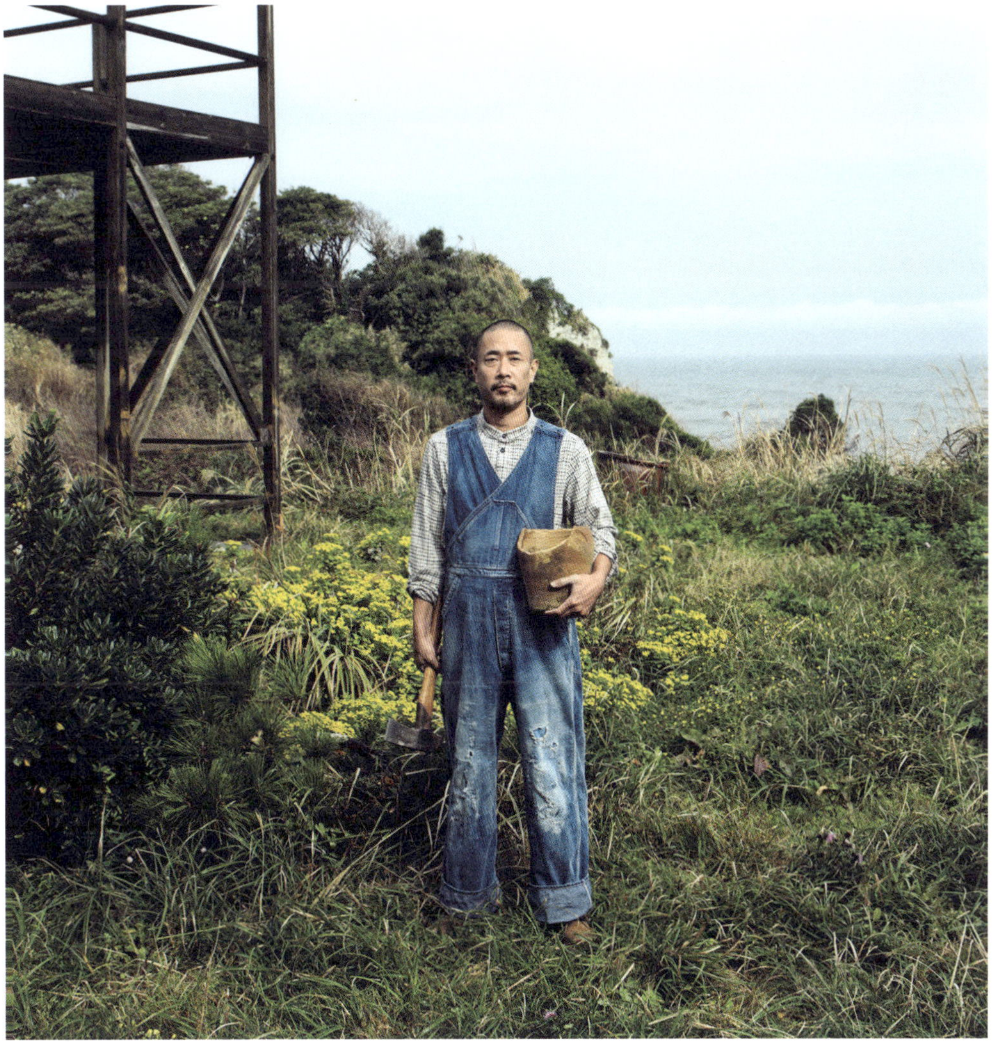

My name is Kazunori Hamana. I make pottery through improvisation. I try to create something according to my intuition.

I live in Isumi, a city in the Chiba prefecture, located in the eastern part of the Boso peninsula, south of Kujukuri beach. My house is built on a hill overlooking the Pacific Ocean. In the morning, I wake up to the rising sun and, at night, I go to sleep looking at the moon. My day unfolds to the sound of waves and the caress of the wind. I grew up in the middle of a concrete jungle and early on I decided, against my parents' advice, to leave my hometown to study at an agricultural high school. The era of mass production and mass consumption had just begun, and the agricultural industry was no exception: chemical fertilizers were used to obtain more efficient and profitable yields. I wanted to learn about sustainable agriculture and study environmental issues, but I was sorely disappointed. So, I went to study in California. After that, my life was a series of ups and downs: I opened a vintage shop in Tokyo, then a restaurant, before leaving it all behind to settle in Isumi and become a fisherman. Today, I no longer fish; I make ceramics and I sell anchovies, as well as my own sauce, called Seguro-no-Kusare, the result of two years of trial and error. When I think back, I realize I have always wanted to establish a close connection with nature and practice a self-sufficient lifestyle. To understand nature, I wanted to do something with my hands. For me, pottery is a way to use my body and be close to the earth.

Although there are many famous contemporary ceramists, I learn more by looking at pieces from the Muromachi and Azuchi-Momoyama periods [c. 1336–1573 and 1568–1600 respectively]. I try to infuse my objects with the same spirit, but the four-hundred-year gap makes comparison difficult. So, I make my pieces with these references in mind and with my own understanding of them. One of the reasons I don't make figurines is that they emphasize the ego and self-affirmation. I prefer to remove this individualism from what I do. In those earlier periods, the ceramist left no personal trace on their pottery. This is probably why I like these antiques—why they always draw my attention.

I use clay sourced from the Shiga prefecture. By nature, it changes and shifts. I follow it, and I embrace its form to avoid fighting against nature. My work, despite my ideas, also depends on the weather and the temperature. Sometimes I redo my work several times to repair certain pieces that I am not happy with. I always repeat these efforts to reach a satisfactory result. On the other hand, creating objects in this manner and concentrating on the piece is, for me, a way of going against mass production and rationalization.

Once the firing process is over, I prefer to leave my works outside, on sunny balconies or in shady bamboo groves. Exposed to the elements, enveloped by plants and sometimes broken, they continue their development, marked over time by the changing seasons. No piece is ever finished: it remains alive, open to the marks and traces of time. Sometimes, a local craftsman specialized in *kintsugi* [the art of repairing ceramics with gold or silver lacquer] repairs cracks.

By respecting and being aware of the nature around you, you can feel the essence of things. In this sense, I see no difference between preparing anchovies and making pottery.

Although I am still learning many things, I try to expand my knowledge in the areas that interest me. Then I give myself a challenge: if I don't succeed the first time, I try again. I would like to achieve my ideal quality through this process of trial and error. By creating, I seek to provoke reflection and encourage the recognition of beauty in unique and imperfect things.

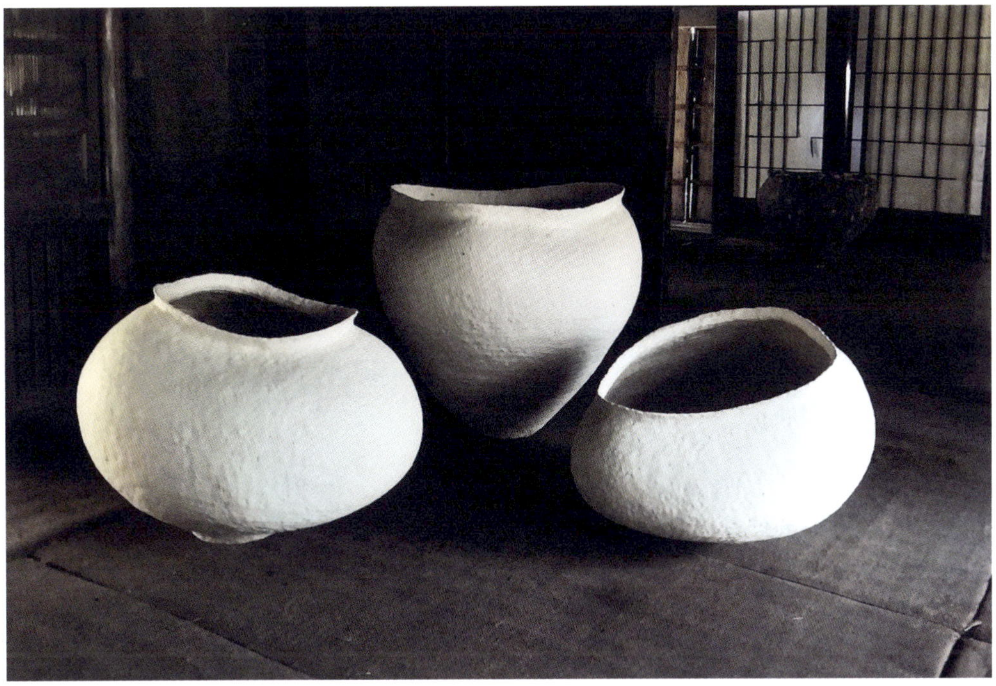

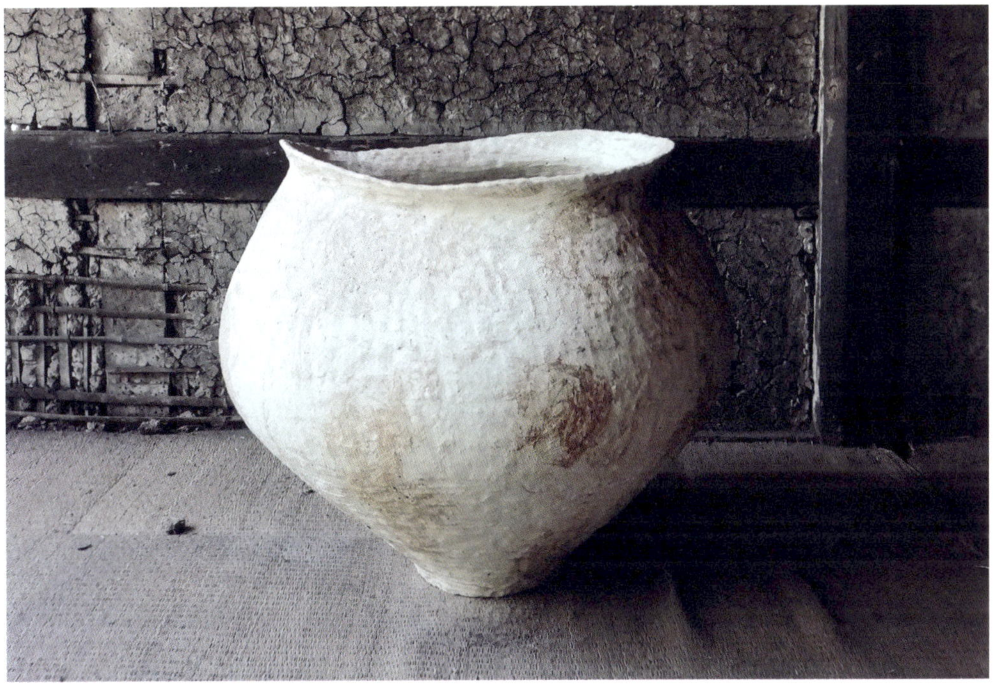

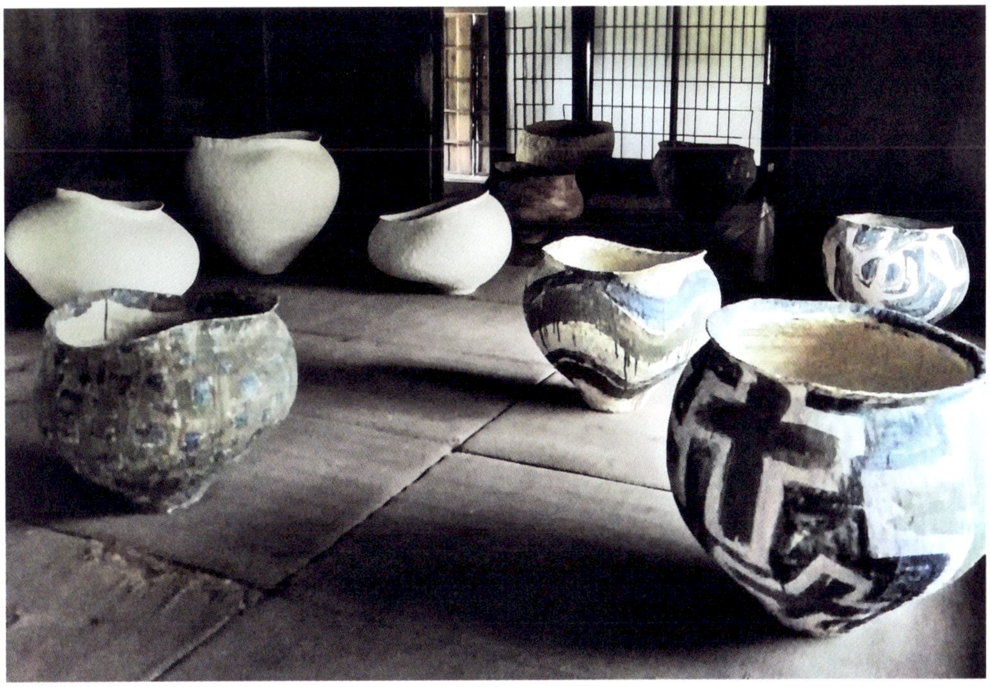

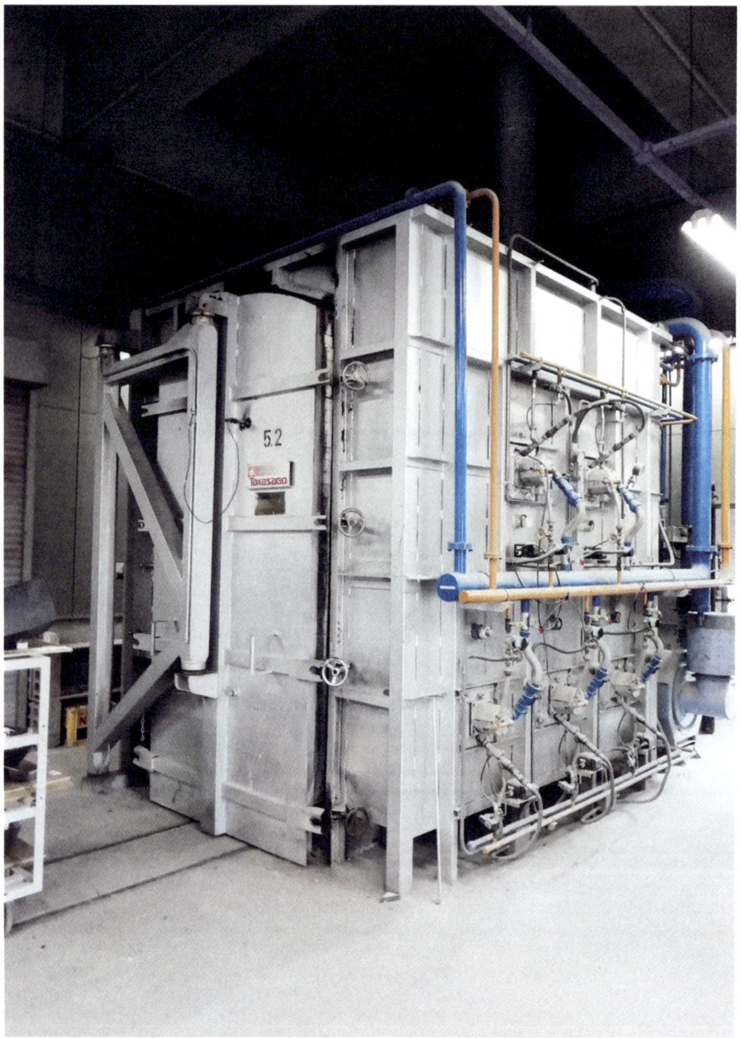
52
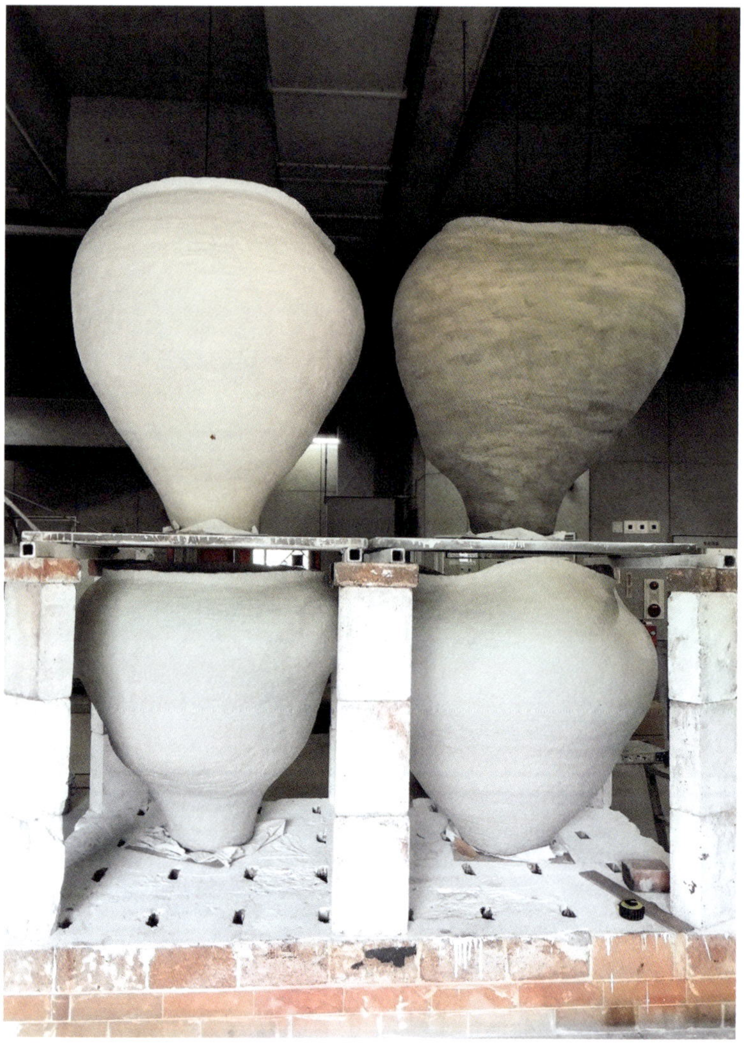

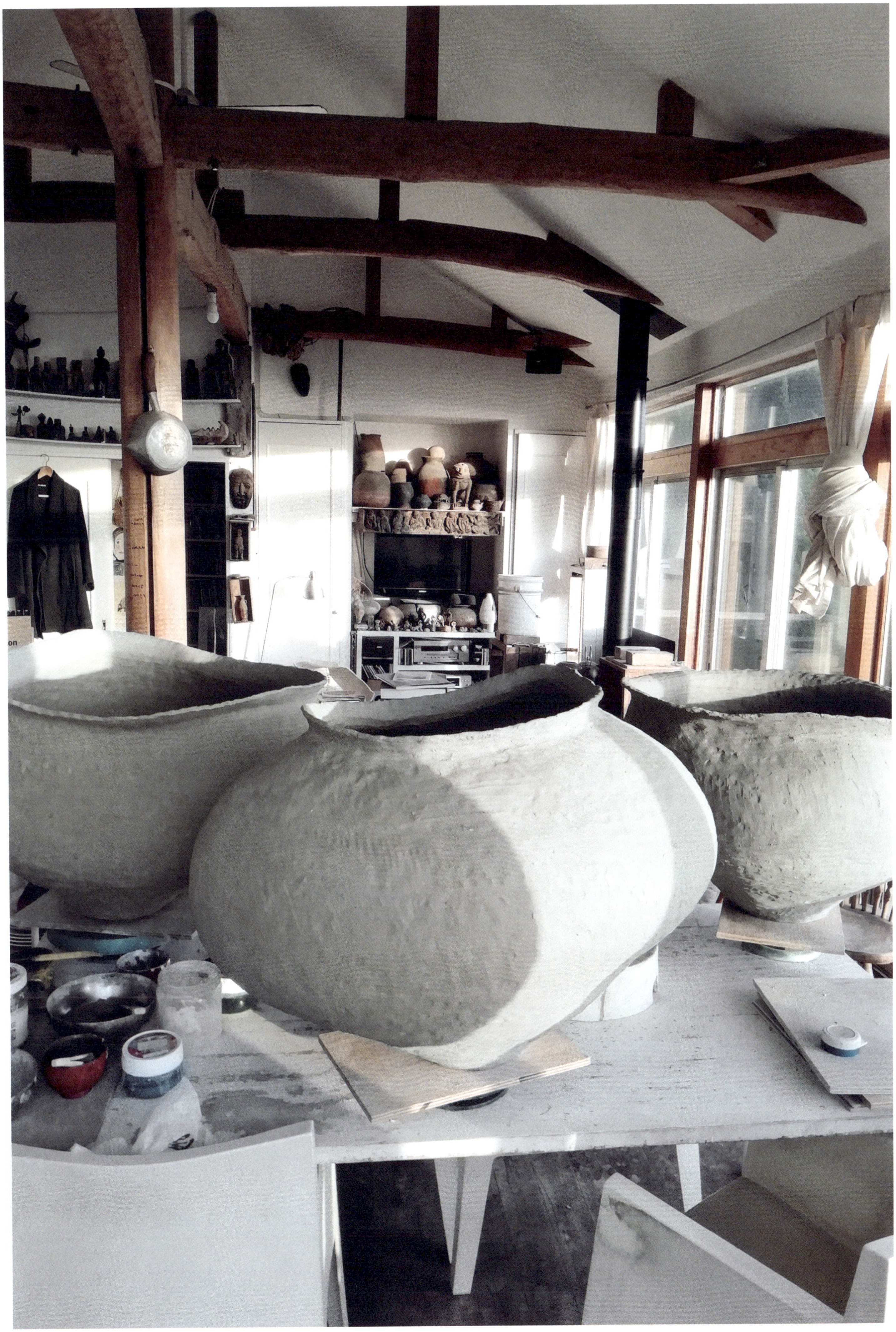

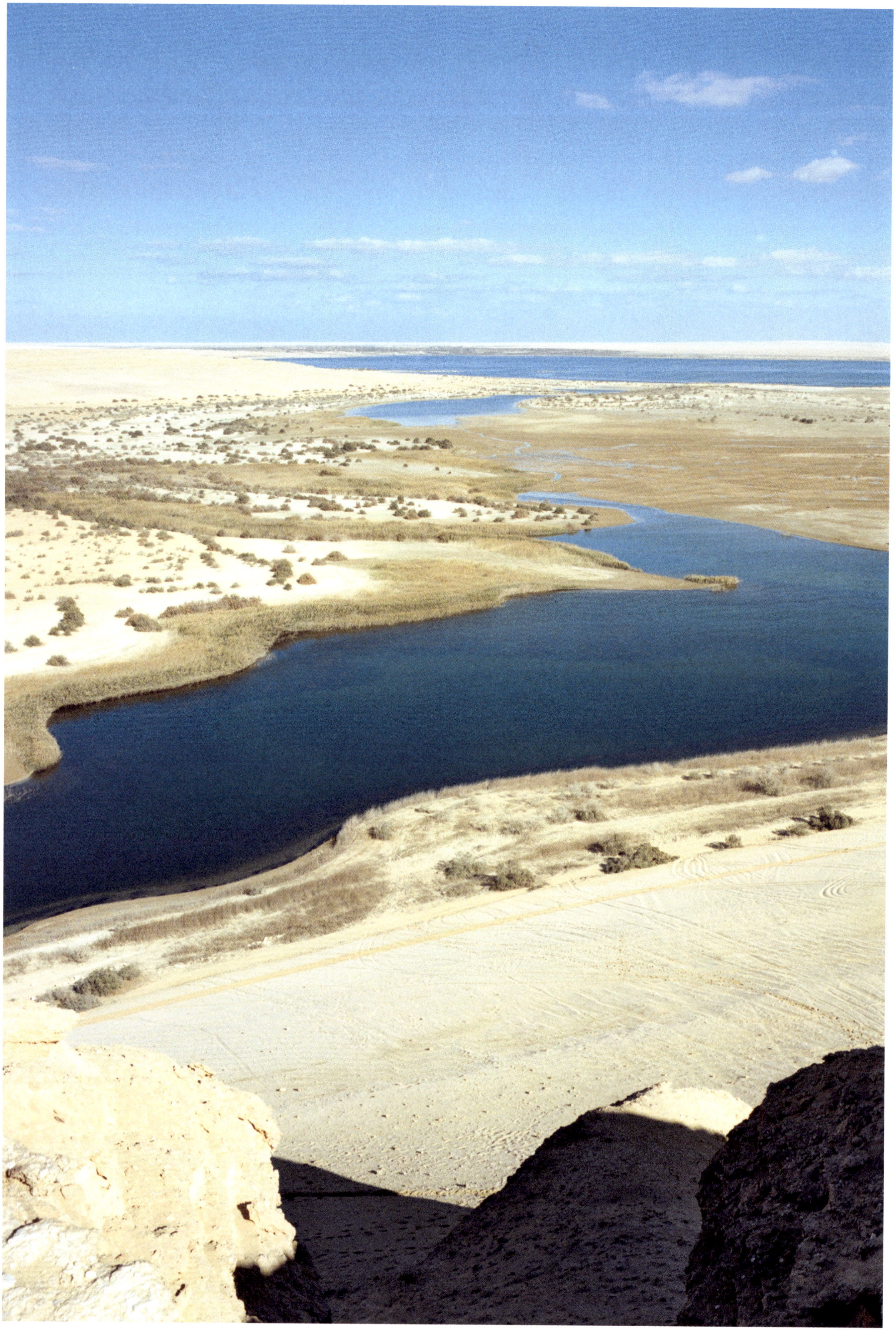

Amel
Mansour Pottery

Potter

Fayoum Oasis, Egypt

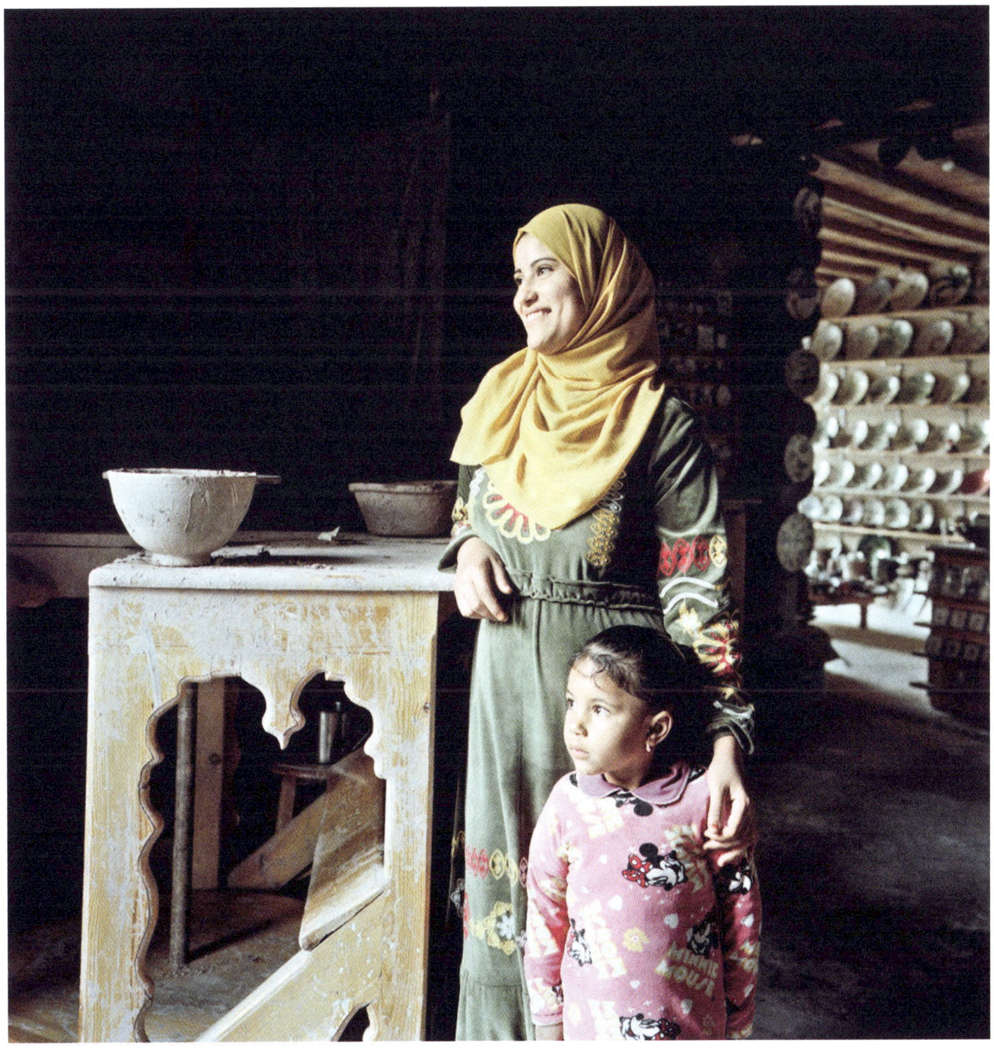

My name is Amel, and my parents were farmers. I grew up in the village of Tounès, in the Fayoum Oasis in Egypt, where I am now a potter.

When I was a child, my parents worked for "Om Angelo" [Swiss potter Évelyne Porret] and "Abu Angelo" [her partner, Michel Pastore]. I remember when I was six years old, I would finish my homework after school, then run to their ceramics workshop where I would make small animals. At that time, twenty years ago, there was no water or electricity in the village. It was a hamlet. Women carried water from the stream in pots balanced on their heads, and the fellahs [agricultural laborers] worked in the fields or fished in the lake.

Om Angelo and Abu Angelo deeply influenced me during my years of training. They taught me how to manipulate clay, to make a plate. But Om Angelo would break pieces she considered unsuccessful, even if I thought what I had made was beautiful.

We use a clay from Aswan that we buy in a neighborhood in Old Cairo. It's a red clay that has to be mixed with other materials before it can be thrown on the wheel. I like this clay; I can feel when it is ready to be shaped.

When I make a piece, the form is important, but the decoration is what I consider to be most important of all. If the piece is a little crooked, the decoration can make up for it. Most of the patterns I create are inspired by things around me: trees, flowers, animals, cows, and buffalo. The decoration is enhanced by a transparent glaze enriched with pigments and oxides. I like the color blue because it goes well with white.

This profession has allowed me to create a future for myself. It seems pointless to me to study when you can make pottery. Today I am married, and the training and support I've received from the local pottery school have made it possible for me to become a craftswoman. Most men don't want their wives to work outside of the home. When I first got married, my husband was also against the idea: he wanted me to stop making pottery and to wear the niqab. I had moments of doubt, but eventually he agreed that I could return to a workshop from time to time. I took advantage of the fact that he was working away from home to say that I had gone to the doctor and he had asked me to stop wearing the niqab because my sight was deteriorating and my eyes hurt. In the end, I persuaded my husband to take up pottery as well, and I've taught him everything I know.

We worked for different potters before gathering enough money together to build a wheel and a kiln, buy clay, and establish our own workshop. Today my husband oversees the kiln, and I throw and decorate the pieces. He loves this work as much as I do, and not only for the financial security. Our pottery sells well, and that's important, but what I love most of all is going to the workshop to open the kiln after a firing. It's a magical moment, especially when I take a piece out of the kiln and I'm happy with it. It's always very exciting.

I welcome the changes taking place in the village. There are more and more workshops being established, and I'm proud to say that I come from Tounès. This place is unlike any other. People travel from far away to visit and buy pottery here. Our pots are also sold in stores in Cairo and sometimes at exhibitions abroad.

In the future, I imagine myself with my husband and our children, in our workshop, surrounded by a new generation of potters who will contribute their ideas and innovations.

I hope that we will continue to produce high-quality pottery. At the moment, some potters are producing poorly made pieces and selling them cheaply, which is detrimental to our work.

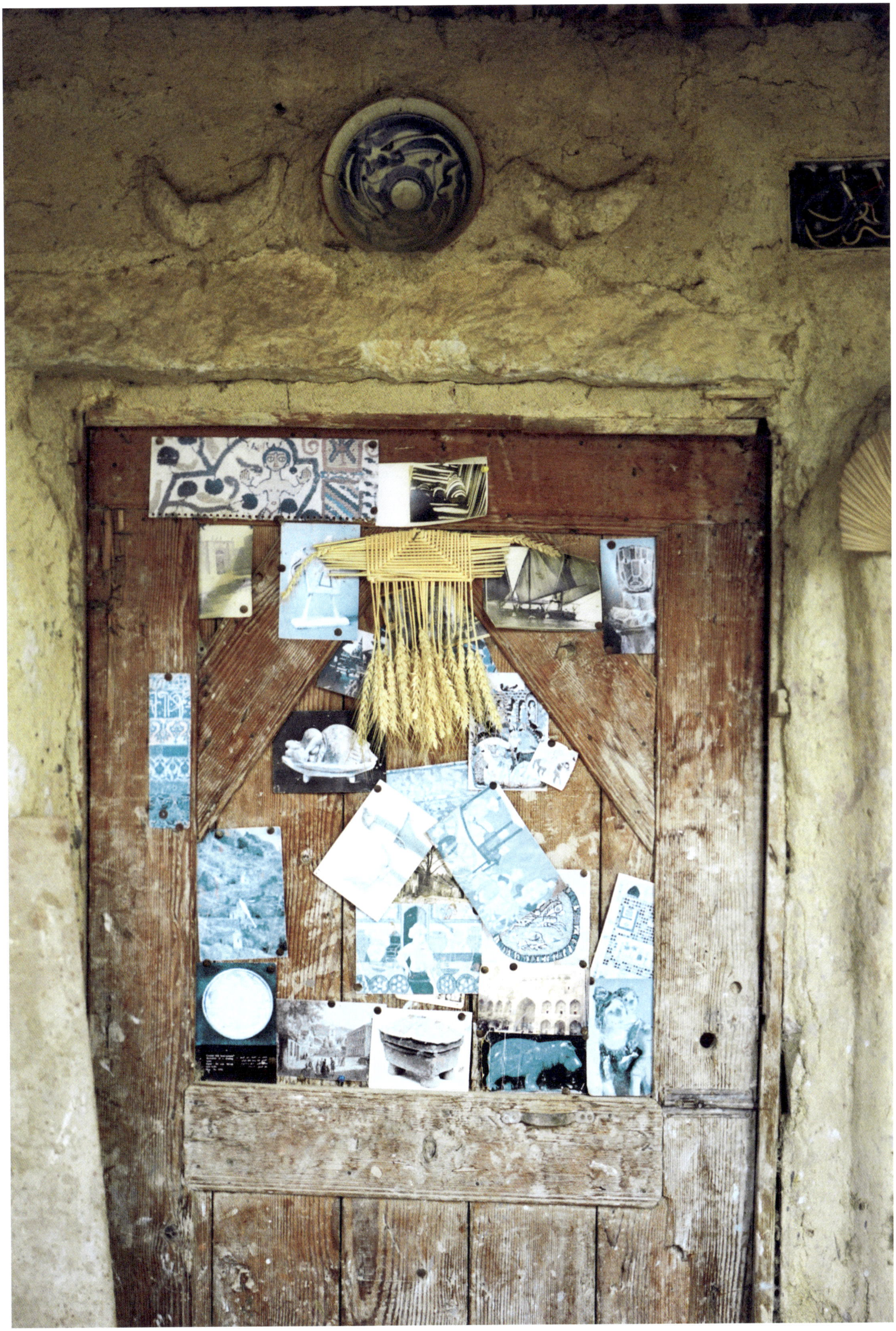

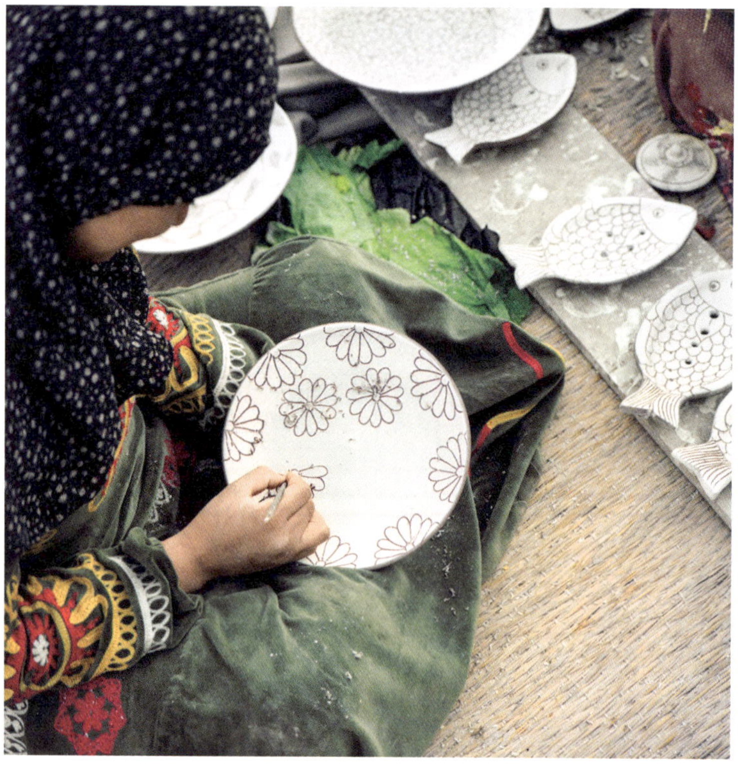

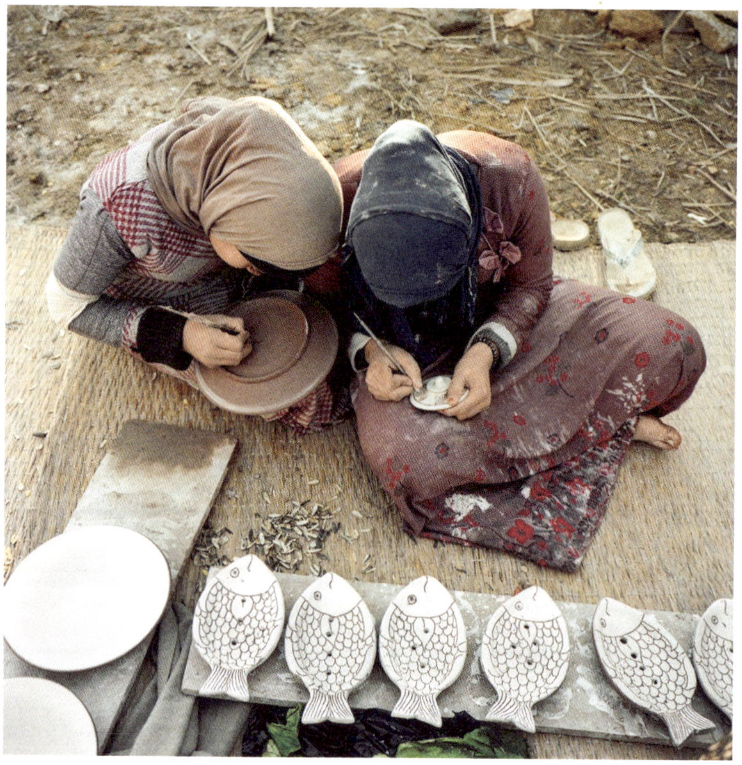

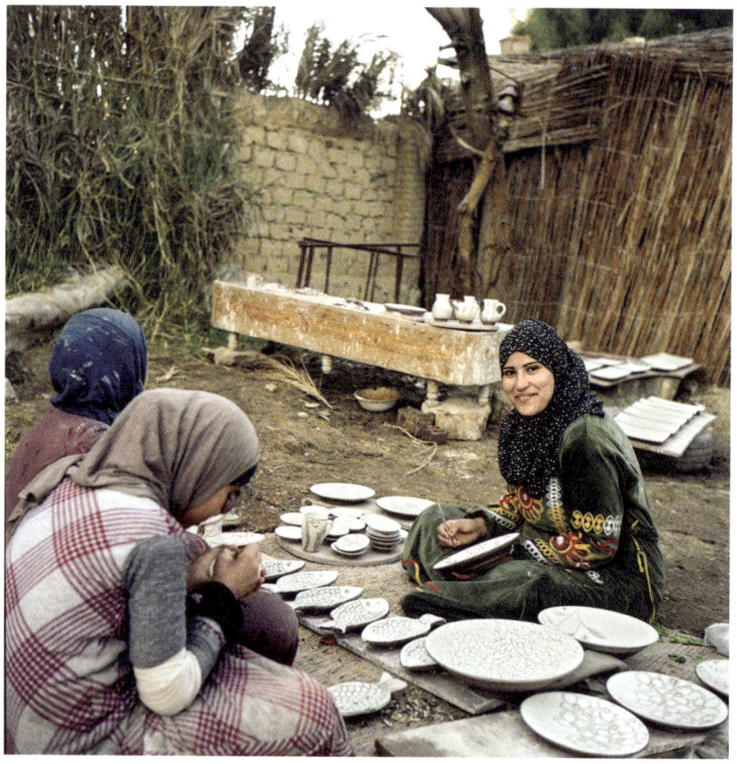

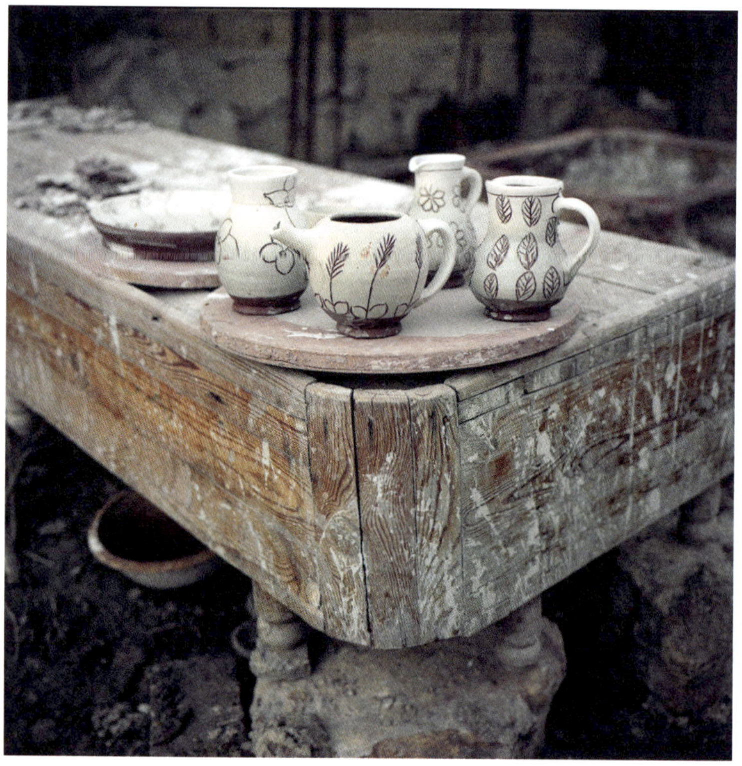

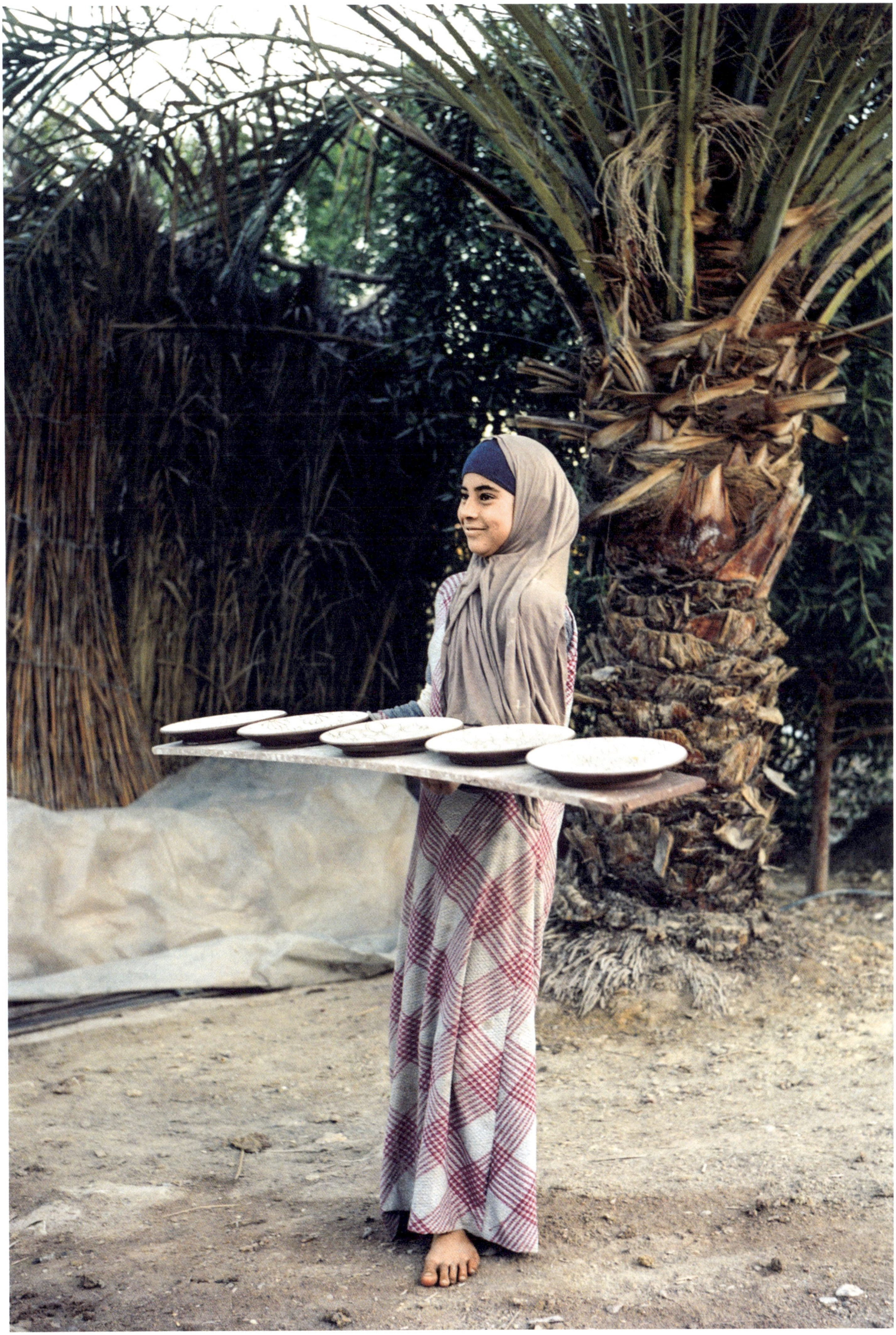

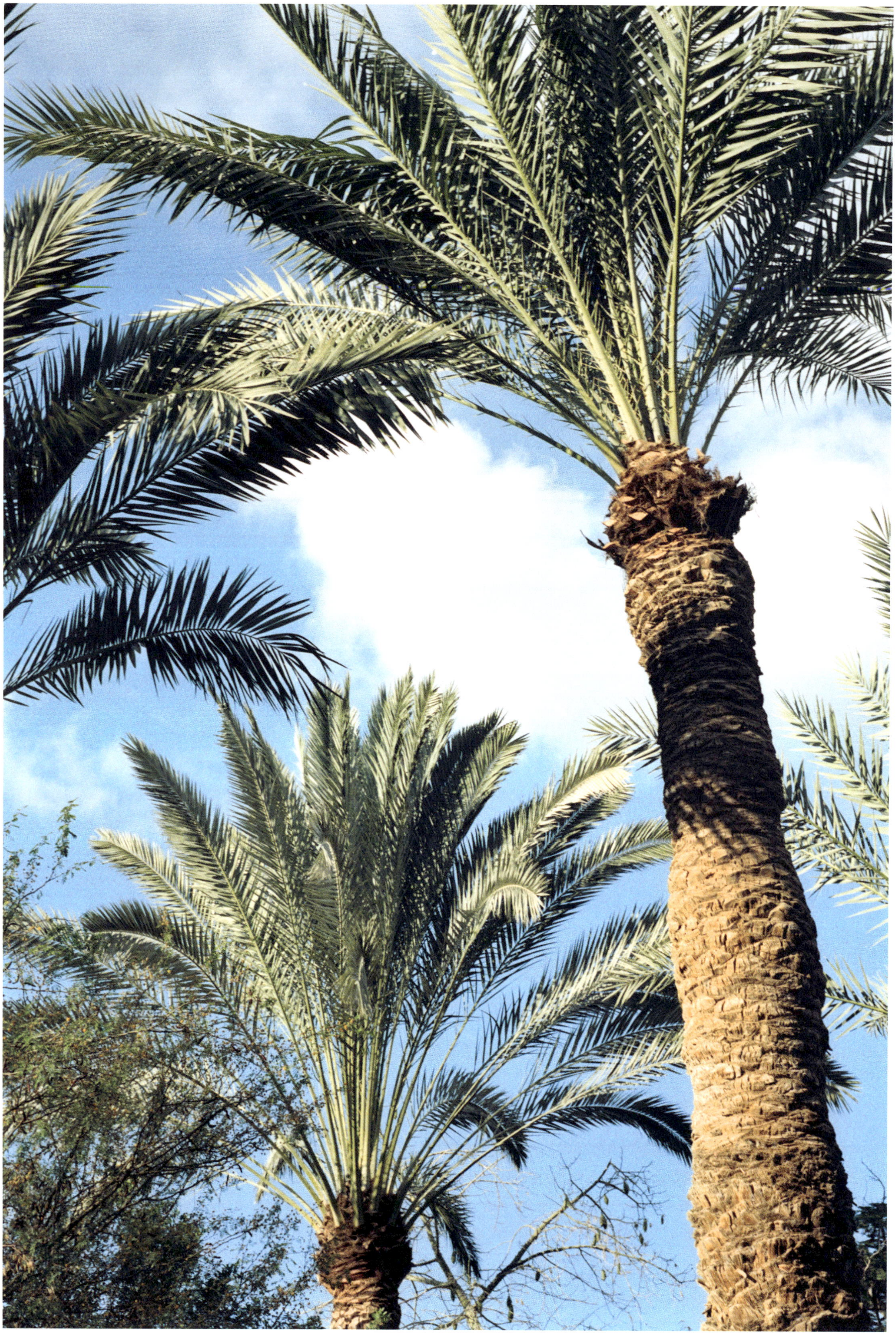

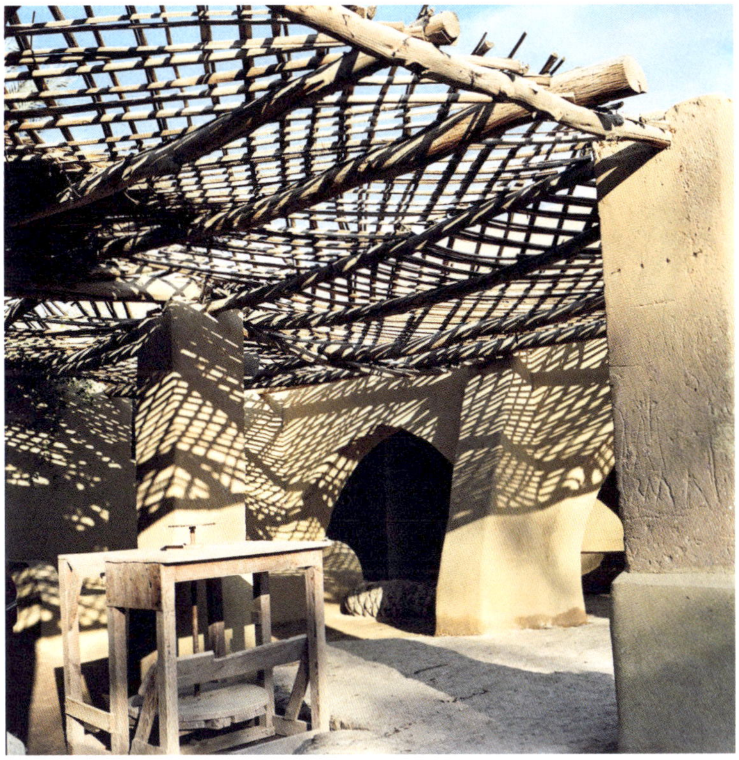

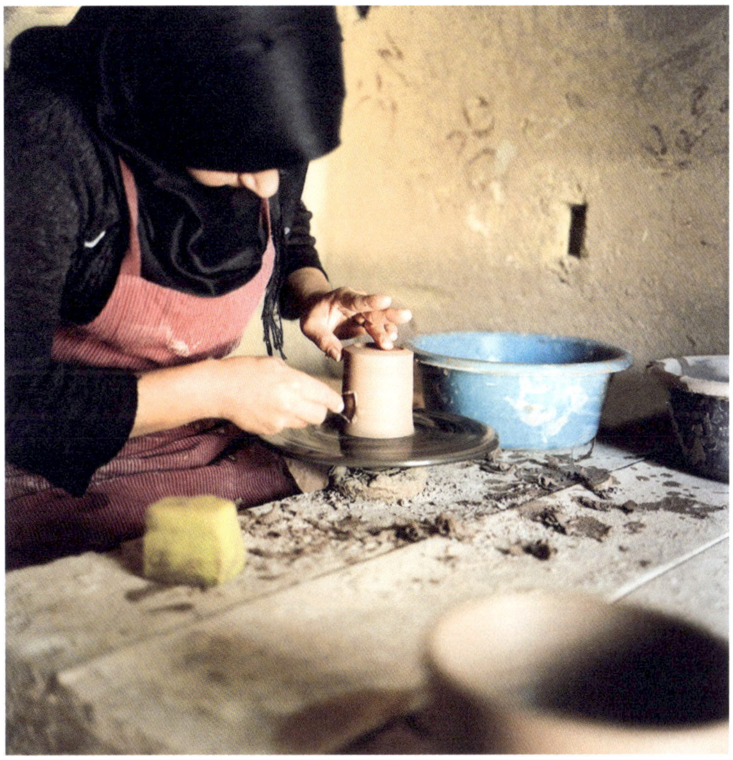

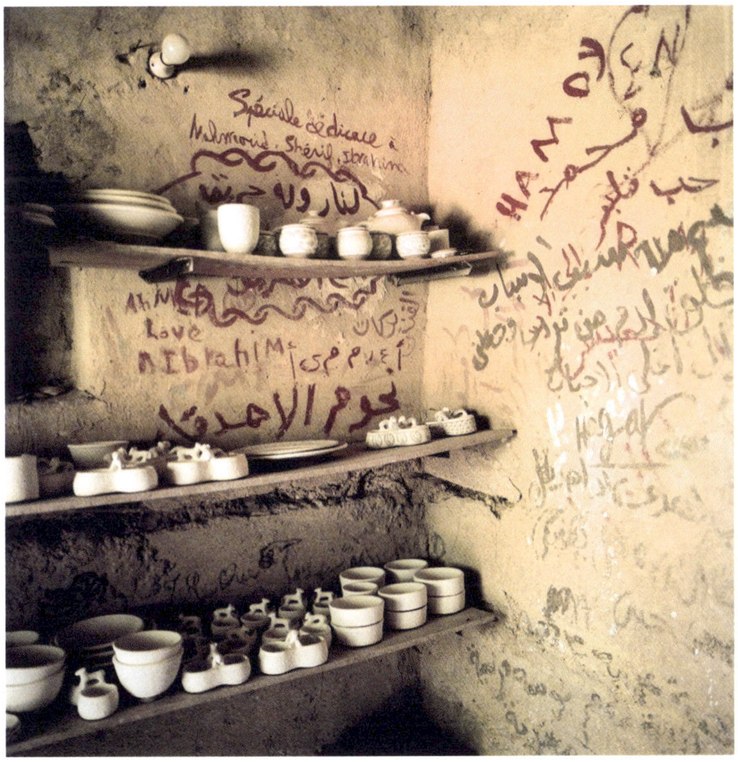
Spéciale dédicace à
Love

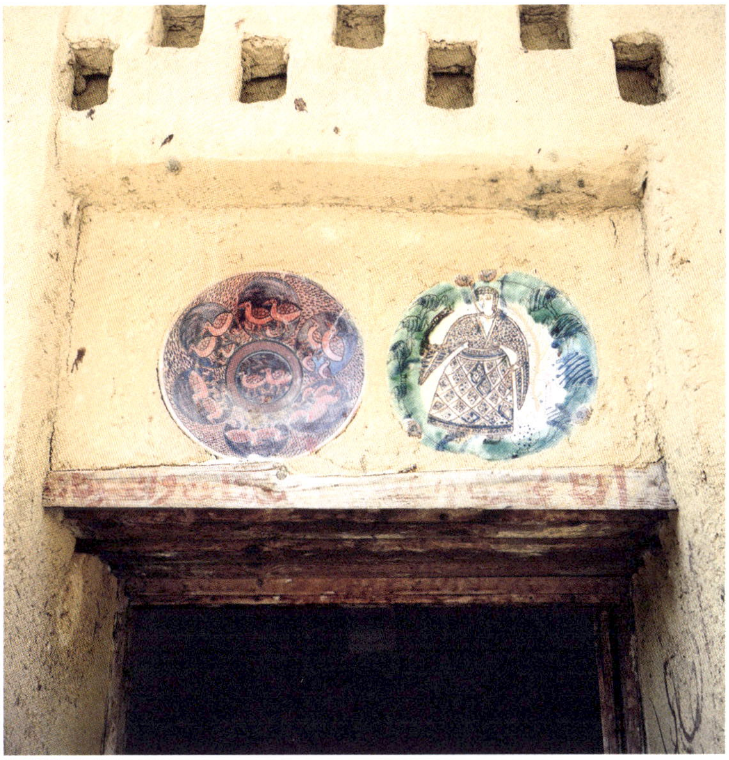

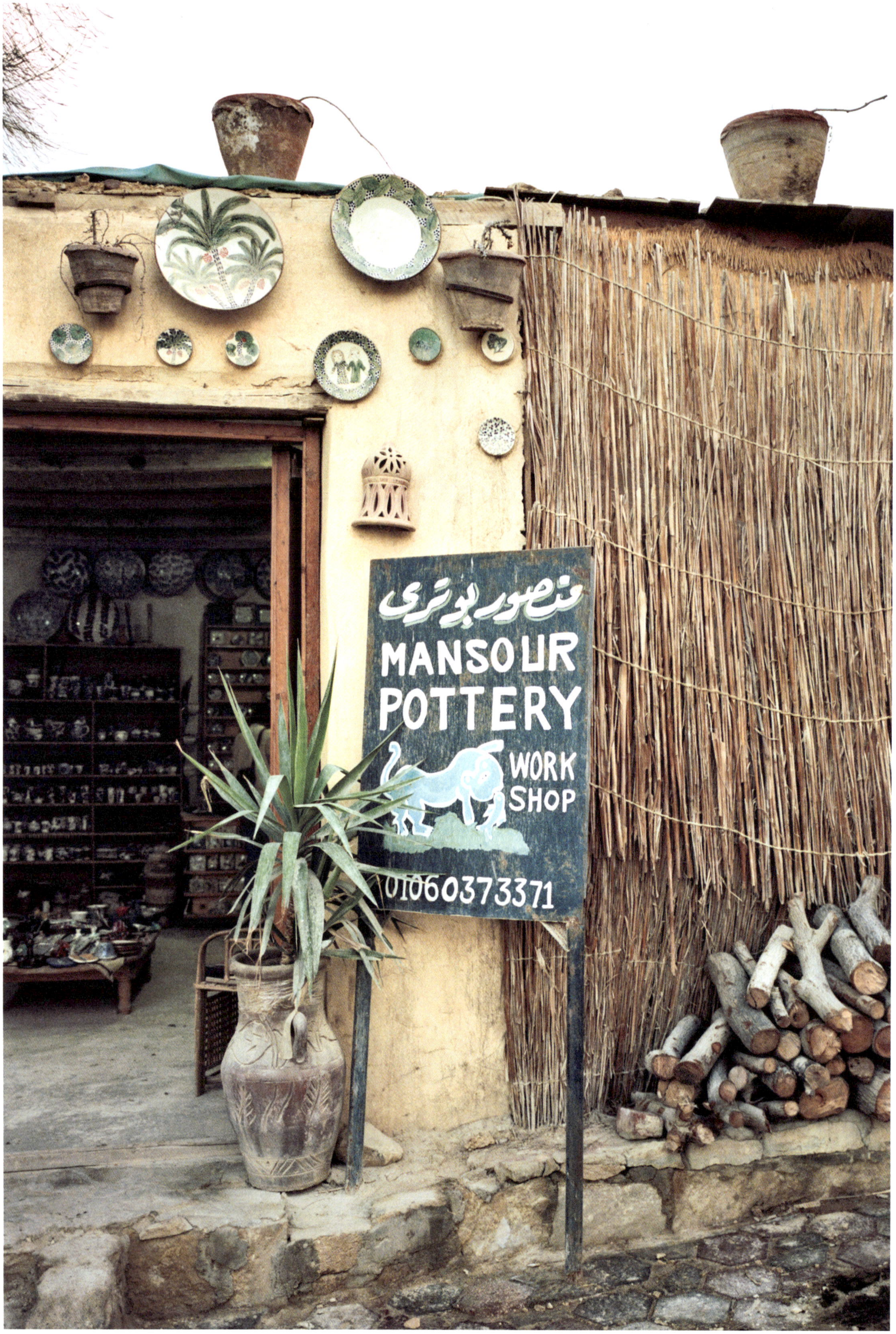
منصور بوترى
MANSOUR
POTTERY
WORK
SHOP
01060373371

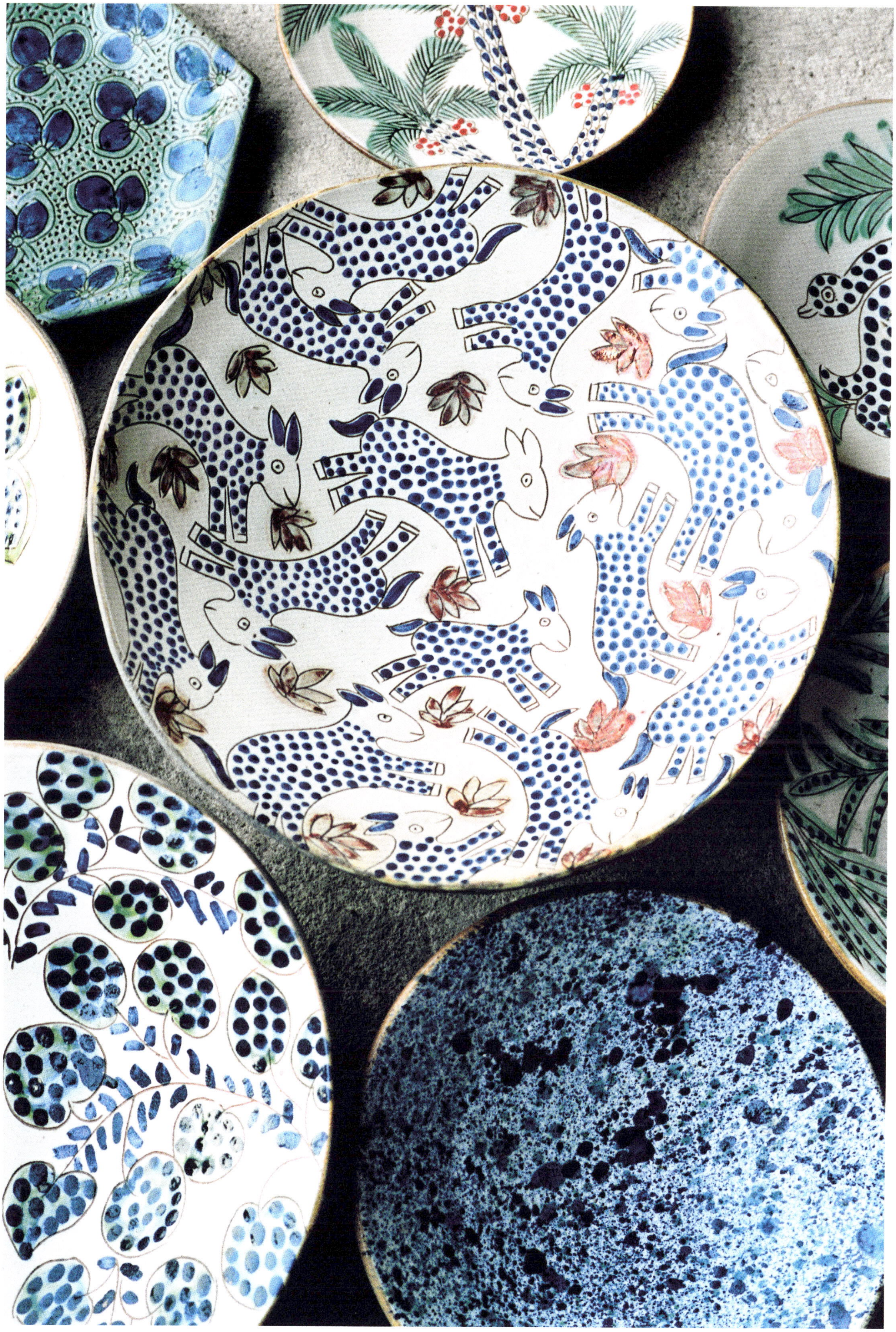

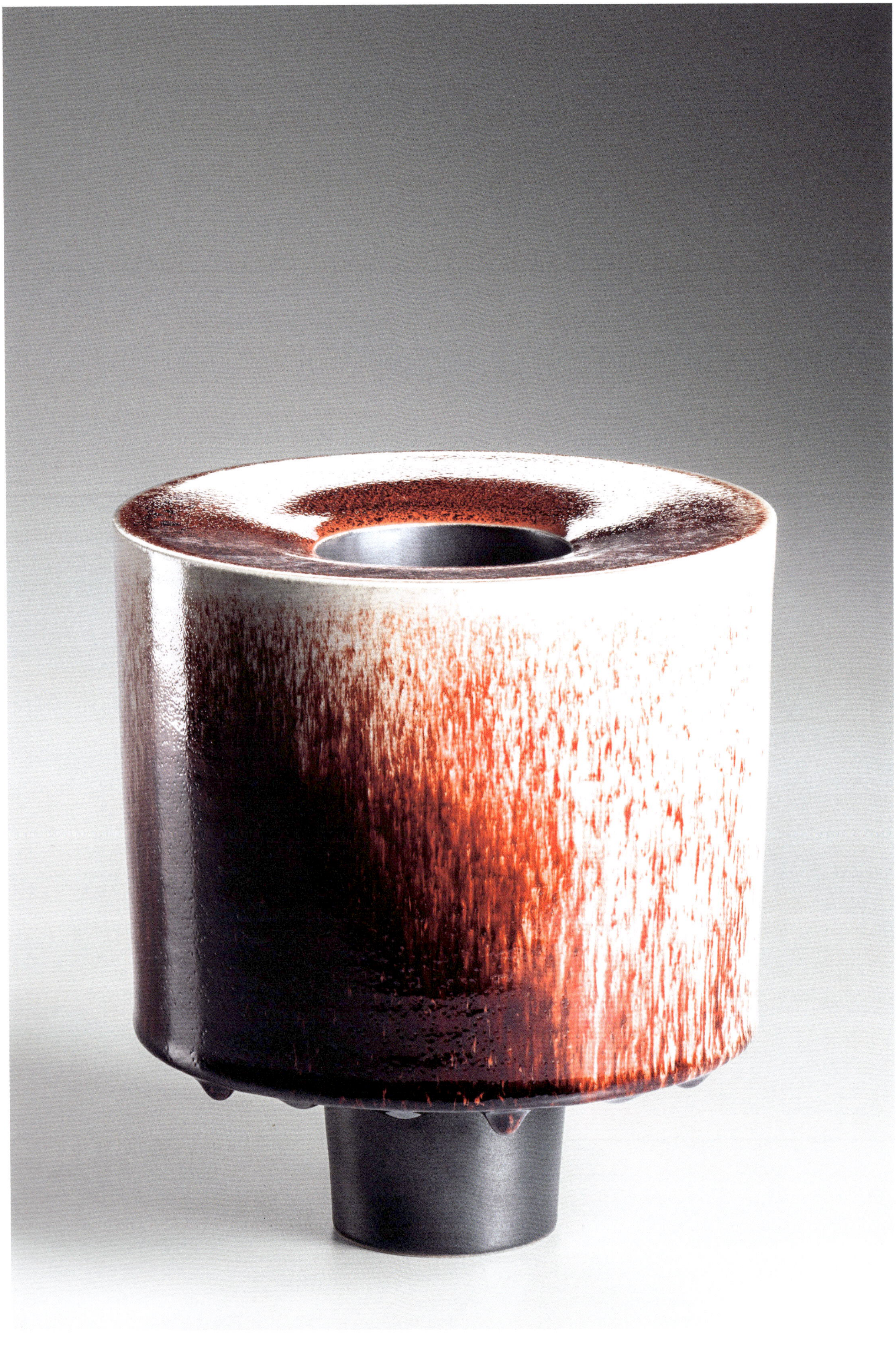

Thomas Bohle

Ceramist

Dornbirn, Austria

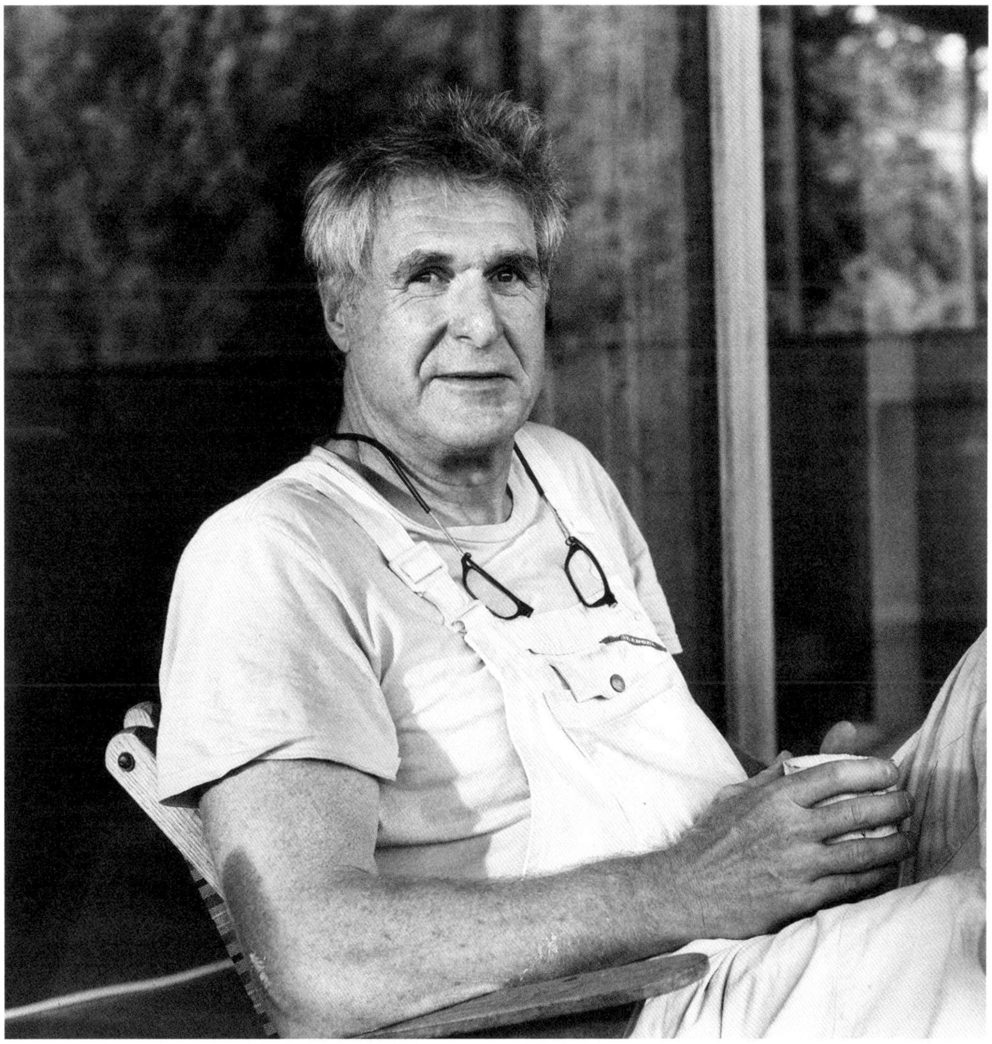

My name is Thomas Bohle, and I'm a ceramist. Working with clay, letting the soft, moist material glide through my fingers and take shape, provides a kind of haptic perception—an experience through touch—and gives me extreme sensory pleasure. This fascination is what keeps me coming back to the wheel.

My work is inspired by ancient forms and glazes. I am as captivated by everyday objects fashioned from clay in rural regions as I am by the fine art of glazing in ancient China. The first objects glazed with a deep oxblood red date to the Song dynasty, a time when glazing was—as it remains today—one of the ceramist's greatest challenges. My work uses ceramics to illustrate the connection between traditional craft and contemporary art. Although my work is based on ancient forms, modern tools offer new possibilities for creating objects.

I grew up in Dornbirn, a small city in western Austria, where I still live today. I trained as a nurse, a profession I practiced for many years. I discovered ceramics when I was twenty-six, in England, where I sat down at a wheel for the very first time. The auditory synesthesia I experienced through the material and the pleasure of creating with my hands spurred me on my artistic path. I finished my apprenticeship when I was thirty and worked in several different studios. After much trial and error and research, I established a solid foundation of traditional lines and forms. Make, make, and make again: that is most important—it's the only way to develop new approaches.

After a study trip to Japan, I felt firmly rooted in the world of ceramics, and my stylistic choices began to lean toward a purity of form thanks to my stay there. In Japan, I learned respect for the material and the ability to see beauty through imperfection.

My first forays into ceramics inspired me to create double-walled pieces. Then, rustic objects from my region and the beauty of Song dynasty vessels compelled me to adopt clay as my material. Today, I use light gray Westerwald clay, found along the right bank of the Rhine, near Bonn, which is covered with a thick blue glaze accented with manganese violet. I like the material's surface and the different degrees of energy required at each stage of the process. For these pieces, I use two distinct and contrasting glazes inside and out or on different sections, such as matte and glossy, or red and black. It's important to find the right glaze for each shape—one that enhances the expressiveness of its line. A poor glaze will have the opposite effect.

In Austria, handicrafts are experiencing renewed popularity, and people are beginning, once again, to look to the beauty of craftsmanship. In my opinion, beauty emerges when the hands work freely, unhindered by the mind. An artist is nothing more than a performer at the moment of creation. Beauty arises from deep within and profoundly moves us.

I consider artisanal objects to be precious and sustainable; they are a corrective to a wasteful society.

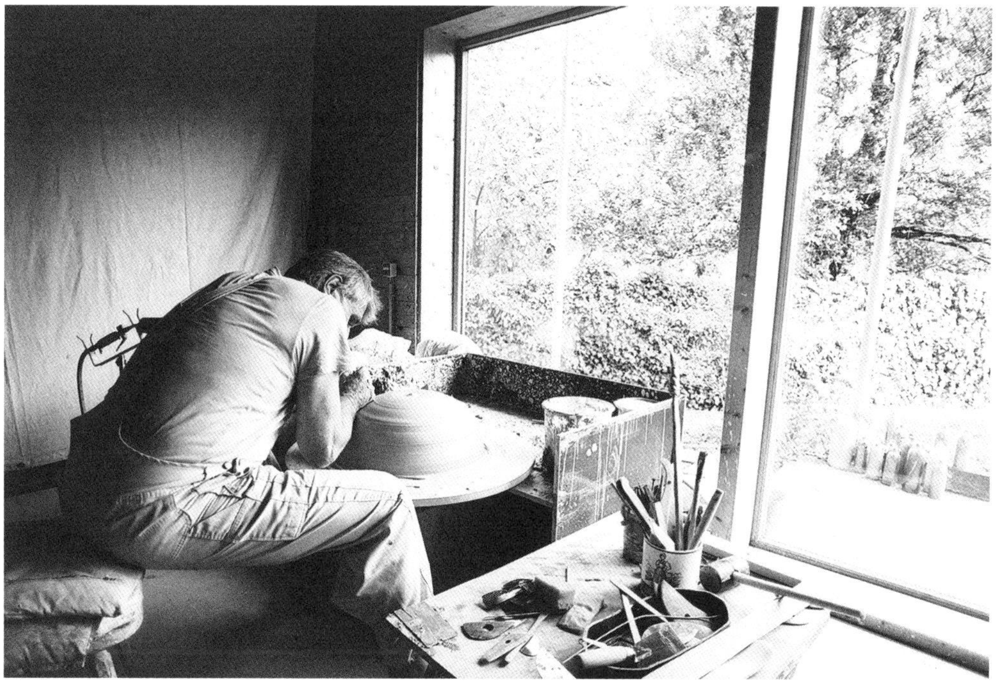

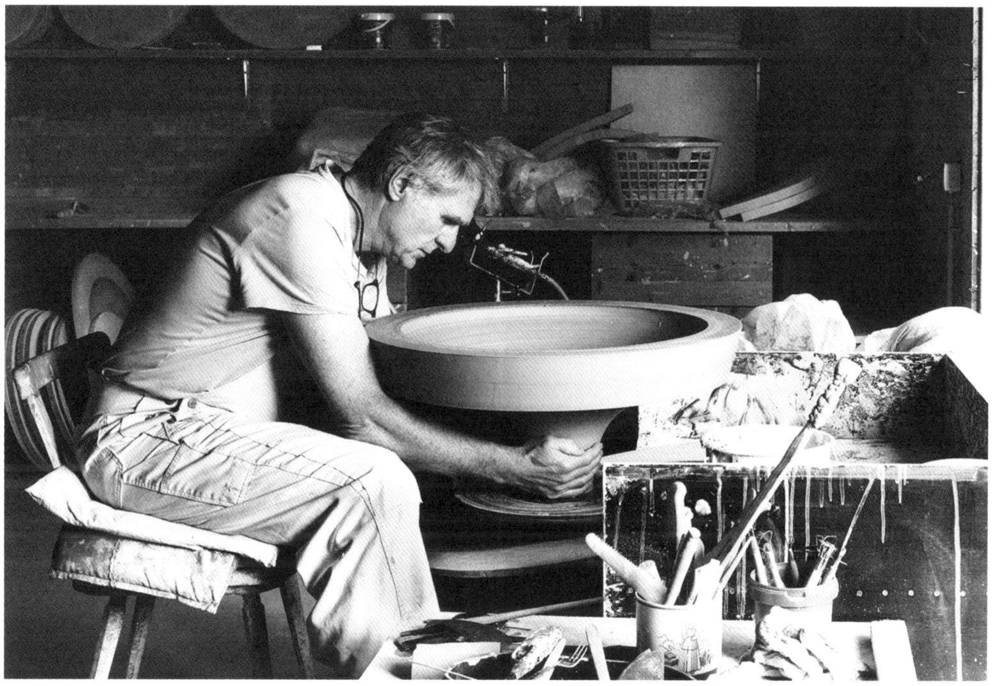

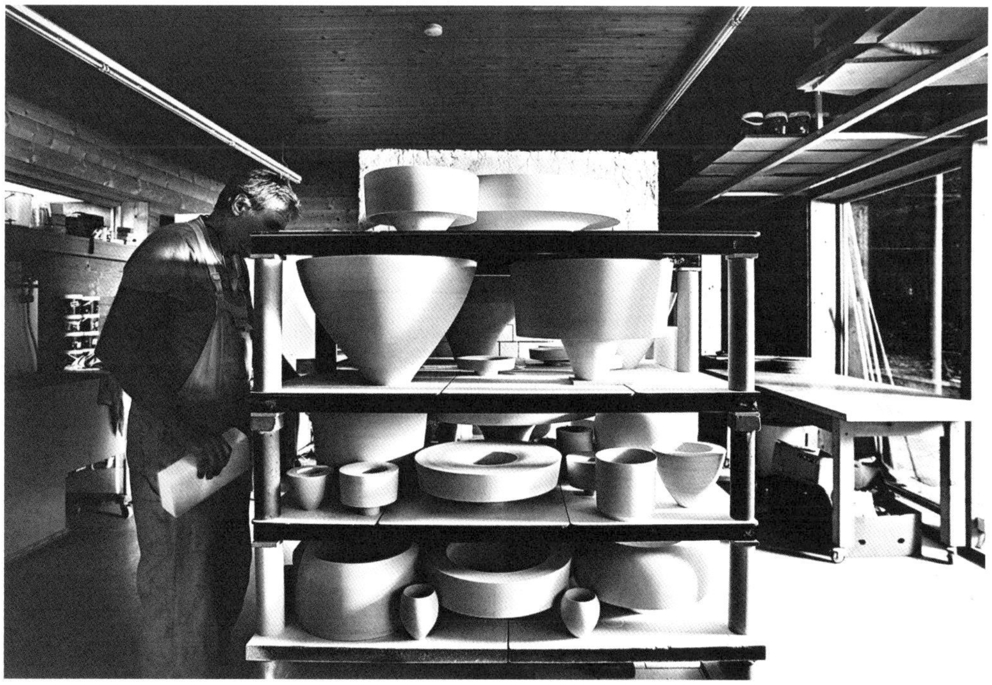

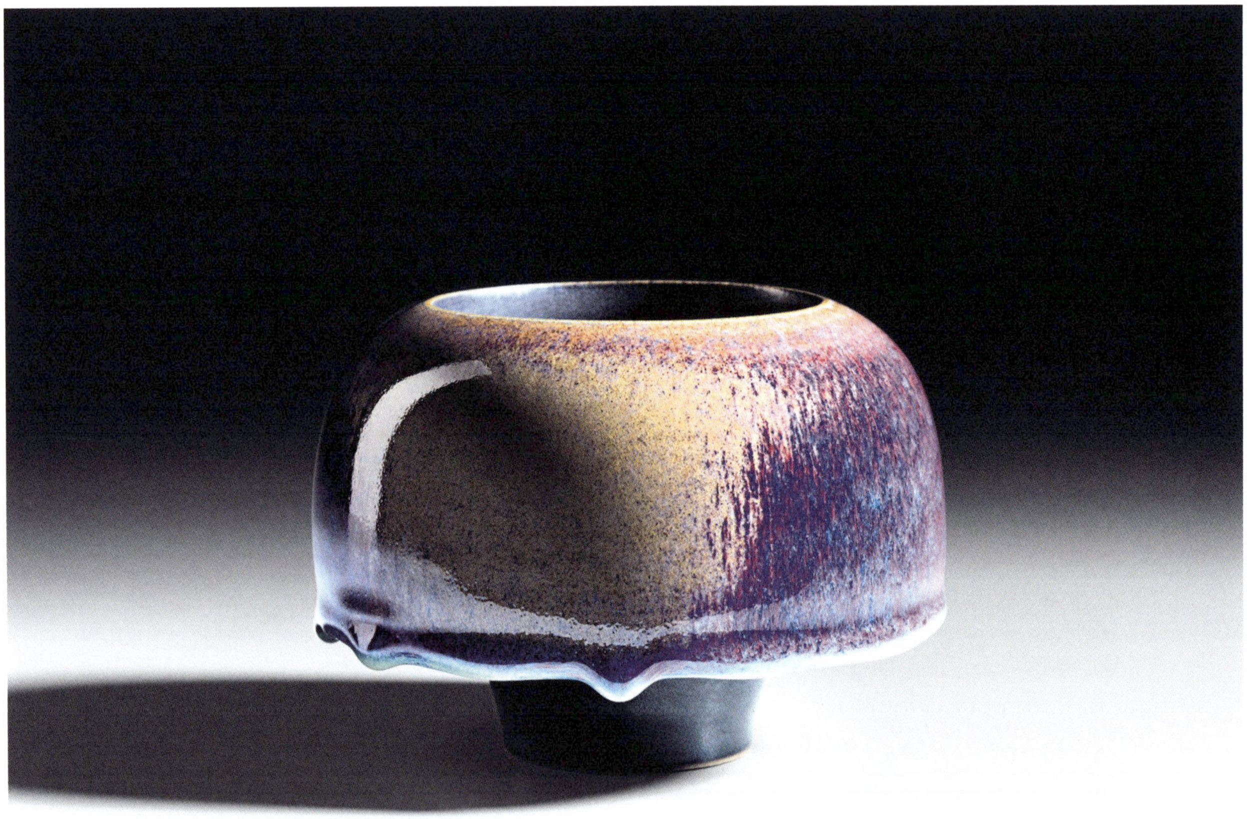

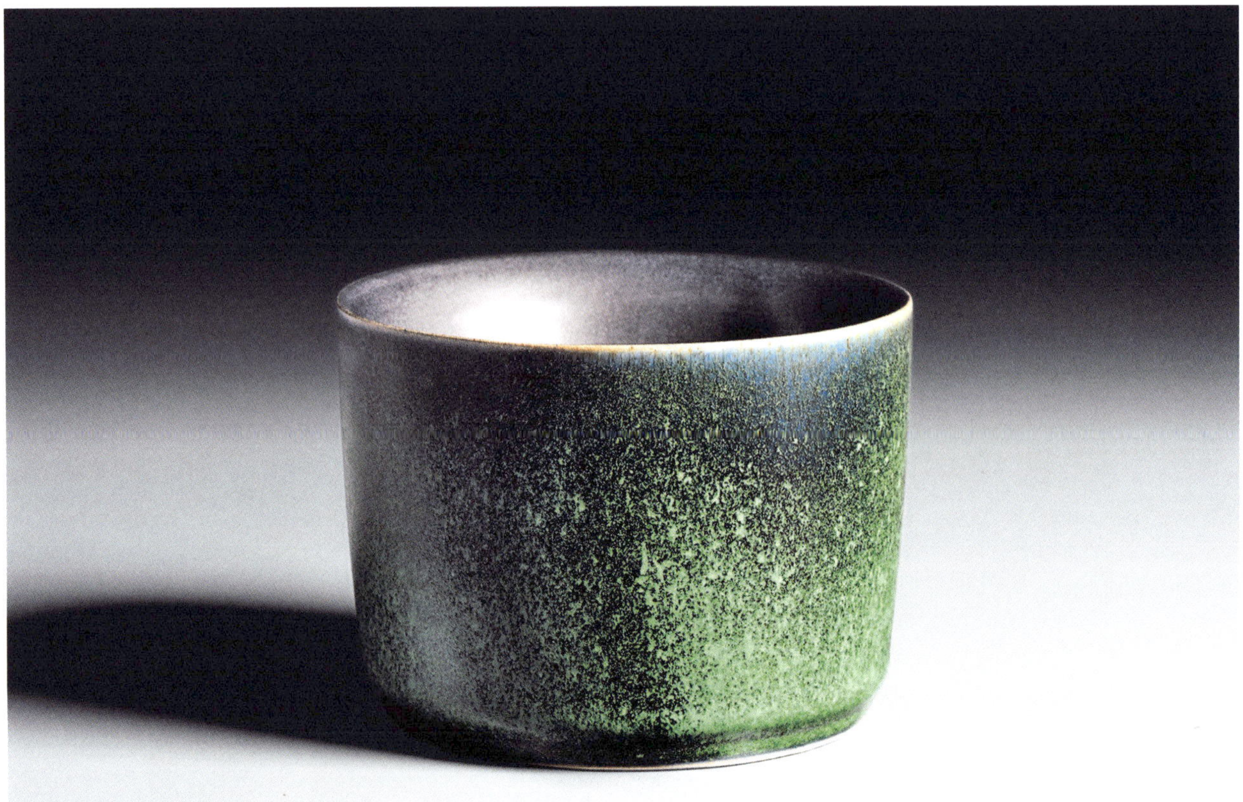

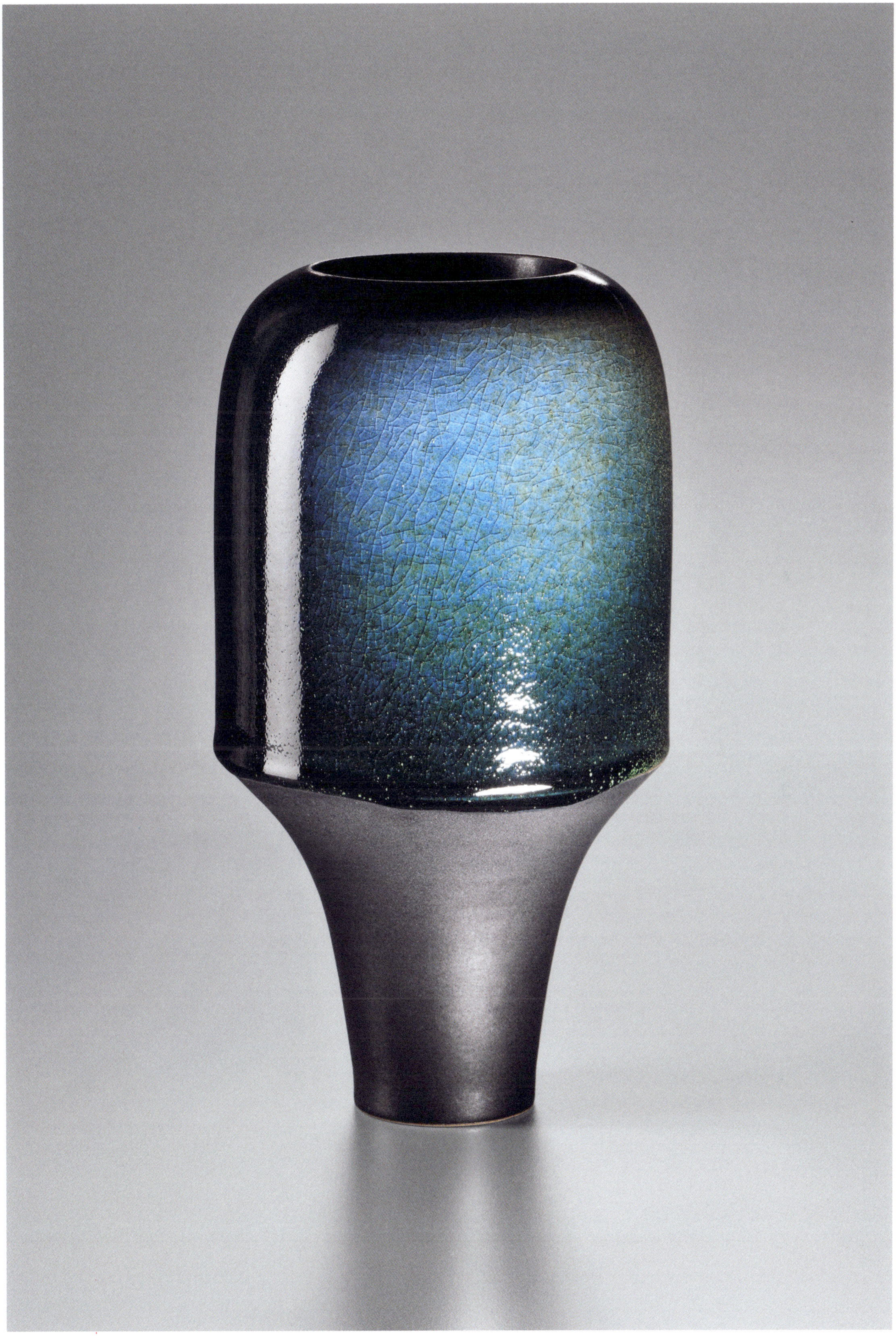

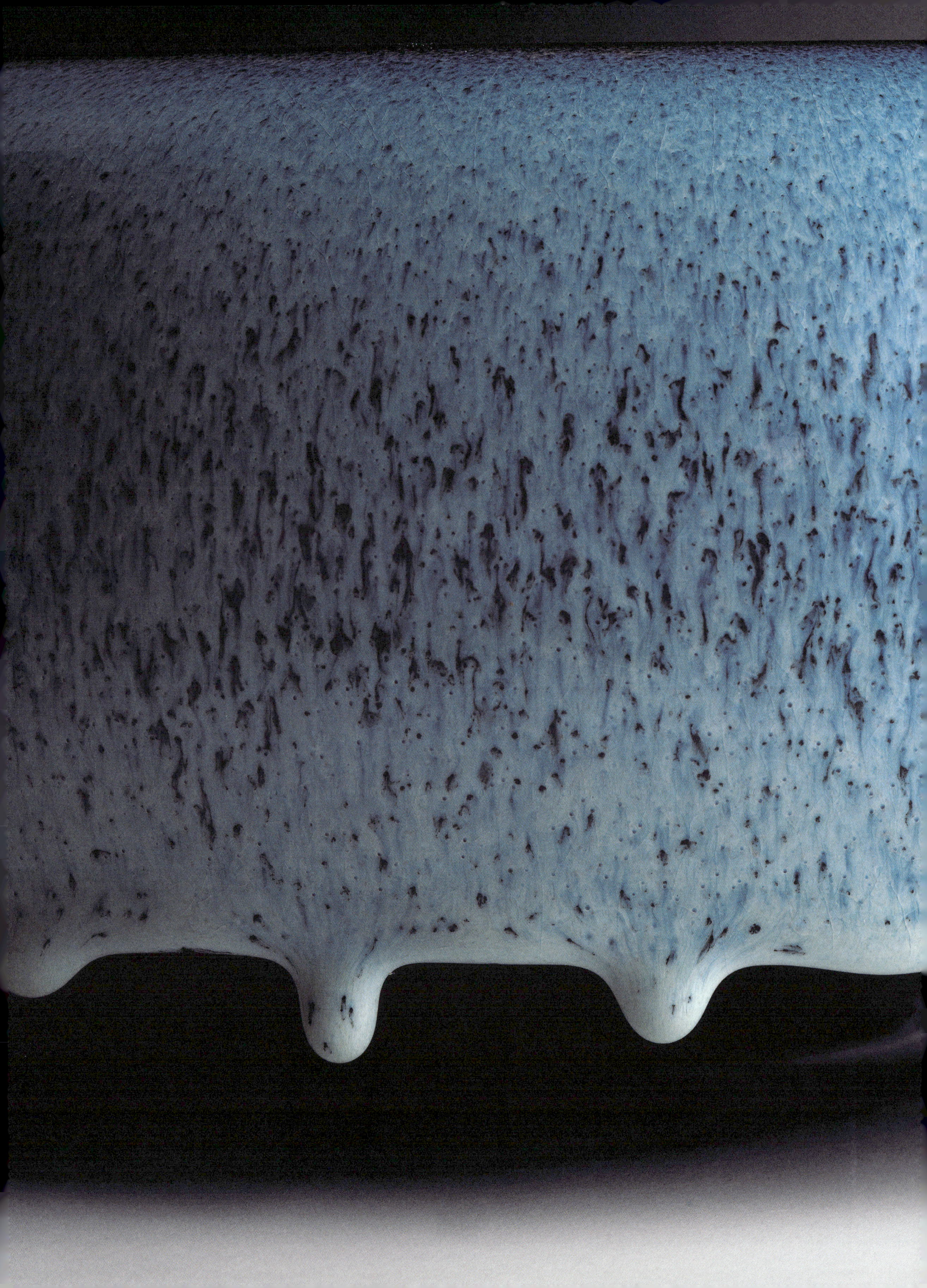

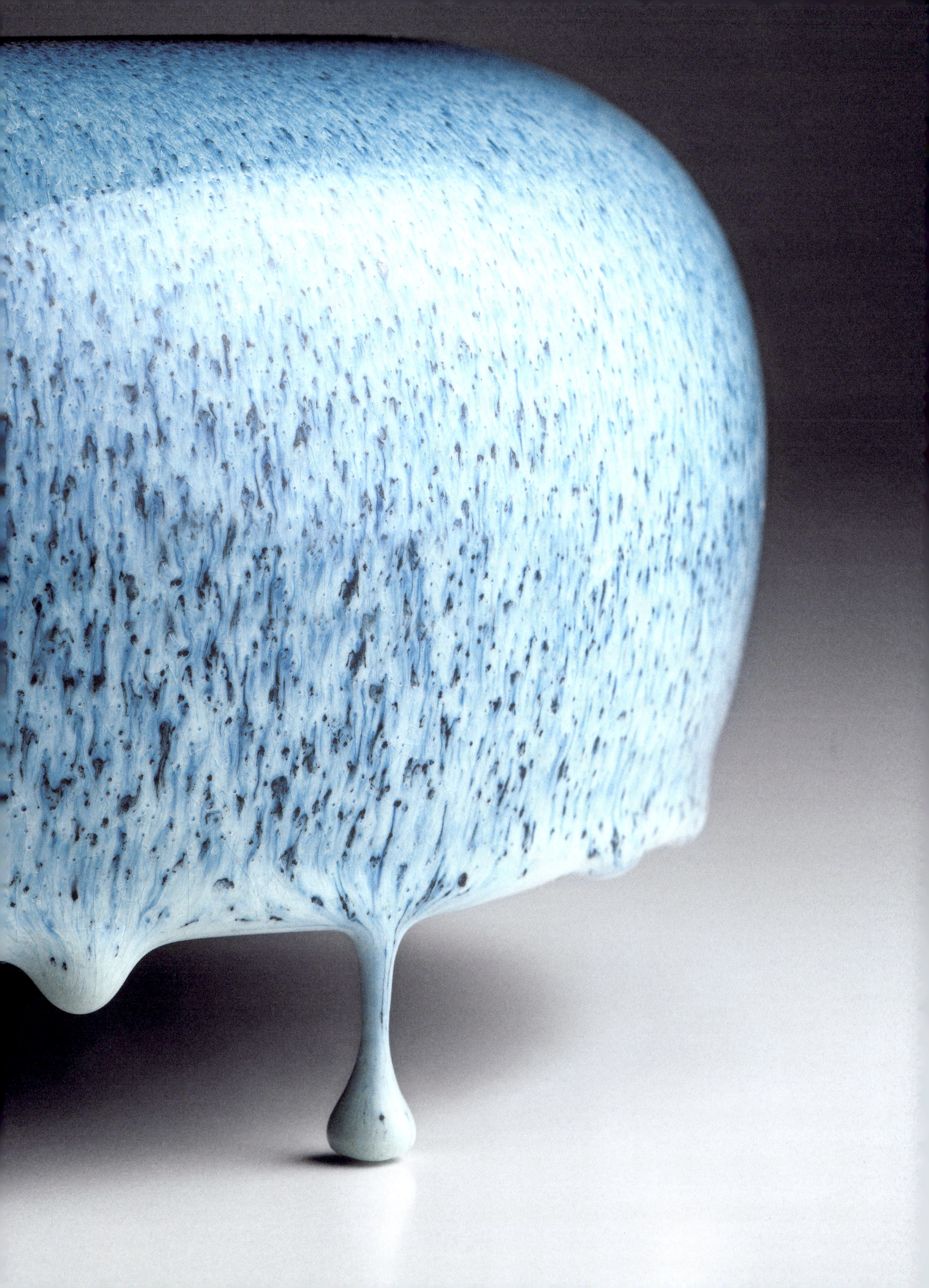

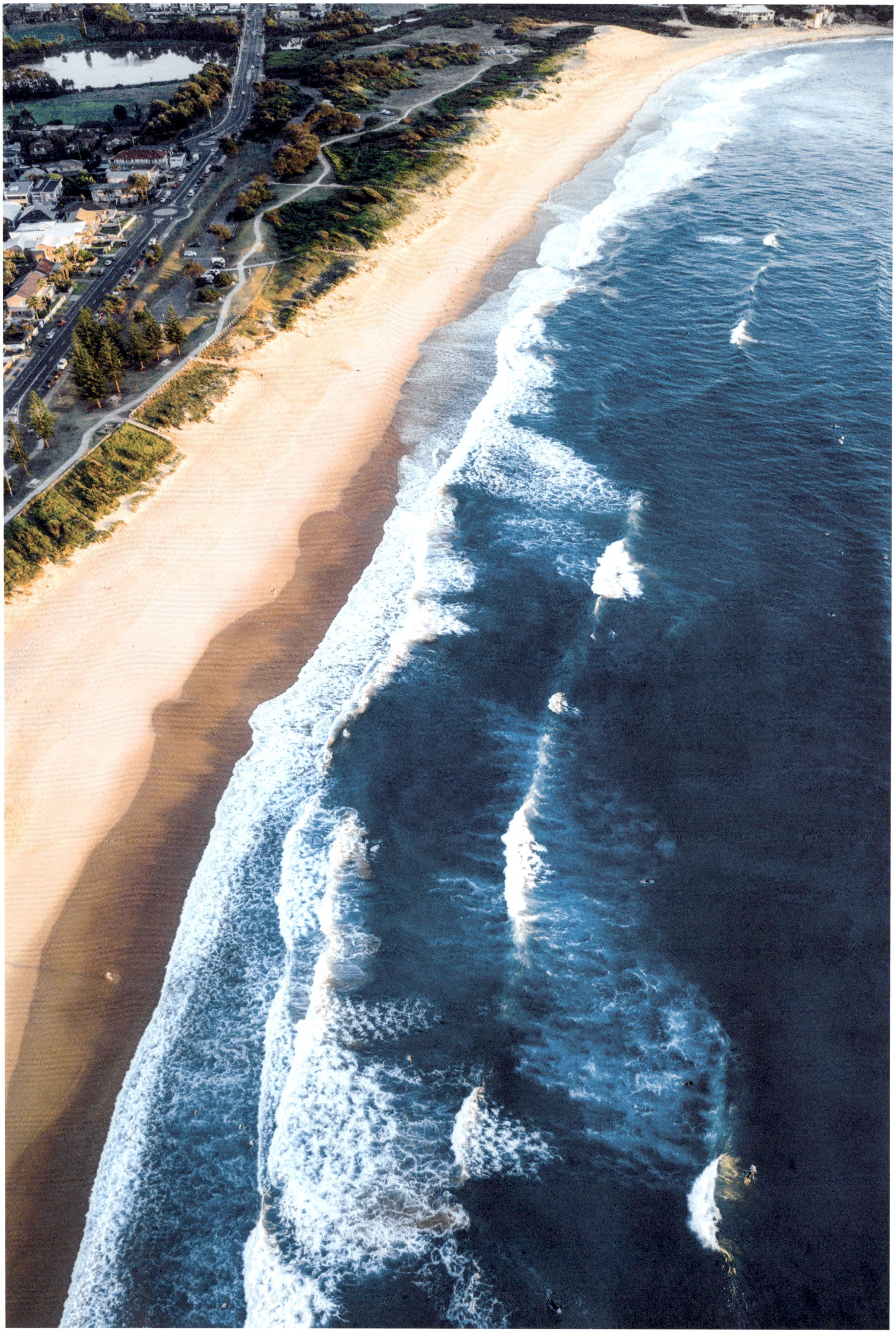

Alana Wilson

Ceramist

Sydney, Australia

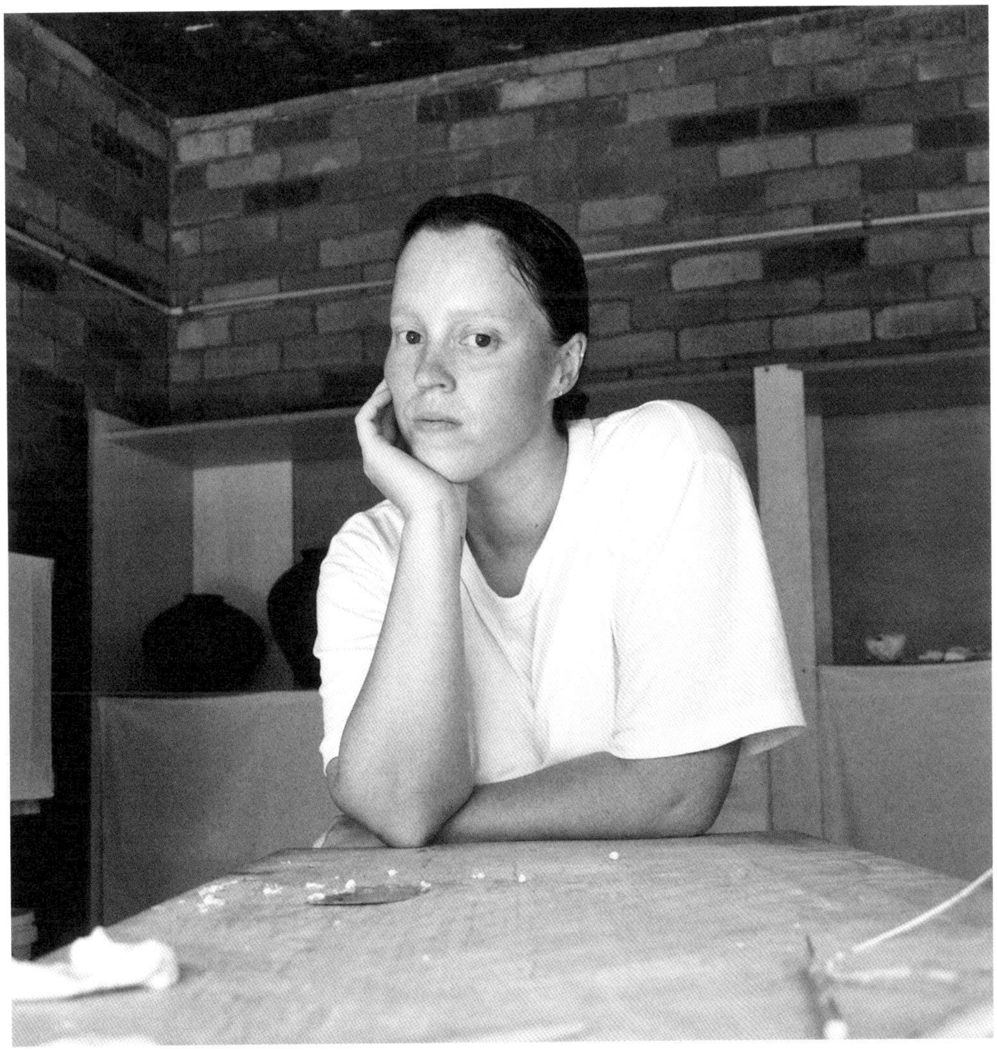

My name is Alana Wilson, and I am a ceramist. My studio is located in Curl Curl, on Sydney's northern beaches. I am an artist currently working across the mediums of ceramics, photography, sculpture, film, and printmaking. My intrinsic nature is to observe, to go against the grain, to seek an alternative angle to most ideas or conceptions. I'm someone who strongly believes in the importance of our connection to nature and our connection to one another.

I was born in Australia but grew up in New Zealand, and so had several family homes in my early years, which meant I struggled to feel a sense of belonging to a definitive place. As a child, most weekends were spent exploring the rock pools or on bush walks. I would collect shells and the bones of small animals, which seemed to me like relics of the fragility of the world.

My first discipline rotation at art school was ceramics. I loved it immediately and never wanted to leave the studio at the end of the day. My mum always reminded me that the key to success was to believe that you could achieve it. I was already committed to following my intuition and natural tendencies, and I continued to choose what I enjoyed doing each day—which was working with ideas, sensitivities, and concepts through various mediums, predominantly clay.

Ceramics is one of the most ancient processes present in human history. The earth is clay, minerals, and oxides. There is no doubting the strength of the connection between ceramics and history. Humans have, for thousands of years, used clay and fire to create utilitarian vessels, and this will not cease. Living and working in the present moment, it is impossible not to draw threads between this history and the contemporary zeitgeist of ceramics.

Ceramics is an immensely tactile medium, inherently dealing with physicality, space, form, and the relation to the human body and the maker. The process of ceramics itself is at the mercy of time and heat, of patience and acceptance. Flaw and failure are inevitable when working with this medium.

I begin by observing, absorbing, and reflecting upon the environment in which I live. Utilizing the physical process and highlighting the movements and cyclical nature of generating work, I have found great inspiration from thinking about gesture, mark-making, imprints, and the remnants or impressions we leave—both intentional and unintentional. I'm also greatly enamored with the work of Brice Marden, Jean Dubuffet, and Agnes Martin—mostly for their processes and in-depth research and exploration, more than for the visual results of these.

The glaze is an integral part of the medium of ceramics; it is an important step in the process and contributes to the finished piece by helping to create a unified whole. One of my main areas of research within the studio is glaze technology and firing. I experiment with the materials' boundaries as well as exploring new tools or alternative methods to give rise to moments of discovery and wonder within the firing process. Glaze layering; material washes; the use of saggars, sand, and salt; and oxide vaporization are all techniques I consistently experiment with. I try to use color as local—natural, fitting, honest—not color as ornament.

In my practice, I often ask myself, what is the boundary between art and craft? I do not have an answer, but in turn I would ask, why do we need to define things as one or the other? Perhaps Western culture is the only one to ask this question. I believe in a holistic balance in the relationship between art and life. Historically, craft evolved from pieces created for their utilitarian value, while art evolved from a representation of cultural values and societal observations. Over time, the two have crossed paths every so often, and I think we are seeing a return to tactile physicality.

I believe our values will evolve to reflect the changes in the environment, the economy, the political climate, and the way we connect. I hope there is more good that comes out of it.

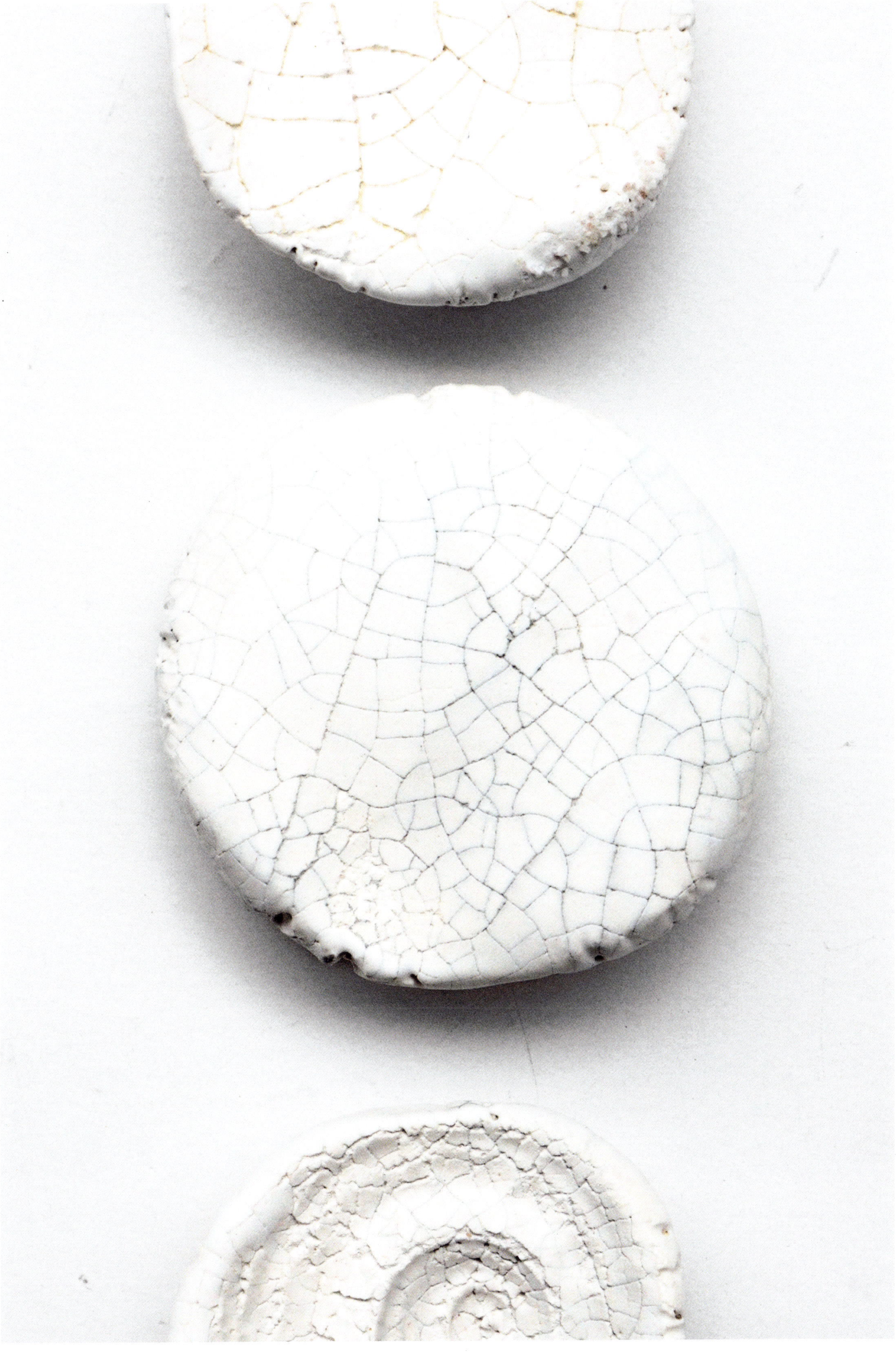

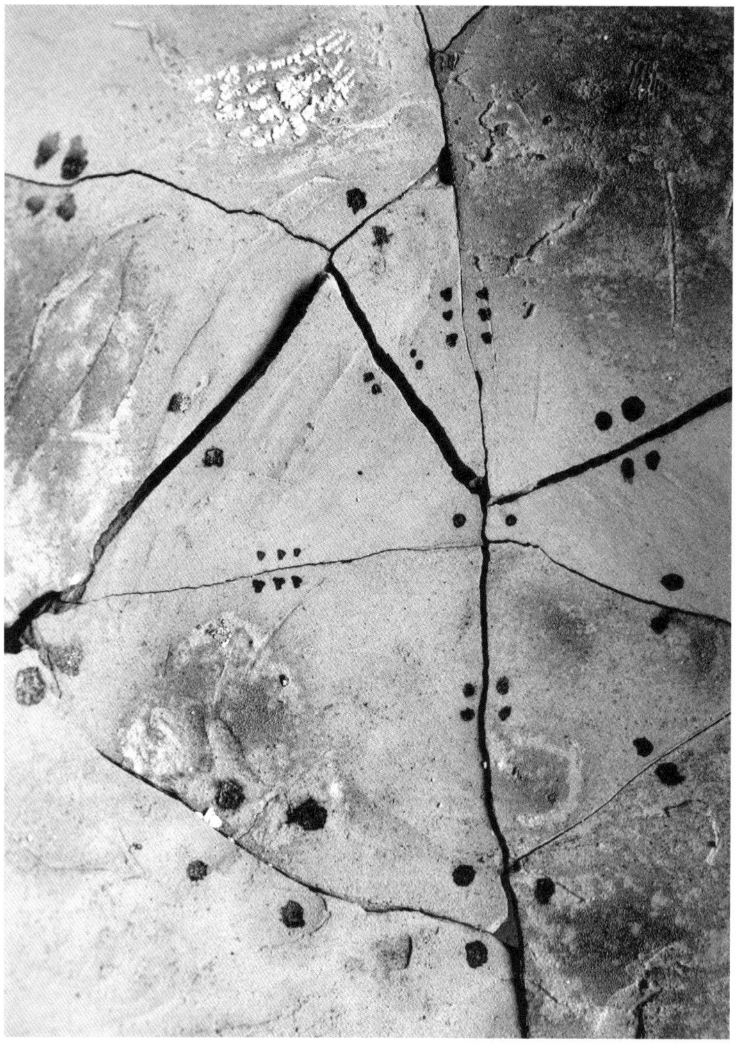

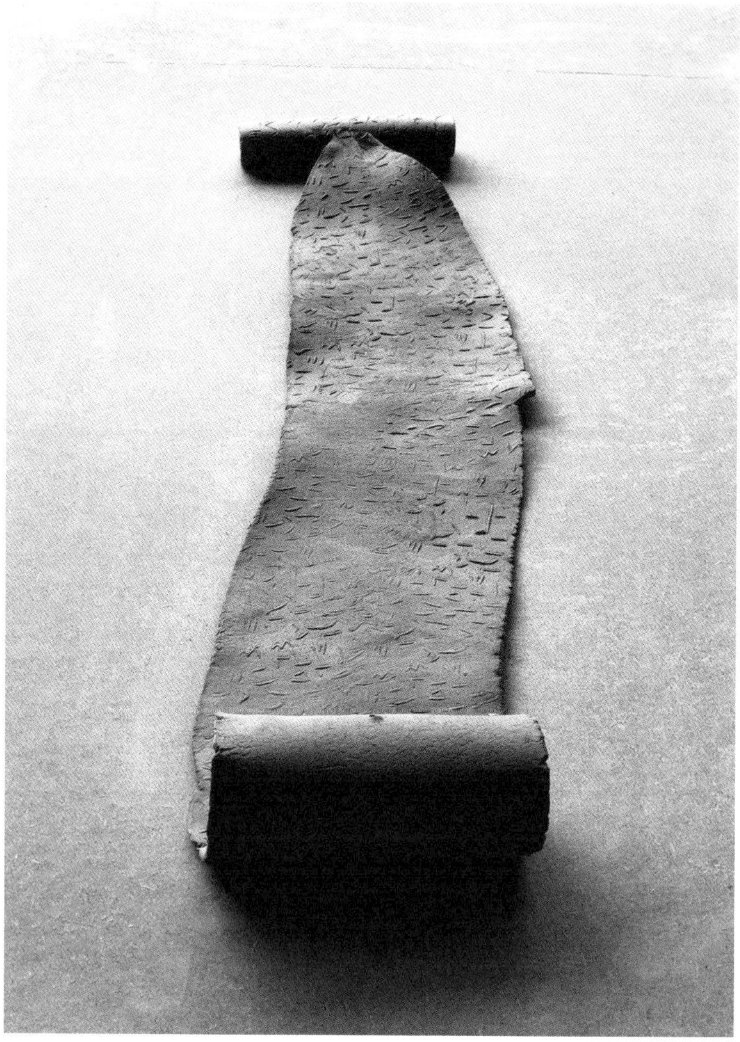

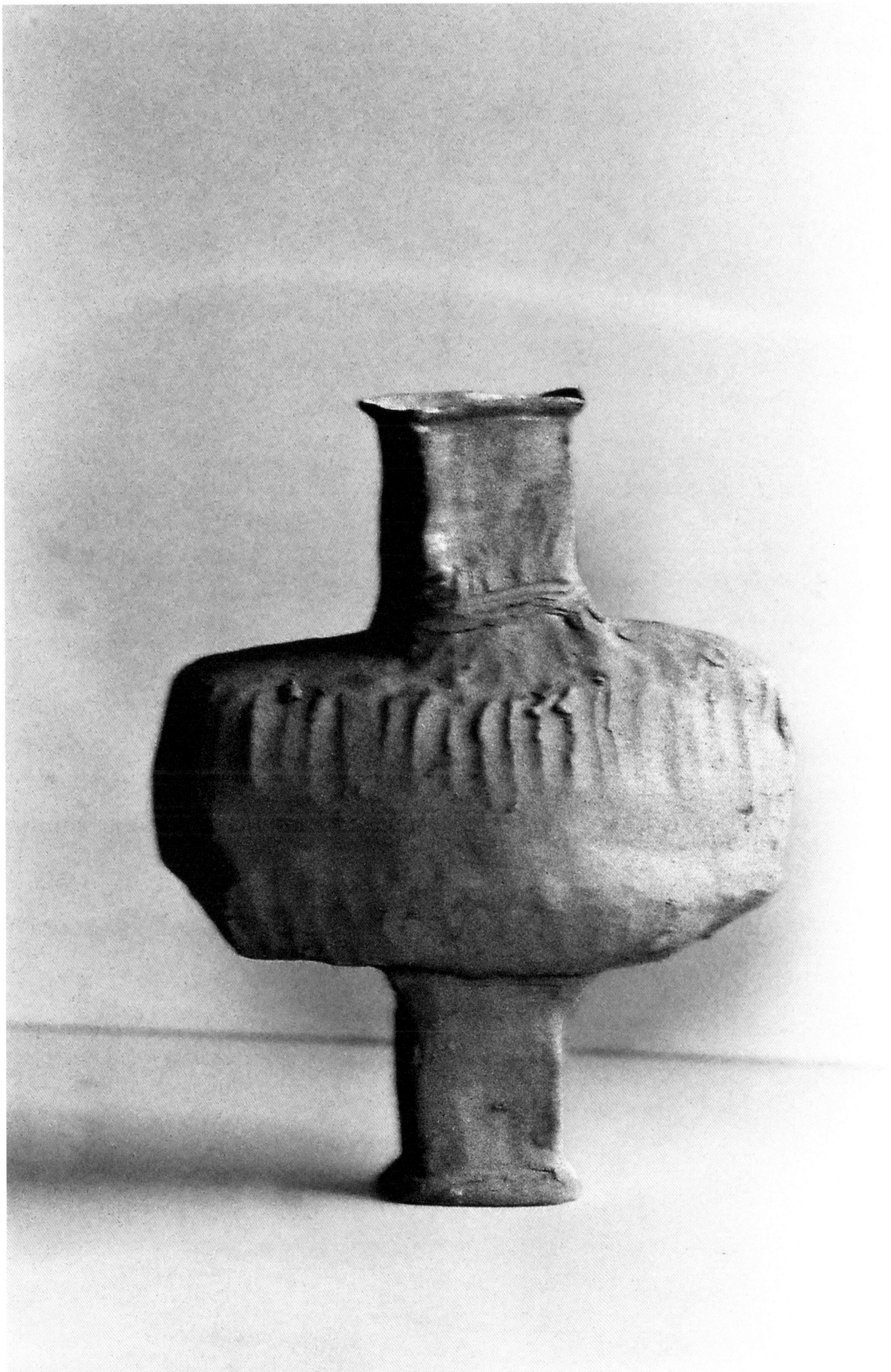

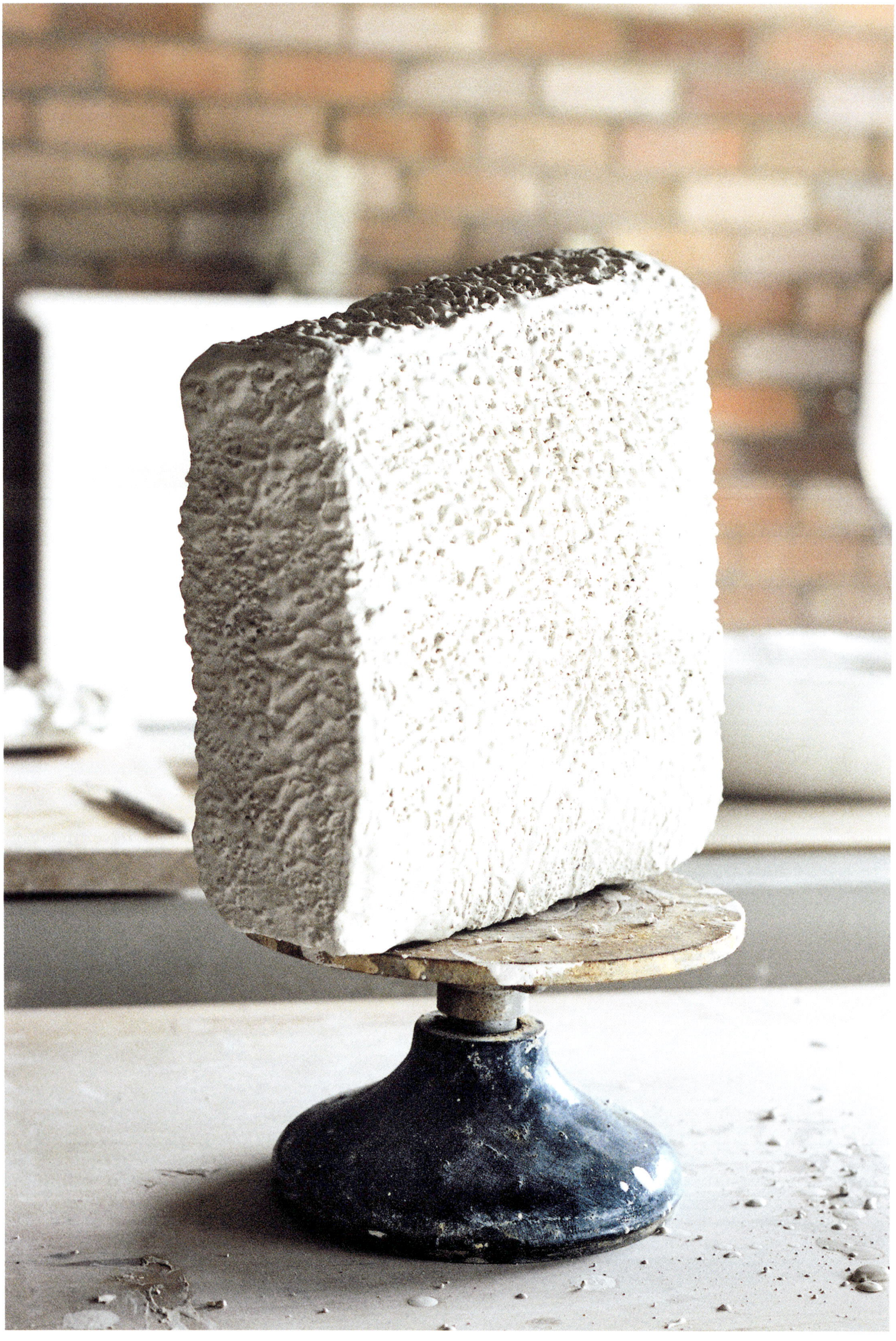

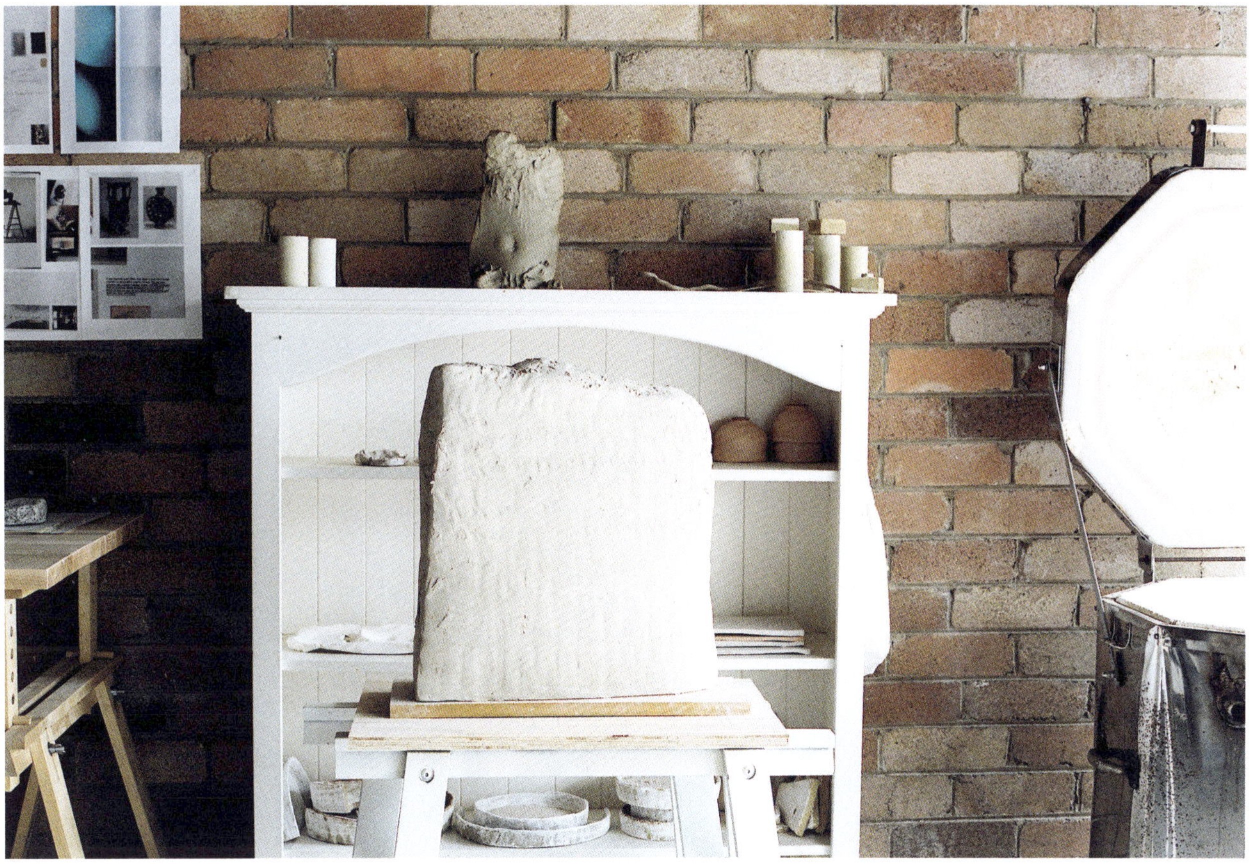

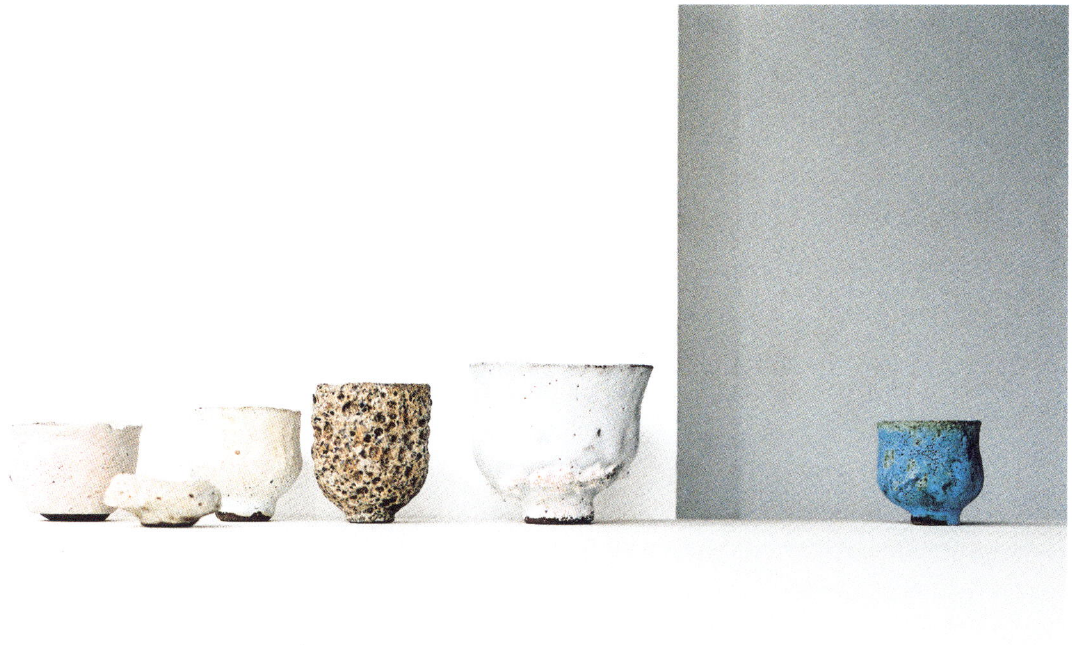

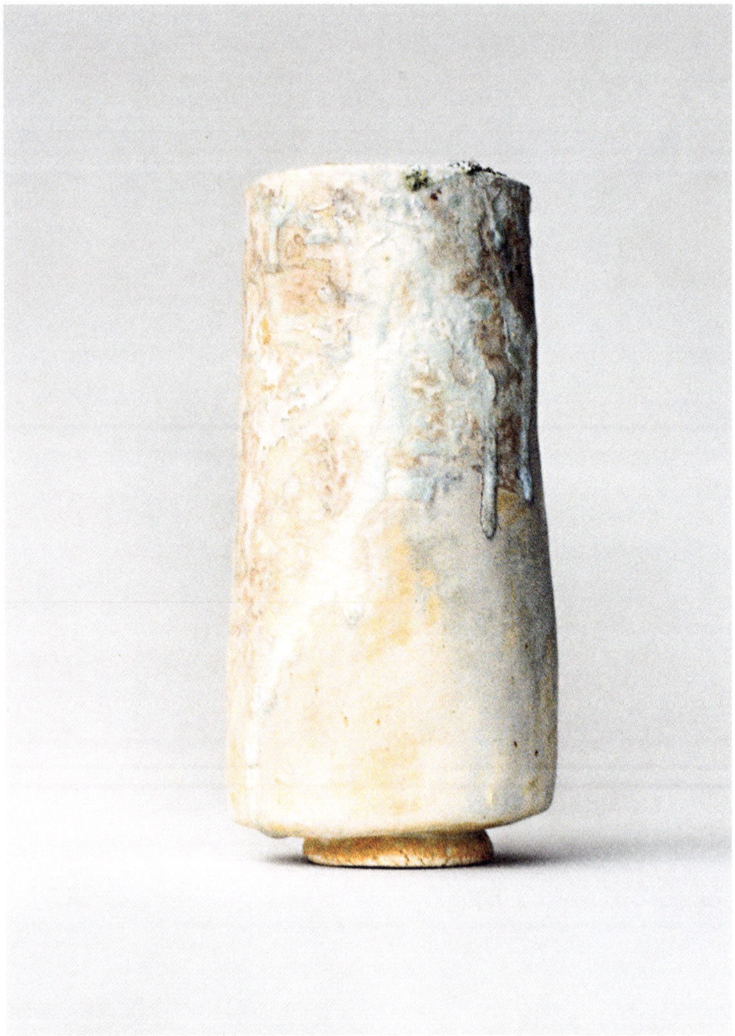

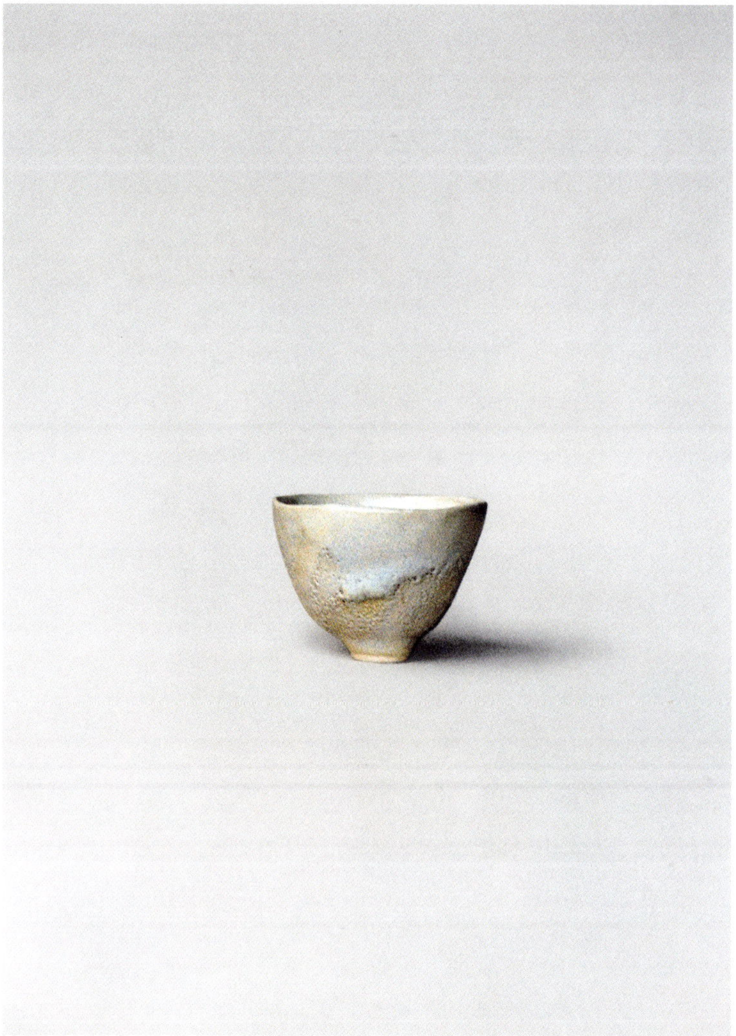

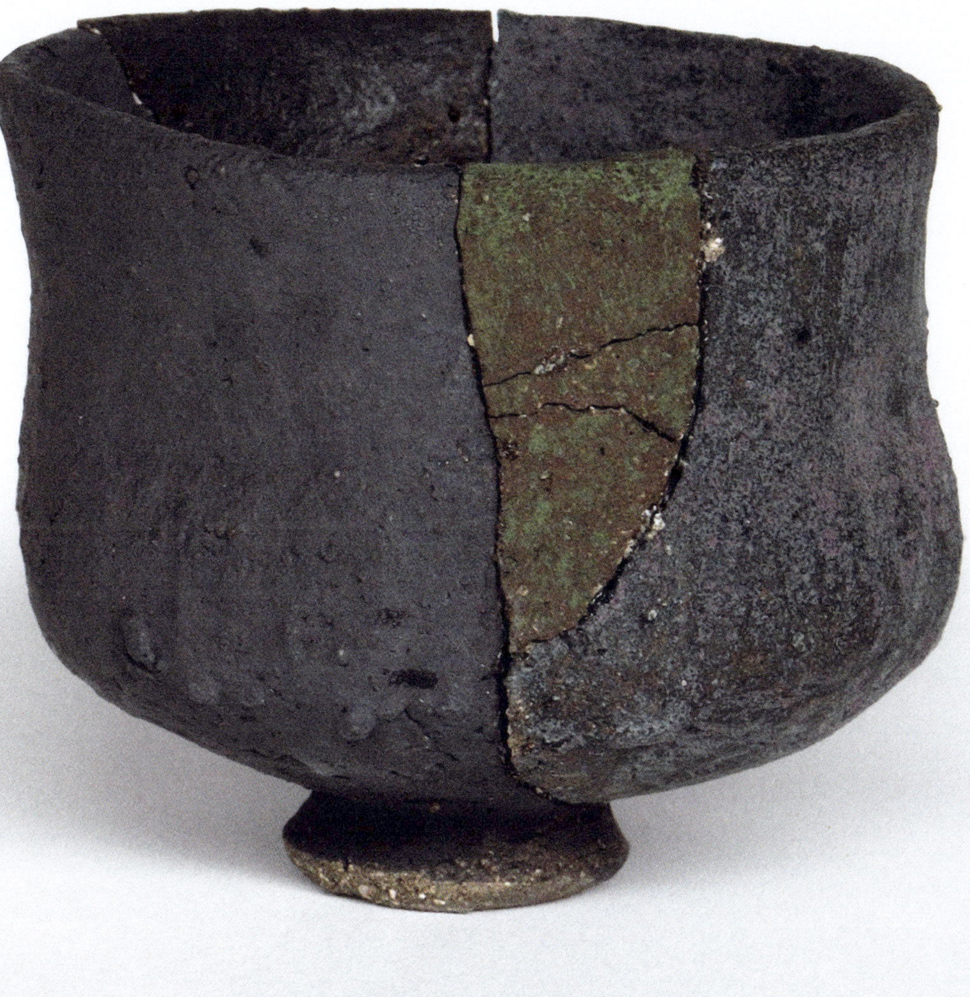

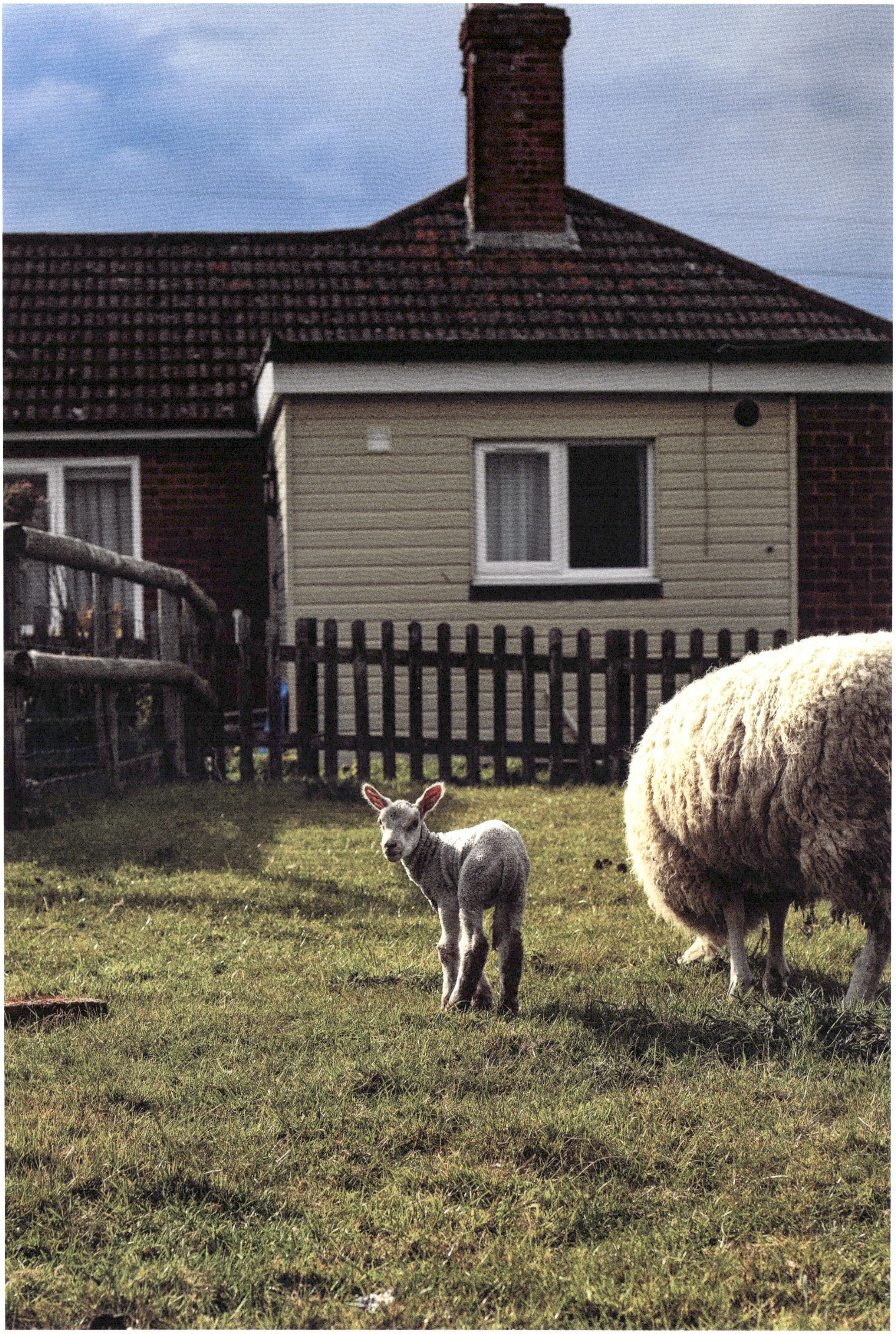

Charlotte Mary Pack

Ceramist

East Sussex,
United Kingdom

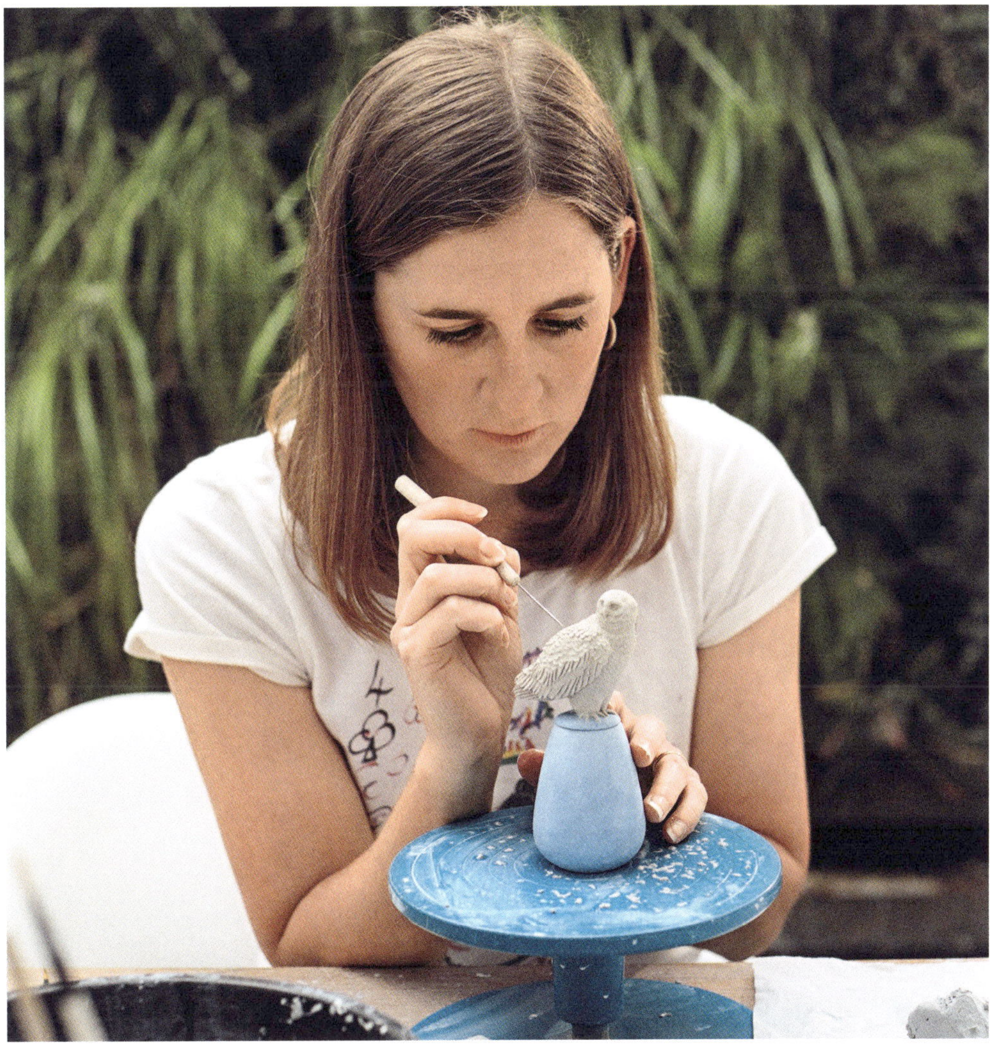

My name is Charlotte Mary Pack, and I am a ceramist. The daughter of farmers, I have a degree in ceramic design: I studied ceramics at Central Saint Martins in London. Today, I live on a lovely farm in Rye Foreign, East Sussex, in the south of England.

I grew up on the family farm with my twin brother, Freddie, and my older sister, Harriet. It was like a giant playground for us. I have vivid memories of sitting under the buddleia bushes in the garden surround by hundreds of butterflies—now I'd be lucky if I saw three or four. Growing up on the farm, where I was free to explore, I developed an interest and admiration for animals and nature from an early age.

From six to ten years old, my brother Freddie and I used to attend pottery classes after school with our very eccentric teacher, Mr. Sparling. He was very strict about what we made and how we made it. One month we'd make a highland steer and another a wild boar, and they had to be a perfect likeness—there was no room for artistic license. In high school, I was lucky enough to take ceramics at A-level, which is when I realized that this was the medium I enjoyed using the most. I drew inspiration from nature and my surroundings, making pieces inspired by my chickens or based on natural objects like twigs, leaves, and acorns found on the farm.

When I am working with clay, I feel self-assured and confident in my ability, challenged, inspired, excited, and, at times, frustrated.

I discovered the Maasai Mara on a trip to Kenya and instantly fell in love with the wide-open spaces. I spent three sleepless nights listening to hippopotamuses brush past my tent and the bloodcurdling calls of lions far too close for comfort. It wasn't until I had experienced and witnessed nature and wildlife on this scale and in its natural habitat that I realized my true passion for it. It seemed an obvious choice for me to follow this passion, too, and I decided to make it my mission to try and help to preserve this wildlife.

My first major piece, *Fading Away*, was for my graduate show. I made all 198 critically endangered mammals on the International Union for Conservation of Nature's Red List. After graduating, I decided that I wanted to see more of Africa. I persuaded my brother and some friends, and we drove 14,000 miles (23,000 km) across nine countries: South Africa, Eswatini, Namibia, Botswana, Zambia, Malawi, Tanzania including Zanzibar, Rwanda, and Zimbabwe. These experiences have been a key influence in my practice.

When I'm working on my animal sculptures, I focus on achieving realism and expressiveness. I use my computer to compile photos of wild animals taken from different angles in order to capture their postures, the way they bend down to drink water, or the expression in their eyes when facing danger. I create my animals in a palette of monochromes. I used to work with earthier tones, but now I just have fun with it; any color goes. I like to display my works together with a full spectrum of colors if I can. In the series *Species Pots*, a back stamp unique to each animal is applied on the underside of each piece and includes the species name and its status in the wild: critically endangered, endangered, or vulnerable. It's important that people are able to identify each animal and have the opportunity to discover the species in detail, as well as the reasons why it is under threat.

On December 4, 2018, World Wildlife Conservation Day, I stayed up through the night to make one hundred porcelain elephants in a twenty-four-hour period—that's one every fifteen minutes! The number represented the lives lost each day to the insatiable and unsustainable demands of the ivory trade. I shared the process live on social media over the twenty-four hours I spent making them, then I displayed the elephants in a spiral formation, from the largest to the smallest in the center. I exhibited them in this way to symbolize their decline in the wild and to create a visual impact that, I hope, provoked a reaction and raised awareness about this ongoing tragedy and our dwindling wildlife.

All the animals that I make are endangered. I don't usually focus on just one. There are thousands of species on the IUCN's Red List. For each animal sold, I donate 15 percent of the profits to animal protection organizations, as well as social projects.

Britain is a nation of animal lovers, so my work is always well received here. My animals have also traveled to Paris, Geneva, and, most recently, to Hong Kong. I hope my work speaks for itself. Some of us may forget, but we're animals, too!

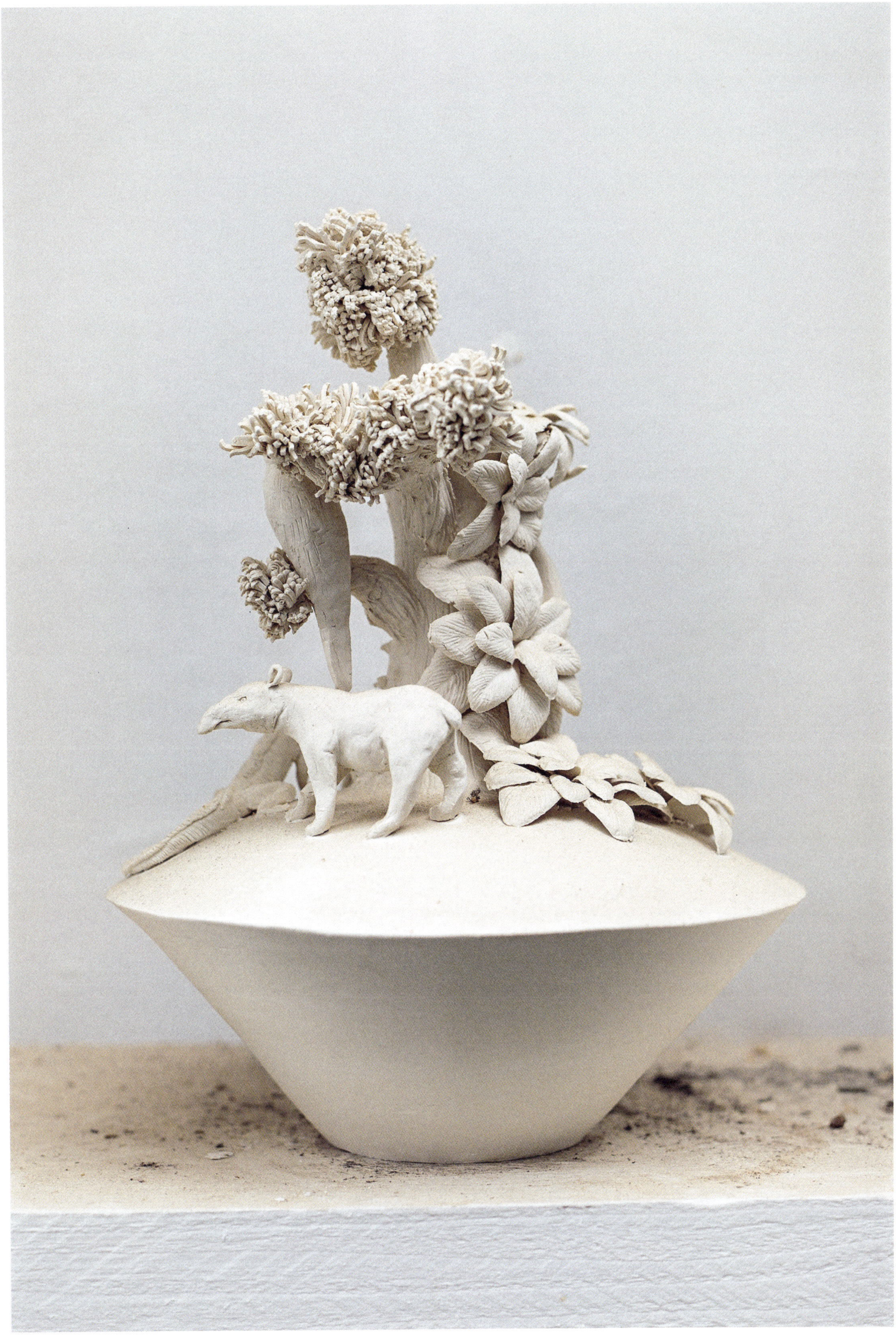

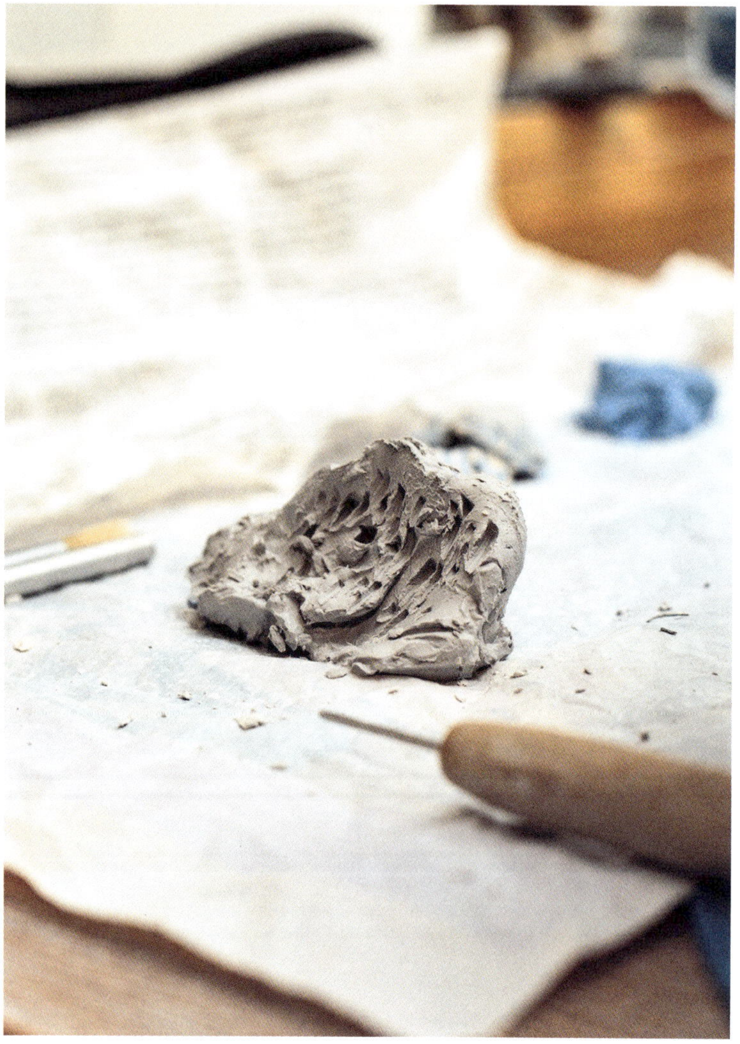
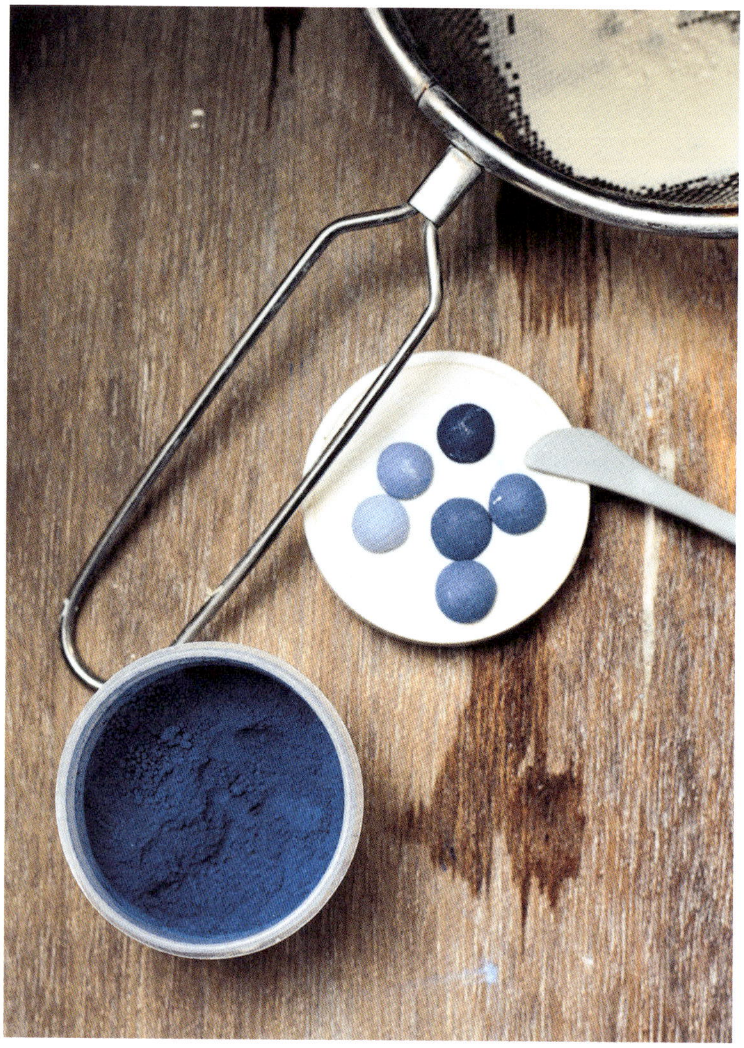

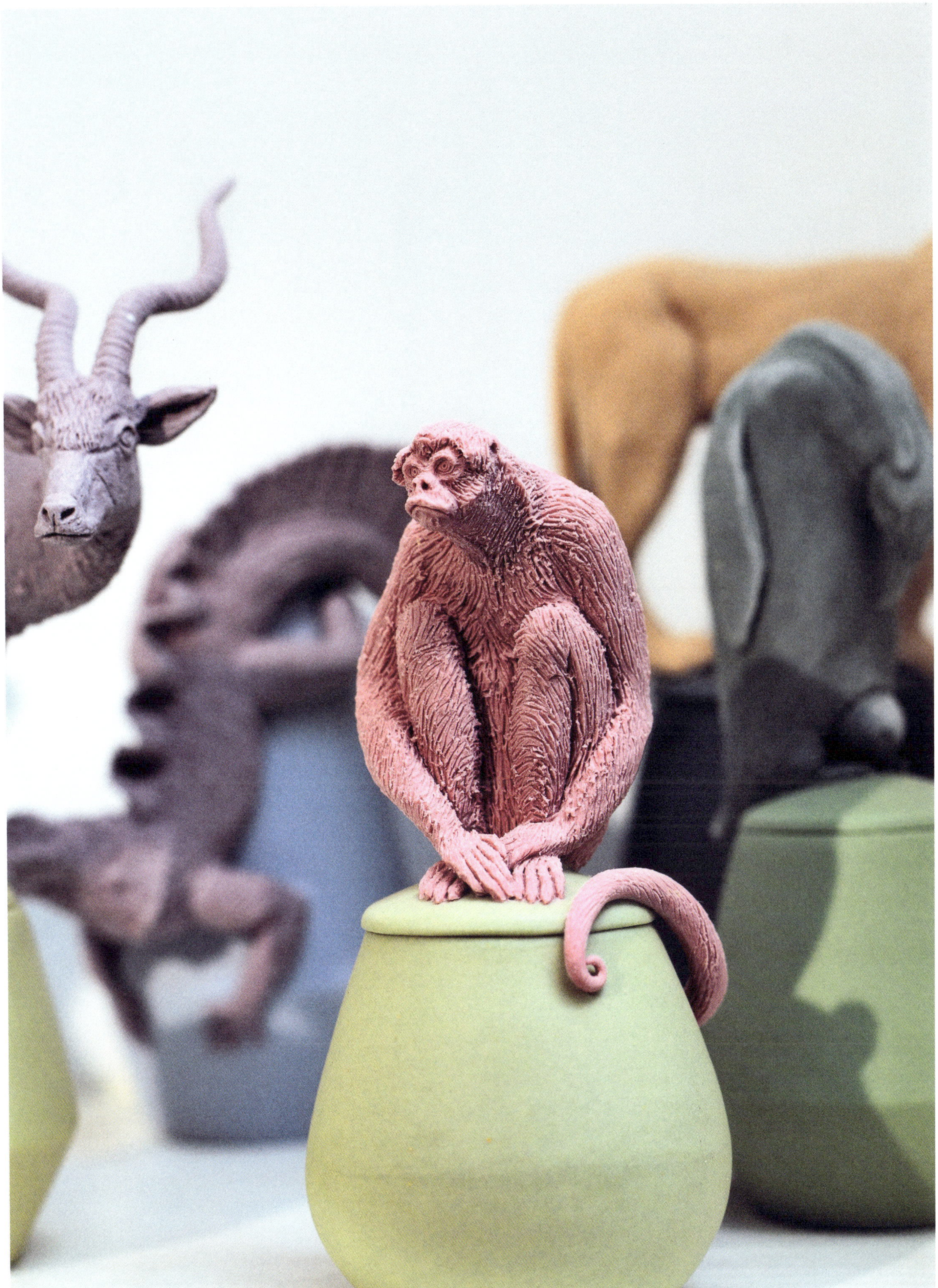

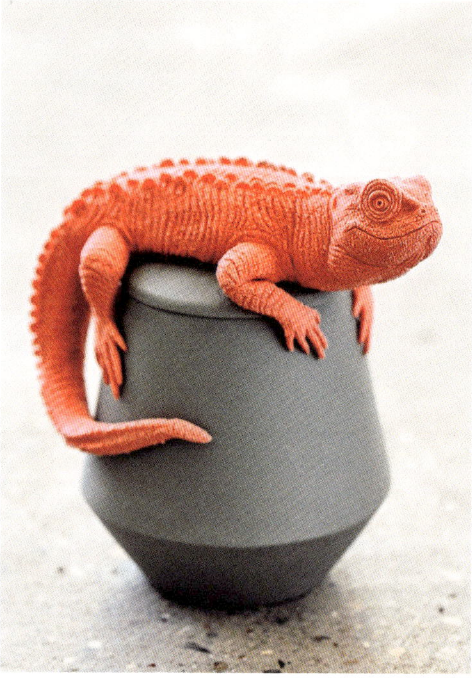
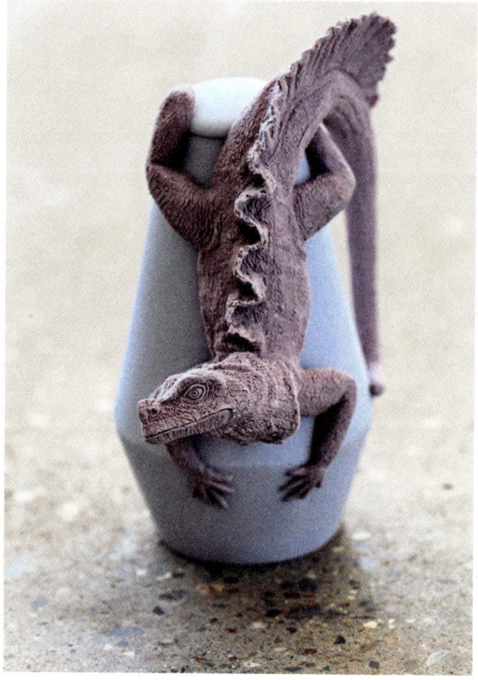
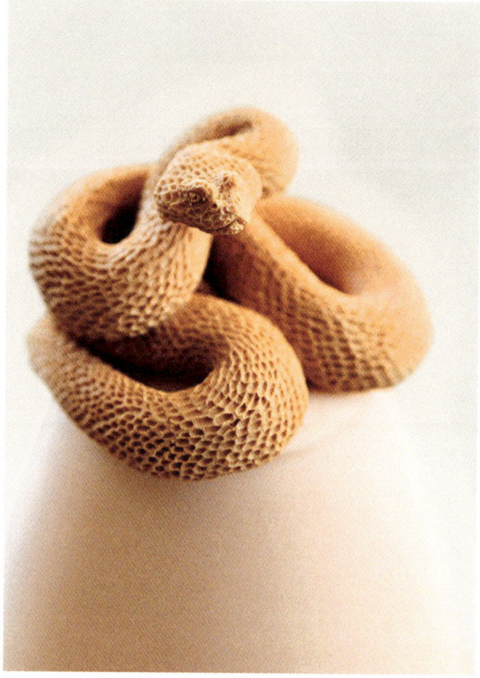
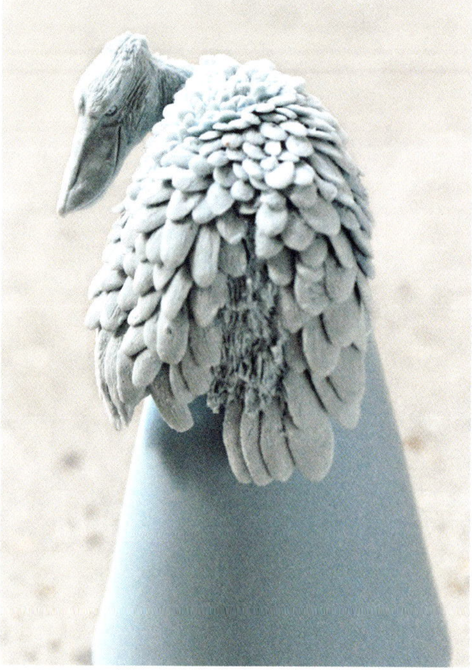
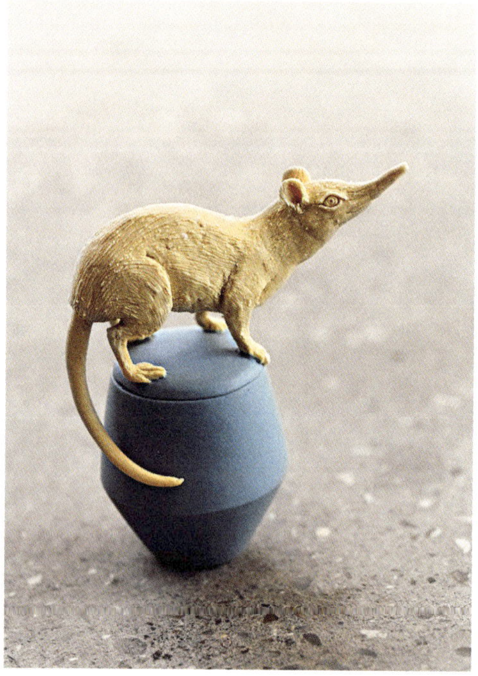
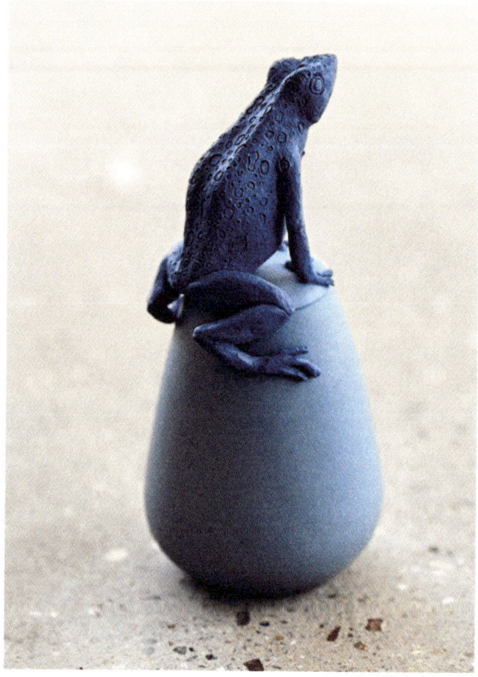
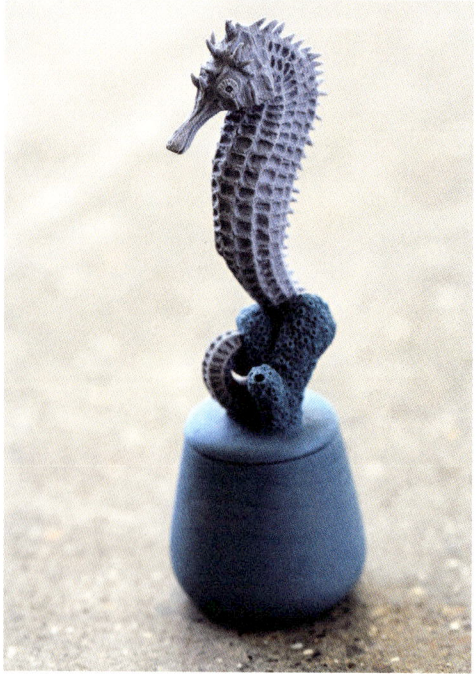
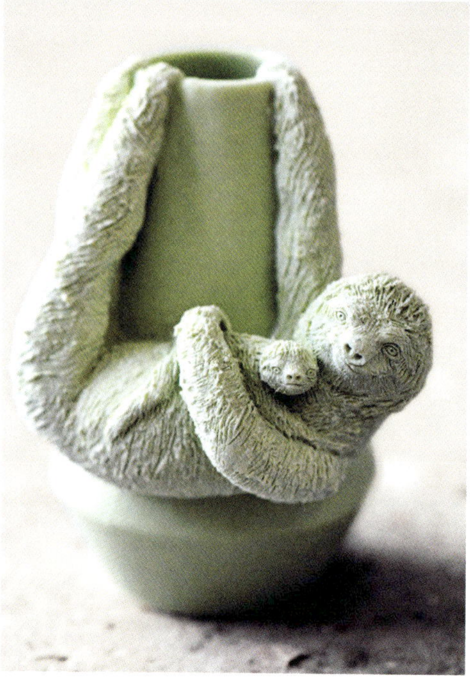
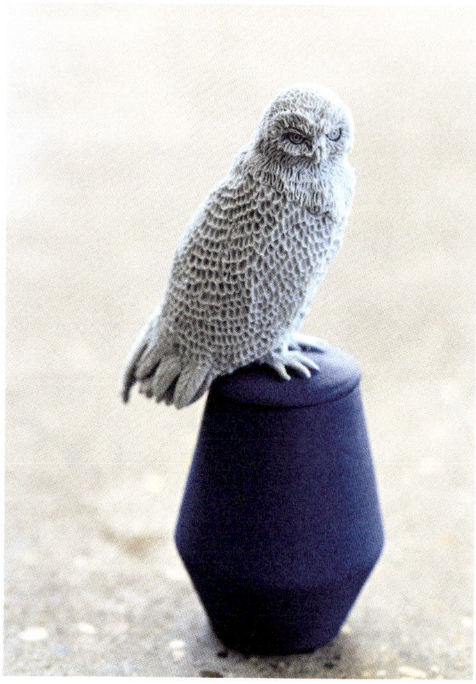

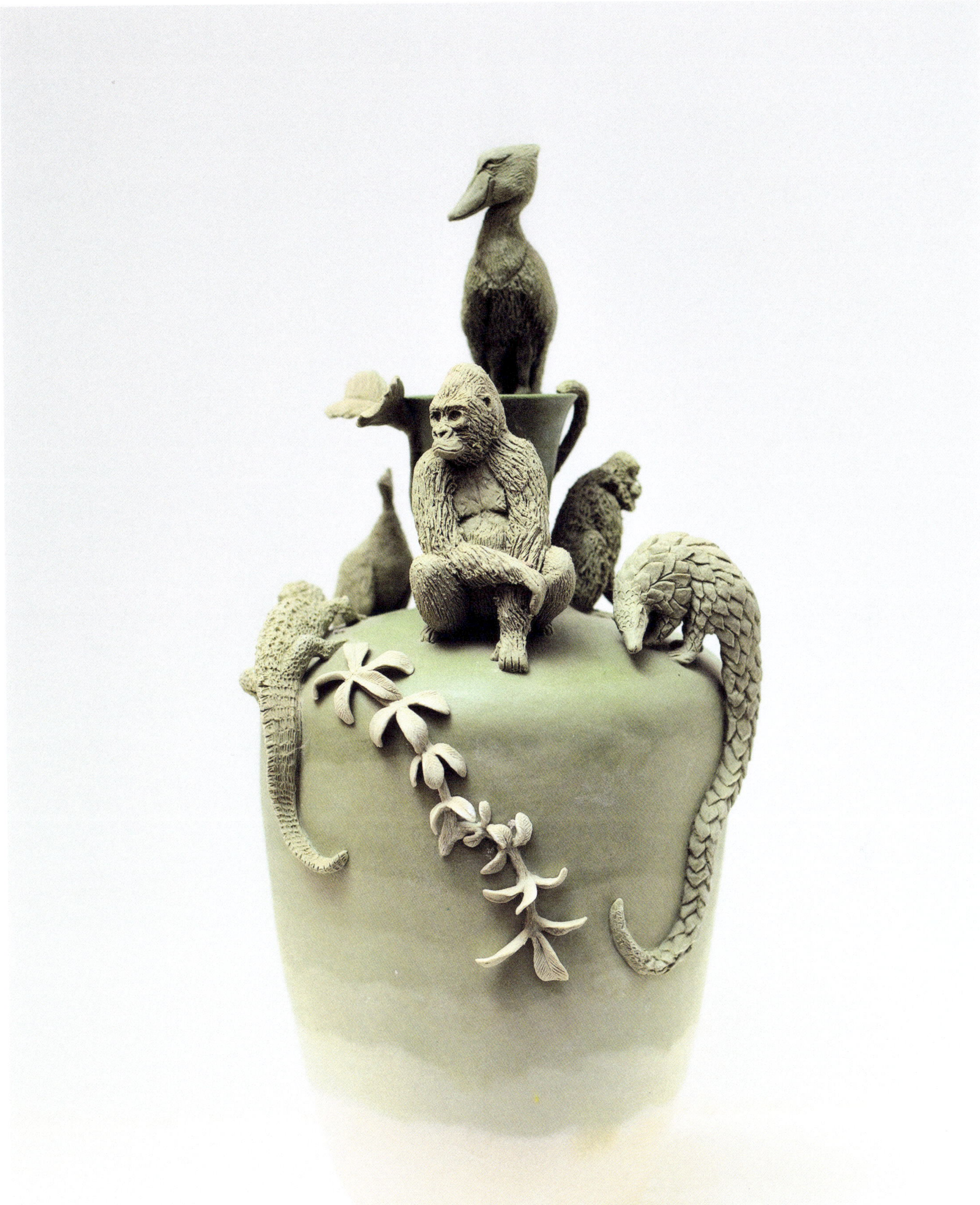

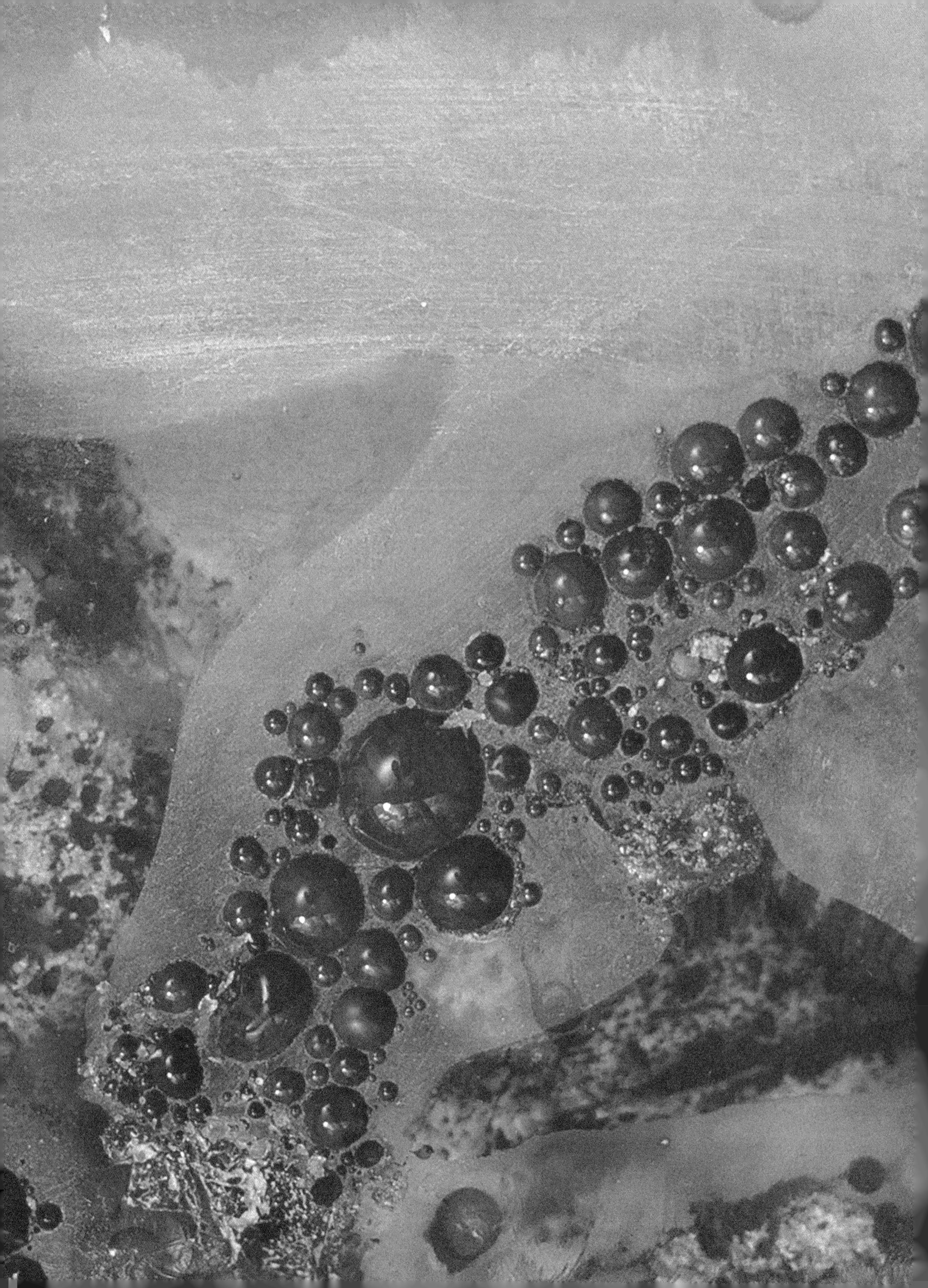

Glass

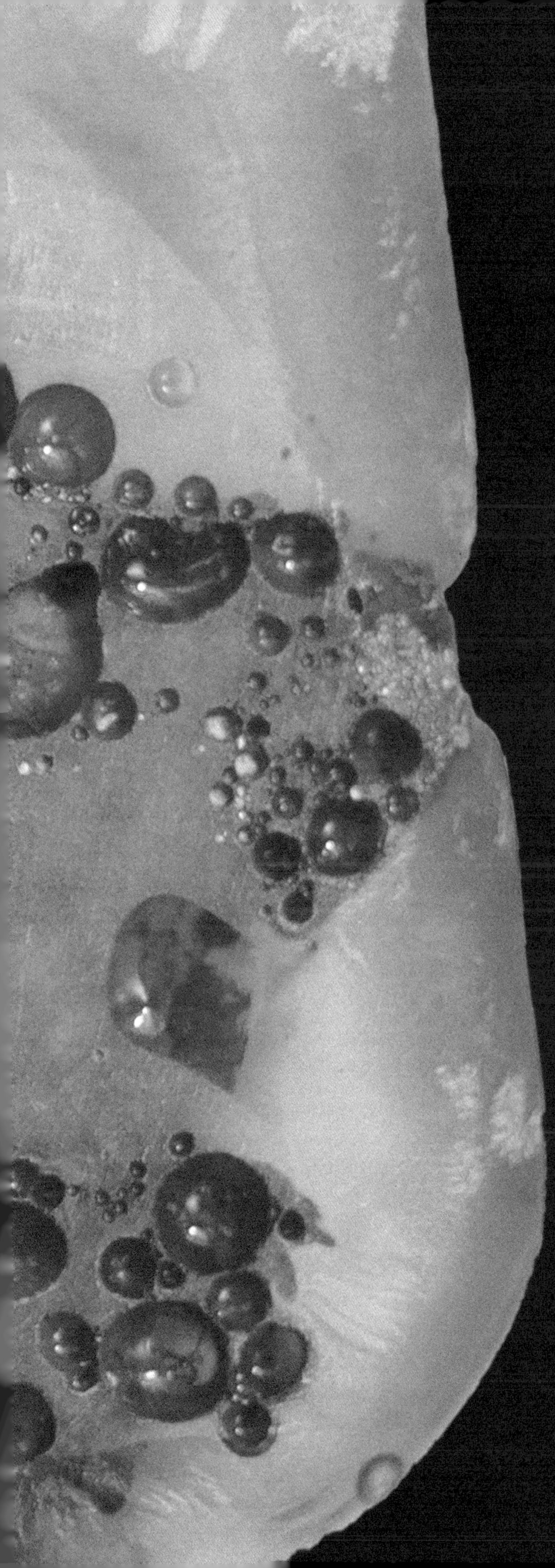

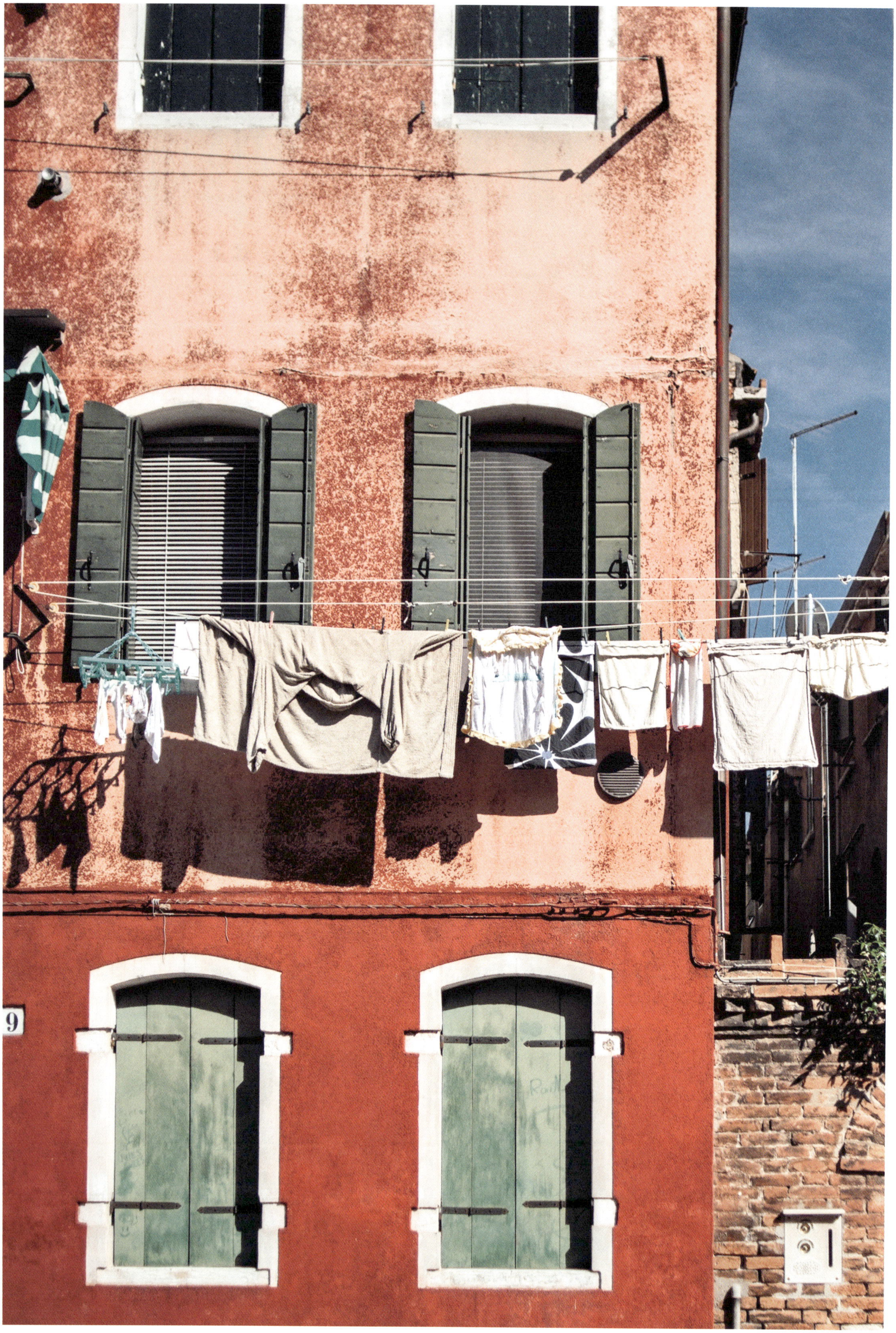
9

Andrea Zilio

Master glassmaker

Murano, Italy

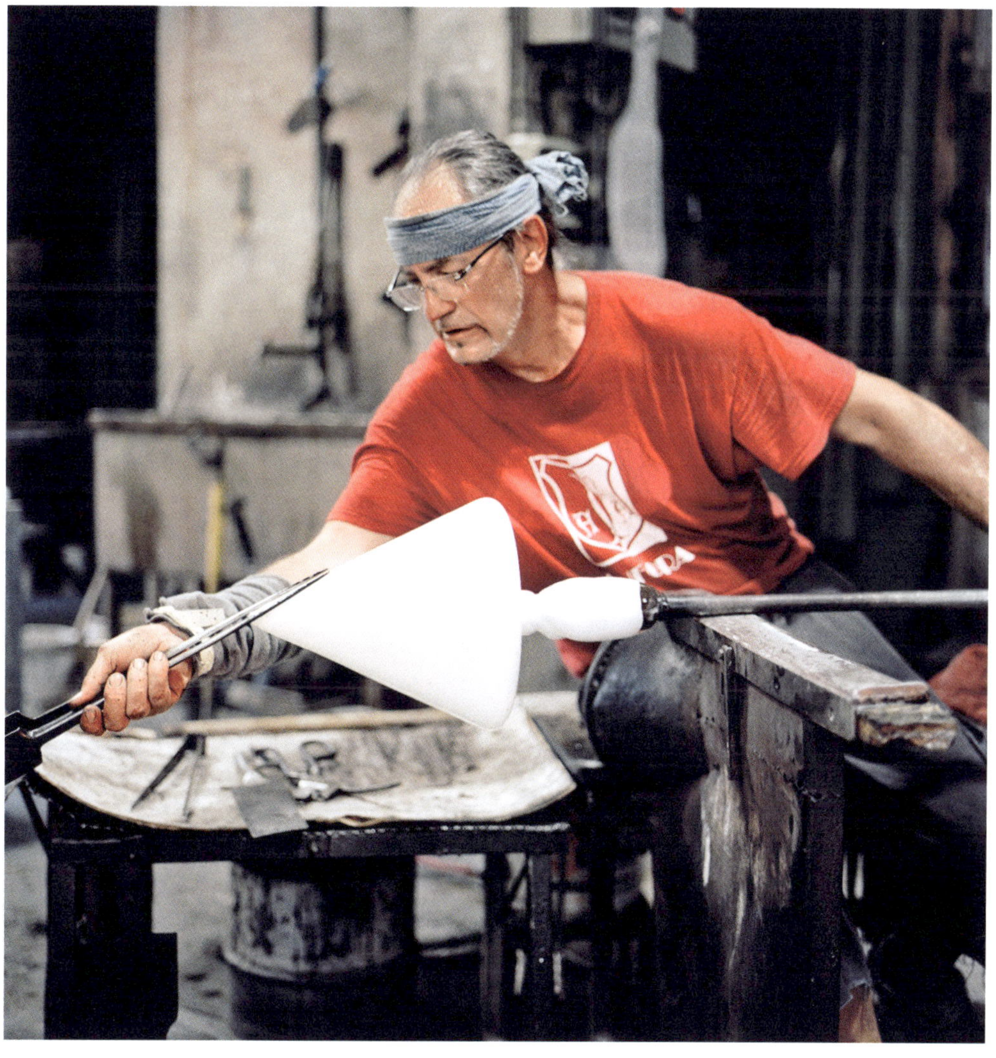

My name is Andrea Zilio, and I am a craftsman and master glassmaker in Murano. I grew up in a modest family in Venice. At the age of seventeen, after training as a carpenter, I entered the *fornace* in Anfora quite by accident: my sister had married the owner. *Fornace* refers to both the building where the furnaces are located and, by extension, the glassmaker's workshop. I never imagined that one day I would be a part of this world; it was a veritable discovery for me. I still love my profession after three decades of working with glass, but, after all these years, I would be lying if I told you that glass still thrills me like it did that very first day.

Glass is made from silica—a white sand that historically came from Fontainebleau, in France—to which soda ash and lime are added as stabilizers, along with other coloring elements. The composition is carefully calculated to obtain a specific color.

The glass has to be worked and blown hot, but it cools very quickly. You have to maintain the right temperature at all times and think about how you're going to create the desired shape. And that's precisely where the difficulty lies—glass work allows no room for errors or doubts and requires intense concentration.

My role could be compared to that of an orchestra conductor: my assistants play their scores around me, while I remain silent. The craft has always been structured in this way: the master works in silence, while a *servente*, as the name suggests, fulfils the role of assistant and prepares the material. Another helper, called a *serventino*, assists both the *servente* and the master.

The creative process always begins with an idea sketched on paper. I often repeat the drawing on the ground in chalk to memorize the proportions. The *servente* uses a long metal blow pipe to gather the molten material—at 2000°F (1100°C)—from the furnace. Then I determine the amount of glass necessary to make each object, and I begin to blow the material. The temperature falls to about 1800°F (1000°C). At 1400°F (800°C), the glass can no longer be shaped, and if it falls below 1400°F (800°C), the glass could shatter. So, we reheat it in order to continue shaping it. The object is then placed in a furnace set to a constant 900°F (500°C), where it becomes rigid and can no longer change shape.

Murano is a unique place: glass was born here, and the island's inhabitants consider it to be a central part of their identity. Murano glass is still coveted today for its rich colors. These, along with shape and transparency, are fundamental to achieving beauty.

In the last several years, I have been carrying out my own research. I traveled abroad, exhibited my work in prestigious institutions, and made a name for myself. Since then, I've been working with designers and artists. More often than not, designers ask me to make a prototype, then they evaluate the result for large-scale production using an industrial technique. For this reason, the creative process is more rigid; you have to respect the measurements and pay particular attention to the drawings, which are very technical. With artists, I have a lot of fun. When we work together, their craziness is infectious and they urge me to create unique pieces that seemed impossible to produce.

In Italy, craftspeople are given little consideration, even though industrial production is a recent phenomenon, while artisanal crafts have existed for centuries. Today, big companies are smothering a large part of artisanal knowledge. As artisans, we feel abandoned rather than supported. When I began, five or six thousand workers stepped off the vaporetto in Murano every day. Now there are only three or four hundred of us left.

I continue to believe that artisans possess a holistic knowledge: they are creative and they understand the characteristics and weaknesses of the materials. I think it is very important that I pass on my knowledge to the next generation, but it is difficult to find apprentices who are ready to learn and to persevere. They are often very impatient, and it takes years to learn to shape glass.

I have experienced much satisfaction working with glass, and I still do. The personal work I've carried out with artists and designers has appeared in books. My children and grandchildren can see my creations in these publications, and that is my greatest joy.

Interview carried out in collaboration with Susanna Pozzoli.

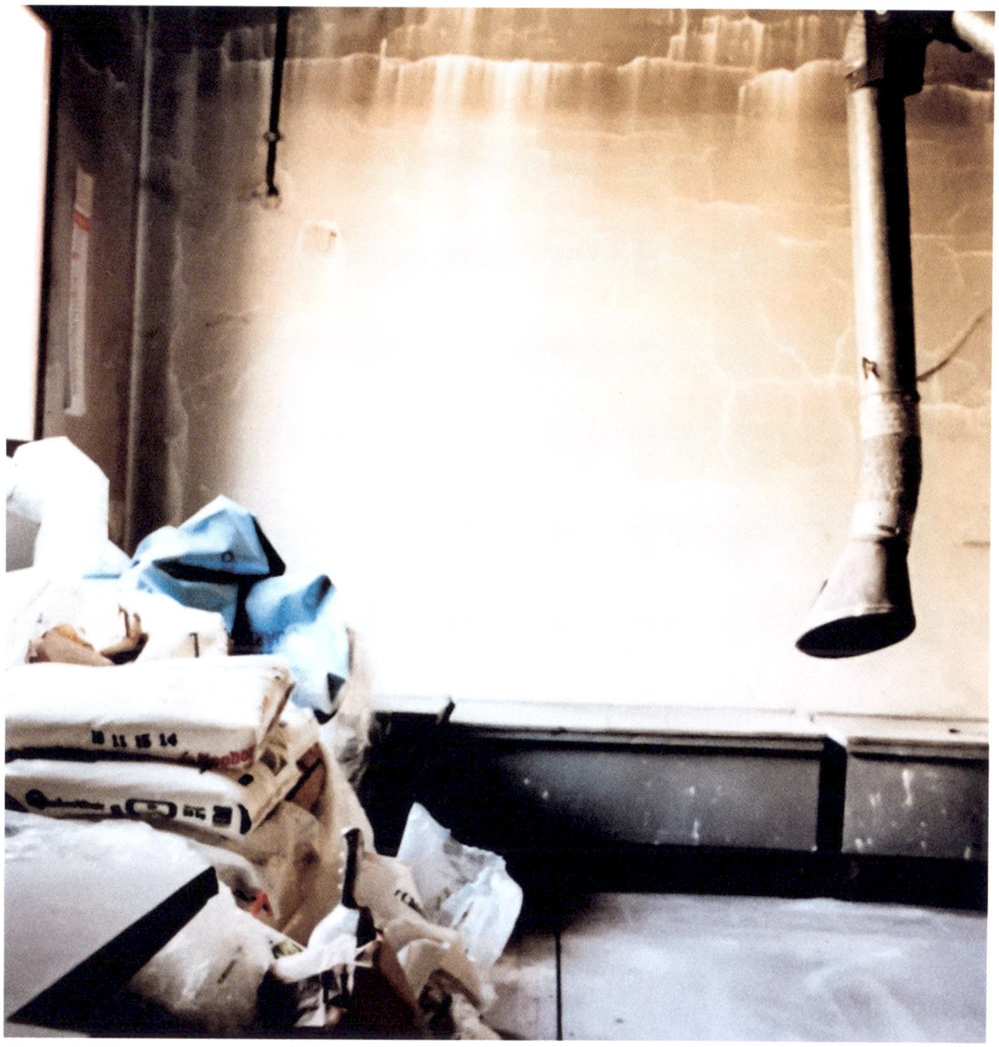

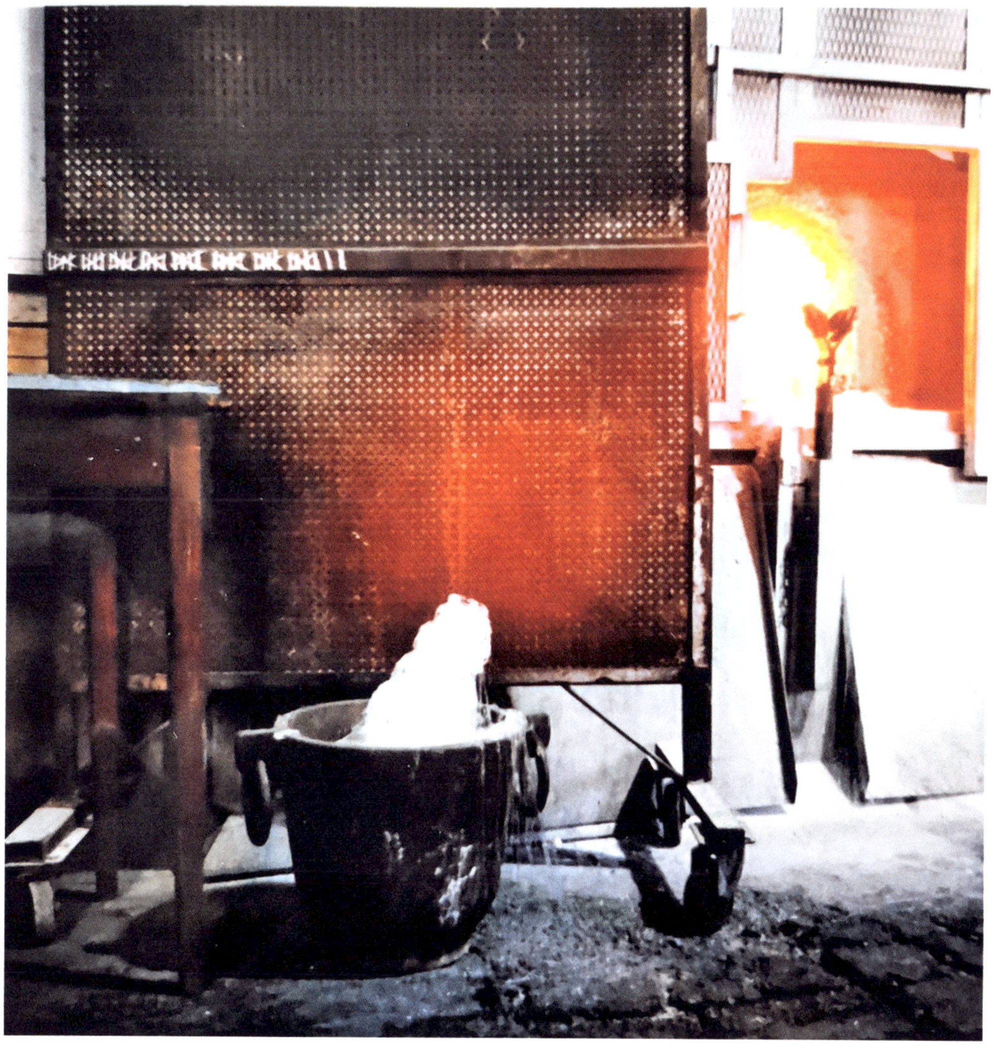

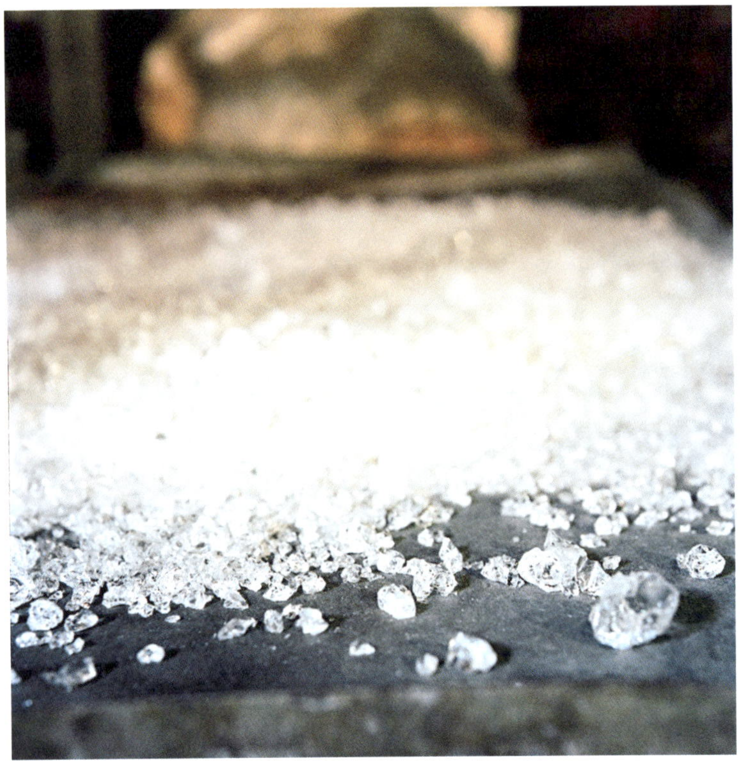
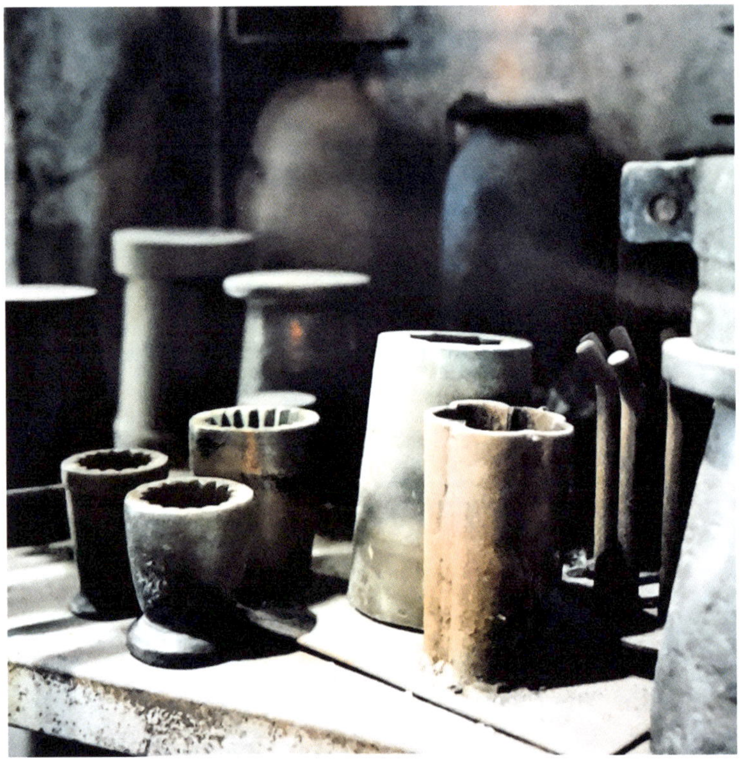
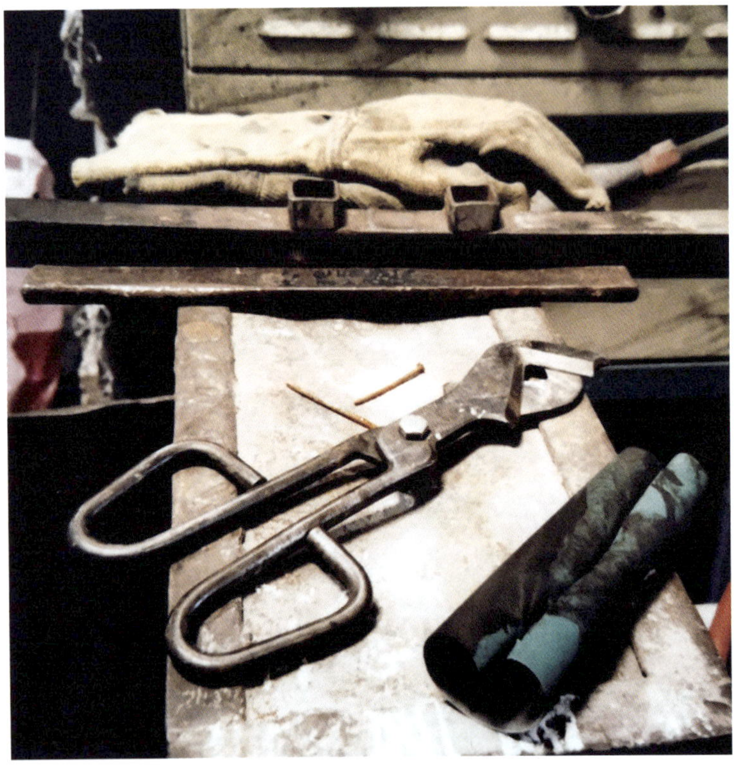
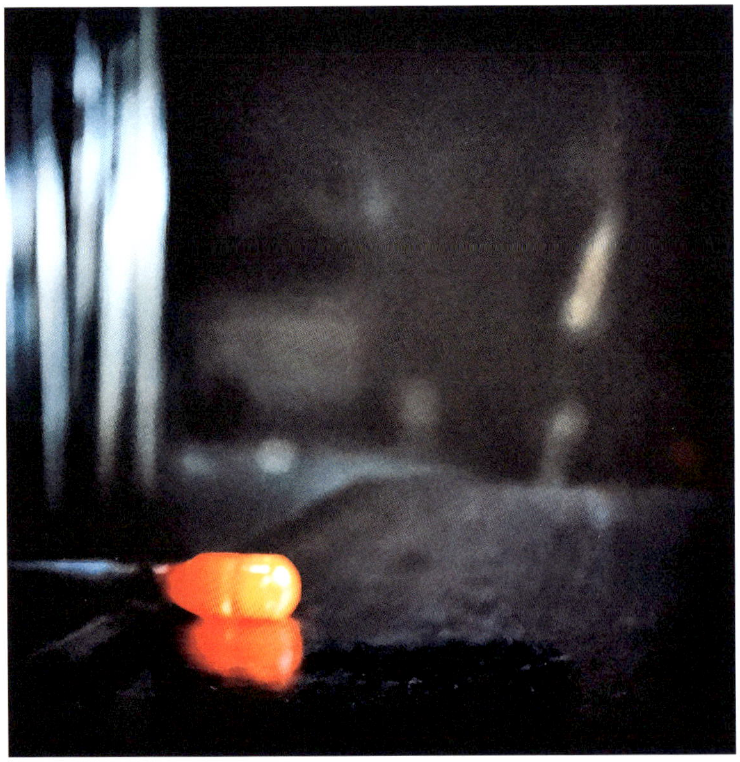

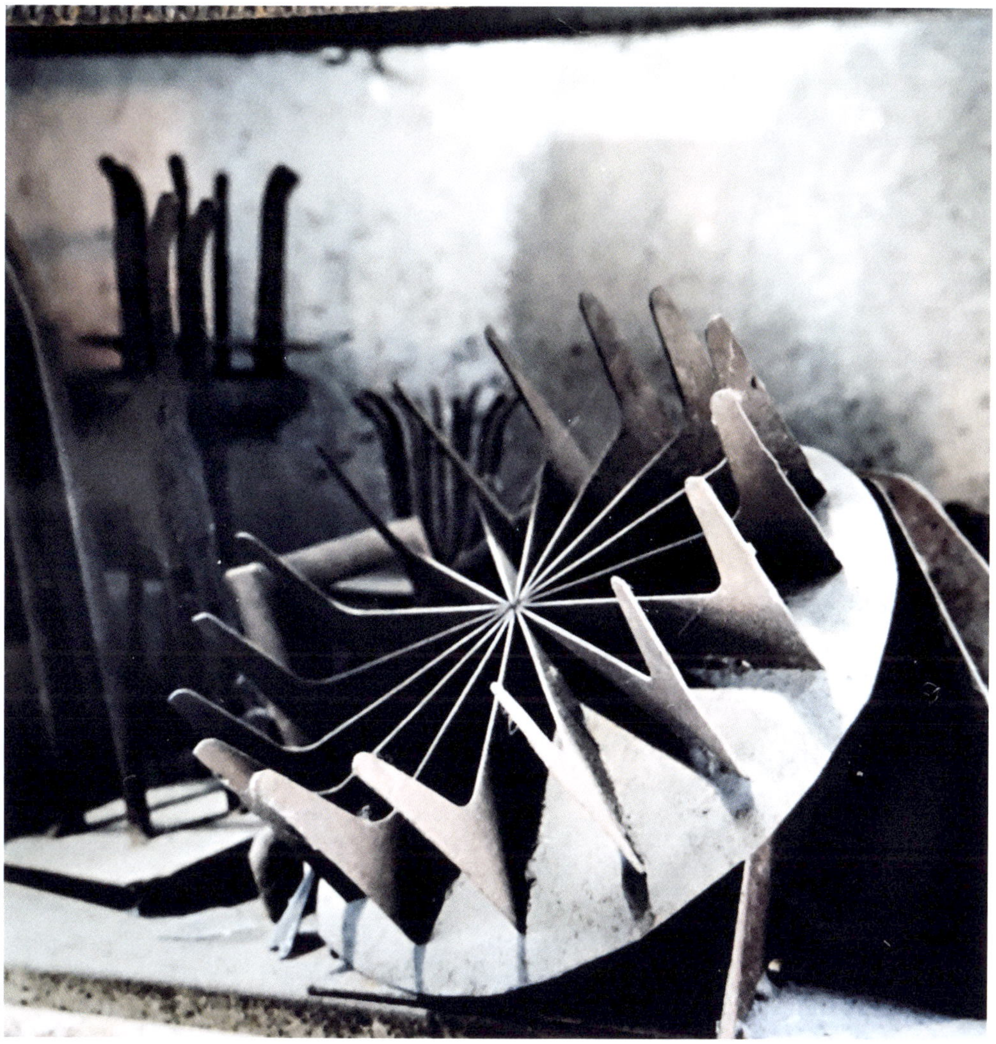

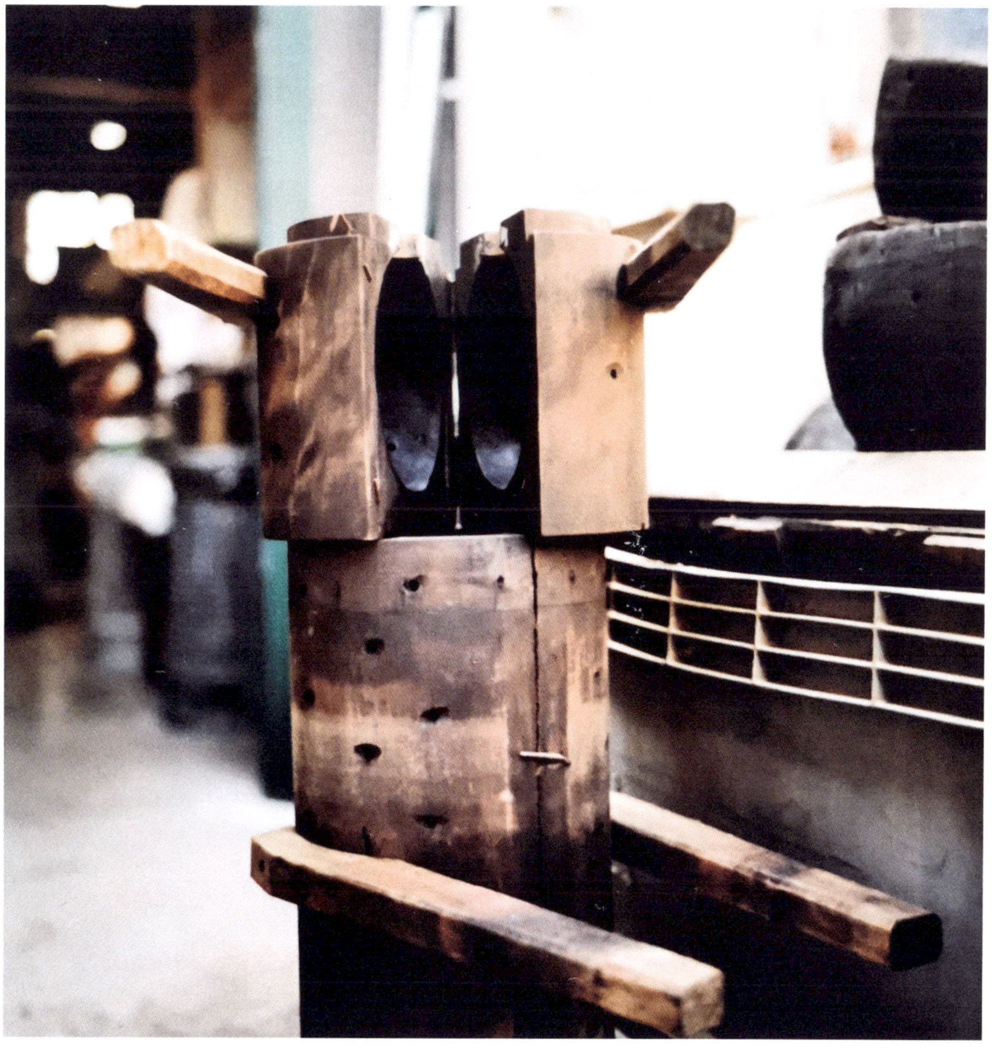

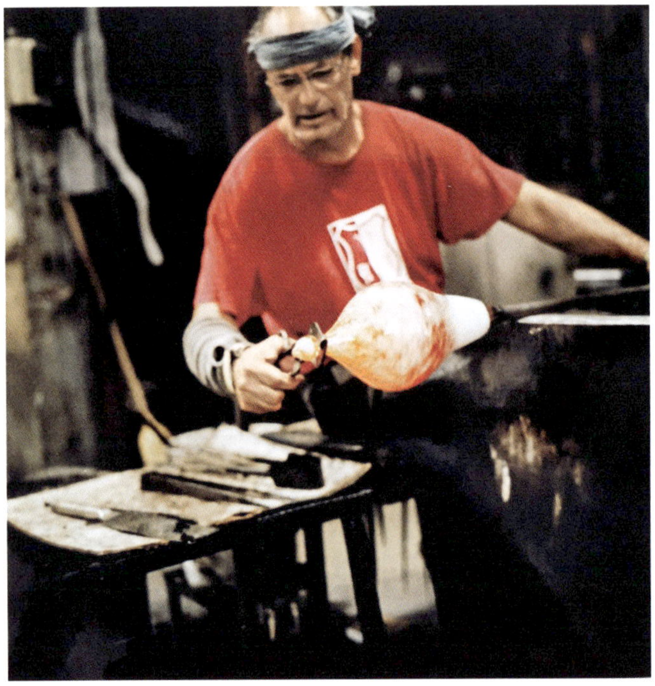
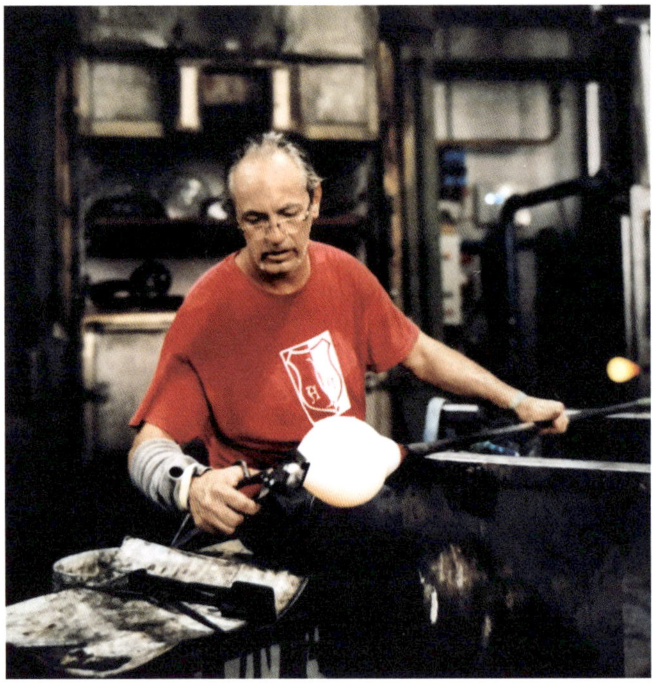
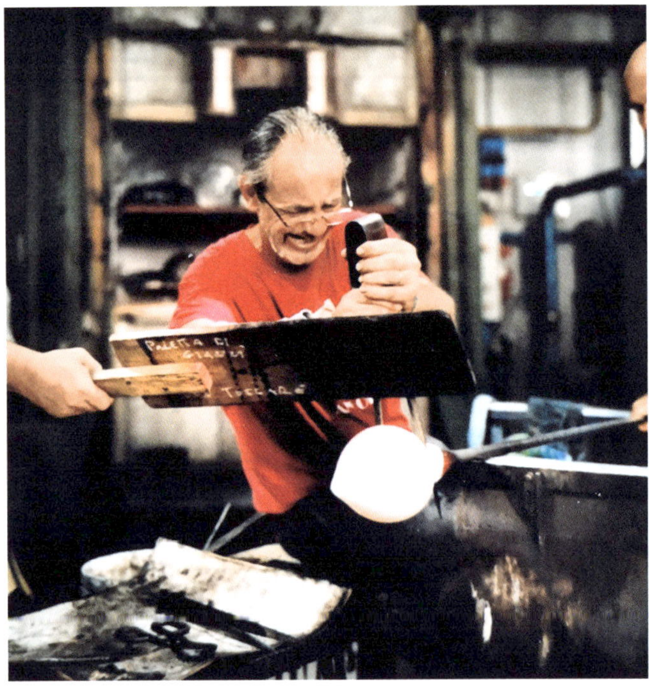
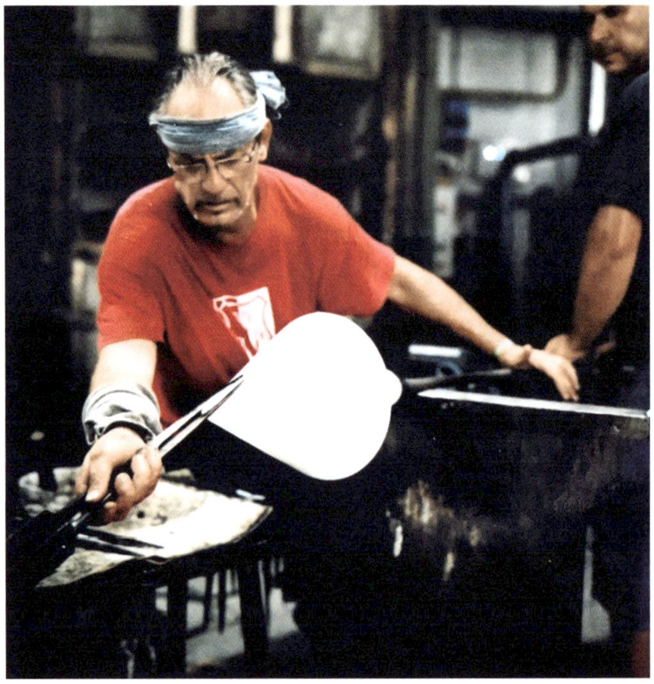
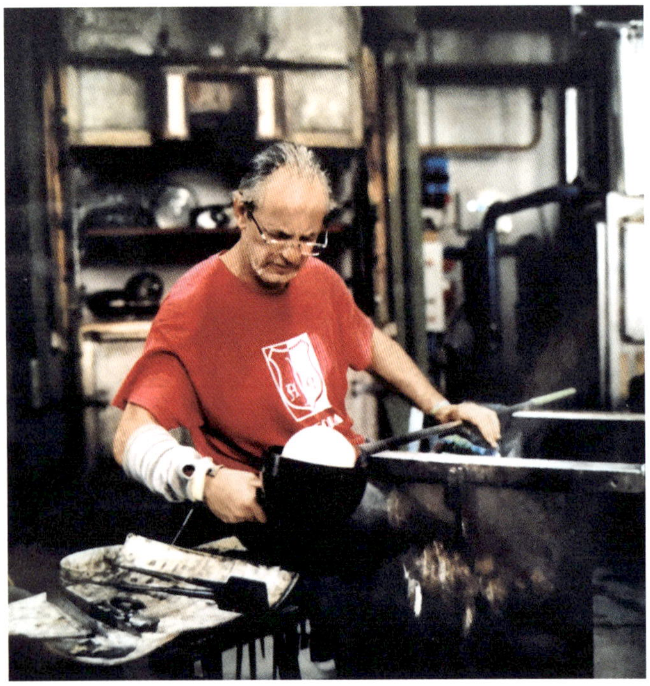
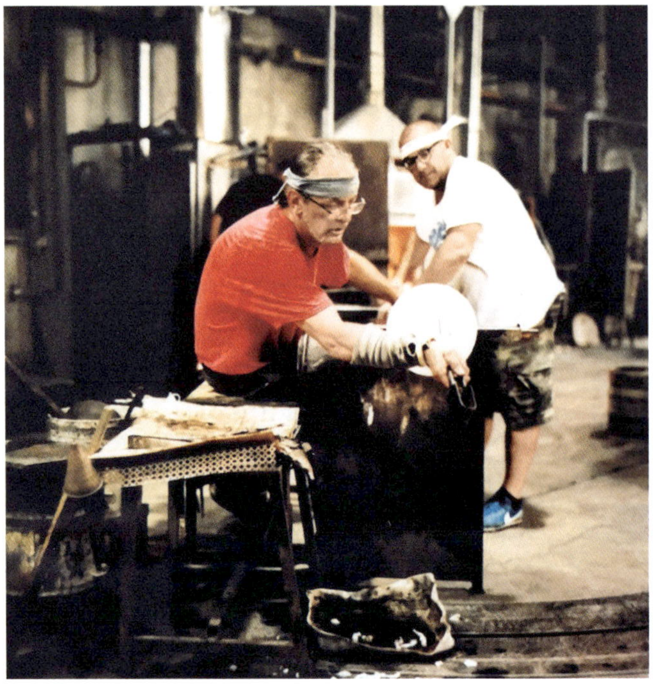

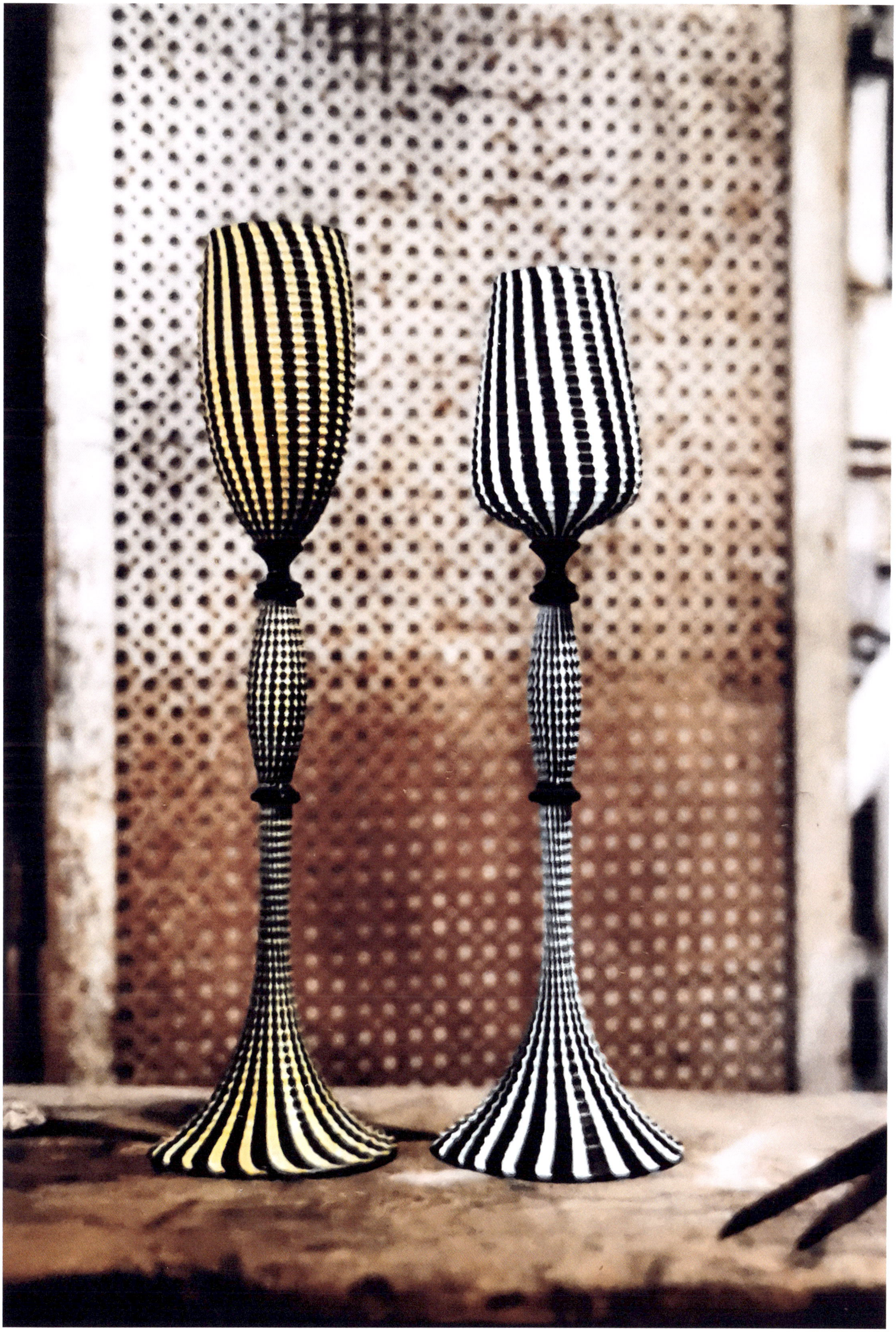

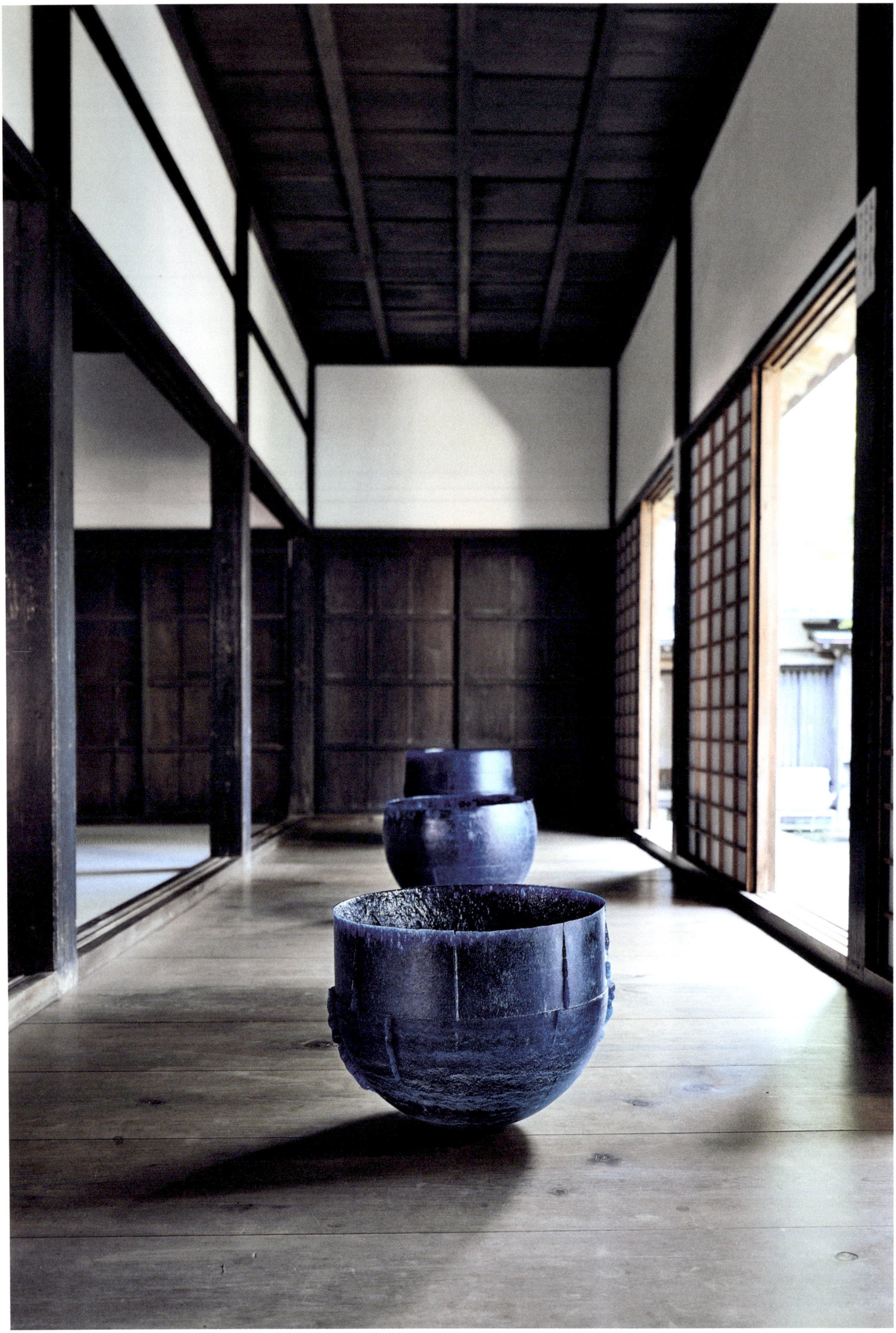

Yoshiaki Kojiro

Glass artist

Takayama, Japan

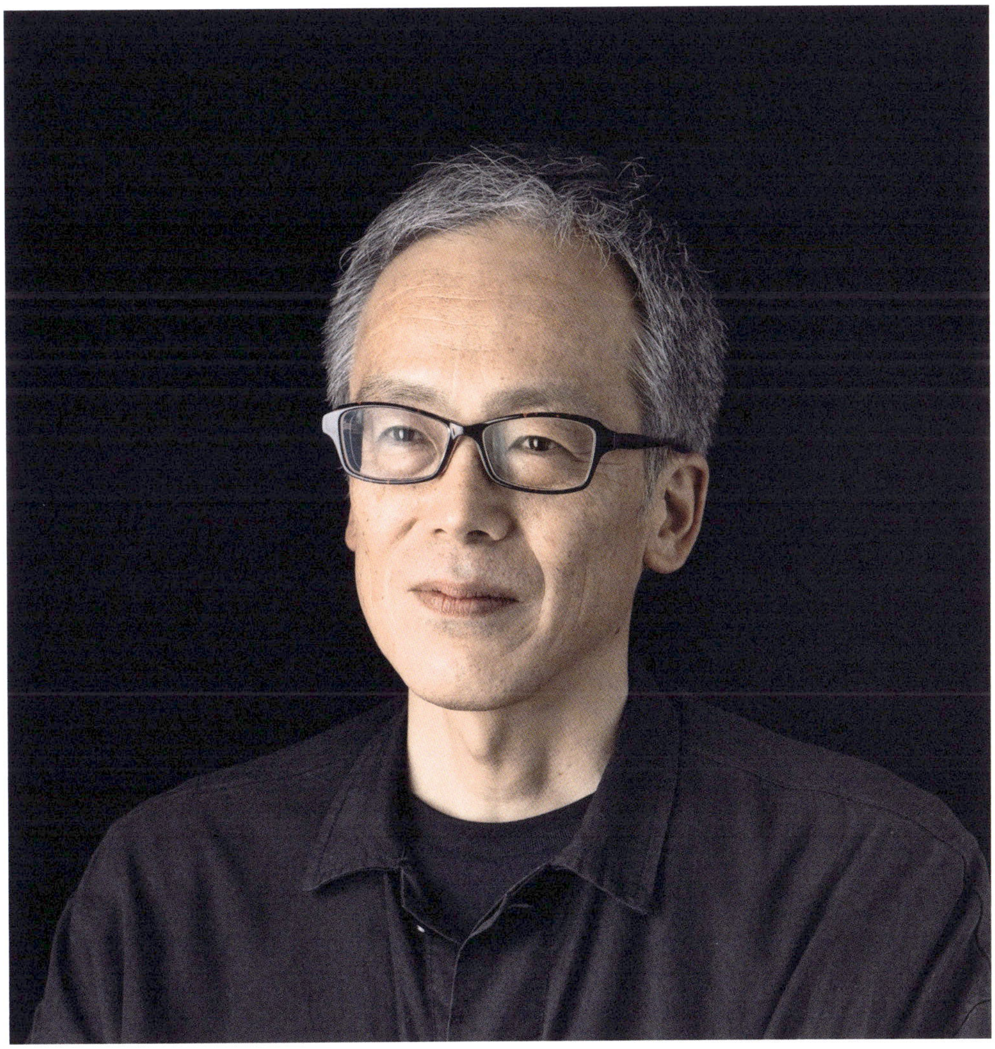

My name is Yoshiaki Kojiro, and I have been a glass artist for twenty-two years. Glass is obtained by fusing refined raw materials from Mother Earth using fire. My work consists of creating objects formed by the interaction of glass, tiny bubbles, heat, and gravity. I seek to shape forms based on the natural properties of glass—forms that best reveal the moment when the surface cracks at high temperature. My work is more about suggestion than description.

I studied architecture, with a specialty in engineering, and art at the Tokyo Glass Art Institute. At the age of twenty-nine, I left the firm where I was working after visiting a glass-blowing workshop in Okinawa. I remember the molten elements taking on the form of a container in an instant. I was captivated by the speed and energy of the material, and fascinated to see the spectacle of humanity's connection to nature condensed in the relationship between the glass and the artisan's gesture.

The material reveals a potential beyond my imagination. I trust it implicitly, and the result is reflected in my work. I combine different materials in my creations. I mix, for example, glass powder with lime or copper powder, then enclose the mixture in a fireproof plaster mold and fire it at 1400°F (800°C); the mold gradually fills with foam glass, like bread dough. The extent to which the glass foams depends on my objective; I regulate the material by cooling it quickly. When the gases are released, the shape of the work changes and areas crack, creating a very dense piece. Foam glass is used not only in art and in craft, but also to improve floors and in insulation materials.

My wife is a sculptor. We used to live in the city, but now we are fortunate enough to live in the middle of nature, in a village surrounded by mountains. Everything here is new to us, and our values have changed. The people who live here need very little. I have come to appreciate the importance of living according to the rhythm of the seasons, and the pleasure this brings with it.

Due to events linked to the Covid-19 pandemic, I spend most of my time in my studio; all the exhibitions that had been planned were postponed. I work at a slower pace, which gives me the opportunity to reexamine the need to create things and to analyze my relationship with the world. I pay particular attention to the natural environment that surrounds our studio, and I observe the changes more than ever.

To be honest, the coming months and years are going to be difficult. Today, we have enough time to rethink the contradictions and problems of this world, to reconsider the way in which we live. I get the impression that many people are already starting to look for solutions. It won't be easy for us to change our way of life, but the crisis hit us so hard that I am convinced it will accelerate this paradigm shift.

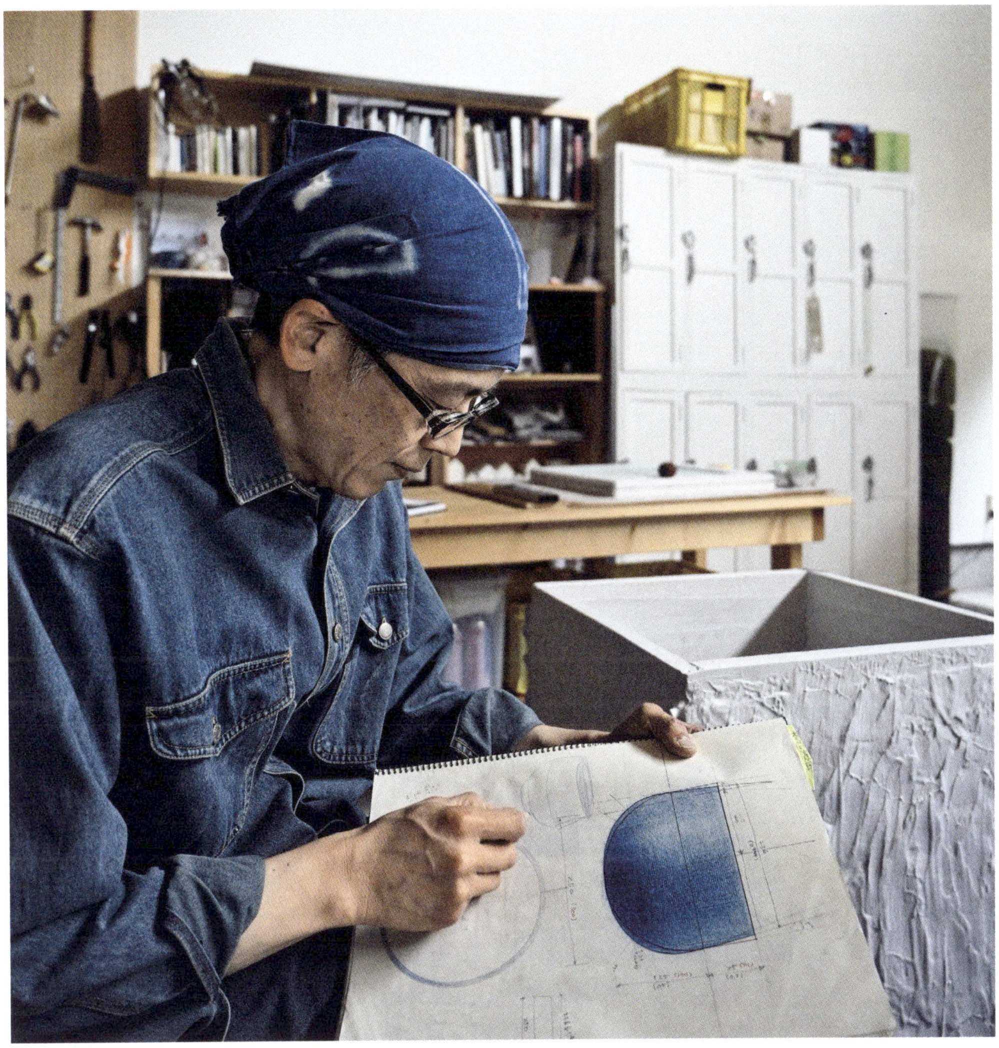

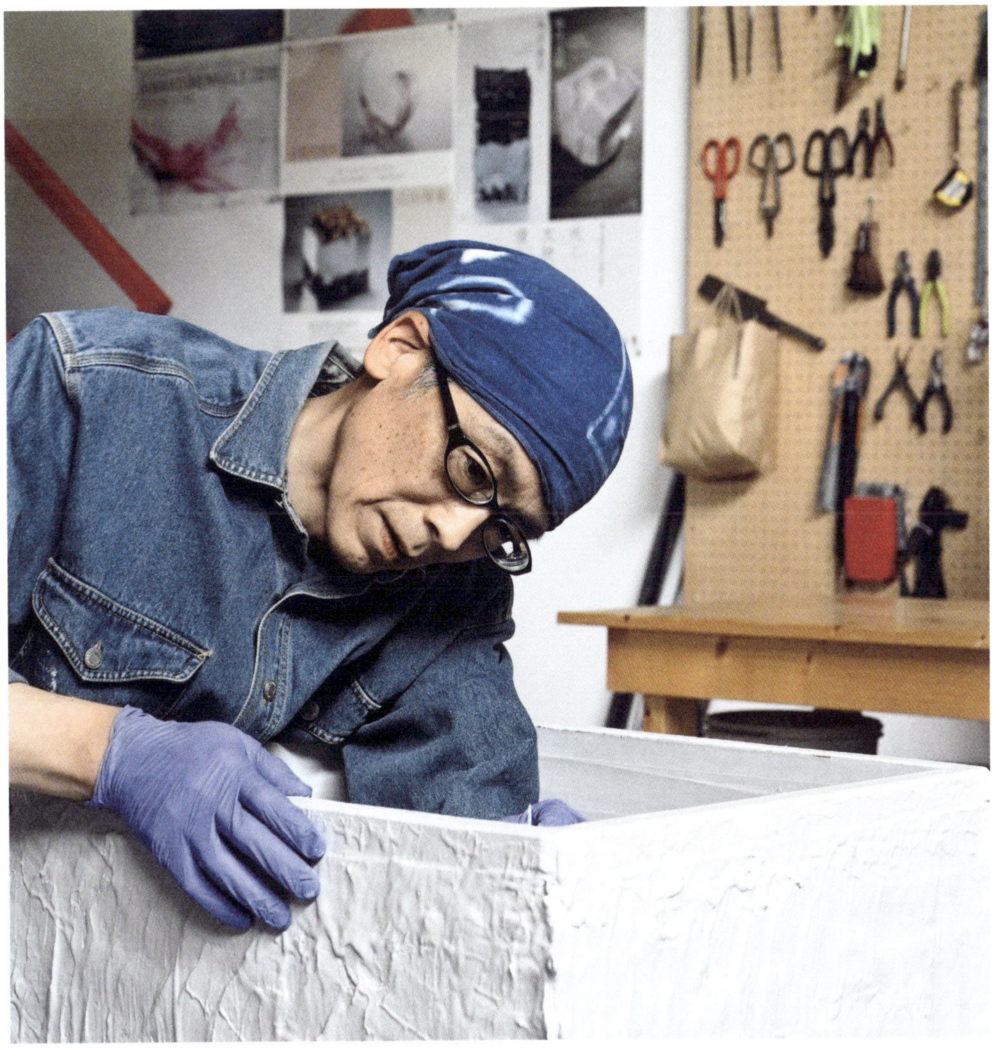

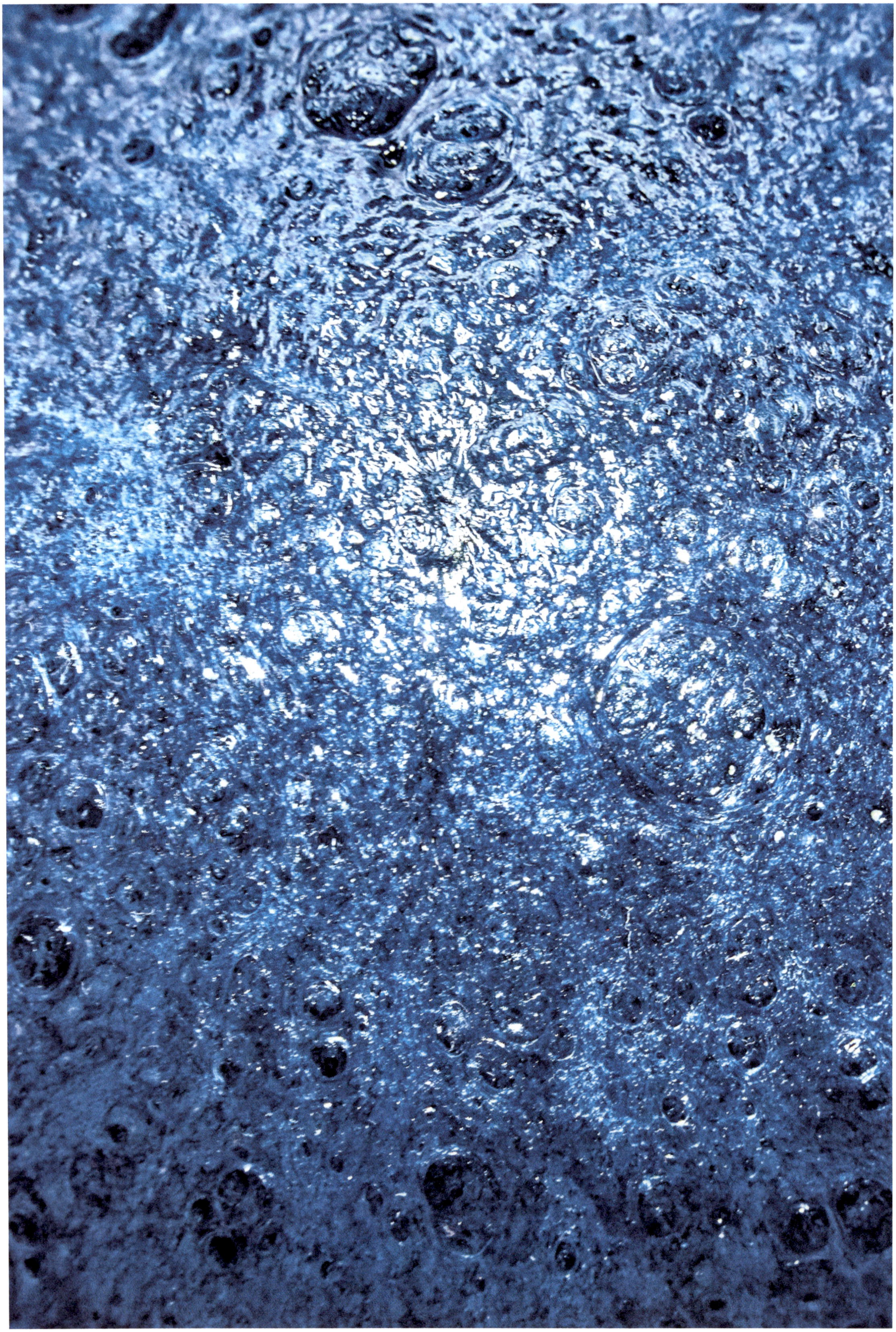

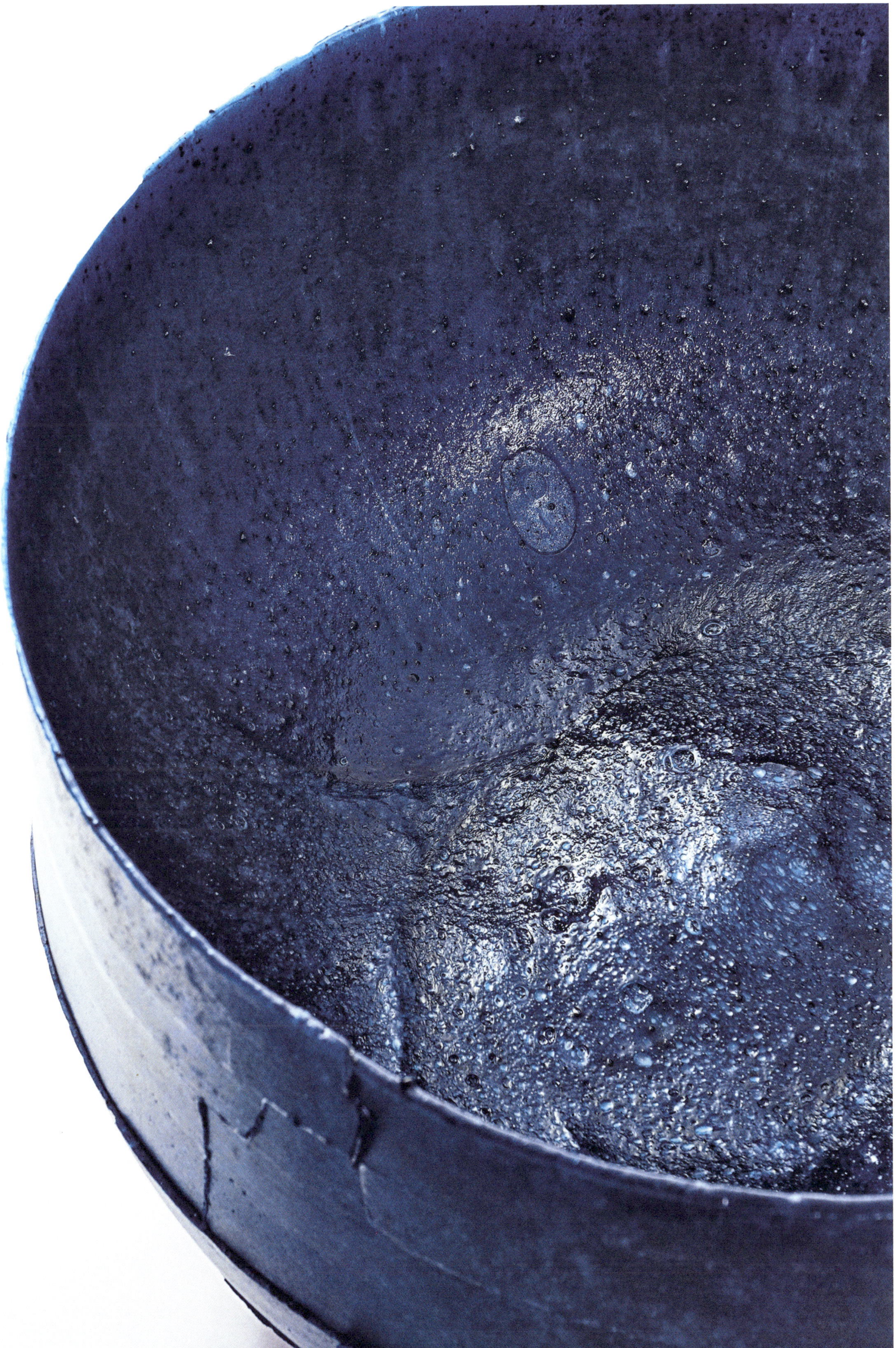

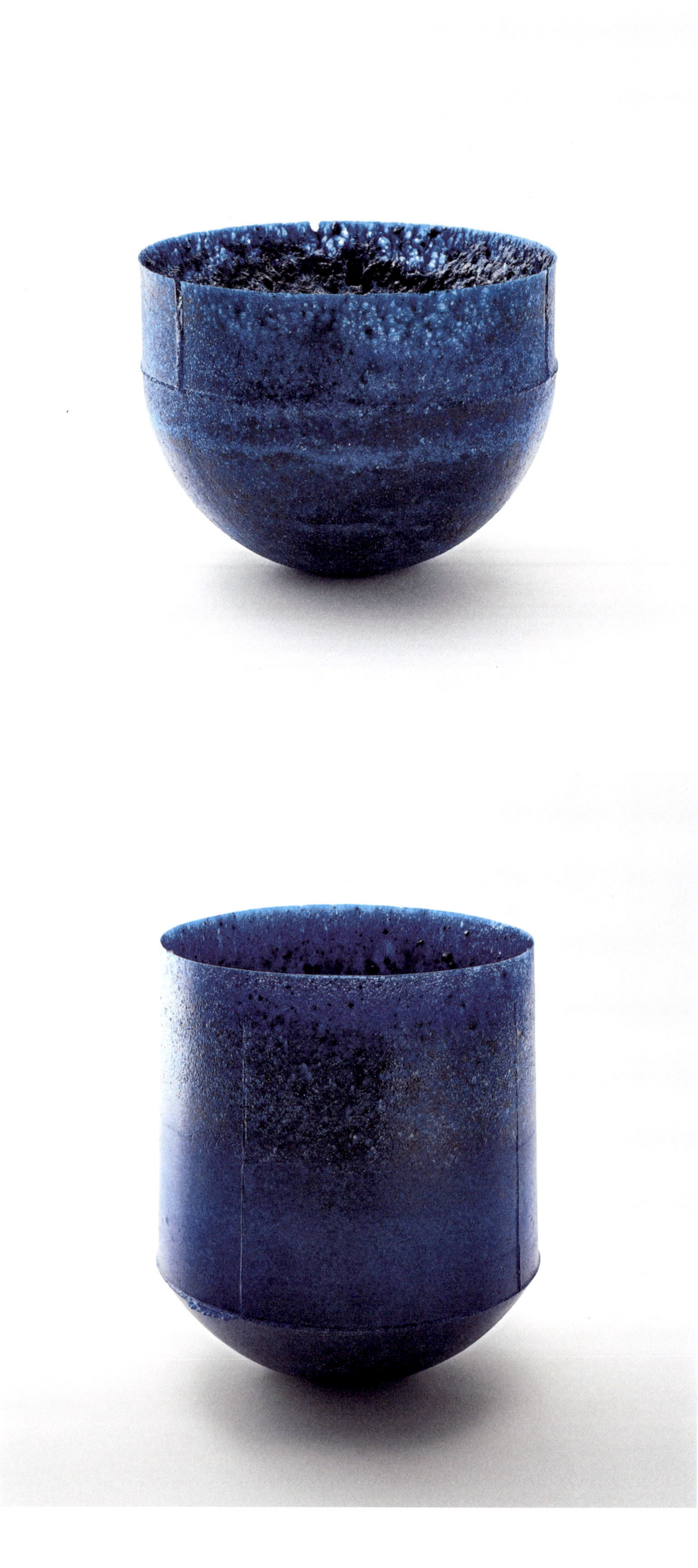

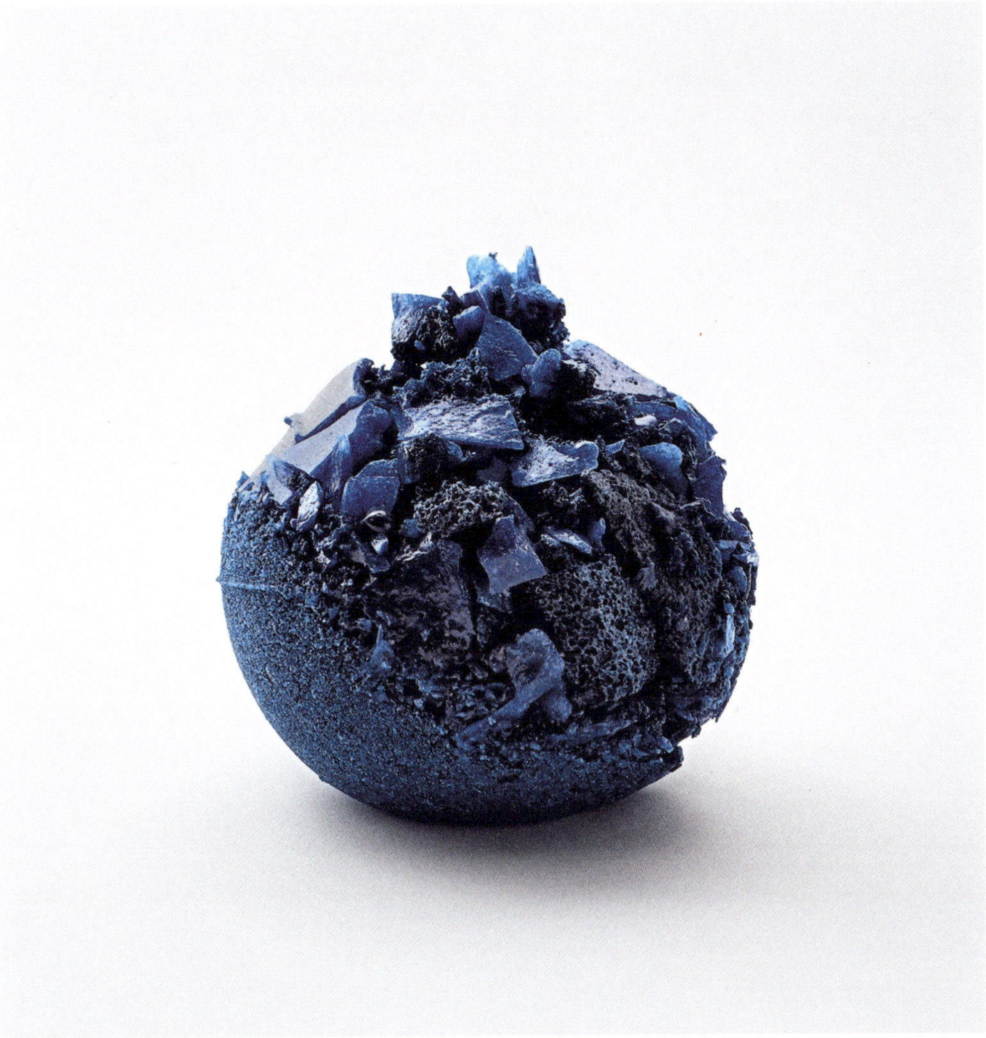

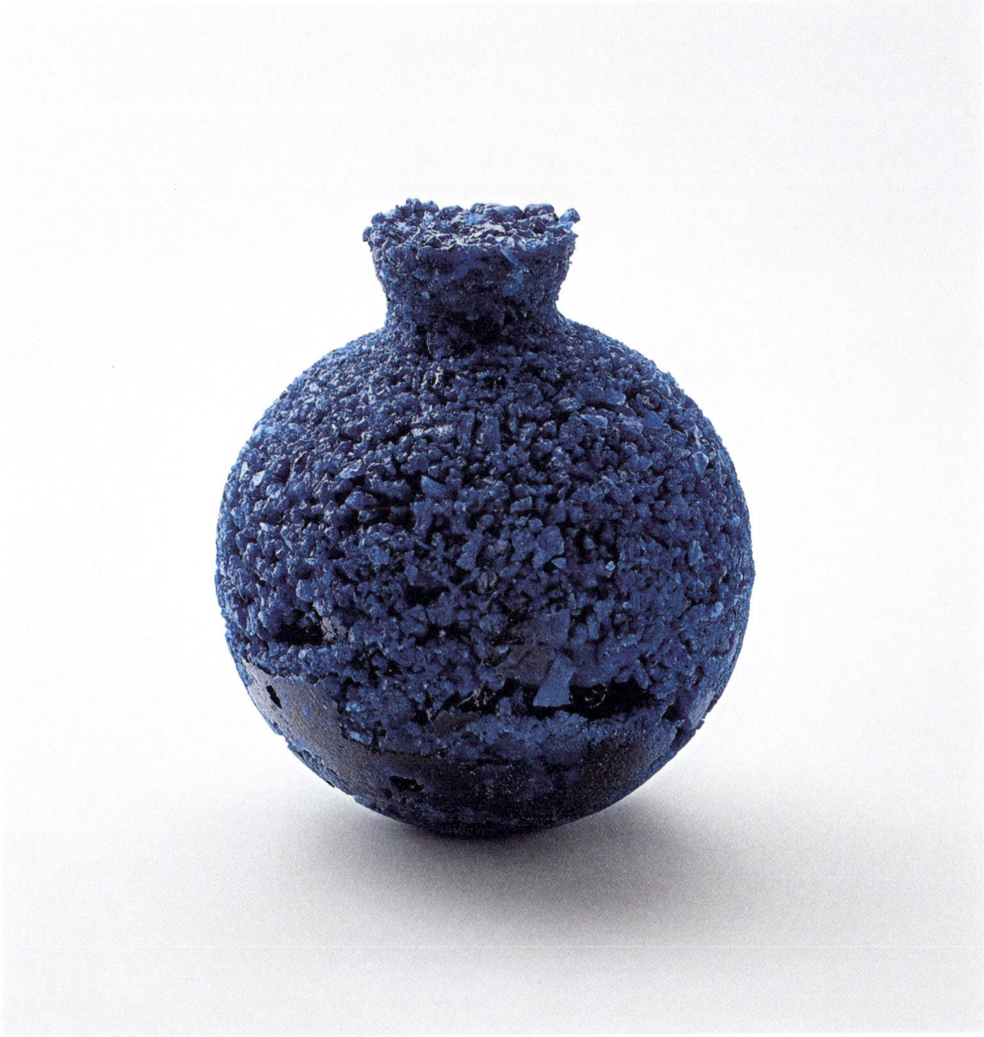

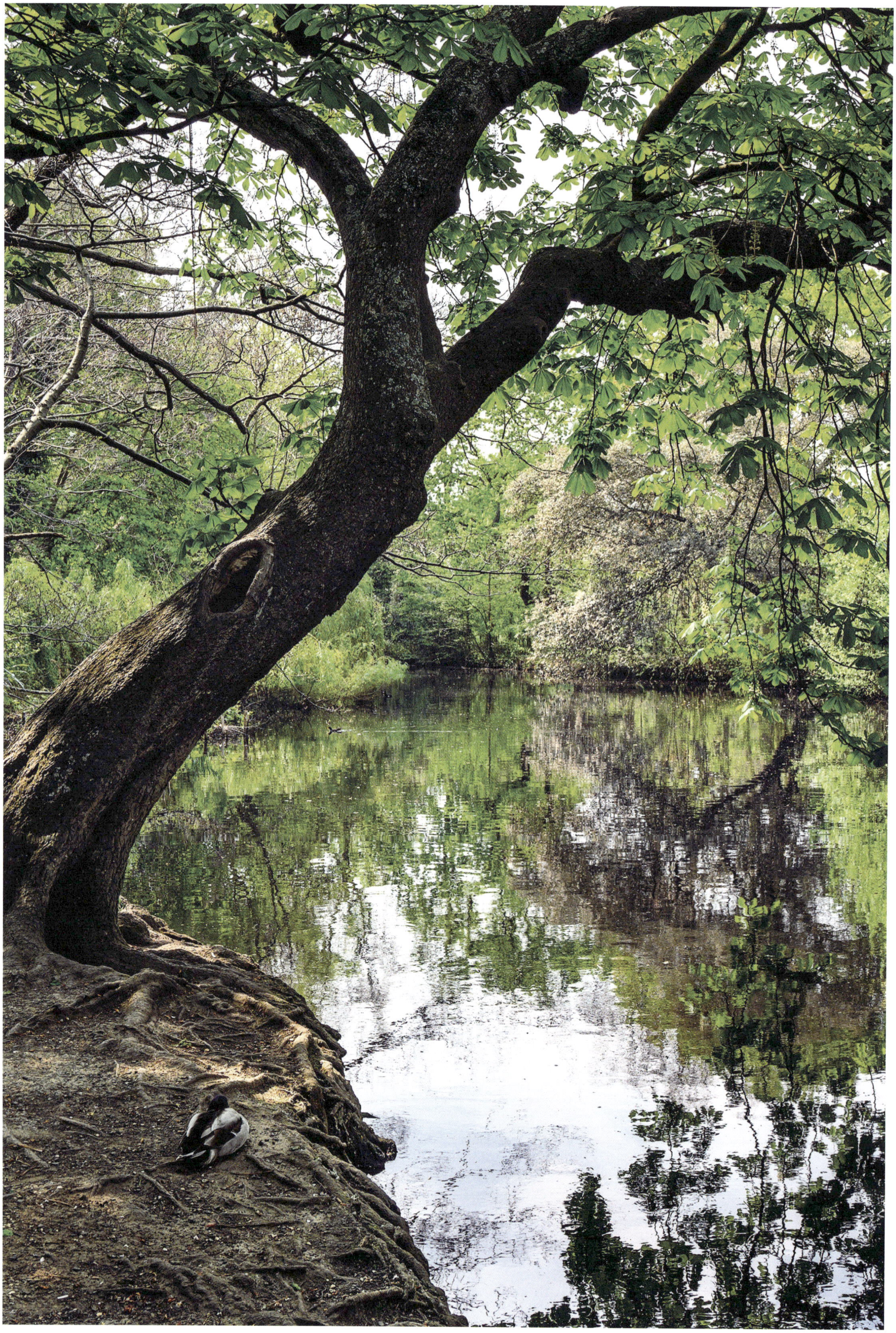

Anna Dickinson

Glass artist

London,
United Kingdom

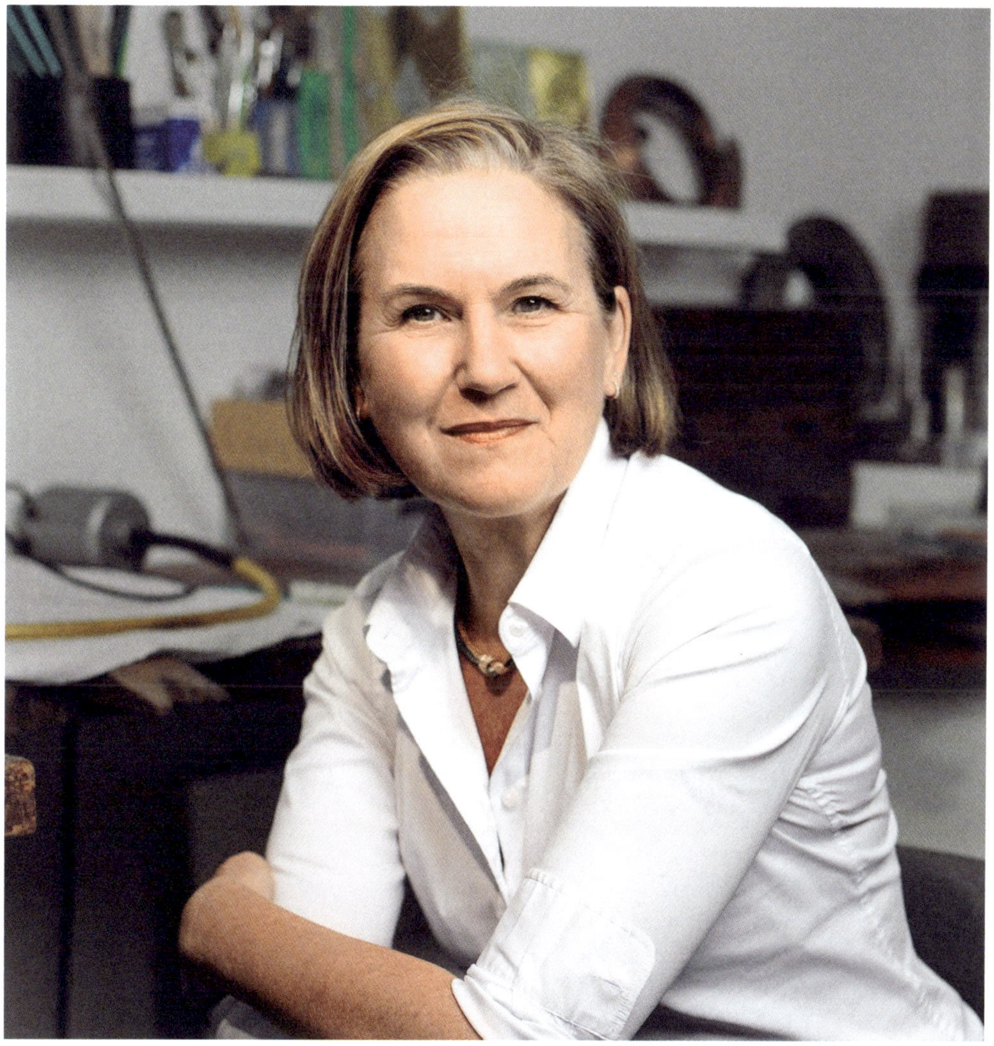

My name is Anna Dickinson, and I am a glass artist. Like many artists who work with glass, I started with clay, perhaps because it is more readily available and less expensive. When I was eighteen, I was introduced to blown glass and was instantly fascinated by the process and the material. I loved the heat, the spontaneity, and the respect required to handle it.

When I use hot glass, I am completely focused and immersed in what I am doing. Technically, glass is a very difficult material to manipulate—it is hard work, both physically and mentally. Even after many years, I feel like it is testing me all the time. Working with glass requires a huge amount of patience and a propensity for problem-solving. Fortunately, I have always been drawn to the challenge, and when everything goes well, the experience is very rewarding. My feelings about glass vacillate between love and exasperation. There are so many qualities within glass to explore: transparency, opacity, color, reflection, thickness, and weight, contrasted with delicacy and lightness. I never tire of the material; there is always something new to discover.

When I begin to make something, I tend to have an idea of what I want. But I am also very open, adapting as I go along. I keep sketchpads, which are for ideas, and notebooks in which I carefully log techniques and everything about the construction of the work. I started doing this when I was young. Now I have pads and notebooks going back forty years that I still refer to.

Every piece I make, I make for myself. Each piece has to excite me and I have to learn something from it, through research and exploration. A sense of achievement on completing a piece is vital. I am interested in the energy created by two or more materials coming together, and I attach great importance to the way in which they are combined to create something different and new.

Color is also extremely important in the creative process. Everything I do is carefully considered, nothing is rushed. There are a lot of colors in glass that I really do not like; I find them brash, garish, and cold. For many years, I just worked with clear and black glass, then I gradually started to explore color. I was drawn to natural colors: earthy, warm tones. I respond emotionally and am attracted to a particular color because of the way it makes me feel. I also have to consider the other materials I will be combining with the glass, as this process brings several colors and qualities together. They have to create a harmonious energy, to complement each other. Glass is also a material that allows you to explore light and shadow.

As I work, I am having a dialogue with the material. So, the time spent handling and working a piece is crucial: without it, there is no dialogue. This dialogue tells me what the work wants or does not want, what is possible or impossible. It can take months to make a piece. When everything is working in harmony, the piece is complete, and each completed work informs the next one.

Working on a daily basis and thinking creatively is very important. My skills are continually improving, and this allows me to consistently produce works to a high standard. I am an artist who makes beautifully crafted works, so perhaps you could say I am both an artist and a craftsperson.

Crafts have become immensely popular in the United Kingdom recently. Several reality television shows based on the subject have raised public awareness. People have embraced the idea of "making," from amateur to professional level. Most people get pleasure and satisfaction from making things.

Creating my artwork is a hugely important part of my life, and I would be lost without it. It is central to my mental and physical well-being.

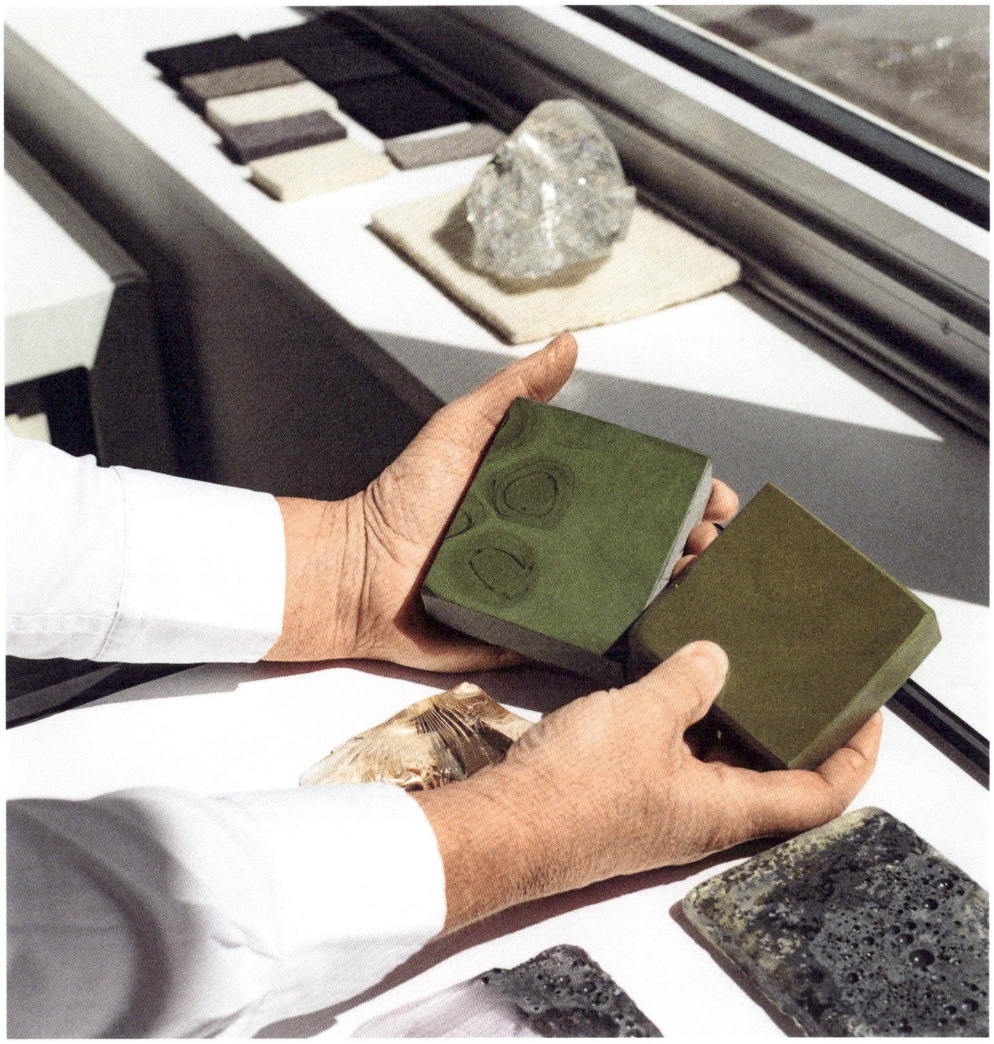

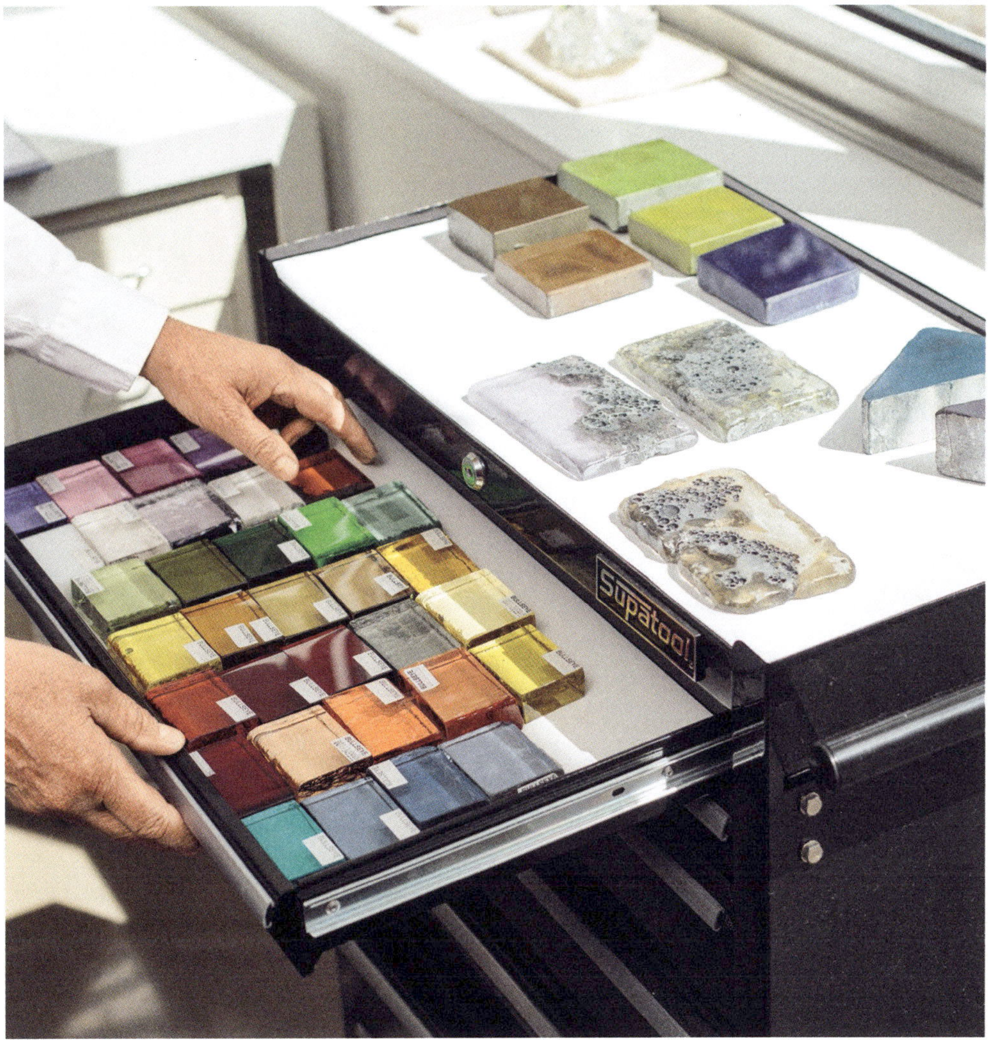
Supatool

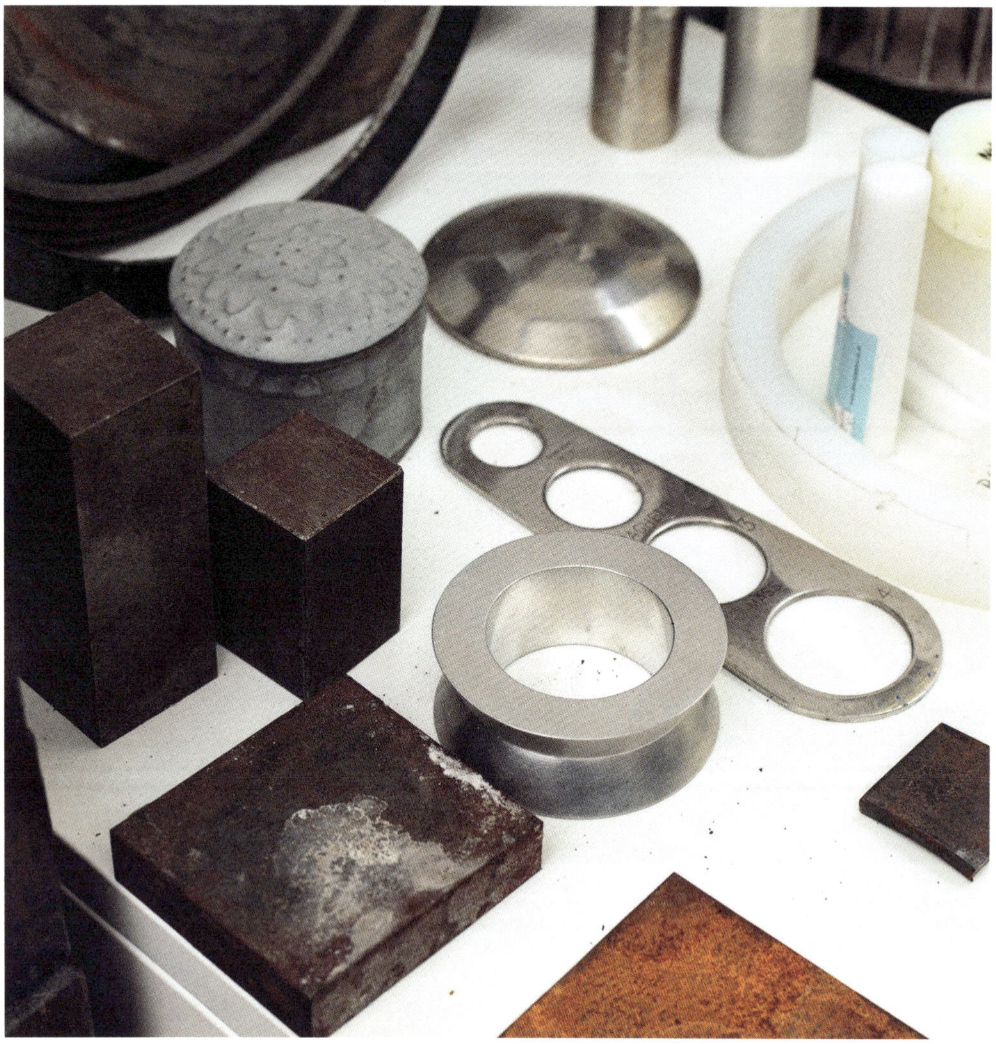

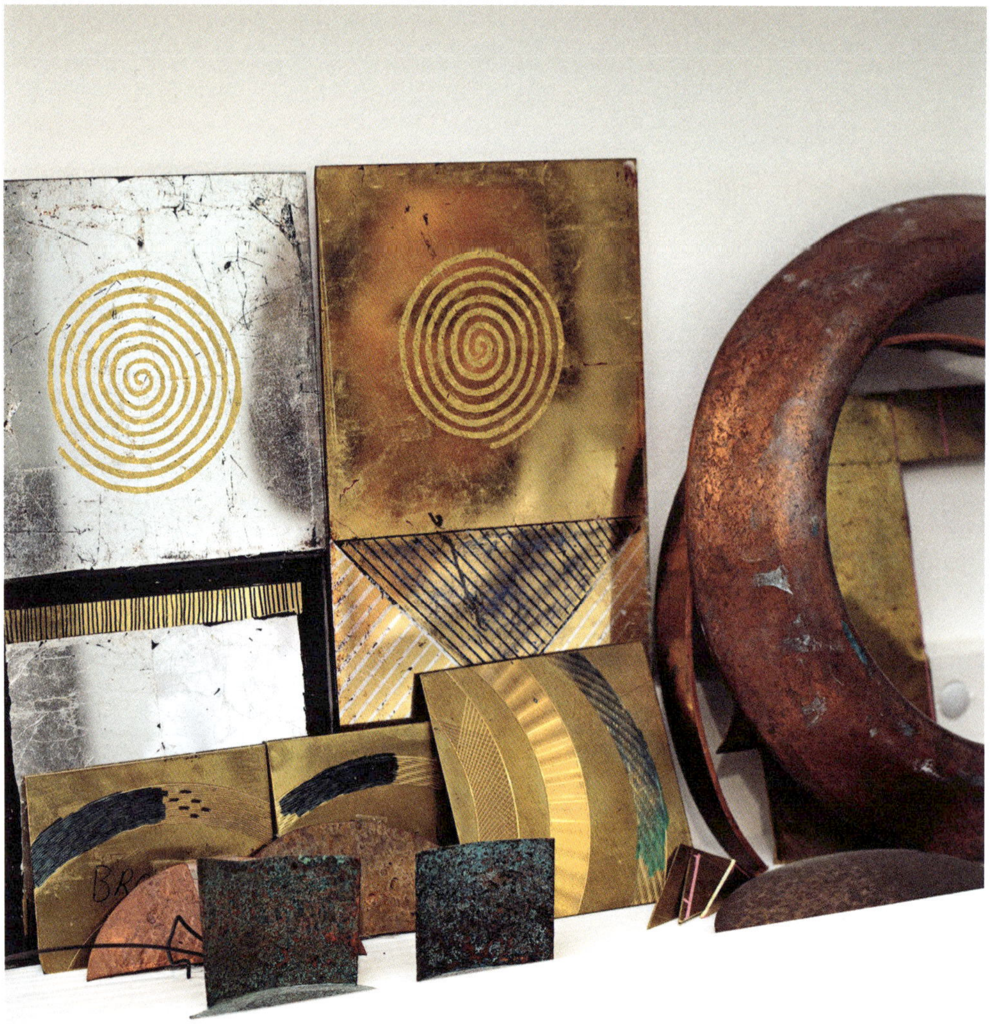

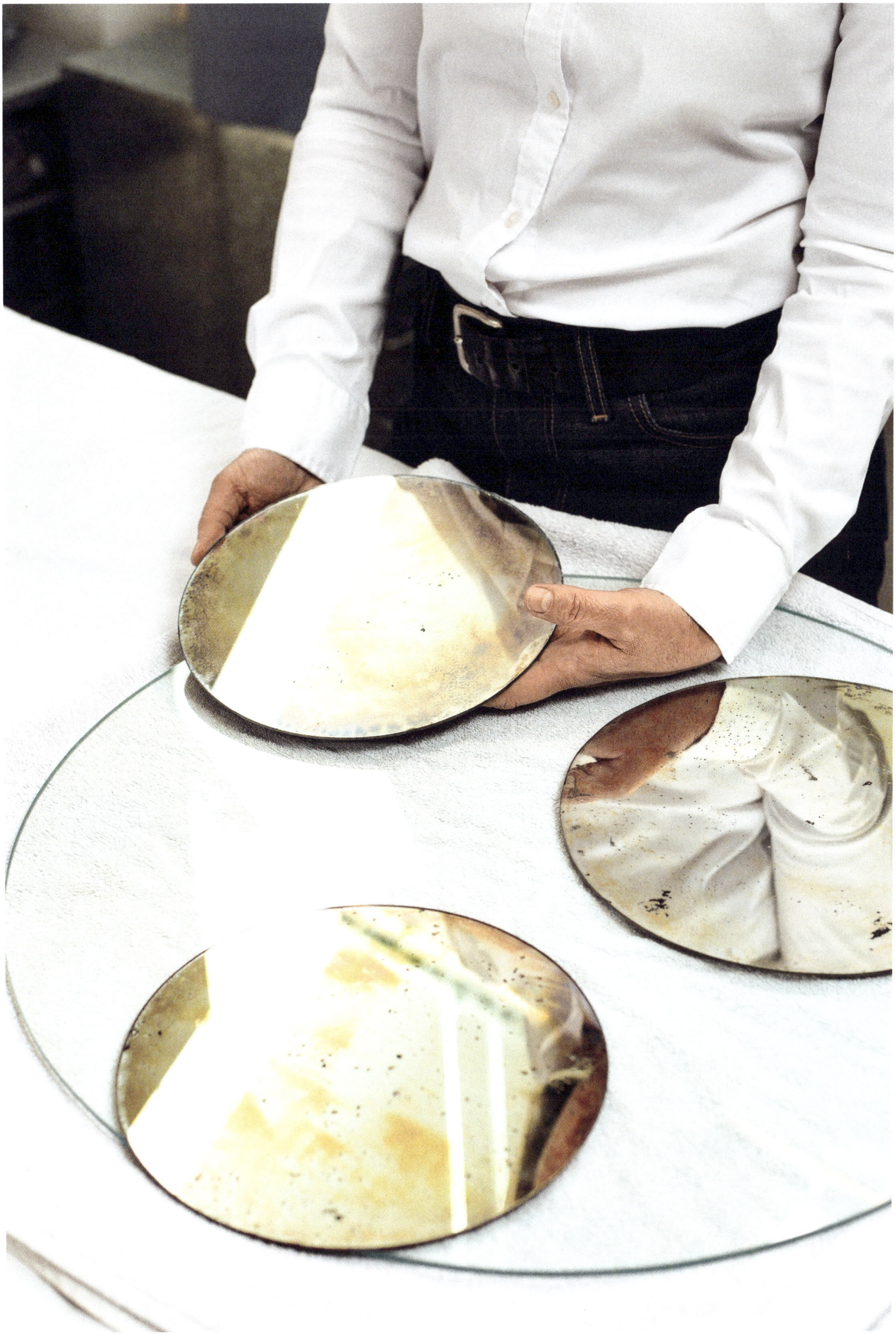

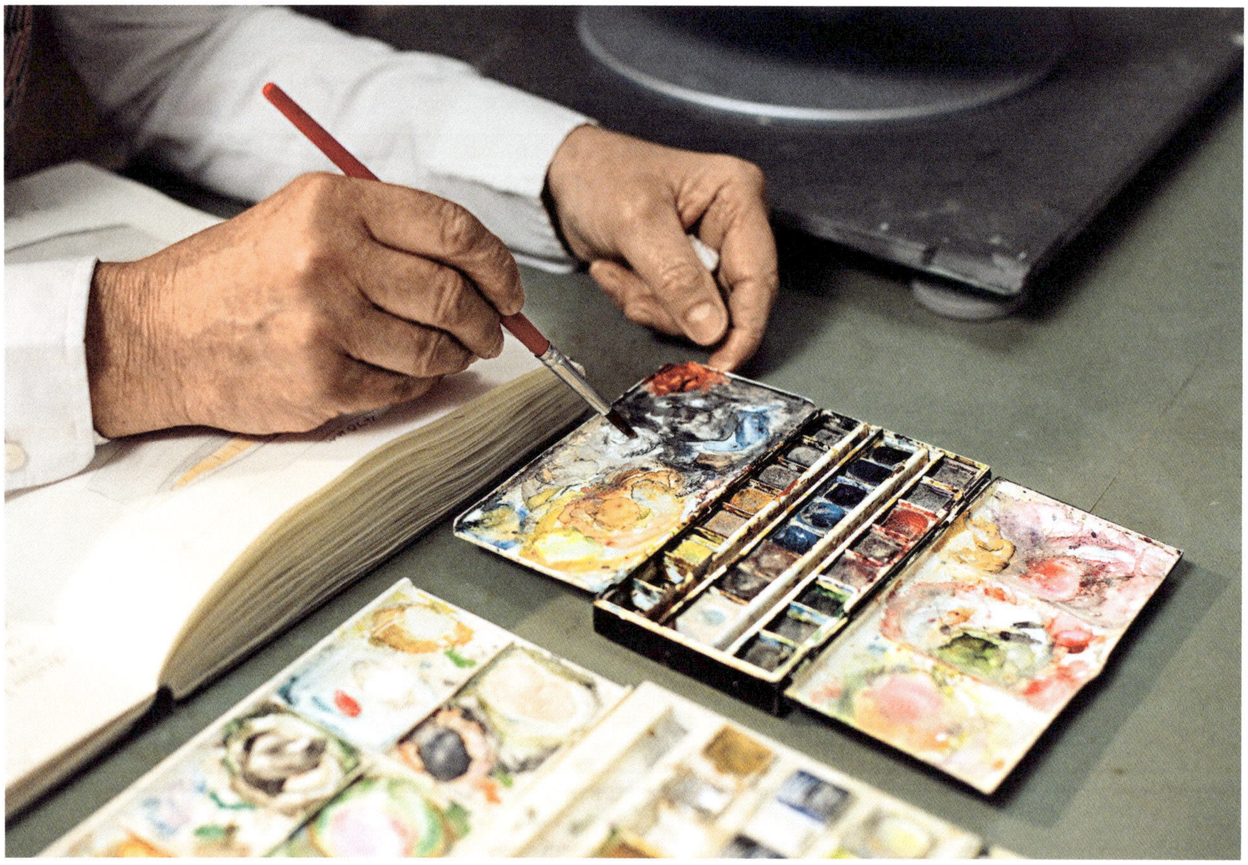

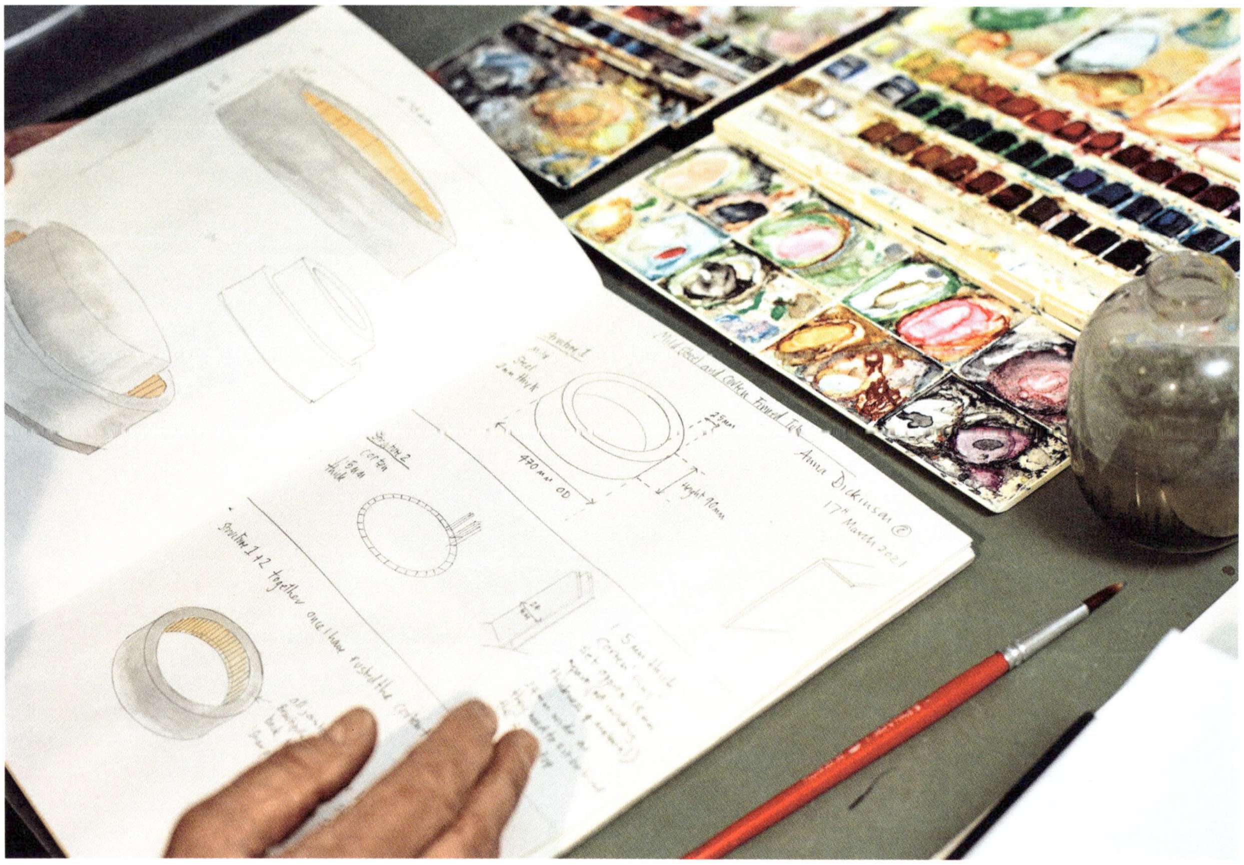
Anna Dickinson ©
17th March 2021

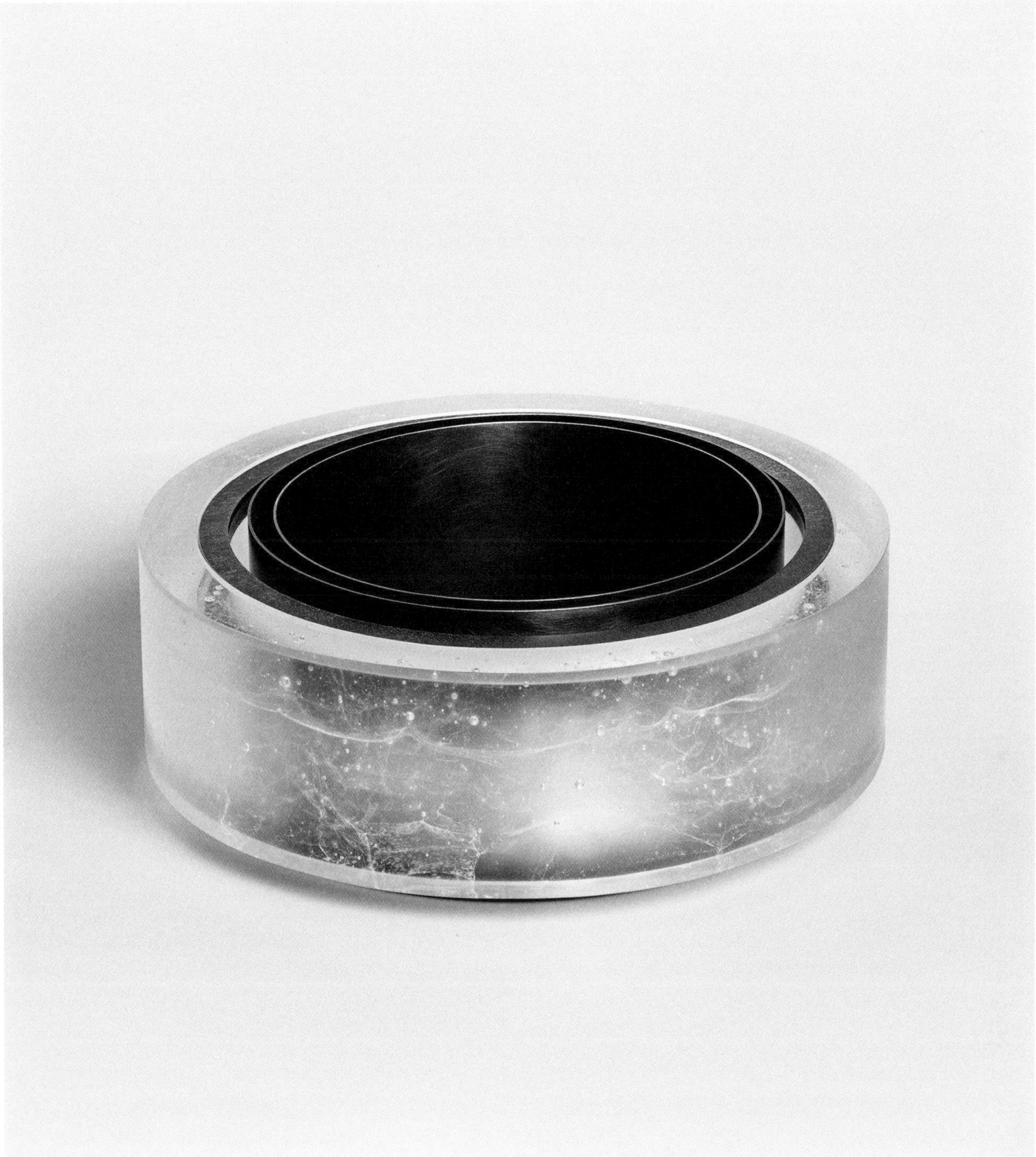

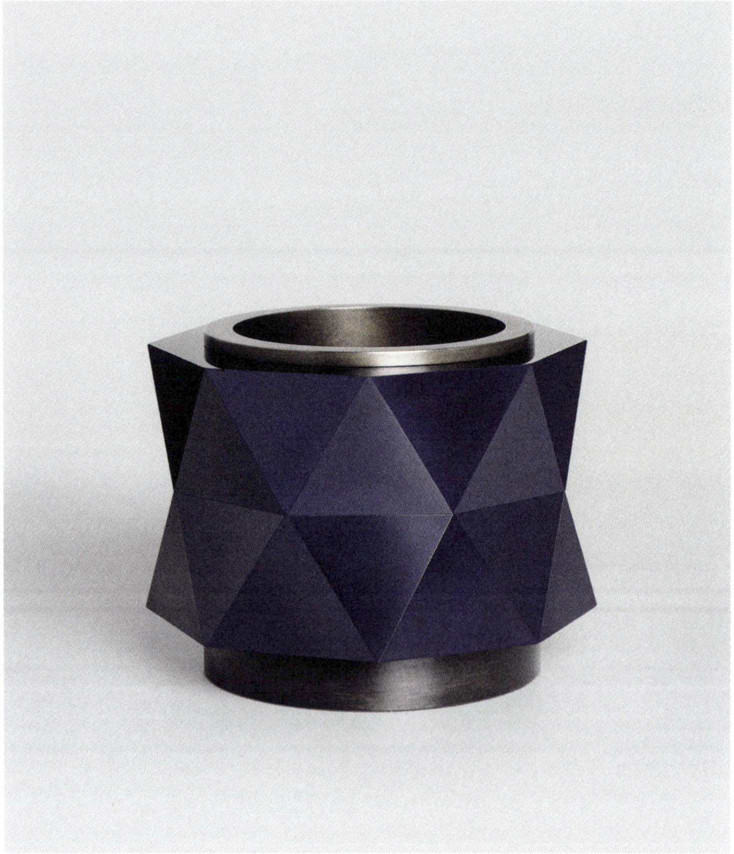
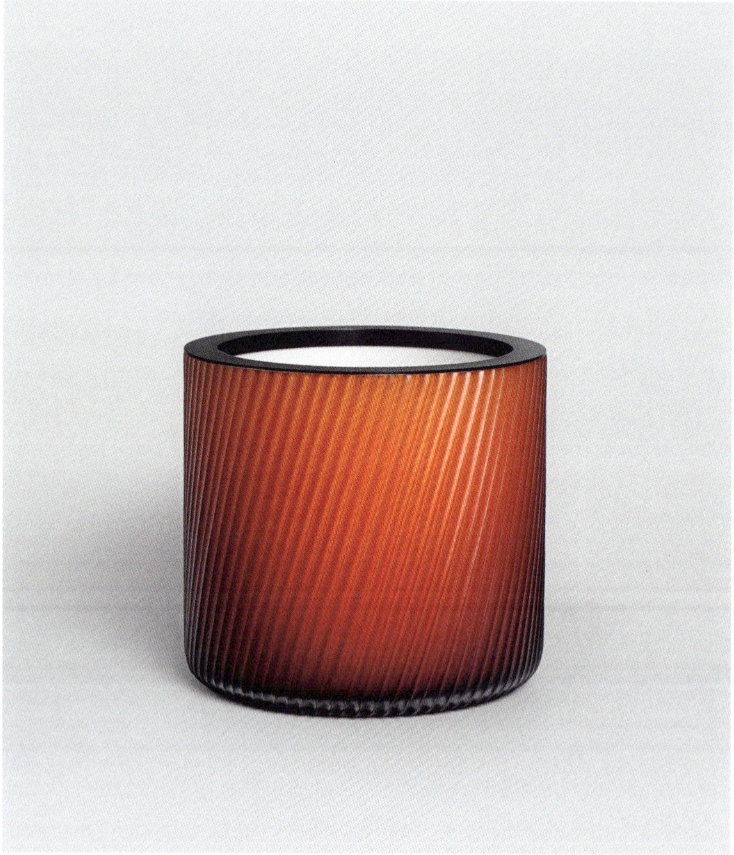
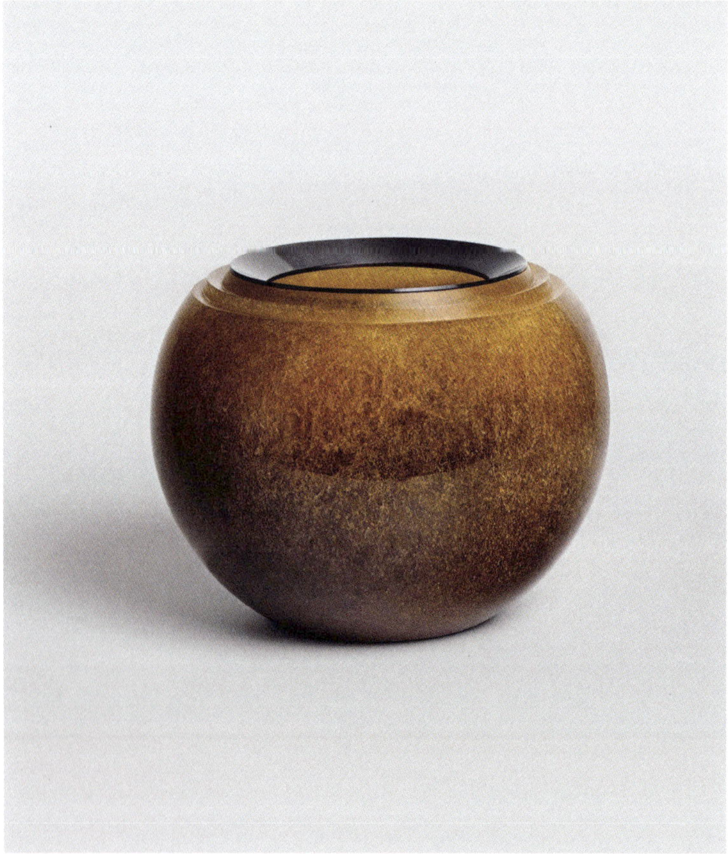
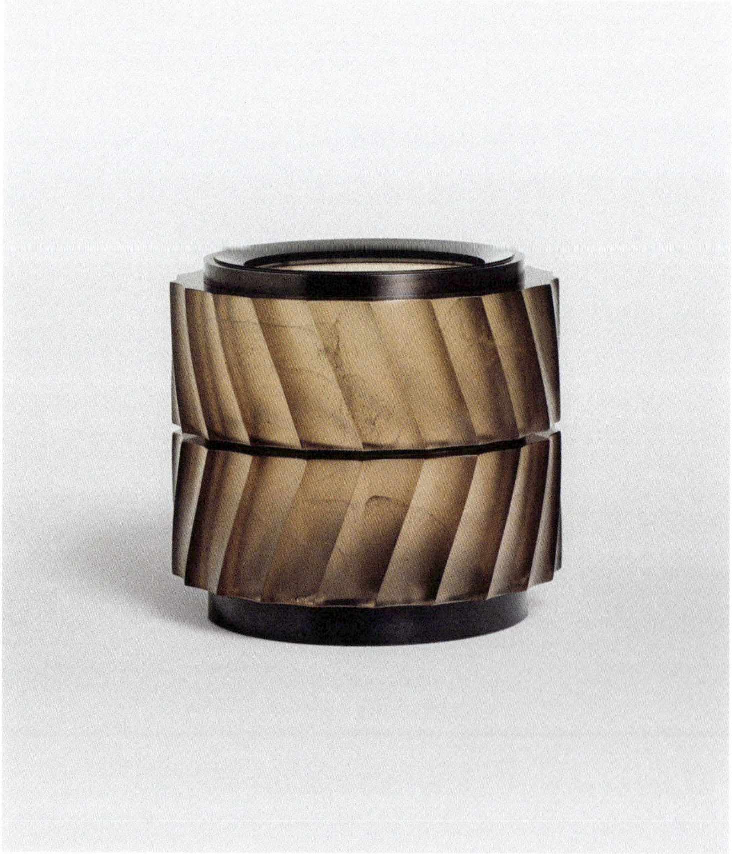

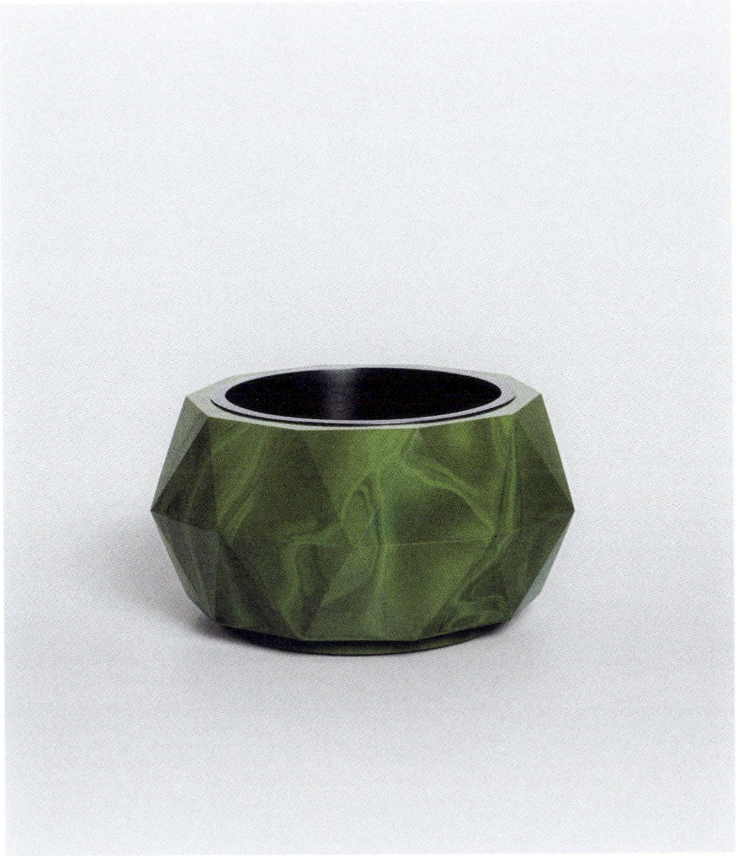
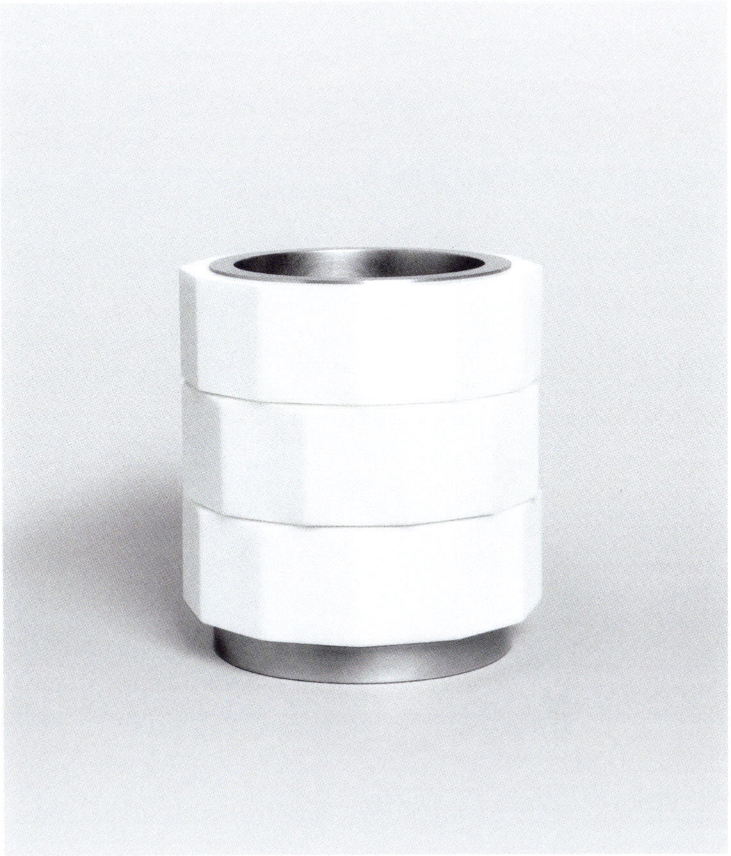
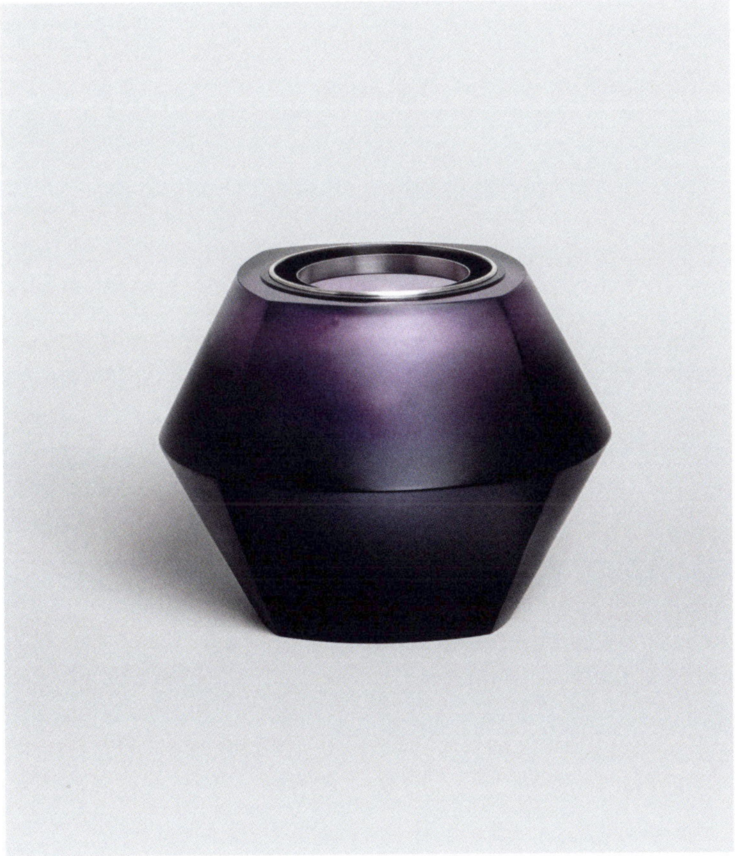
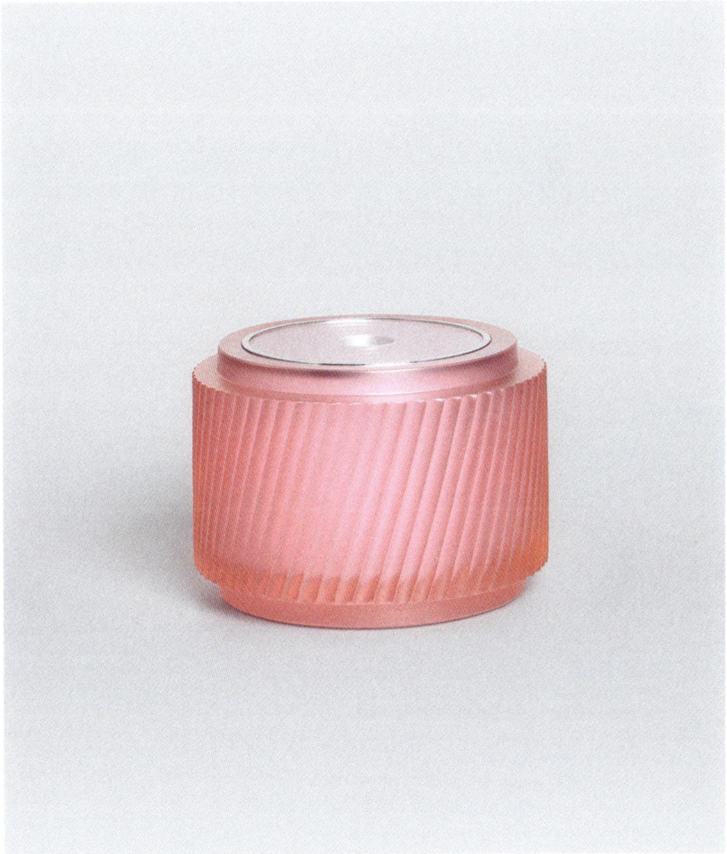

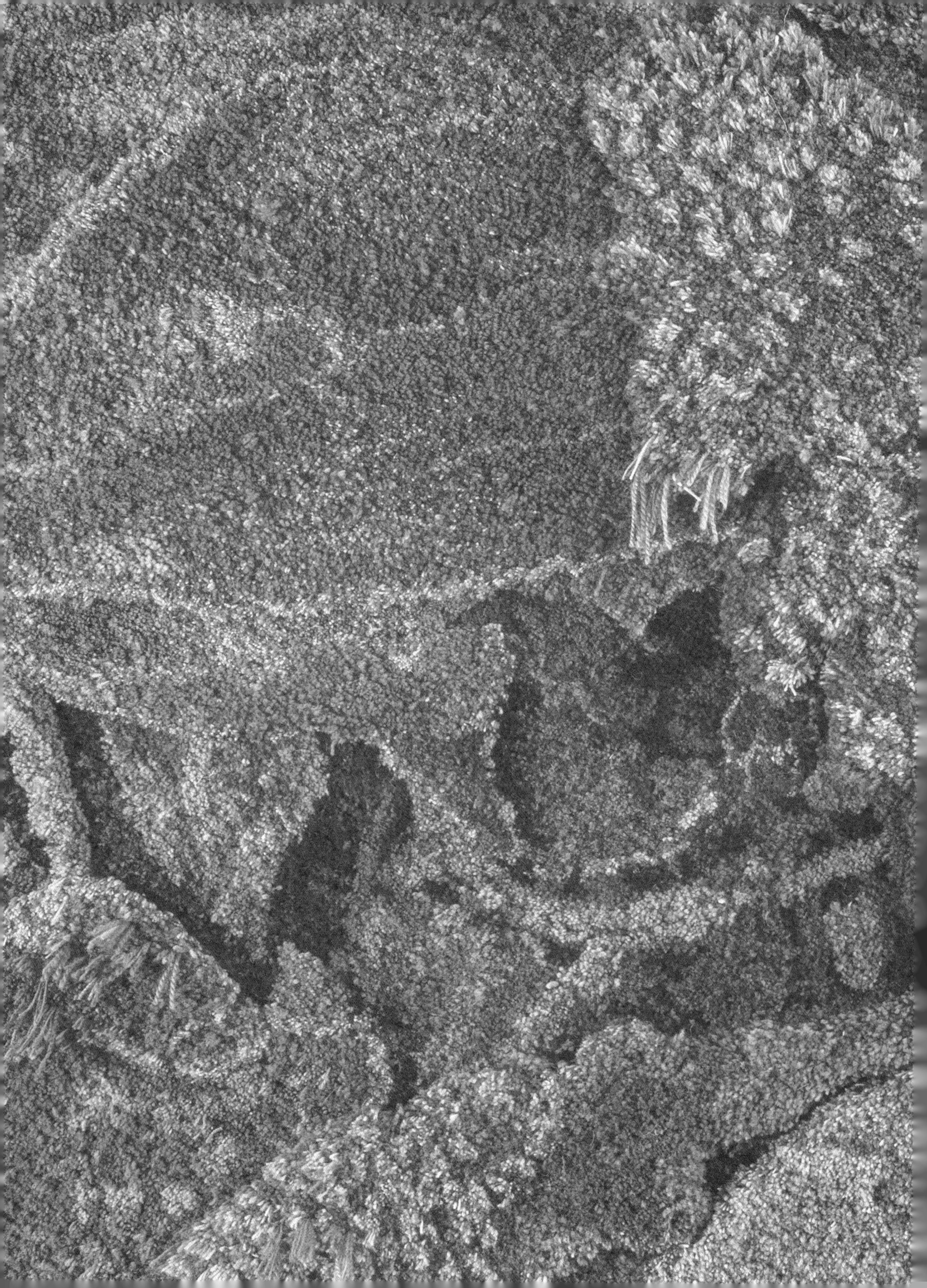

Textiles

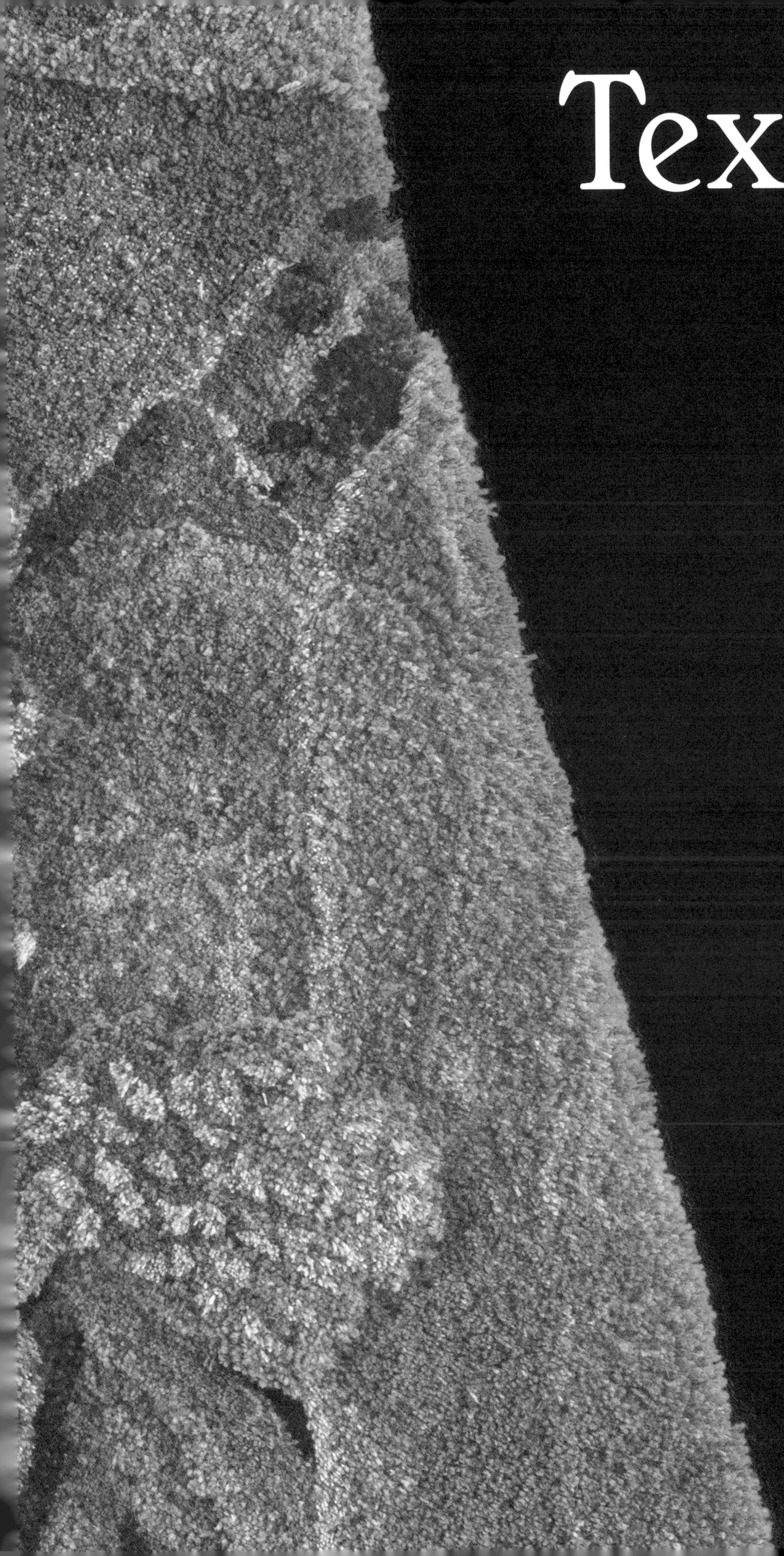

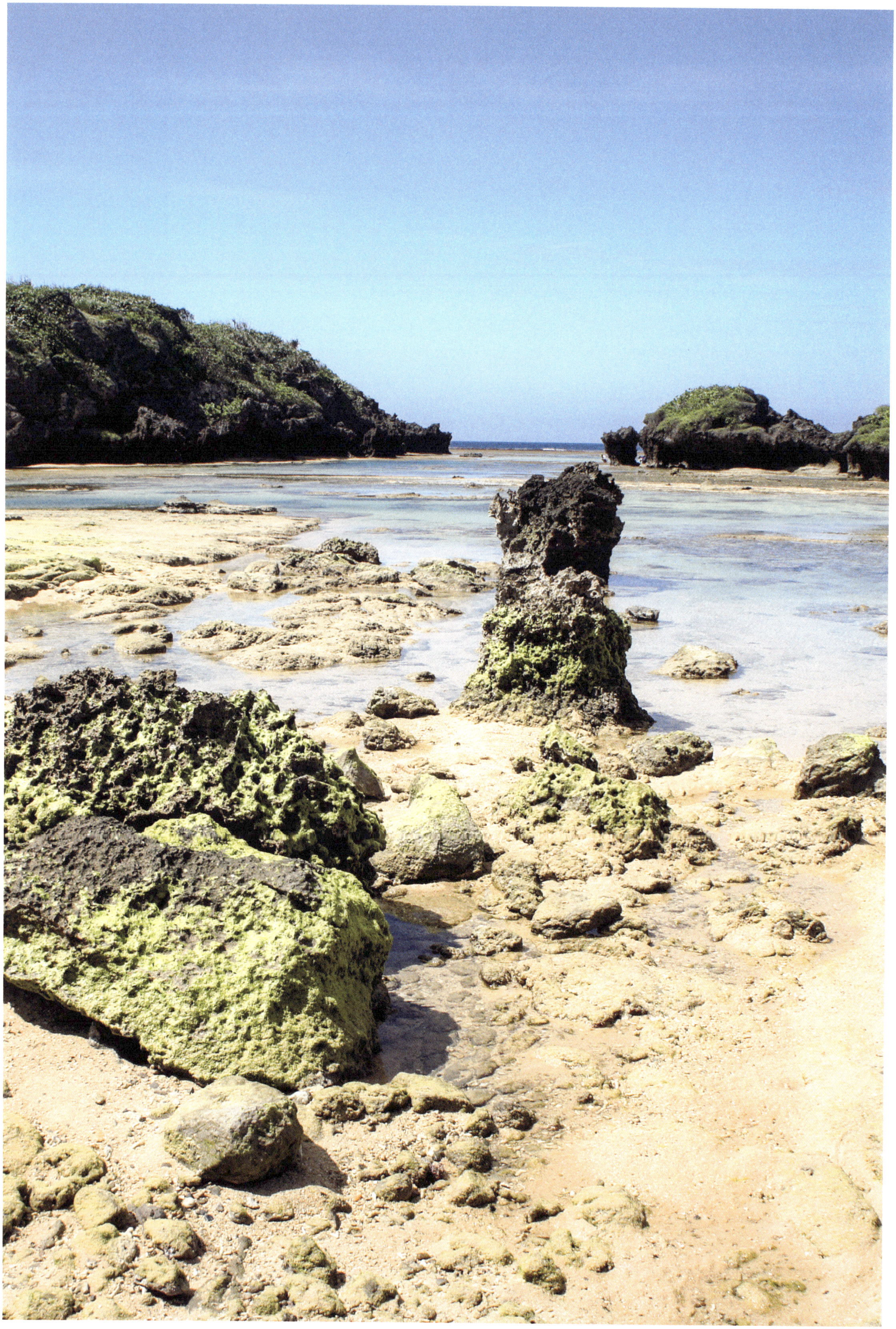

Akiko Ishigaki

Dyer and weaver

Iriomote, Japan

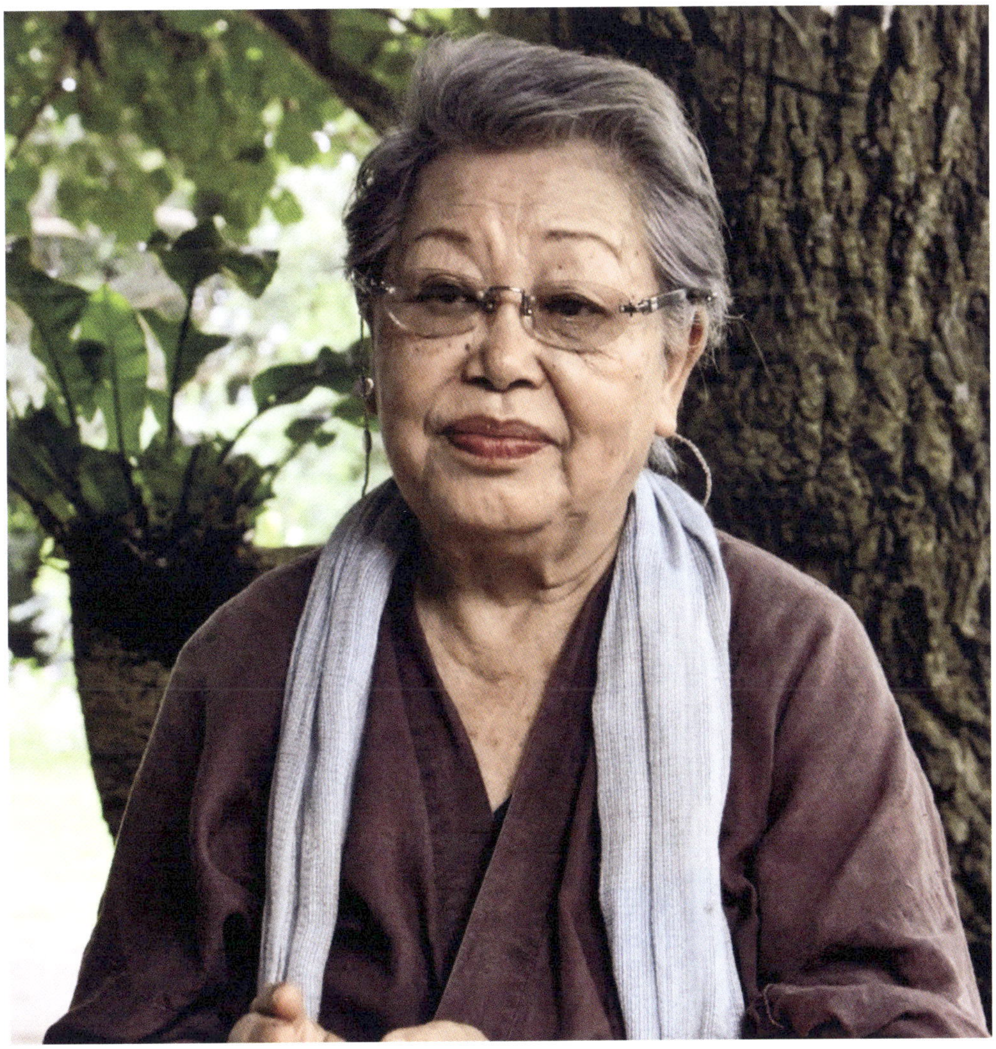

My name is Akiko Ishigaki, and I am a weaver and dyer. I was raised by my grandmother on the Japanese island of Taketomi, one of the islands of Yaeyama, in the southern part of the Ryūkyū Islands archipelago. My grandmother was a weaver and taught me everything I know. When she died, her most precious pieces were donated to the Japan Folk Crafts Museum in Tokyo. A few years later, when I saw her kimonos again in the museum's collection, I realized how extraordinarily talented and skilled she was. I understood at that moment that she had set me on a path—one I have followed all my life.

For a long time in the archipelago, clothes were woven from Chinese nettle or banana fiber (*bashô*)—it was part of island culture. But when I moved to Iriomote with my husband, Kinsey, no one was weaving anymore. The locals worked in the coal mines to earn a living. I remember that there was nothing, just bamboo. Kinsey sourced banana trees from the west of the island, and together we started planting them around the workshop he had built on his ancestral land. That was more than thirty years ago.

Today, in Iriomote, we have everything we need to create textiles—yarn, fiber, and dye—because we have the mountain, the river, and the ocean. We are surrounded by a wonderful natural environment, protected by the gods. In my garden and in the forest around the house, I grow mulberry and banana trees, and indigo plants. I can watch over them and take care of them. The plants tell me when they are ready to be harvested. People here have always lived in tune with nature, and I try to do the same, which means I have to make an effort to stay in shape.

There are three kinds of banana trees: one for flowers, one for fruit, and one for fiber. Before weaving, there are many steps to follow. When your mind is too occupied, the *bashô* gets upset, grumbles, and breaks. It took me ten years to understand this. Compared to other natural fibers like linen or cotton, *bashô* requires a great deal of attention. The fiber is extracted from the trunk. To obtain it, you need to choose the right tree, with a trunk covered in leaves from top to bottom, and cut it at the right season. The leaves are removed and are left in the field as compost, and the trunk is peeled. To make high-quality thread, the third layer is used; it is dried and then boiled in water mixed with ash. There is no standard recipe: the result varies according to the size of the *bashô*, the water, and the weather. After these steps are complete, I give the fiber to the elderly ladies of the village to make the thread, which is a time-consuming and demanding process. You have to stay focused and be nimble with your fingers to twist the threads one by one and bind them together. When I examine a textile under a magnifying glass, I can tell where it comes from—Yaeyama or elsewhere. To weave a single kimono, I have to cut down a hundred banana trees from my fields.

I was introduced to dyeing by Master Fukumi, in Kyoto. Here on the islands, the plants are different; each has its own color. I base my work on four tones: brown, which exists in all plants; yellow, from the *fuguki* tree; gray, from the *tsurubami* tree; and indigo. I understood the mystery of indigo through Japanese painting and literature. It is the most interesting color—it offers a world without limits. With yellow and blue, I can make green, which no plant can produce. The color green is very mysterious: it is only perceptible in the indigo jar. Green is said to be the color of another world.

At eighty-five years old, I continue to make fabrics using ancestral methods. Most of the young people to whom I pass on this knowledge come from Tokyo and Kyoto. After several months, each of them tries to live at nature's pace, far from the hustle and bustle of the big cities. If they leave serene and at peace, it is not down to me—it is thanks to the power and emotional force that nature exerts upon us.

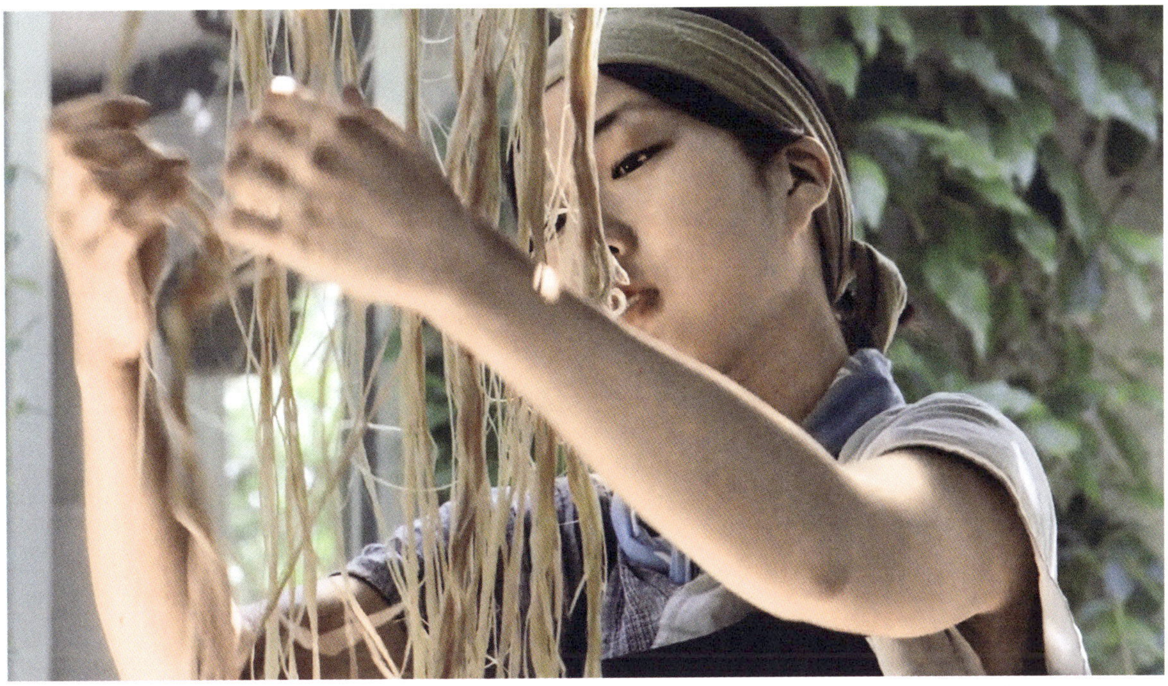

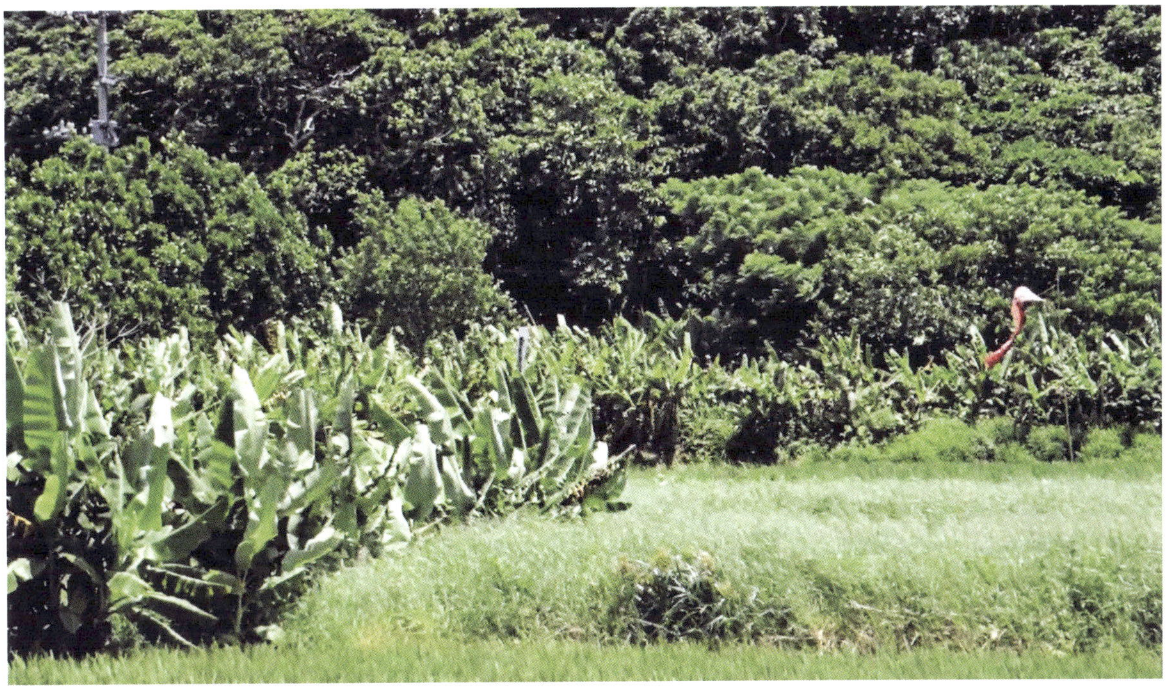

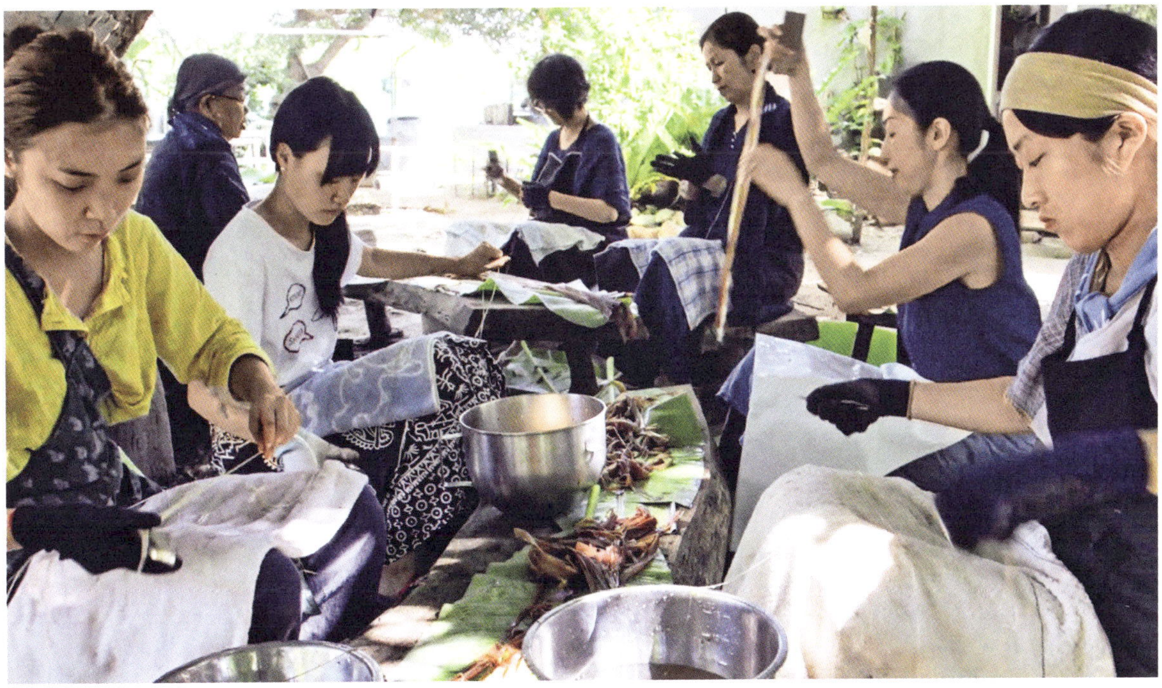

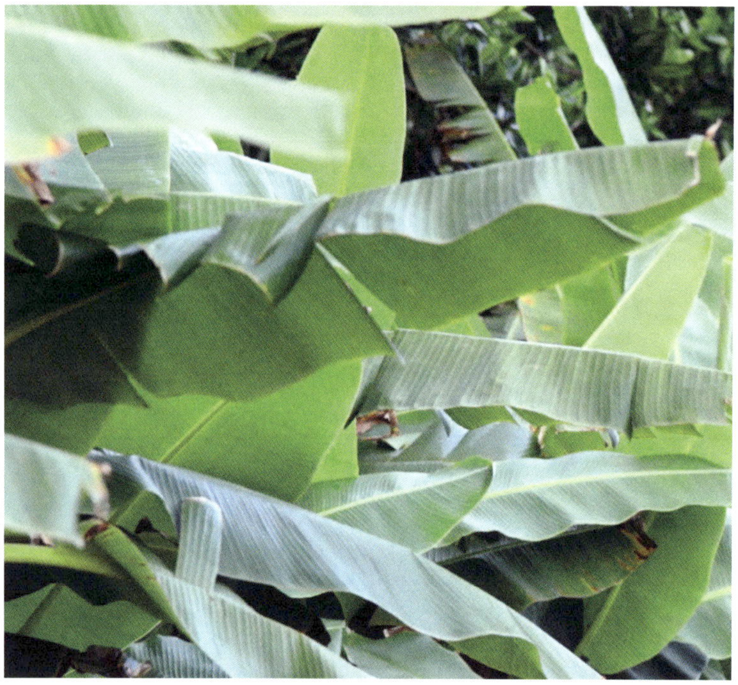
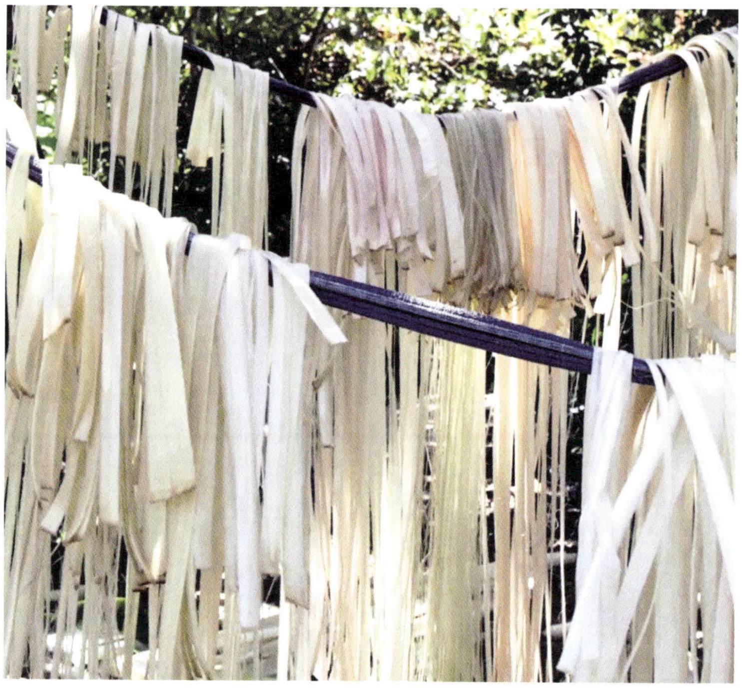
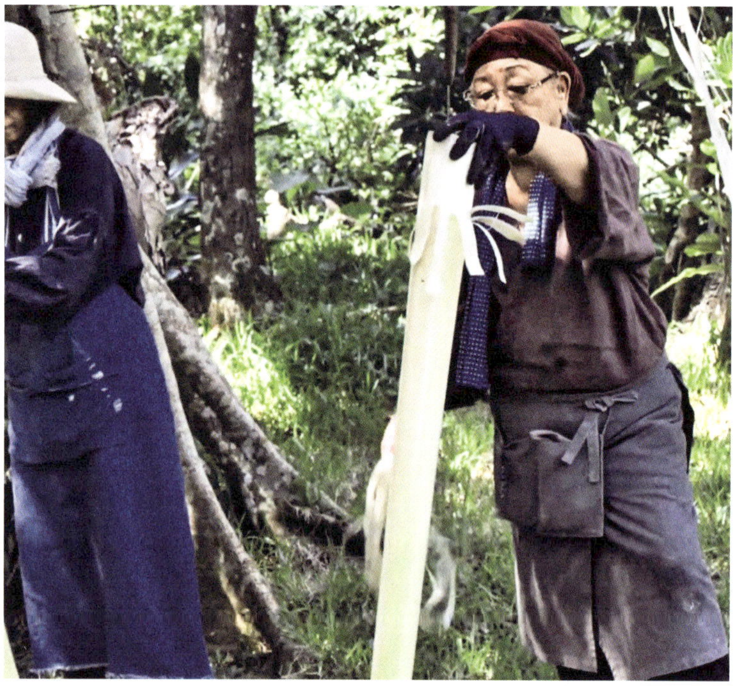
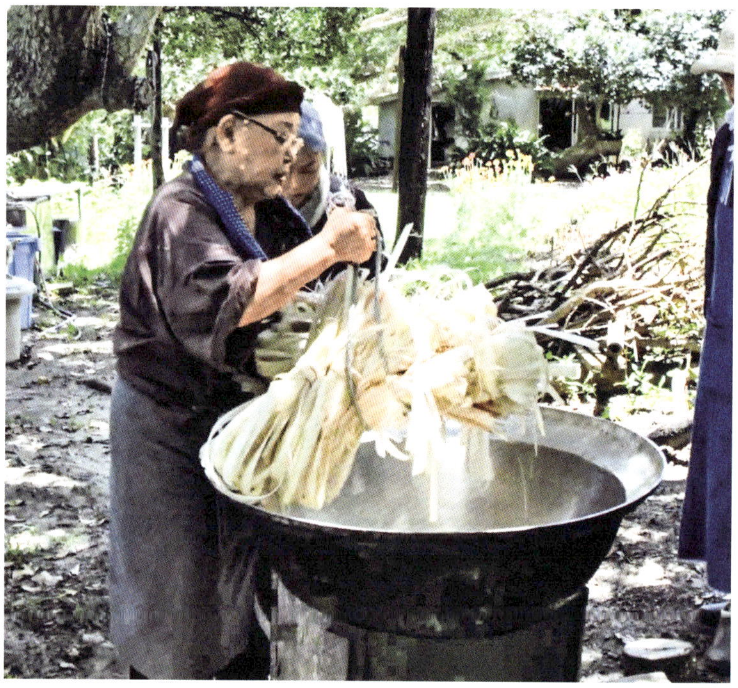
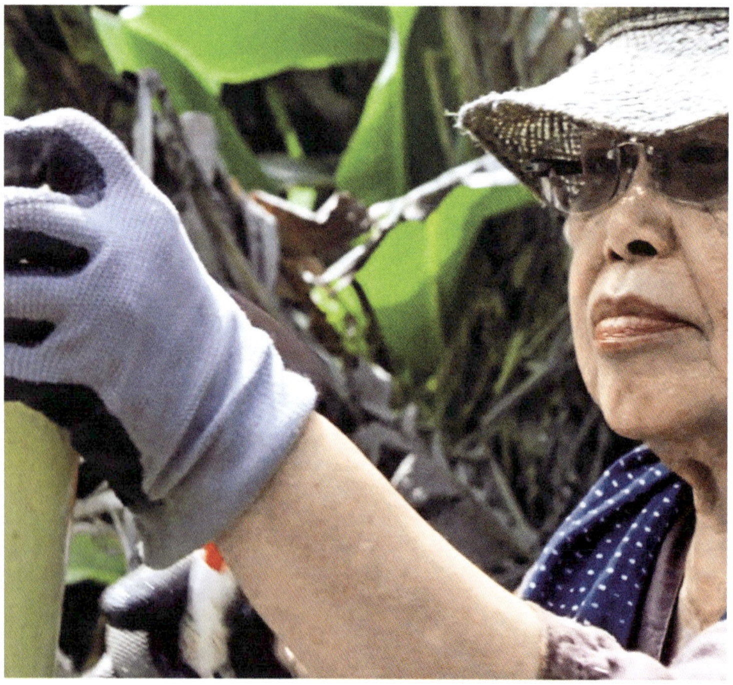
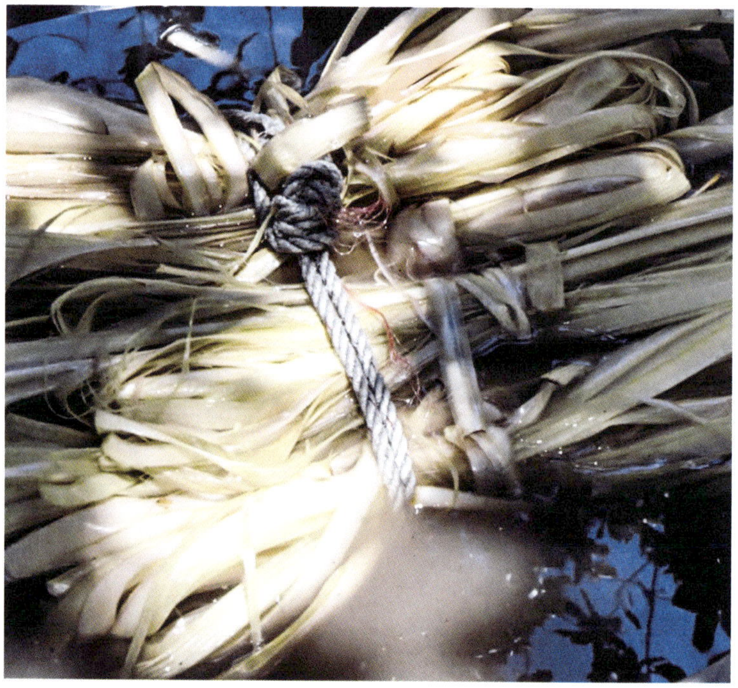

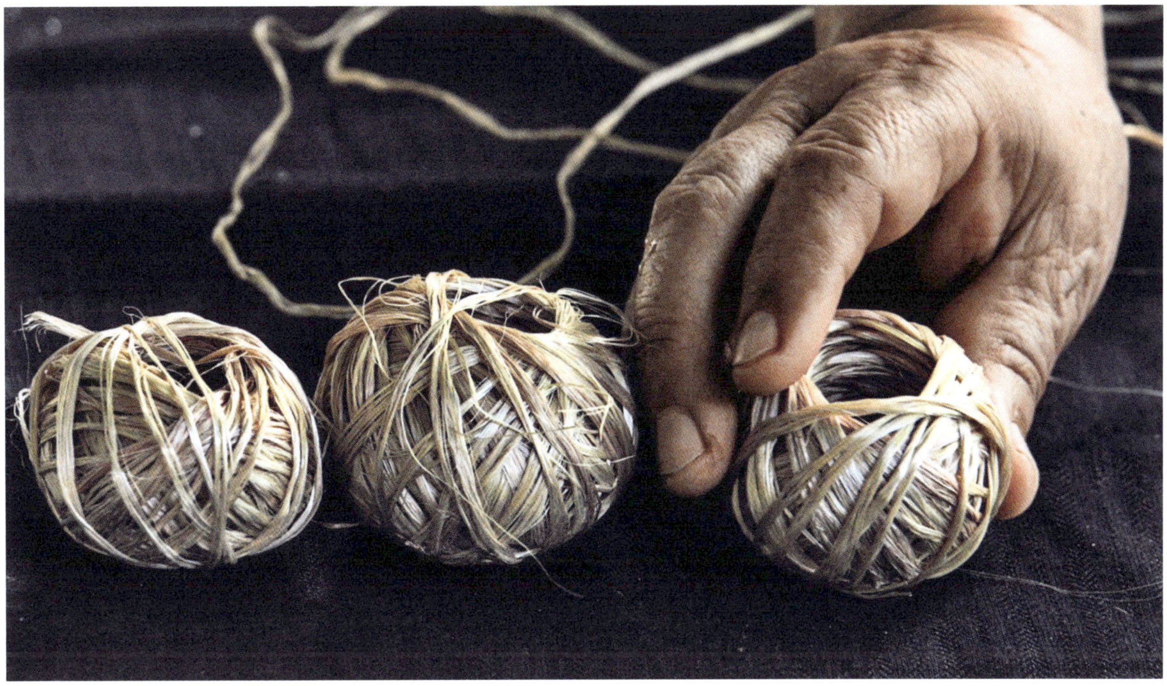

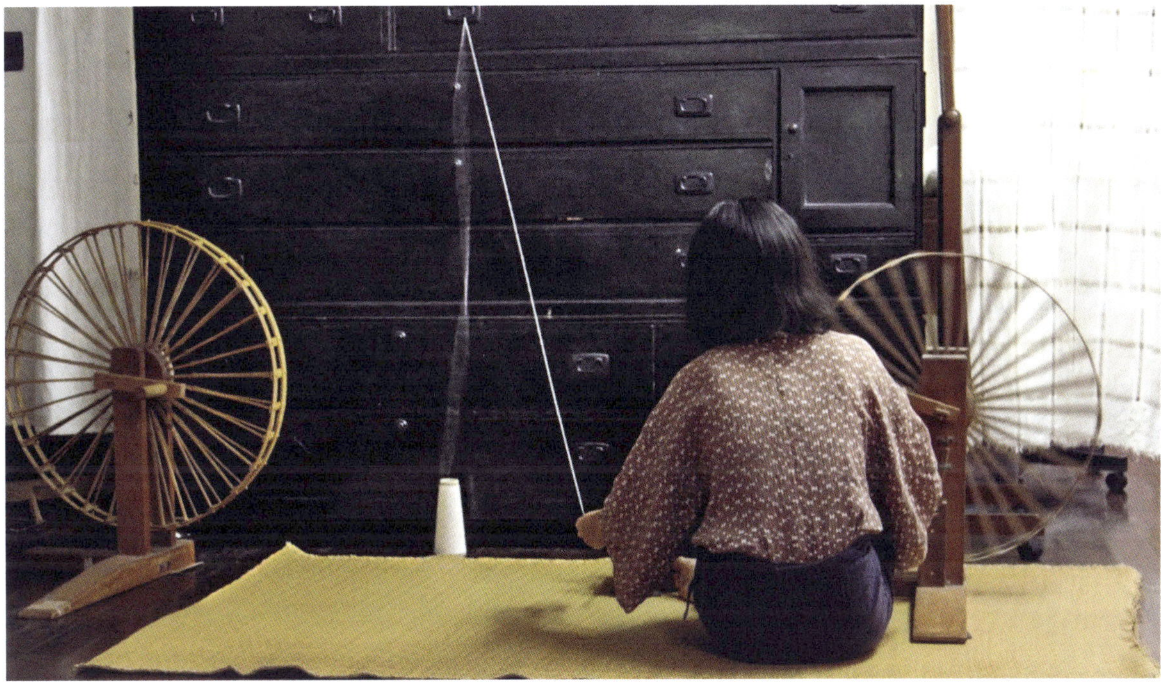

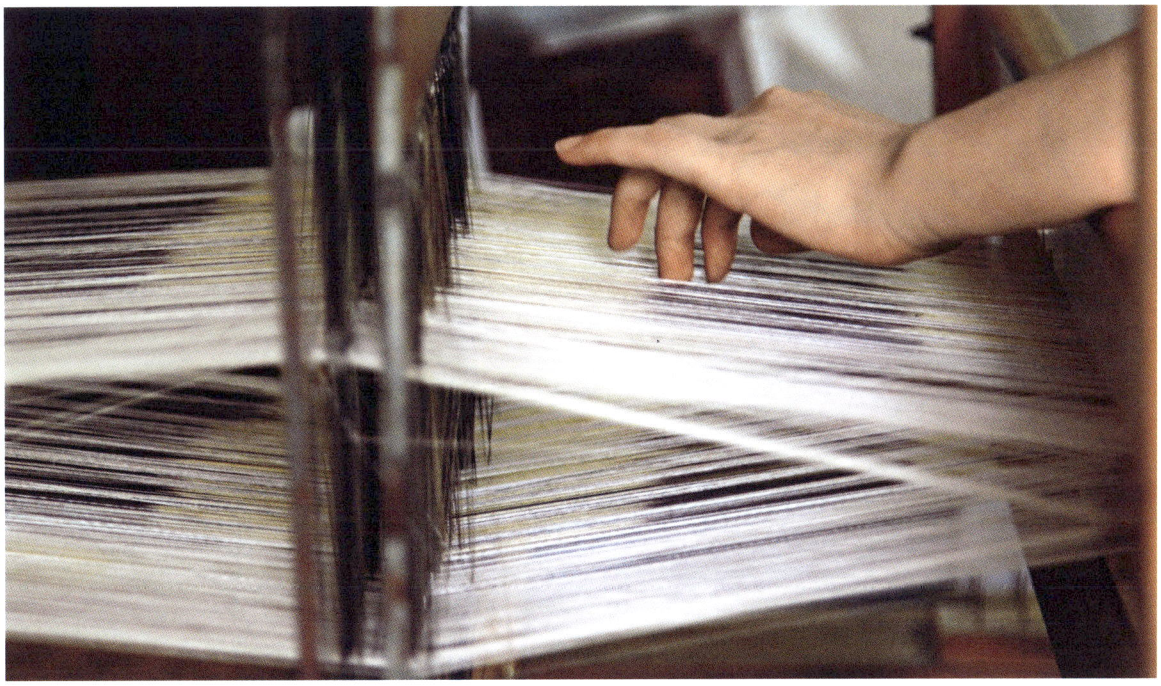

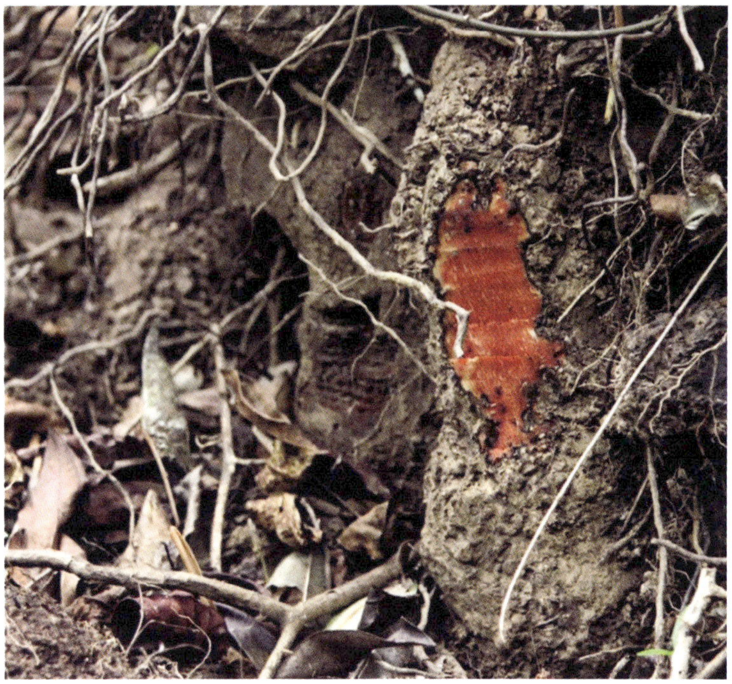
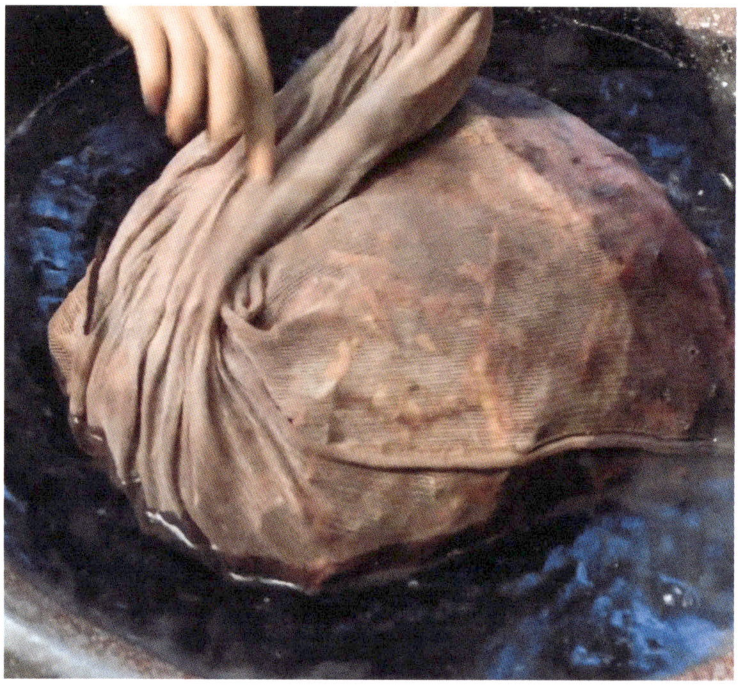
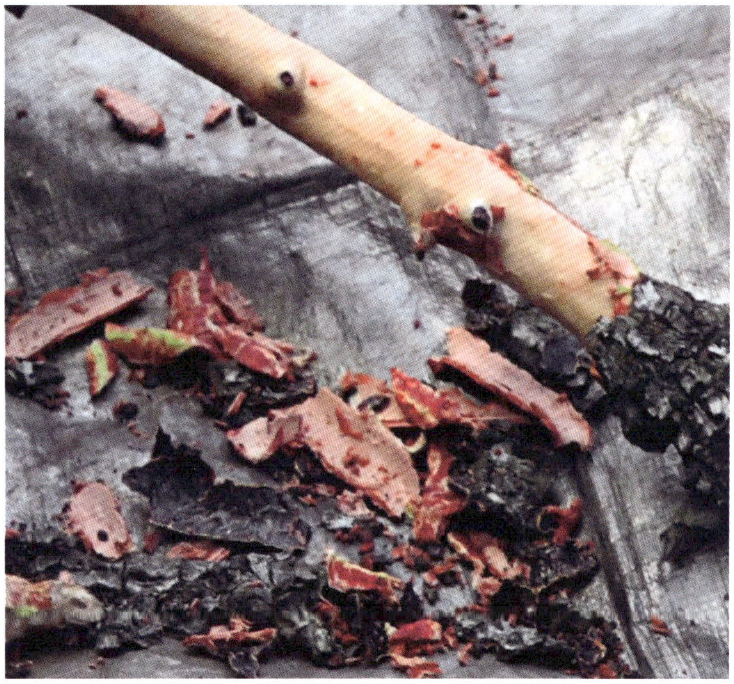
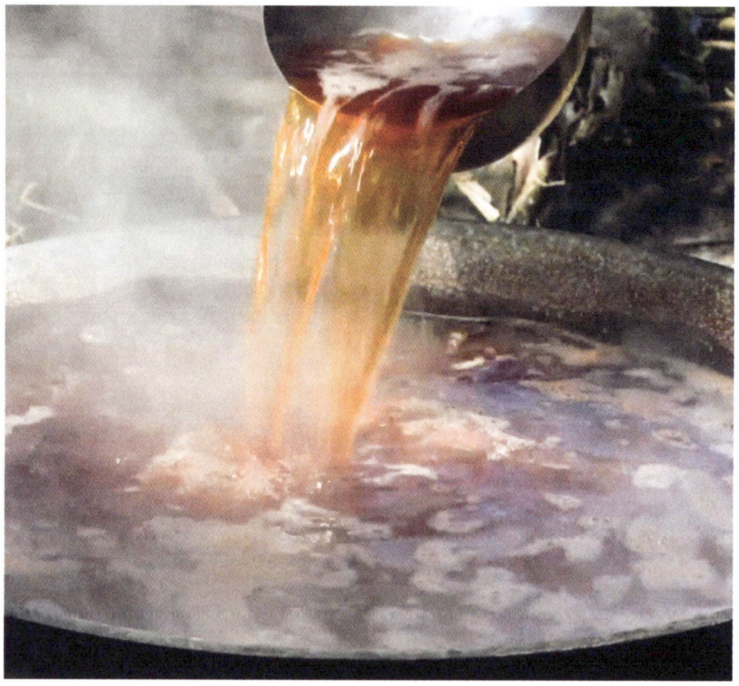
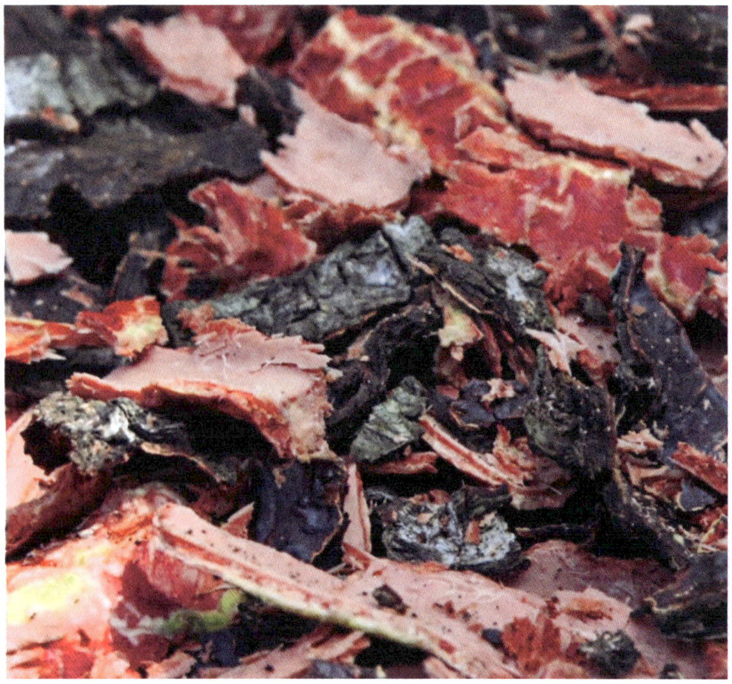
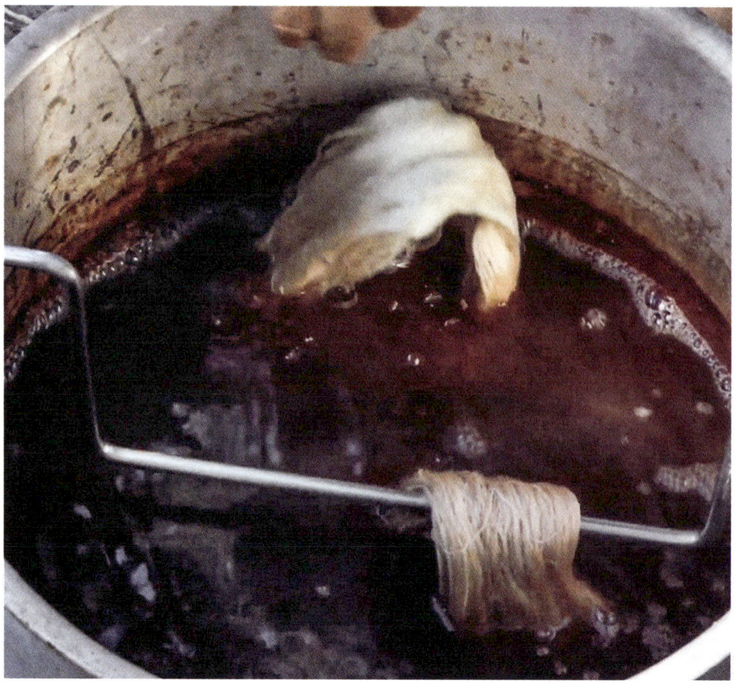

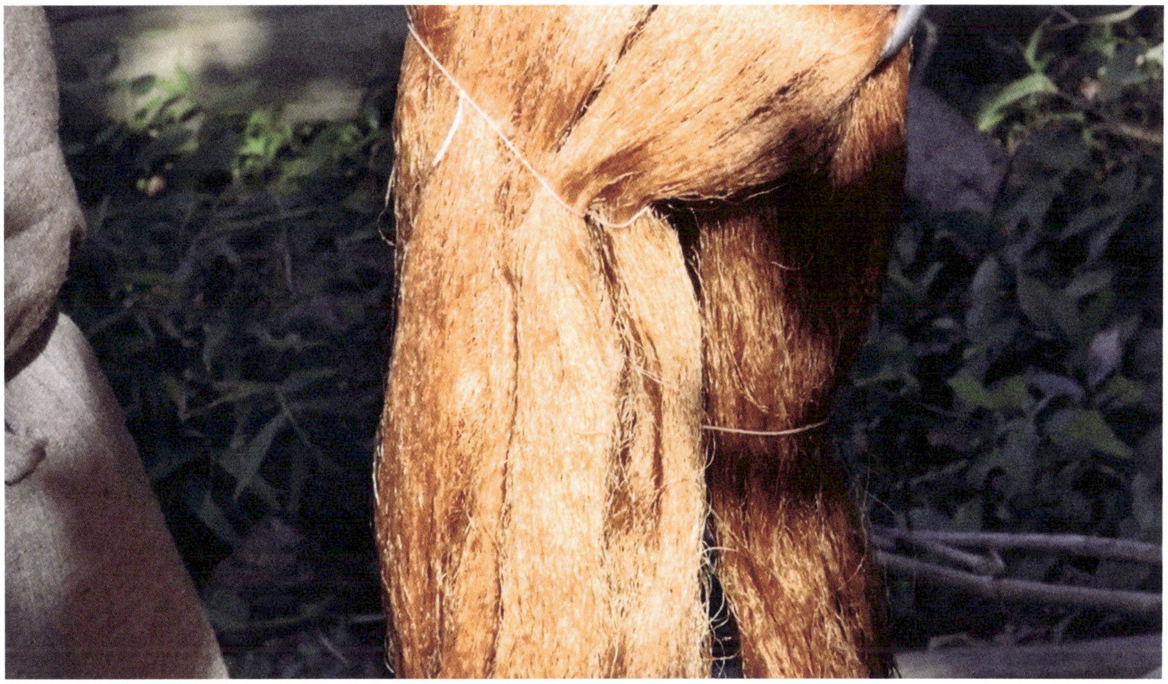
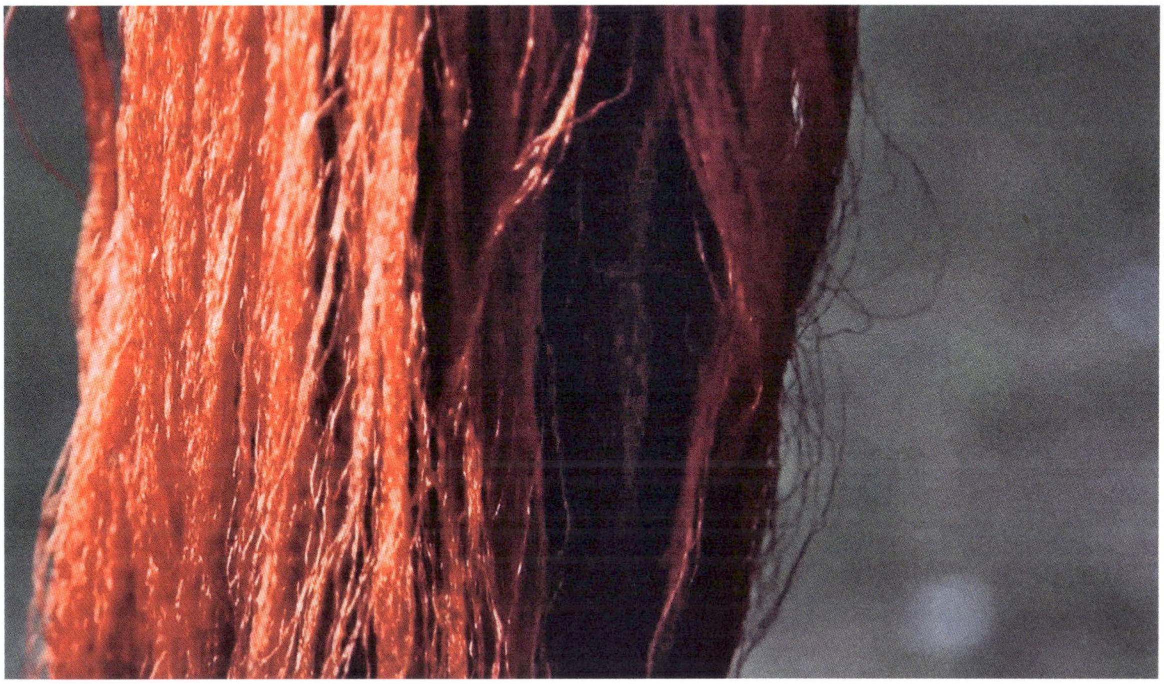
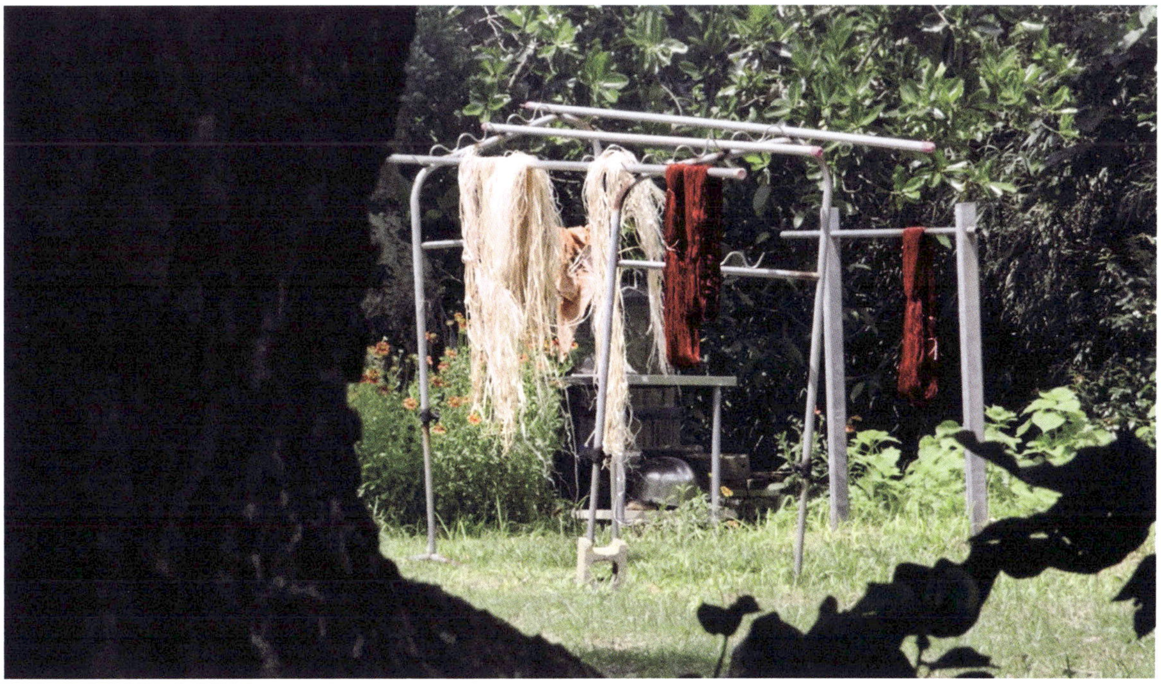

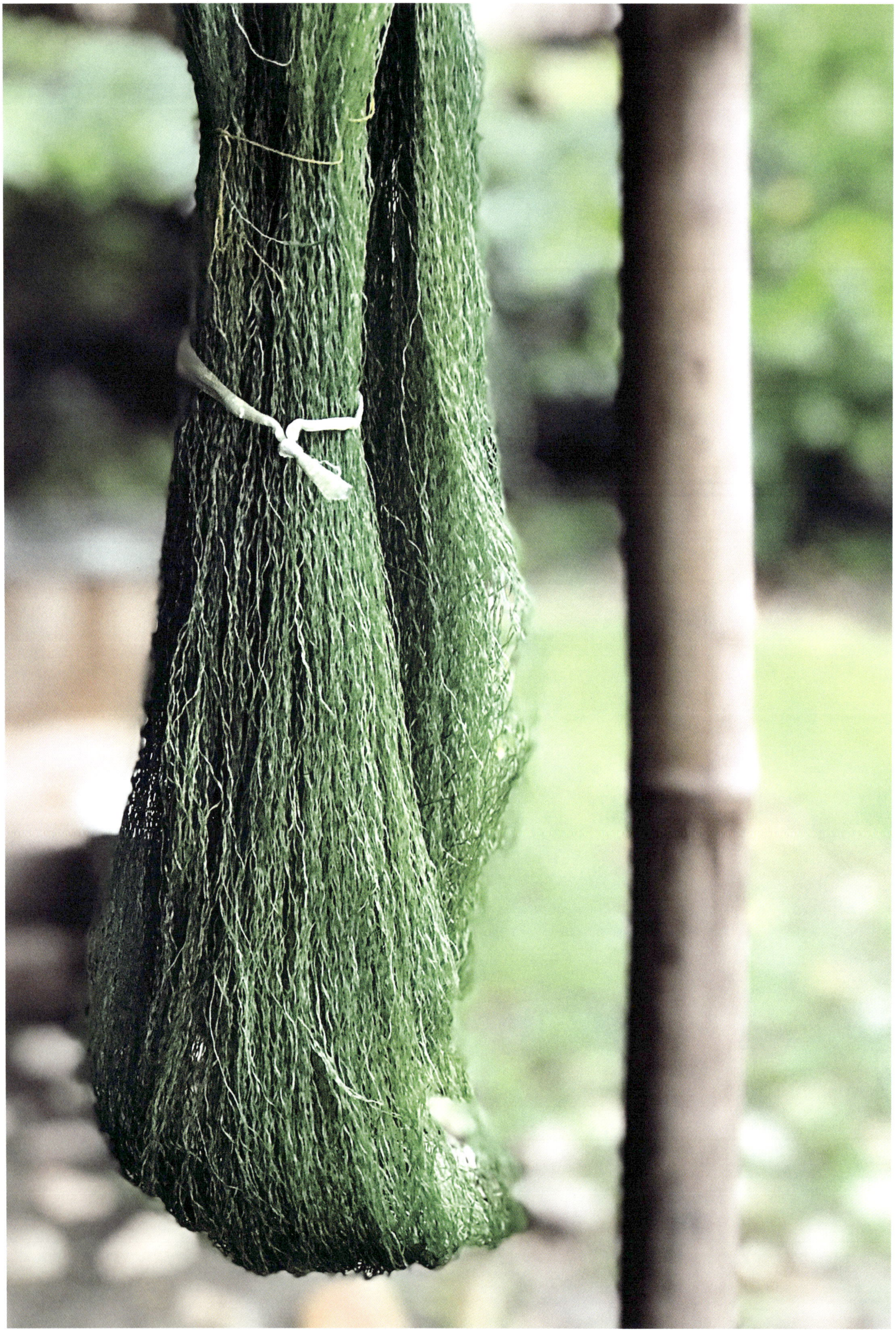

Chiaki Maki

Dyer and weaver

Bhogpur, India

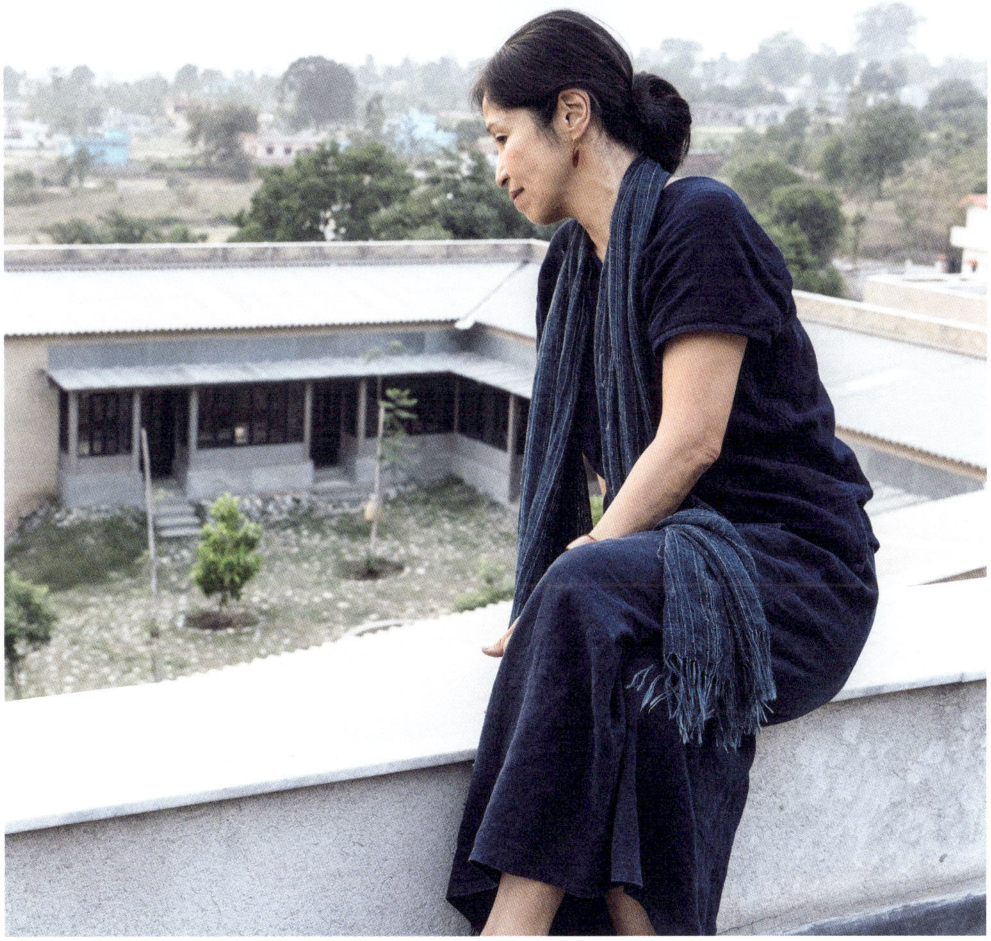

My name is Chiaki Maki, and I create textiles with craftspeople, using my hands and my heart. I was born in Japan, but since 2013 I have split my time between Akiruno, Japan, and my Ganga Maki workshop in the foothills of the Himalayas, in Bhogpur, India.

I grew up in the suburbs of Tokyo, where nature was still very much intact. My mother was an artisanal basket maker. She was particularly fond of banana fiber (*bashô*) and hand-woven textiles. From early childhood, I was familiar with the words "spinning and weaving," "kimono," and "*bashô*," and the idea of making things by hand was like a mantra for me.

I studied art in Japan and the United States. In the 1980s, the attraction of Japanese fashion was so great that I returned to my country. But I was not happy in the industry. So, I traveled to Eastern Europe, Central America, Indonesia, Thailand, and China, before arriving in India. There, I met many craftspeople. I was fascinated by natural materials: they existed because the traditional Indian way of life had been preserved. I began to forge a strong bond with these artisans so that I could realize my dream: to make textiles for everyday use while respecting nature's cycles.

At an exhibition in Tokyo, I met the Indian architect Bijoy Jain (Studio Mumbai)—an encounter that would prove decisive. My studio, located about twelve miles (20 km) from the current site, had become too small. For more than a year, I developed my new studio with Bijoy; it took three years to build. In this 15,000-square-foot (1,400 m^2) workshop, we can produce silk, wool, cotton, and linen textiles, all dyed and woven on site. We mainly use silk hand-reeled at the Ganga Maki studio from cocoons sourced from a local silk farm in Dehradun. Our textiles are enriched with other materials such as wild (or tussar) silk, eri silk, hemp thread, and wool. Some plant fibers, such as *bashô* or ramie, are harvested around the production site, or elsewhere in the country, and used to make thread.

The material is the most important element in my dyeing and weaving work. It has to be meticulously made. During cocoon production, the silkworm winds a thread around itself by shaking its neck. To reel the silk by hand, the thread is extracted from the cocoon with the fingertips, without using any tools. As it dries, the thread takes on a beautiful, powerful shape. I am convinced that the material speaks to me: it inspires how I dye and create textiles. The thread tells its own story, including the climate in which the cocoons grew and their state of health. When I touch it, I can see the shape I want to create.

Weaving is done according to the North Indian climate. Hemp, *bashô*, and ramie must be used in the monsoon season, while hand-spun wool is woven in the dry season.

Color is fundamental, and is derived mainly from the plants we grow around the workshop; these include indigo, marigold, henna, and madder. Color is also life. Seeing, listening, touching, smelling, tasting—awakening the five senses: that is what beauty is all about.

Nowadays, I am often asked what I want or really need. Imagination is a joy. My pleasure comes above all from making and sharing. As Bijoy Jain says, "Many of the craftspeople employed in the workshop are descended from generations of skilled textile workers. Our project is about embodying and cultivating the cyclical relationship between work and life, the sun and the moon, thus bringing together the past, the present, and the future."

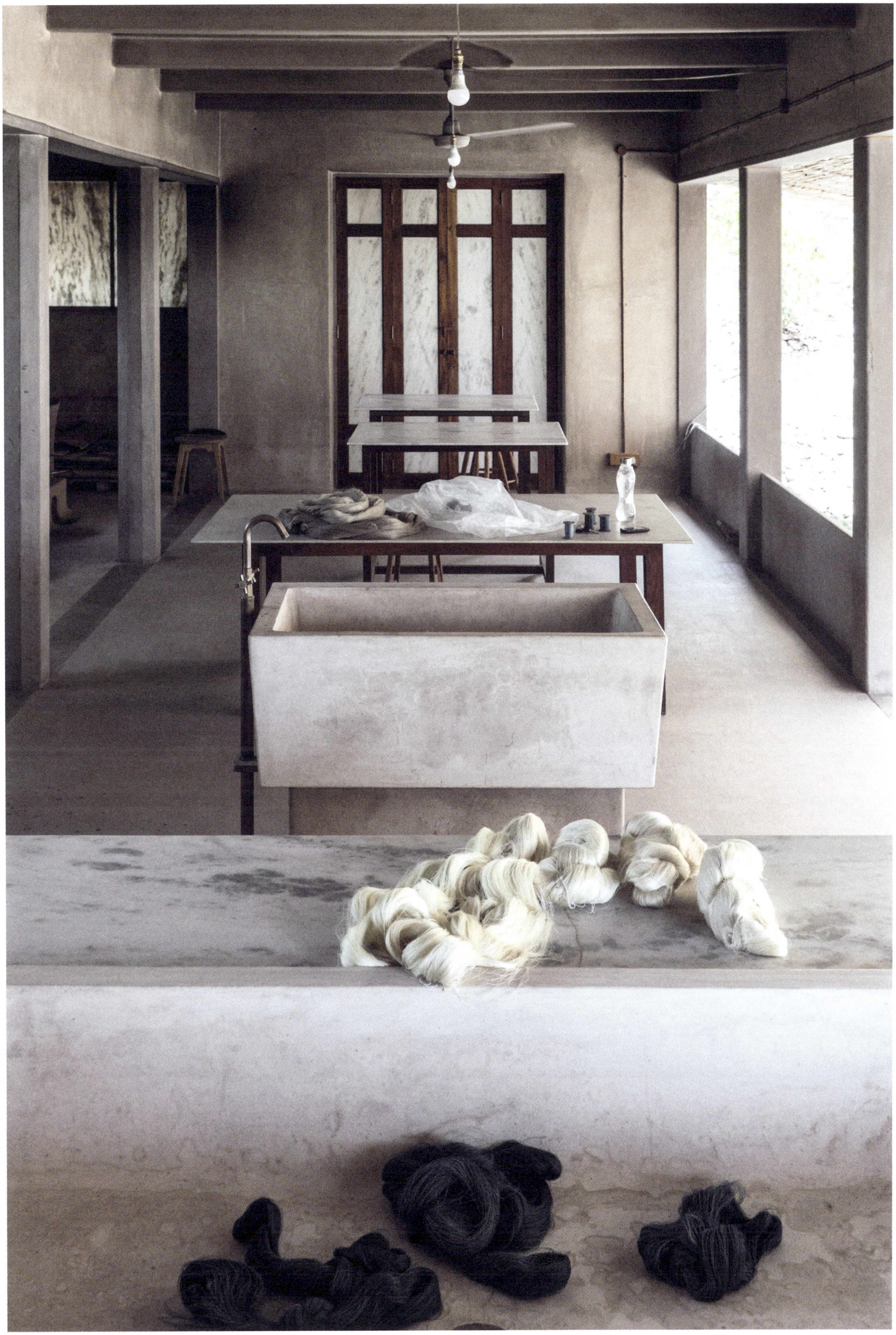

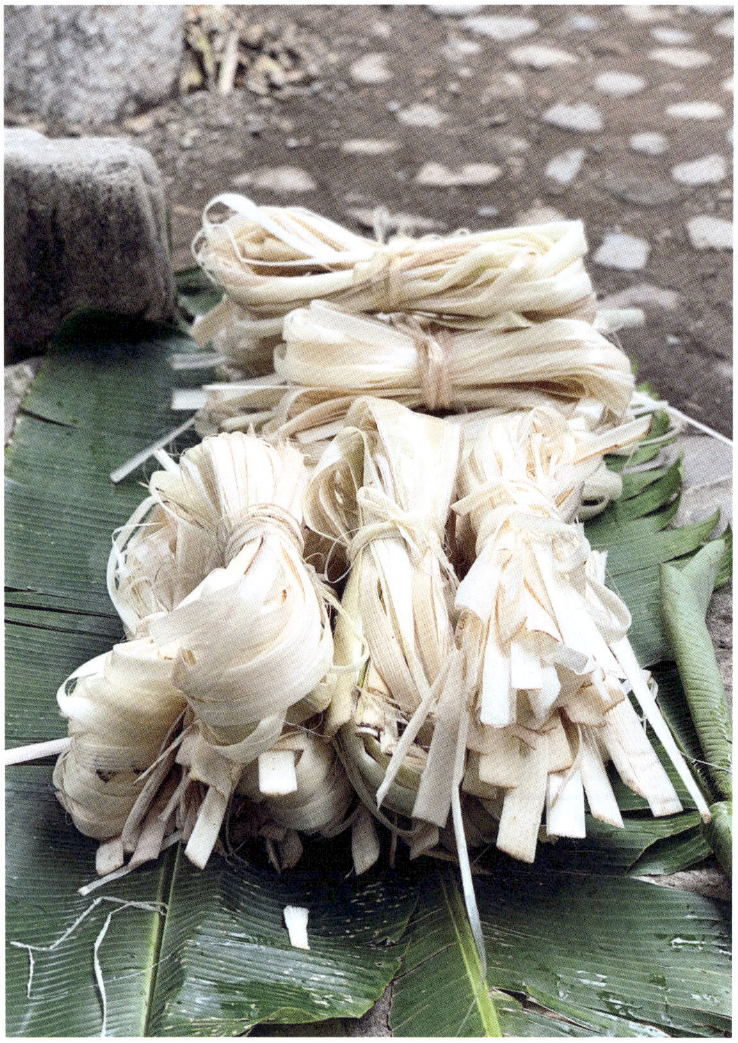
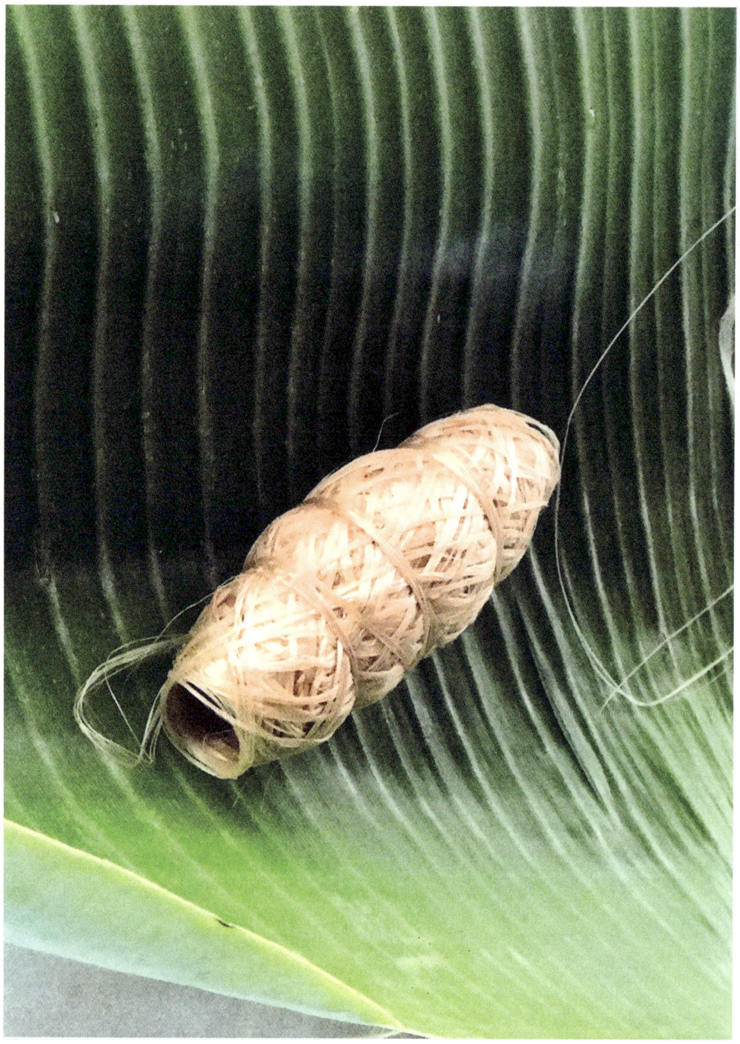
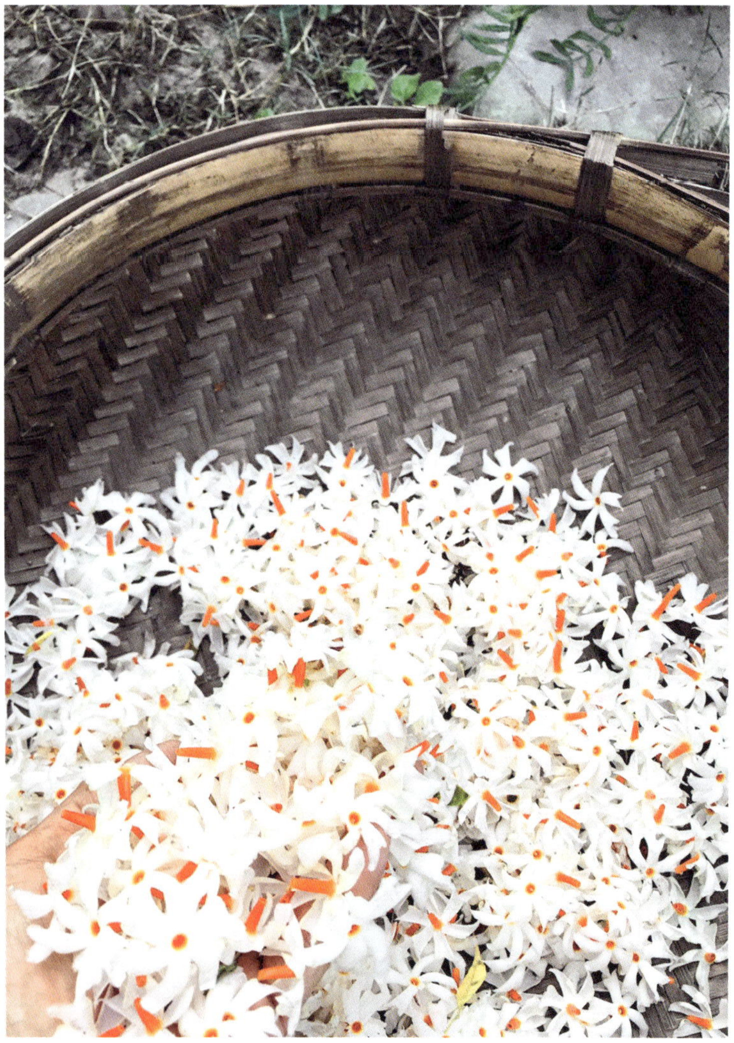
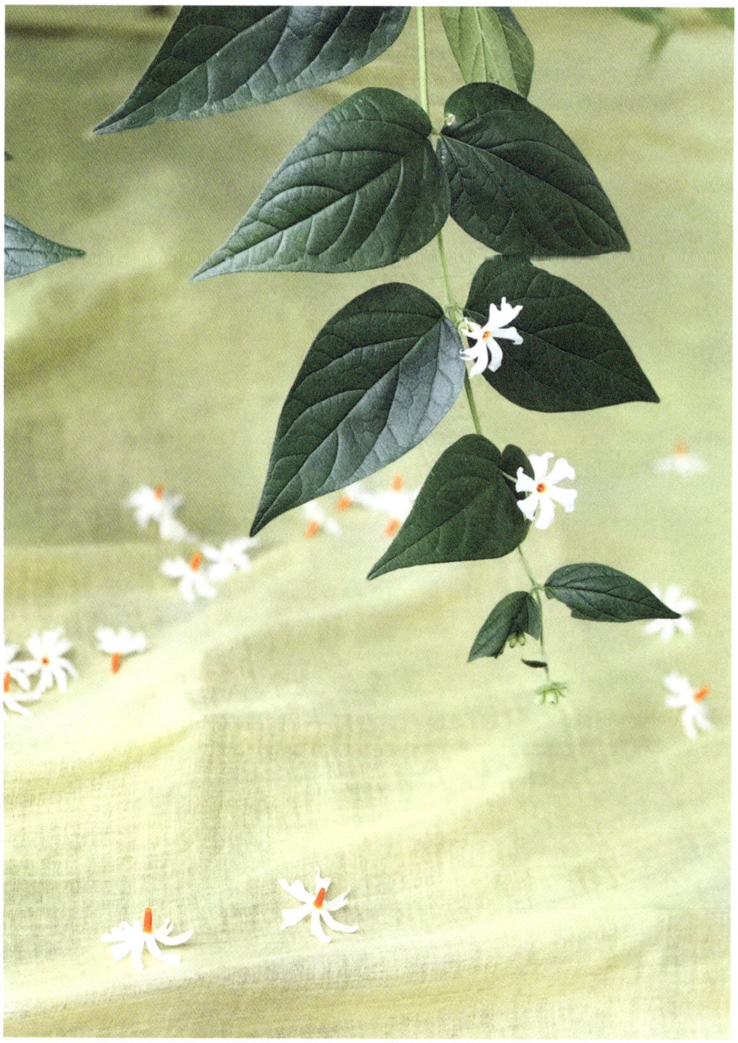

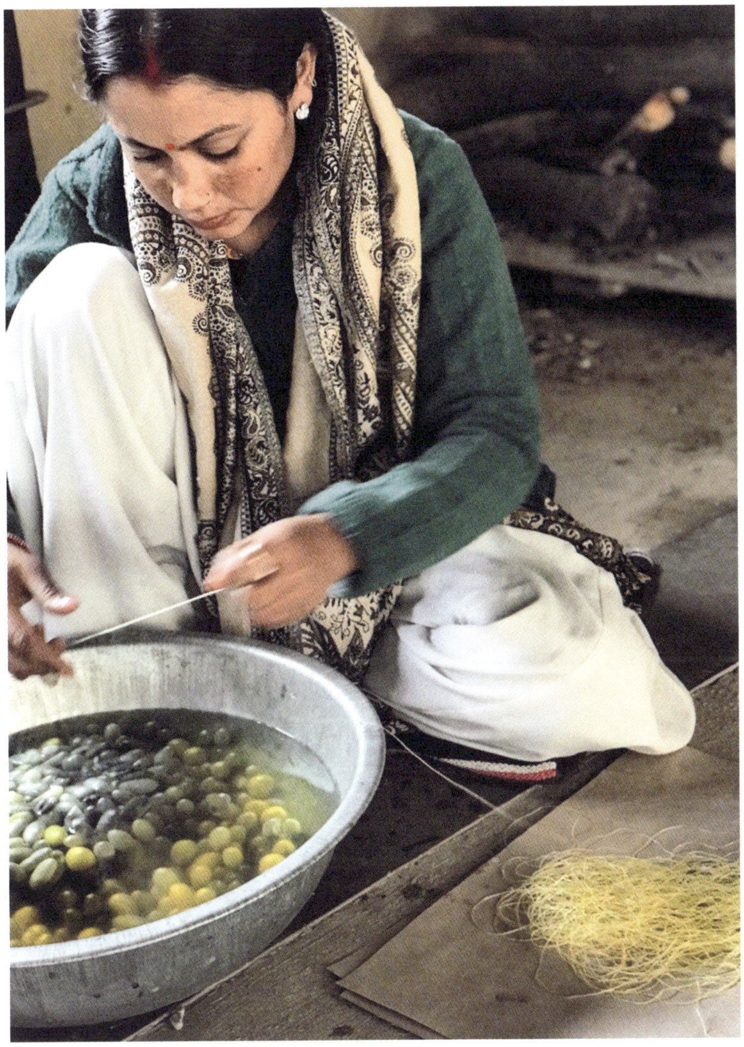
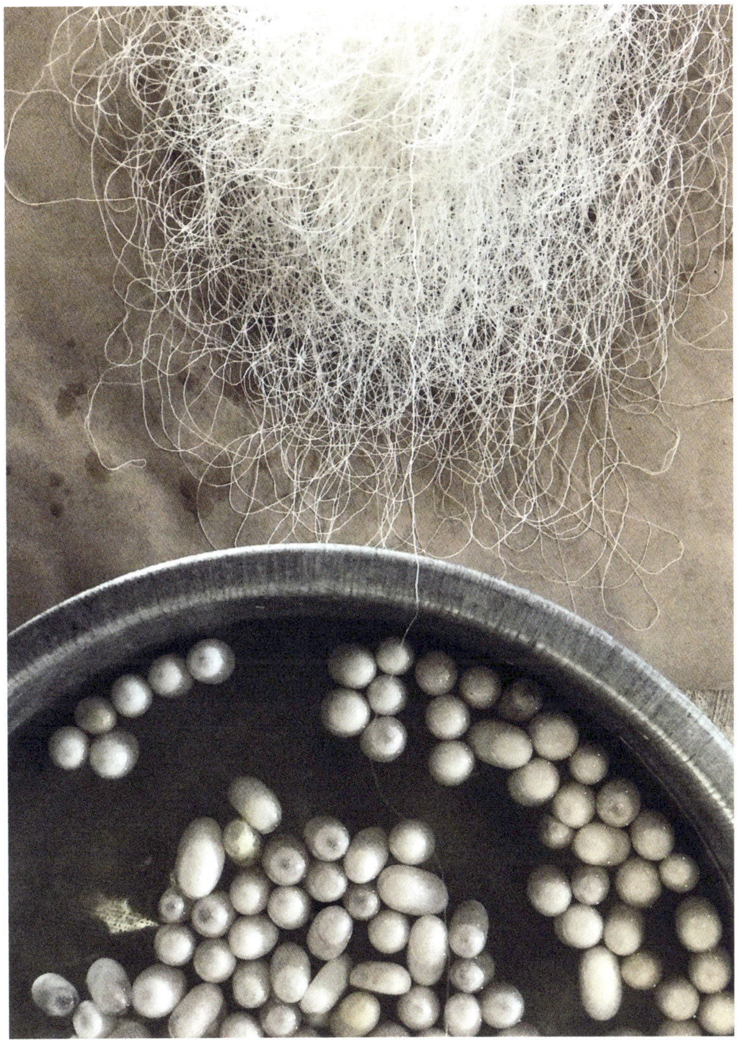
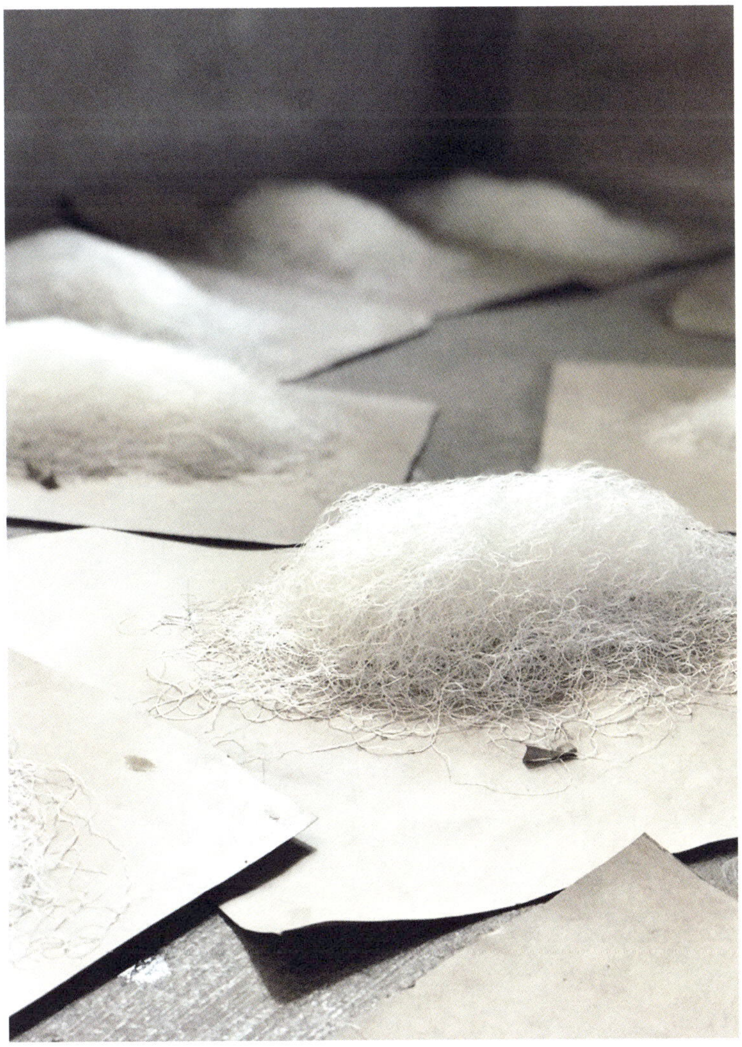
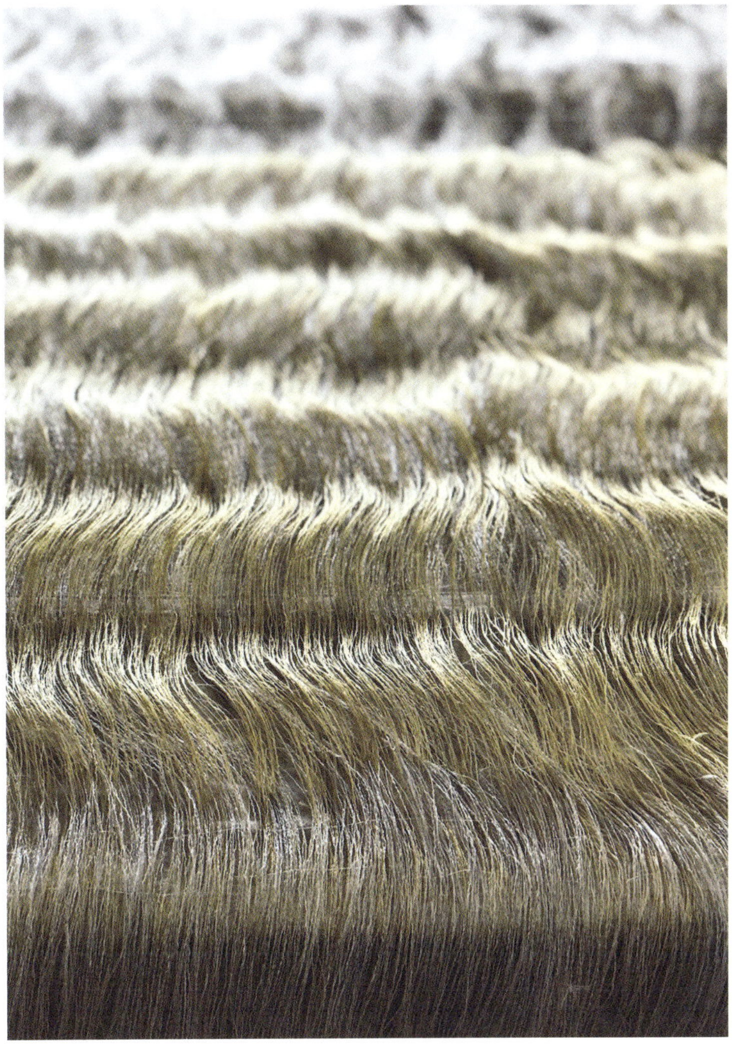

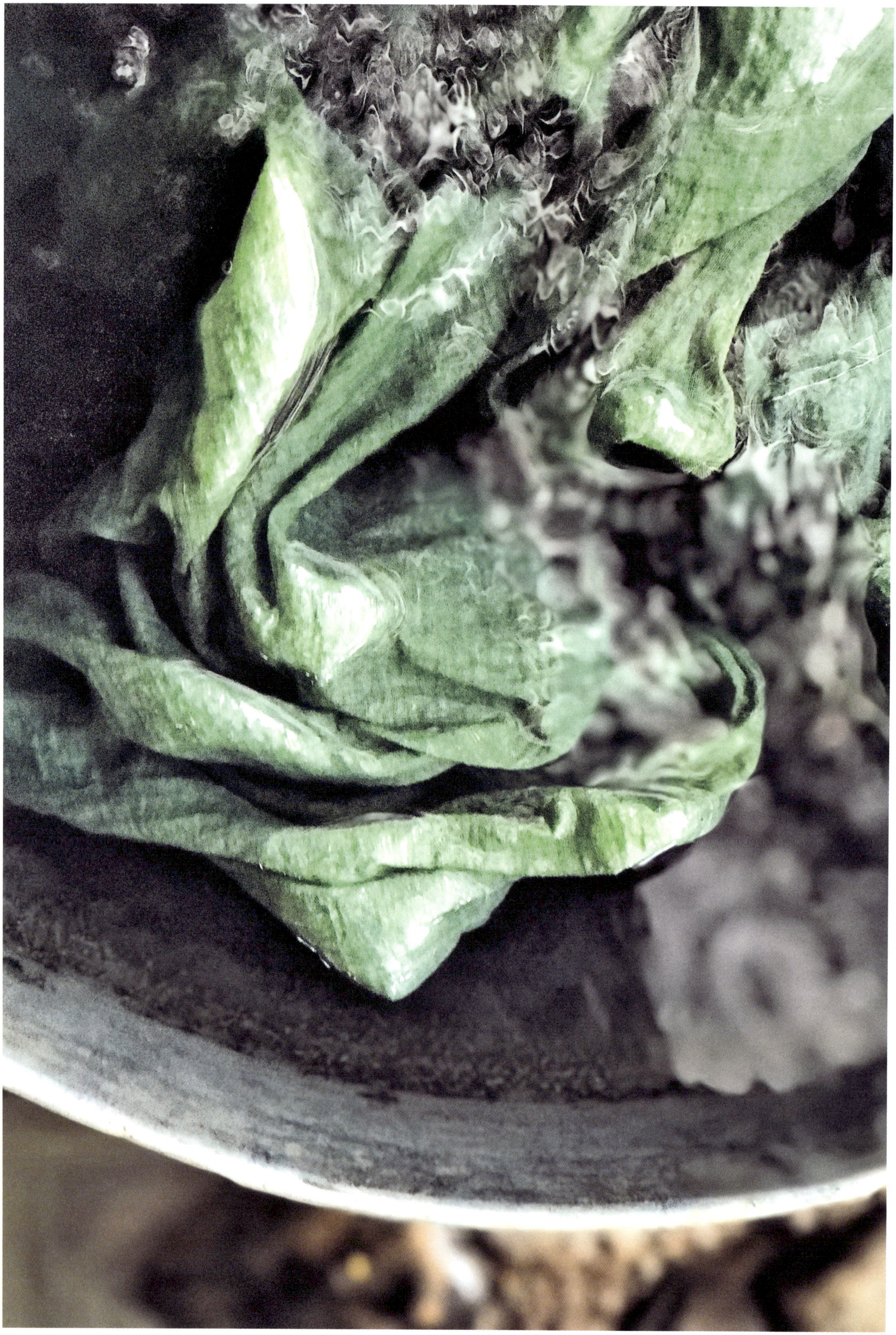

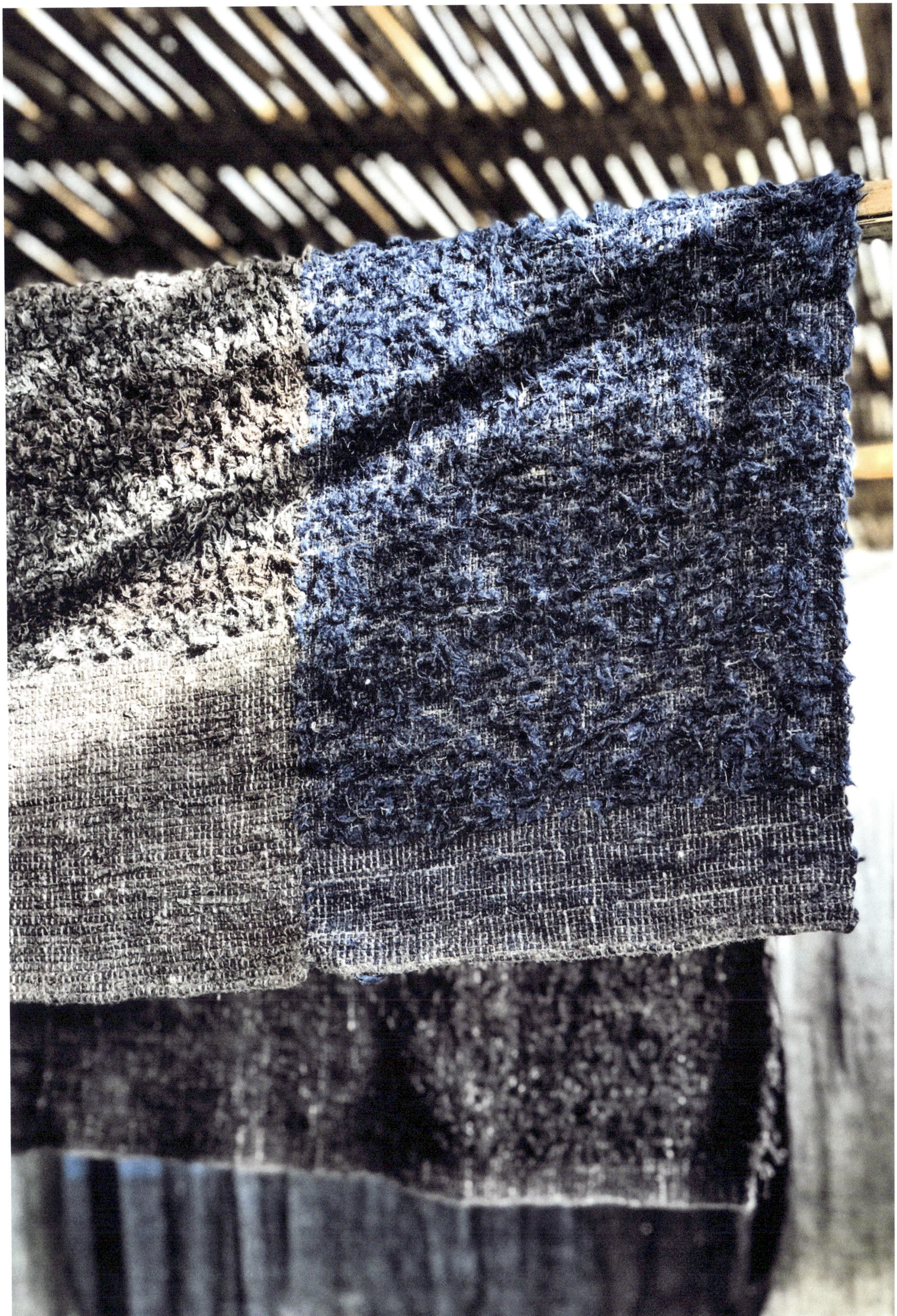

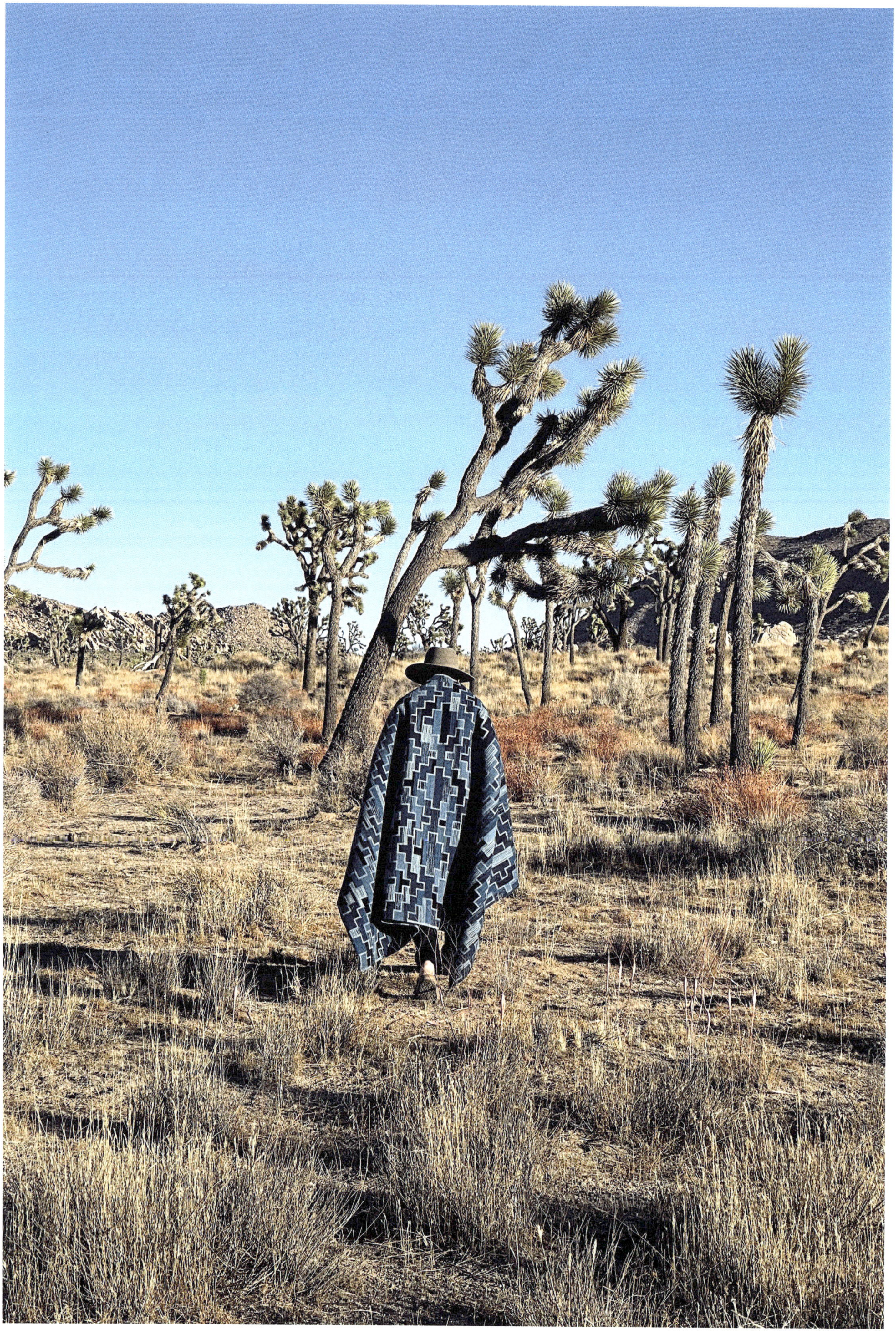

Porfirio Gutiérrez

Weaver

Ventura, California, United States, and Teotitlán del Valle, Mexico

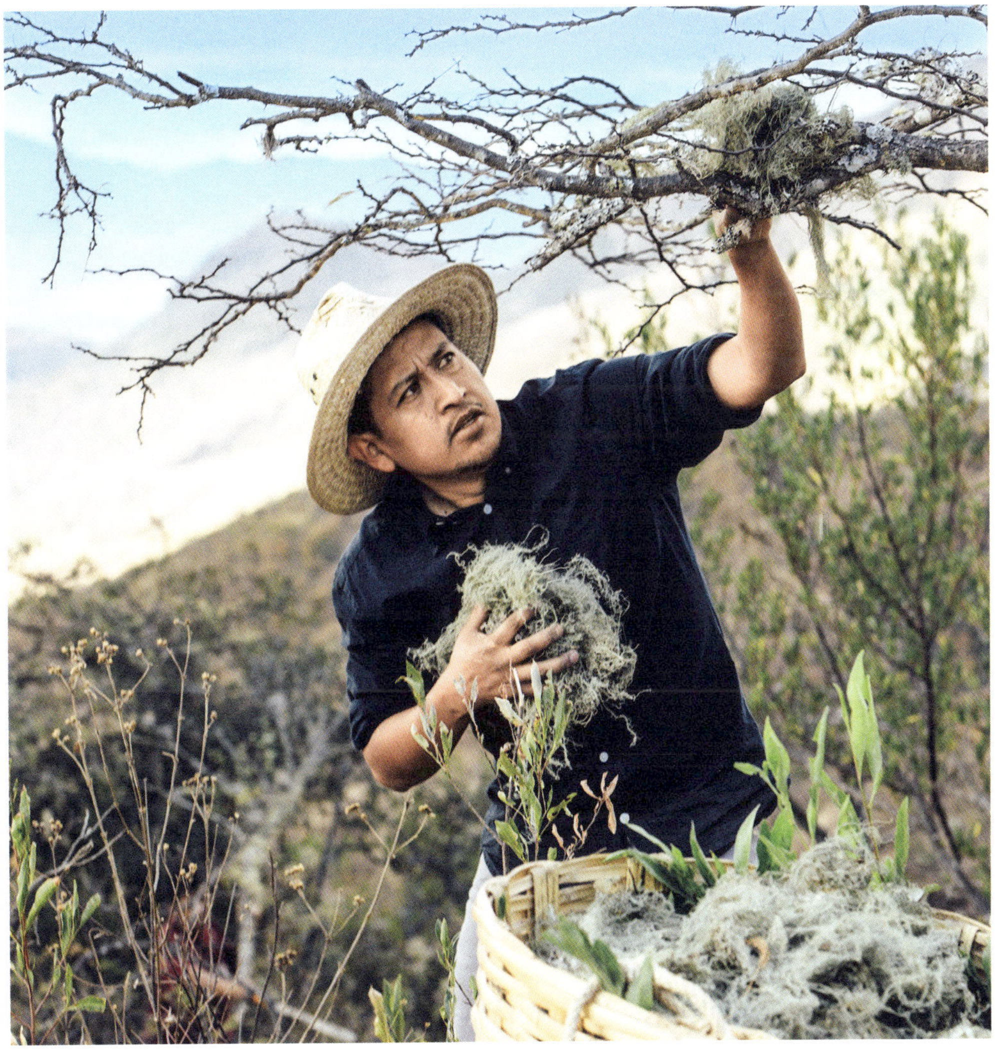

My name is Porfirio Gutiérrez, and I am a textile artist specializing in traditional weaving. I split my time between California and Teotitlán del Valle, in the state of Oaxaca, Mexico. I am descended from a long line of weavers who belong to the Zapotec people: a thousand-year-old civilization whose culture is based on spirituality, with an affinity for divinities associated with fertility and agriculture.

Our workshop, located in the family home, employs around thirty people, mainly women from our community. I work with my sister, Juana, a specialist in natural dyes; her husband, a weaver; my nephew, Javier; and my parents, who are over seventy. My parents married very young, and one of the first things they did was to acquire a loom, a spinning wheel, and materials (sheep's wool, palm leaves, silk, and agave fiber) to set up a workshop that would allow them to feed their family. They managed to raise eleven children, supported by their humble craft.

When I was twelve, my mother taught us how to spin and dye, and my father taught us how to weave. I remember when I was a child, they would wake me up at dawn, and I would follow my father into the mountains, looking for plants to extract color from. What he taught me—over and above the coloring qualities of each plant, the places where they grow, and their seasonal nature—was respect for all living things, the attention we need to pay to the material, and our sense of belonging to this earth. My parents cultivated in us an awareness of the divine and the spiritual nature of what we do.

The natural colorants we use for dyeing are extracted from local plants, as well as from minerals and insects such as the cochineal: a parasite that feeds on the prickly pear cactus. Juana masters the subject perfectly and has created a much wider variety of tones than the ten shades our family had been using: she is able to produce almost two hundred, with an infinite number of variations. For her, using natural dyes means giving back to the earth what we take from it. Today, only a dozen families in our community work with natural dyes. It takes the knowledge of the dyer to extract the color from the plants, and the vision of the weaver to translate it into a design.

Each textile is a medium for artistic expression and tells a story through symbols as old as our civilization. These symbolic representations are the same as those found on Zapotec archaeological sites, the walls of our church, and the nearby ruins of Monte Albán and Mitla. They also reveal the blending of Native American and European traditions; the fusion of these two cultures has led to new modes of expression in textile art.

Weaving is my language. I learned to weave at the same time as I learned to speak. It is a way of life; it's in my DNA. I have realized that our work does not stop at craftsmanship; it goes far beyond that. We are custodians of our traditional culture, and we have to share our knowledge with the new generation. I am convinced that I was born to be an artist and to bring attention to this craft. When I create a fabric, it is not a personal piece—it is the work of an entire people expressing itself. Above all, I am here to write a new chapter in the history of my community with my creations. Through these works, I would like to be the voice of this ancient culture.

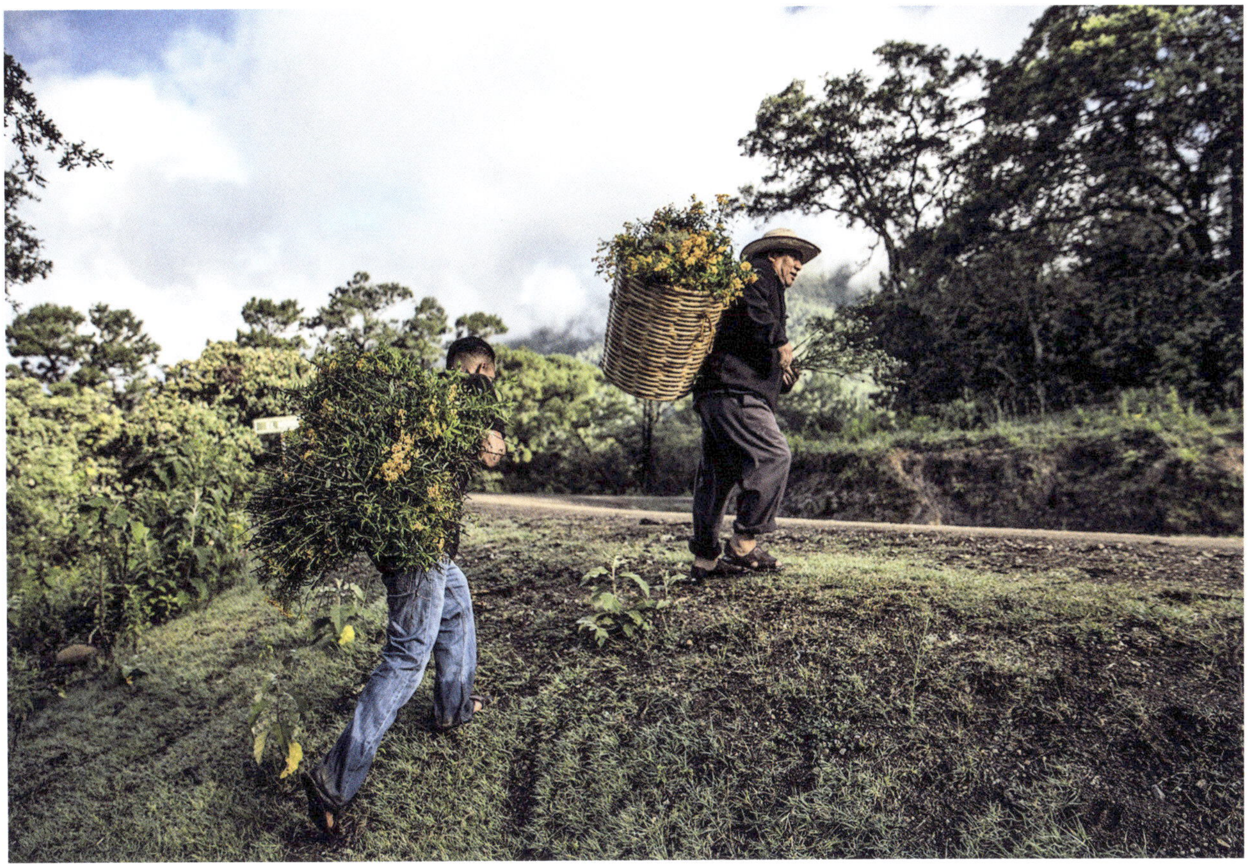

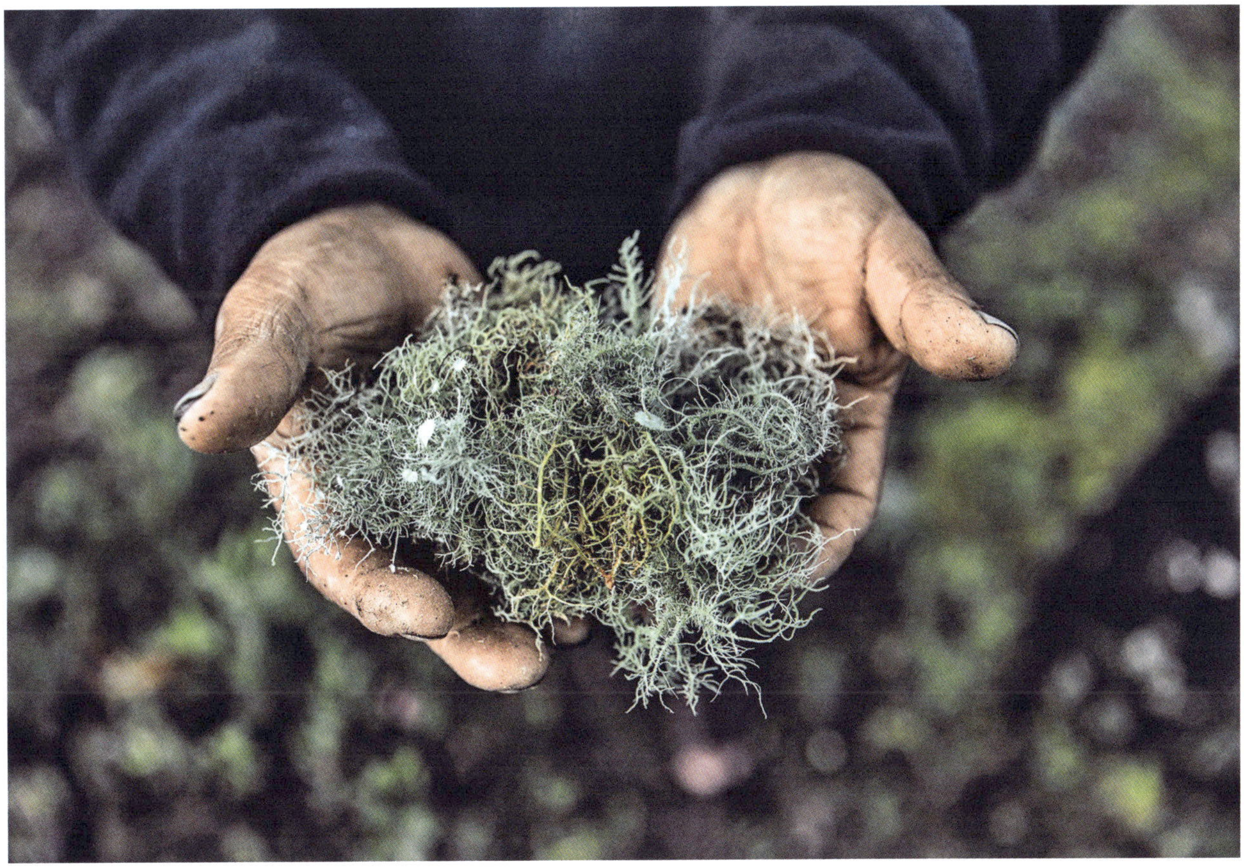

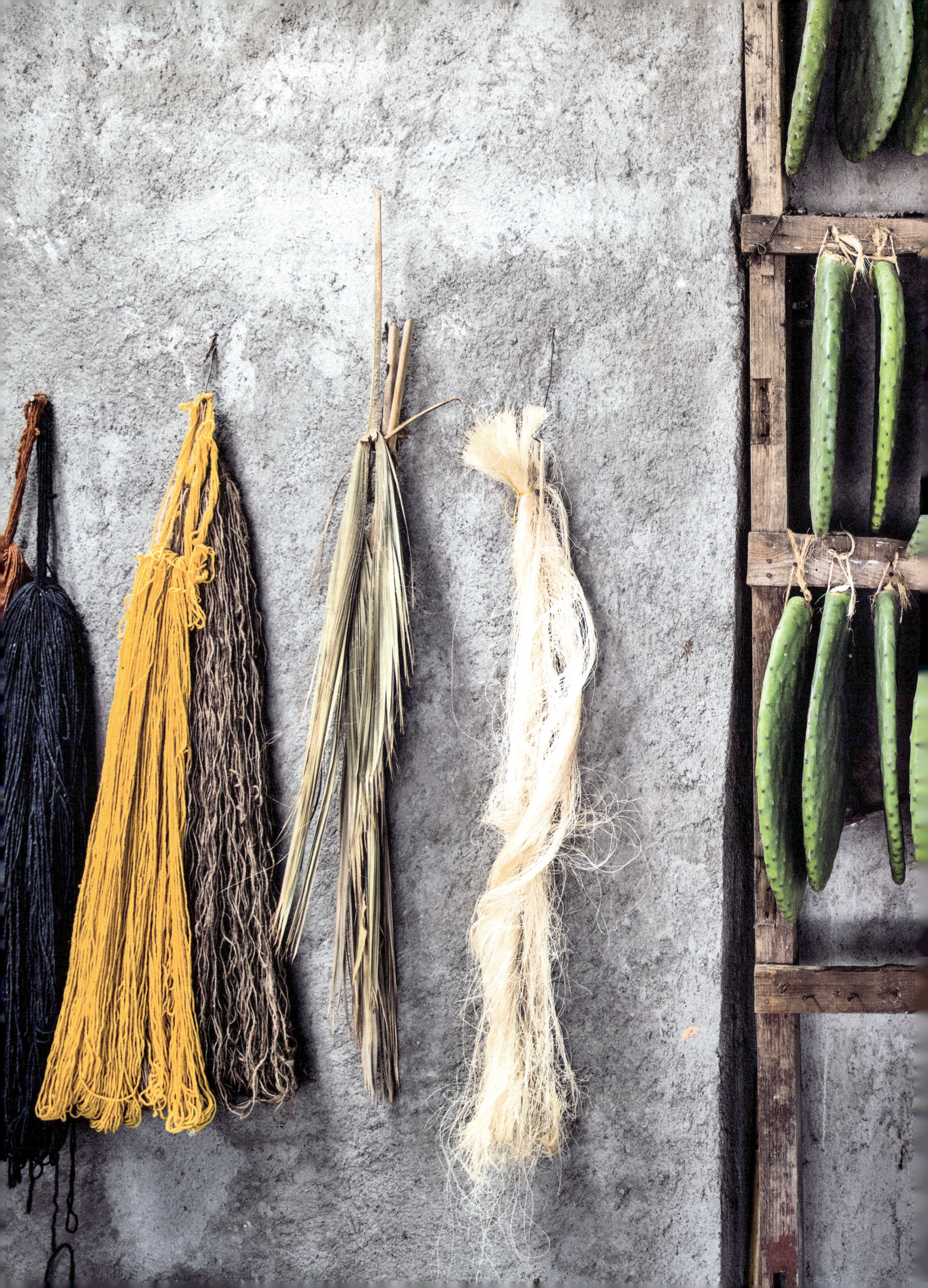

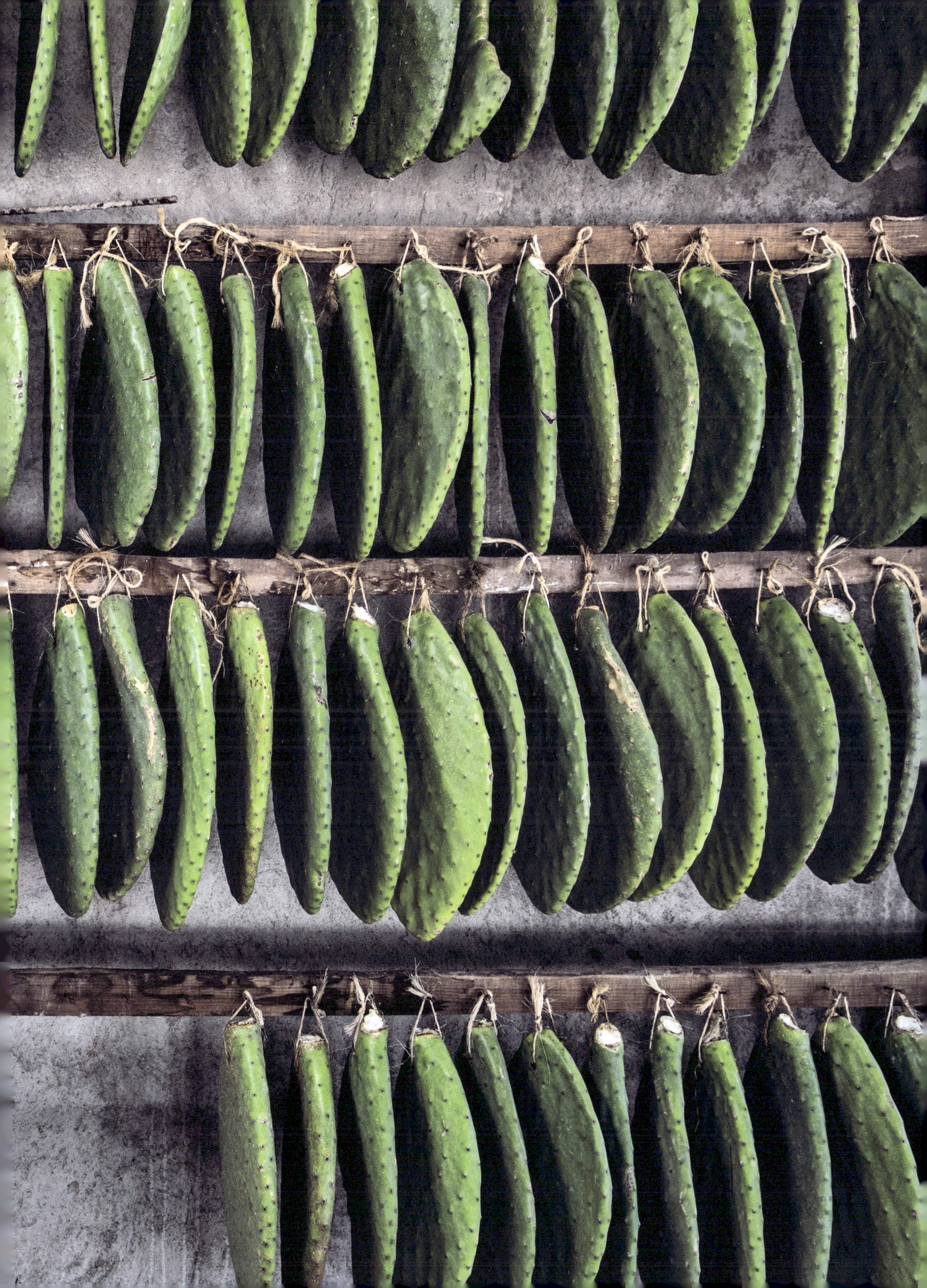

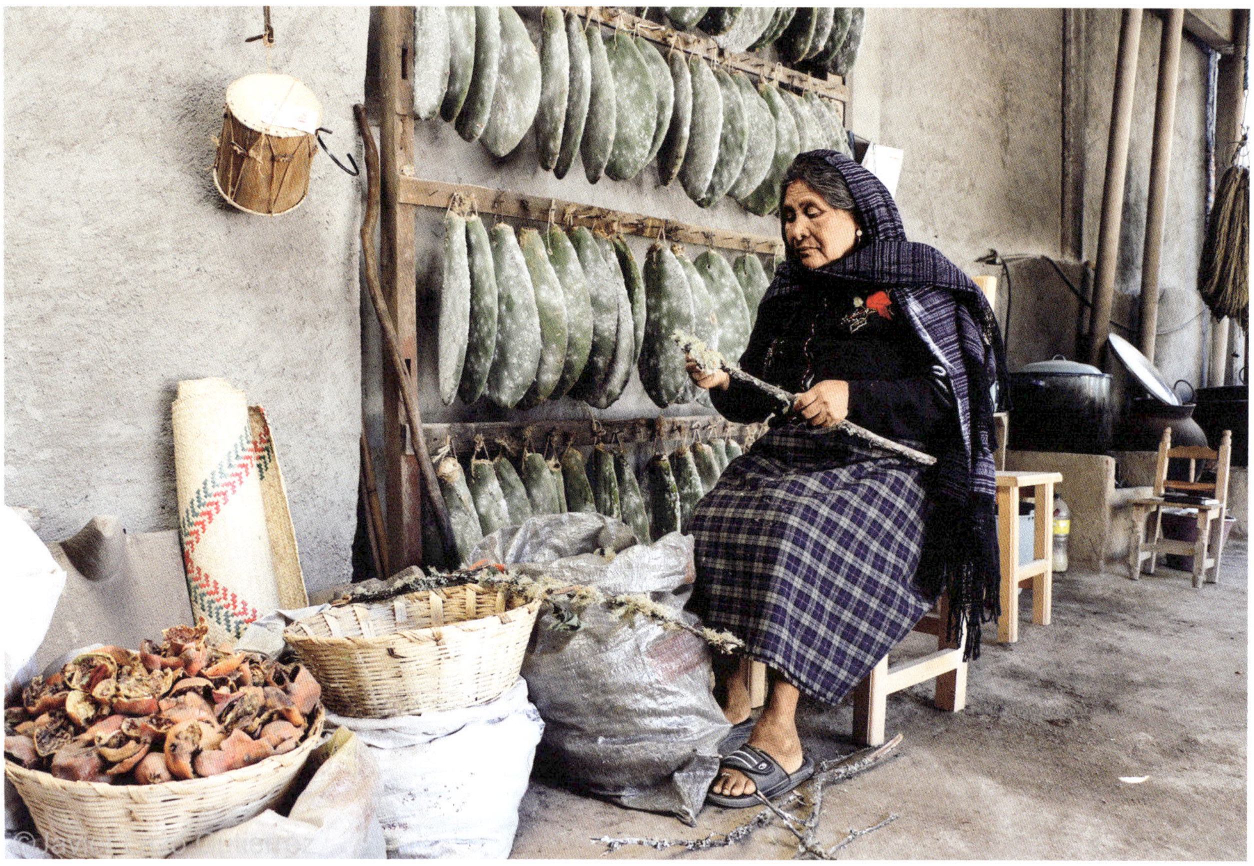

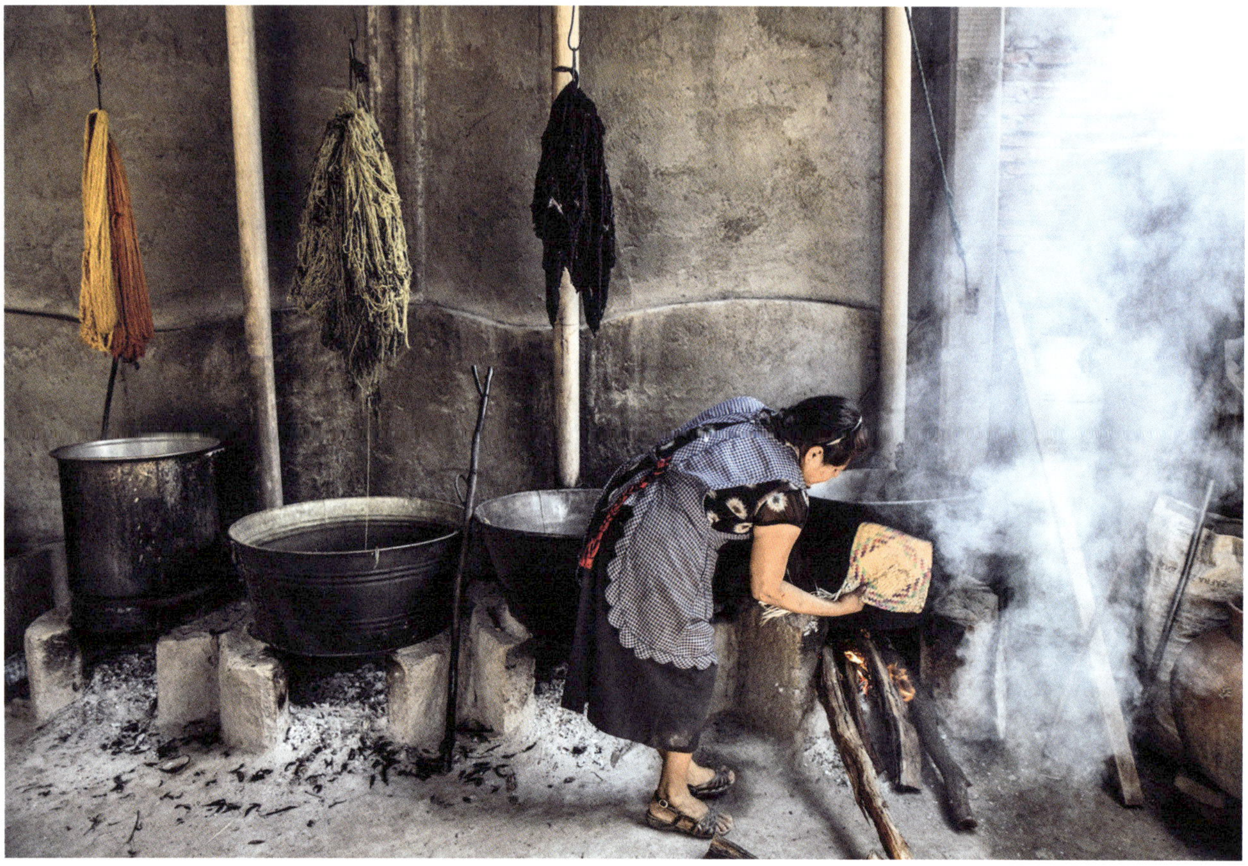

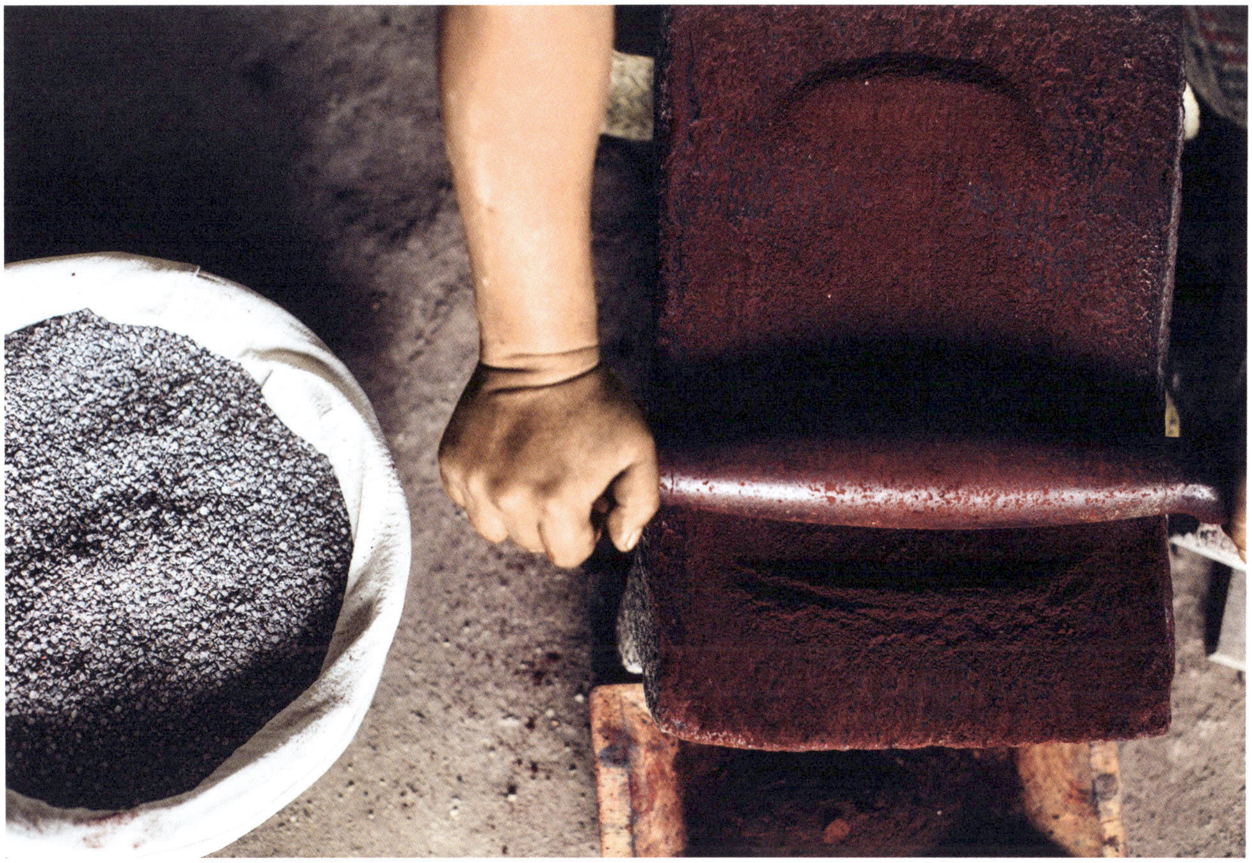

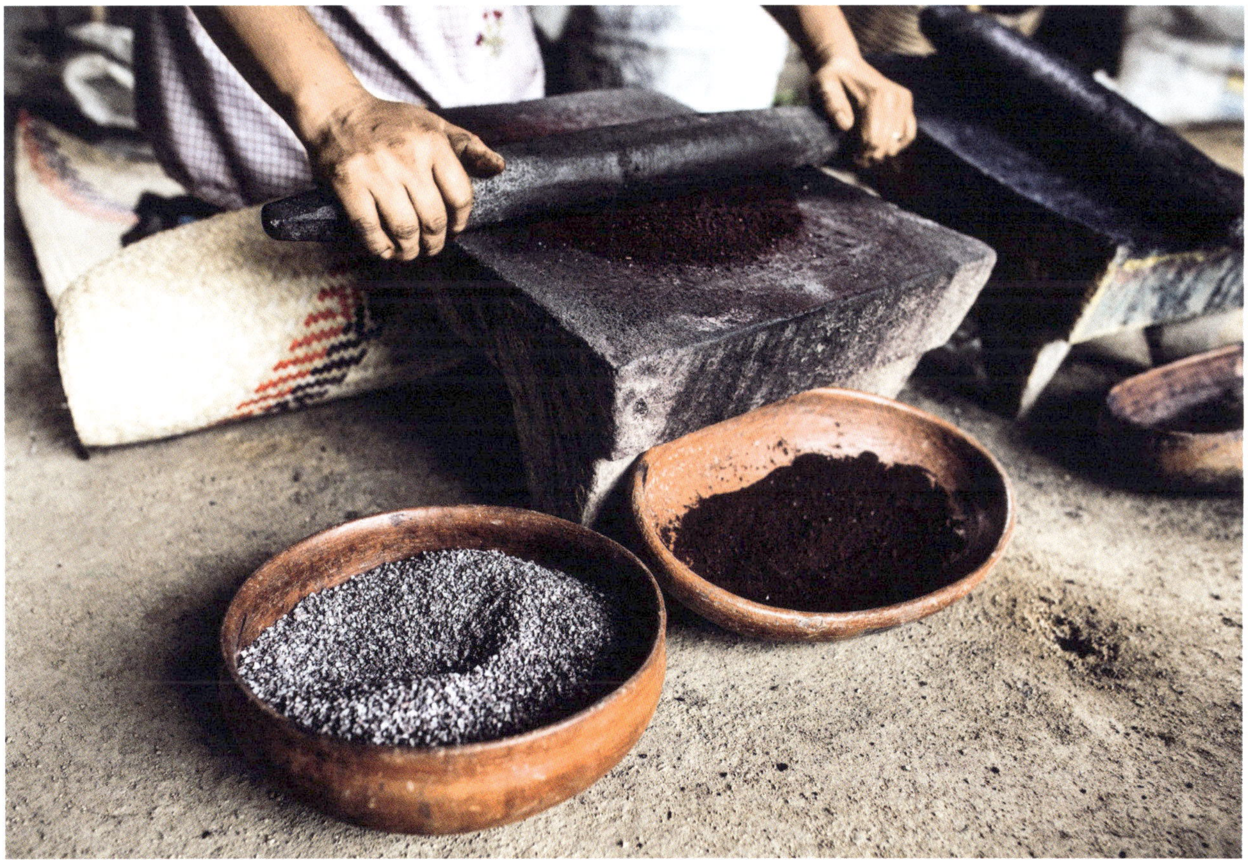

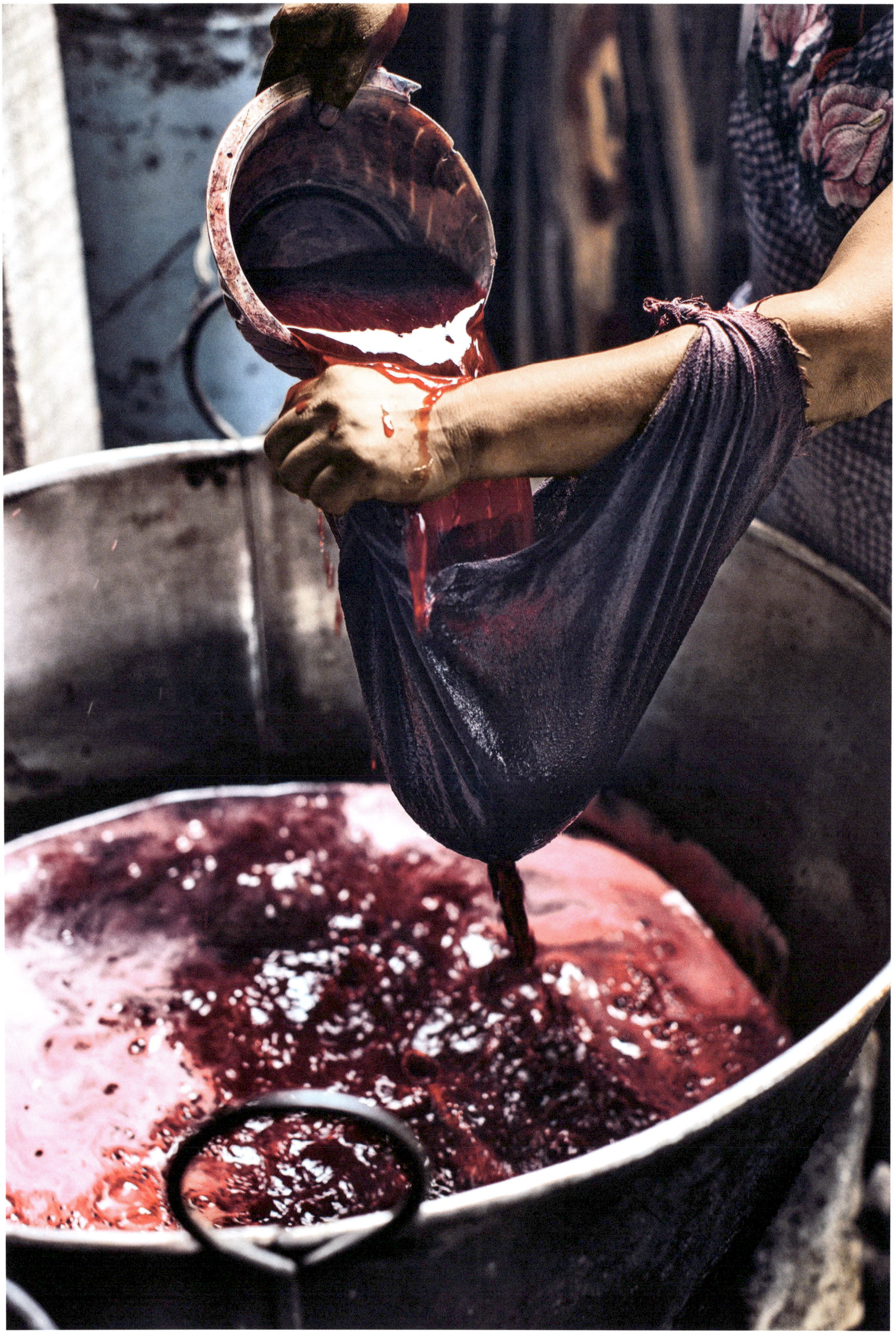

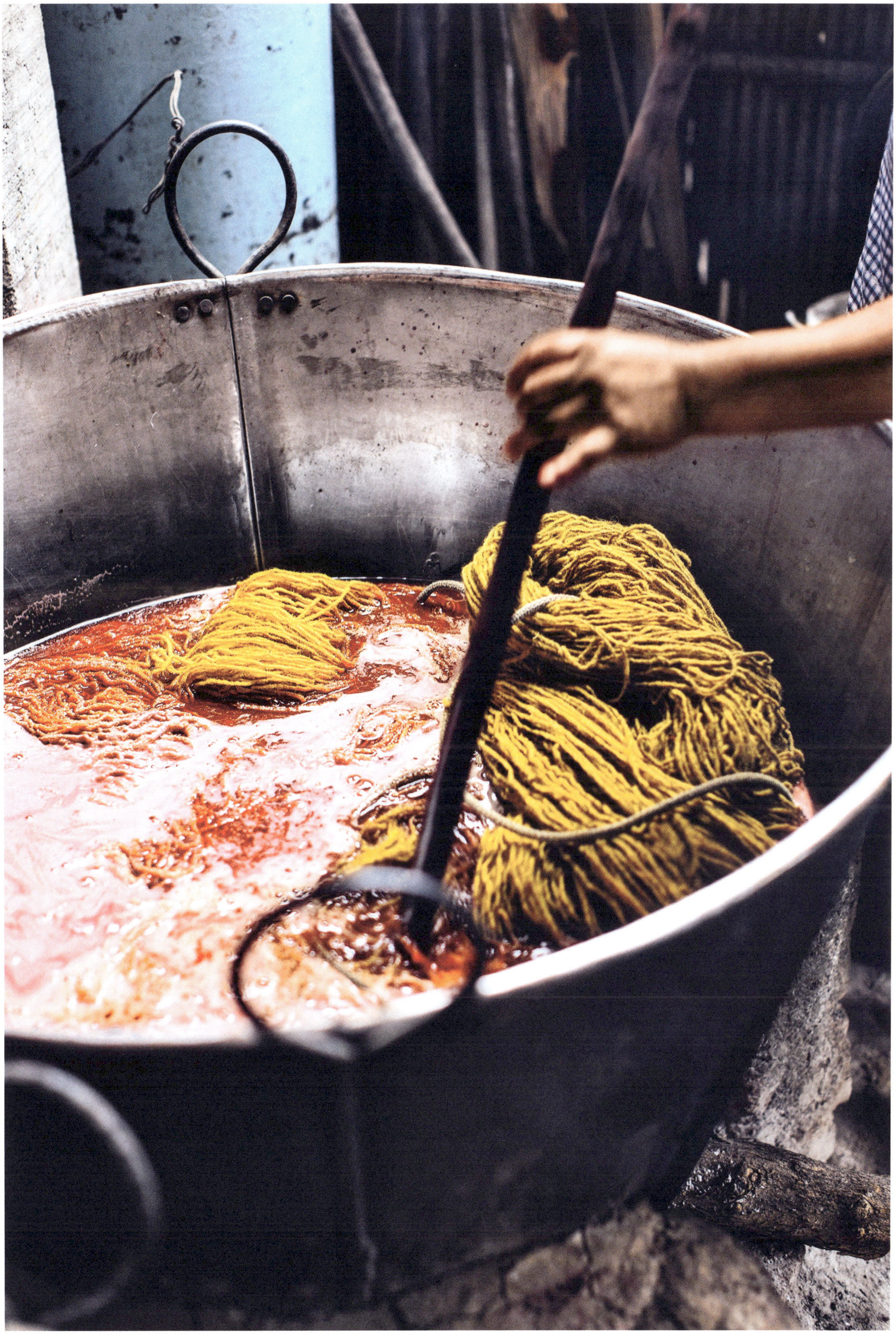

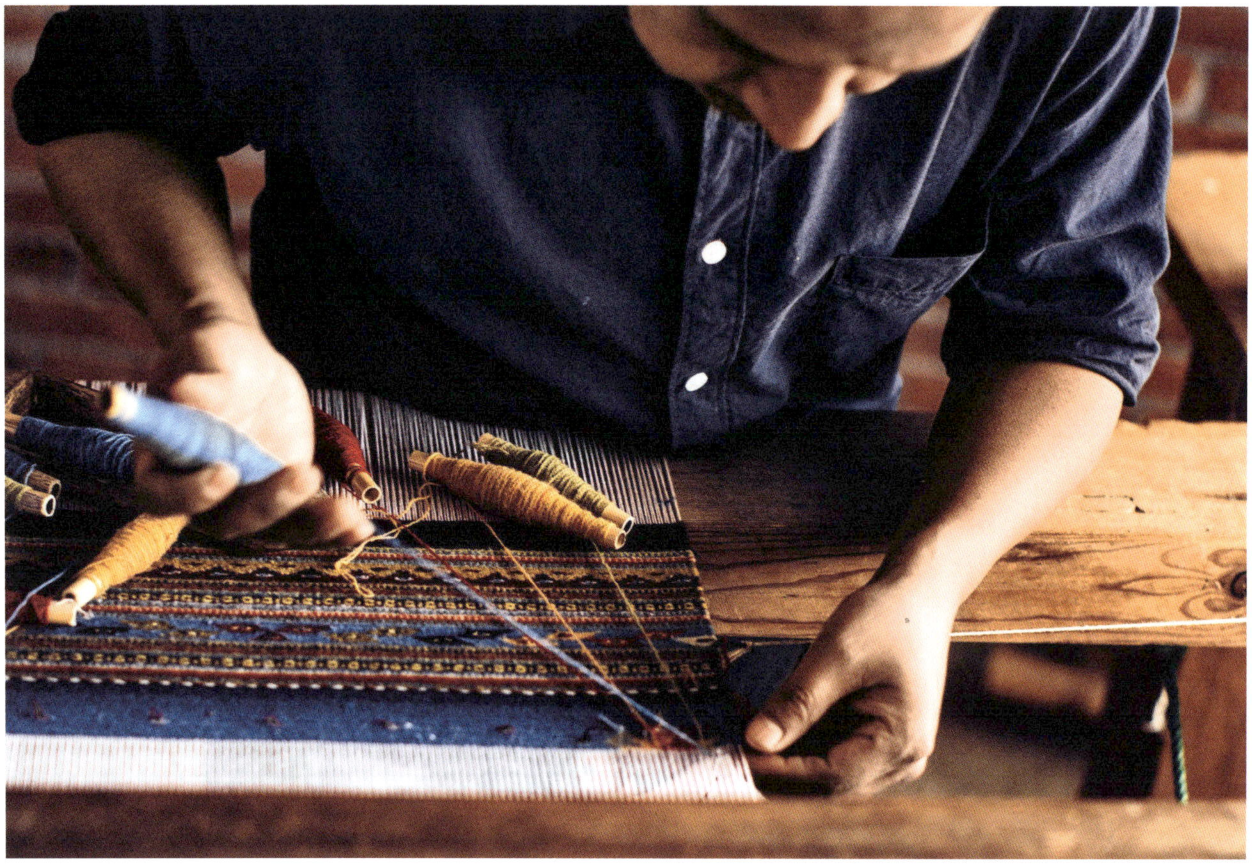

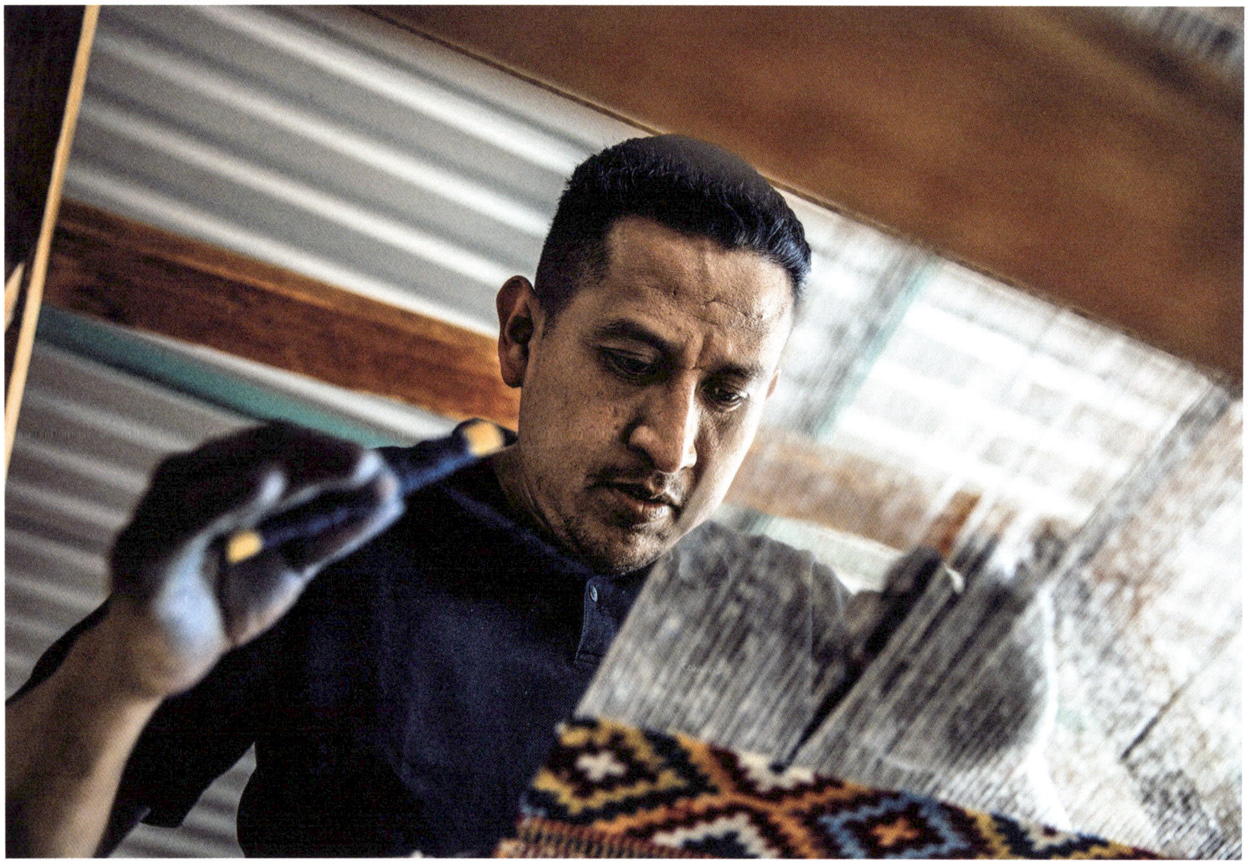

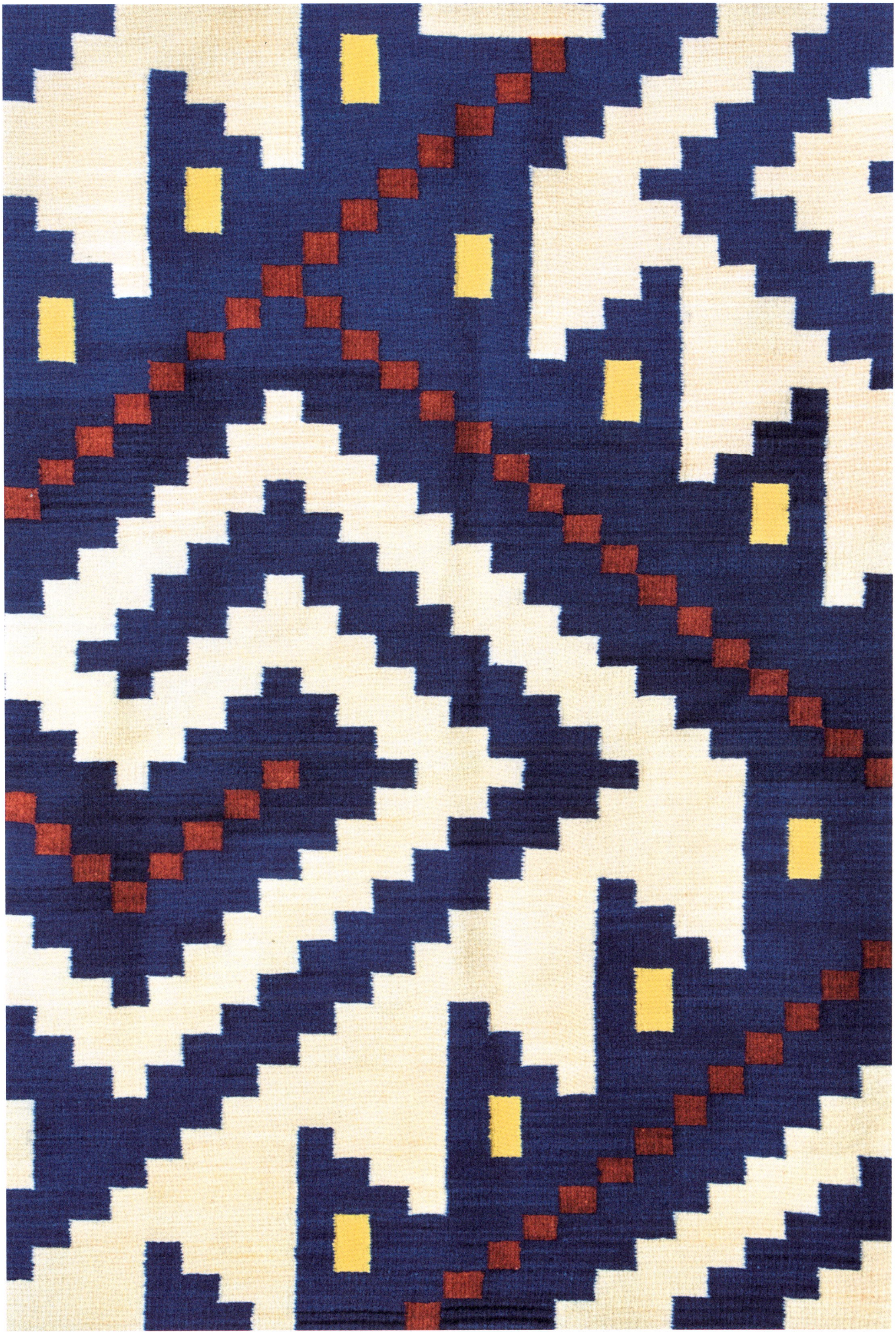

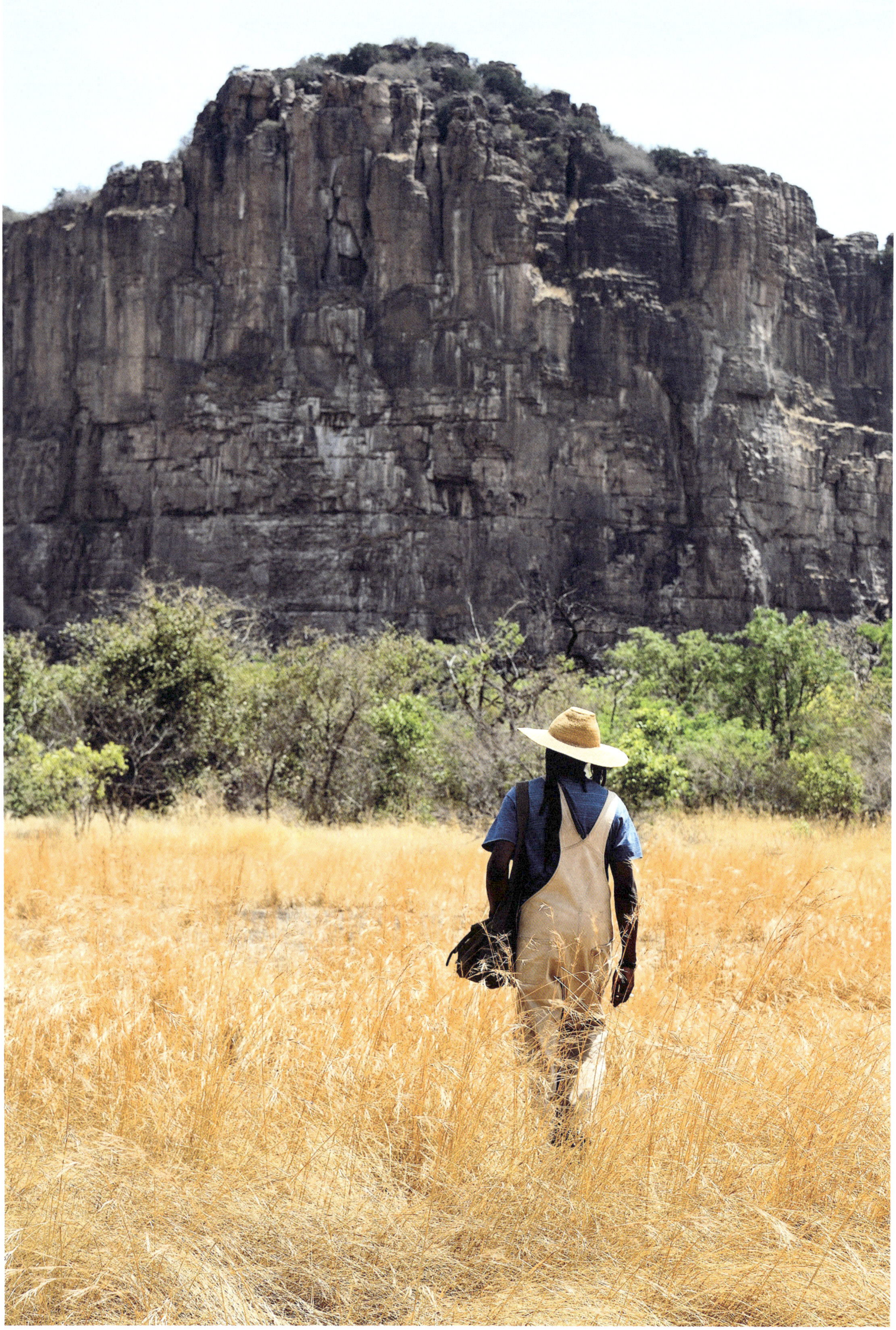

Aboubakar Fofana

Dyer

Bamako, Mali

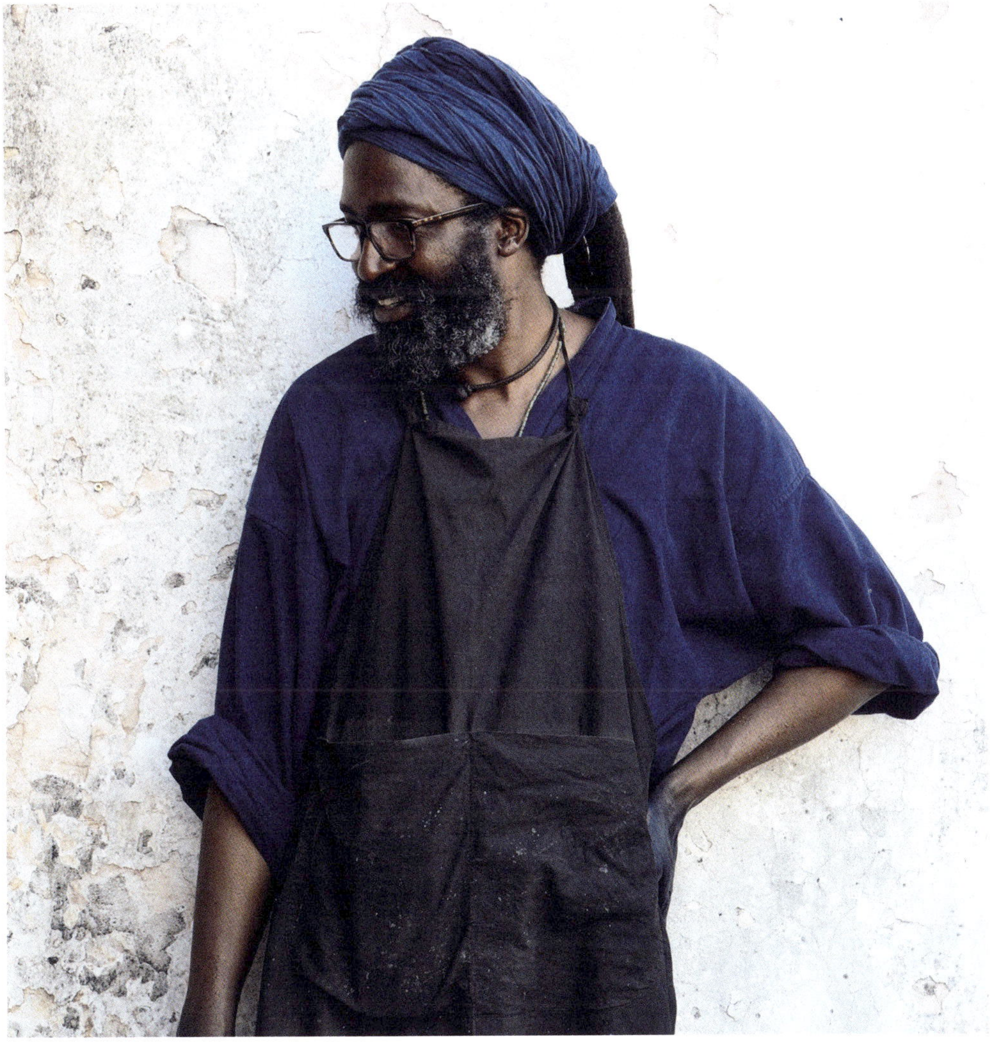

My name is Aboubakar Fofana and I am a textile artist. I see artisans as initiates. We receive a heritage, and it is our duty to pass it on. In our Mandinka culture, transmission is essential. I am a descendant of the Fofana line, and I exist through my ancestors. This heritage is rooted in a cultural identity; it involves taking the impersonal and turning it into something personal. I was born in Africa—in Mali—and came to France at the age of twelve. Today, I divide my life between the two continents.

I have lived with several different family members: with my grandmother, my aunts, and my sisters in the Guinean forests. I am self-taught, and I owe much to my grandmother, who was a healer and herbalist. She had a special relationship with nature. She comforted both body and mind. In those days, all the plants I knew were medicinal. Certain tannin-rich plants were mixed with clay and used to dye clothes. In this way, textiles became therapeutic garments. Indigo, for example, has anti-inflammatory and antiseptic properties.

A garment dyed with indigo carries heavy symbolic weight; it is worn at various ceremonies, to protect a child, an adult, or a deceased person during their passage to the other world. I remember my first revelation: I was seven years old. I discovered that the leaf of the wild indigo tree I held in my hand was oxidizing, revealing an intense blue liquid. It was fascinating. This visual shock cultivated my sensitivity to color, and I developed a deep interest in this shrub. "Blue," my grandmother told me, "is what the plant shows. To get there, it has to give its spirit and soul. What you cannot see is just as important as what you can."

No one in my family was a dyer. In Mali, the use of natural dyes was being lost; synthetic dyes were taking over and expertise was dying out. My first challenge was to reappropriate this art in order to pass it on.

Becoming a dyer is a long process. It took me fifteen years to understand what I was doing, because I could not find a master to teach me this craft. There was a lot of trial and error. I traveled extensively in West Africa, listening to the stories of the elders. Most of them told me, "We mainly use synthetic dyes. In one day, we can dye fifty loincloths, whereas our mothers only dyed around ten fabrics a week." Then I traveled to Europe, Japan, and the United States to collect first-hand accounts and recipes.

Dyeing is closely linked to the material being dyed. I use cellulose fibers, traditional cotton strips, which reveal their true nature once dyed. To broaden my range, I also use old fabrics, lengths of linen and hemp from Europe. Mali is the leading producer of cotton on the African continent, but only 5 percent is processed locally. Even if the amount of yarn processed by the communities of women who work with me is but a drop in the ocean, it is important to keep this added value within my country.

Today, I run a five-person workshop in Bamako. I trained some of the craftspeople more than twenty years ago. Around 2013, I also set up a sixty-one-acre (25-ha) farm in Tabou, in the municipality of Siby. At first, the soil was unproductive, and everyone told me that nothing would grow. It took me years to make this land what it is today. To provide the raw material for the Bamako workshop, we planted two species of indigo trees: *Philenoptera cyanescens*, the West African indigo vine, and *Indigofera arrecta* (known variously as Bengal, Java, or Natal indigo). We grow tomatoes, eggplants, onions, and chilies as well, to supply the two nearby villages. My work is also a commitment to this community. This farm is a lifetime's work, and I approach it as an artistic creation that I initiated but will not finish. A hundred men and women are involved, and a new generation will carry it on.

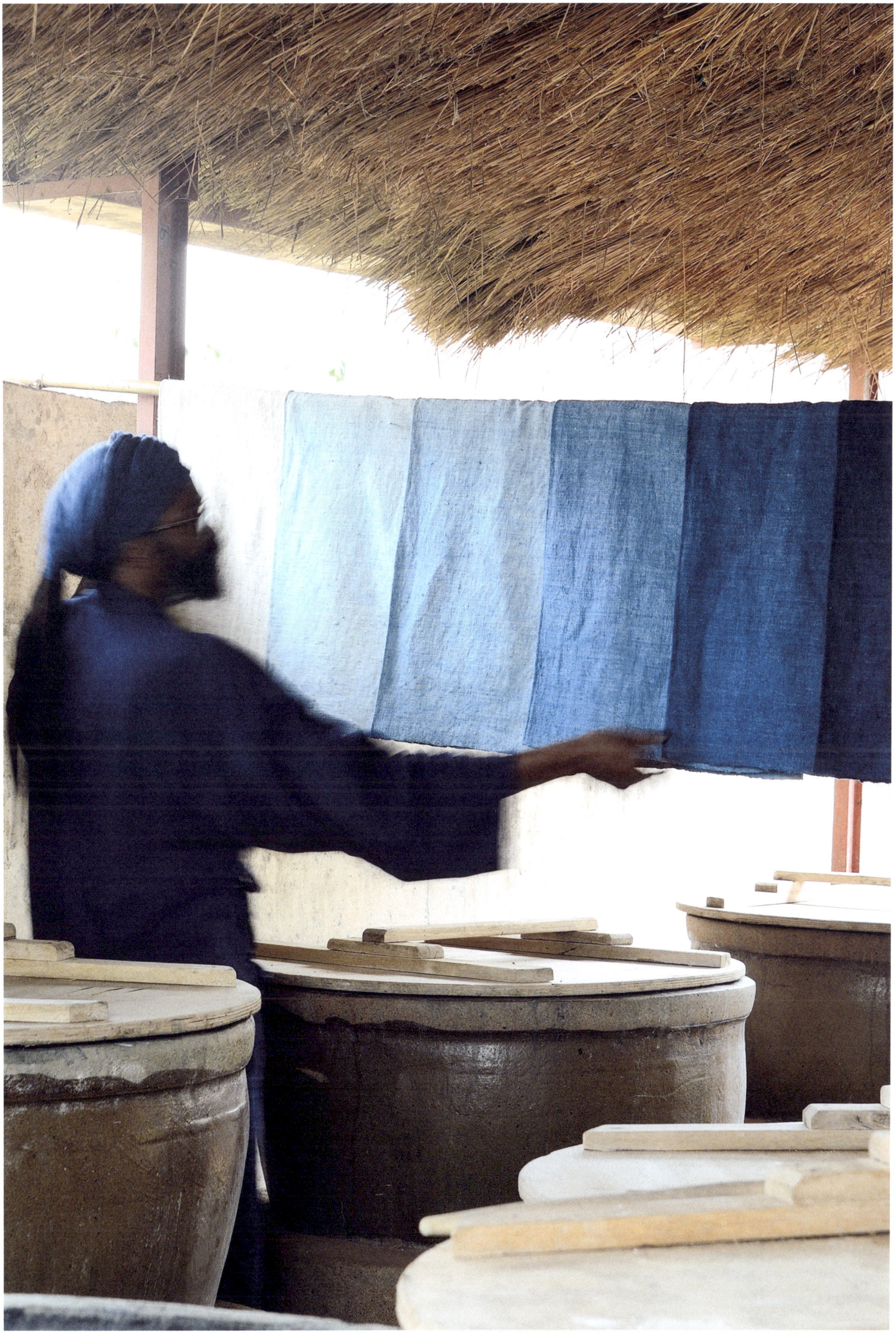

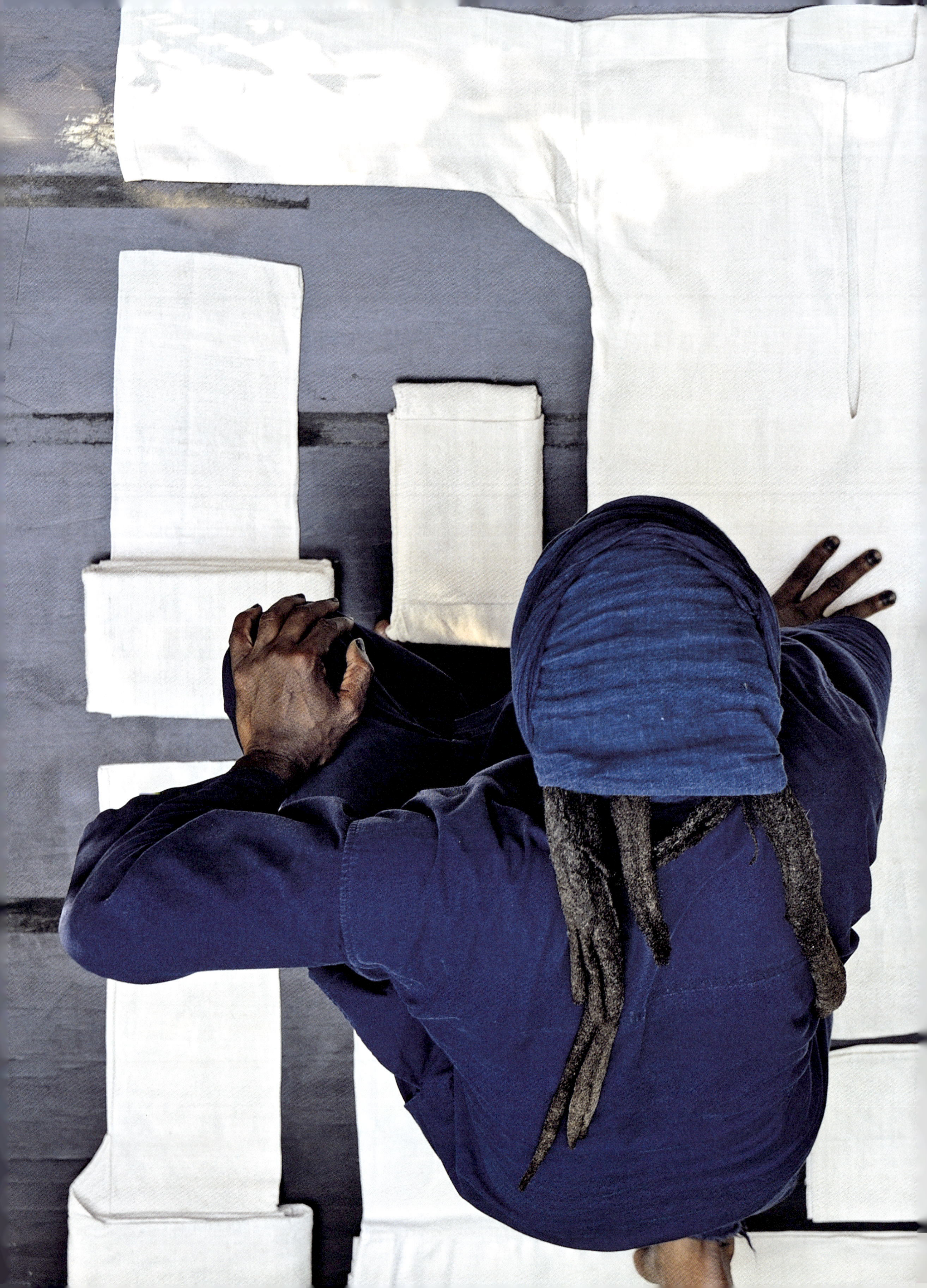

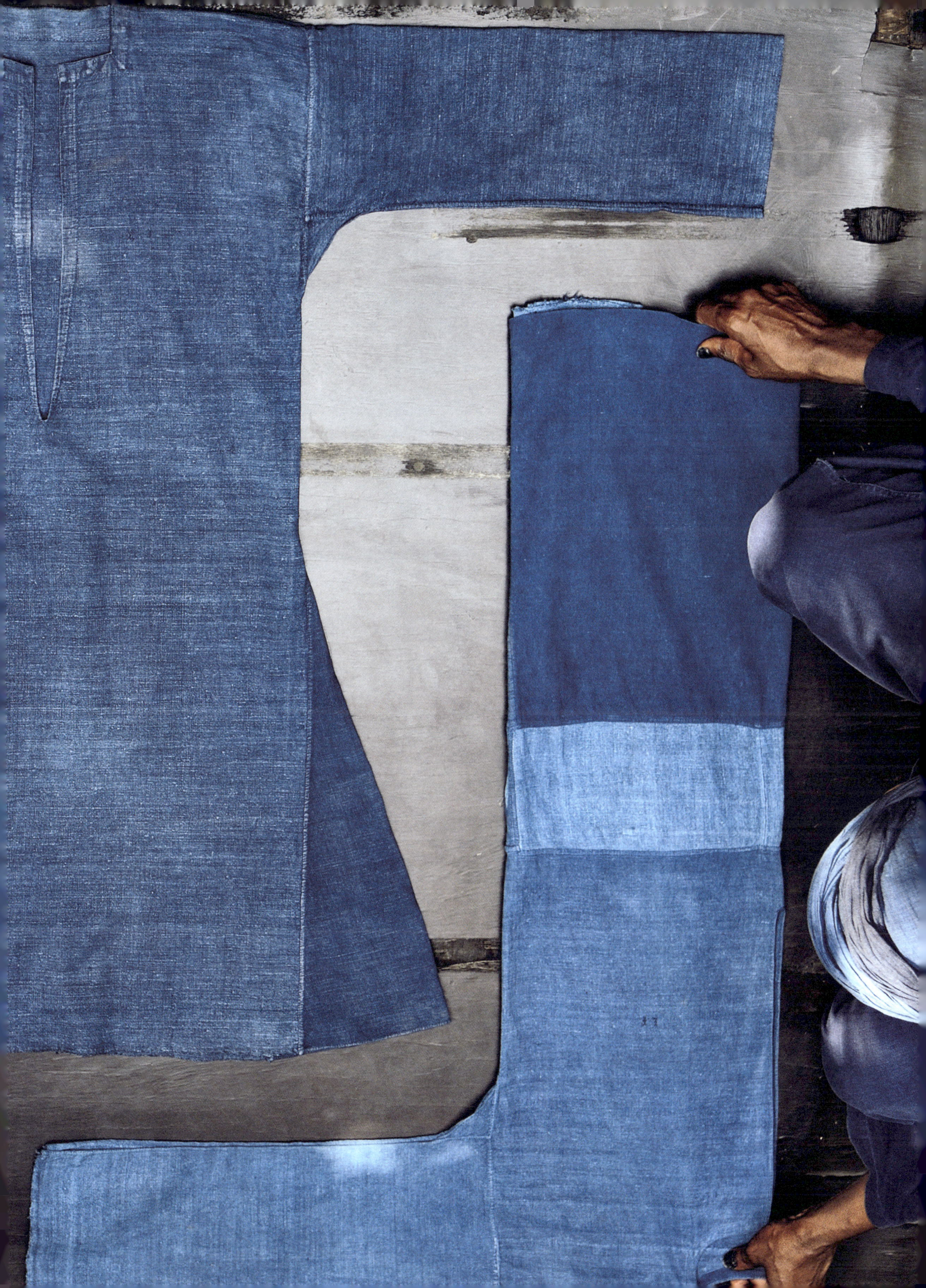

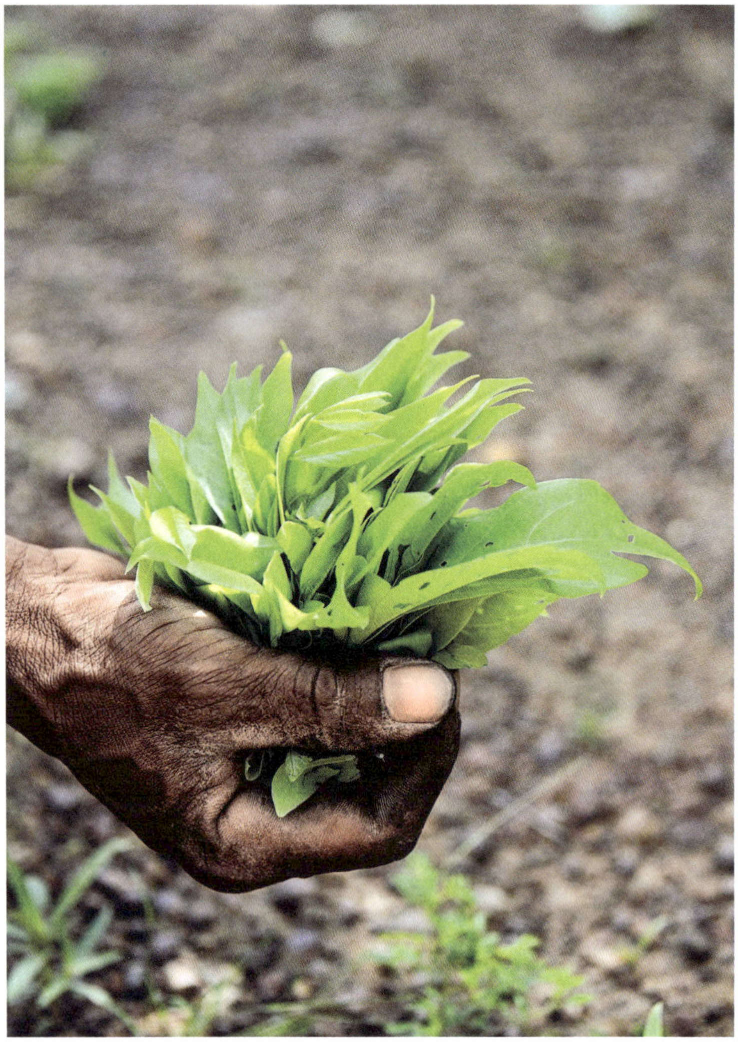
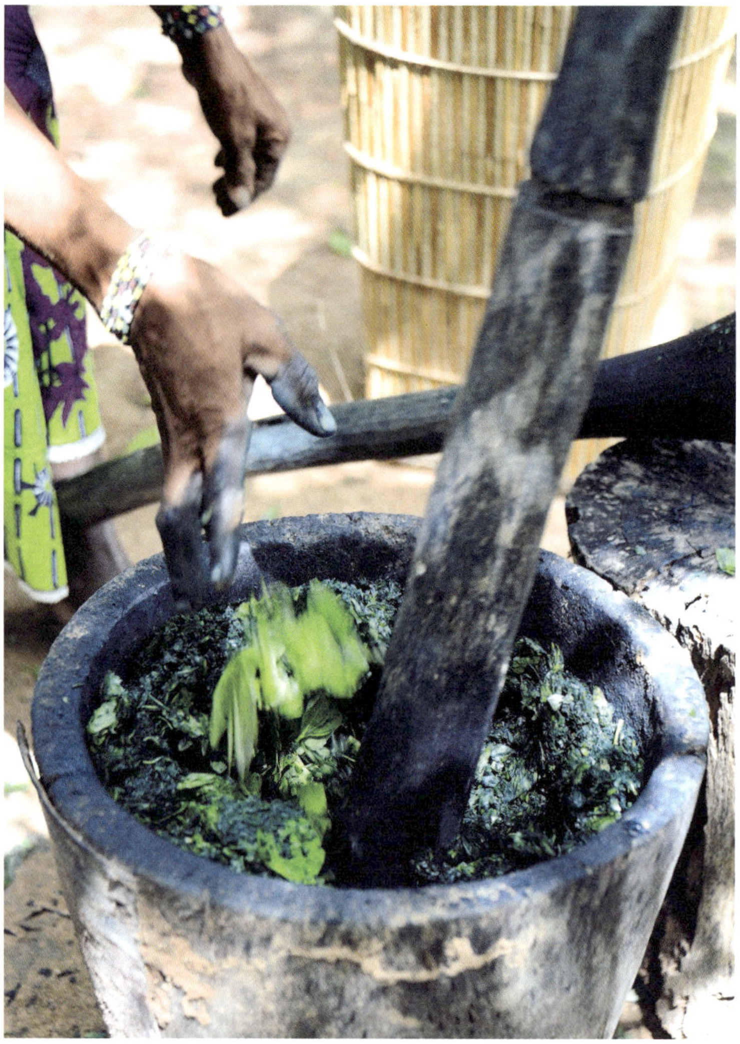
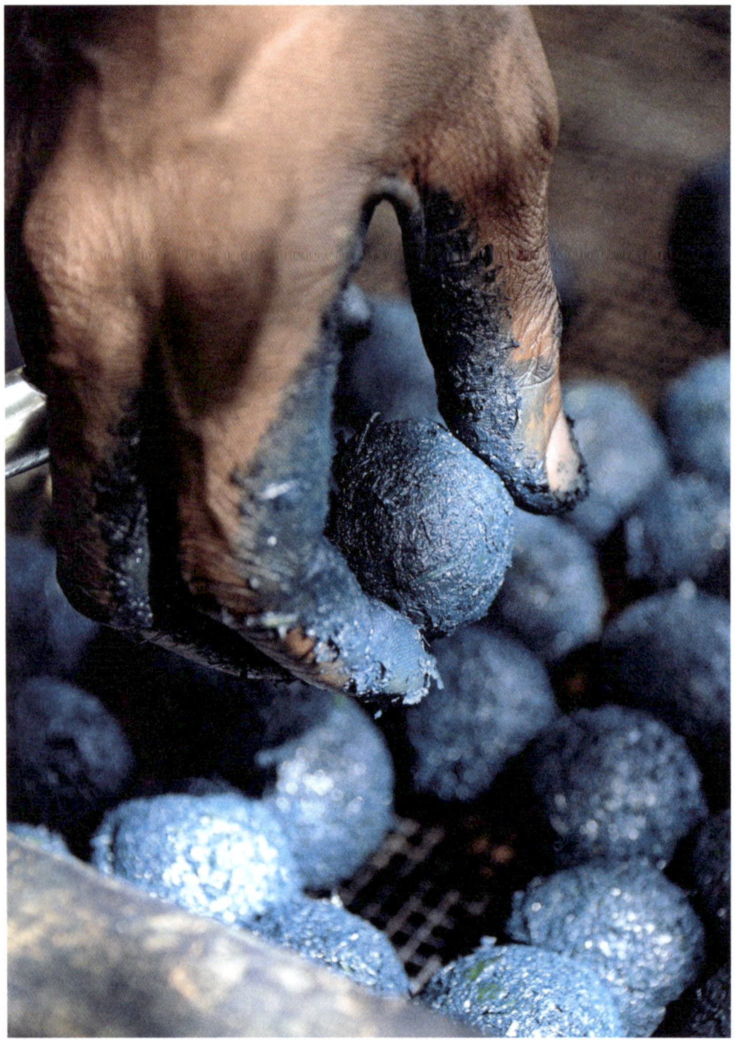
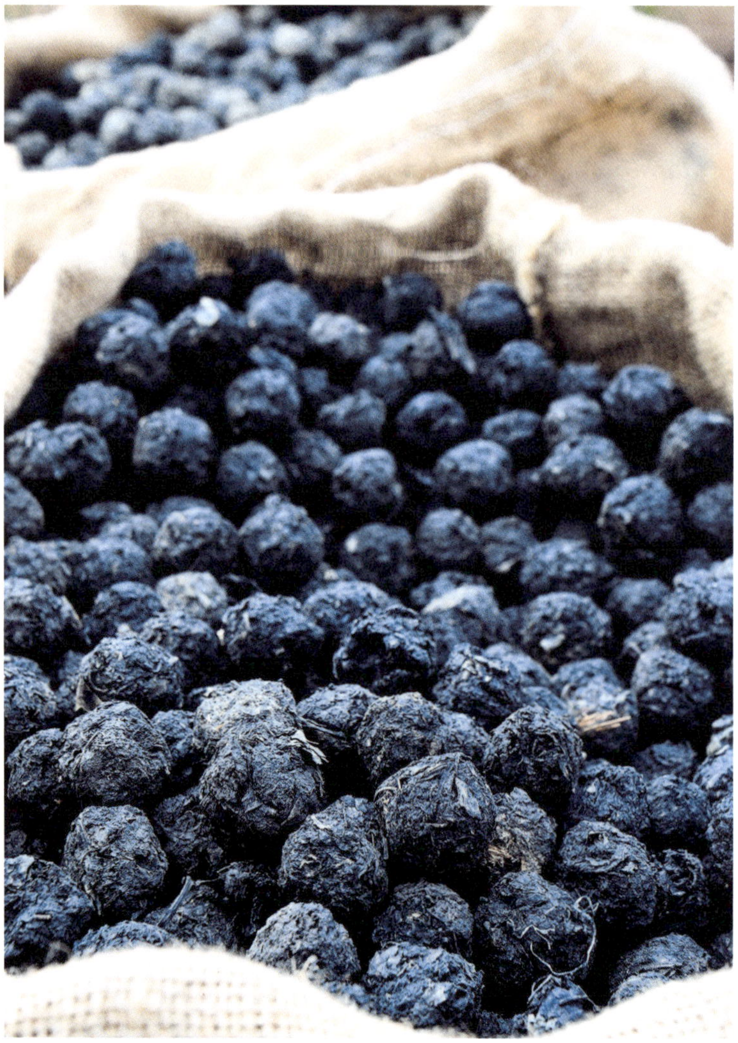

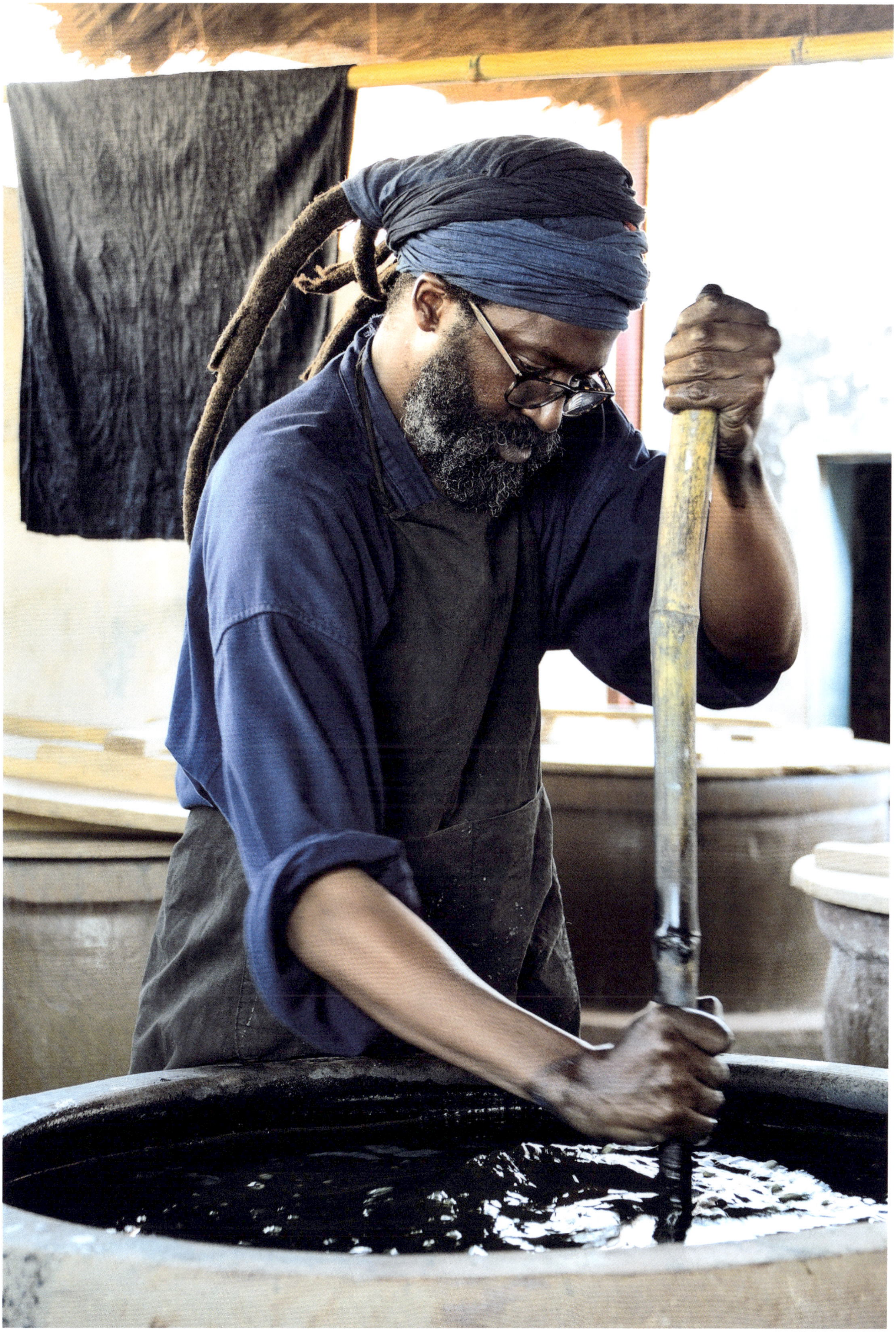

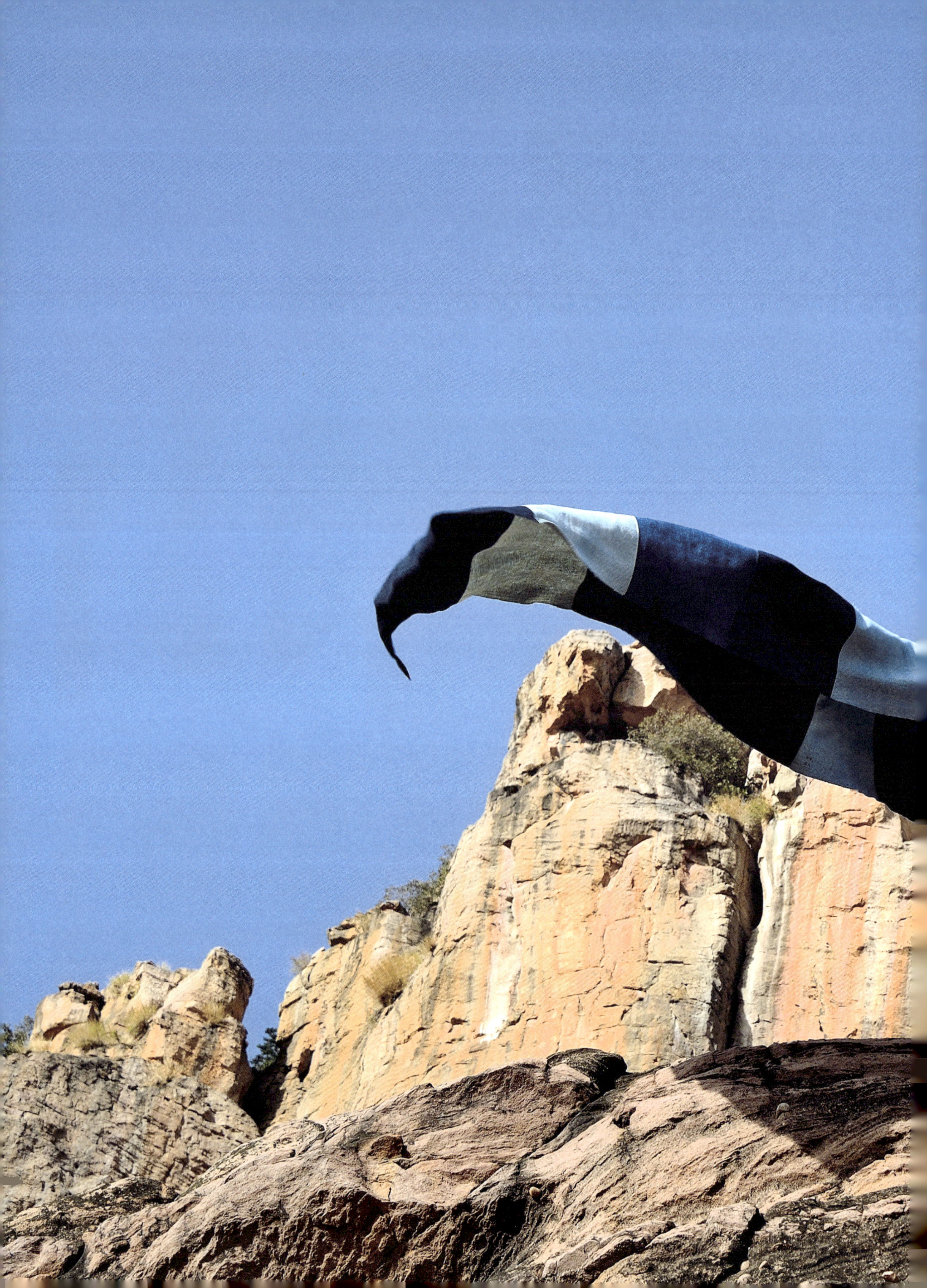

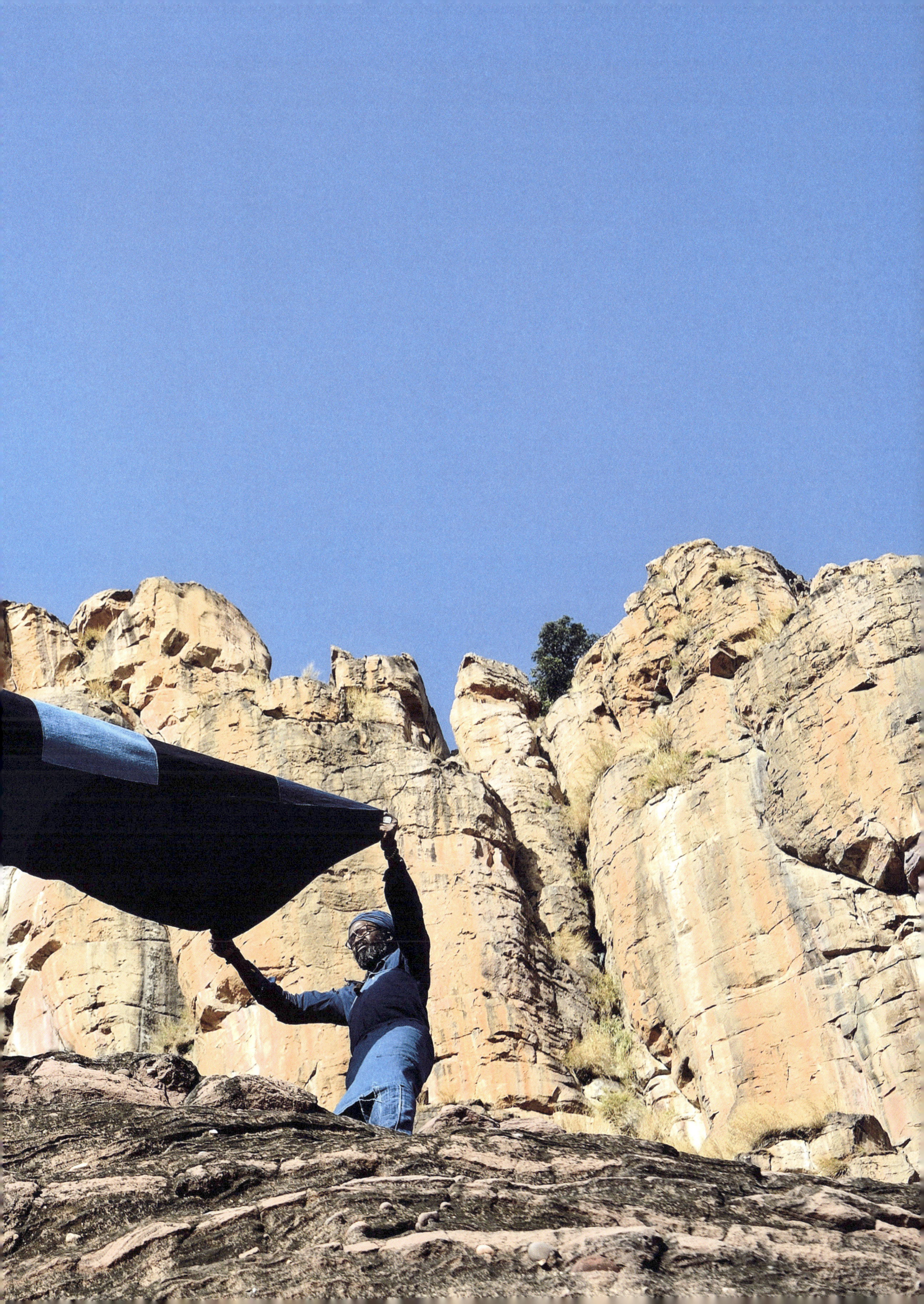

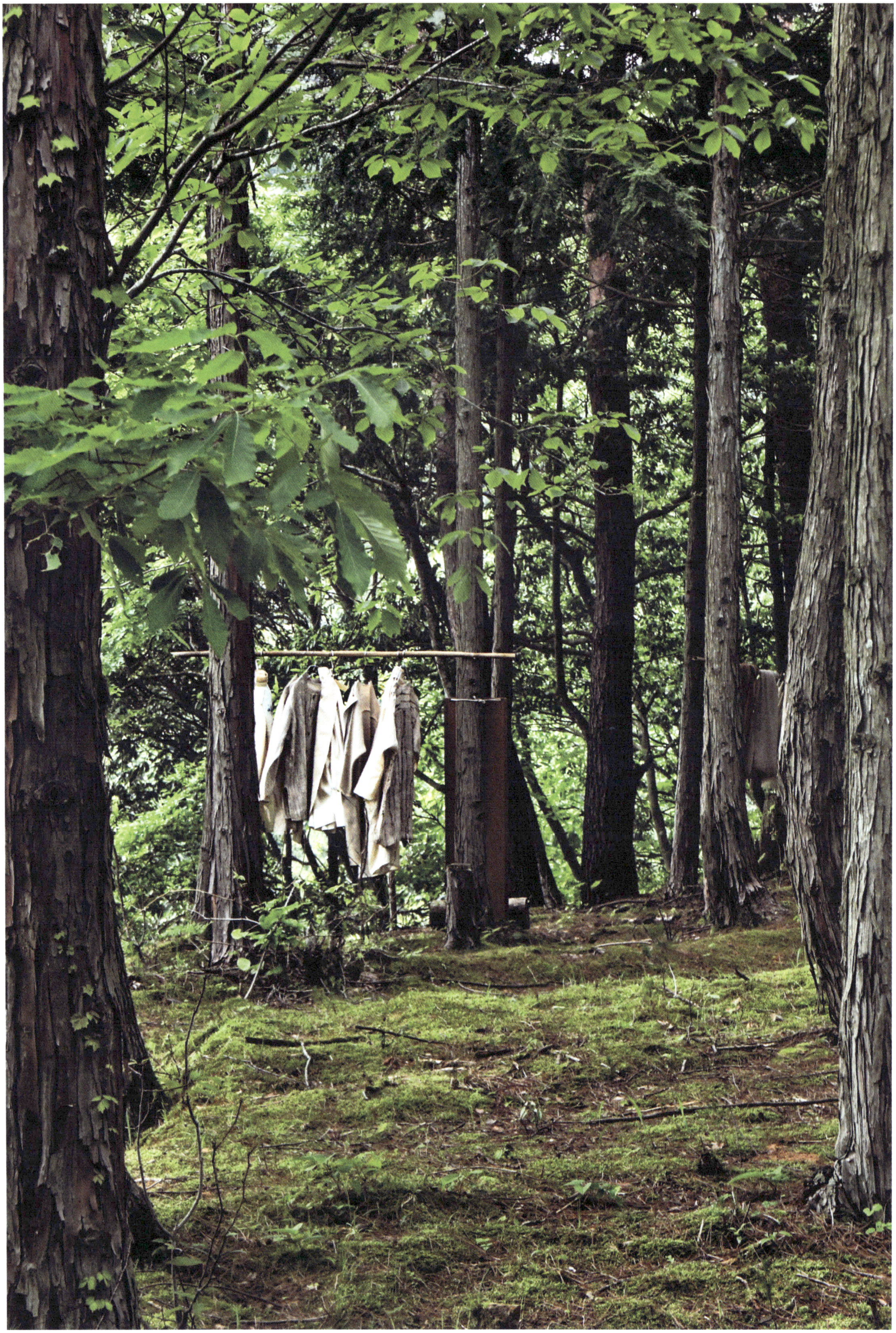

Taiki Iai

Dyer and fashion designer

Fukuchiyama, Japan

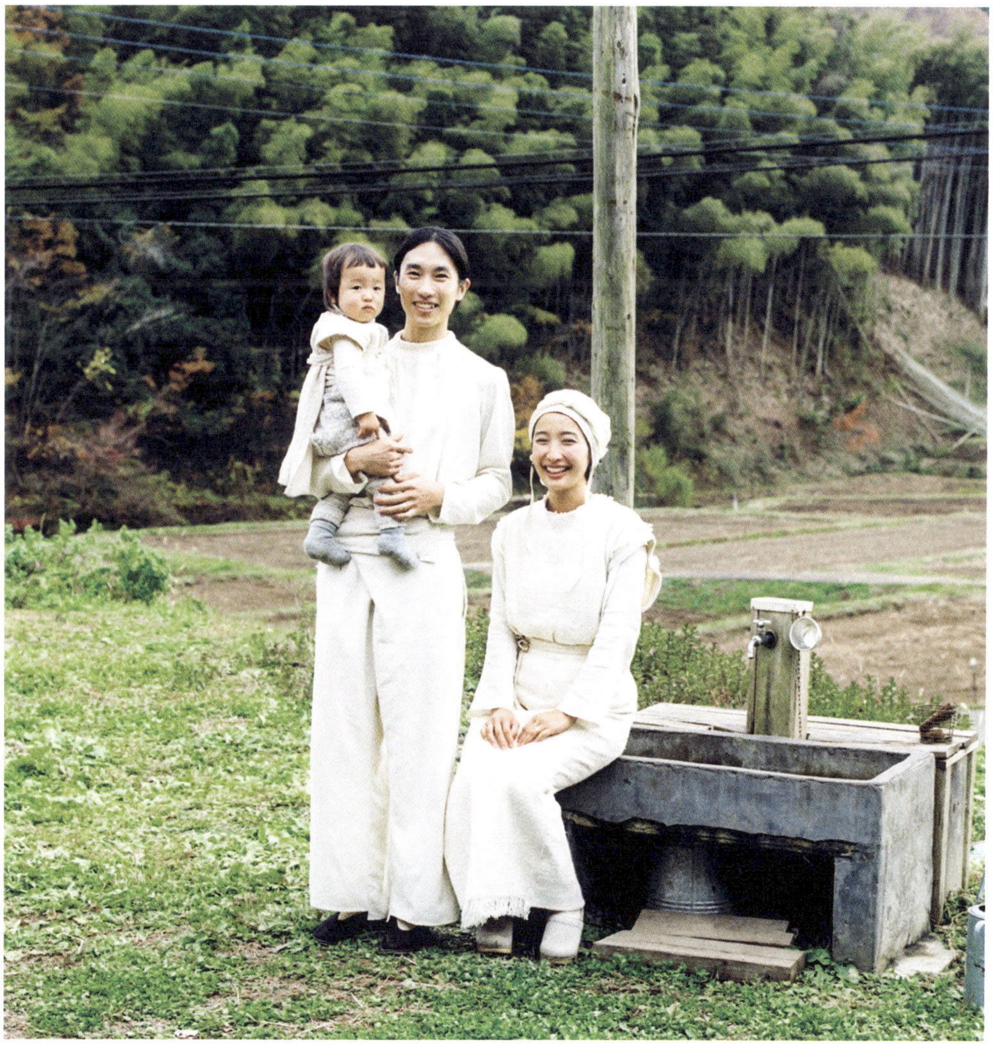

My name is Taiki Iai. I was born in 1991, in Fukuchiyama: a small mountain village located a two-hour train ride from Kyoto. As a child, on my way to school, I would sometimes cross paths with stags, birds, frogs, insects, and flowers; I realized at a very young age that the planet is home to an incredible variety of living beings.

I trained as a firefighter and worked for several years in the fire department in Tokyo's Shibuya district. On March 11, 2011, the day the earth began to tremble, I had just turned twenty. I was sent north to help the many victims of the earthquake. We never imagined such a catastrophe could happen. This tragedy changed my life. I left everything behind to return to my native village with my wife and adopt a lifestyle more in tune with nature. I relearned how to feed, shelter, and clothe myself. It was then that I decided to follow my childhood dream of becoming a textile dyer and clothing designer.

As a boy, I was fascinated by clothes. On Sundays, I would put on my favorite outfits and go to the fashionable Harajuku neighborhood in Tokyo to pose for street photographers. I bought my first sewing machine when I was nineteen, but I really entered the world of clothing design and dyeing when I moved back to Fukuchiyama.

My home-atelier is located on a century-old farm surrounded by rice fields and a few isolated wooden houses. I completely renovated it. The production area takes up about six tatami mats of space; just in front there's a garden and a sunken walkway where you can hear the babbling brook. The mountain, grass, flowers, trees, and twenty-eight villagers in this hamlet all feed my imagination.

For my collections, I use only natural materials: cotton, hemp, silk, old Japanese fabrics, Indian silks, and hand-woven Chinese ramie fabrics.

I taught myself how to recognize the plants in my garden and extract color from them. The colors of the mountain, of golden wheat dancing in the terraced fields, flowers, and the sky at dusk: everything has a unique rhythm and breath. The hues vary according to the humidity in the air, the quality of the water, and changes in the climate. Color highlights the season. I like "hazy" tones, like ash, tea, and rose. A beautiful color is like a wave containing hundreds of different shades.

I don't intellectualize the process of creating or dyeing my garments. Instead of thinking, I just let my hands guide my work. That's why I never draw designs; I touch the fabric, I put it on my body, and I begin to sew.

Today, I make custom clothing for the residents in my hamlet to wear while working in the fields. I also hold several sales each year and communicate via Instagram. I want my garments, like light, to be a part of people's lives forever.

At the moment, the world's major powers are having an enormous impact on nature and are provoking uncontrollable situations. We must take care of those around us. A small village in Japan, or even a simple movement created by each one of its inhabitants, can be enough to resist the storm.

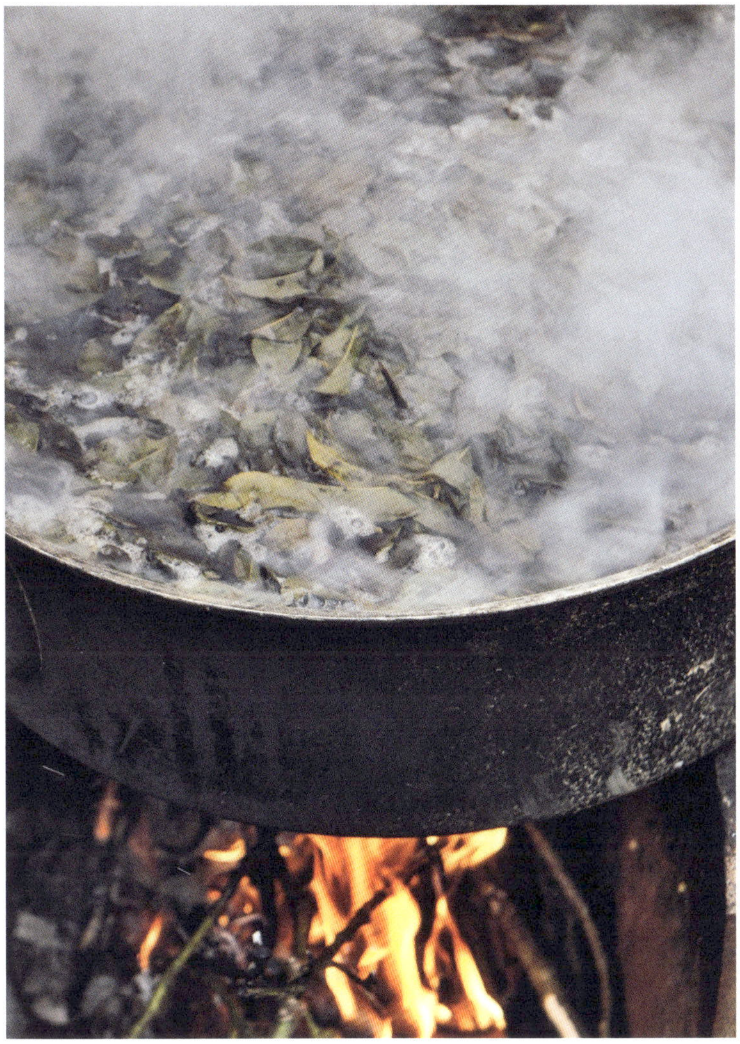
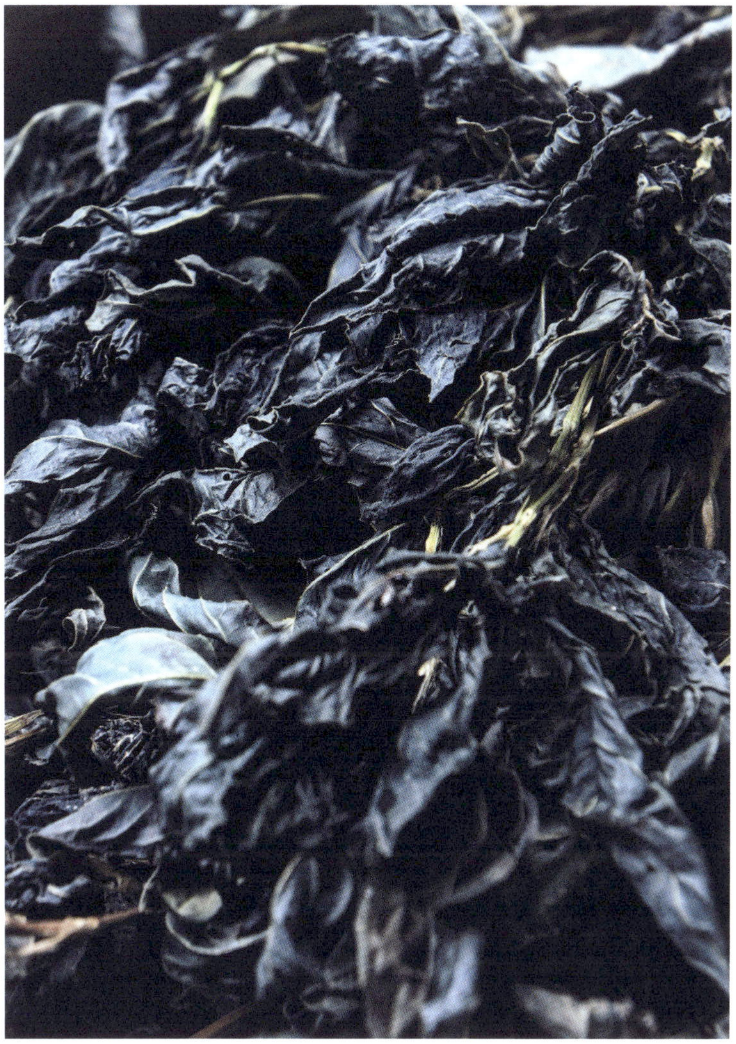
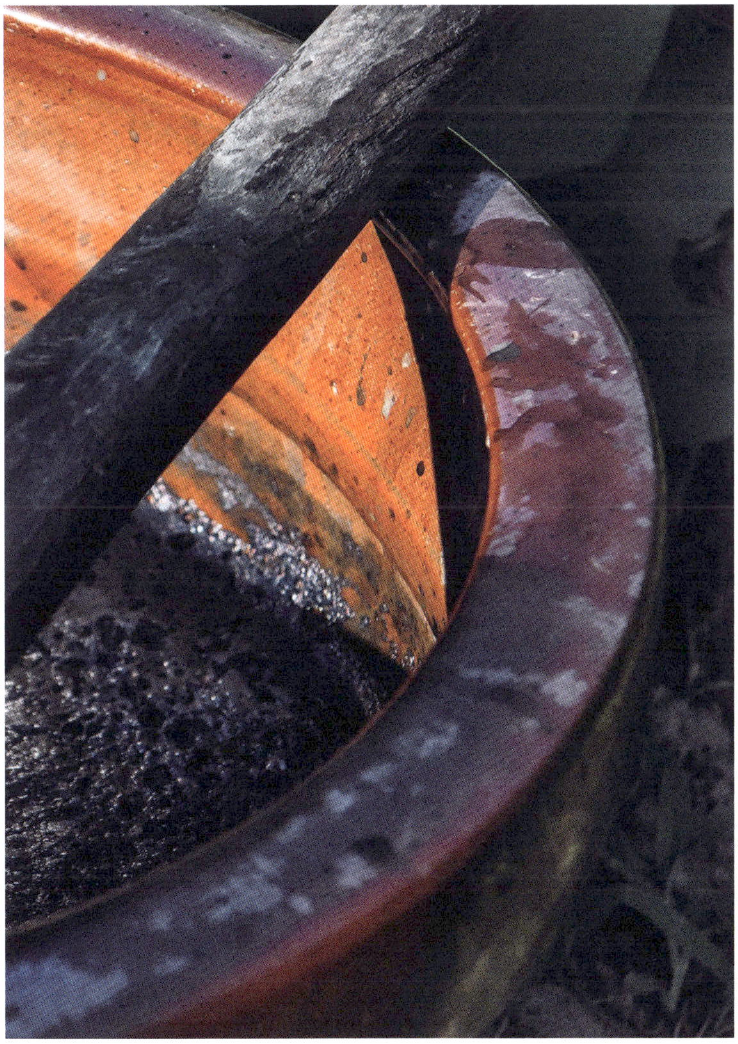
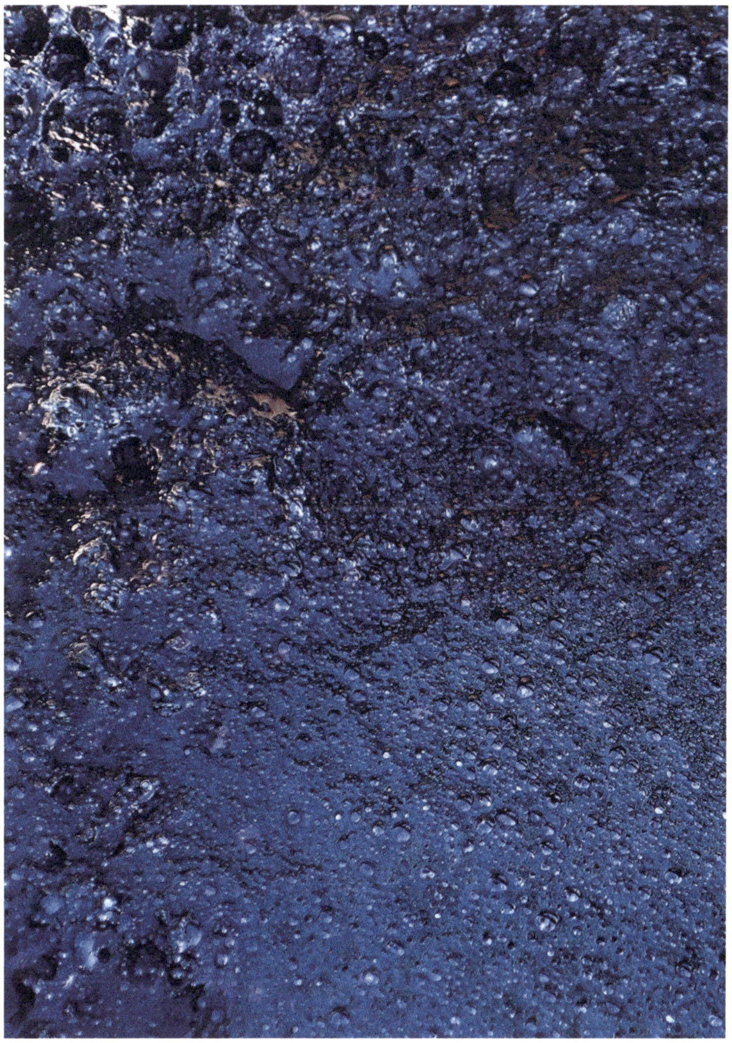

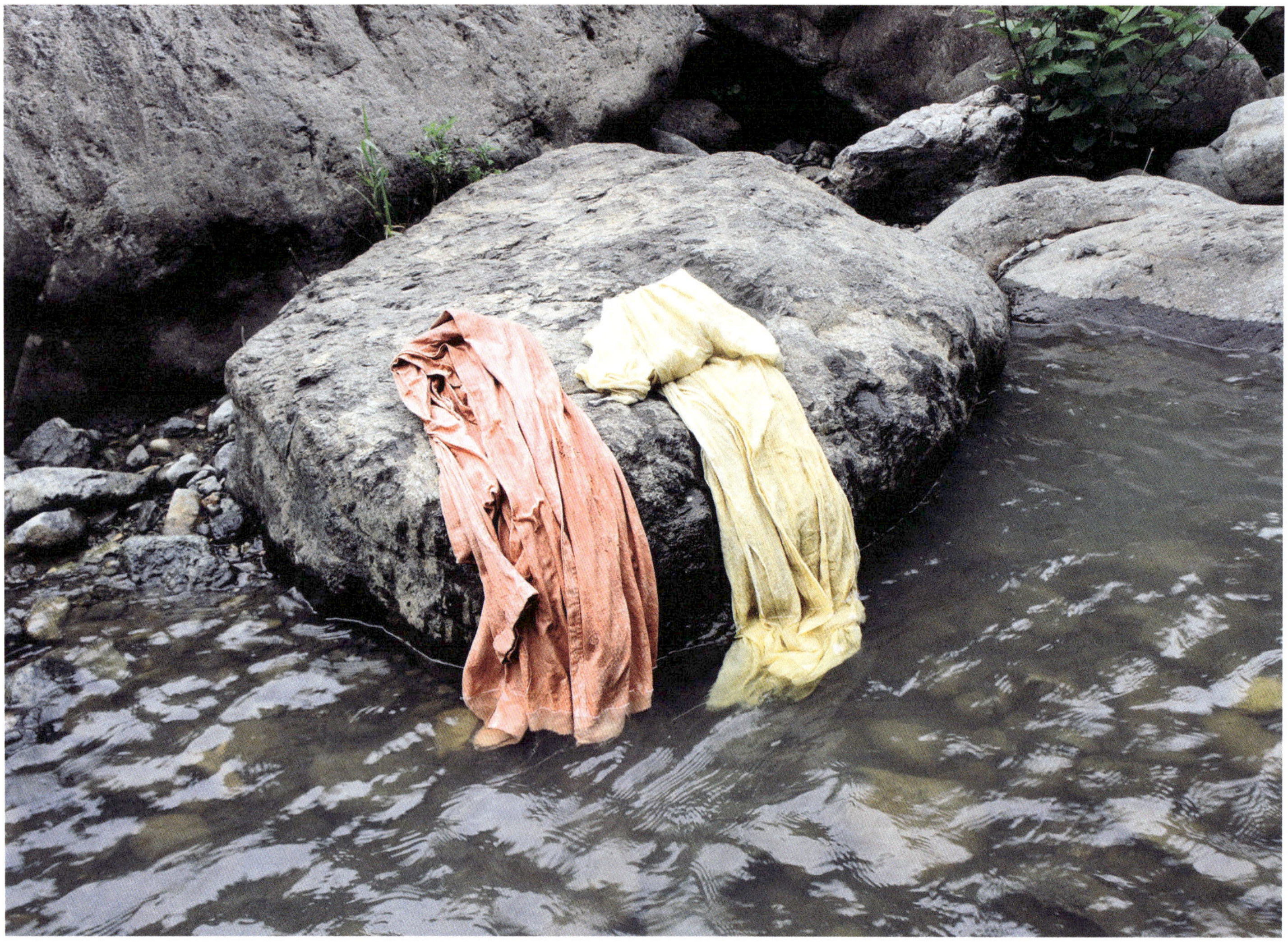

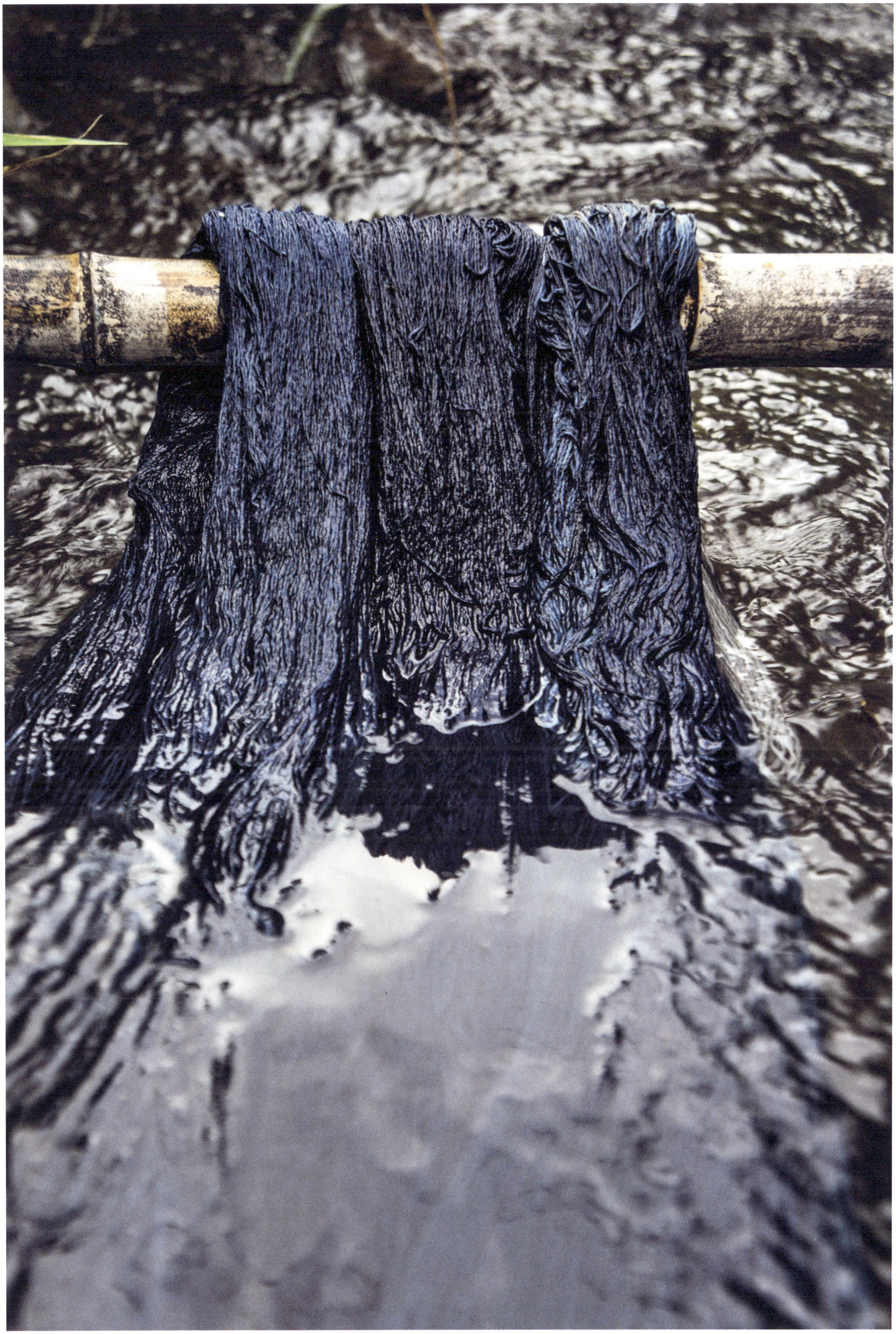

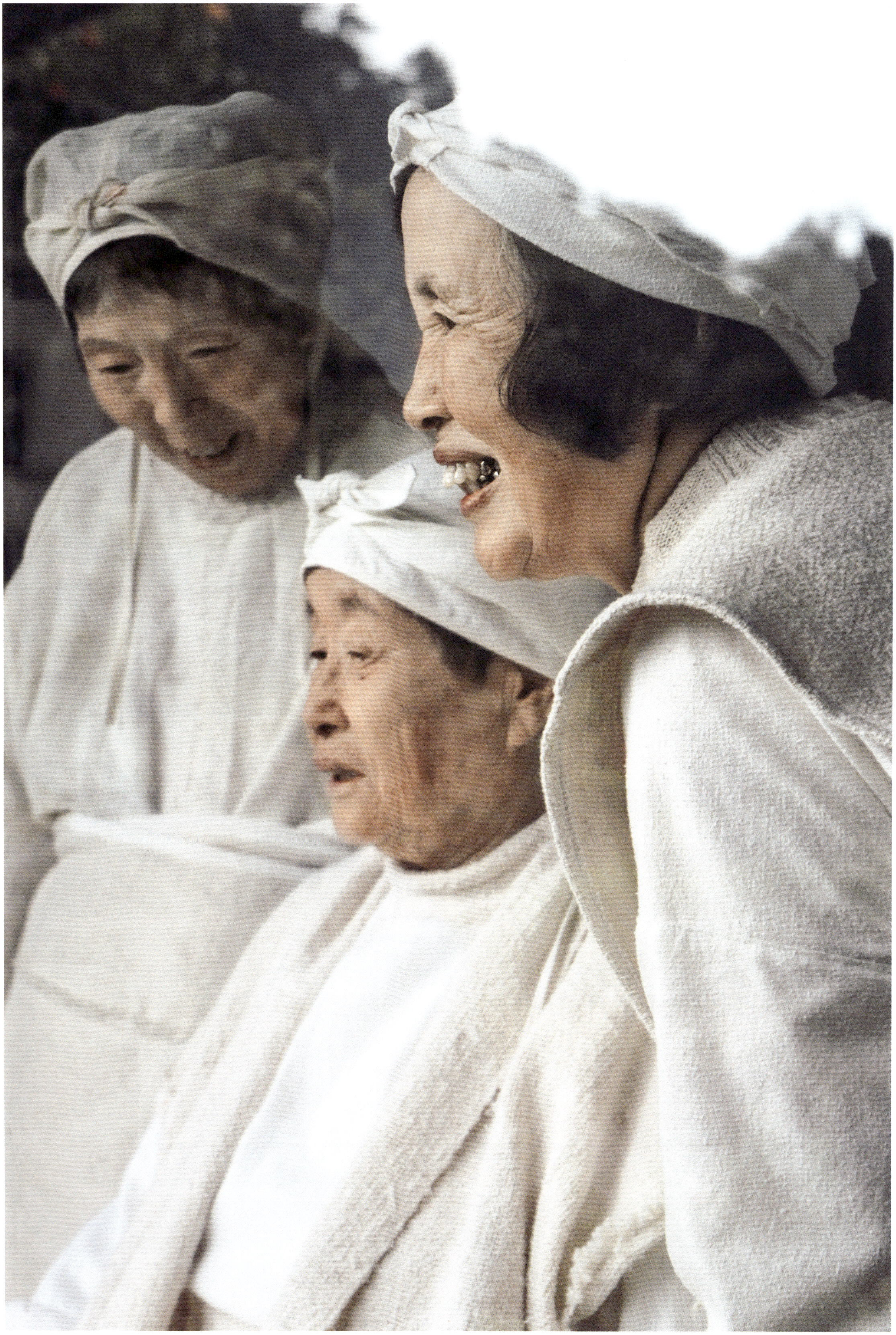

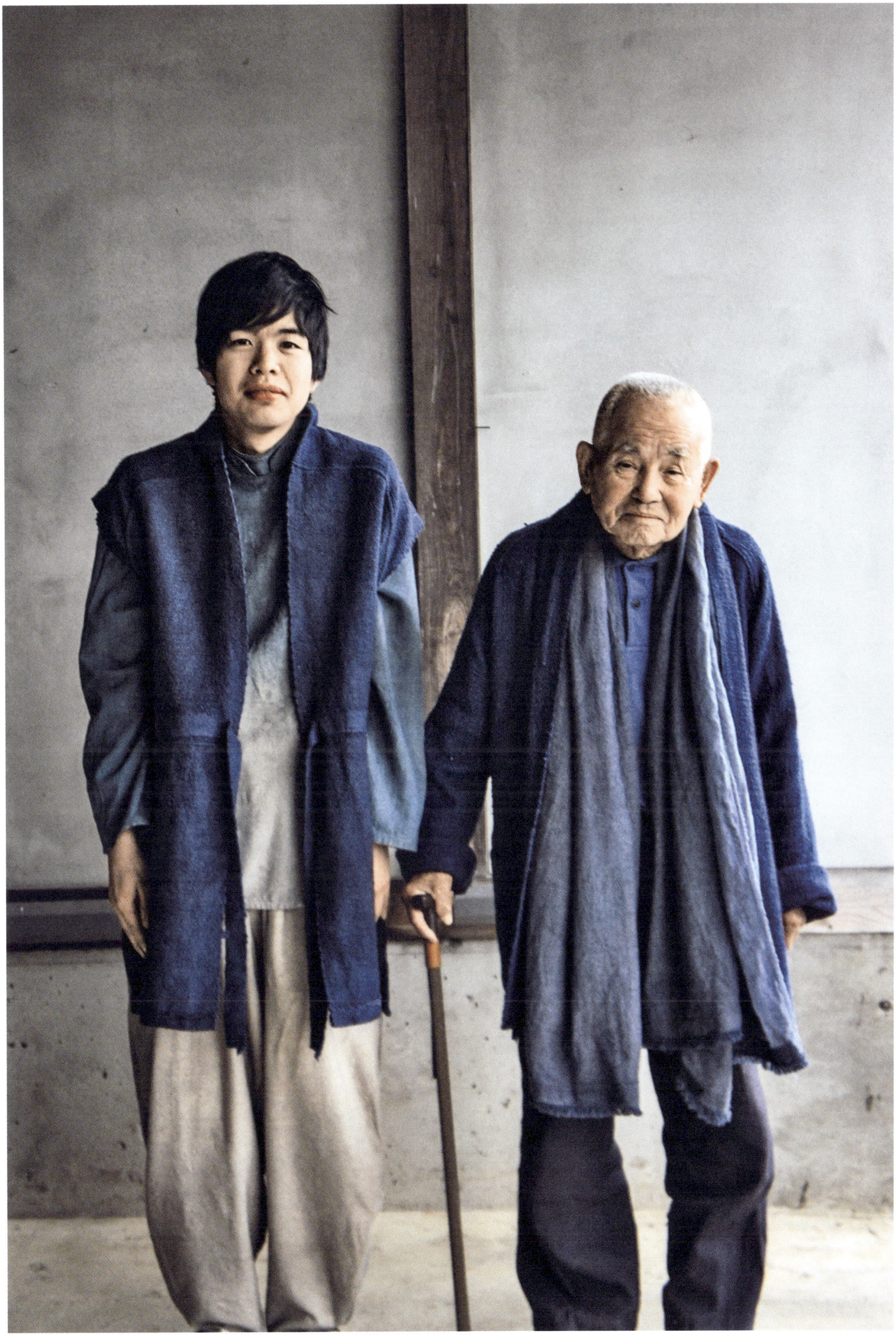

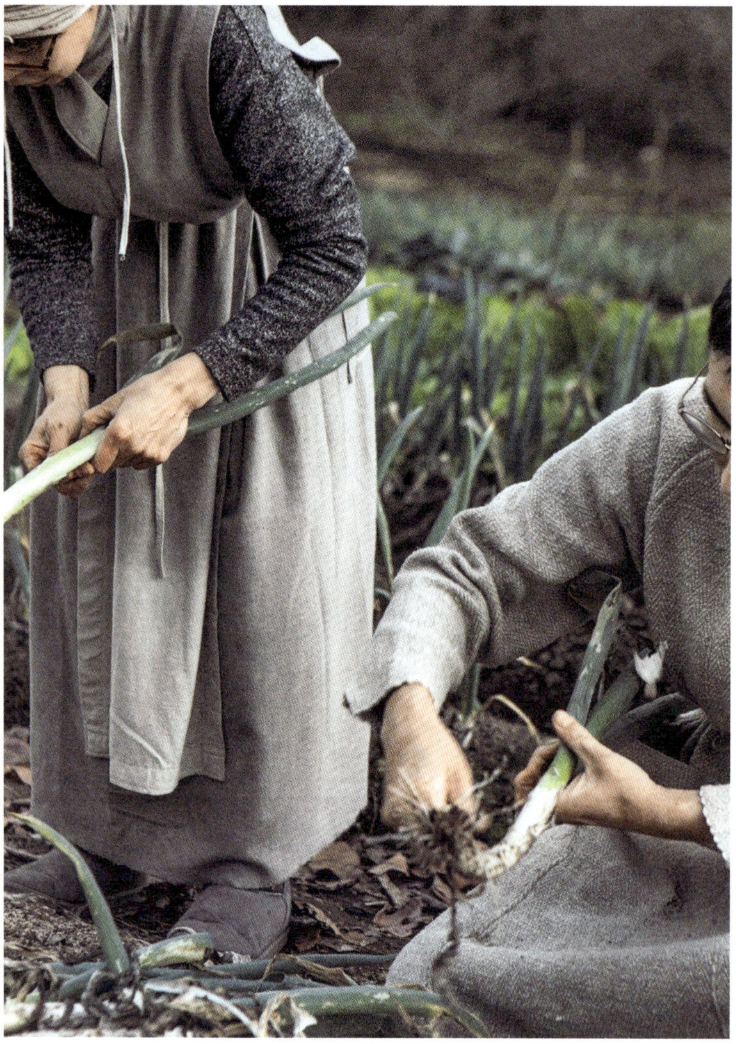
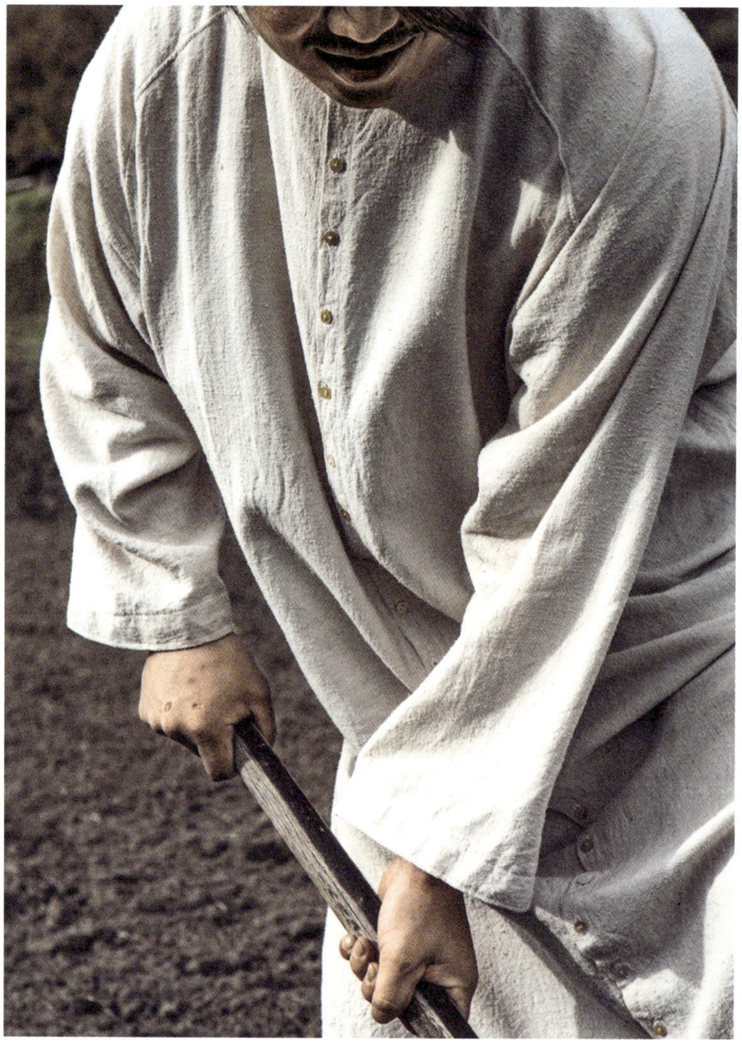
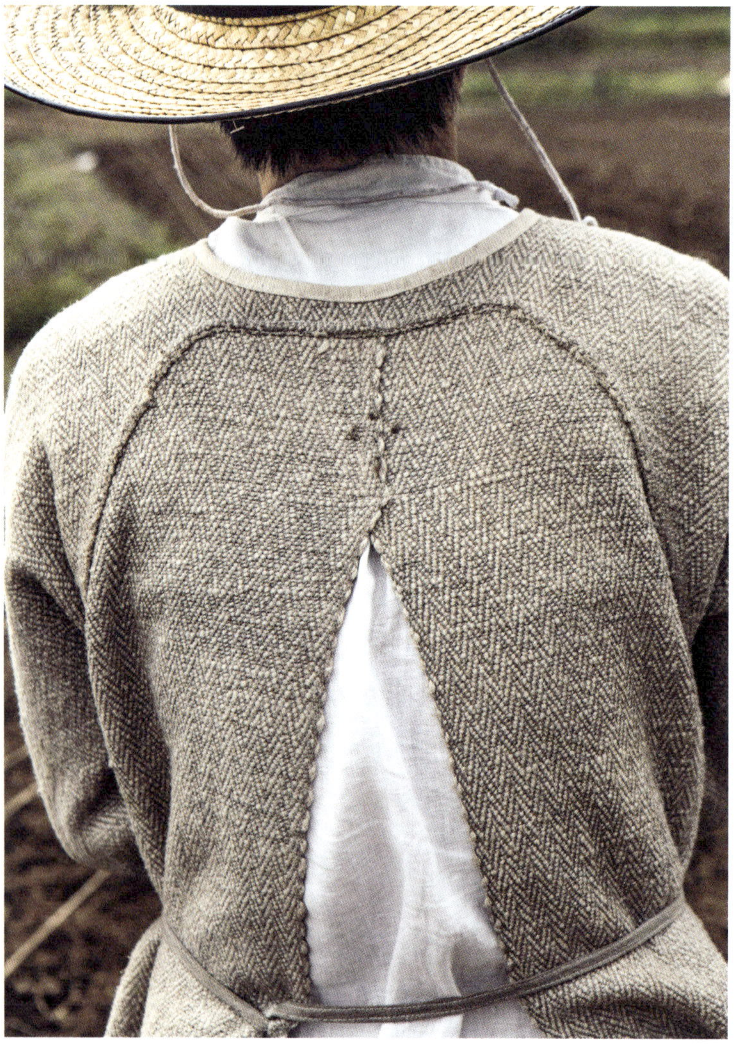
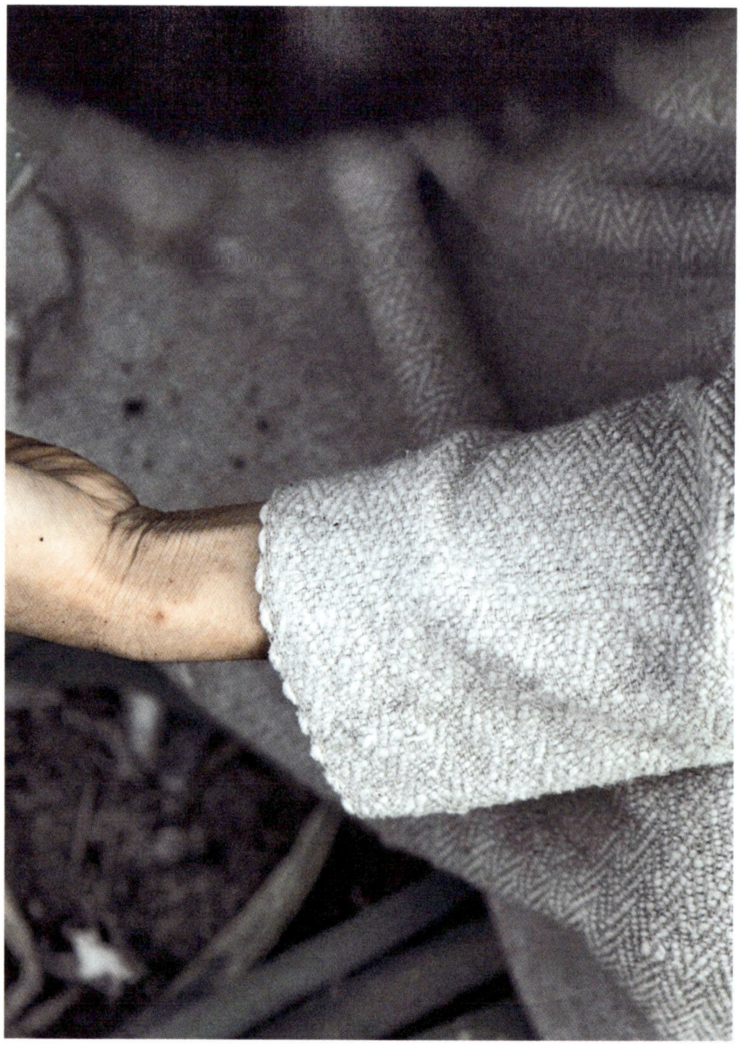

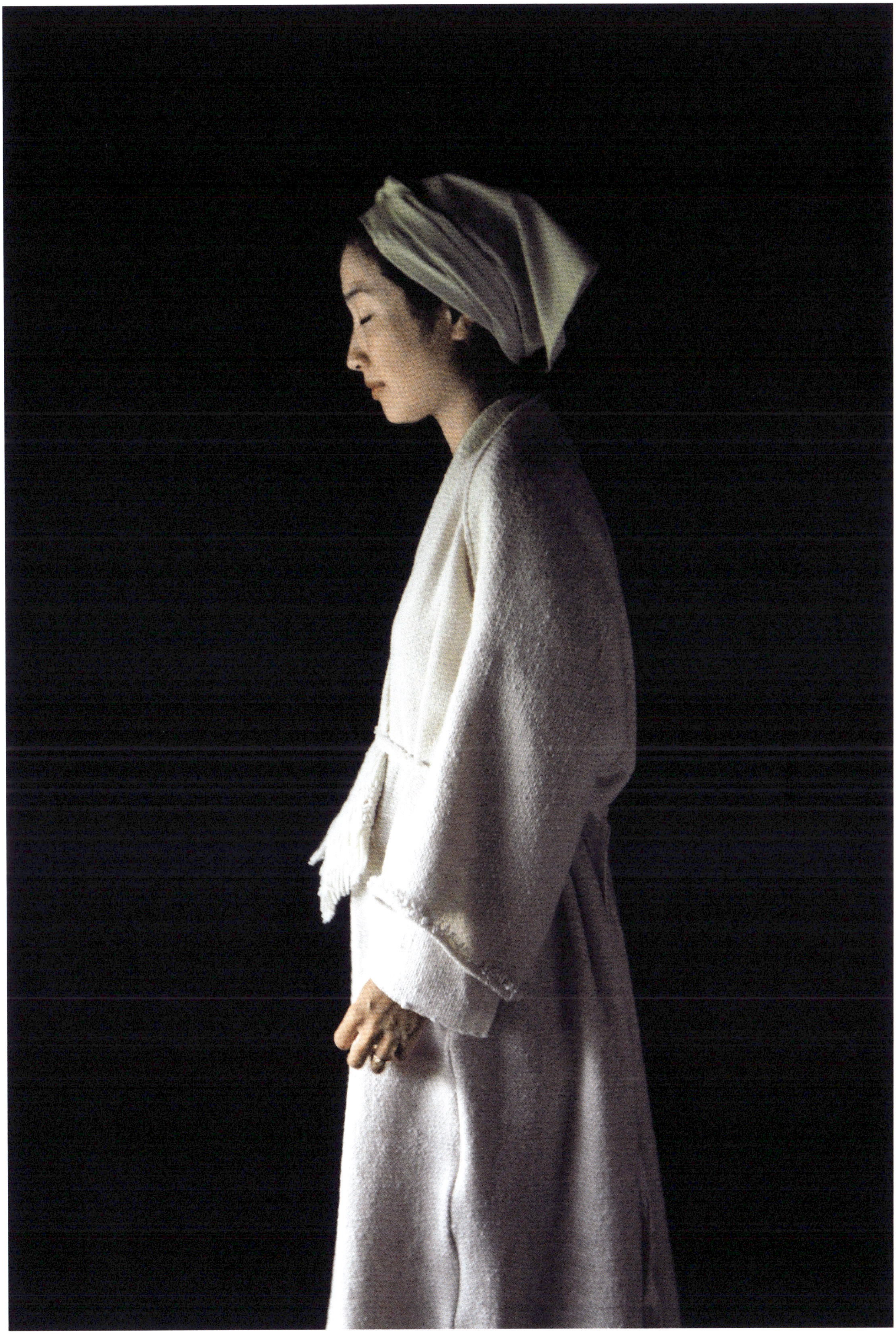

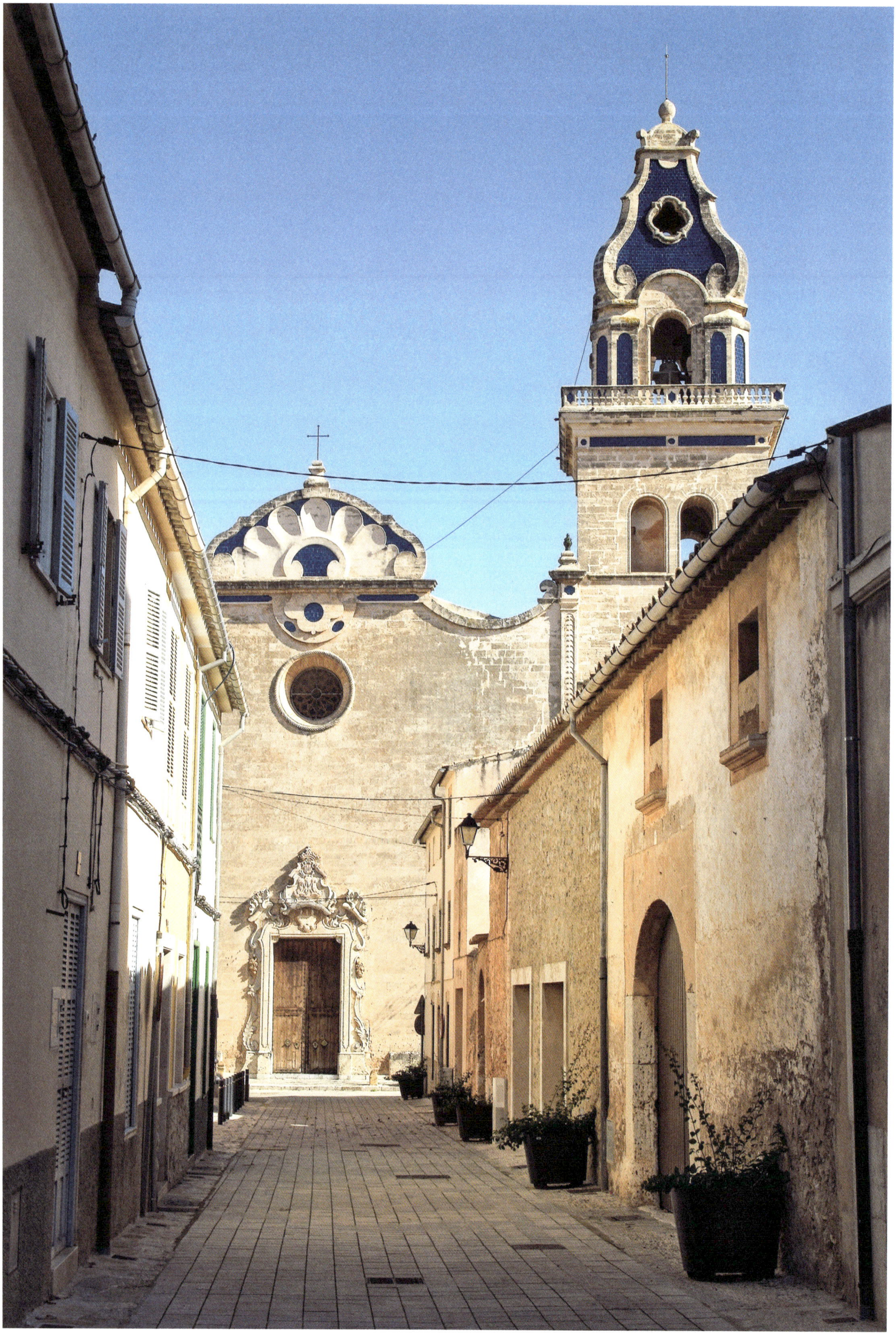

Guillermo Bujosa

Dyer and weaver

Santa Maria
del Camí,
Majorca, Spain

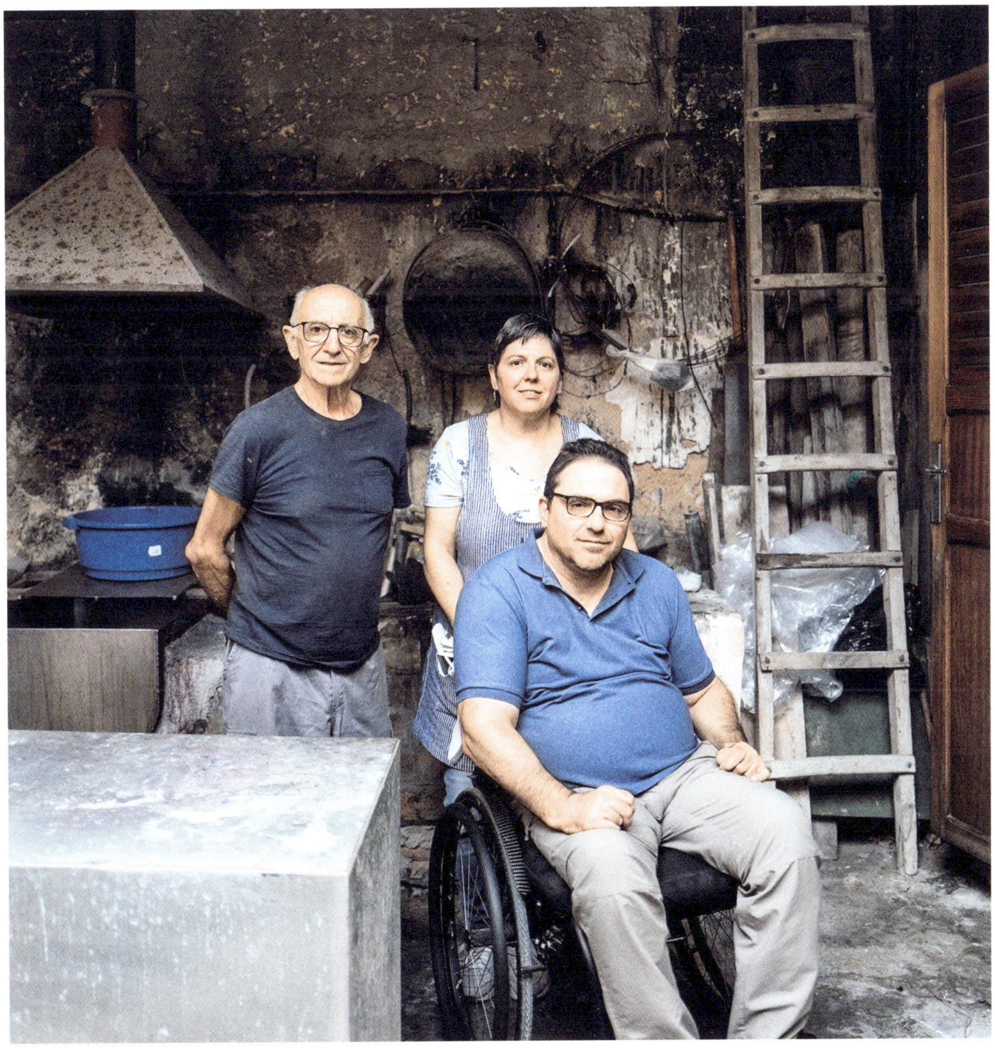

My name is Guillermo Bujosa. I live in Santa Maria del Camí, a small village near Palma, the capital of Majorca. I oversee dyeing and weaving in the workshop that my grandfather founded in 1949. My sister, Maribel, and I are the third generation to manage our small company.

Family is the most important thing in my life. My grandfather and father taught me the profession and passed on a great many things, and they both significantly influenced my work. I also did a lot of research: I read specialized texts and listened to the advice of textile artisans. Deepening my knowledge is fundamental for me.

At the start, we had a number of obstacles to overcome. We worked hard to preserve designs from Majorca, because it is becoming increasingly difficult to maintain this living craft tradition on the island. Now, in the workshop, we try to connect past and future by combining older, typical designs from the island with contemporary ones, by giving them new interpretations, or by collaborating with artists like Miquel Barceló.

Traditional Majorcan fabric, locally known as *tela de lenguas*, is dyed and woven using the ikat technique. Its "blurry" edges resemble flickering flames, which inspired the Catalan term for the fabric, *flàmules,* in the early eighteenth century. Ikat is a dyeing and weaving technique practiced throughout the world, especially in Asia and South America. *Tela de lenguas* is said to have its origins in Asia, which is quite possible, considering that Majorca was once a stopover for ships sailing the trade routes between Asia and Europe. Asian ikats are actually very similar to Majorca's *telas de lenguas*, whose designs are achieved using a unique dyeing process that requires great agility: the thread is hand-dyed before weaving, and the design is gradually revealed as the fabric is woven. This gives the textile an irregular, imperfect quality that distinguishes it from industrially produced equivalents.

To make our Majorcan fabric, we use 100 percent natural materials like cotton, linen, and silk that we source from Barcelona and northern Europe. Blue, extracted from natural indigo, has always been the traditional color, but now the palette we use is infinite. To me, a beautiful color is one that inspires feeling.

Majorcan craft is going through a difficult period, because it is hard to find skilled artisans. Today, most Majorcans are turning to industry or tourism. However, I think that crafts contribute to preserving our origins, and to keeping our culture alive for future generations.

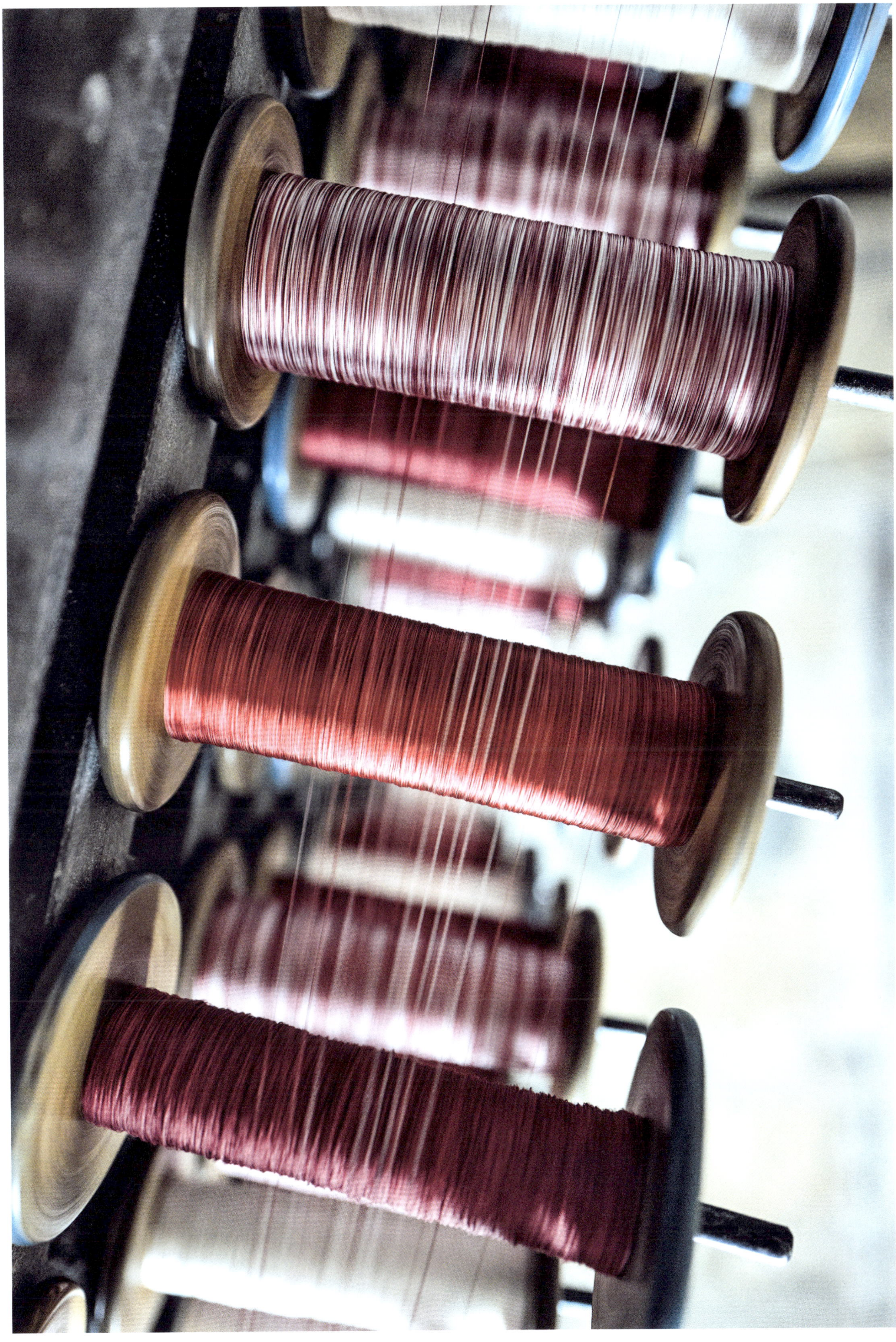

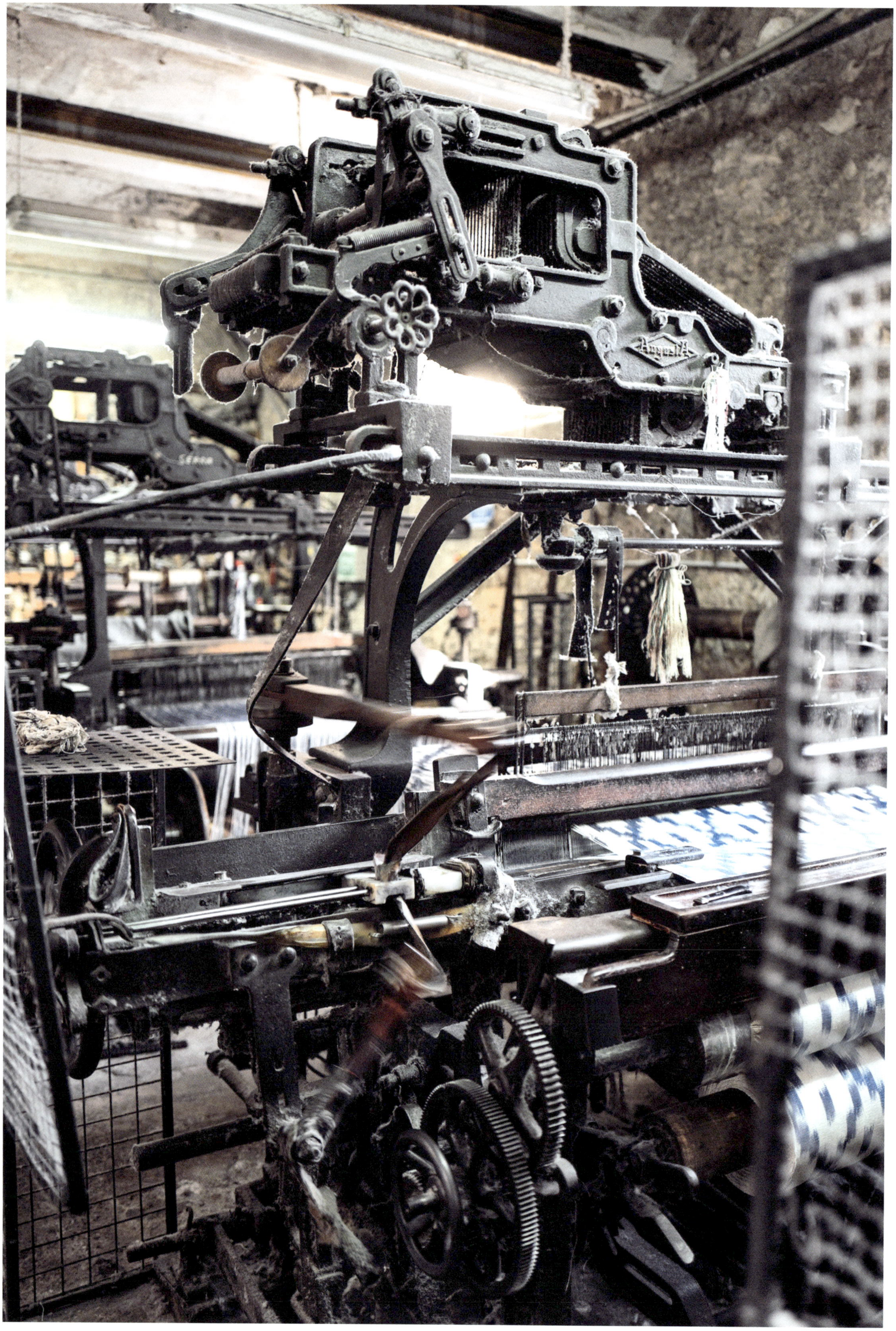

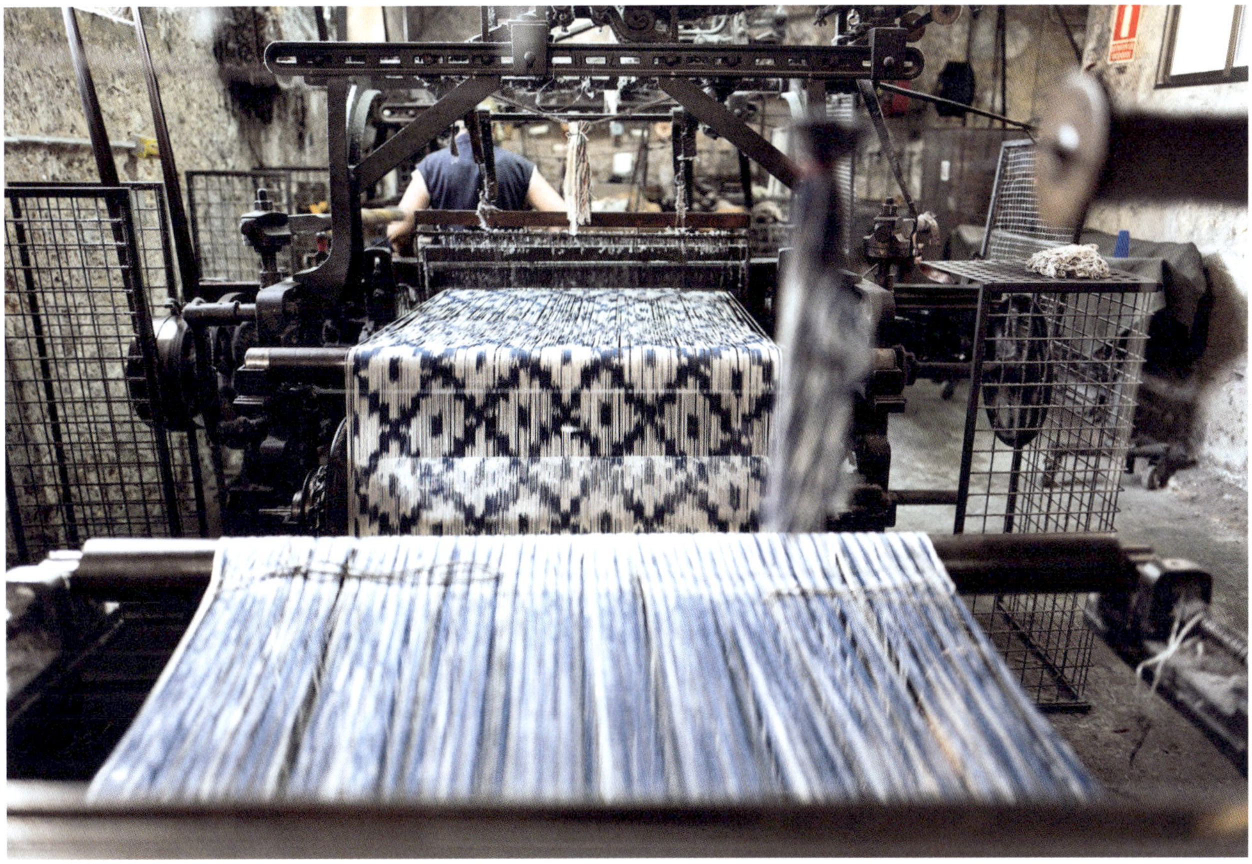

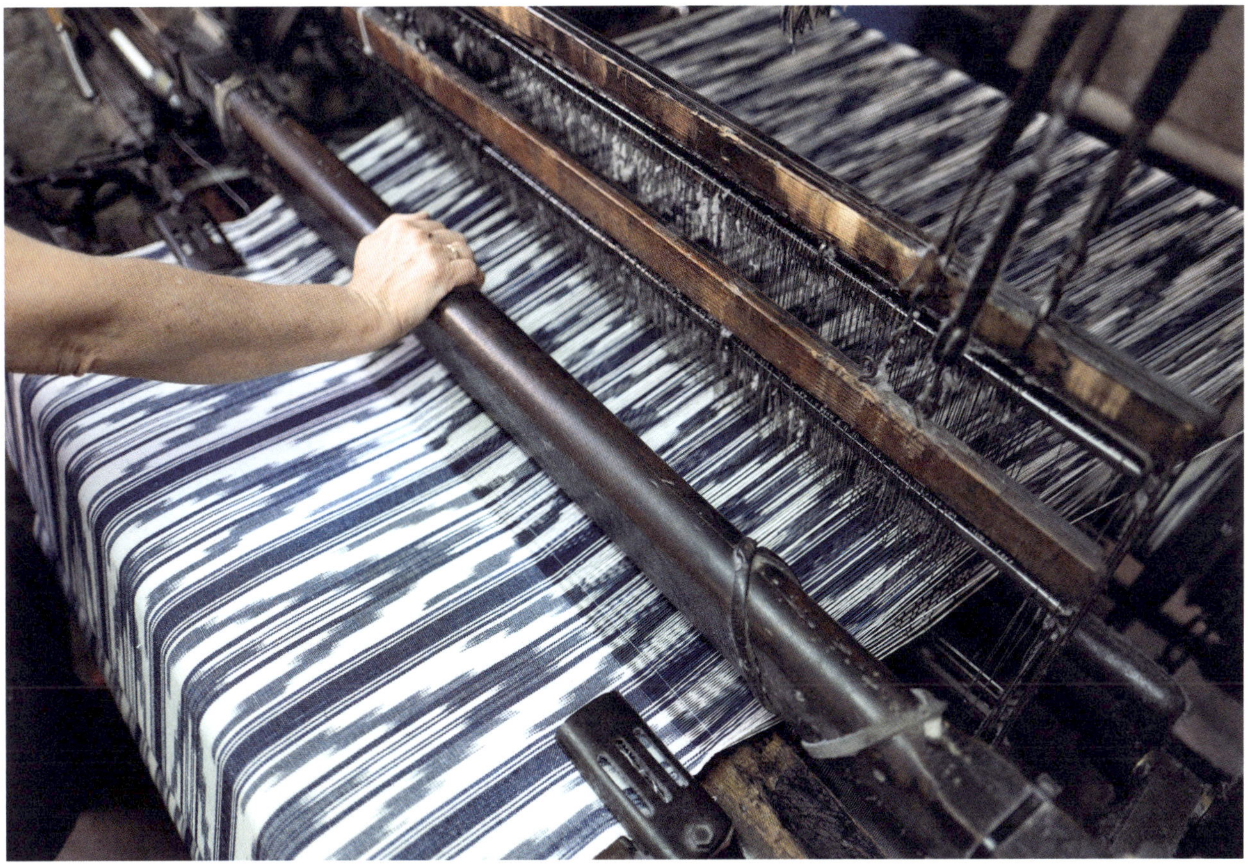

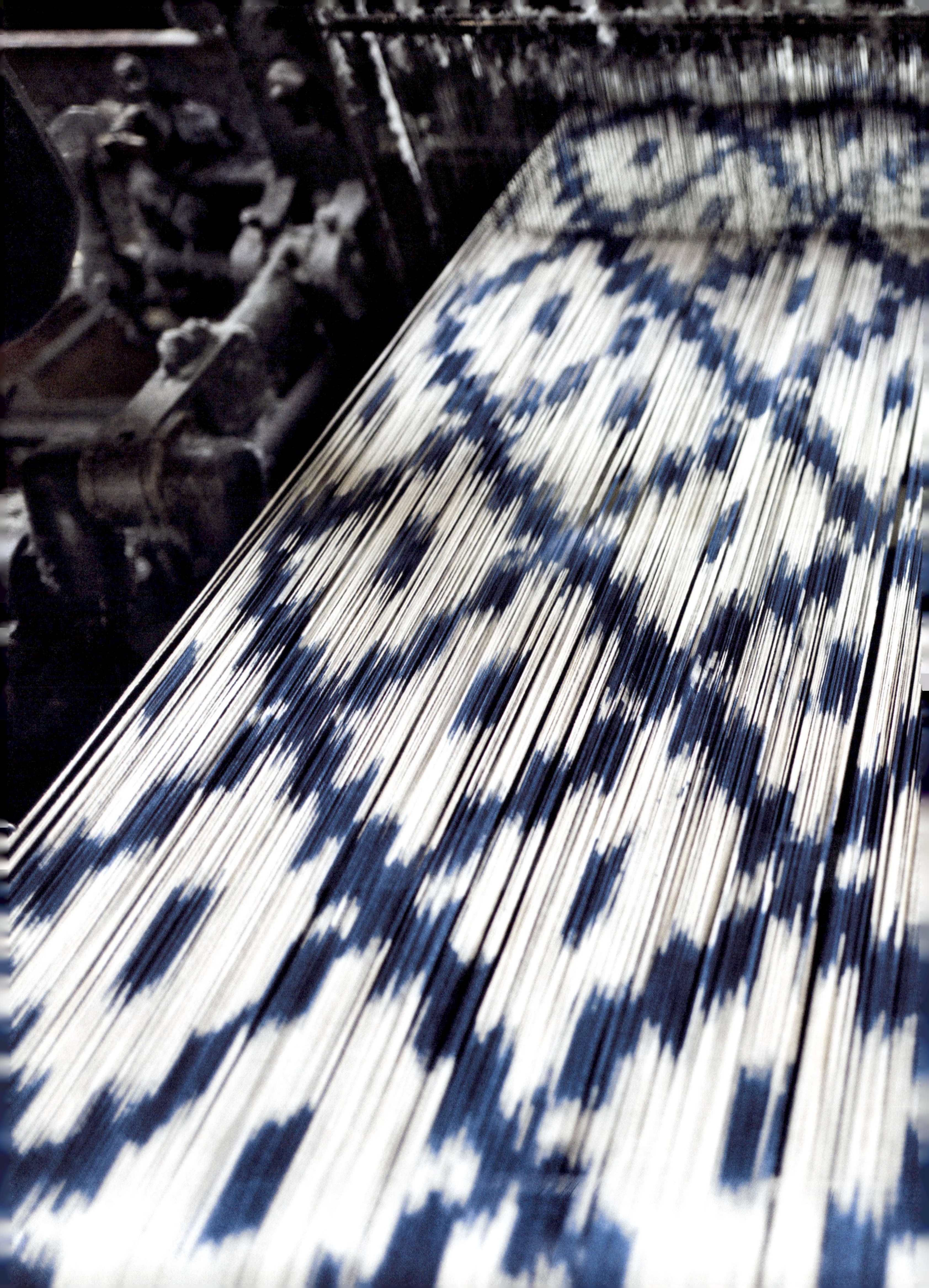

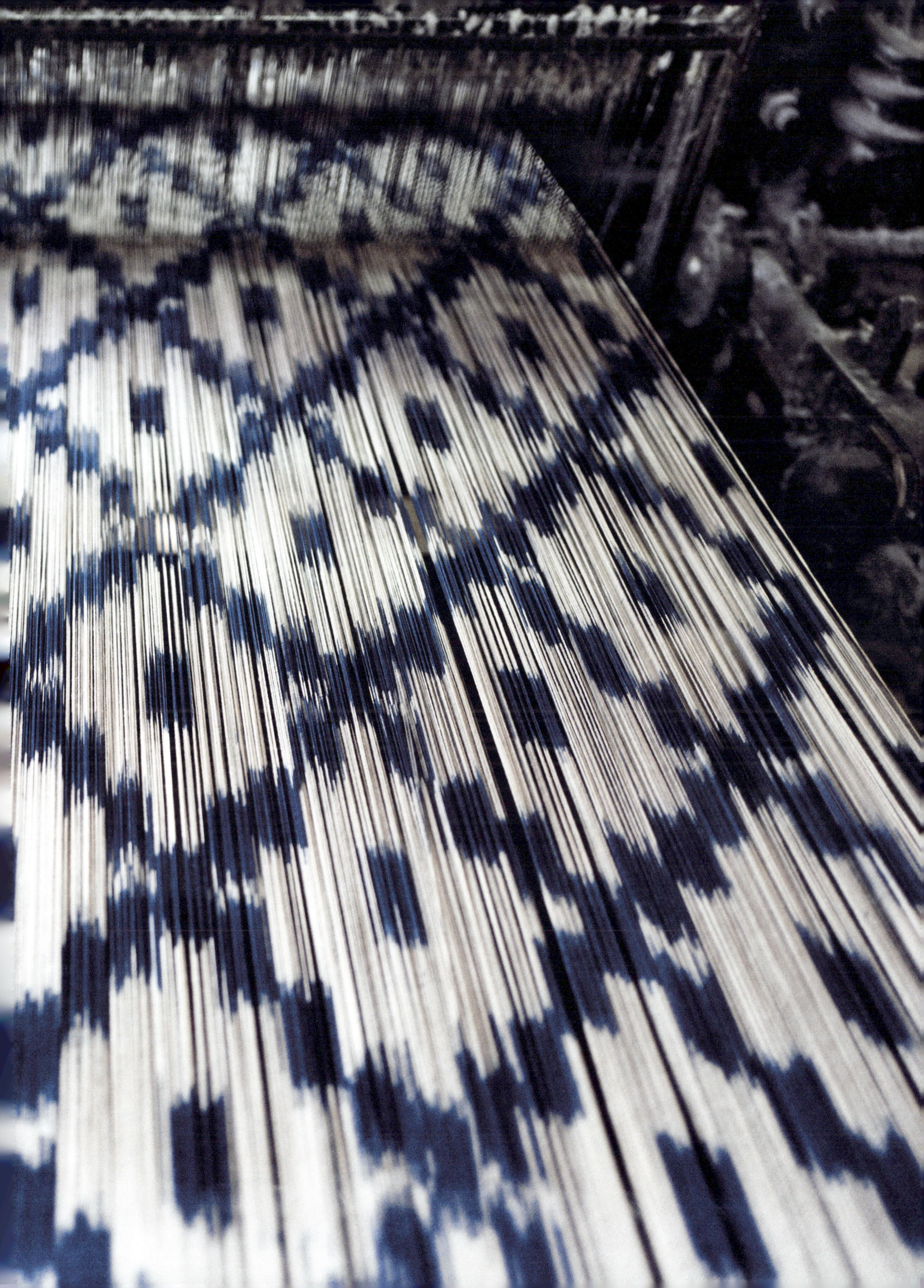

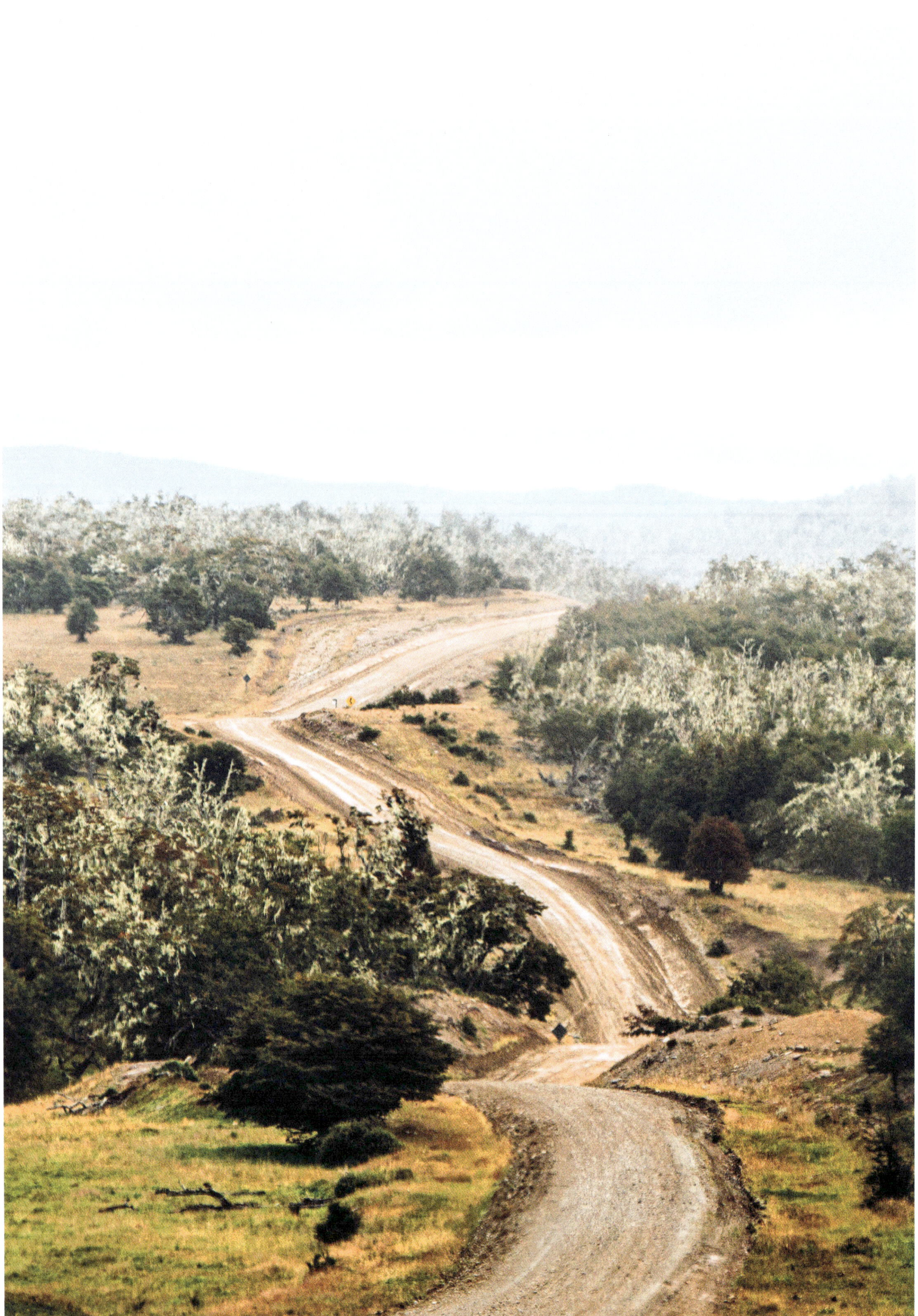

Alexandra Kehayoglou

Textile artist

Buenos Aires, Argentina

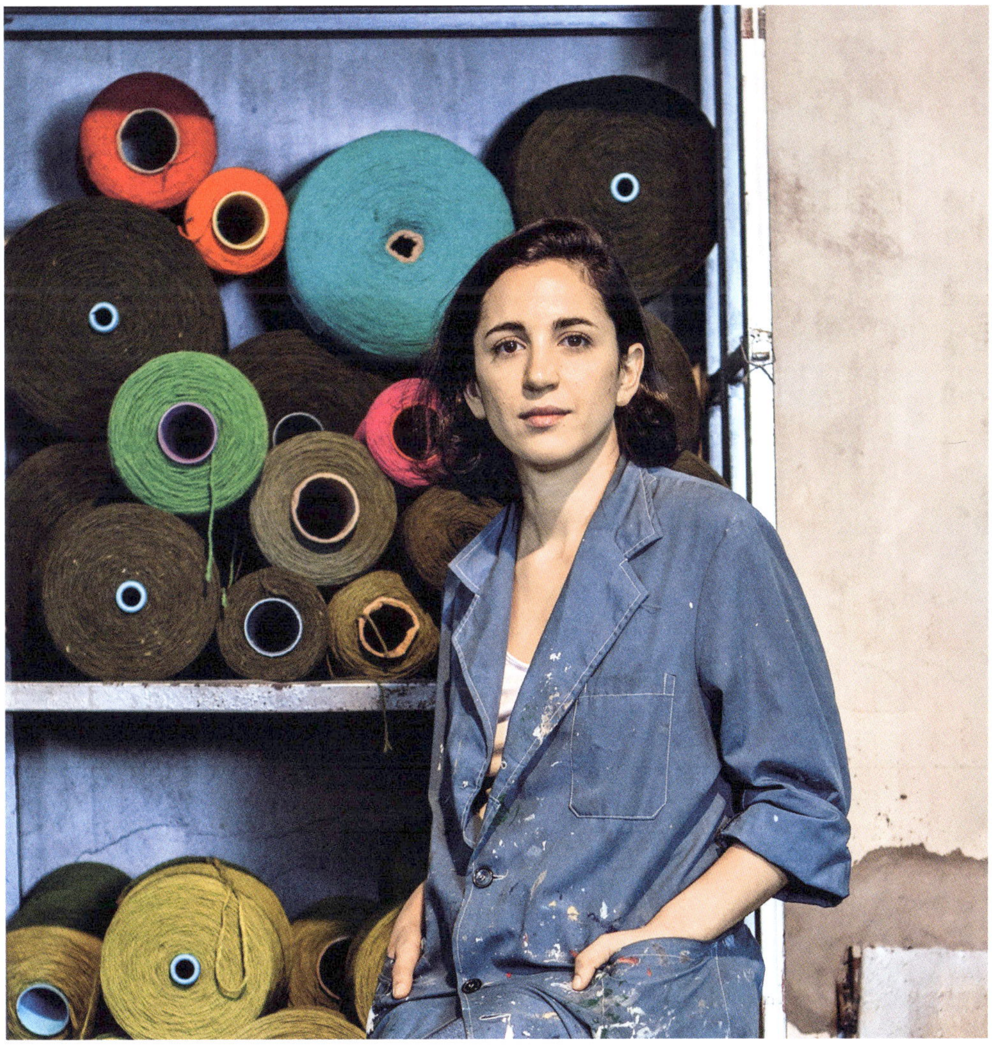

My name is Alexandra Kehayoglou. I live in Buenos Aires, near the Río de la Plata. My father has Greek heritage and my mother is Polish, Basque, French, and Native American. I attended art school, where I studied painting, and I developed a strong interest in photography, which I still use in my work. At the time, I was attracted to art as a means of communication, and this artistic feeling has made me who I am. My interest in craftsmanship began in art school, but I'm convinced that this attraction has always been there.

My ancestors were Greek and came from Isparta, in Turkey—a town specialized in the manufacture of carpets and the cultivation of roses. My grandmother was forced to leave the country in the early twentieth century due to the Greco-Turkish War and traveled by boat to Buenos Aires, where she entered an arranged marriage. In Argentina, her loom saved my family from the tragedy of exile. It is important for me to honor my Greek origins, and their influence is very present in my work. Greece is a precious land where I return each year to pause and think about what I am doing, and connect with my ancestors.

My father has been an inspiration for me. He encouraged me to find a use for all the surplus wool stored in his factory. So I started experimenting; I was finishing art school at the time, and I had the urge to include this material in my work. I also think that something deep inside draws me to it.

In recent years, I have become known for my hand-tufted, natural wool carpets that explore our relationship with nature and with the landscape that surrounds us. I create the carpets by hand, using a tufting gun to weave the material into the frame (a canvas stretched on a vertical loom). I discovered that it is possible to sculpt carpets: I weave in the threads, leaving a maximum pile height; then I sculpt the wool using scissors and razor blades. A portion of the wool, which I dye myself, comes from Argentina and the rest from New Zealand and Spain. In the beginning, I made all of my work using industrial surplus from the family carpet factory; today, I still use some of the wool that my father gave me.

Textiles carry information. Threads are like veins, or bridges, or cables. For me, this information is connected to the trauma of my family and the idea that the material comes from nature. Wool is a living material that humanity has used for millennia; I believe that it is intrinsically connected to nomadism. And it has a social dimension that connects people; the tapestries of Chilean artist Violeta Parra also come to mind.

In 2013, I began collaborating with my husband, the artist José Huidobro. Working together has made more sense to me than many other things. We do not always complement each other; we are rather explosive. We spend hours discussing things—work and crazy ideas—and we both hope to continue this fruitful artistic collaboration.

Personally, I work to provoke reactions, not only when the work is finished, but also through the process of investigating the memory behind the landscapes that I depict, or the stories of the people I recount in relation to a particular place.

In Argentina, my work is often not received as I intended it to be. When I began addressing the theme of aboriginal land, few people seemed to agree with my approach. This country is very political, and I think it is easier to show non-political works.

Today, humanity is facing a crisis, and our relationship with the environment is proof of that. I think we can see very clearly in the environment what we need to change in ourselves. And we urgently need to change, because we are growing ill and so is the land.

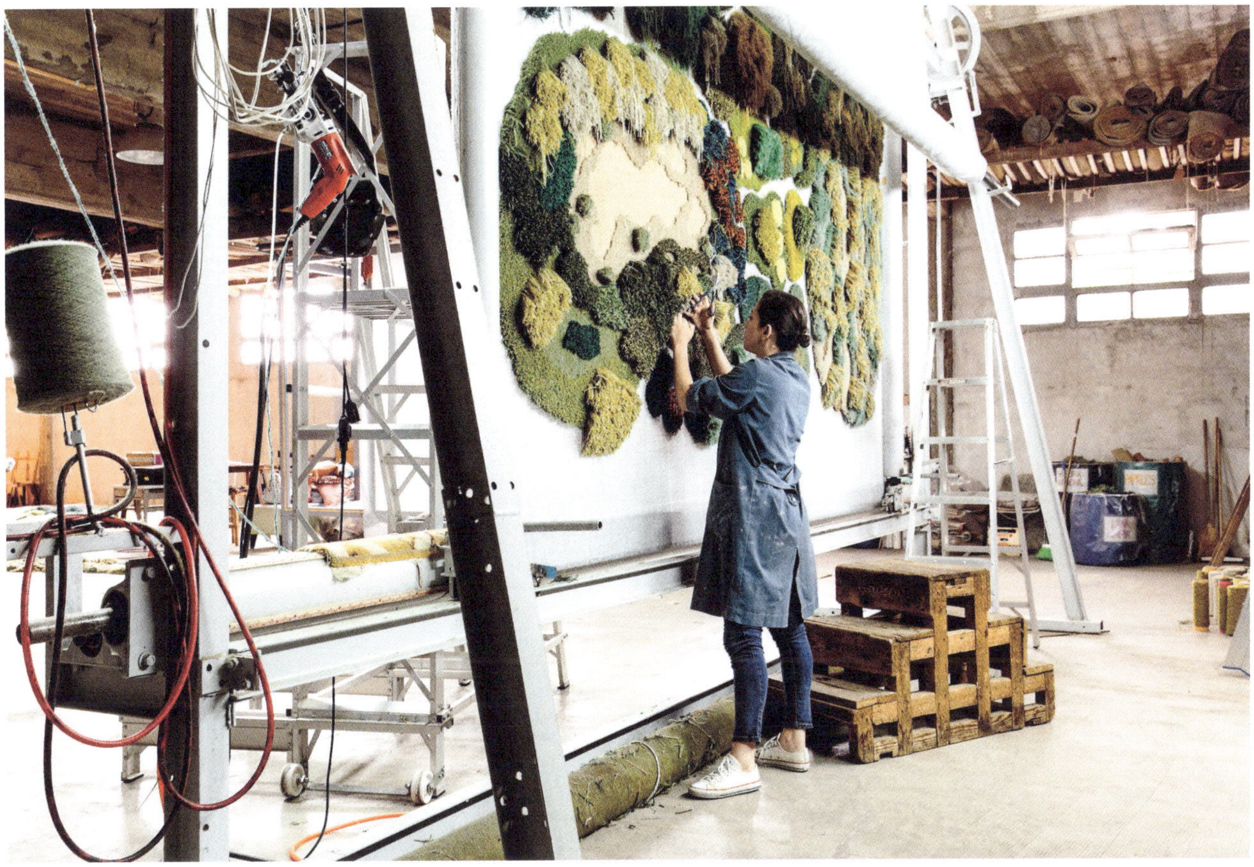

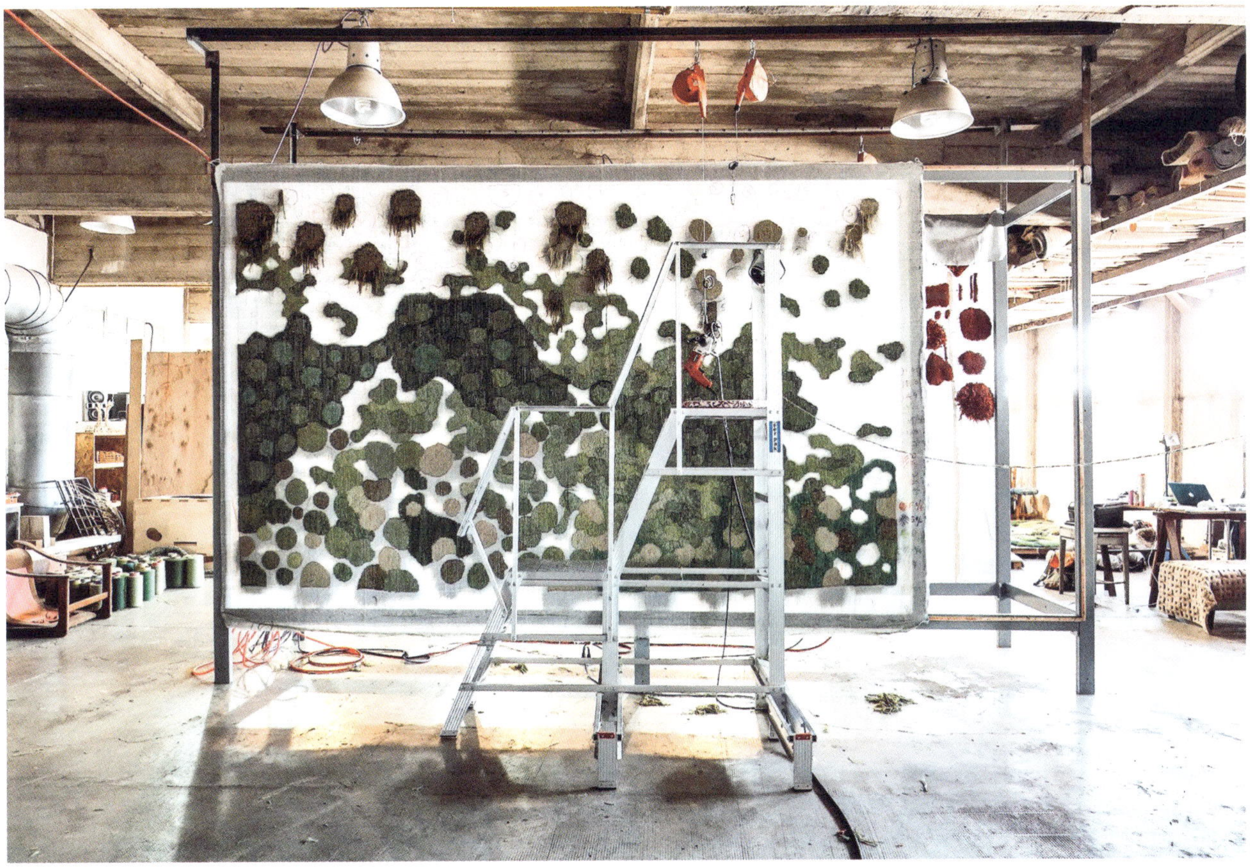

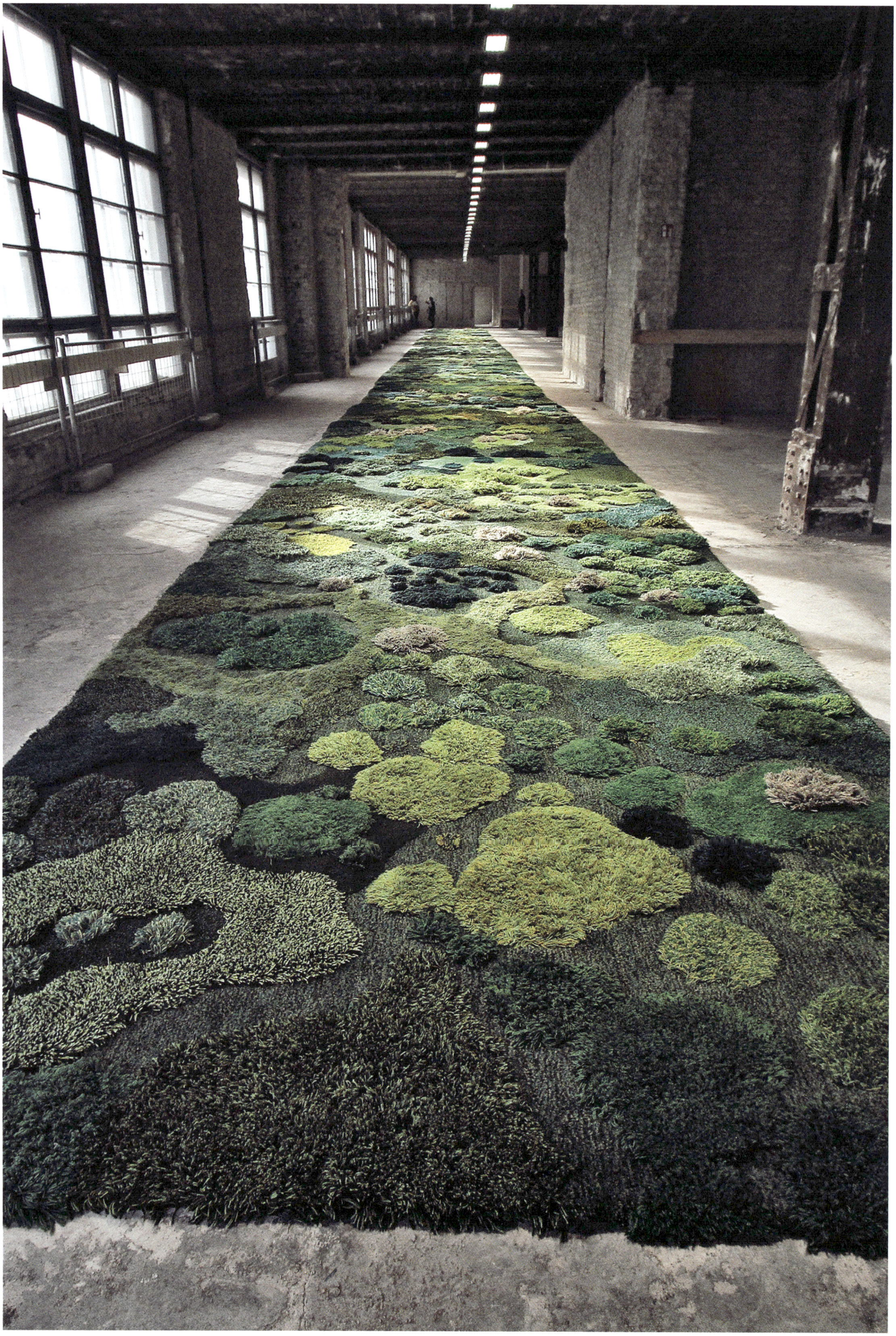

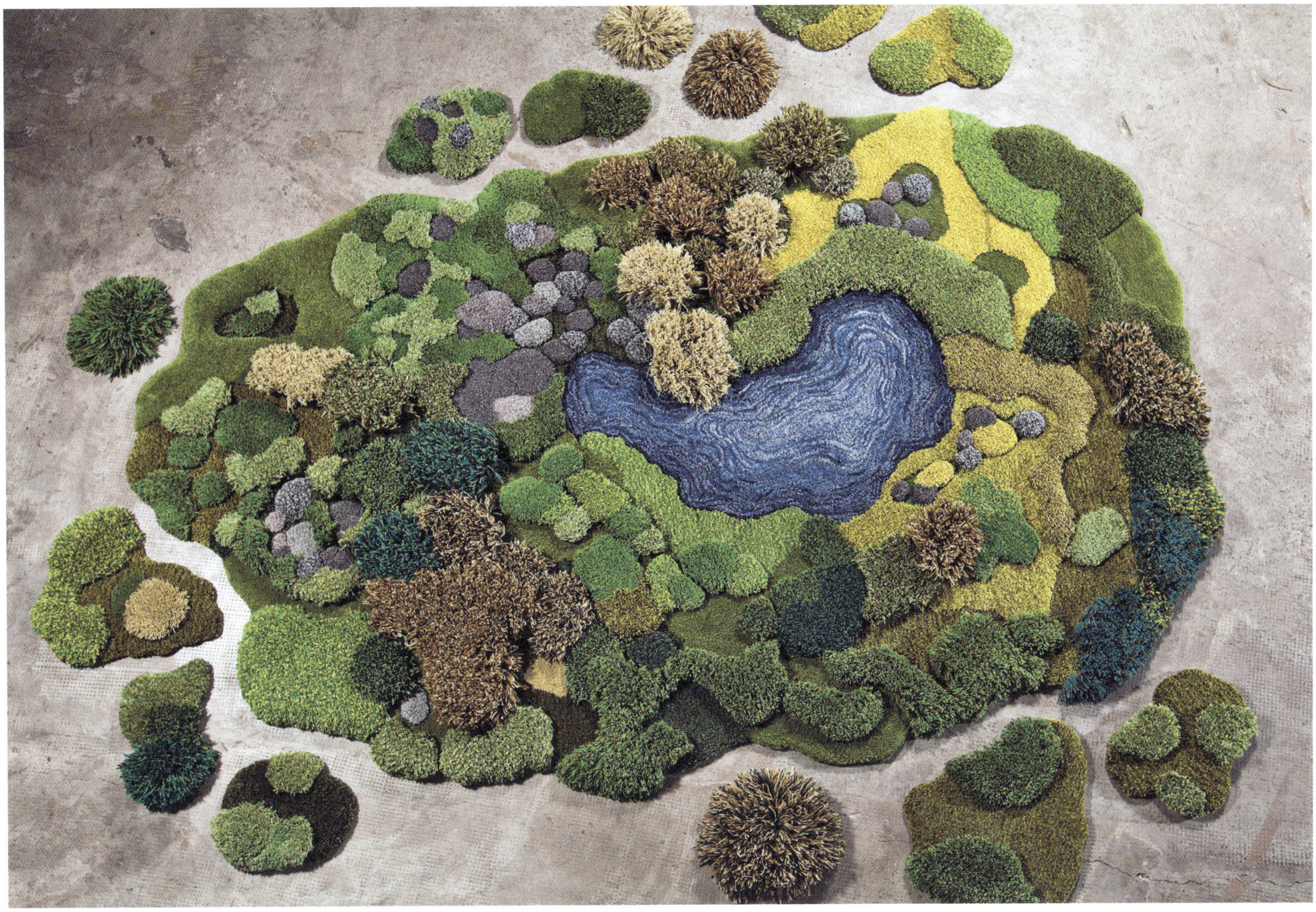

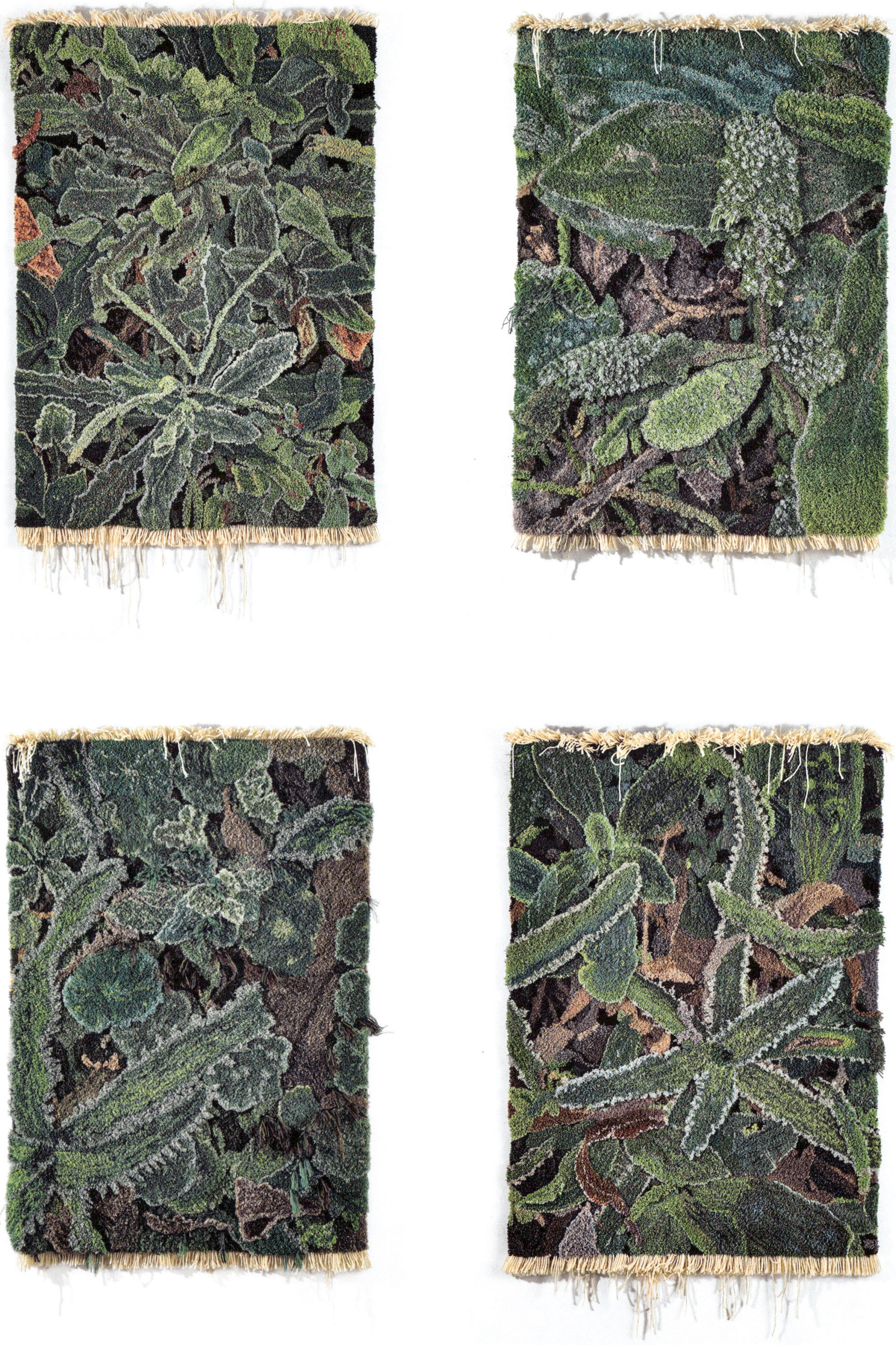

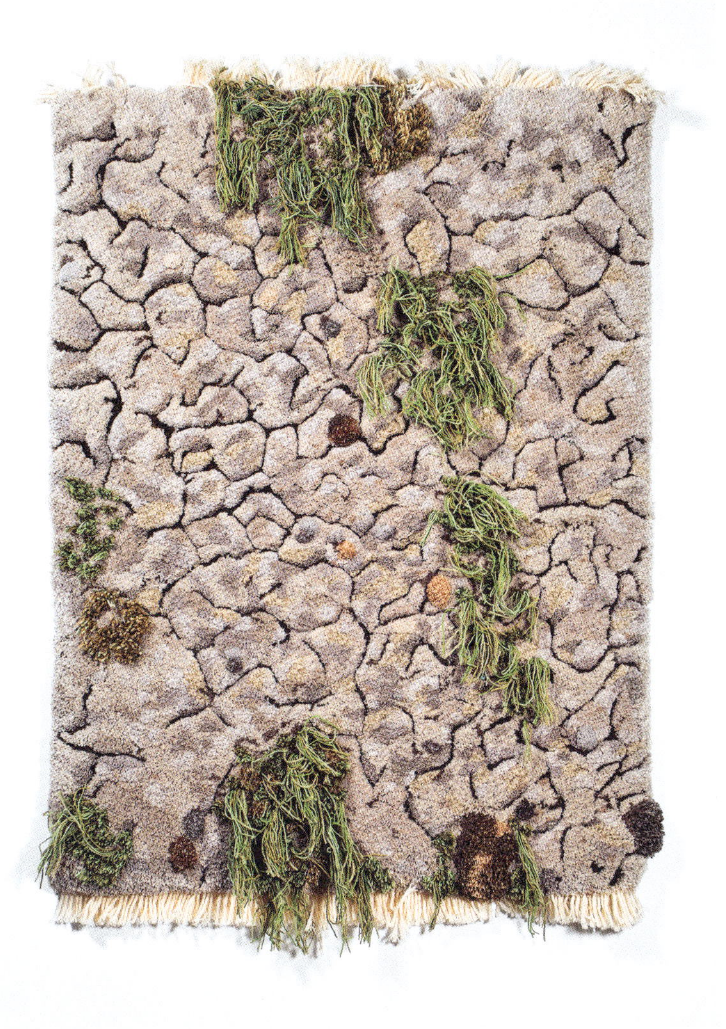
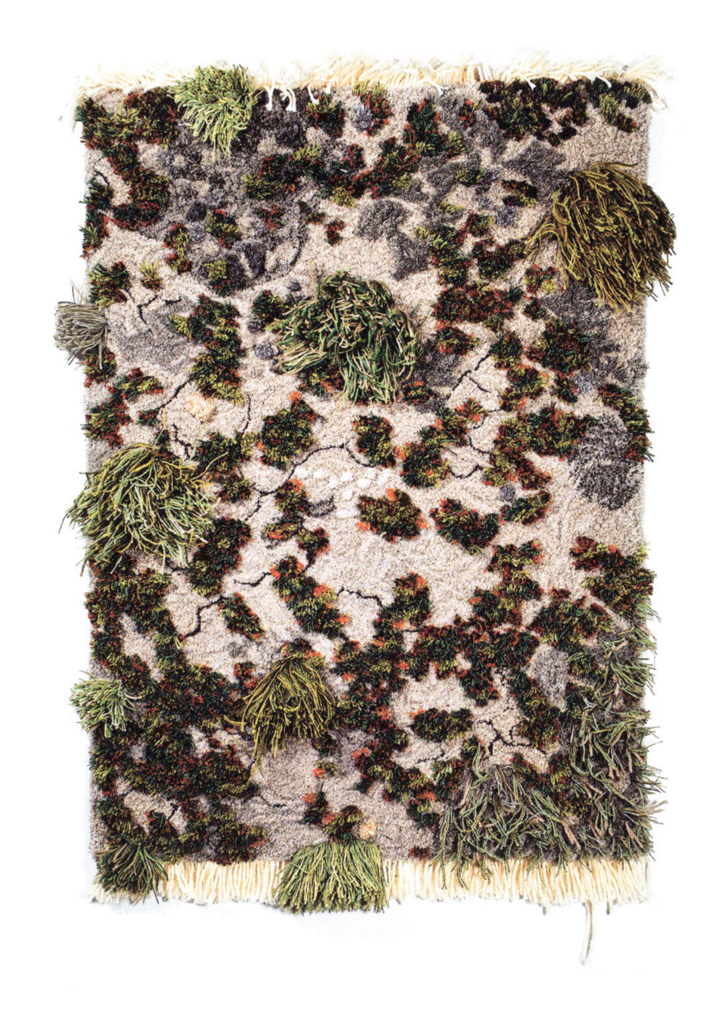
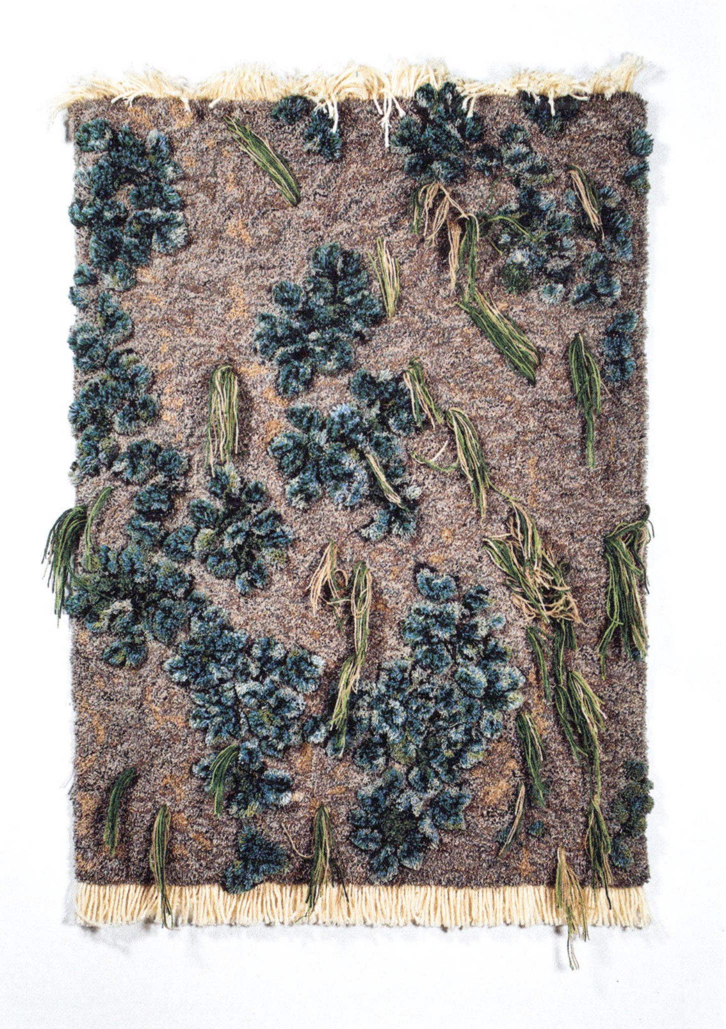
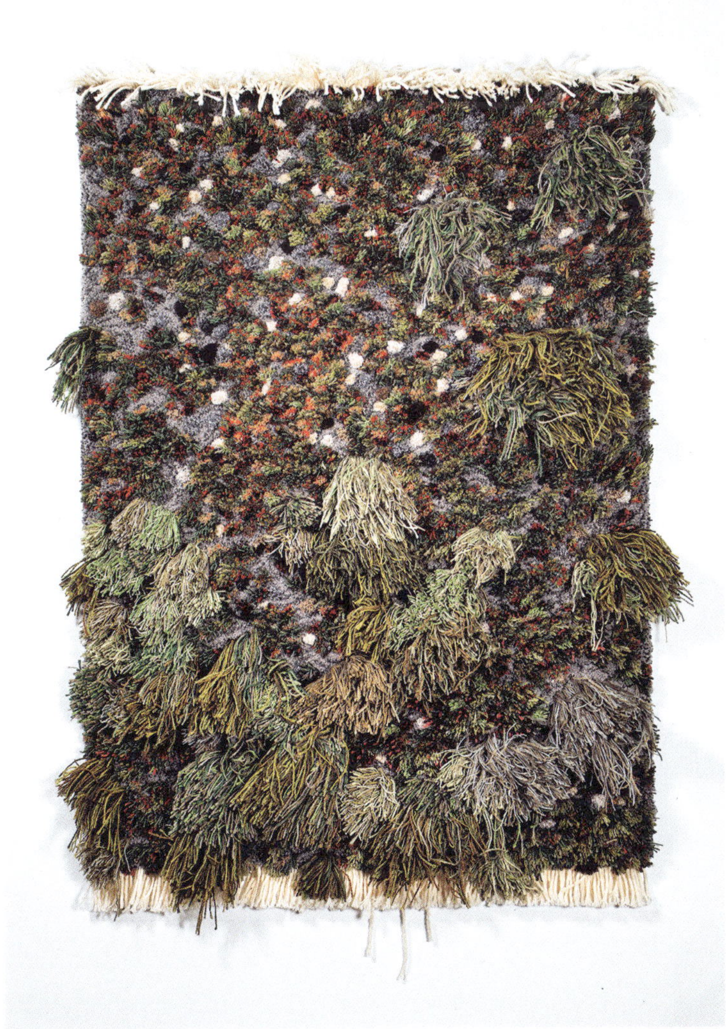

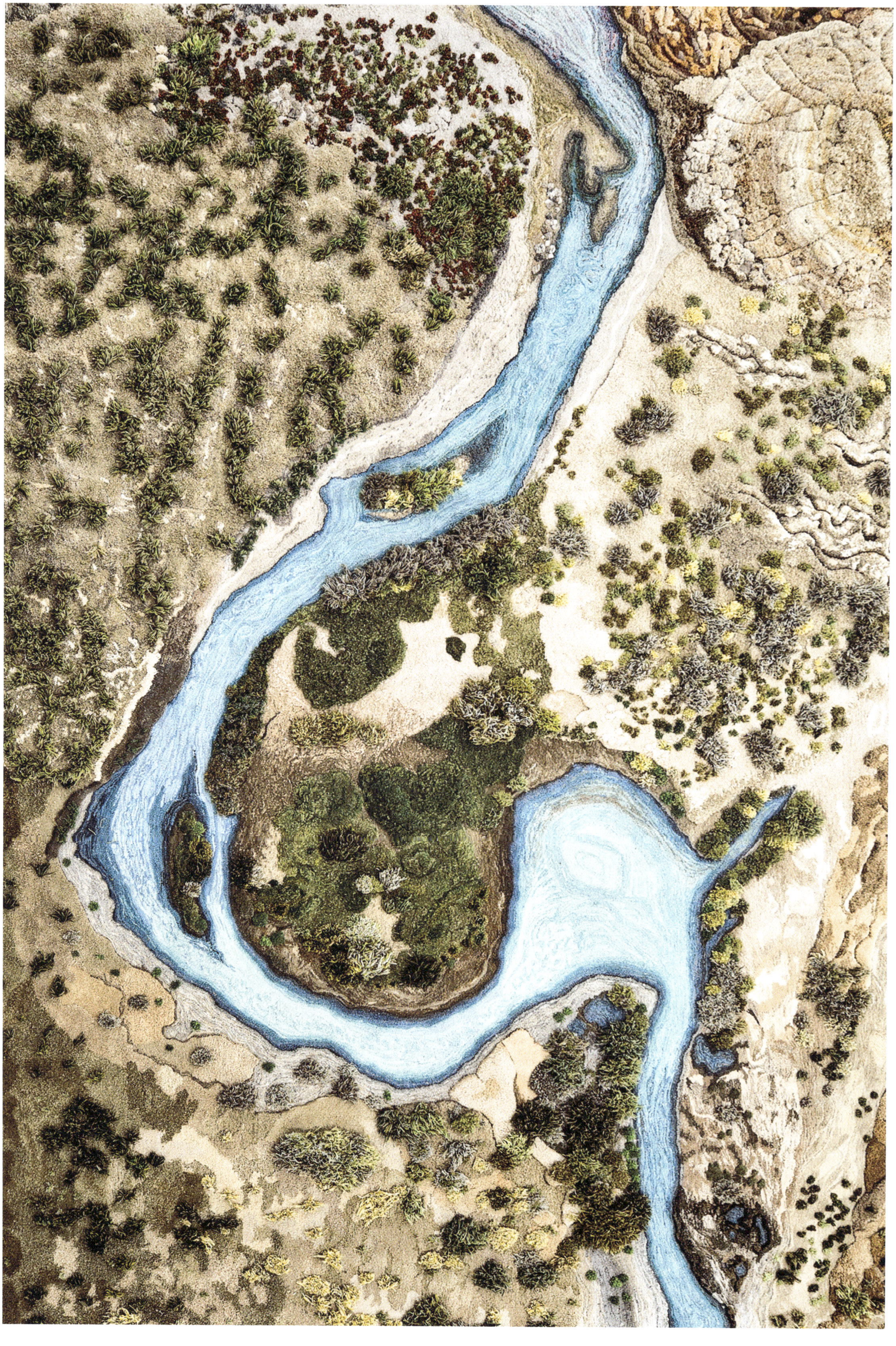

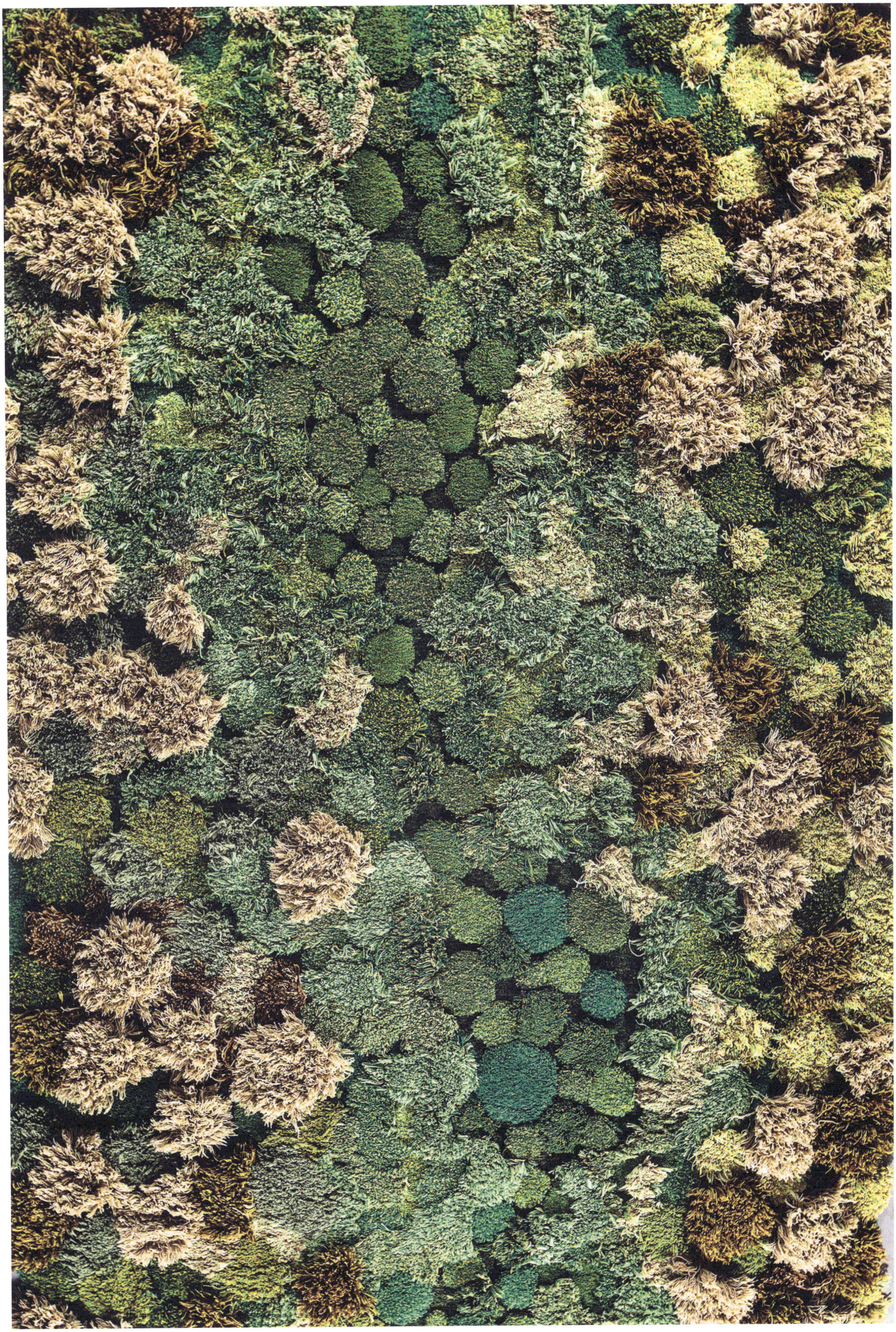

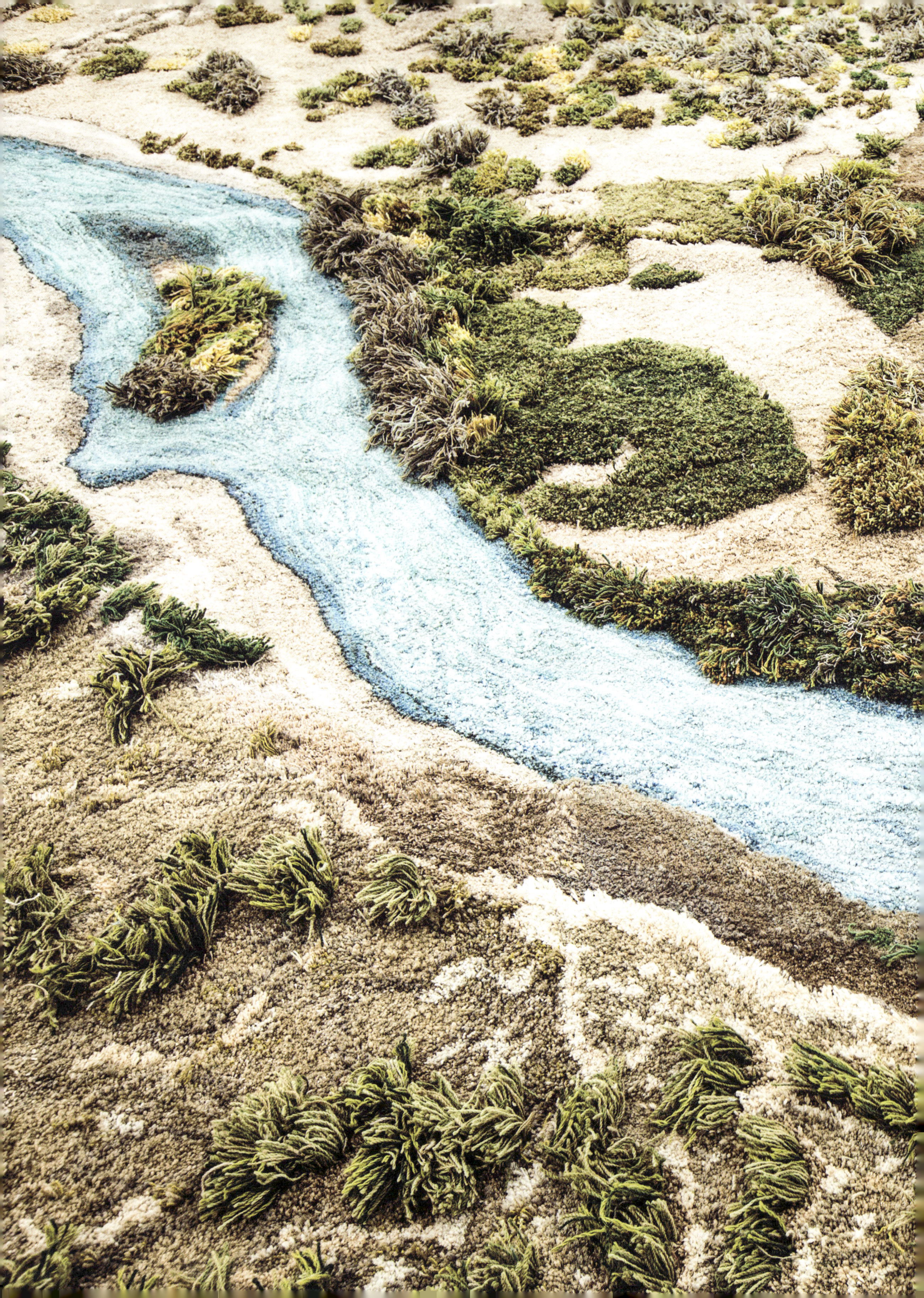

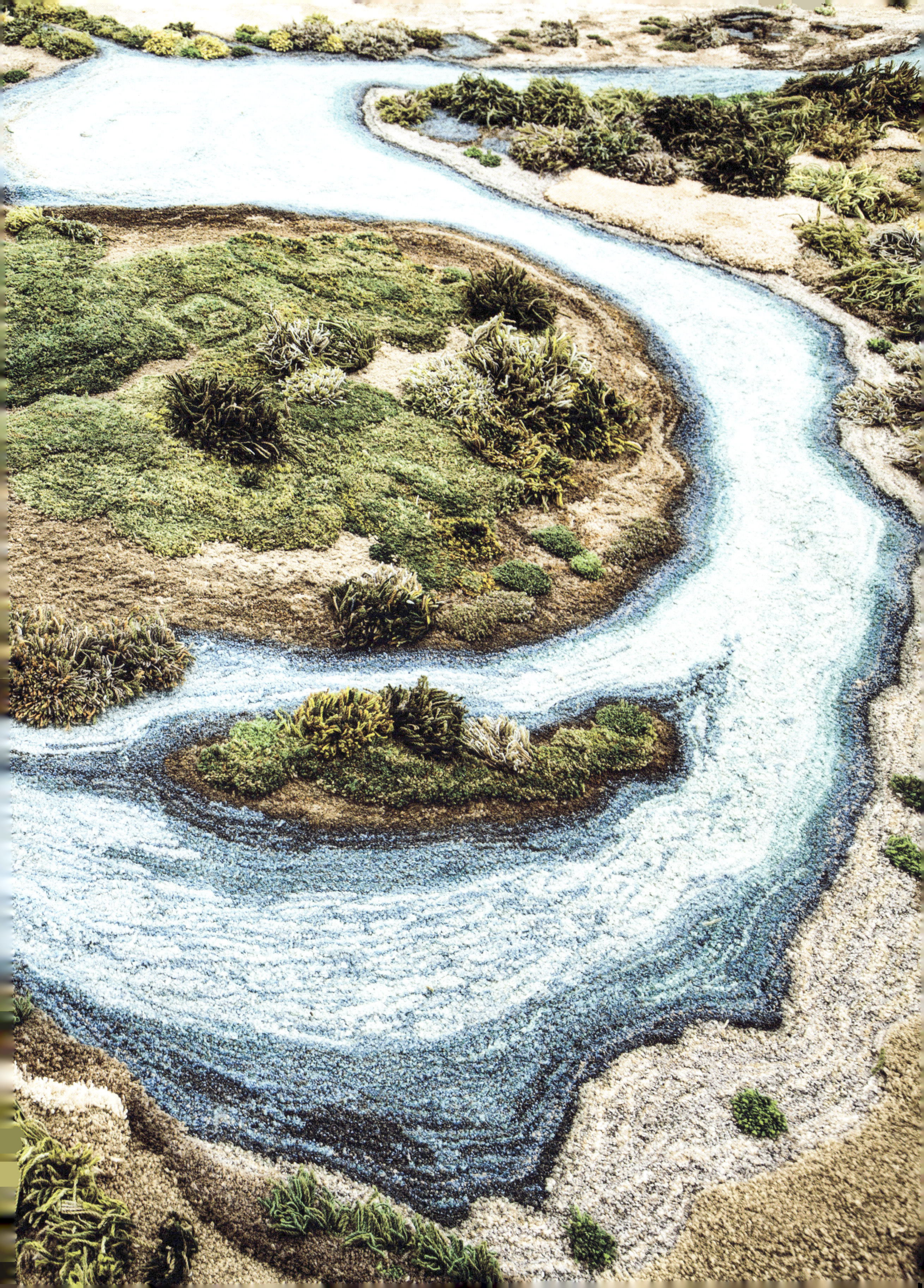

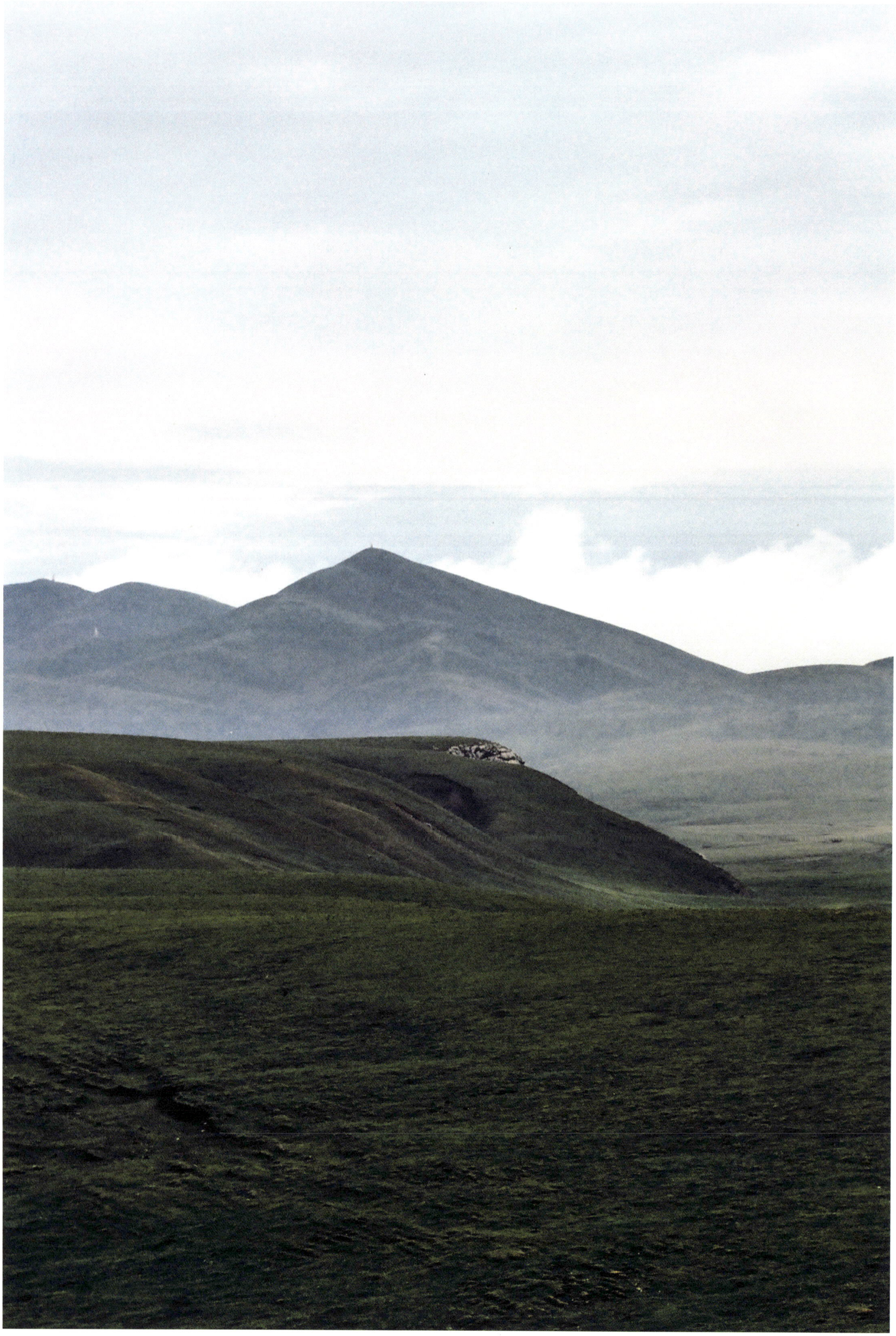

Wandi Kyi

Weaver

Ritoma,
Tibet Autonomous
Region, China

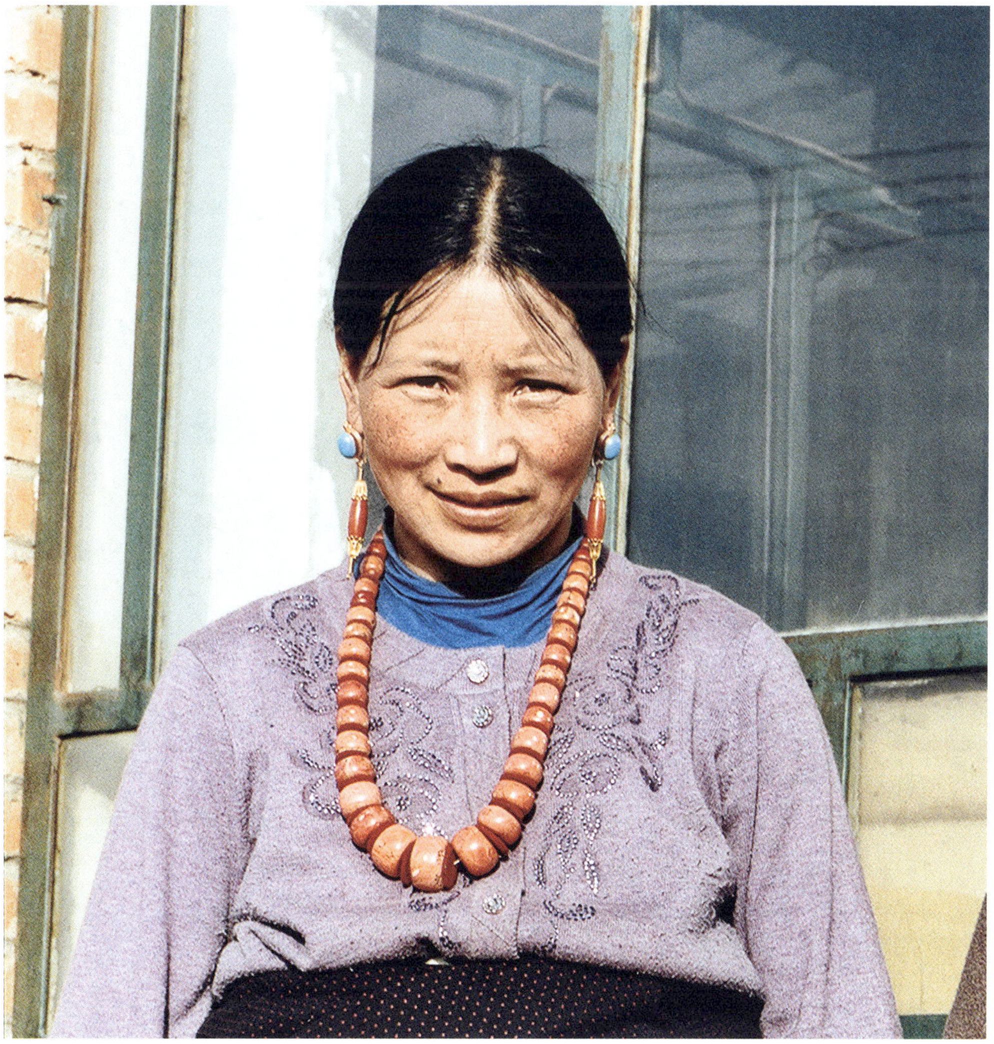

My name is Wandi Kyi, and I am a weaver and mother to three children. I am forty years old. When the Norlha workshop was created in 2007 by Kim and Dechen Yeshi, it had only ten employees. I began with spinning, then turned to weaving. Before the workshop was built, we worked in tents set up across the river. Weavers bear heavy responsibilities, but this profession suits my character.

From the age of five or six, I grew up in the pastures year round. My older brother and I stayed home to help our parents. My younger brother went to school, but I never learned to read or write. A nomad's life is difficult, but I look back on it fondly. I was lucky to live in wide-open spaces.

My older brother still works with my parents and looks after the animals. It is our custom that boys inherit the herd and girls are married off to other families or sent to school to get a job later. Twenty years ago, people in Ritoma were forced to sell their animals and become migrant workers in order to support their families. Traditionally, women also held a low social status. My parents didn't want me to marry young, and when Norlha was established, they were eager for me to work there. Half of the two hundred families in our village have one or more family members working at Norlha.

It was difficult when I first started learning to weave on the hand looms, because I could not read, or take notes. But I worked hard with the foreign experts who had been hired to train us. For the past two years, I have been learning how to weave with Jacquard looms.

In the workshop, we weave with yak wool called *khullu*. This is a soft under-down that grows beneath the yaks' long top coat and protects them from the cold in winter. I quickly took an interest in *khullu* because I grew up with yaks. I remember when I was a child, my mother had a felt cloak. It was waterproof, so when it rained, we wore the cloak during milking to protect us from the cold mountain climate. Now, when I work with yak *khullu*, I feel this connection with the pastureland, and it gives me a feeling of warmth and comfort.

Once a weaver has mastered the weaving process, they no longer need to count the steps and are free to recite prayers and mantras, which is exciting for a Buddhist. I think that Tibetans should not only believe in the Buddha, but also practice Buddhism in their daily lives. The most popular prayer is the six syllable mantra "Om Mani Padme Hung," which our elders recite every day. Regardless of what they are doing, the mantra calms them. Tibetans have a saying that no one teaches you this mantra: it comes down to you from your elders and fills your life, without having to be learned. In the workshop, the weavers work to the rhythm of the creaking looms and the soothing chants. Sometimes, however, I encounter technical problems—I worry about becoming less efficient or losing my reflexes, and I dream about it at night.

For the last ten years, I have had a stable income. I met the man who became my husband, I had children, and we built a house. These ten years have been a turning point in my personal life, one that took me from the pasturelands to the weaving workshop, and from being single to starting a family. I laid a foundation and have built a life for myself.

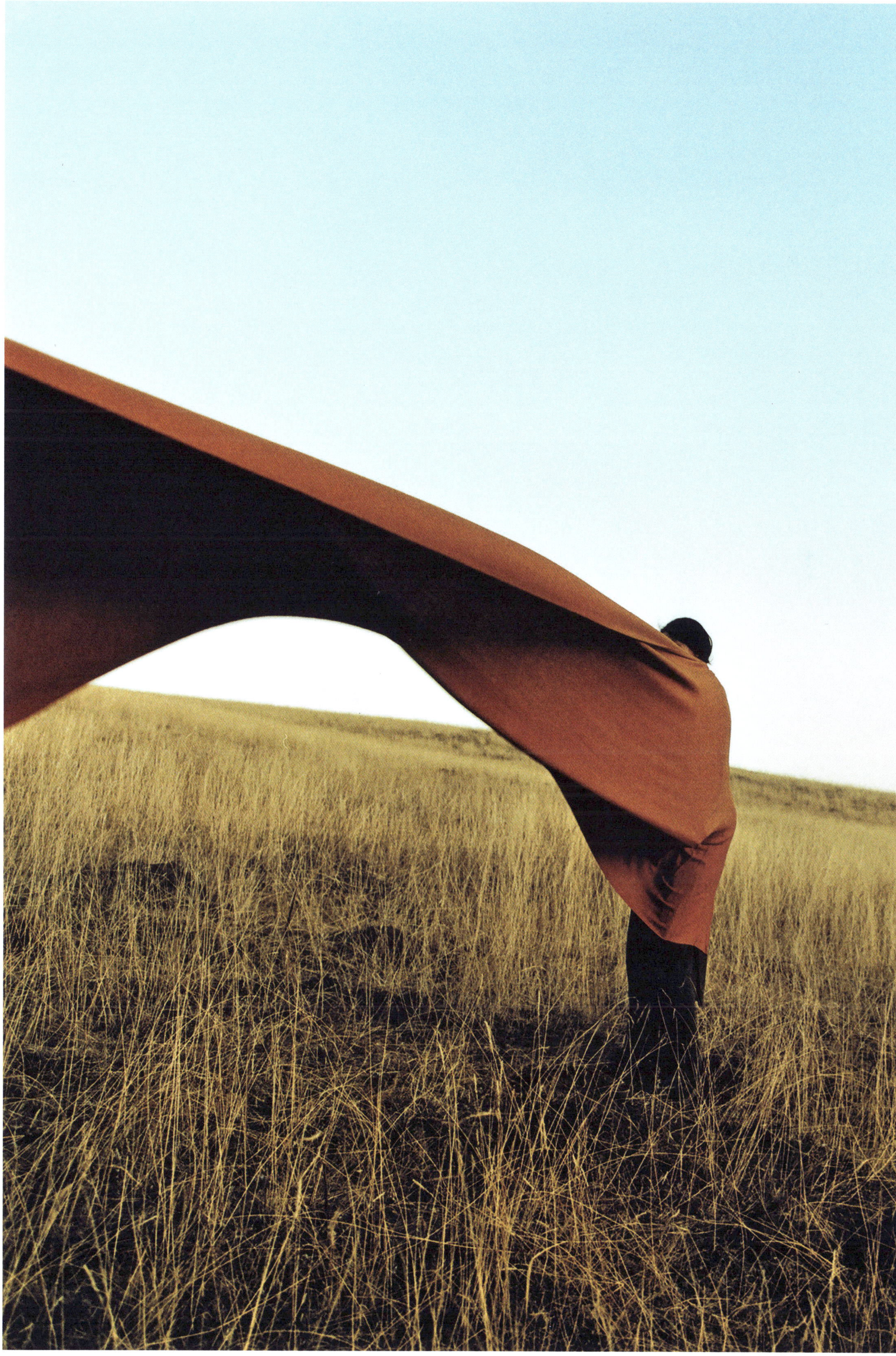

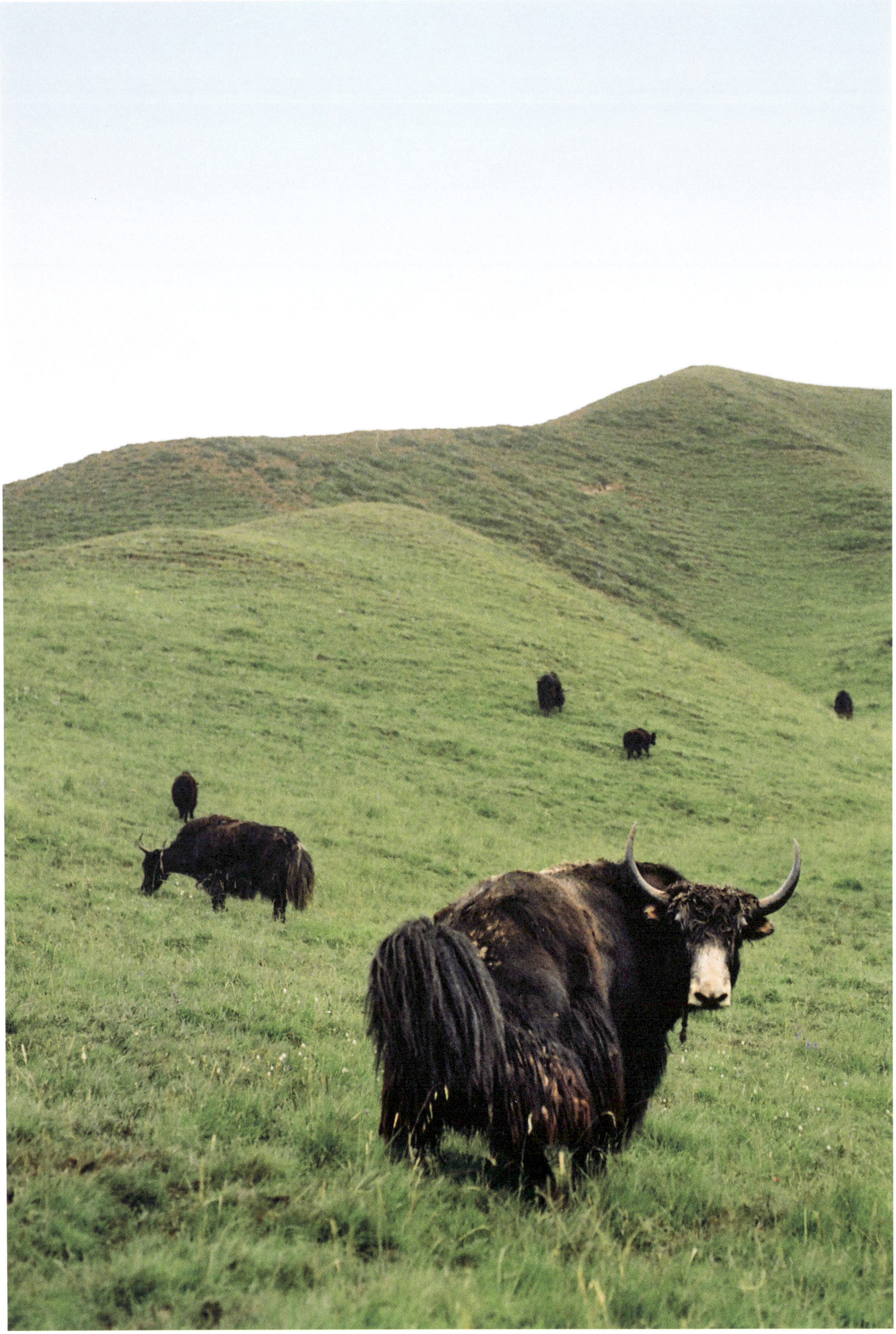

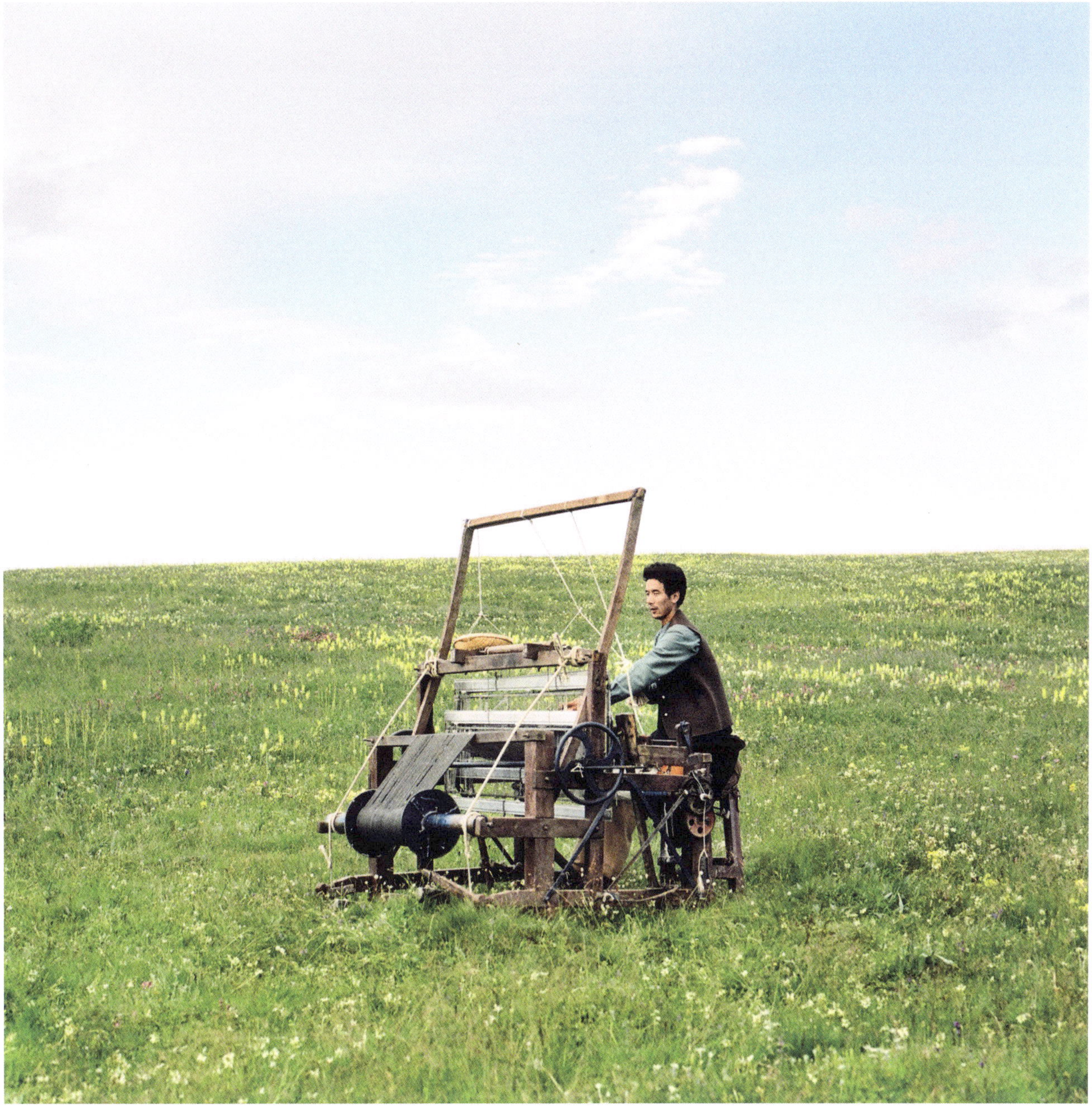

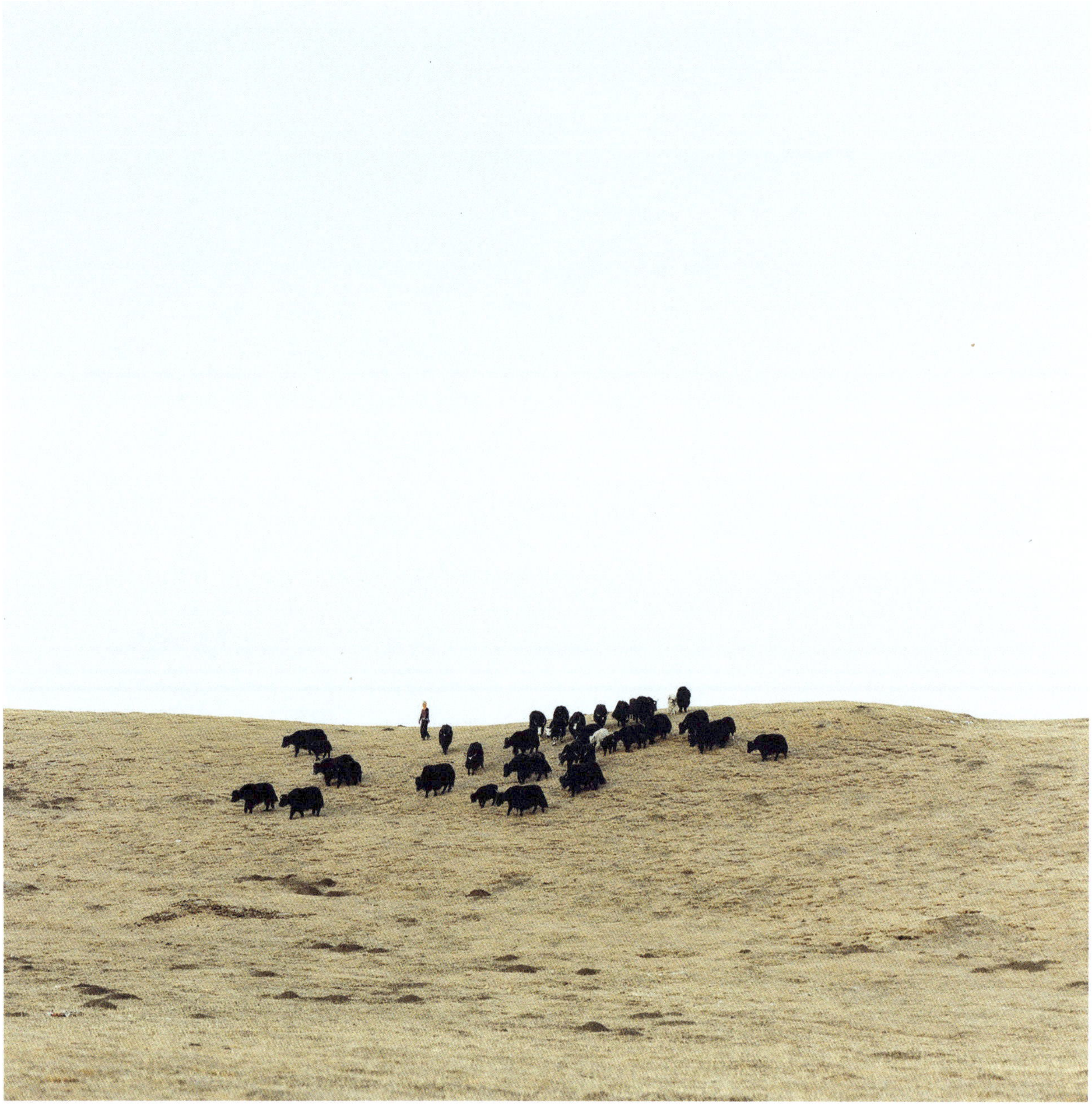

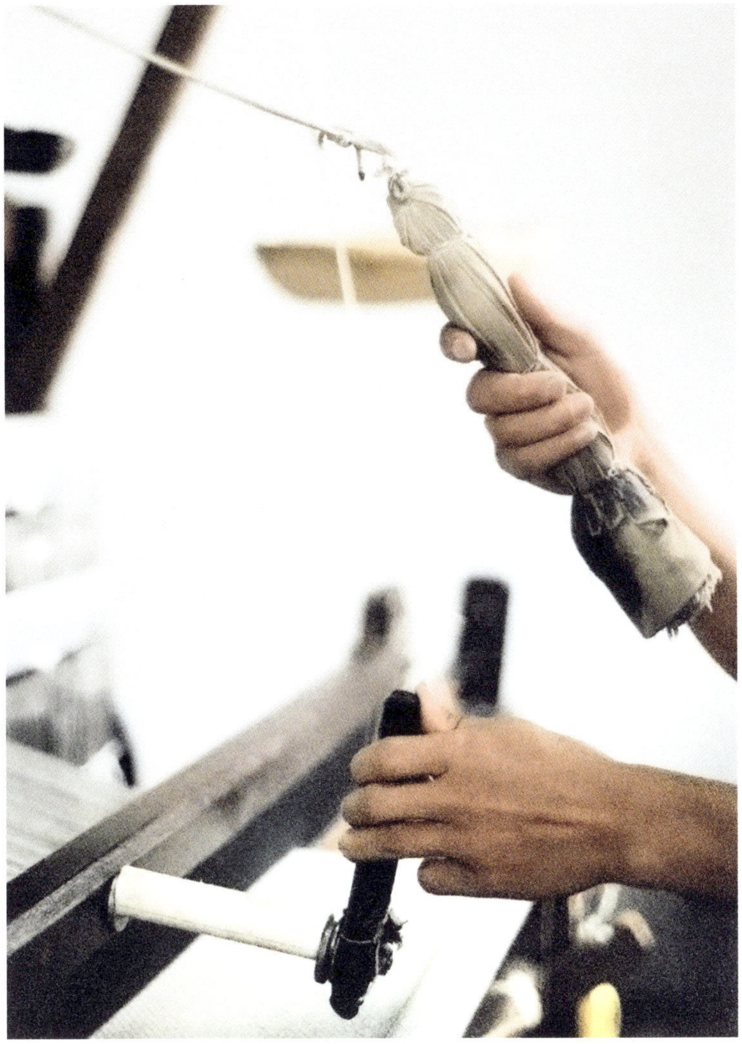
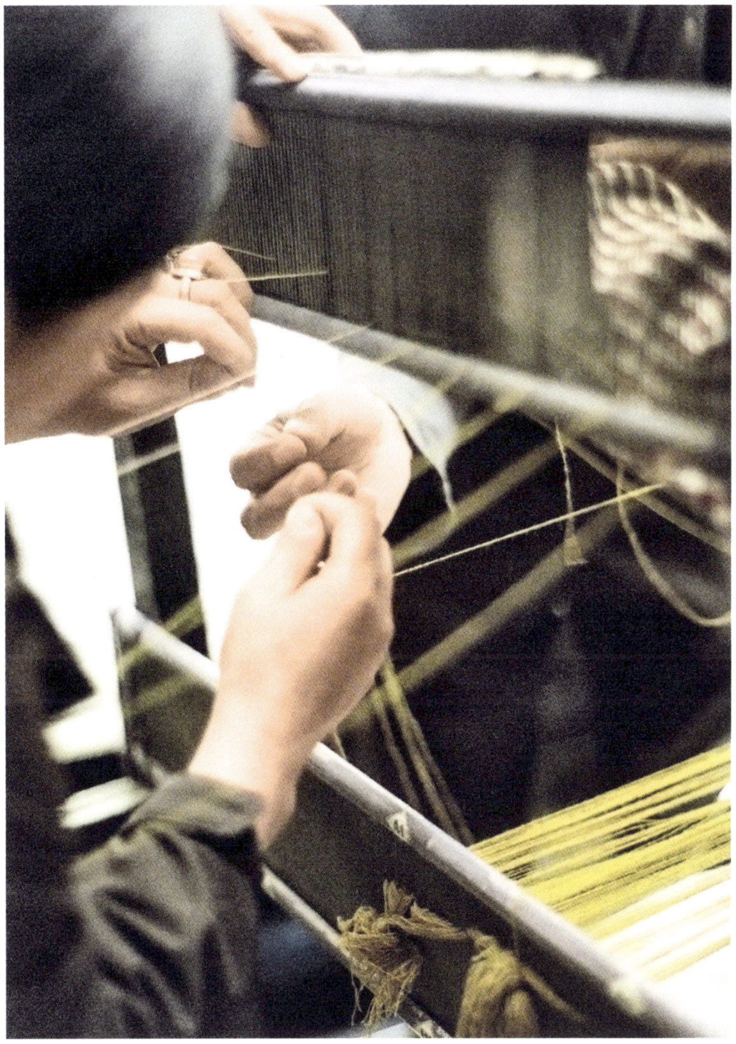
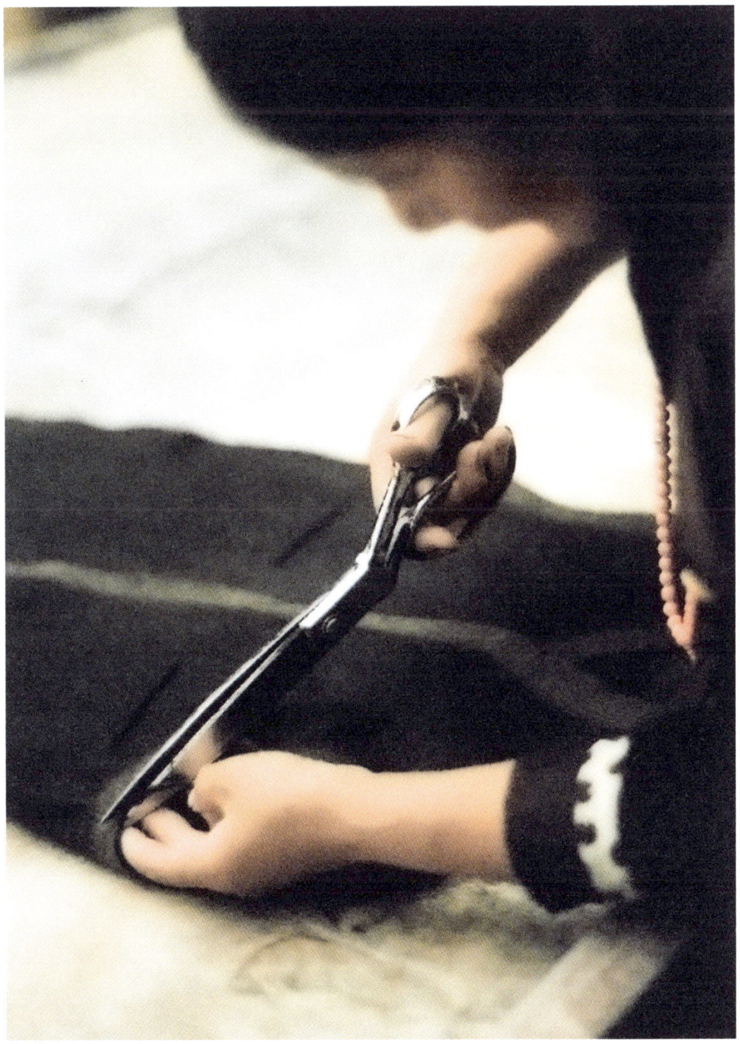
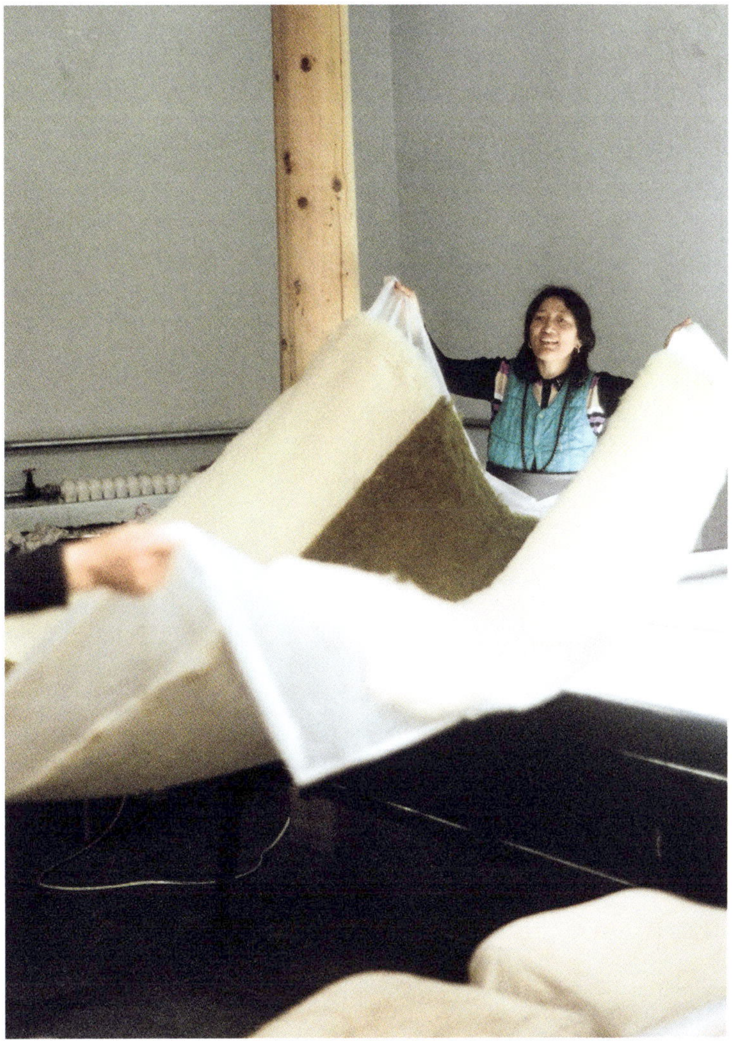

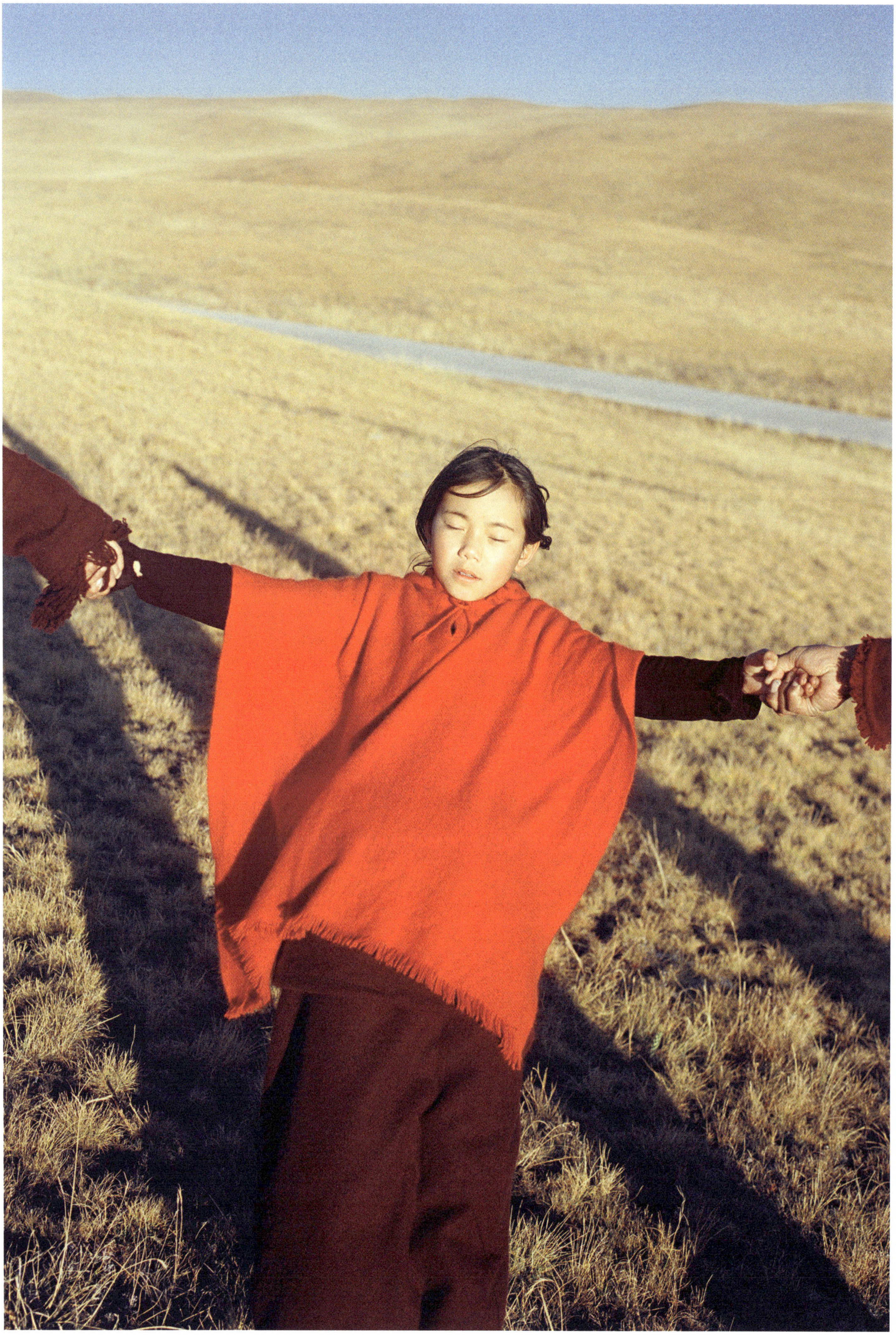

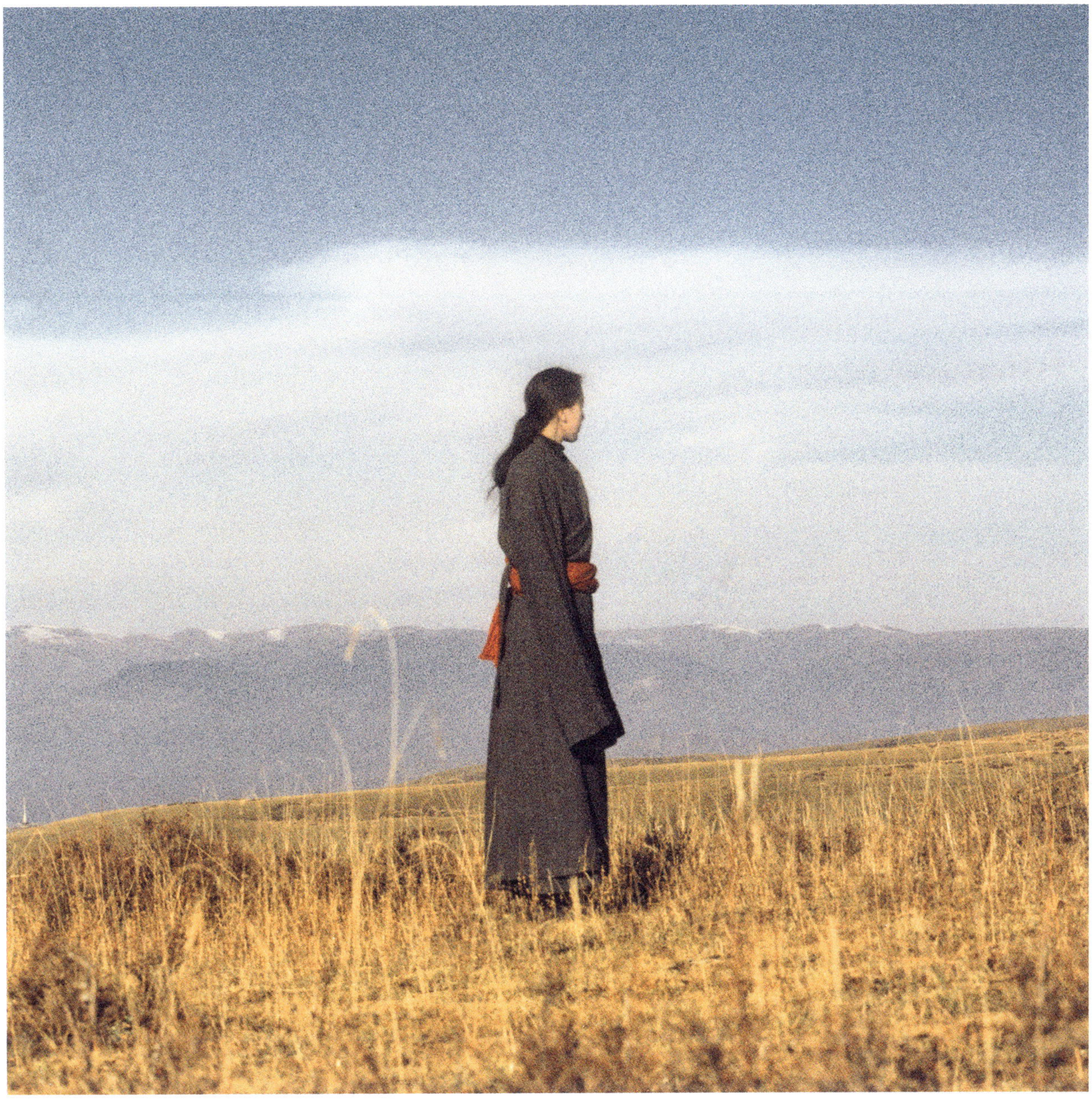

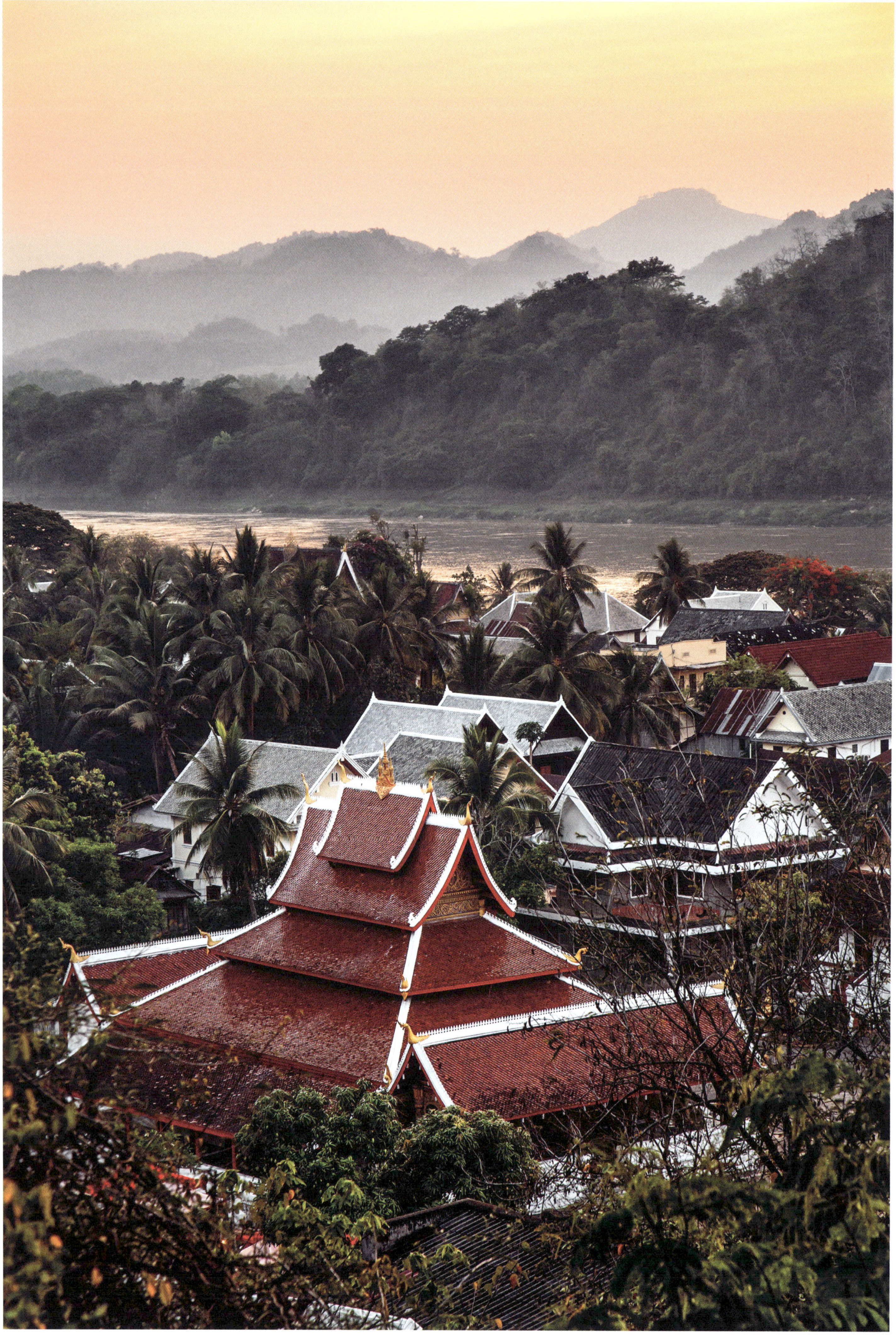

Tiao Nithakhong Somsanith

Embroiderer

Luang Prabang, Laos

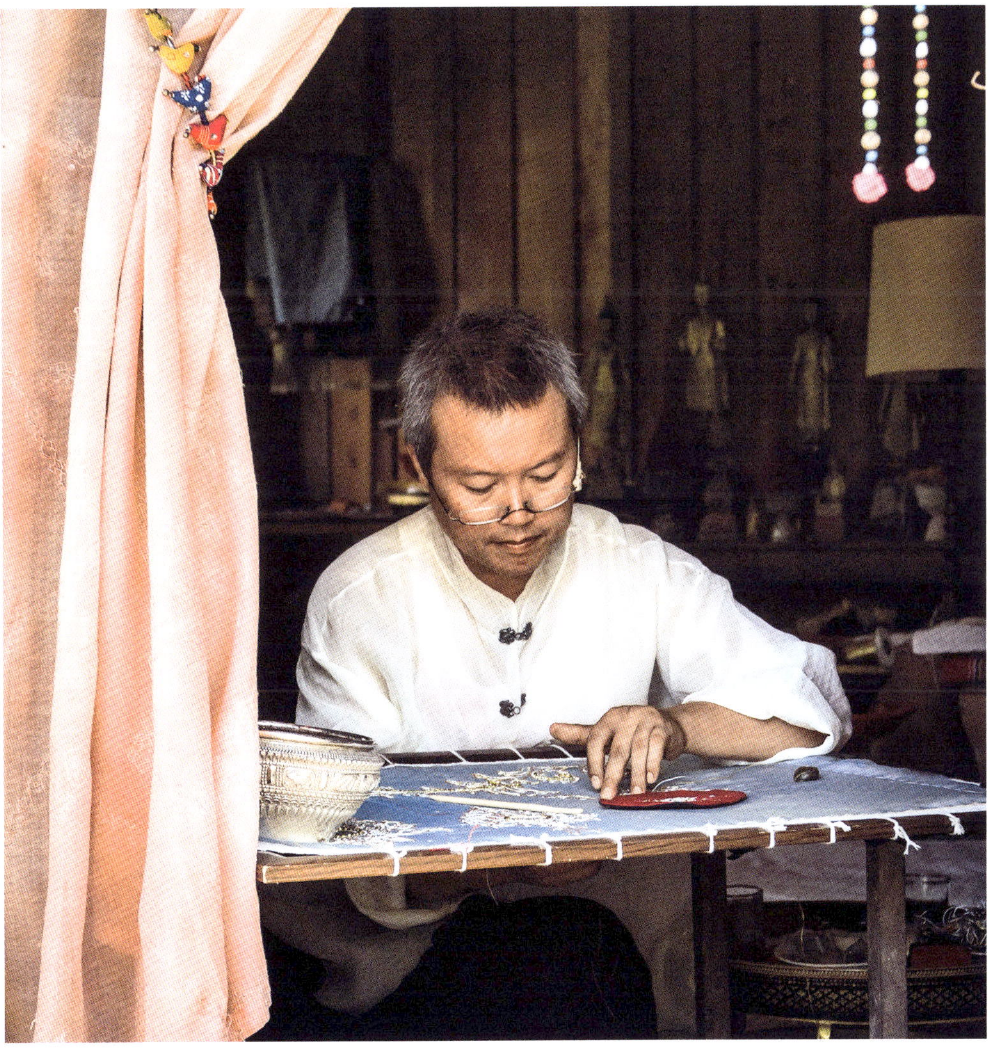

My name is Tiao Nithakhong Somsanith, and embroidery is my reason for living—and probably for dying. A skilled embroiderer cultivates a desire to embroider, out of necessity and out of pleasure, to become one with their work. To be an embroiderer is to have a humble understanding that the spirit begins and ends at the fingertips. There is no such thing as a "good" embroiderer!

As a child, I lived in Luang Prabang: a mysterious city full of paradoxes and animated by rituals and beliefs in "another" world. In Laos, embroidery is not a profession, it is a way of life—a way of thinking in stitches, thread, and needles. We embroider, just as we cook, to create together or, just as we garden, for well-being. The arts are all connected: embroidery, gilding, fresco painting, lacquer, flower arranging, to name but a few.

The art of embroidery was passed down to me from my mother, grandmothers, and aunts: they all belonged to the royal court. As a young boy, I accompanied them to the embroidery workshop, and I learned by watching them work. Today, I repeat their movements when I embroider.

In Laos, embroidery is women's work, but men create the patterns. Forms cut from tissue paper serve as words and symbols for the composition and arrangement of a work. Apprentices and masters use them as guides. I learned this technique from artisans at the royal palace when I was four years old. A pattern is alive and fragile, like life. For contemporary works such as the series *The Impermanence of Life*, I work directly on tree leaves in various stages of decomposition. The "thing" is already present and is in itself enough, providing the only framework that I need.

Creating the outline is like dancing with the gold thread: the needle sets the rhythm and the body follows along. If you try to pull on the thread, it resists. Embroidery is a living art. Mastering it requires you to be in harmony with the forces of nature and the hereafter, to venerate Buddha and the ancestors, the spirits of places, the earth, and water. Freedom of movement comes when you are no longer yourself and you succeed in forgetting the objective, when the needle and thread become one and exist in symbiosis with us. When you feel like you are floating, and you feel the Master's hands guiding your own.

In Laos, we have always preferred sparkle over shine; that's why we darken the thread, so the gold settles to the bottom of the silk and acquires a patina over time. Just as wrinkles are a sign of wisdom, patina is the mark of nature and highlights the events of a life.

Today, this craft is in jeopardy, partly because of tourism and partly because of fashion and vain desire.

I left Laos in 1984. The suffering experienced by exiles such as me comes not so much from losing our country or homeland, but from losing everything that makes us "us": the small things we love, the affection of those who raised us, the fragrance of secret gardens, the scars from childhood antics, the taste of our personal "madeleines."

Laos has seen many conflicts. These force us to realize that salvation lies in learning to live from day to day. Building your life on the tangible is a utopian concept. During all these years, embroidery has enabled me to overcome exile. Gold thread is my umbilical cord; it connects me to my parents and to my ancestors. Today, my workshop is my home: between France—land of exile, exchange, identity, and existence—and Laos, a wellspring of inspiration and fertile ground for my creations. This back and forth is vital and essential for me.

To this day, I am proud to be able to think in embroidery and live according to the rhythm of the stitches.

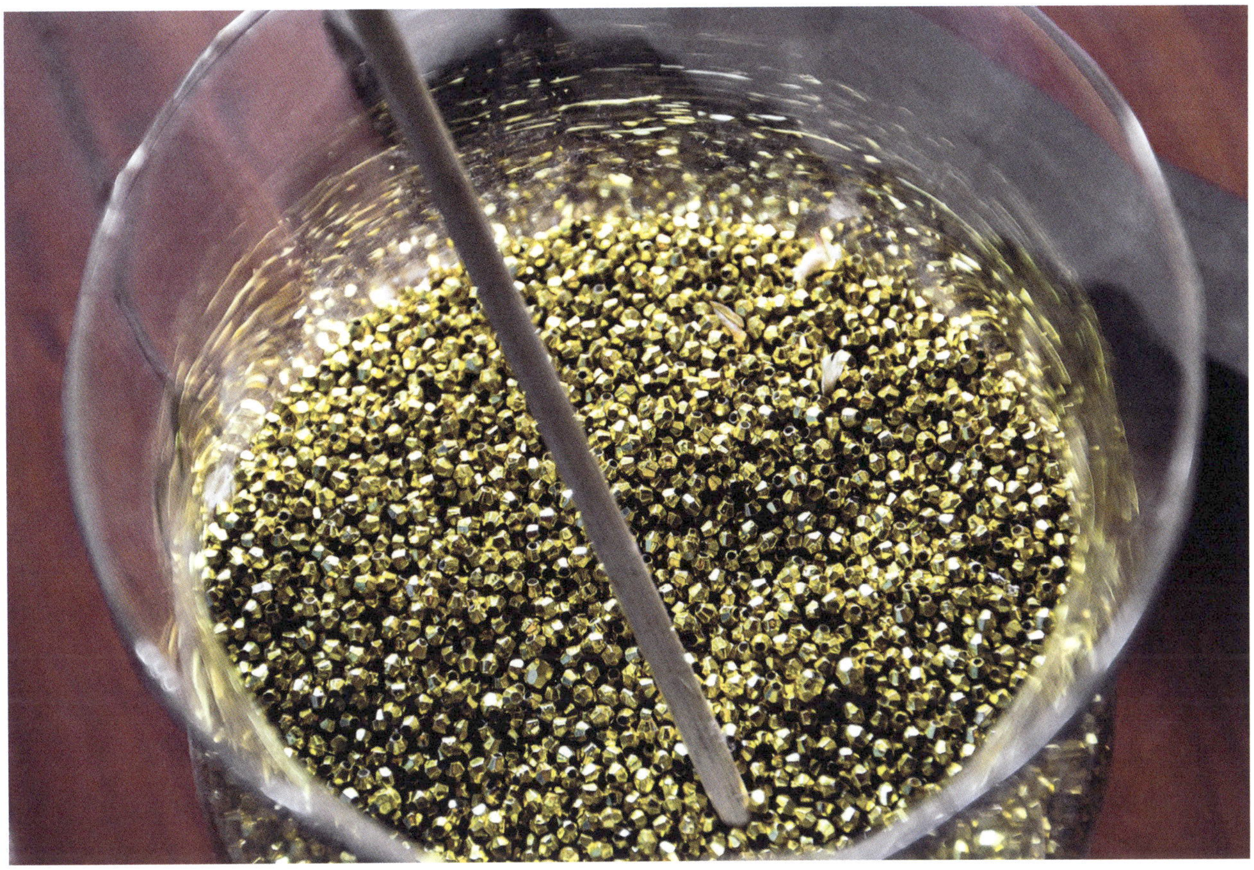

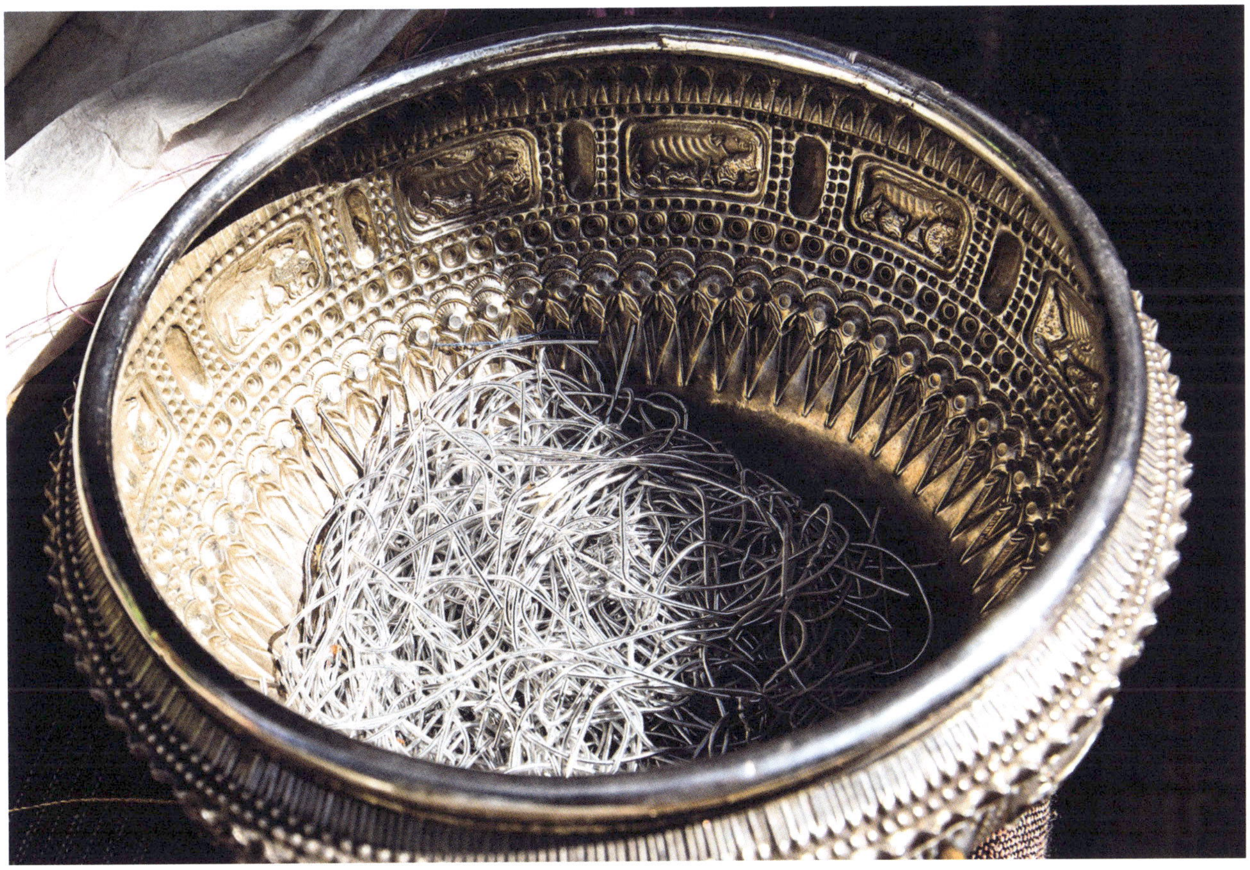

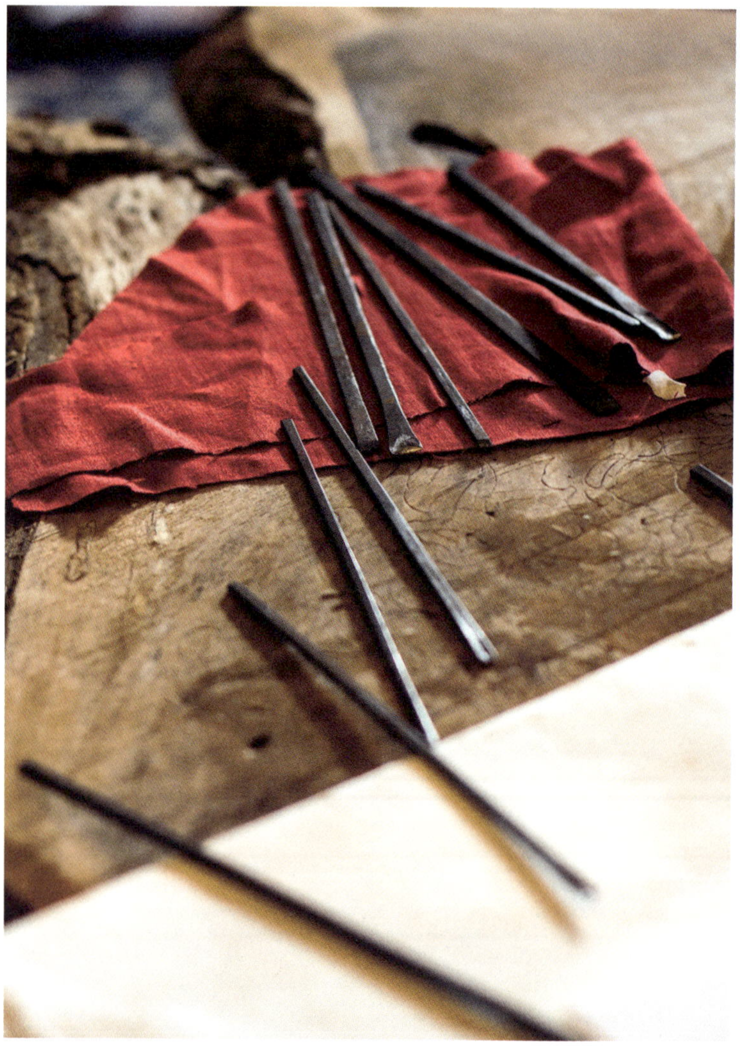
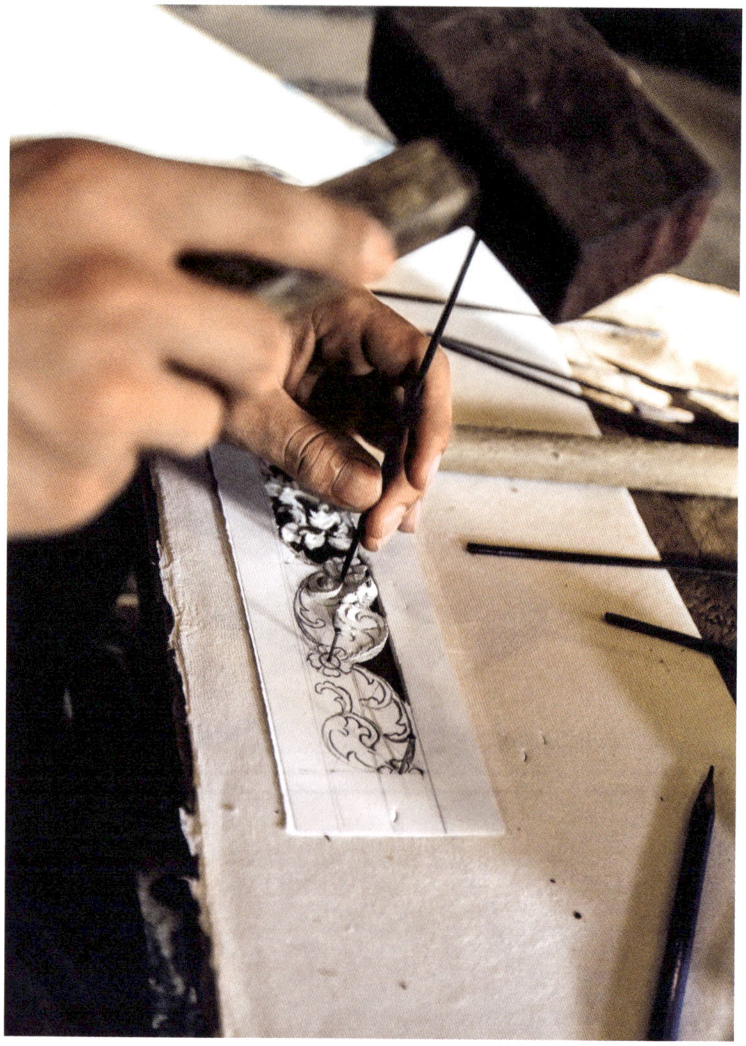
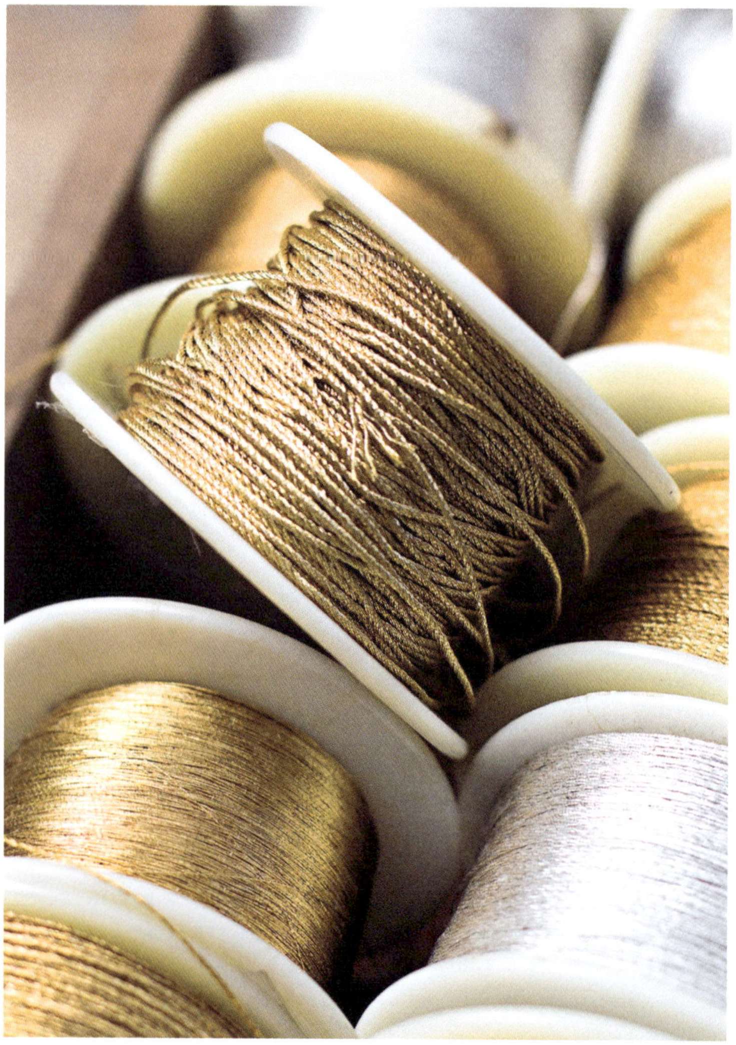
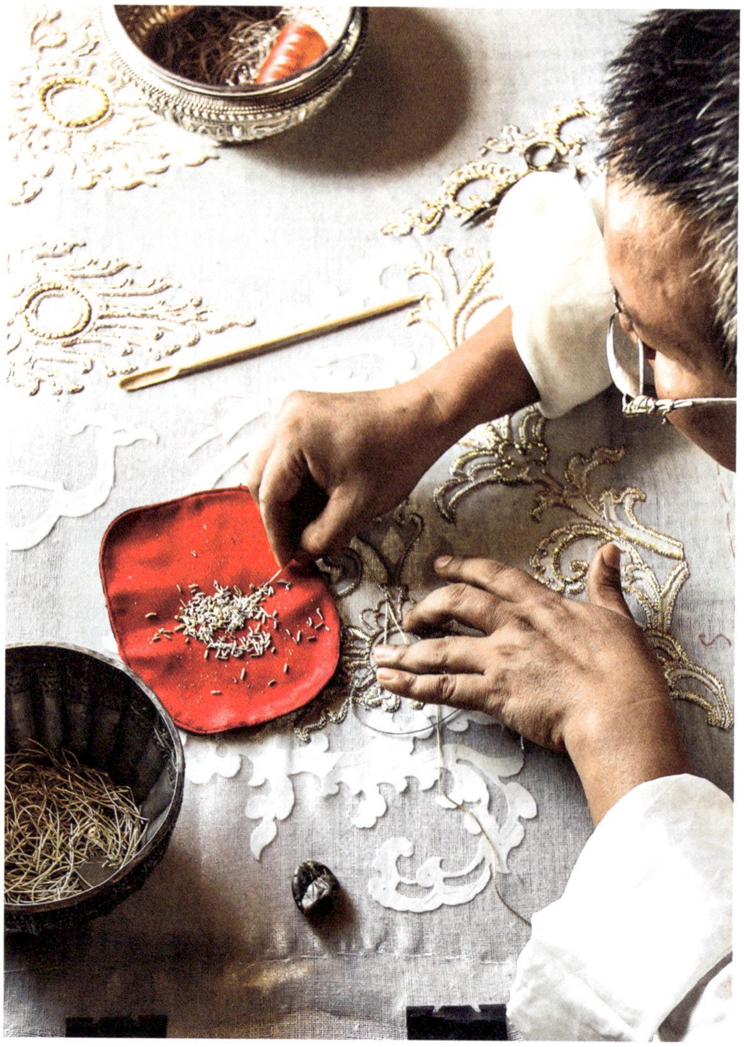

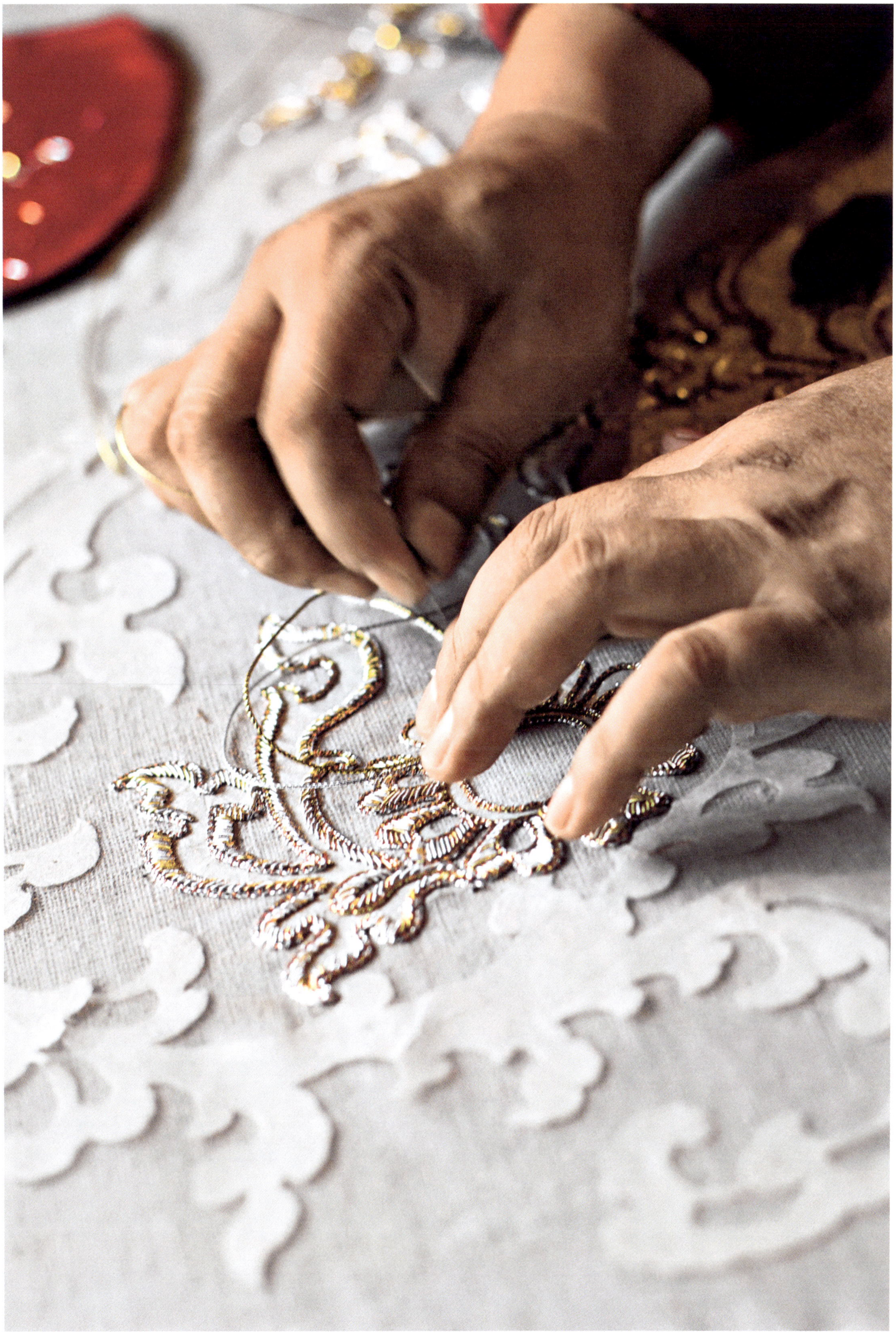

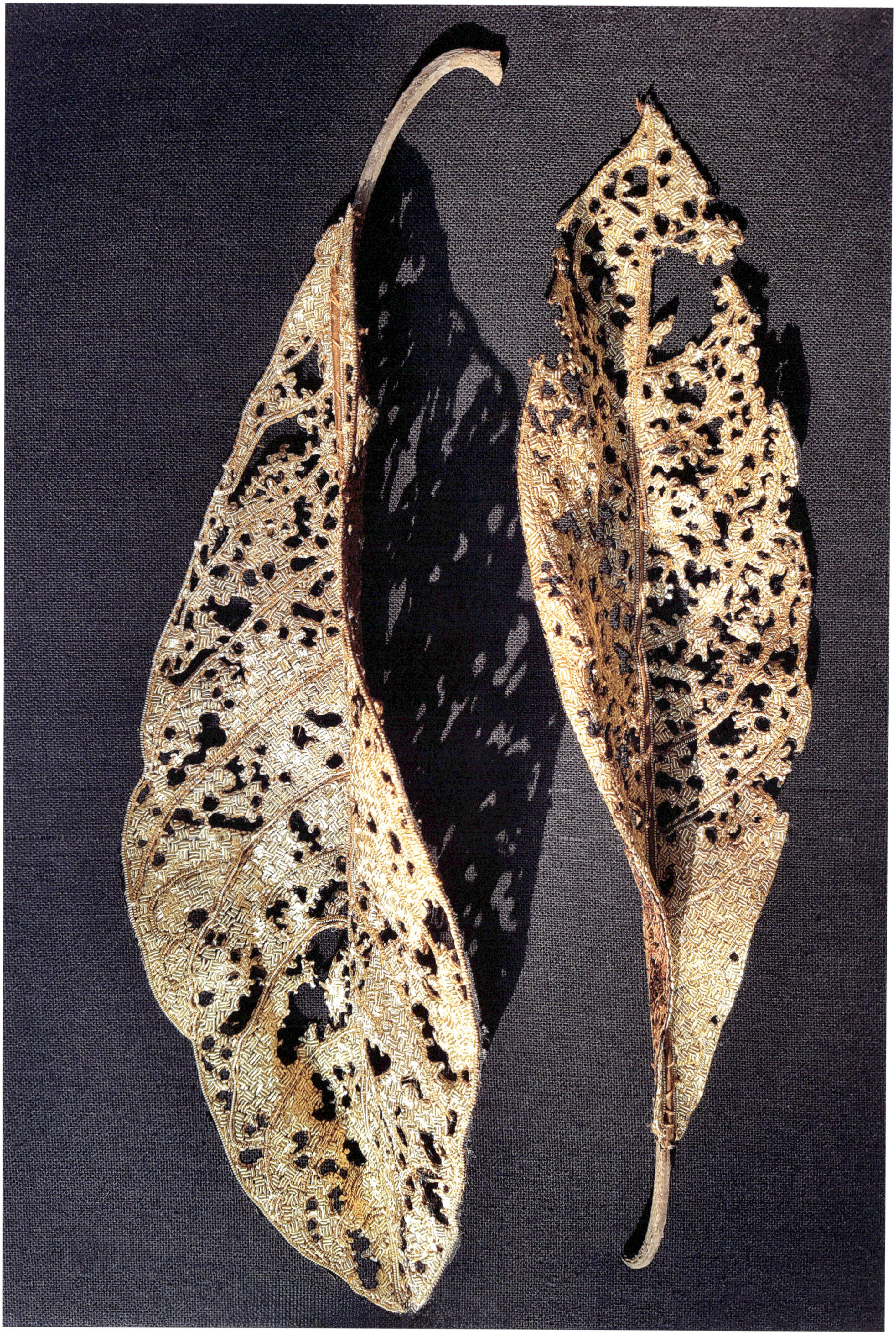

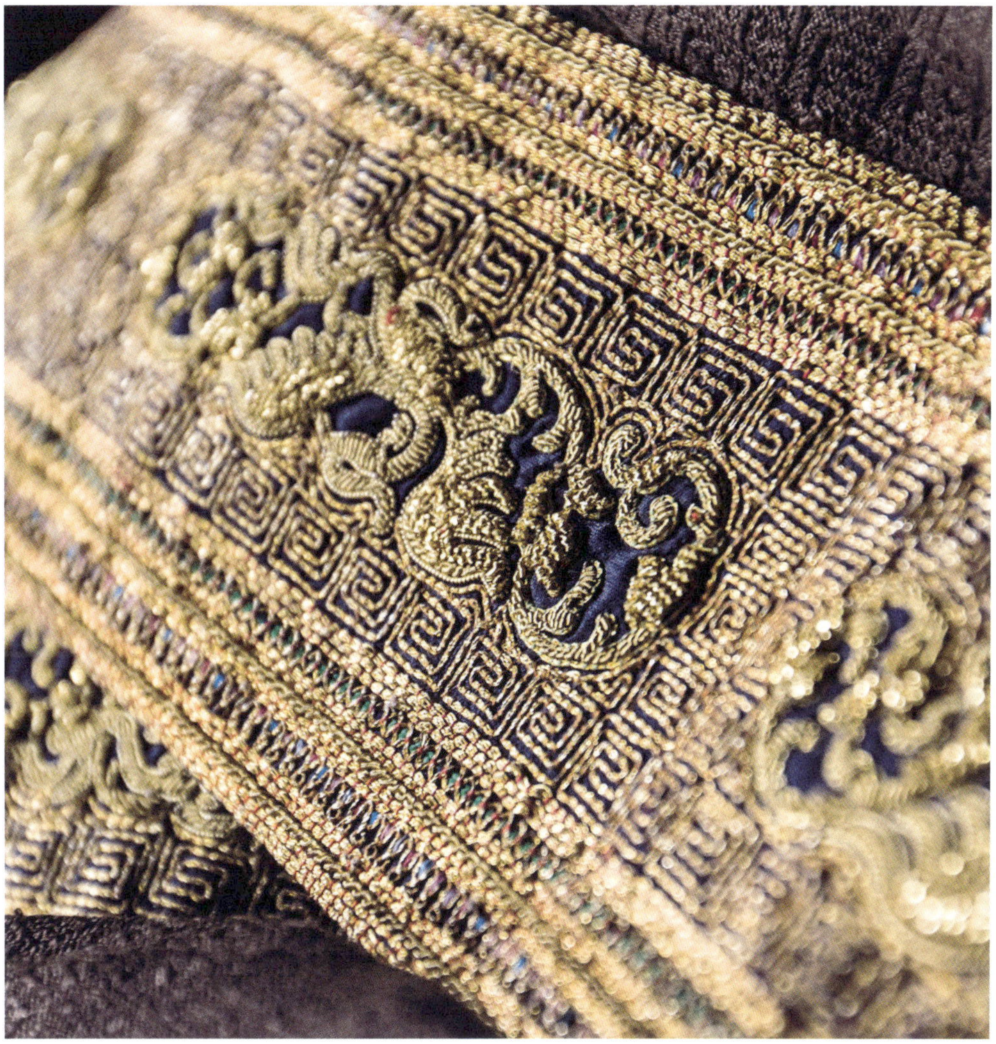

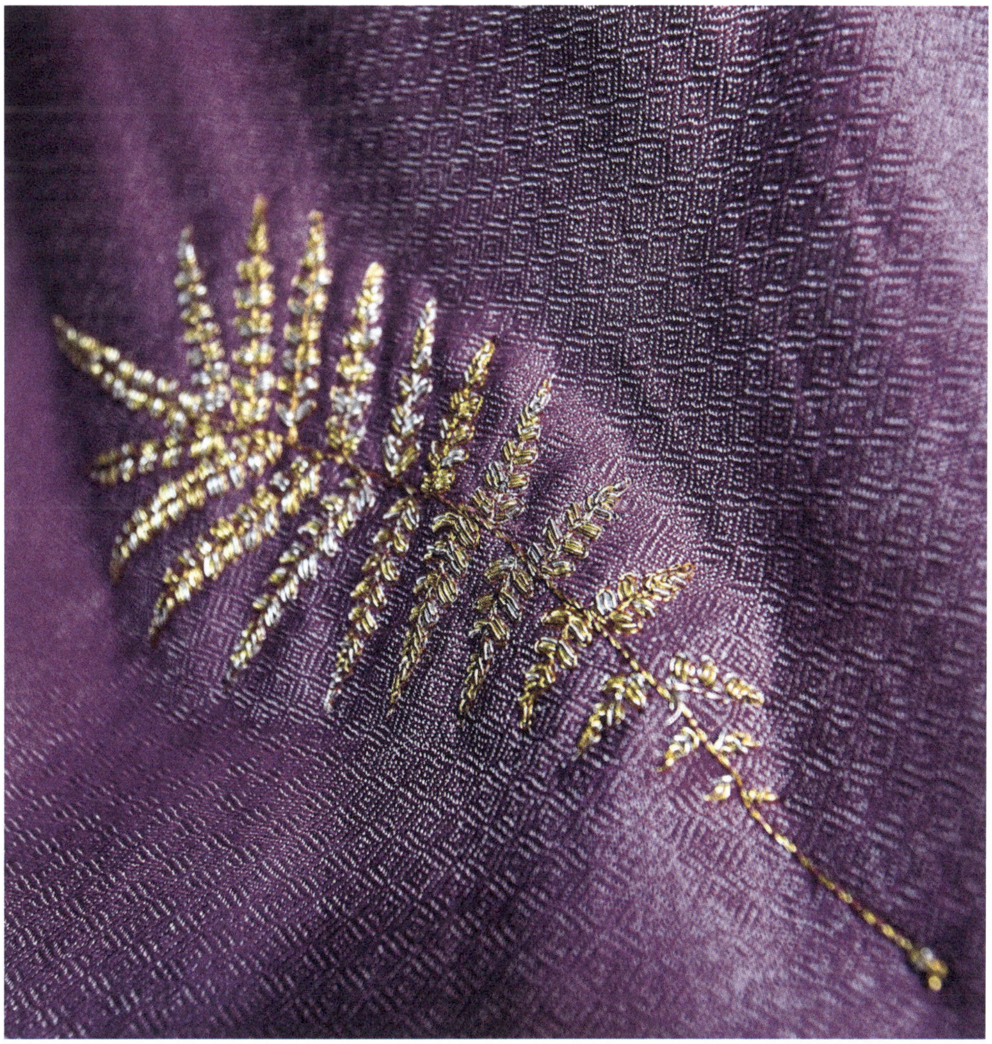

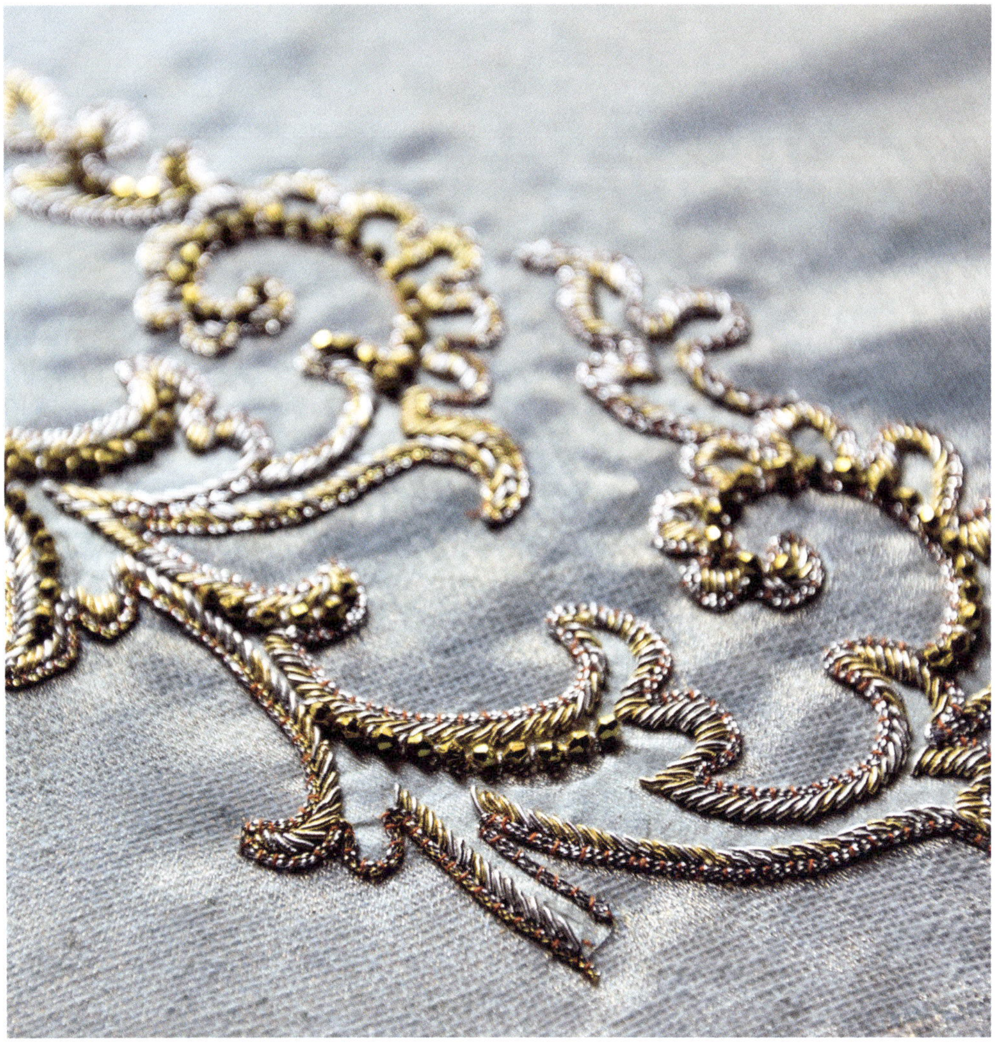

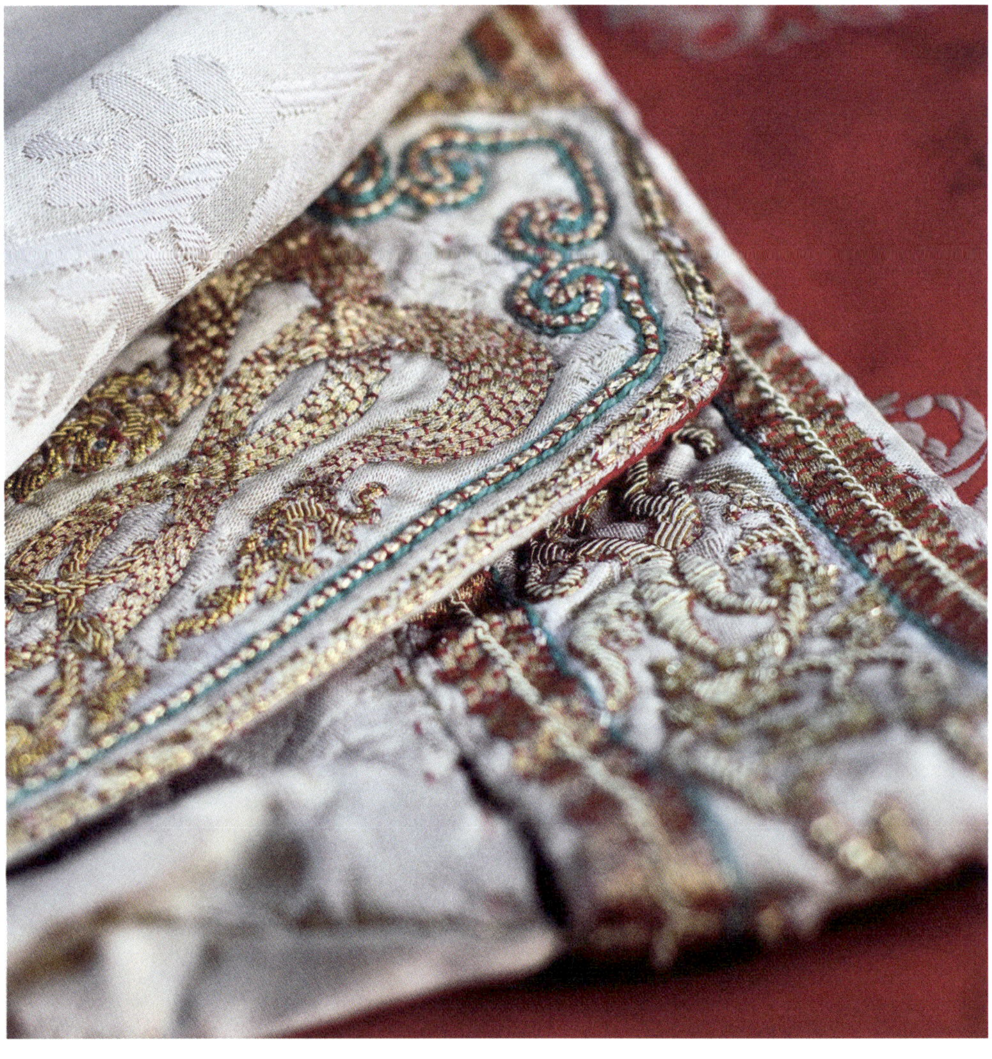

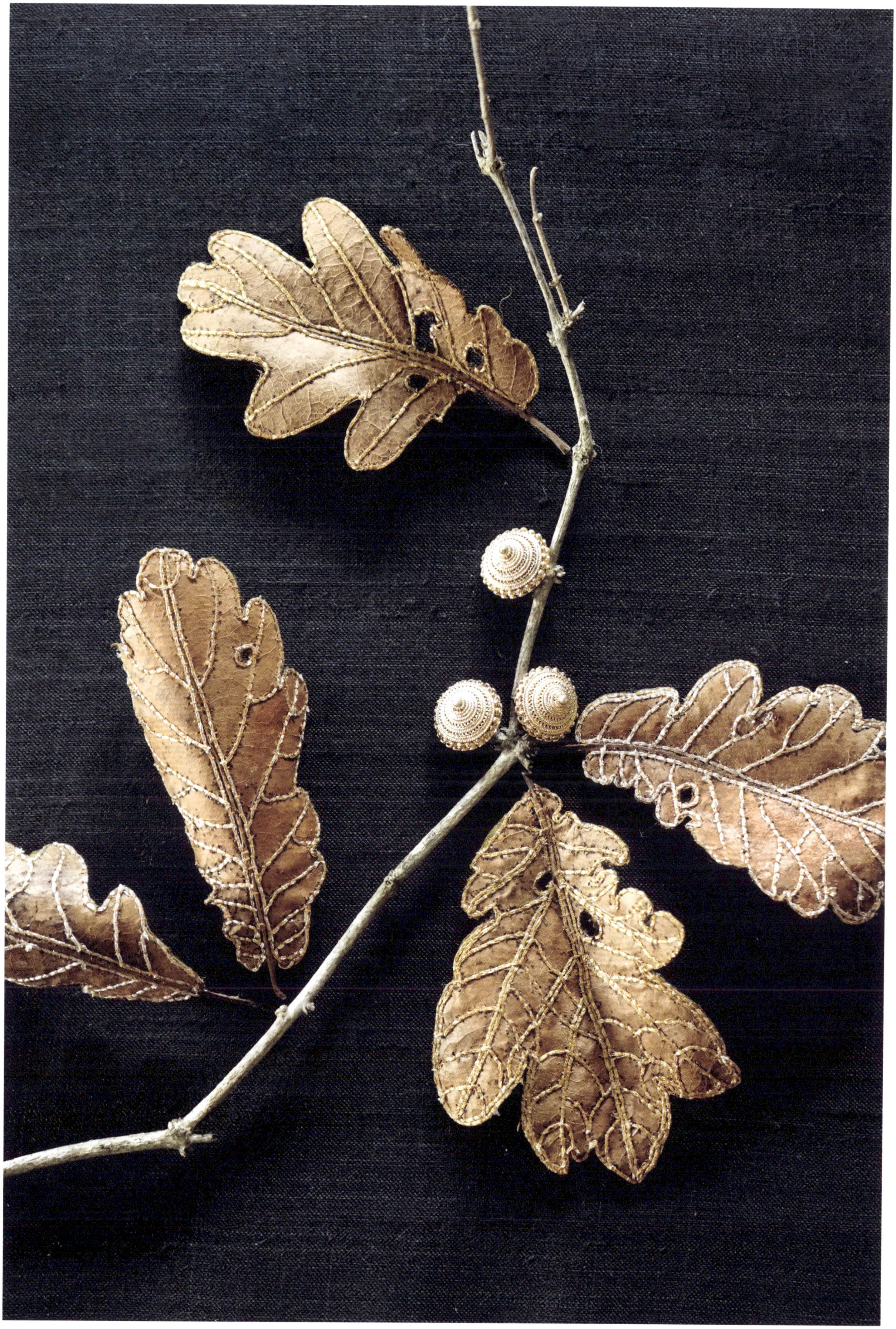

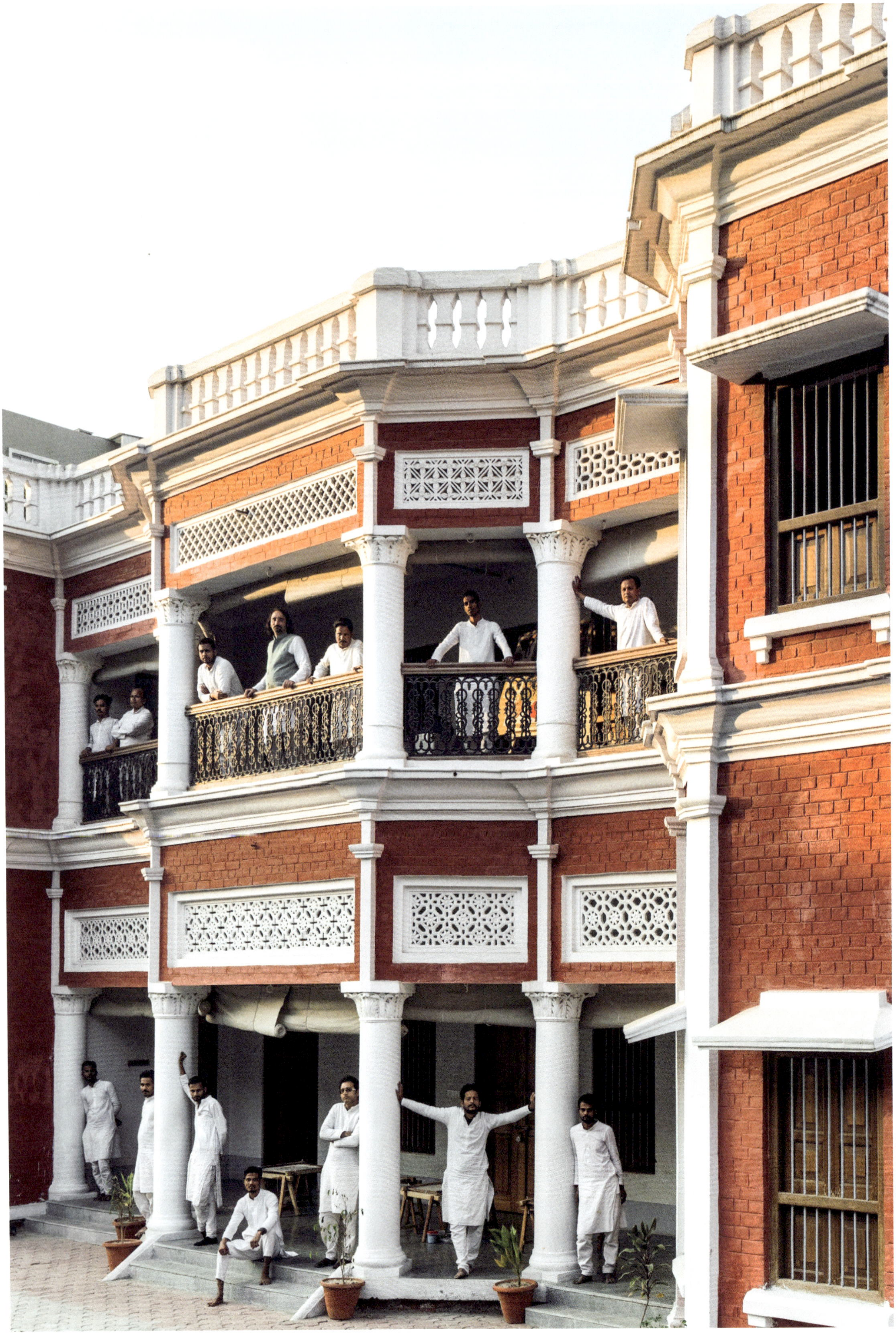

Maximiliano Modesti

Kalhath Institute

Embroiderer

Lucknow, India

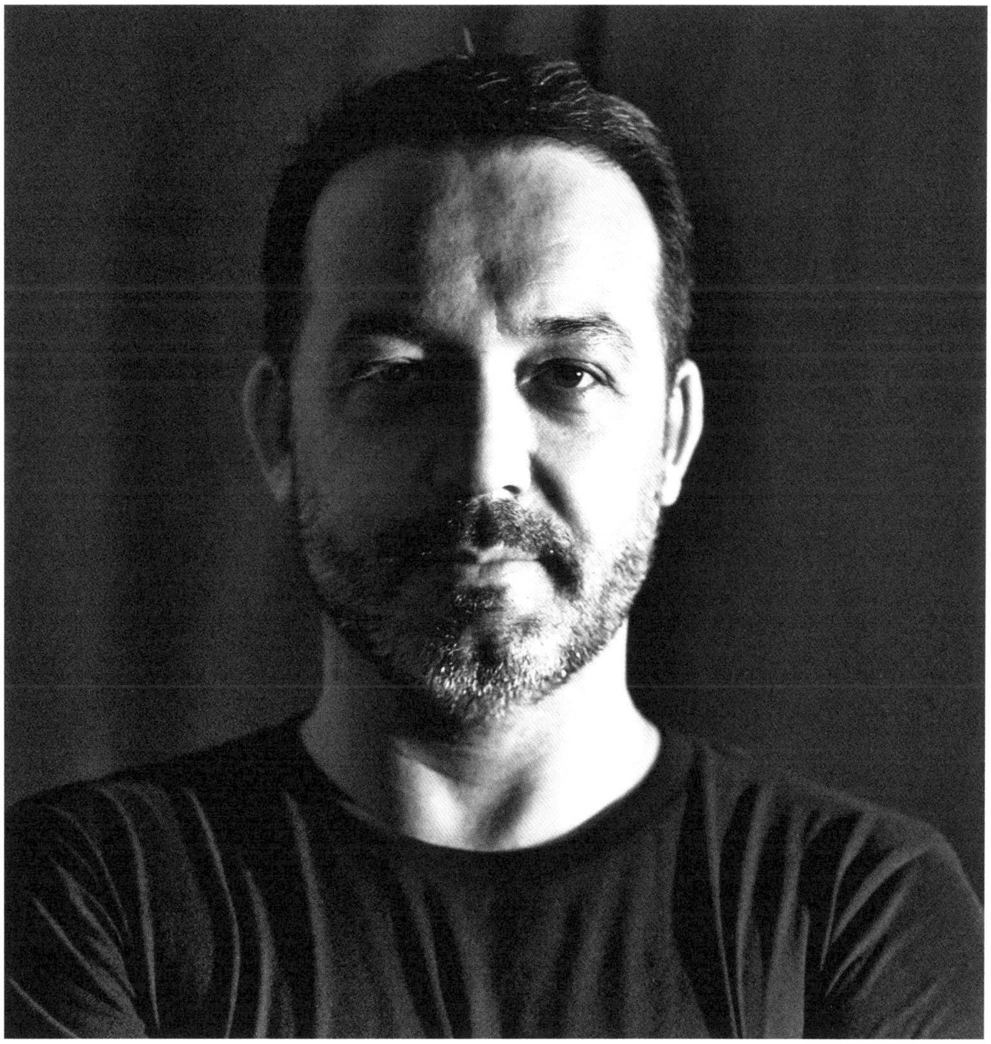

Embroidering is an incisive act: you mark time, you leave your imprint on something as ordinary as a scrap of fabric, but this imprint remains and will always remain.

My name is Maximiliano Modesti. I always say that I lead an orchestra between India and France, but, in a much more down-to-earth sense, I am an embroiderer. I have lived and worked in India for more than twenty-seven years.

When I was a student at the Institut Français de la Mode, I took a study trip to India, where I visited workshops for weaving in Varanasi, embroidery in Bombay, block print in Jaipur, and tie-dye in Gujarat. Of all these techniques, embroidery offers me a world of possibilities that the other crafts do not.

From 1992 to 1996, I worked with Azzedine Alaïa. Those four years changed my life. One day he said to me, "You're not a great designer, you're a great decorator of dresses." I liked this idea. On March 1, 1998, I took a one-way flight to Bombay. I discovered the embroiderer's trade with Master Liakad. He trained me and taught me how to communicate with Indian artisans before I opened my first workshop. Today, I work with six hundred embroiderers spread across two production sites—in Bombay and Lucknow, in northern India—which supply international luxury fashion brands.

In order to build something sustainable, I had to abandon the system by which embroiderers are paid a daily wage, and live, sleep, and work in the same space. To support their training and earn their recognition, I offered them salaried work and guaranteed a certain level of stability to encourage them to develop their skills and become entrepreneurs themselves. In India, most artisans, and their children, abandon their craft for lack of sufficient income; they can make more money driving taxis than embroidering.

In 2016, Mohammed Amine Dadda and I cofounded the Kalhath Institute, an embroidery school in Lucknow. Each year, around fifty students enroll at the school, which is directed by Jaspal Kalra. The students are between twenty-one and fifty-five years old, and must have at least five years' experience to apply. Women and men are equally represented. We have diplomas in *chikankari*—an embroidery technique from Lucknow that uses white thread—intended for women, and another in *zardozi* needlework for men.

The institute's objective is to educate, train, and support embroiderers in the state of Uttar Pradesh, in northern India. Most importantly, we strive to promote and preserve their skills, and to enable craftspeople to increase their income and break free of the conditions they have been confined to for decades. We also want them to be able to understand what we are asking of them, beyond their skills as embroiderers. When they complete their studies, they receive a diploma recognized by the Indian government and are given the opportunity to work for Indian fashion brands or NGOs, or to join the artist residency that we created, which has incredible international influence.

The Indian artist T. Venkanna was in residence at the institute for several months. Of all the work they have done, the students are most proud of these collaborations between artists and artisans. A single piece contains the entire spectrum of skills, and everyone works hand in hand—which is the true success of this residency program.

Finally, the diploma is open to different craft skills: silk weaving in Varanasi, stone work in Agra, block printing in Jaipur, and, in ten years, its influence may have spread even further, allowing even more students and craftspeople to benefit from this training.

Today, it is but a drop in the ocean of the one hundred thousand embroiderers practicing in Lucknow and the surrounding region, but it is just the beginning. For now, the most important thing for me is to see this project succeed.

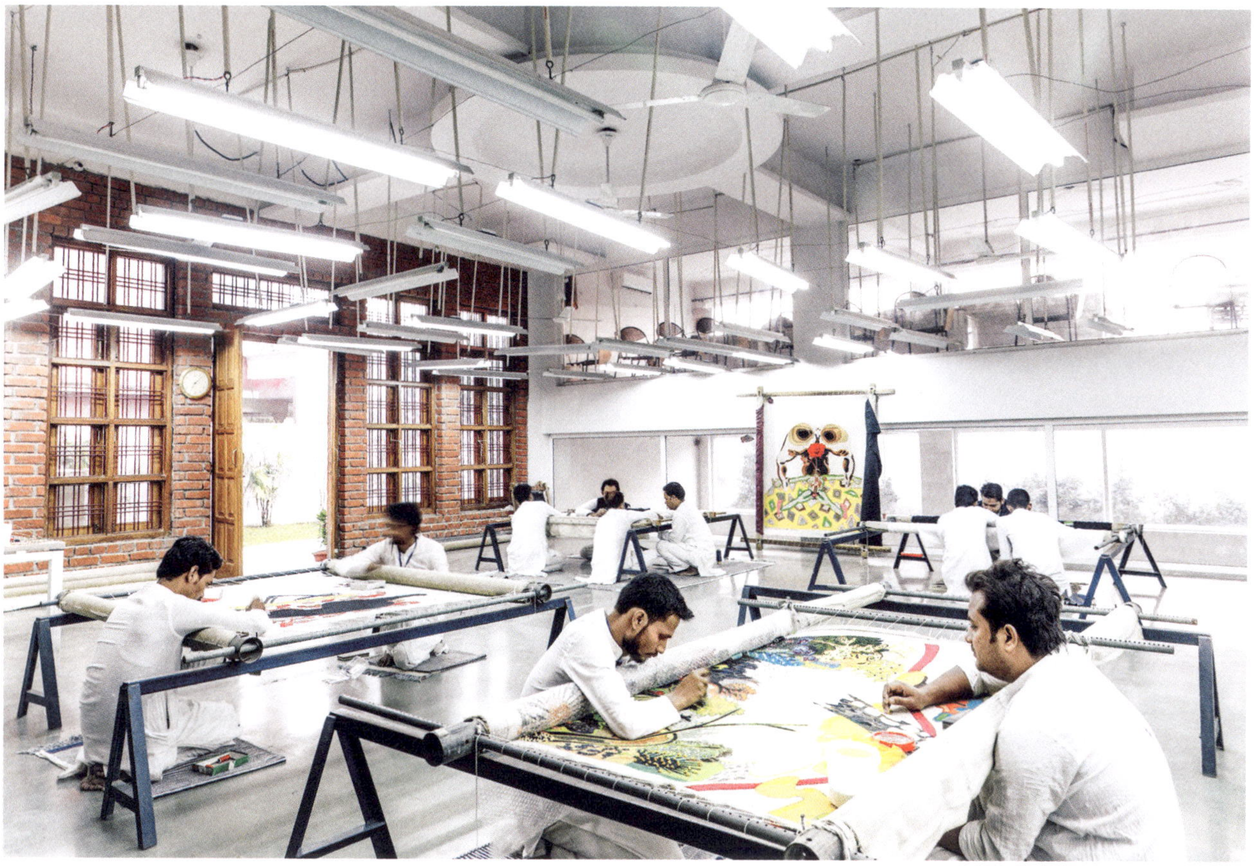

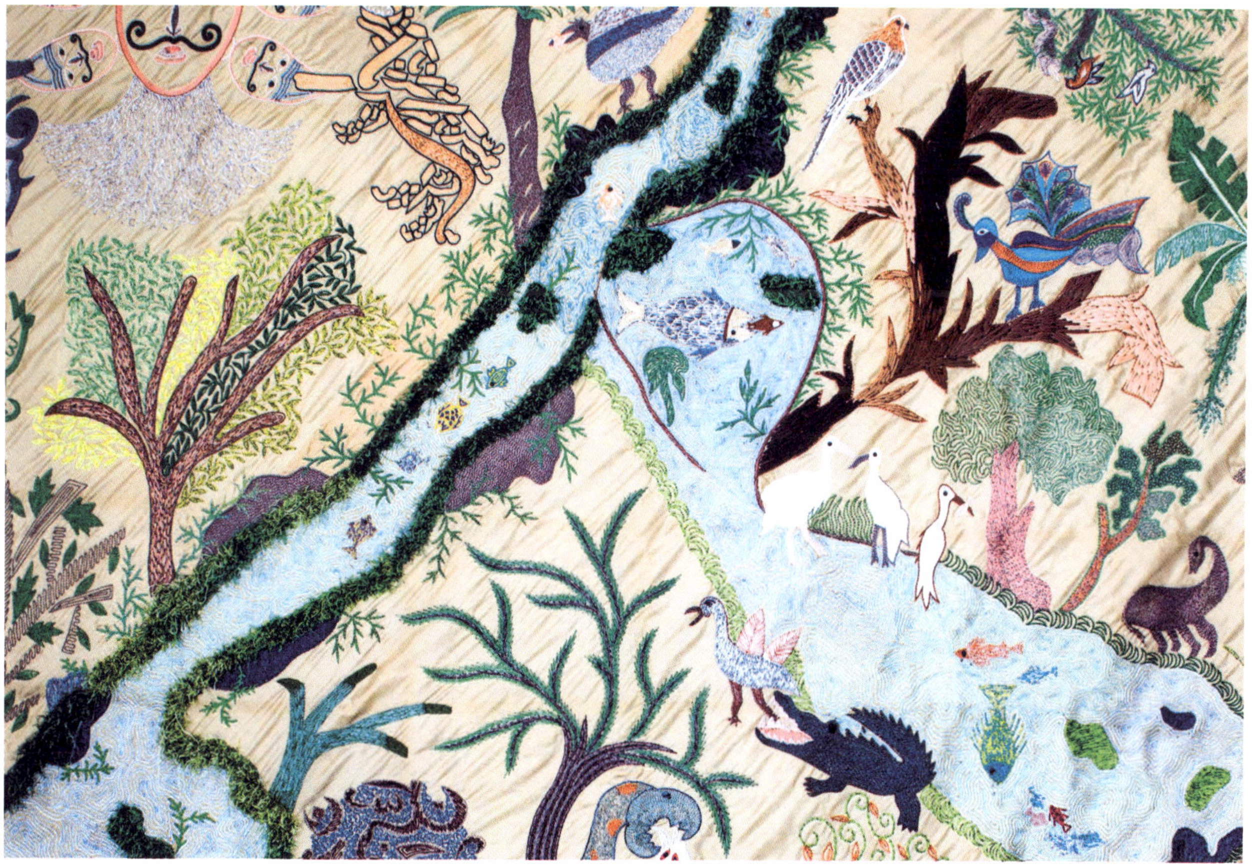

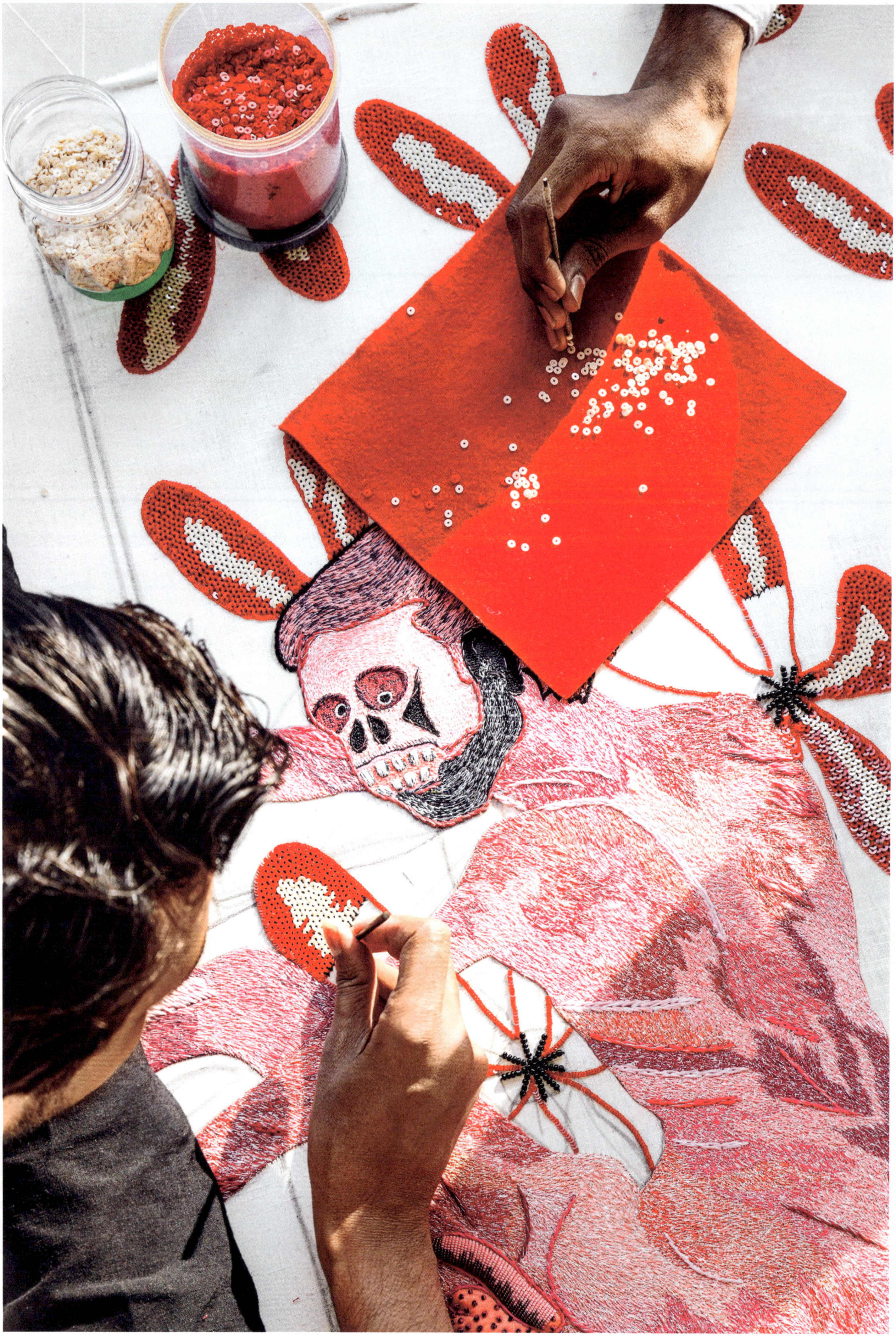

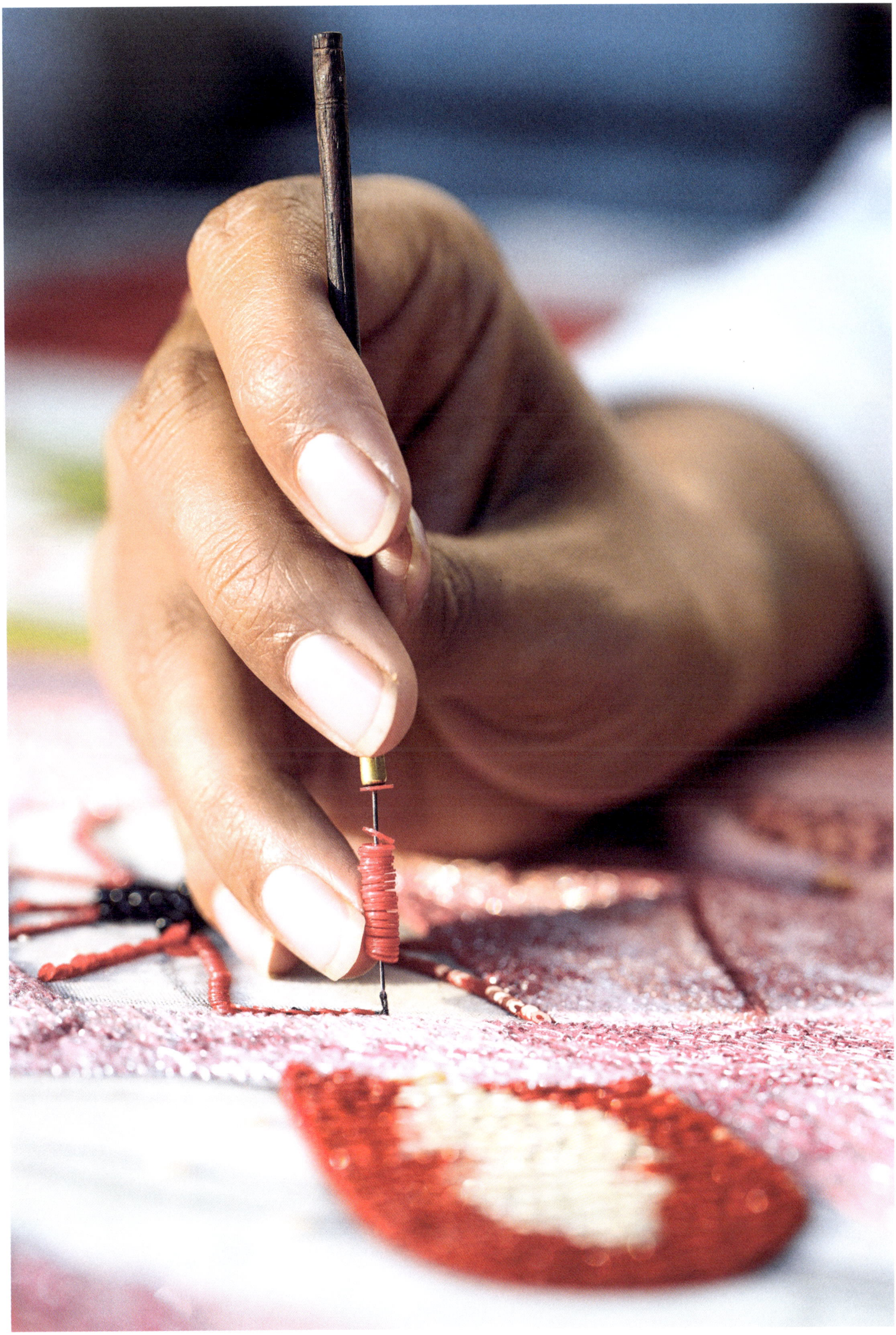

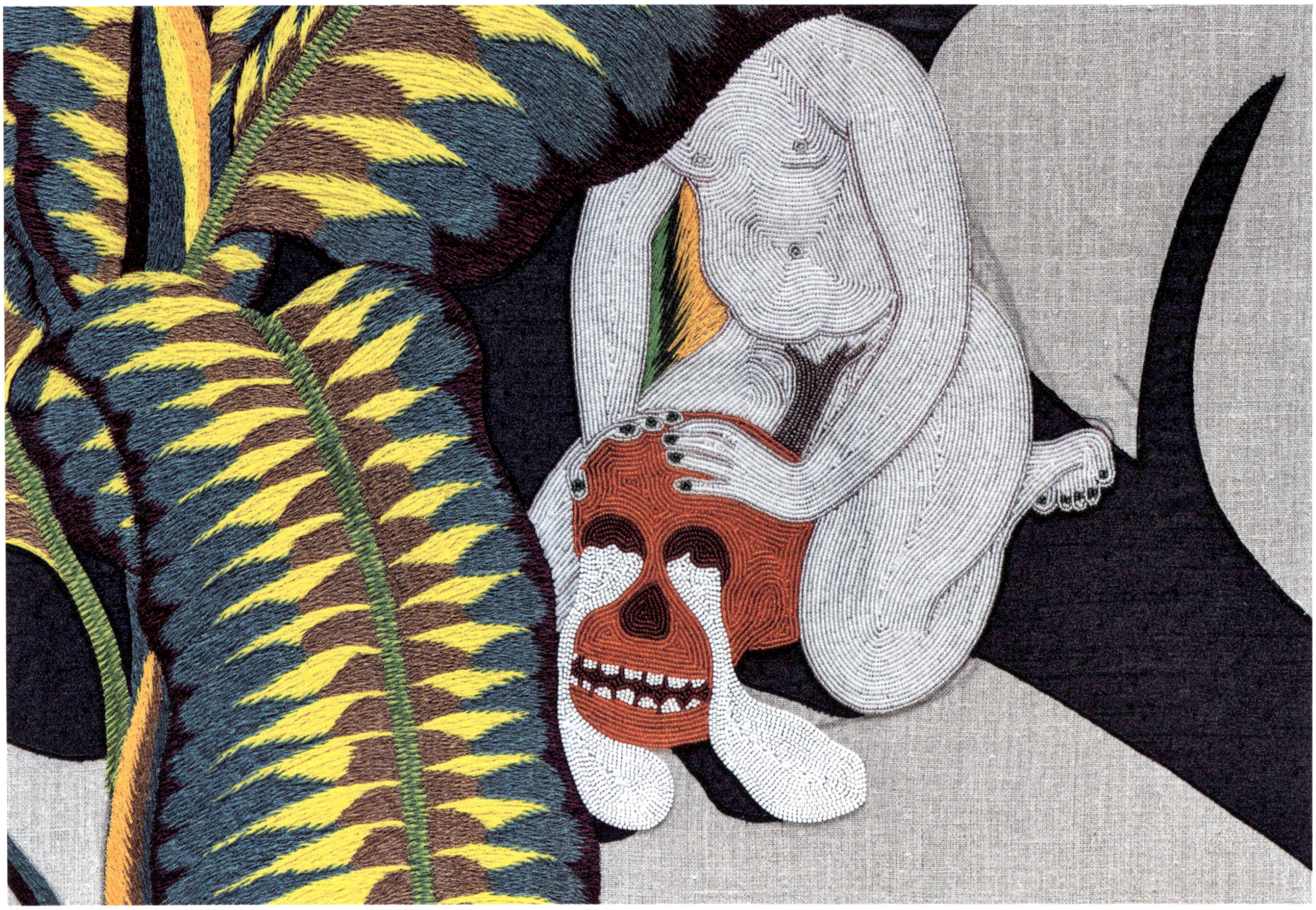

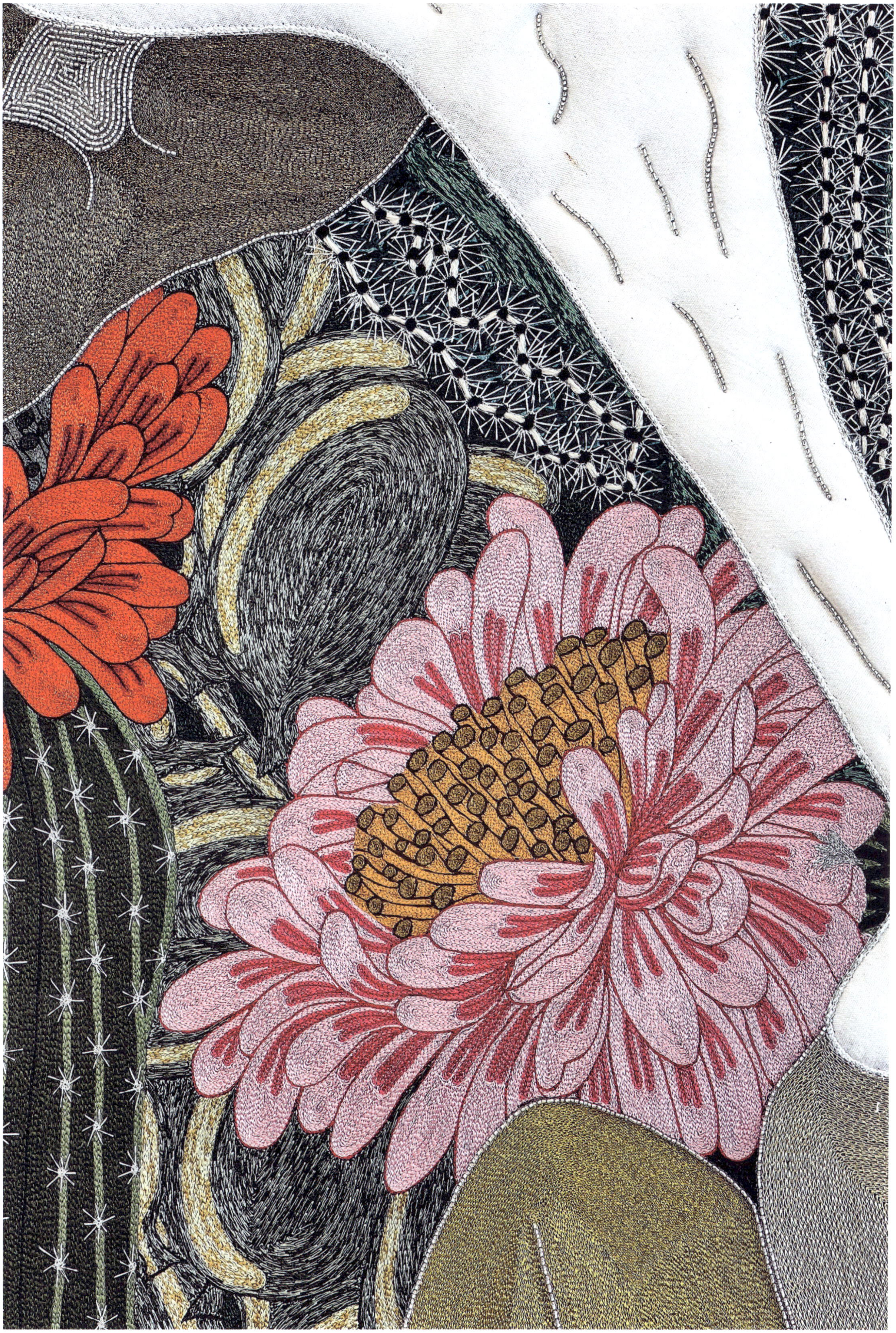

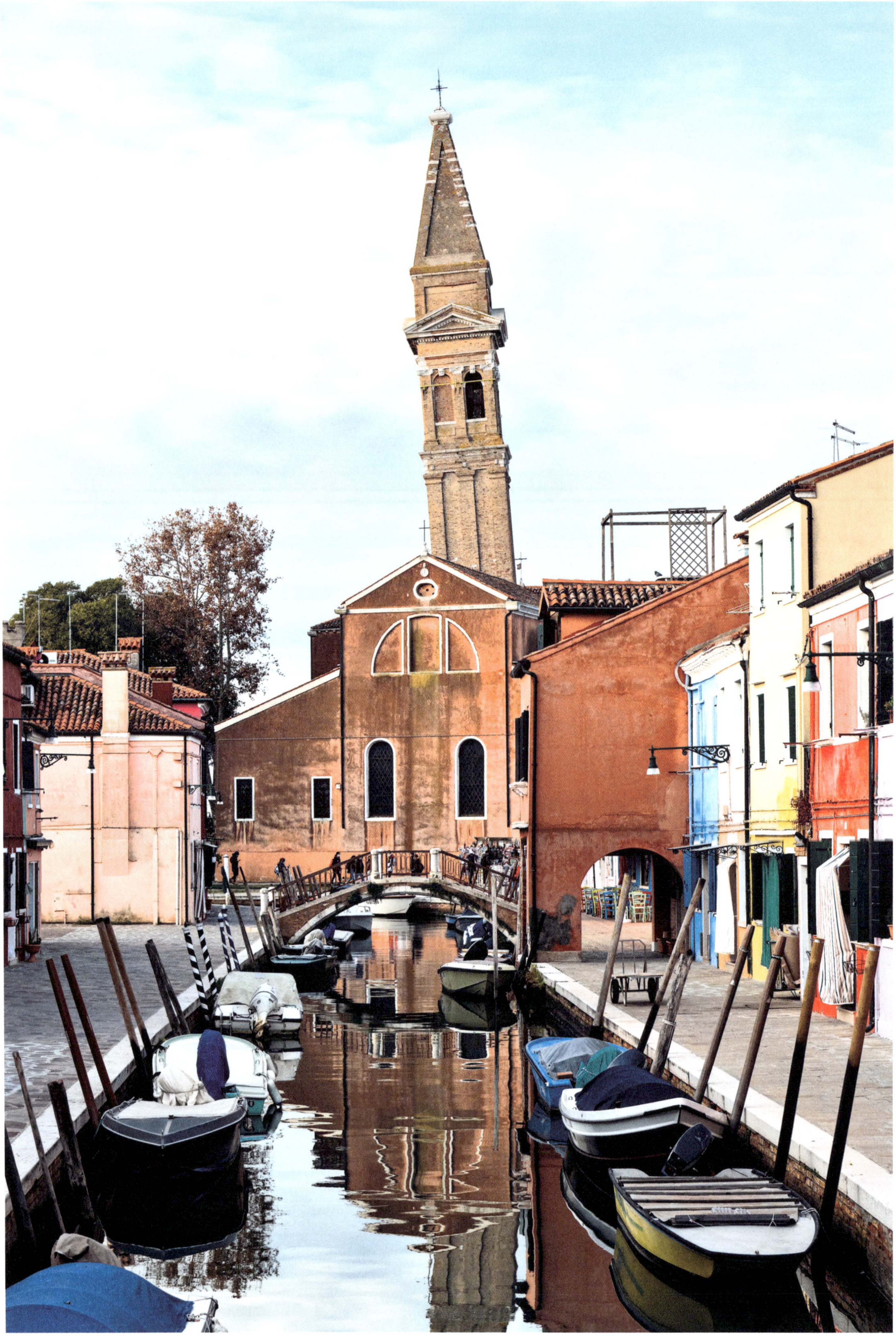

Lucia Costantini

Lace maker

Burano, Italy

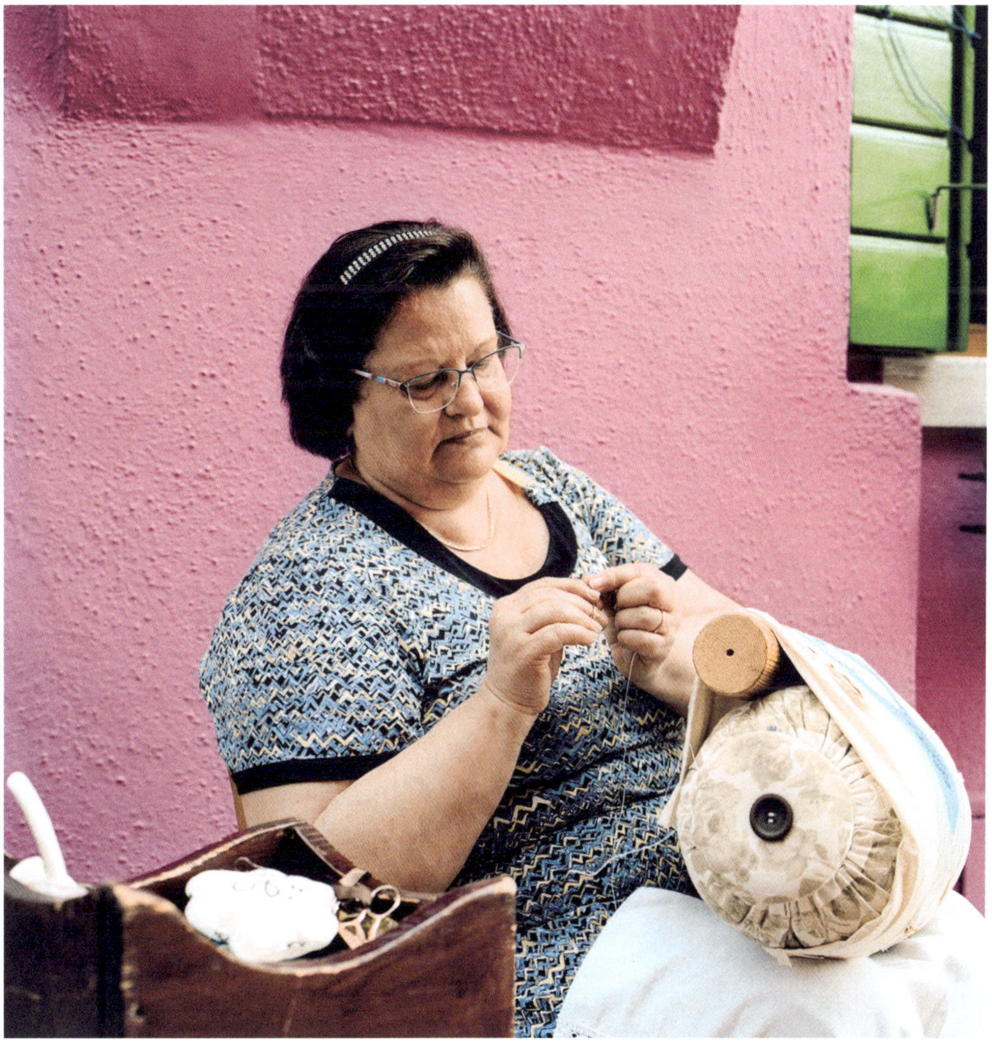

My name is Lucia Costantini, and I am a lace maker. For me, this traditional craft is a personal journey of artistic exploration.

In Italian, the words *merletto*, *pizzo*, and *trina* are all synonyms to define handmade lace woven using a bobbin or needle. The bobbin is used for weaving and the needle for knotting the thread. Lace is impressive in its variety: the more stitches in a pattern, the more complexities intertwine, and that requires lace makers to have a clear vision of the project as a whole. Unfortunately, this craft has long struggled to carve out a place for itself. Today, foundations like the Fondazione Andriana Marcello in Burano, the Fondazione Cologni dei Mestieri d'Arte in Milan, and the Michelangelo Foundation in Geneva work to promote a contemporary perspective on lace making. Much has been done, but there is still a way to go.

Lace making is not a hobby for me; this practice takes commitment, determination, and ongoing training. In my family—and on the island of Burano in general—almost every woman does lace work. We meet in the square in the cool hours of the day. Each of us brings a small pillow called a *strinsiola*. The one I use once belonged to my grandmother and is very dear to me.

I am the eighth of eleven children. My training began when I was eleven years old. I was taught by nuns who gave us long, difficult, and meticulous tasks; in fact, it was a nun who, looking me straight in the eyes, decided my future. Many young women like me were forced into this training because they had no other options. The local population never left the island, especially not the women. The day when that became a possibility, women's salaries increased fivefold.

I also left the island. I began selling glass in various prestigious locations. A whole new world opened before me. Despite those years of intense work, I felt a strong desire to undertake a personal project involving lace, to innovate within this field which could be enriched by what I was discovering, learning, and reading. I thought back to an almost abstract painting depicting a lion's head that required careful observation to decipher the outline. However, I didn't want to repeat stitches and patterns; I wanted to invent something new for each work, to find a sense of freedom. To do so, I had to interpret each project, visualize it, then transform it into stitches and test new threads. I was no longer simply observing and repeating what I had learned or could do with my eyes closed.

In 1983–84, I added color to my work. It was revolutionary at the time! White was then the hallmark of wealth and embodied the idea of preciousness. Color could not be used for work as exquisite, complex, and slow as lace, for fear of making the piece too commonplace, and I received plenty of criticism. But I live on a multicolored island where vibrantly painted houses are reflected in the water and where color is always present. And when we, the inhabitants of Burano, travel to the mainland, we see a world of black and white compared to the wealth of hues on our island. Color is an intrinsic part of my work.

The way a piece is presented is also of fundamental importance. You have to find unusual ways to enable viewers to perceive a new vision. I think Peggy Guggenheim was one of the first to emphasize the importance of exhibiting and enhancing a work within a given space. In a room, a single painting on a colored background is observed with greater attention.

Today, I dream of having a team of local artisans to create unique objects inspired by a web of traditions. Over the years, my work has resonated abroad, such as when I taught in the United States and collaborated with other designers. I thrive on these experiences. However, designers have a hard time grasping the difficulties inherent in lace work, and understanding the specificities, complexities, and dimensions of this craft. It's not about creating large-scale pieces. For a collaboration to work, connection is essential—the more you understand each other, the better you work together.

Interview carried out in collaboration with Susanna Pozzoli

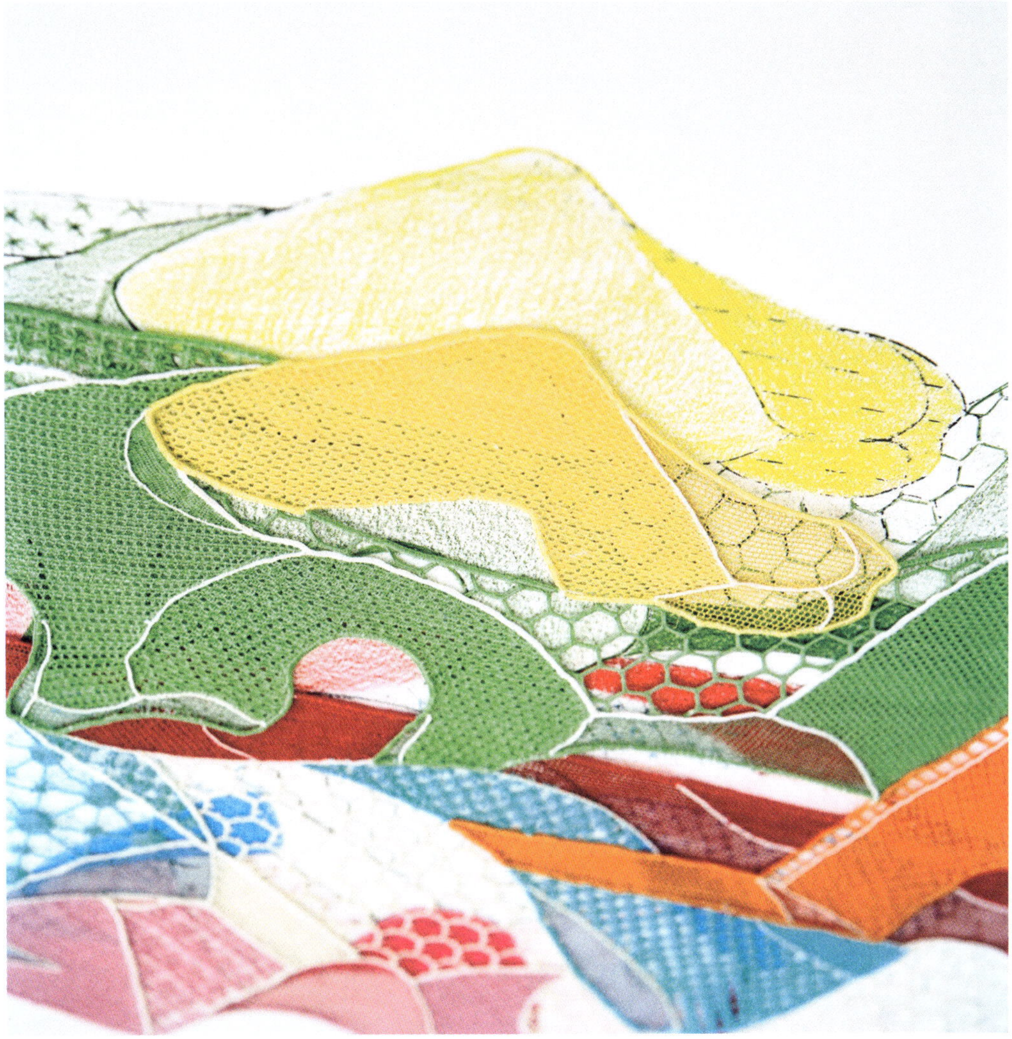

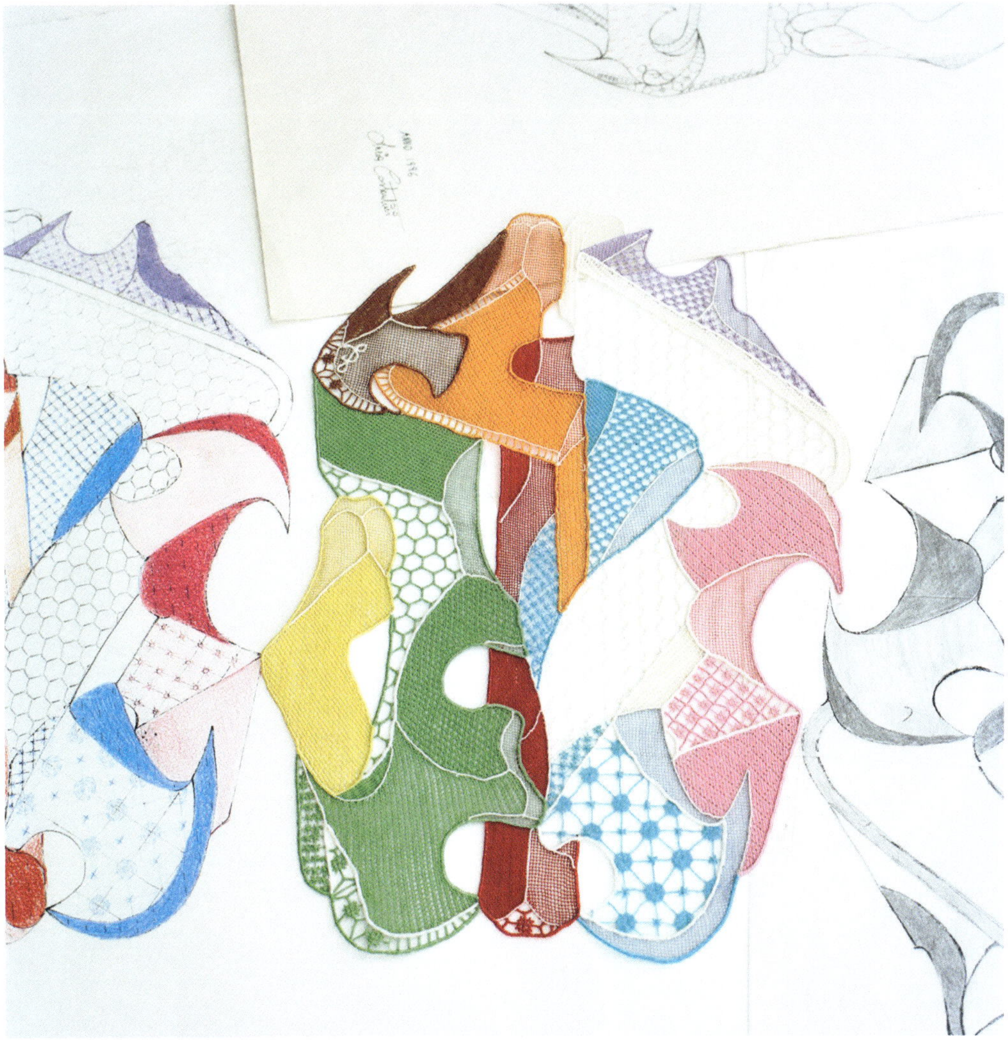

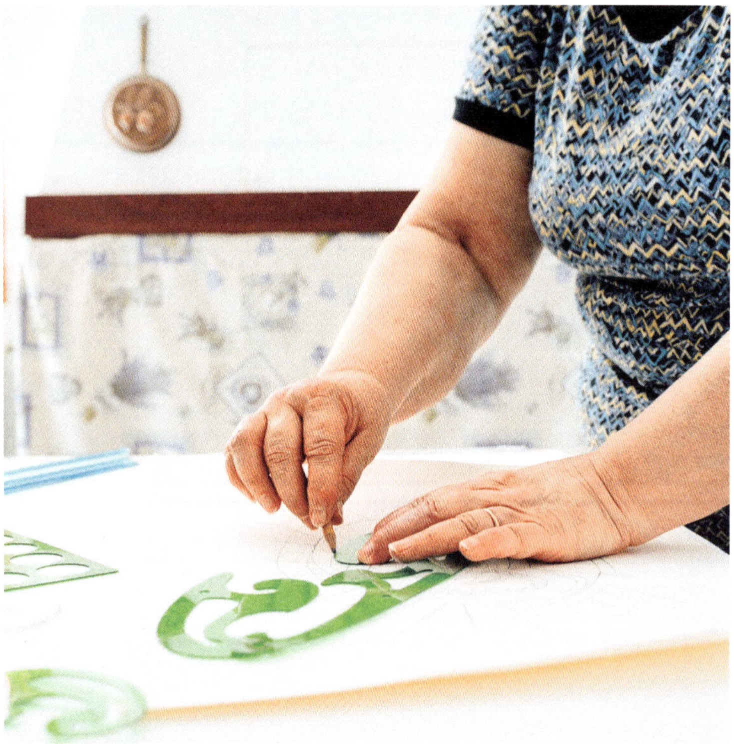

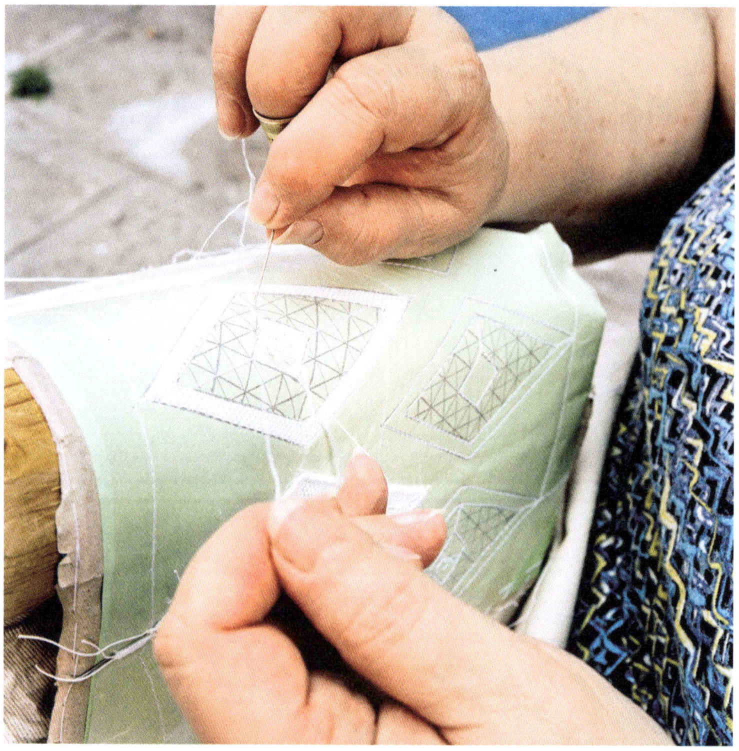

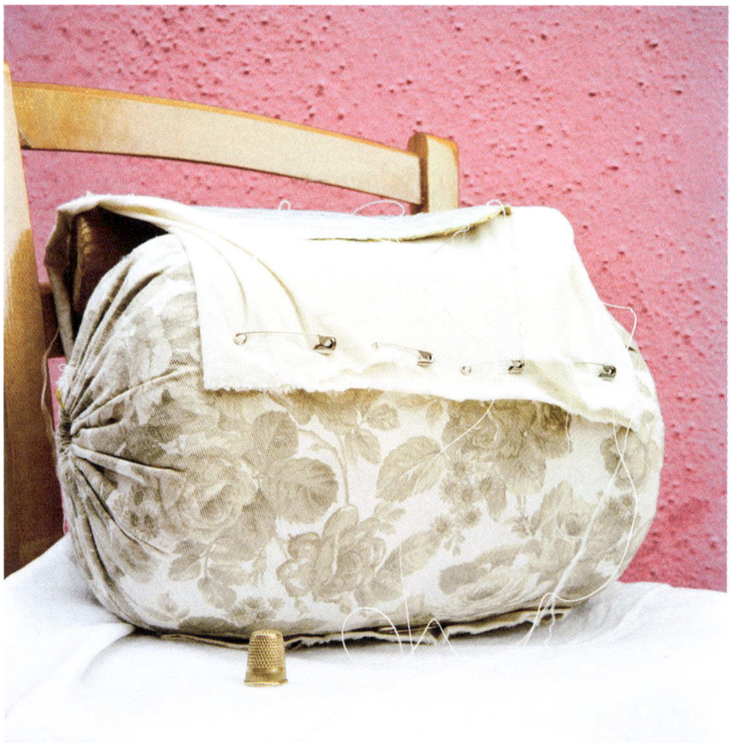

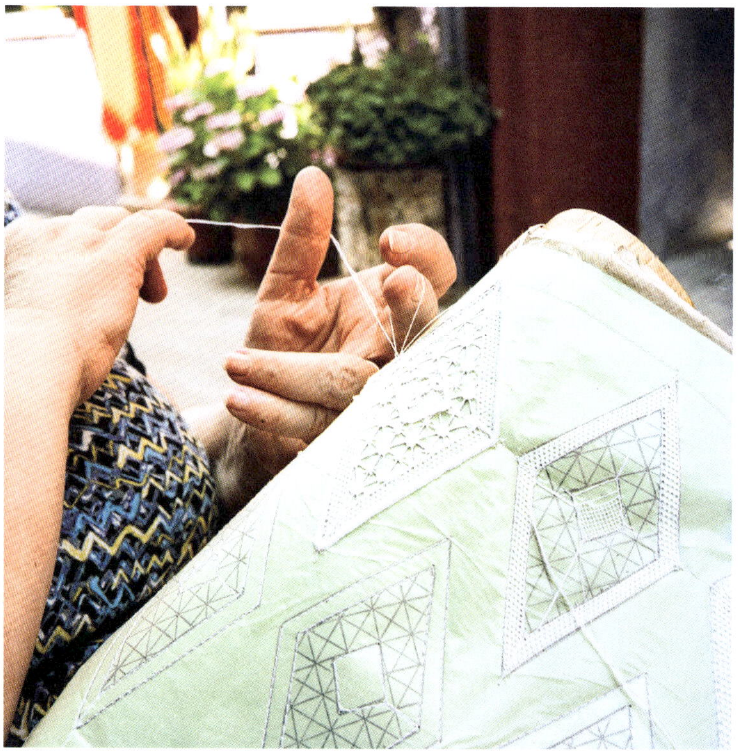

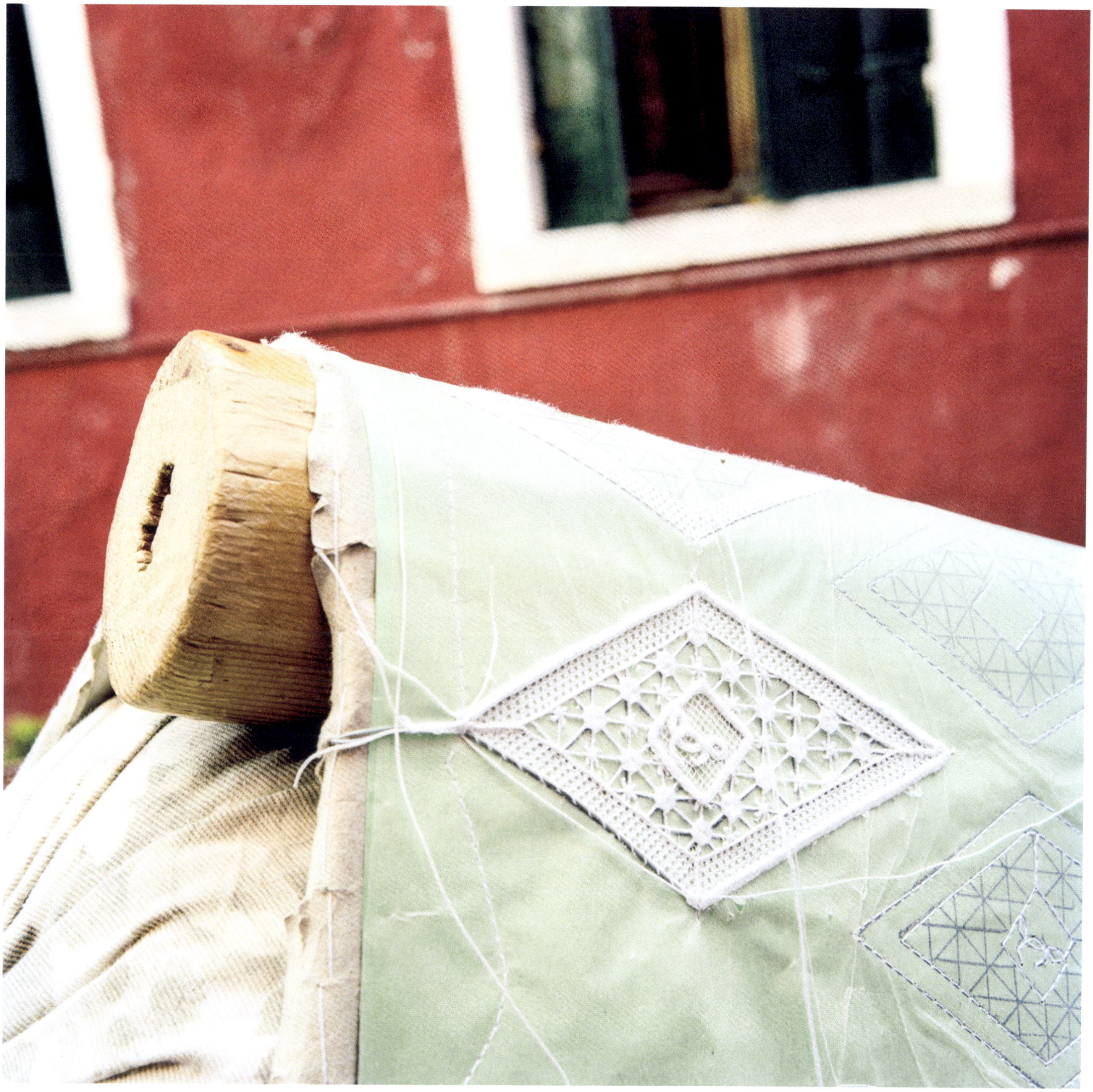

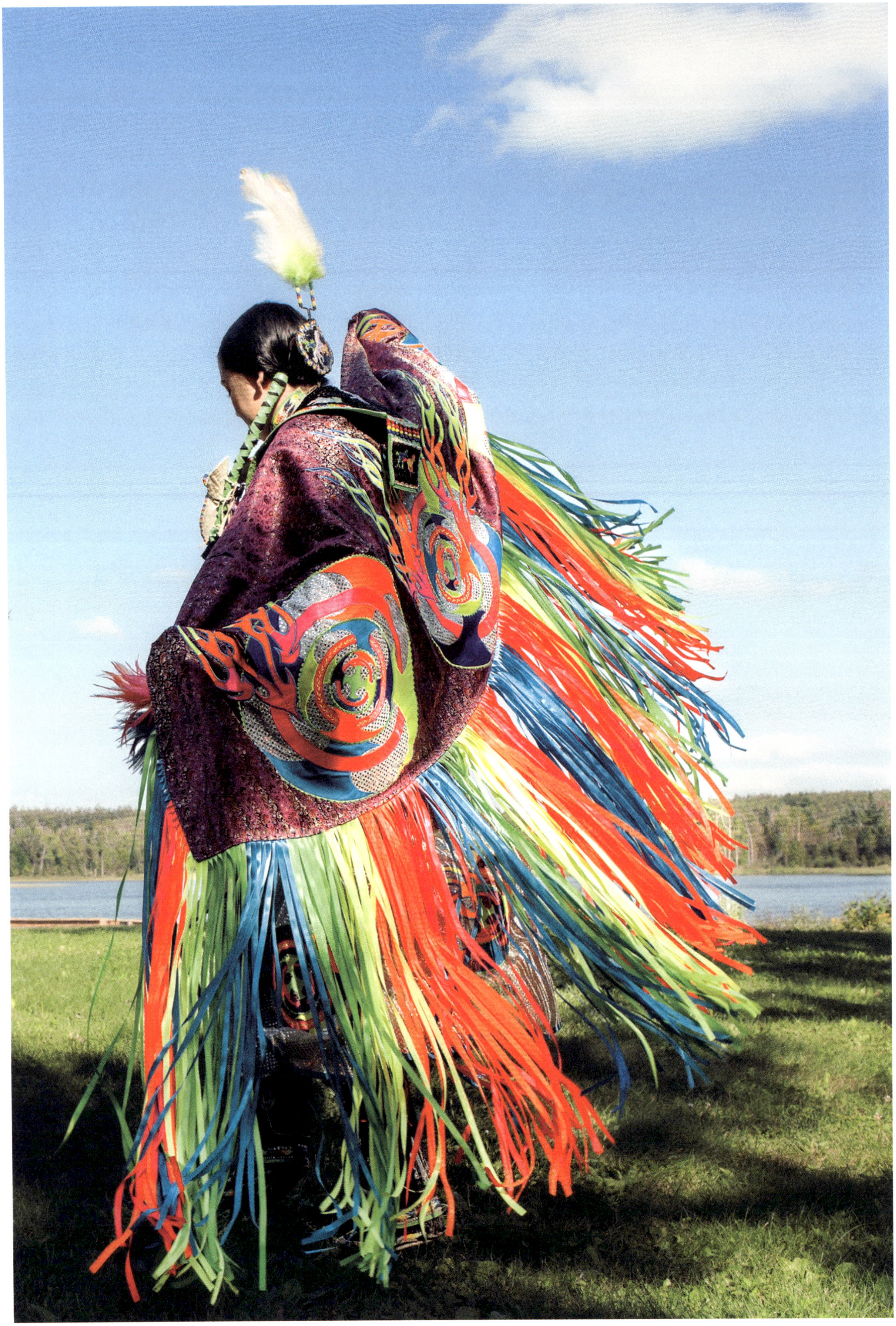

Dana Goodwin and Dennis Williams

Beaders

White Earth Reservation, Minnesota, United States

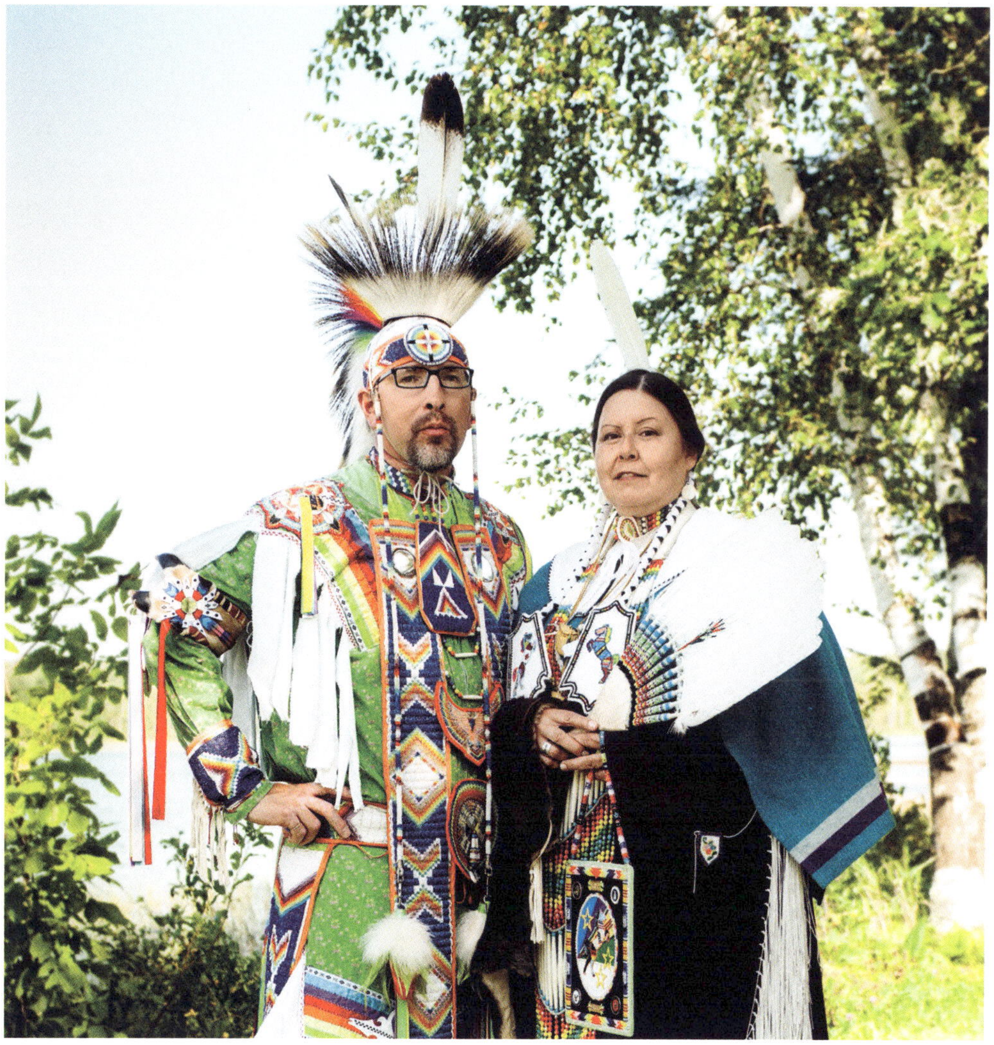

My name is Dana Goodwin, and my husband is Dennis Williams. Together, we create traditional Ojibwe clothing. Although we are very different, Dennis and I were attracted to each other thanks to our shared attachment to Ojibwe culture. We both belong to this Native American tribe—the third largest Indigenous group in the United States, after the Cherokee and the Navajo.

I grew up in an Ojibwe family and we practiced crafts and needlework as a way of life. My great-grandmother and aunts made quilts, rugs, and baskets, and they embroidered. As a child, I loved drawing and I dreamed of becoming an architect or a fashion designer. Today, I design regalia for powwows—Indigenous dance competitions—using what I learned about color at university and, above all, my creative instincts.

Dennis and I live and work with the children of our community on the White Earth Reservation in northwestern Minnesota, where I am a teacher and Dennis is in charge of an after-school program for students from kindergarten to twelfth grade. We spend our free time making powwow costumes. Dennis is an artist; he beads and works with feathers. I make dresses with a patchwork of appliquéd motifs.

Leading a healthy lifestyle, attending powwows, reconnecting with our native language, and educating our children is our way of revitalizing this Native American culture that has suffered decades of federal assimilation policies. In 1880, our children were taken away from their families and sent to off-reservation boarding schools to convert our people to American culture. Generations of Native youth were brutally separated from their parents and made to forget their language. Traditional ceremonies were also banned until 1978.

In embracing his Native culture, Dennis discovered that previous generations of women in his family had created specific beaded flower designs for their lineage. Beadwork generally reflects the environment of each nation and traditionally reveals where we come from. The Plains or South West nations use many triangular designs representing tipis or mountains. We have hills, vines, and a particular flora. We are Anishinaabe.

Dennis taught himself beadwork, with the help of a craftsman, Michael Knapp. He started by creating a headband, then made moccasins for our children. Making beaded shoes for powwows is challenging for several reasons: the moccasins have to be perfectly designed and stand up to wear and tear. In general, he starts by assembling the skin and beads, then he lets his imagination run wild. Some parts, like the beaded harnesses, can take ten months to complete.

We sew the garments by hand, just like our ancestors, who decorated them with great care. In those days, clothing had a function in the community; it had meaning. Some dresses, like the Jingle Dress, also known as the Prayer Dress, are worn by women during a dance that brings healing to the sick. The dress is adorned with small metal cones, which were originally made from tobacco tin lids, sewn close to the cloth; they produce a chiming sound that is both soothing and eerie. When competing, a Jingle dancer is judged on her traditional footwork and the ornamentation of her dress. Feathers, on the other hand, are a decorative element subject to strict rules. To be given the right to wear eagle feathers, you have to wait years and go before a commission to prove your origins.

Today, it saddens us to know that there are so few of us sewing and maintaining the skills associated with Native arts. Very few people speak our language. I think we need to use what we know from the past to move forward into the future. I hope that my children will preserve this knowledge—that they will know who they are and take pride in their identity.

Interview carried out in collaboration with Anne Laure Camilleri

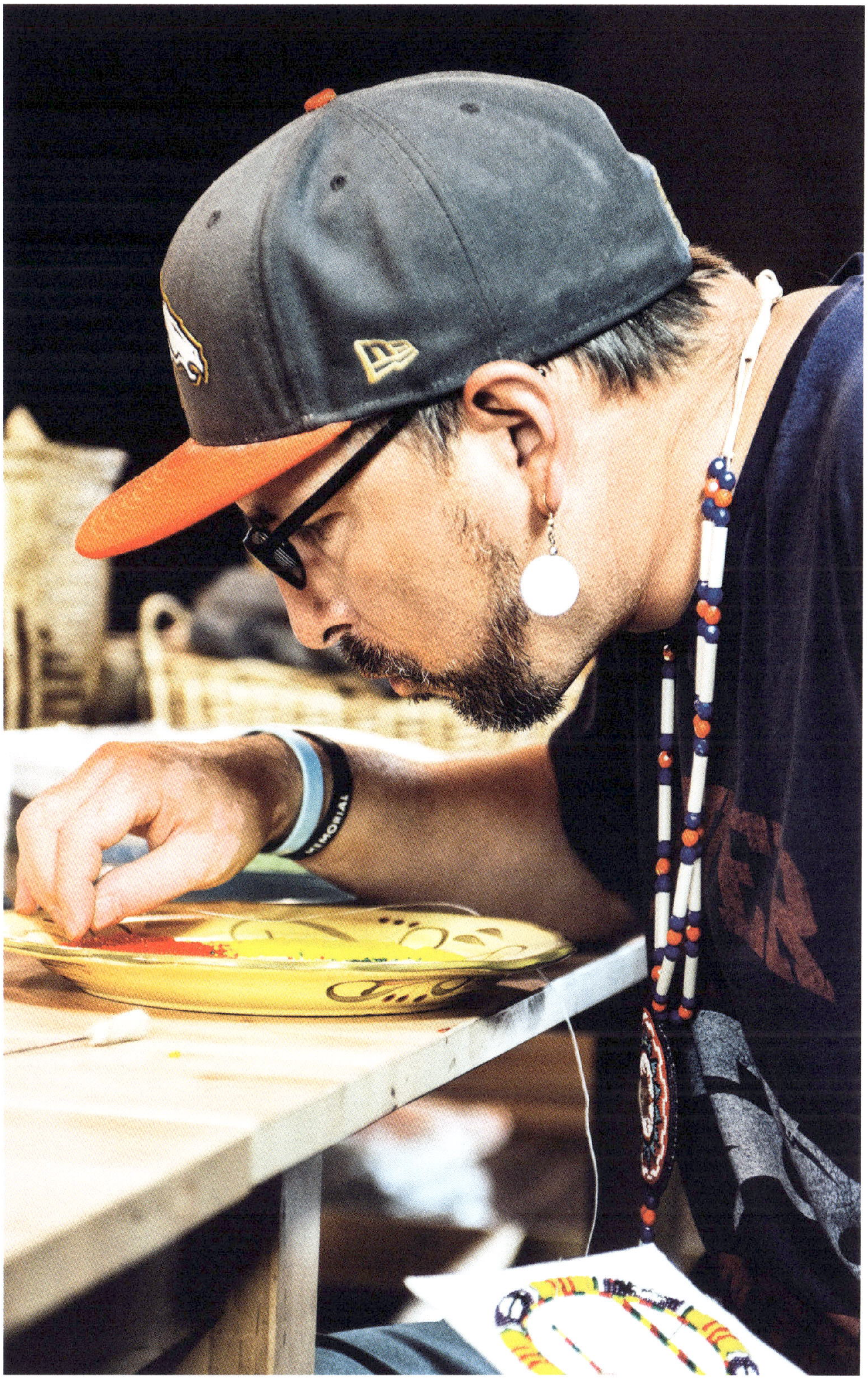

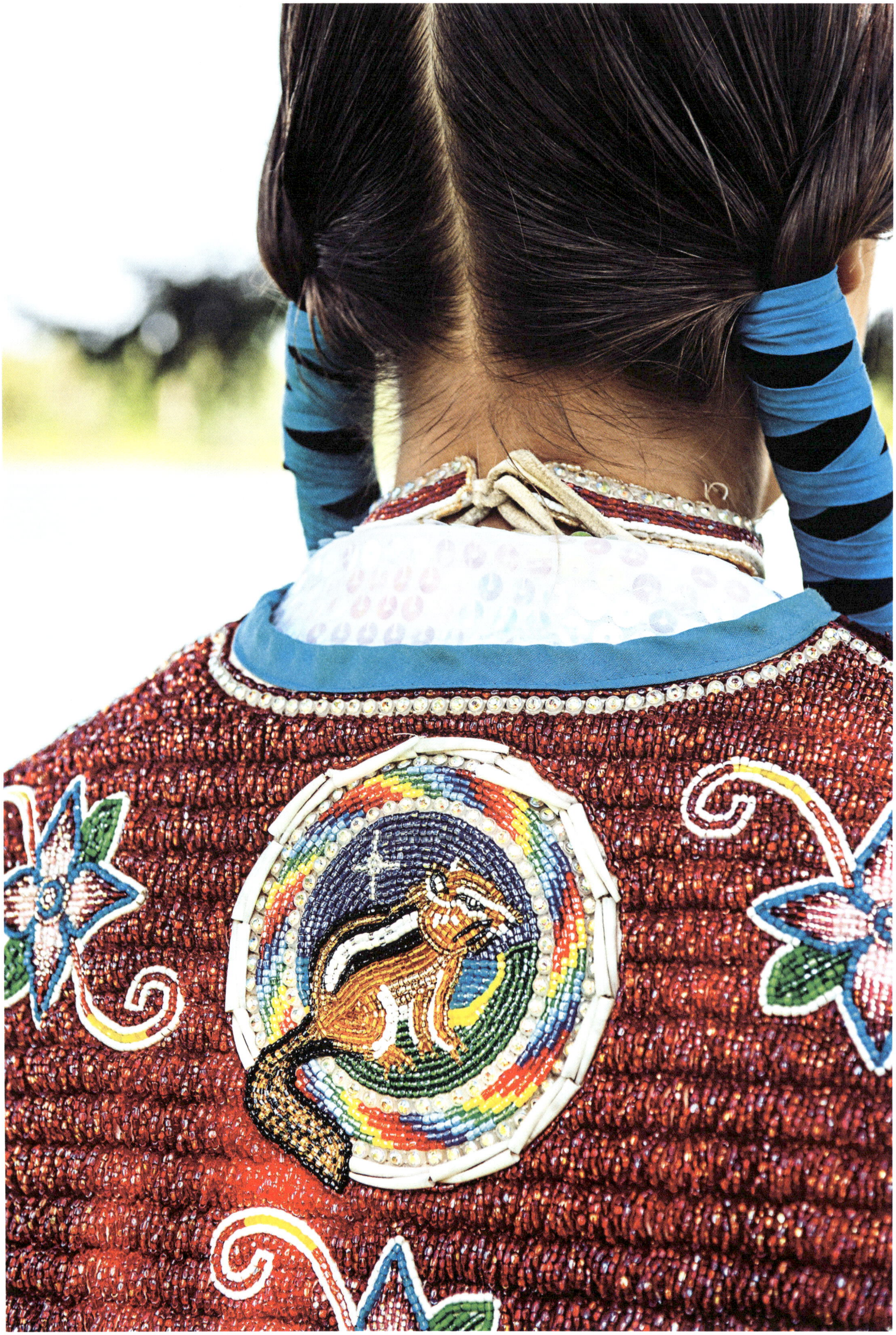

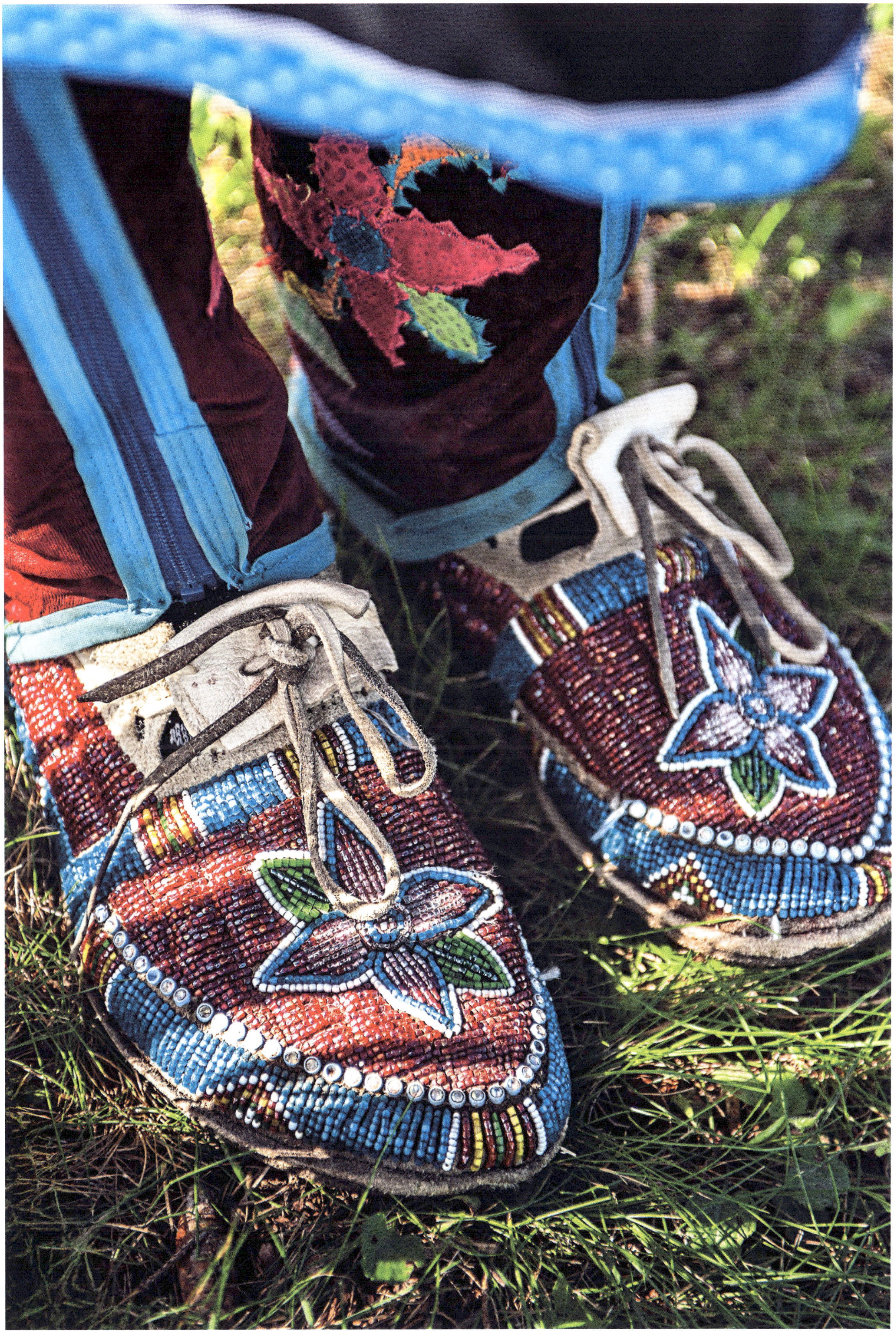

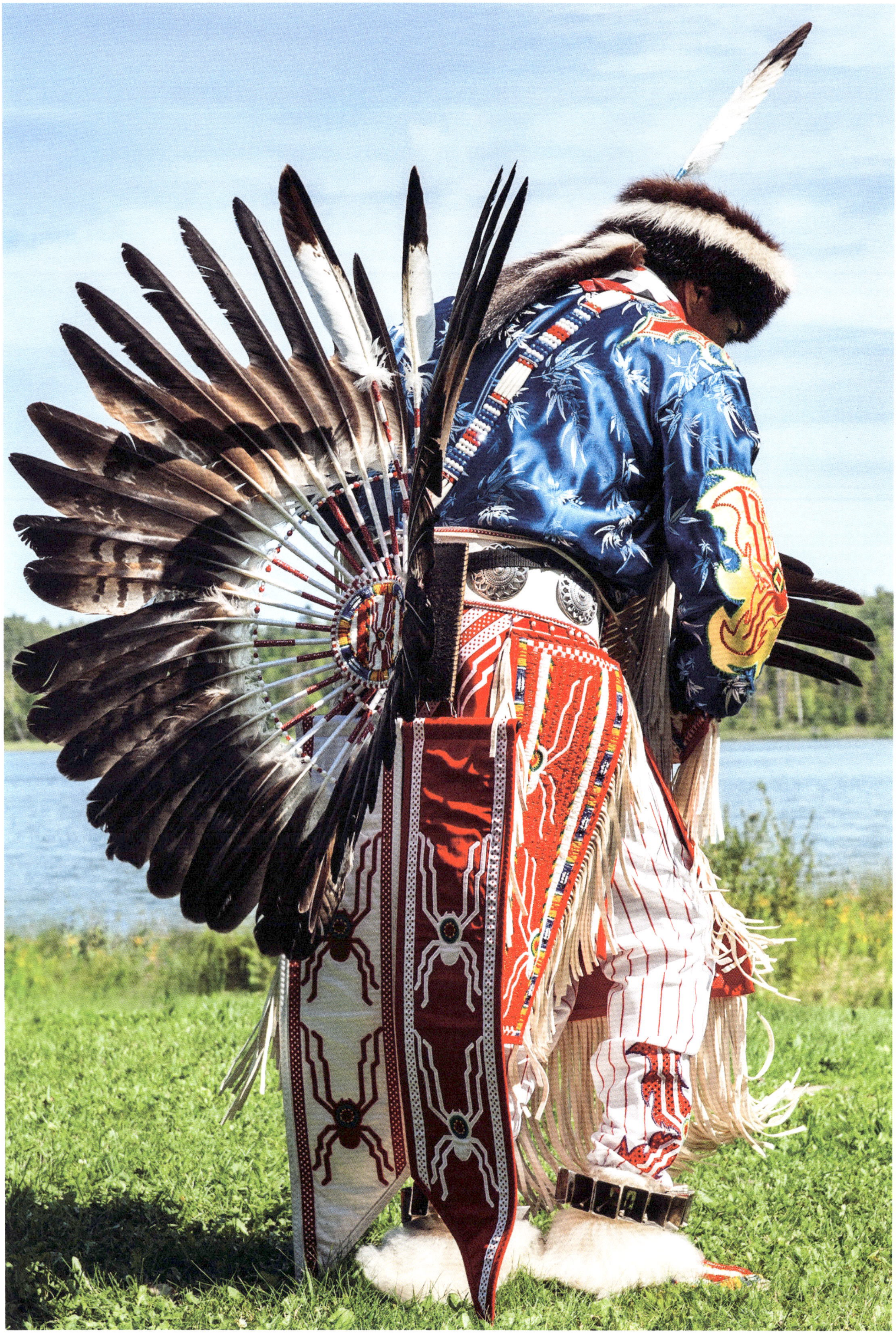

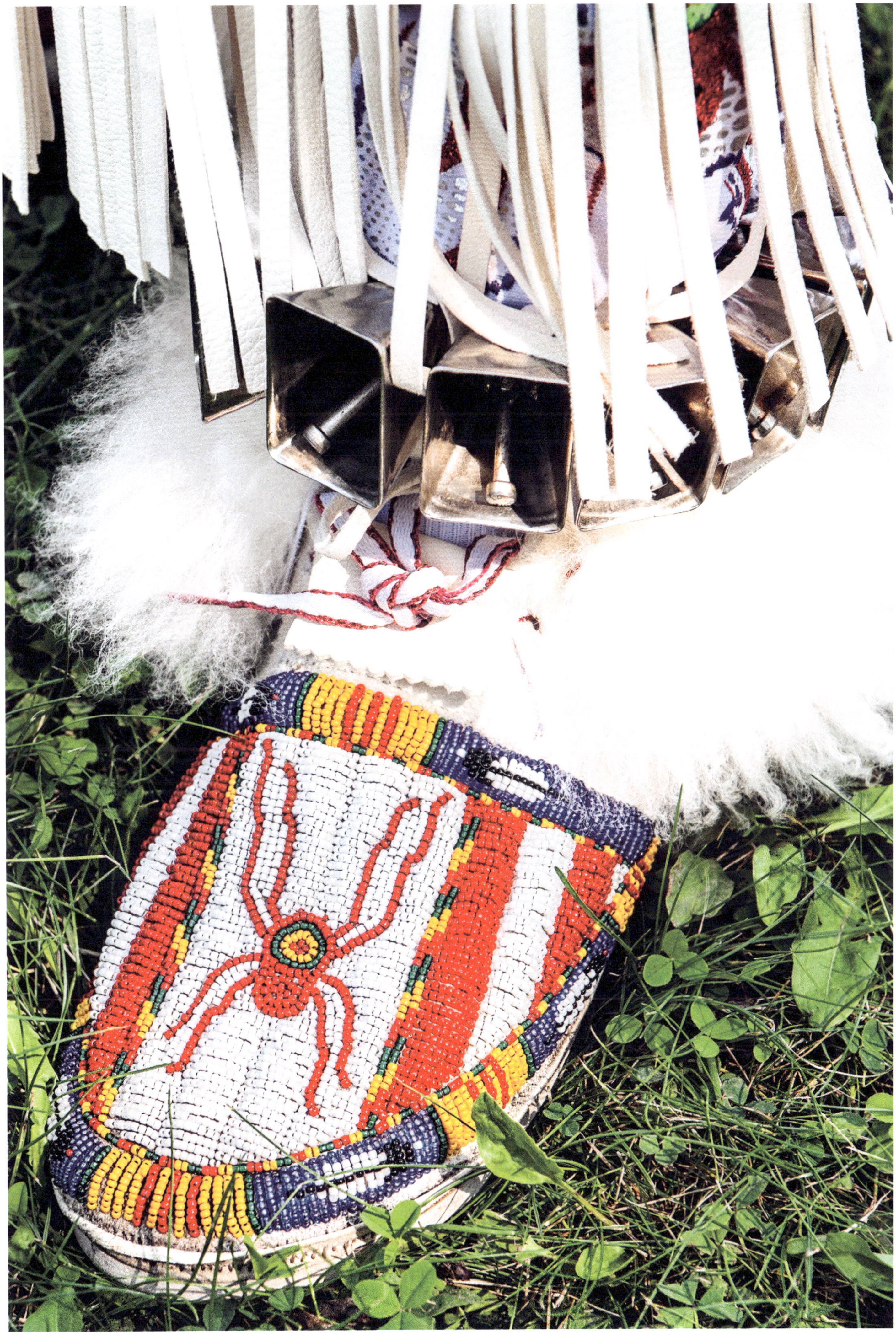

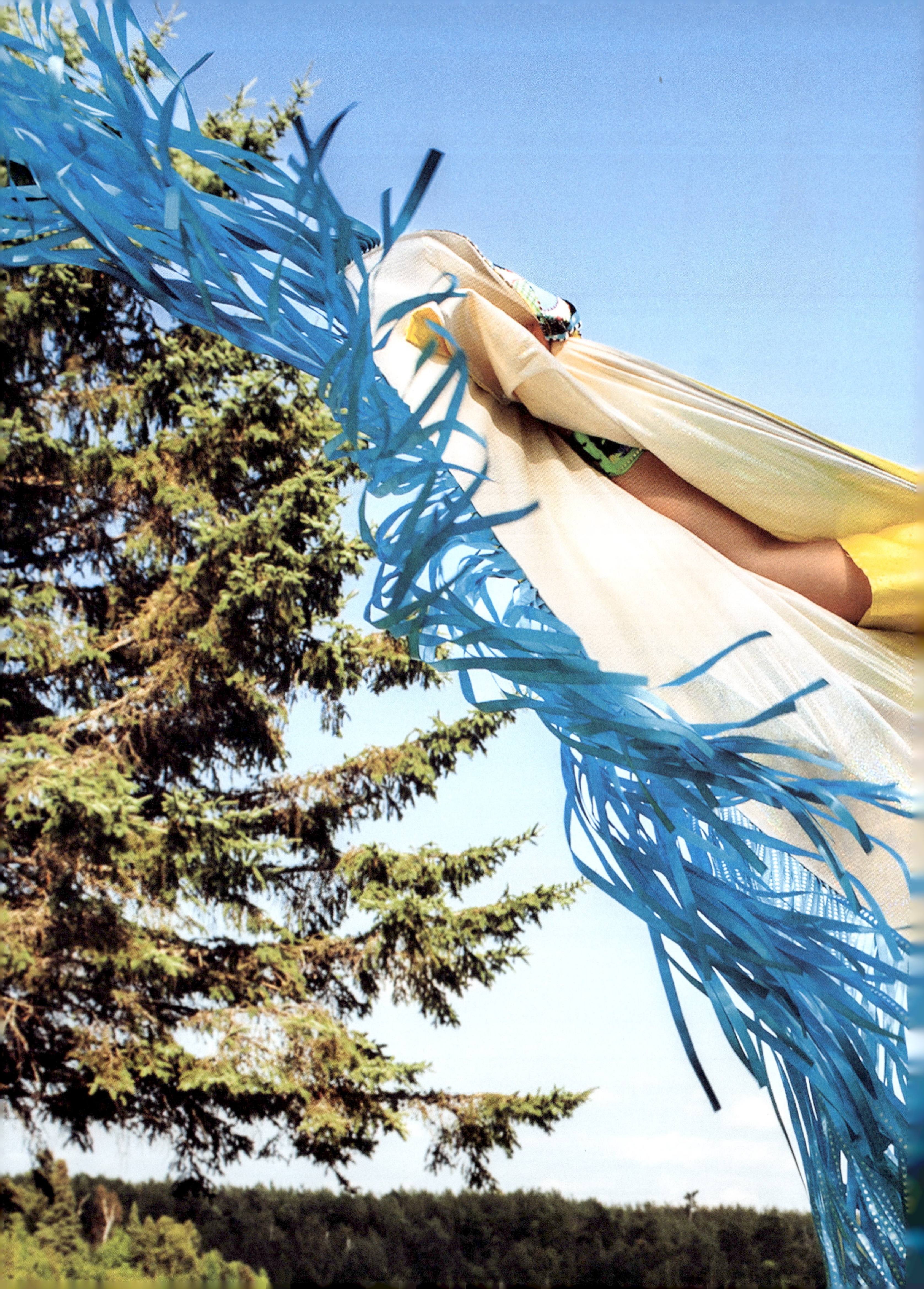

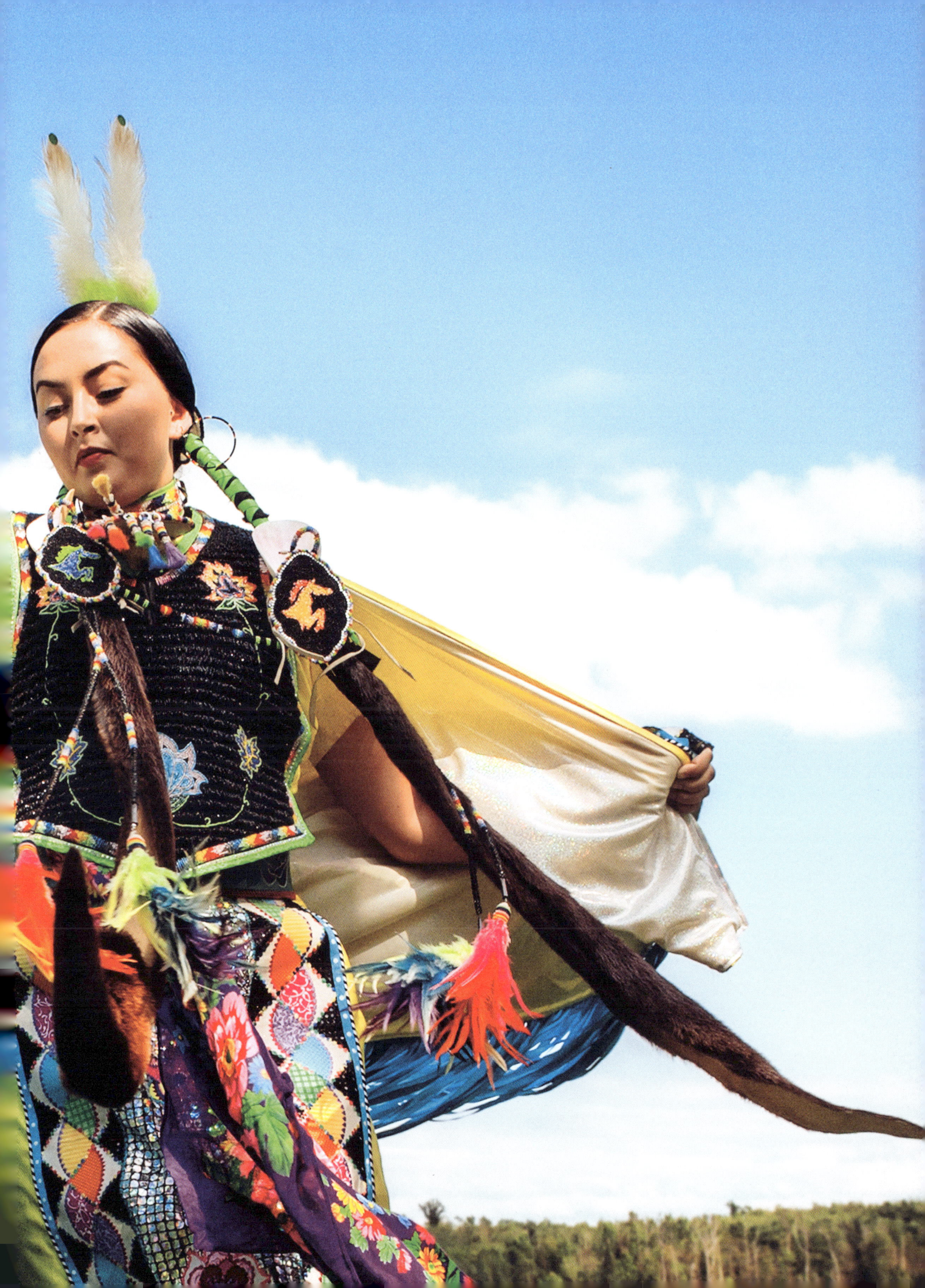

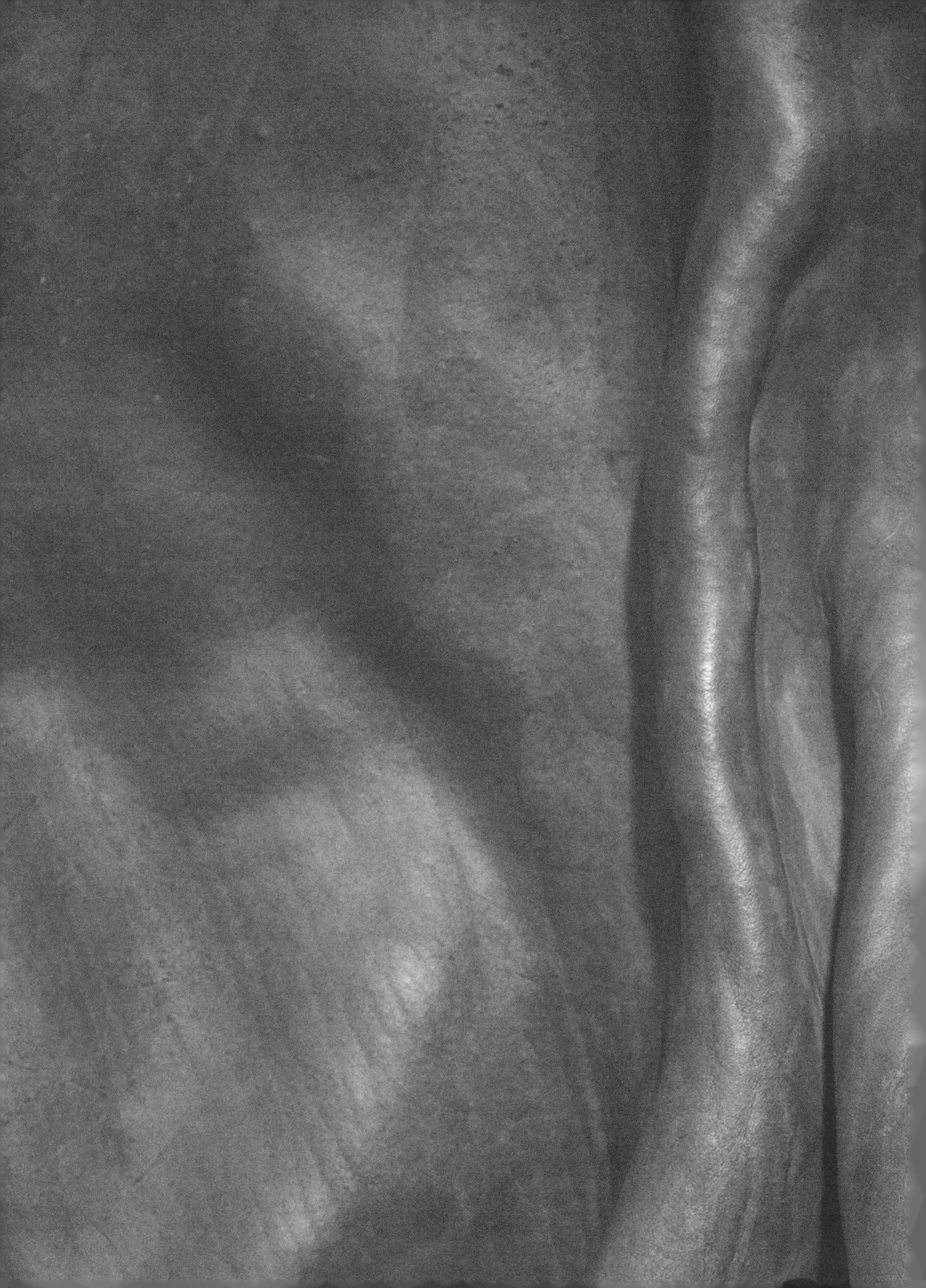

Leather

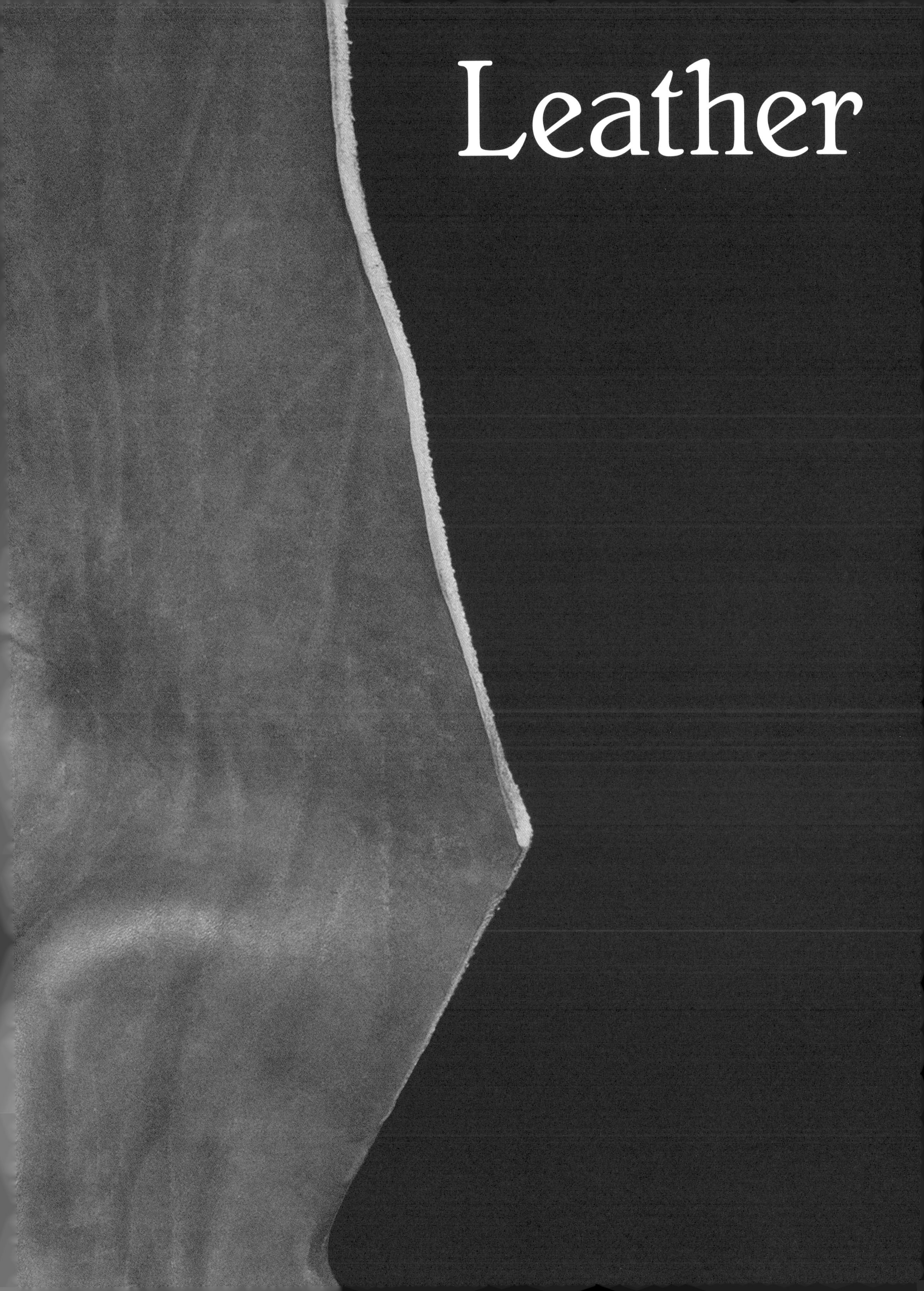

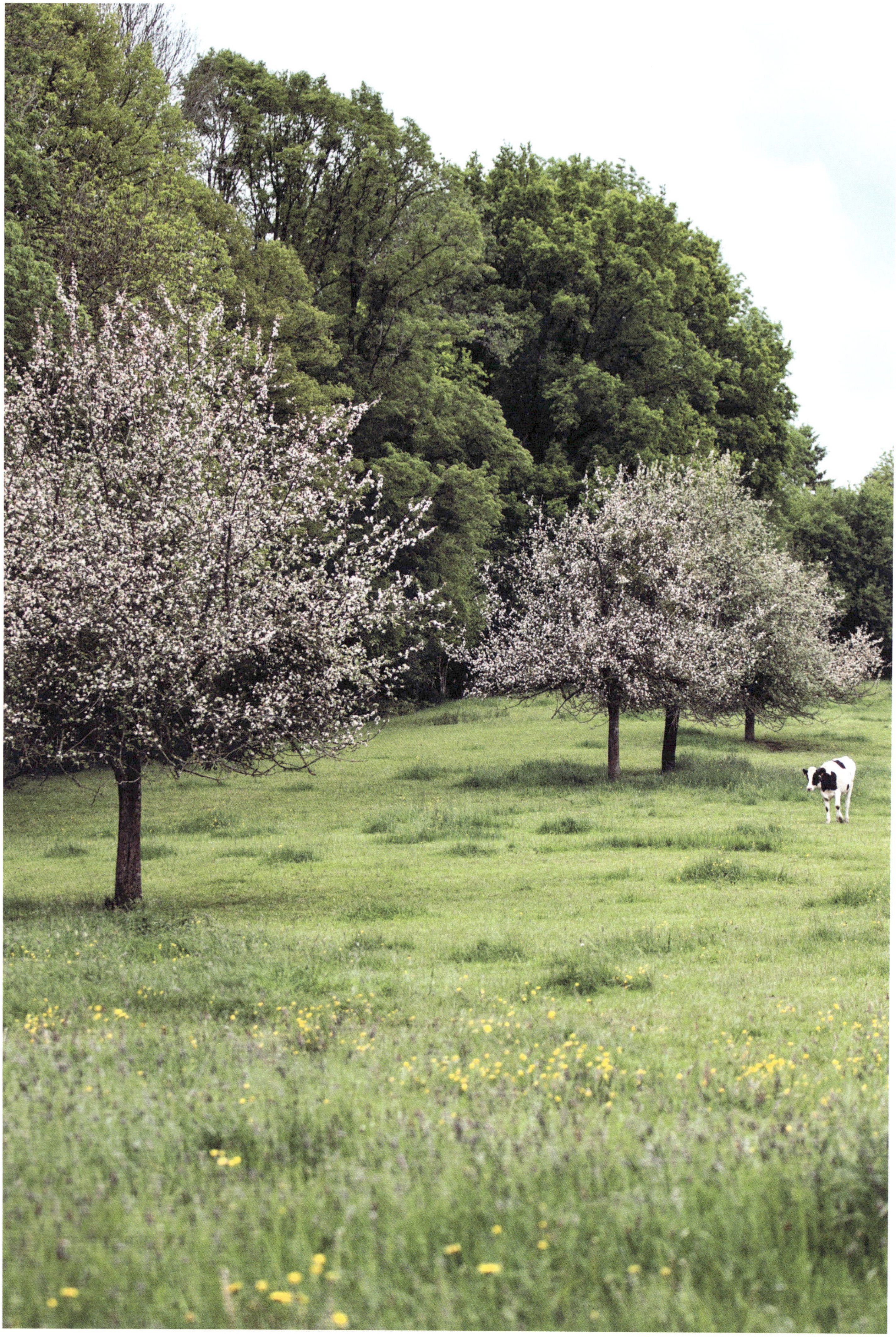

Élise Blouet

Leather restorer

Normandy, France

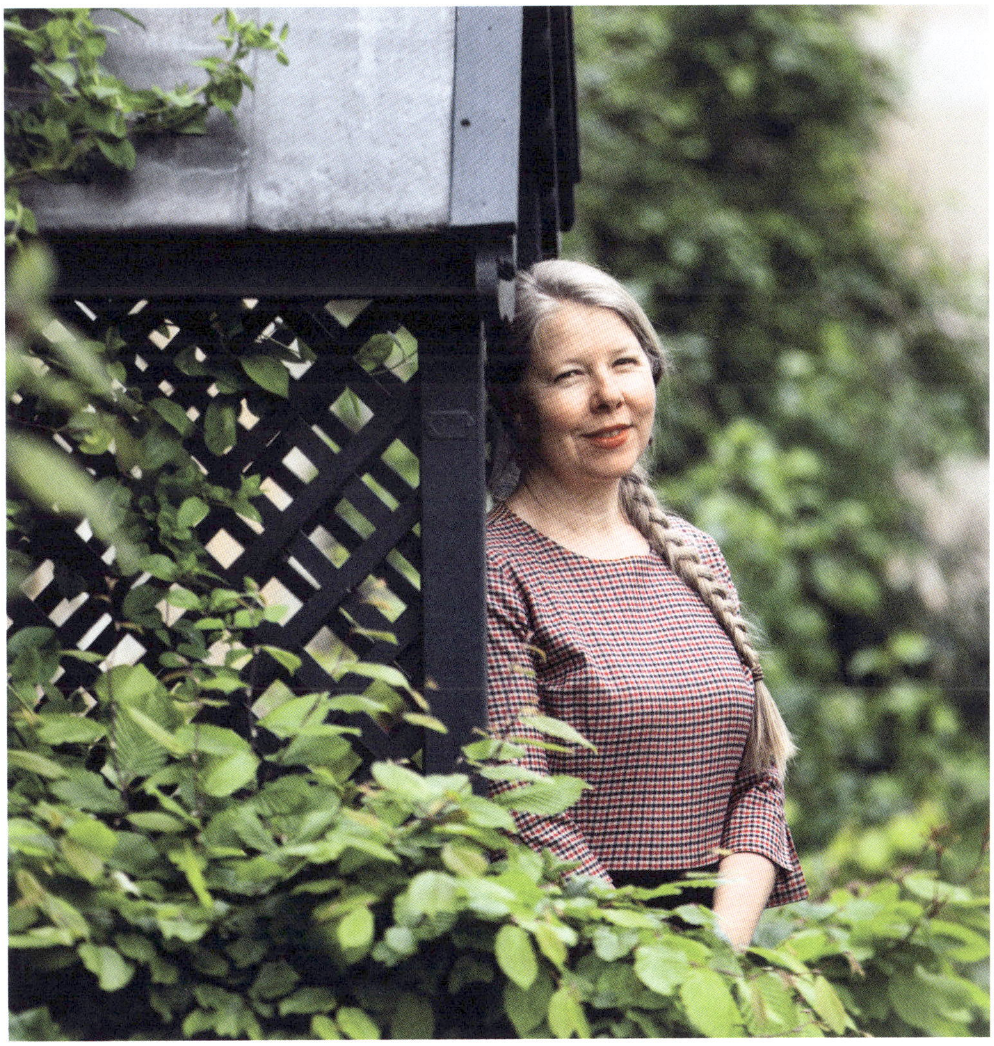

My name is Élise Blouet and I work with Russia leather. As a child, I loved tinkering with old objects, like a World War I bicycle that I restored. After studying science, I learned about conservation-restoration: an academic discipline that combines art and history. When I was twenty-one, I met Antoine Mannella, who agreed to give me an apprenticeship at his workshop for the conservation and restoration of antique weapons in Sainte-Croix, Switzerland. For three years, he treated me like his protégée and taught me how to work with my hands. I learned to file, forge, weld, hammer, dismantle, and reassemble sixteenth-century armor. He sent me to the workshops of his artisan friends to learn other skills, including stained-glass restoration, cabinetmaking, clock restoration, and marquetry.

At Mannella's, the armor often had deteriorating leather straps. I started asking myself questions about this material but found very few answers. After researching leather, I fell headlong into the subject. I ended up spending a year working with leather specialists and doing an internship at the Leather Conservation Centre in Northampton, in the United Kingdom. One day, at the center, Roy Thomson, a former tanner, brought me a sample of Russia leather.

A few years later, a friend of mine sent me a sample of the same type of leather from the wreck of the *Catharina von Flensburg*, found off the coast of Plymouth in southwest England. Although it had spent more than two hundred years under the sea, the fragment of Russia leather was in perfect condition. Normally, classic leather can be preserved in seawater, but in the open air it will shrink, dry out, and become brittle. However, the Russia leather from the shipwreck had simply been rinsed with clear water and could be used as it was. This leather was known in the past for being rot-proof—a fact that has now been confirmed.

Russia leather was traditionally made from mammal hide that was rinsed and prepared, then placed in a vat with a decoction of tree bark. The tannins in the bark slowly penetrated the hide over a period of months, transforming it into leather. In France, tanners mainly used oak and chestnut bark. In Russia, they used willow and birch, and it was this difference that gave Russia leather its distinctive qualities.

The first mentions of this leather appear in customs texts dating back to the seventeenth century. Czar Peter the Great wanted to open Russia up to Europe, so he organized numerous trade exchanges, and exports of Russia leather increased. The Russians sent their "first choice" leather to Western Europe, where only the best craftsmen could afford to buy this exceptional material to make high-quality objects. The reputation of Russia leather dates back to this period, and attempts to copy it in France and England were unsuccessful. Then came the Industrial Revolution and the Russian Revolution, and the recipe was lost.

To rediscover the composition, I relied on ancient texts: I sailed up rivers in Russia with travelers during the reign of Catherine II, explored the world with Marco Polo and his *Book of Wonders*, and retraced the history of the royal tannery in Saint-Germain-en-Laye, west of Paris, which had attempted to produce Russia leather using French techniques.

I was fortunate enough to be given access to many museum storerooms in order to study examples of Russia leather. Scientific analyses helped define the type of tannin used. For this project, a "nose" was indispensable: I will always remember the magical moment when, bending over a seventeenth-century binding in the Bibliothèque du Théâtre at the Château de Chantilly, Mr. Guichard, a perfumer for Givaudan, succeeded in identifying the willow and birch that had been used to tan the leather, down to their exact proportions.

Today, we are taking a global approach to get back to "virtuous" or responsible leather. Recreating leather "the old-fashioned way" is not a step backward—it is a vision for the future based on a durable, high-quality material. During my research, I learned patience, and I have wholeheartedly adopted this tanner's saying: "To make leather, you need time and tanbark."

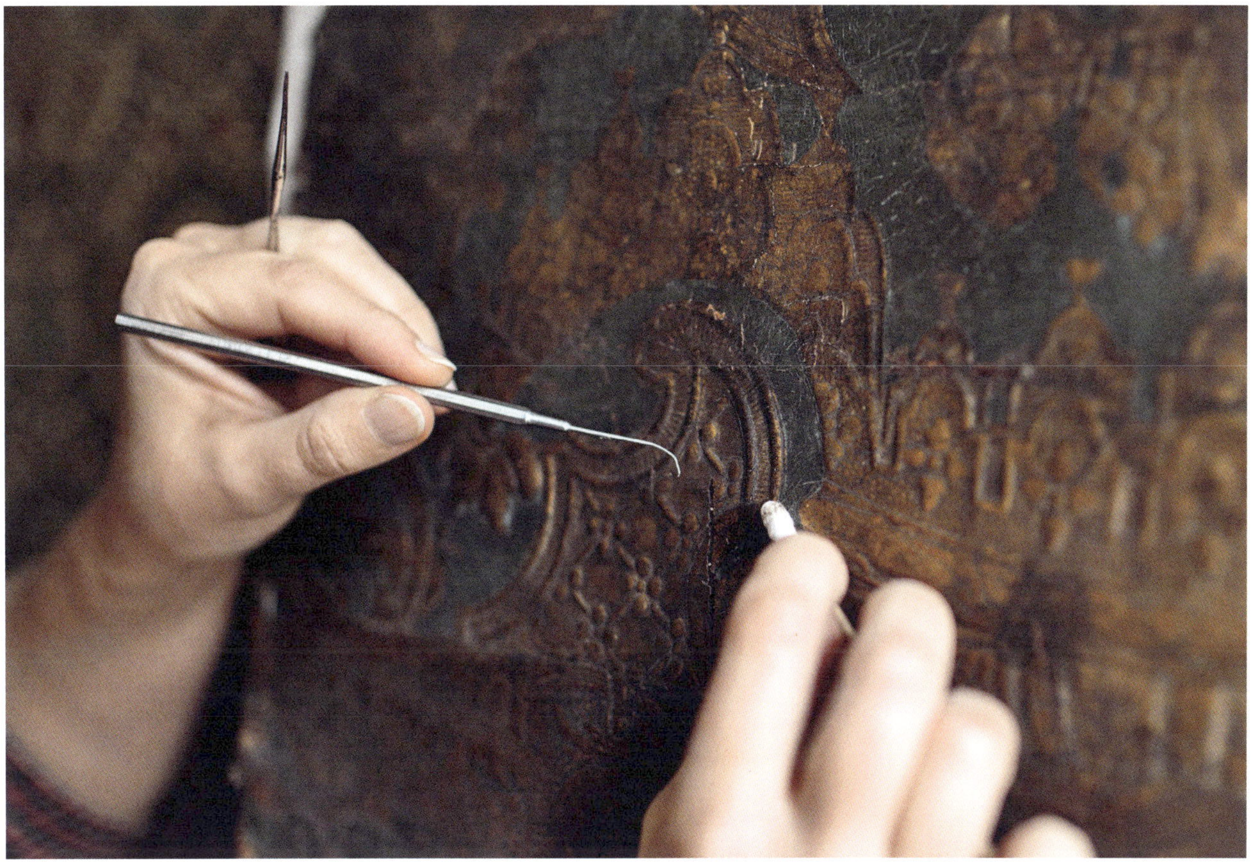

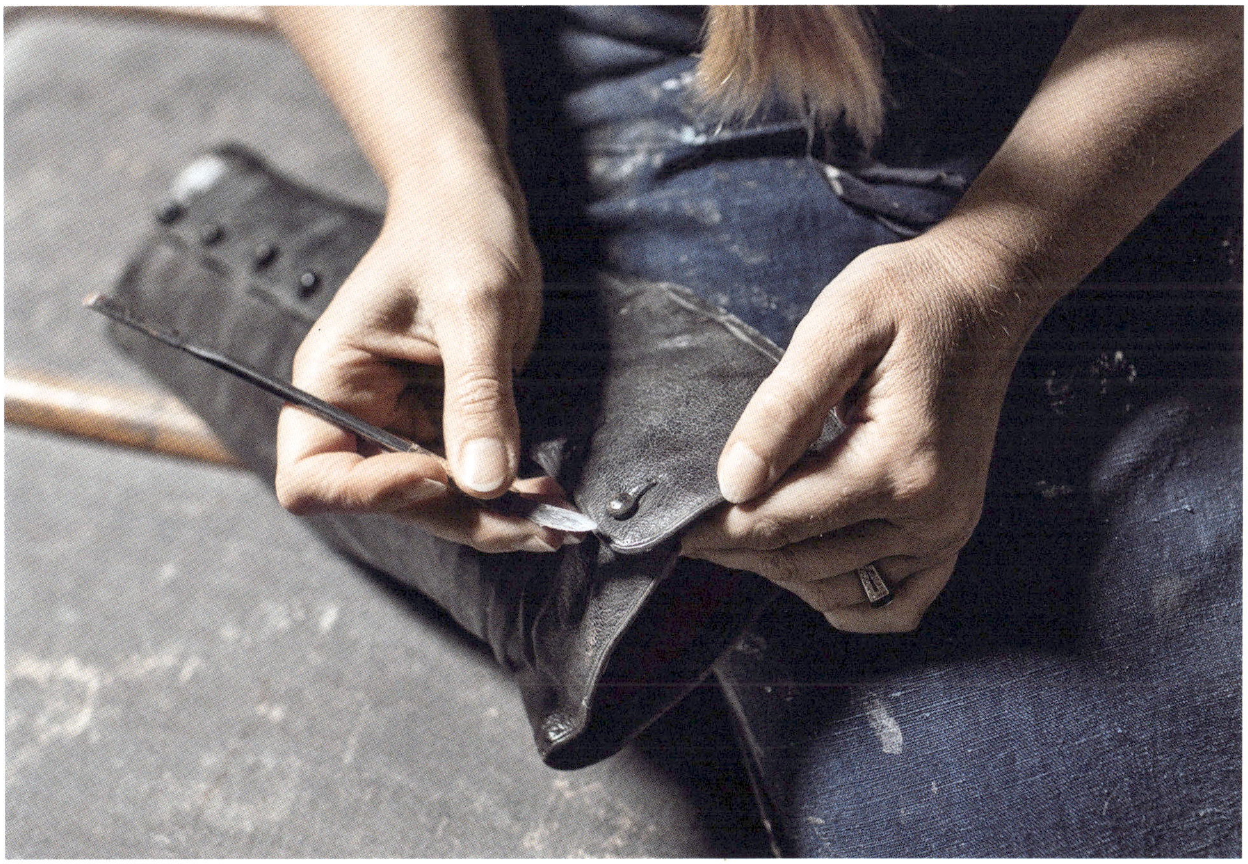

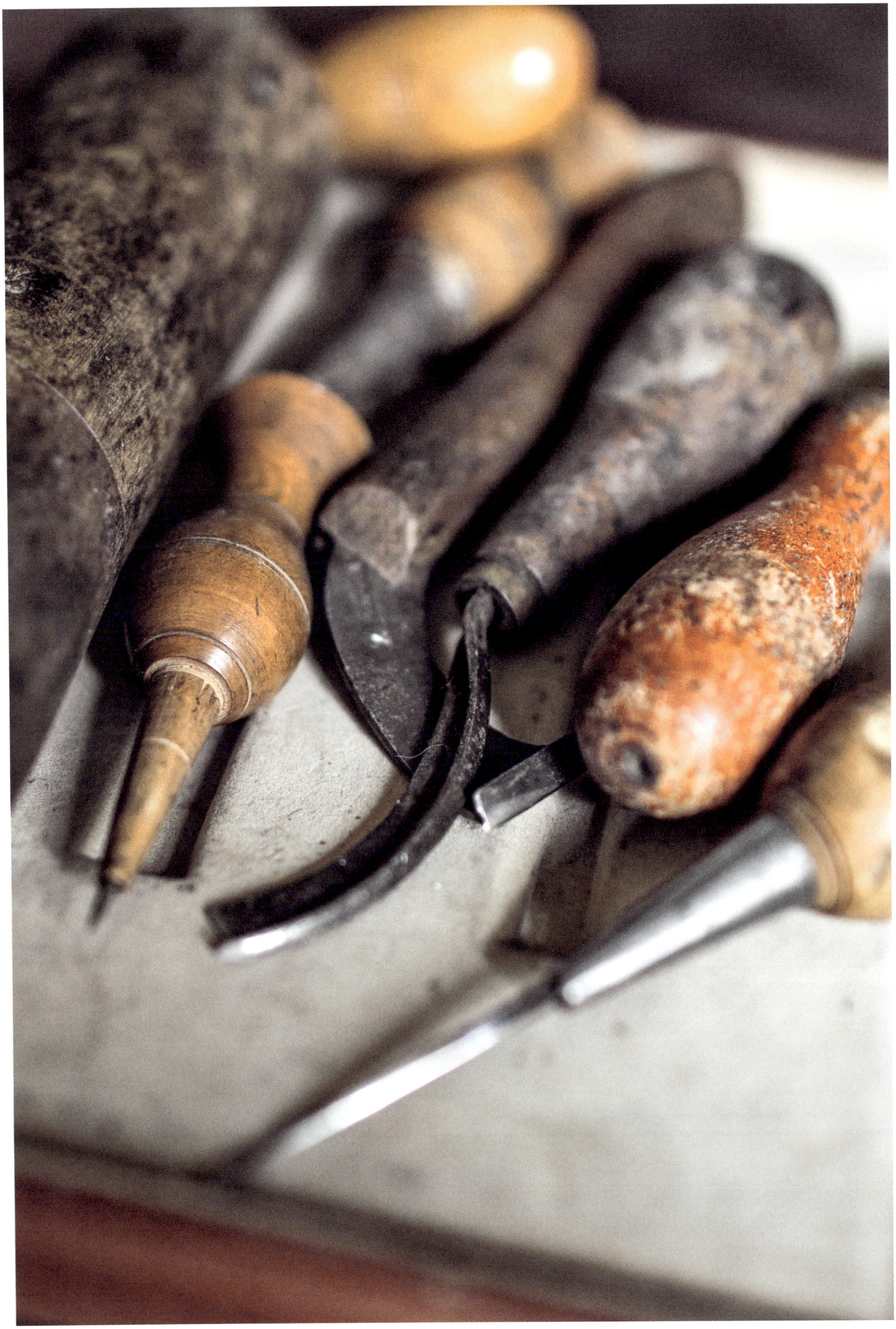

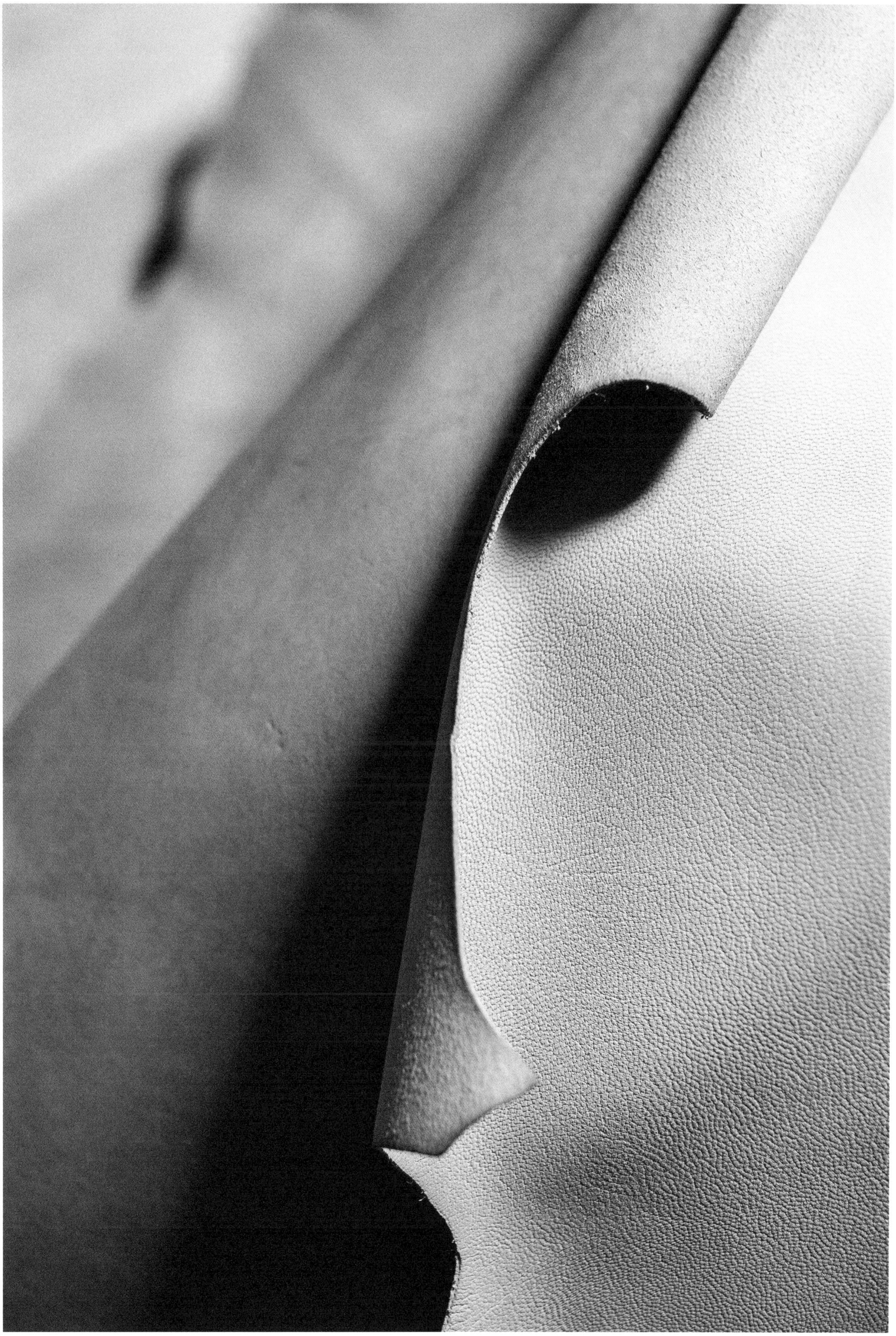

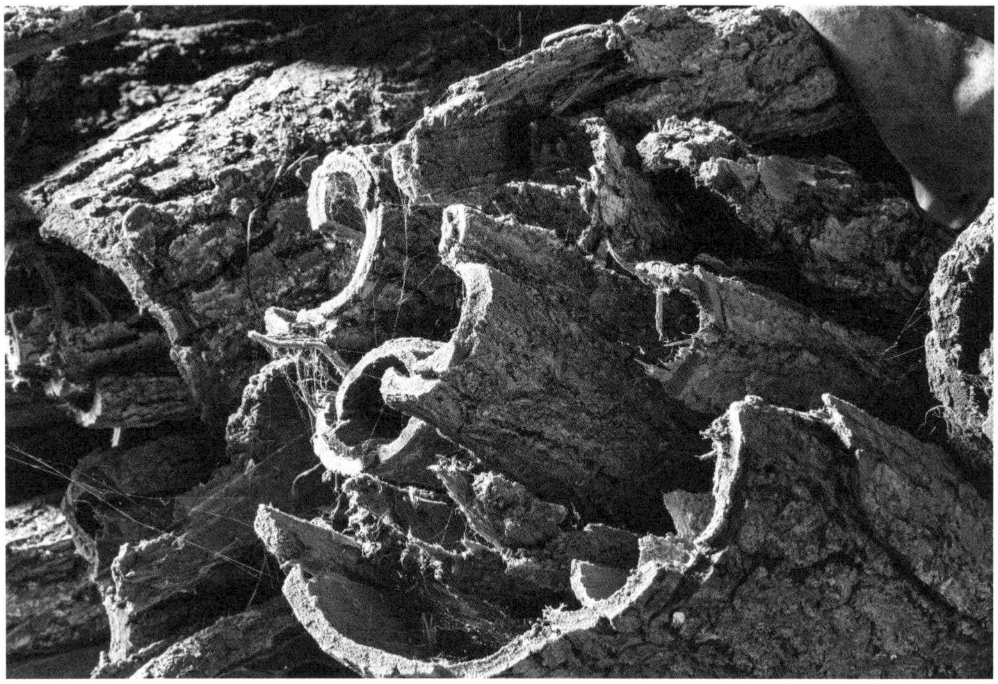

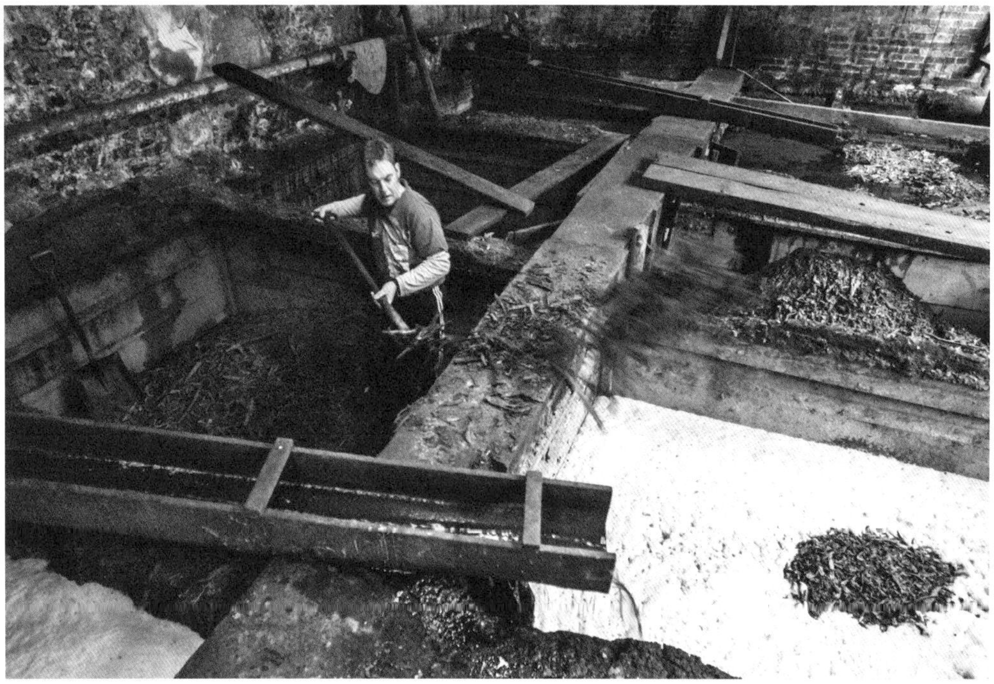

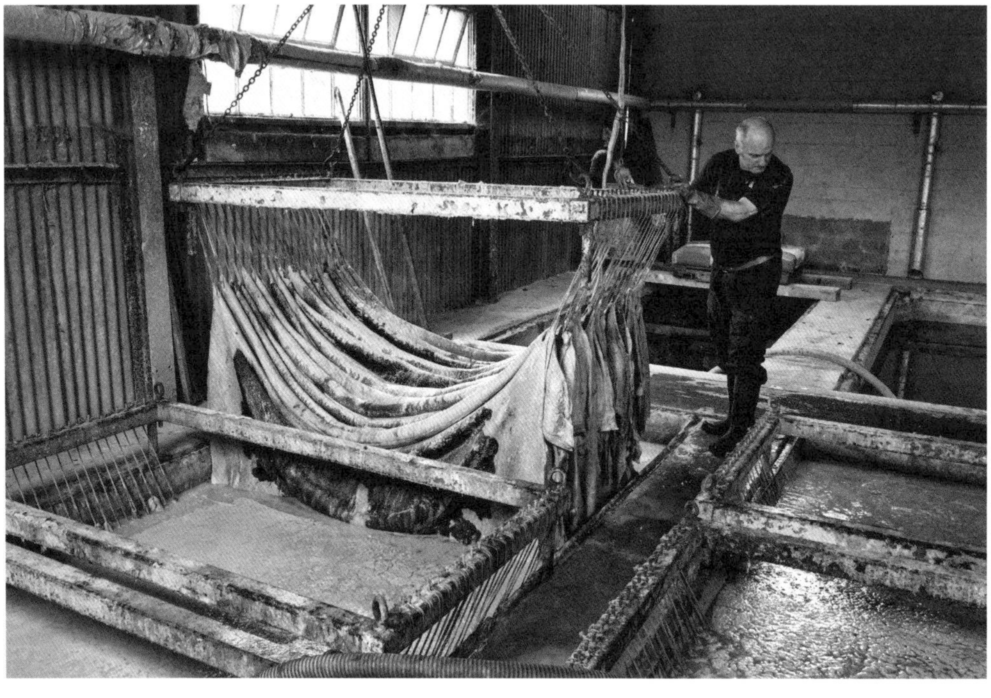

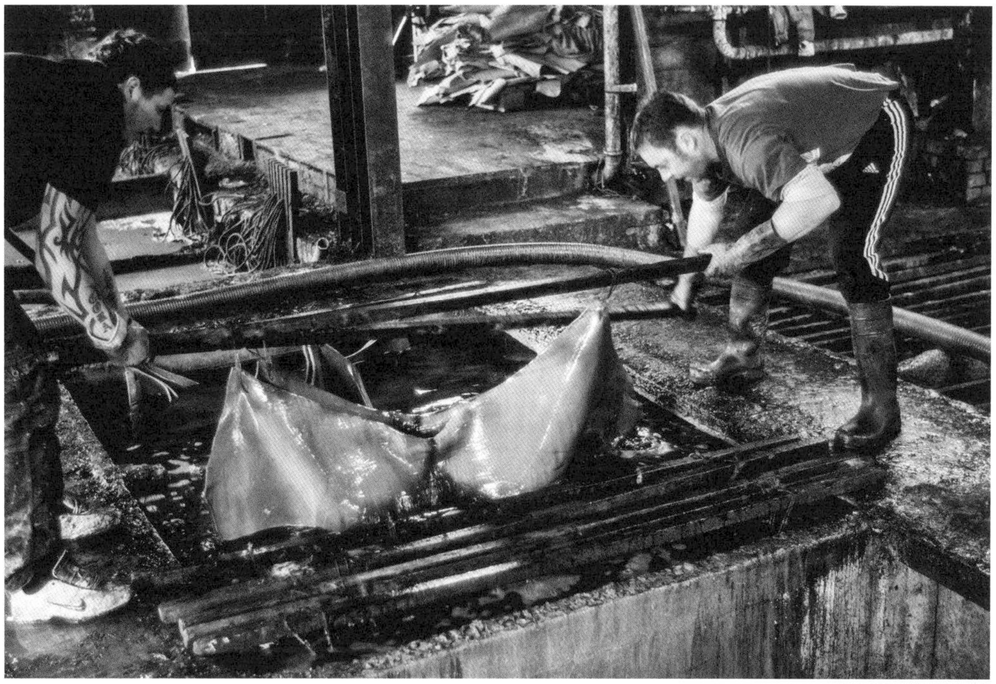

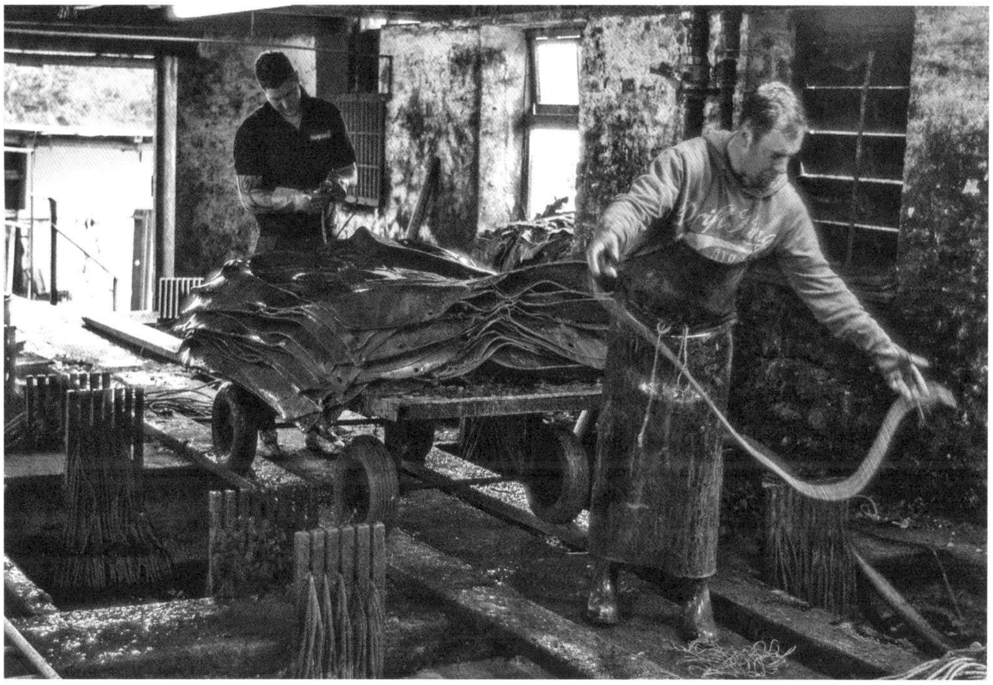

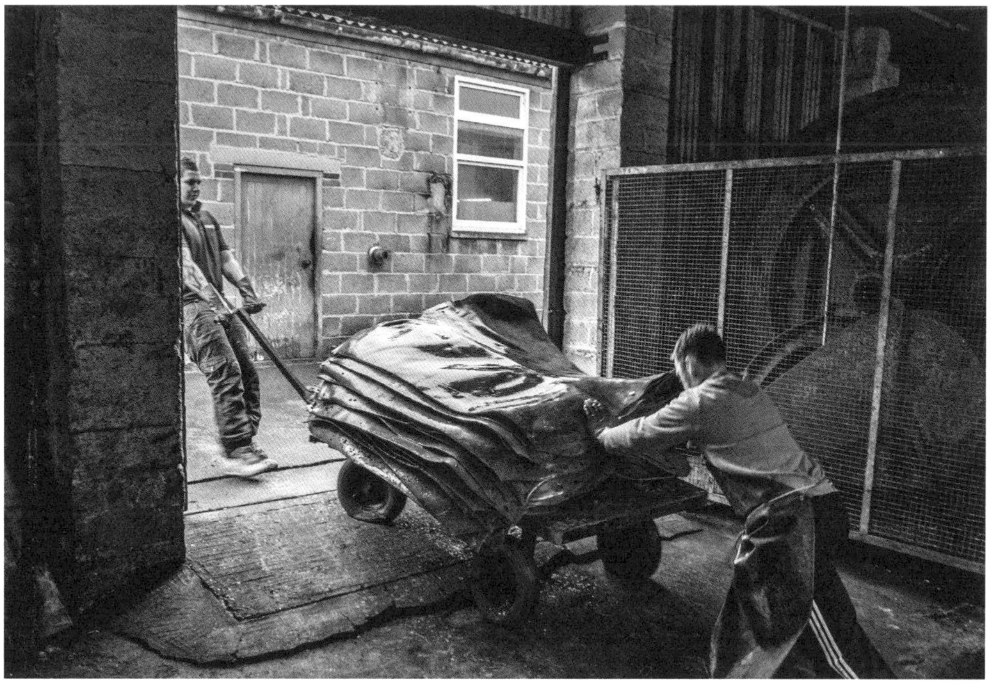

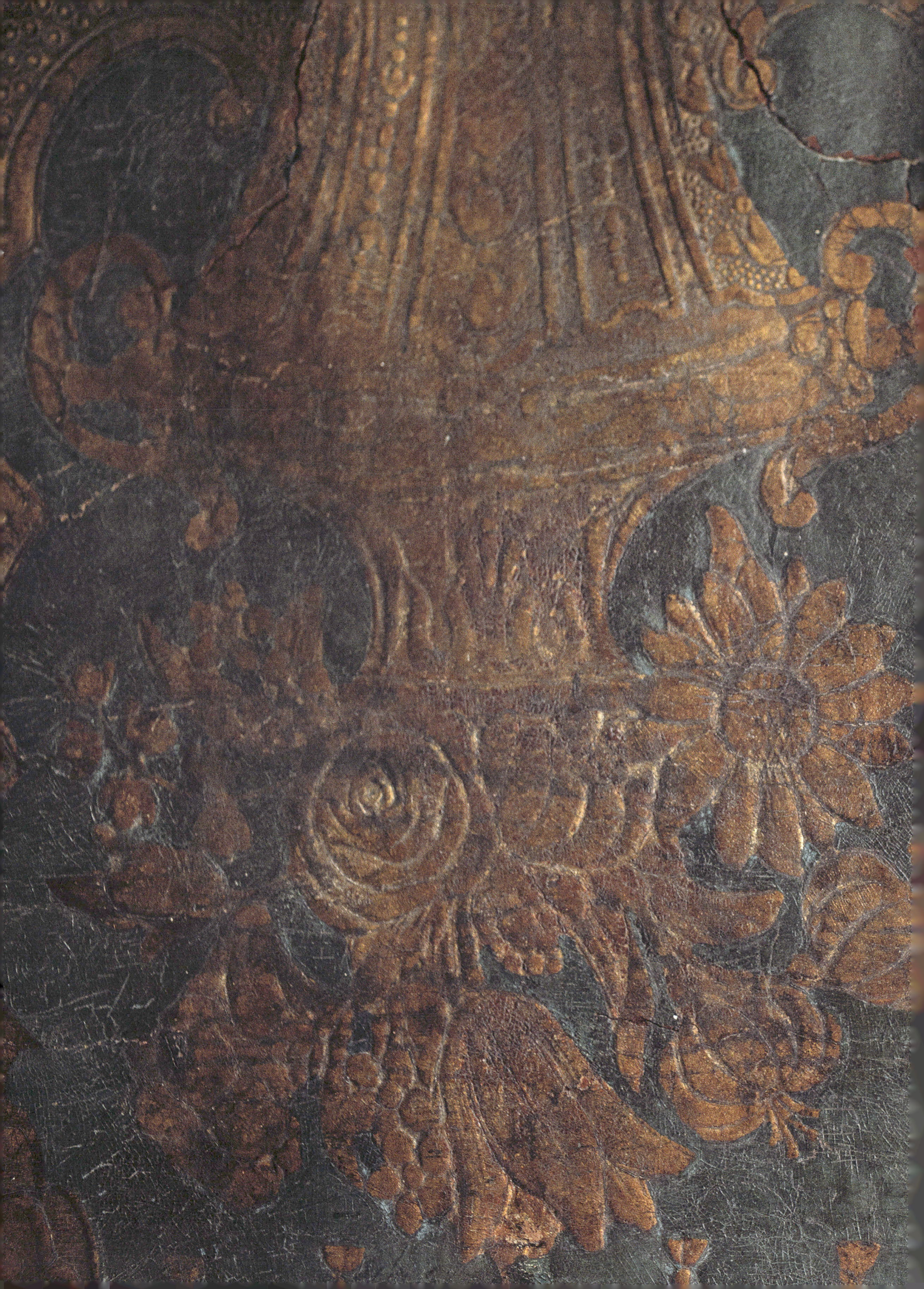

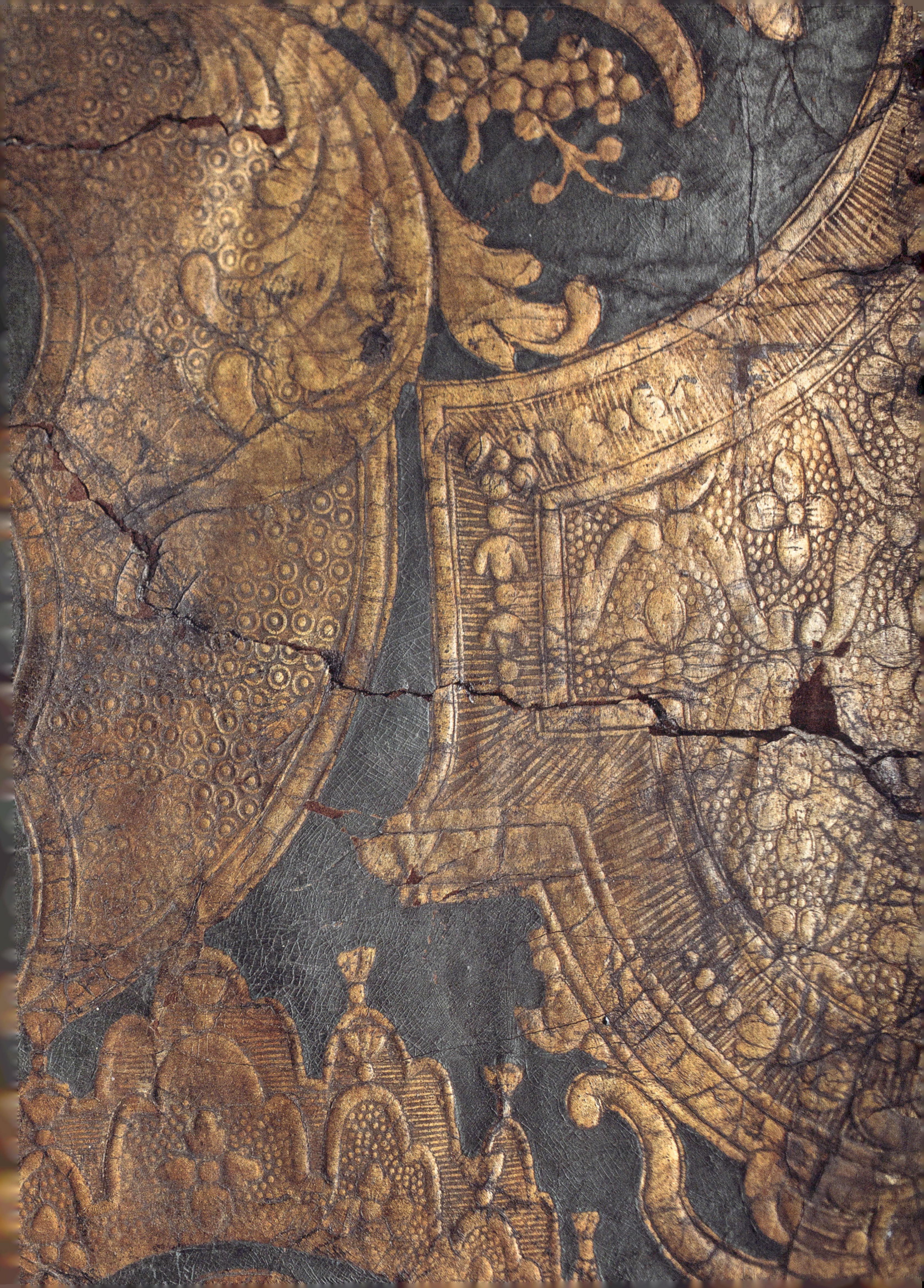

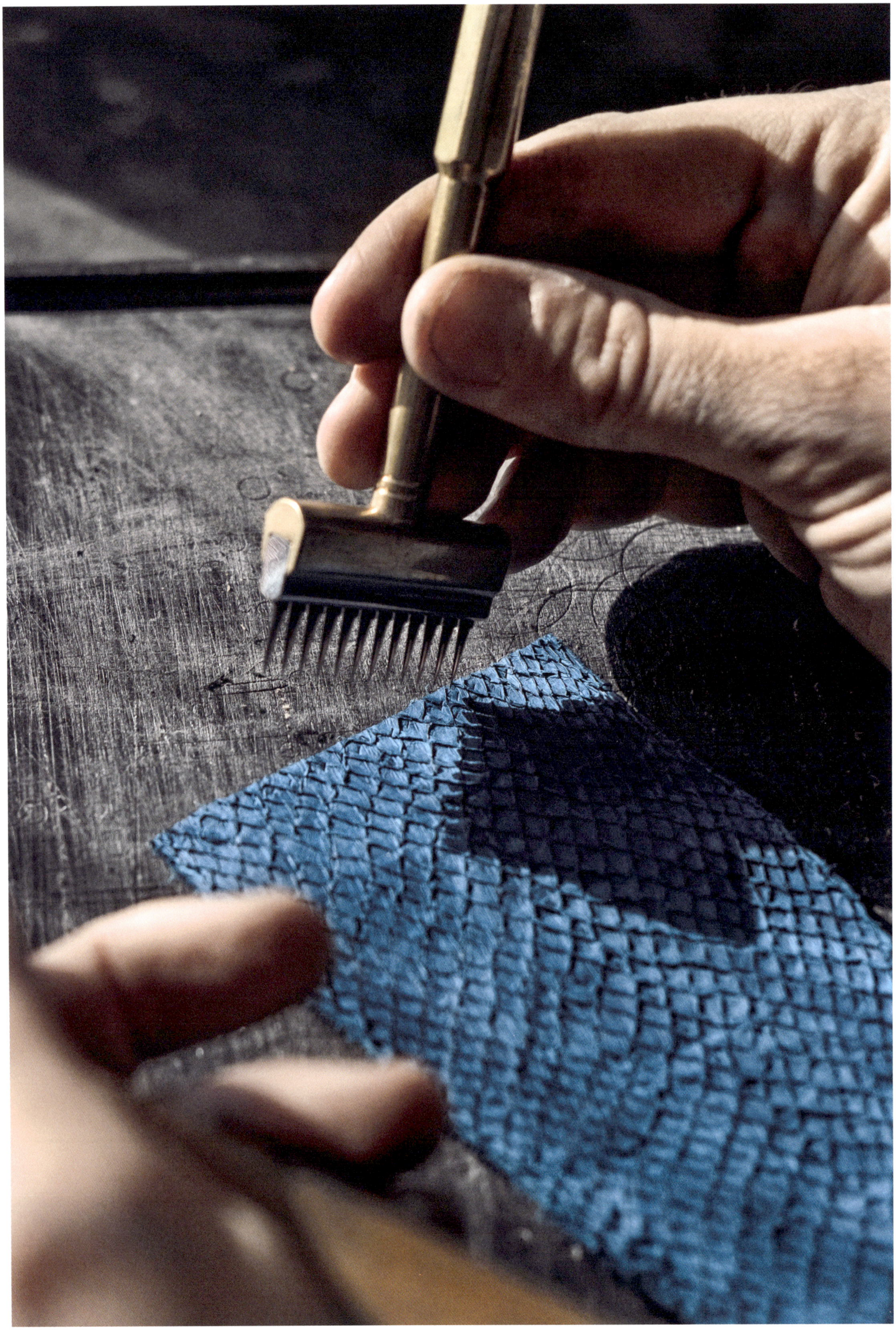

Daniel Ankarstrand

Leather craftsman and designer

Stockholm, Sweden

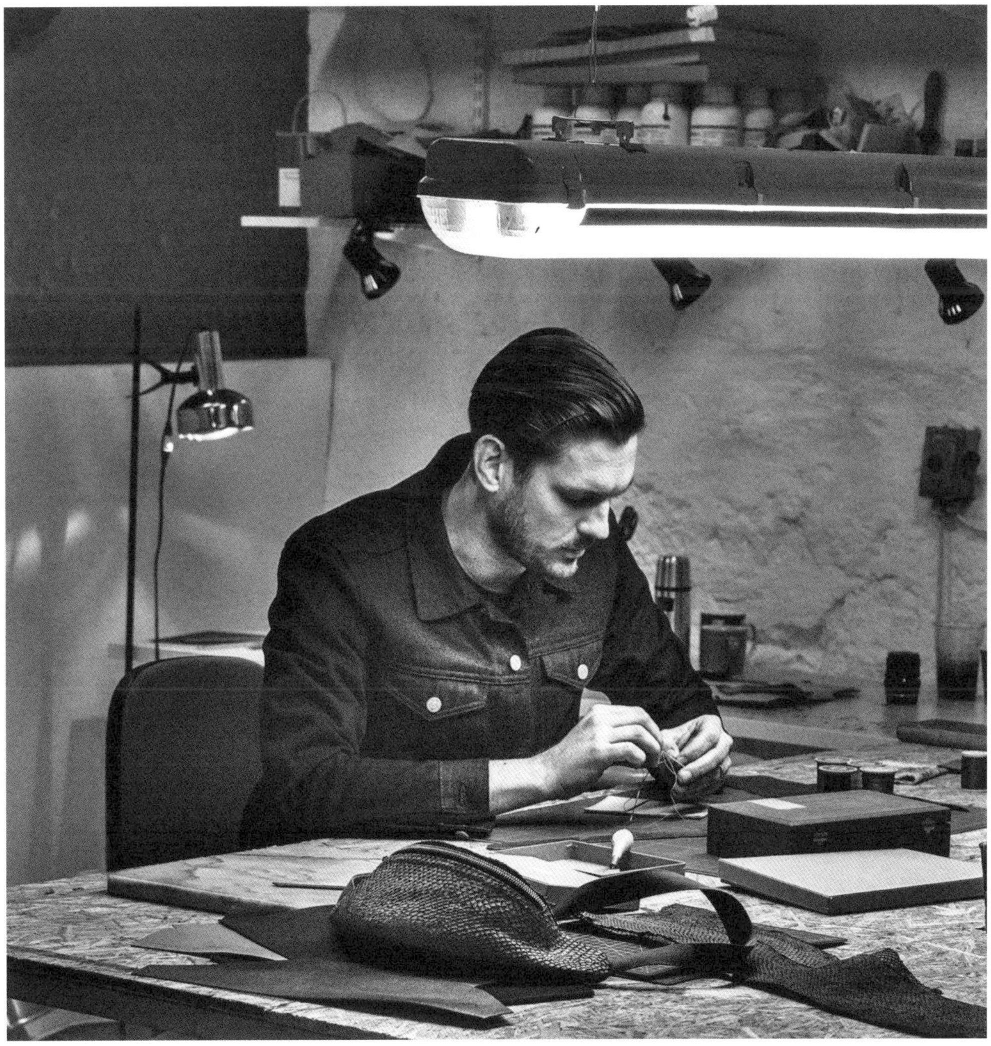

My name is Daniel Ankarstrand, and I am a designer and leather craftsman. My grandfather was an inventor and could fix everything with anything. My father had the same skill, and I have always enjoyed repairing broken objects.

I am a trained therapist, but I have always had a creative activity on the side. When working with people, you never really see the final result, because humans are continually evolving in one way or another. But when a wallet is finished, you see the end result of your work. That distinct difference always offered me a welcome relief when working with people in difficult situations.

If I were to take on a title, it would be "saddler." I have a great respect for this profession, and I'm trying my best to master the craft. I didn't know anything about the field when I started out; I am entirely self-taught. I have always struggled with the feeling of not being a "real" artisan—that my work lacks depth and is not as legitimate as that of someone who has received formal training. But at the same time I feel free, without any boundaries, because I simply don't know the rules yet. One of the advantages of not knowing anything is that you don't realize how hard it will be.

It all started in 2011, when my mother-in-law gave me an iPad case for Christmas. I didn't like it, but instead of just getting another one, I wondered how difficult it would be to make one myself. To learn the necessary skills, I read books from the 1930s and watched videos online to see how professionals worked with leather. I was immediately drawn in by the craft and spent an incredible amount of time refining my techniques. I spent several months practicing stitches before I even made my first product; I wanted the slope and length to be perfect. I was obsessed. As for materials, I was determined to source them ethically. I came across salmon leather accidentally; after ordering some samples, I instantly fell in love.

I really enjoy working with large skins, where the pattern repeats itself. If the skin is too small, you don't get the impression of wildness. I like when you can follow the pattern from the belly to the back. Salmon skin has a suede-like texture, so depending on which direction you look at it, you'll see something different. If you look at the skin from the head down, it looks flat and streamlined, but seen from the caudal, or tail, fin, it appears more wild and interesting.

Icelandic salmon leather has an irregular pattern that I really like. It brings out the animal quality. The natural texture is visible: smaller scales on the stomach give way to bigger ones, like mountain peaks, on the back of the fish. You won't find that on other skins.

I always use high-quality leather, and I want to know where it comes from. I work with a tannery in Iceland. The leather's origin makes it more appealing and gives me a great feeling of pride.

Today, I think we have to change our lifestyle to preserve the environment and our future. The way we treat our planet isn't working anymore. Salmon leather was long considered a mere byproduct of the fishing industry, but now it's starting to gain ground in the luxury exotic skins market. I feel that I am at the forefront of a new material that is both sustainable and contributes to changing how we look at luxury products.

Artisans have been a dying breed for many years in Sweden. However, despite modern technology and a loss of interest in the "handmade," Swedes have begun to appreciate and value artisans once again. But being a craftsperson today takes more than just being good at your job. You have to be a storyteller and explain why it takes so much time to learn the craft and make the final product. And you have to master social media, which may be the hardest part.

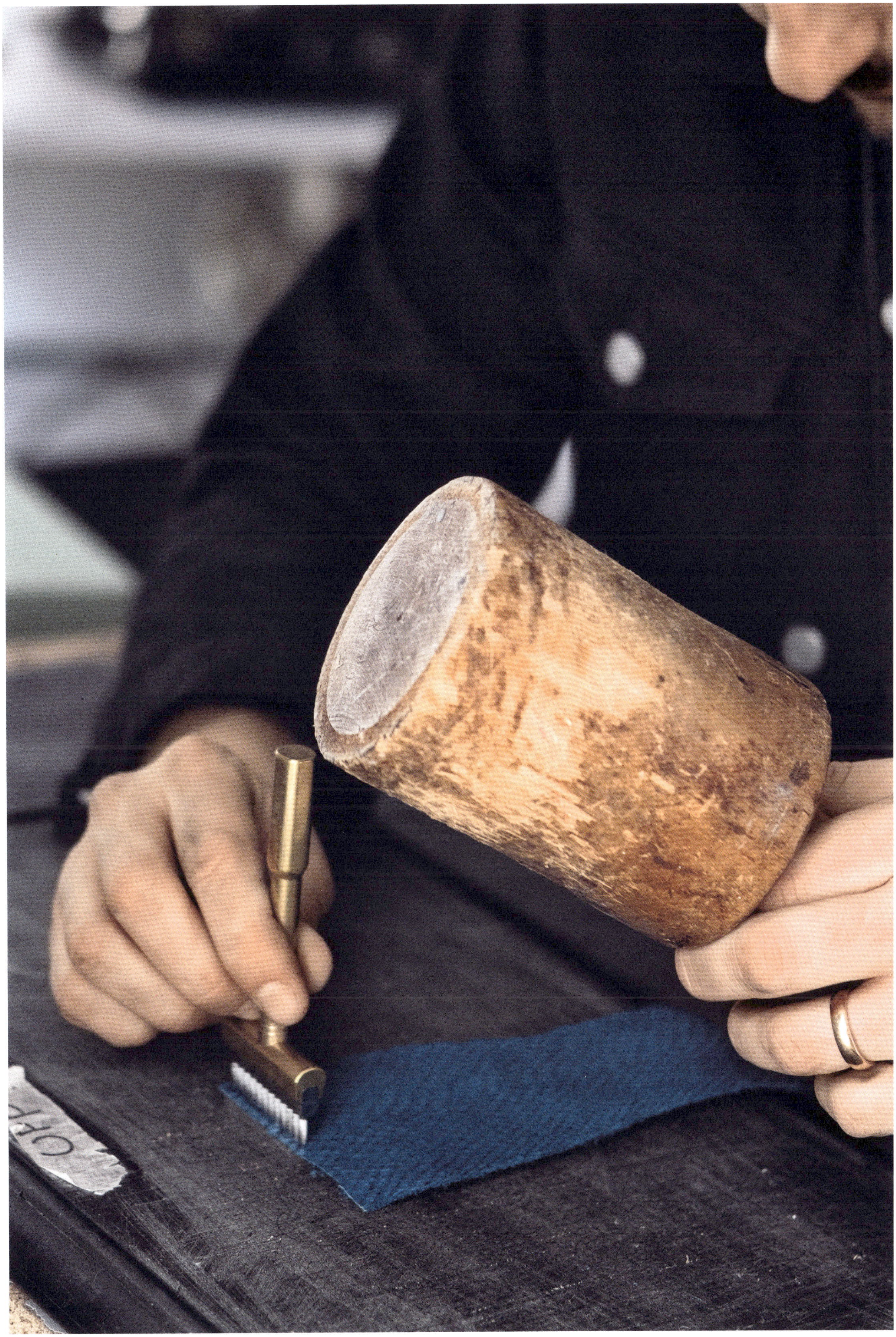

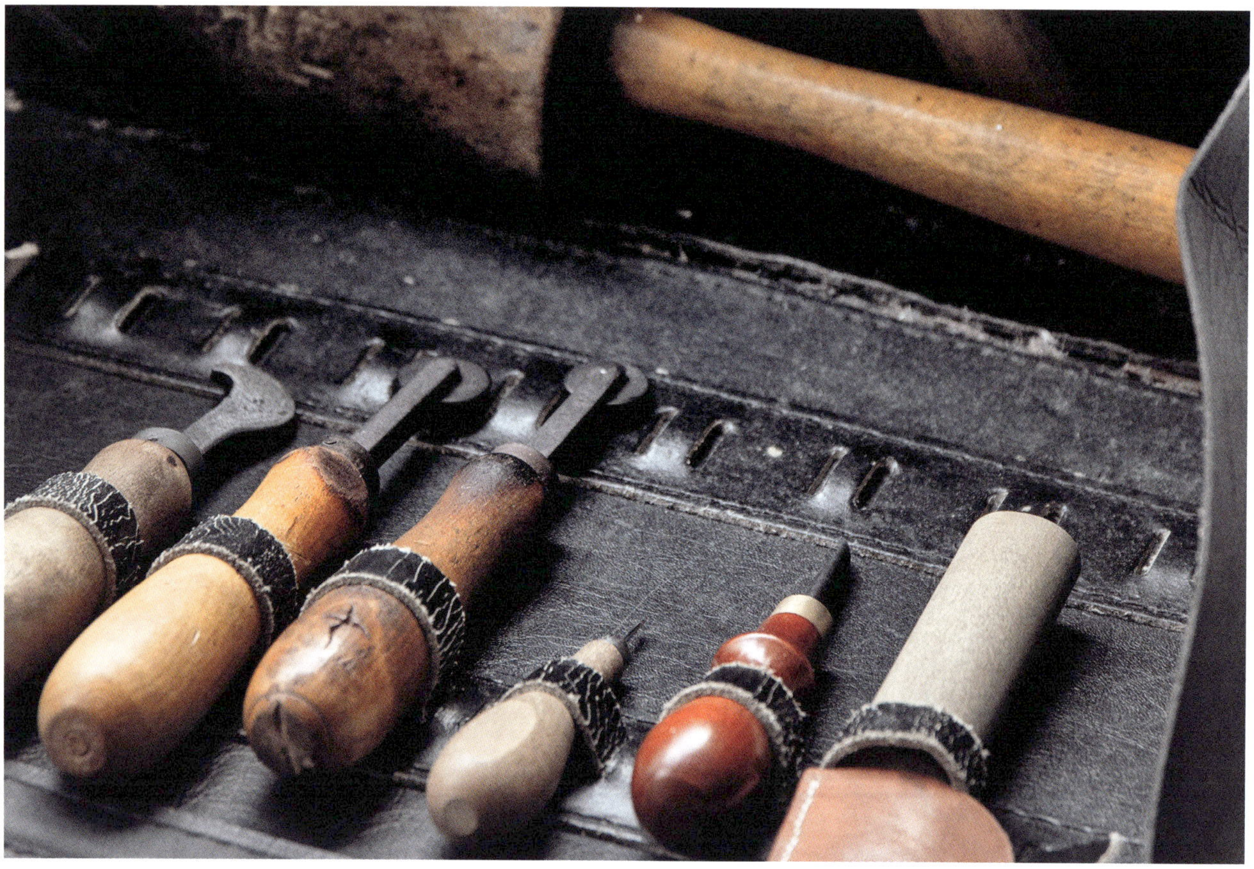

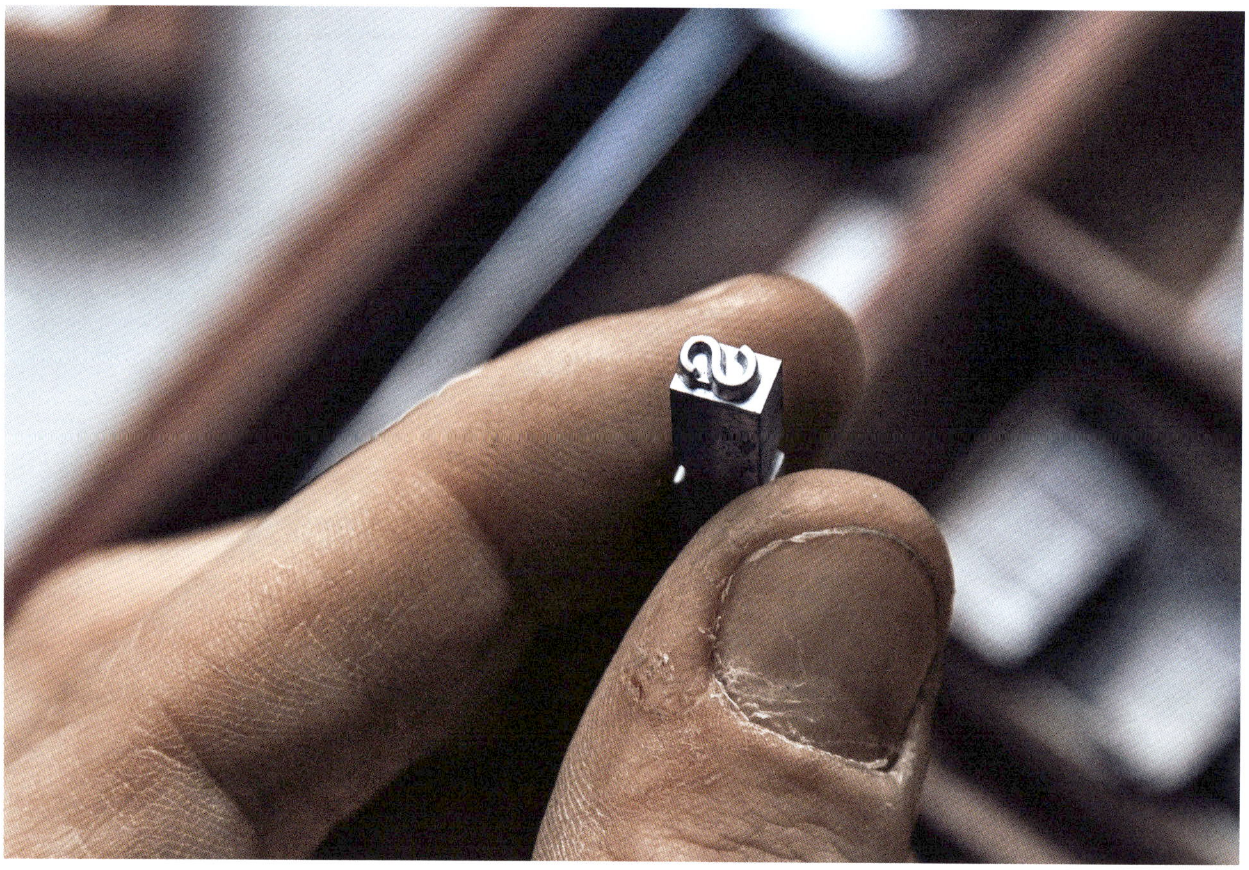

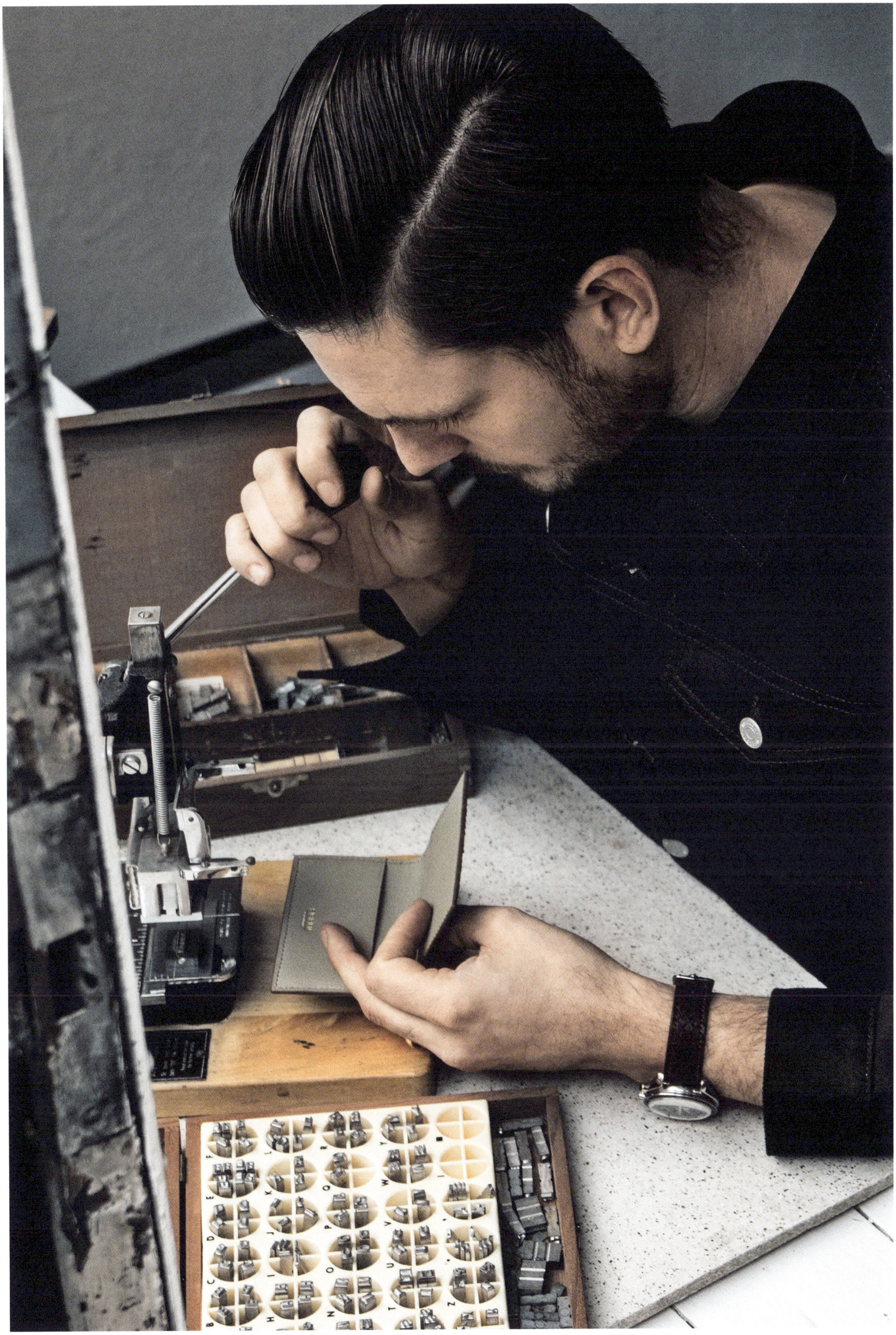

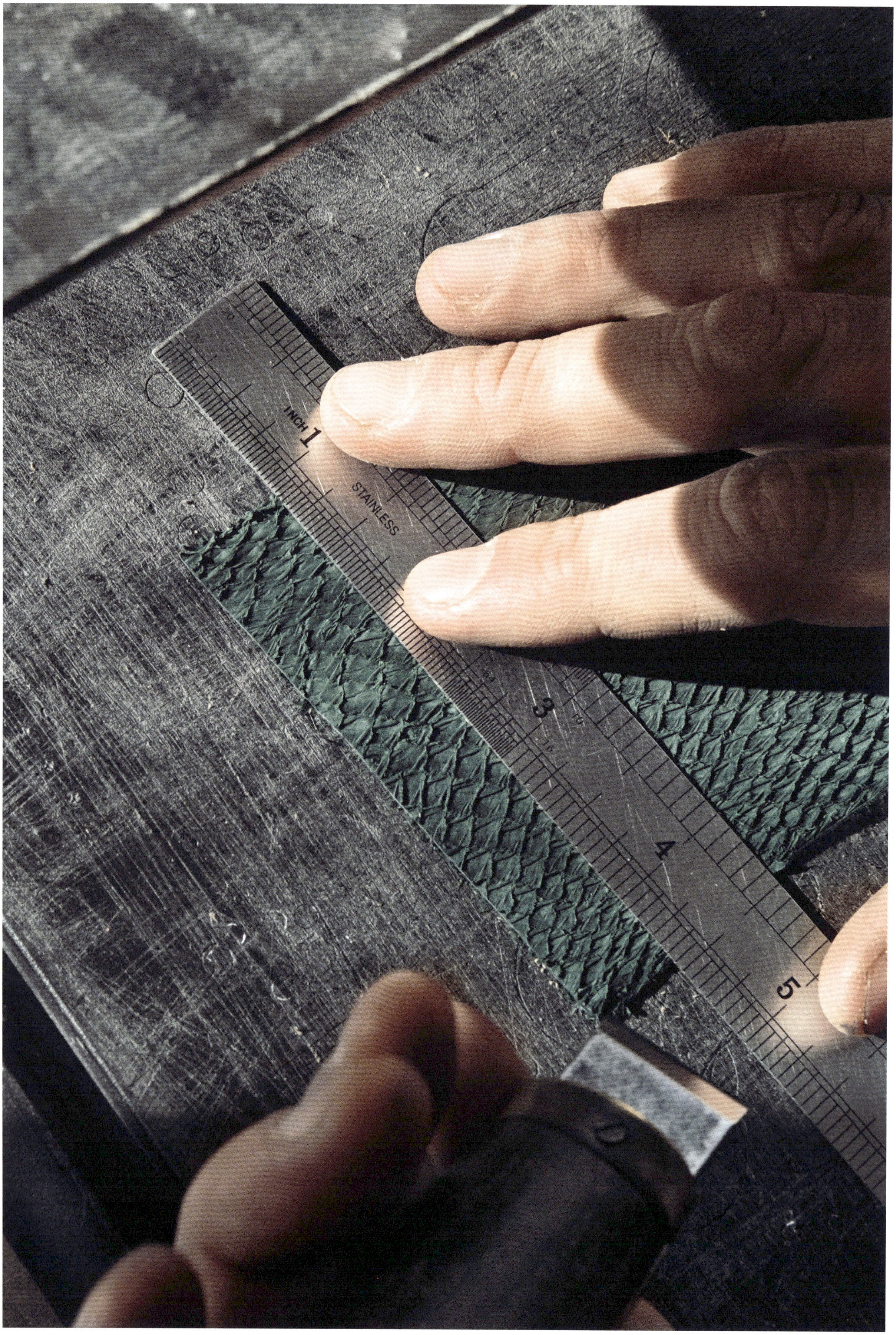
INCH 1
STAINLESS
3
4
5

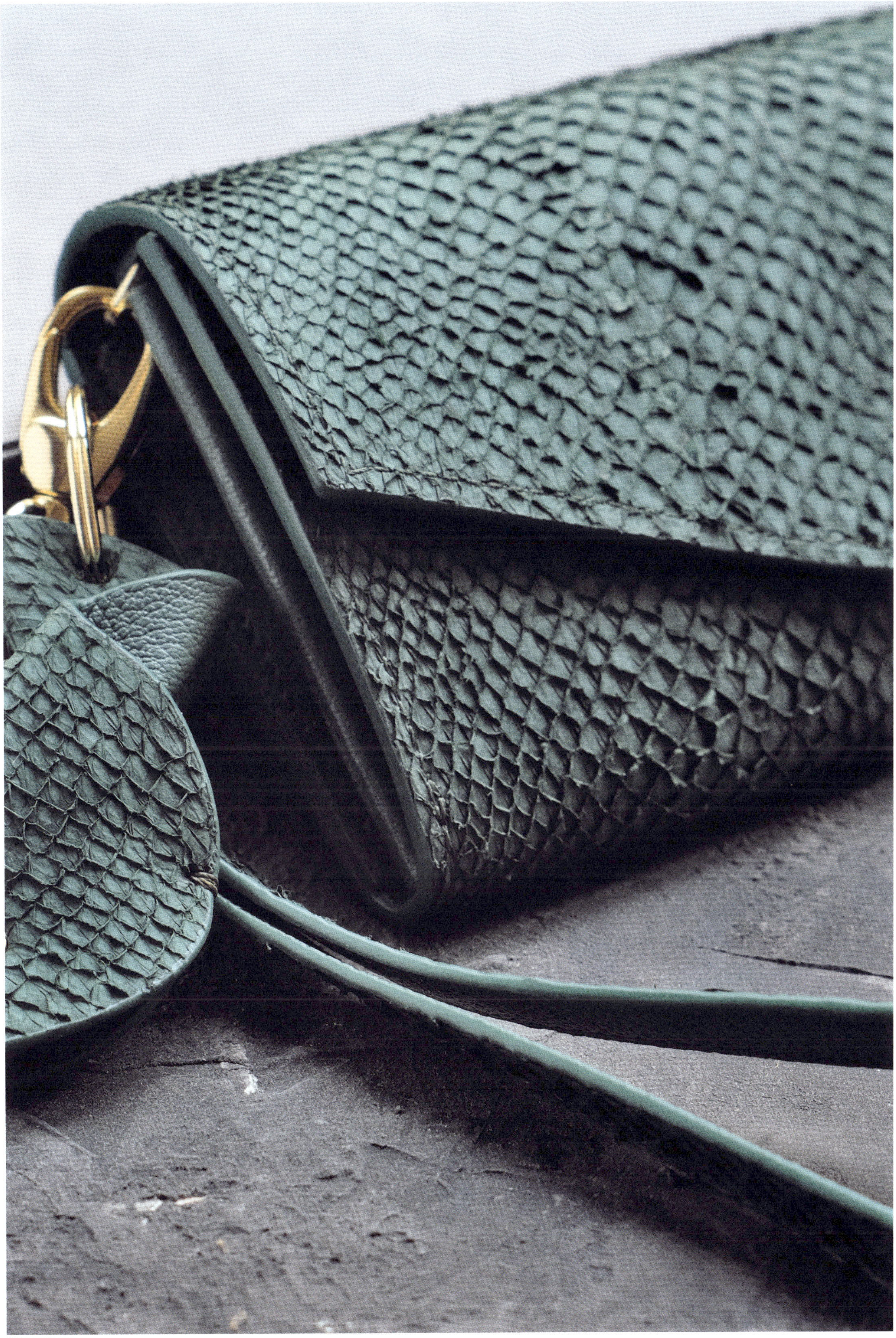

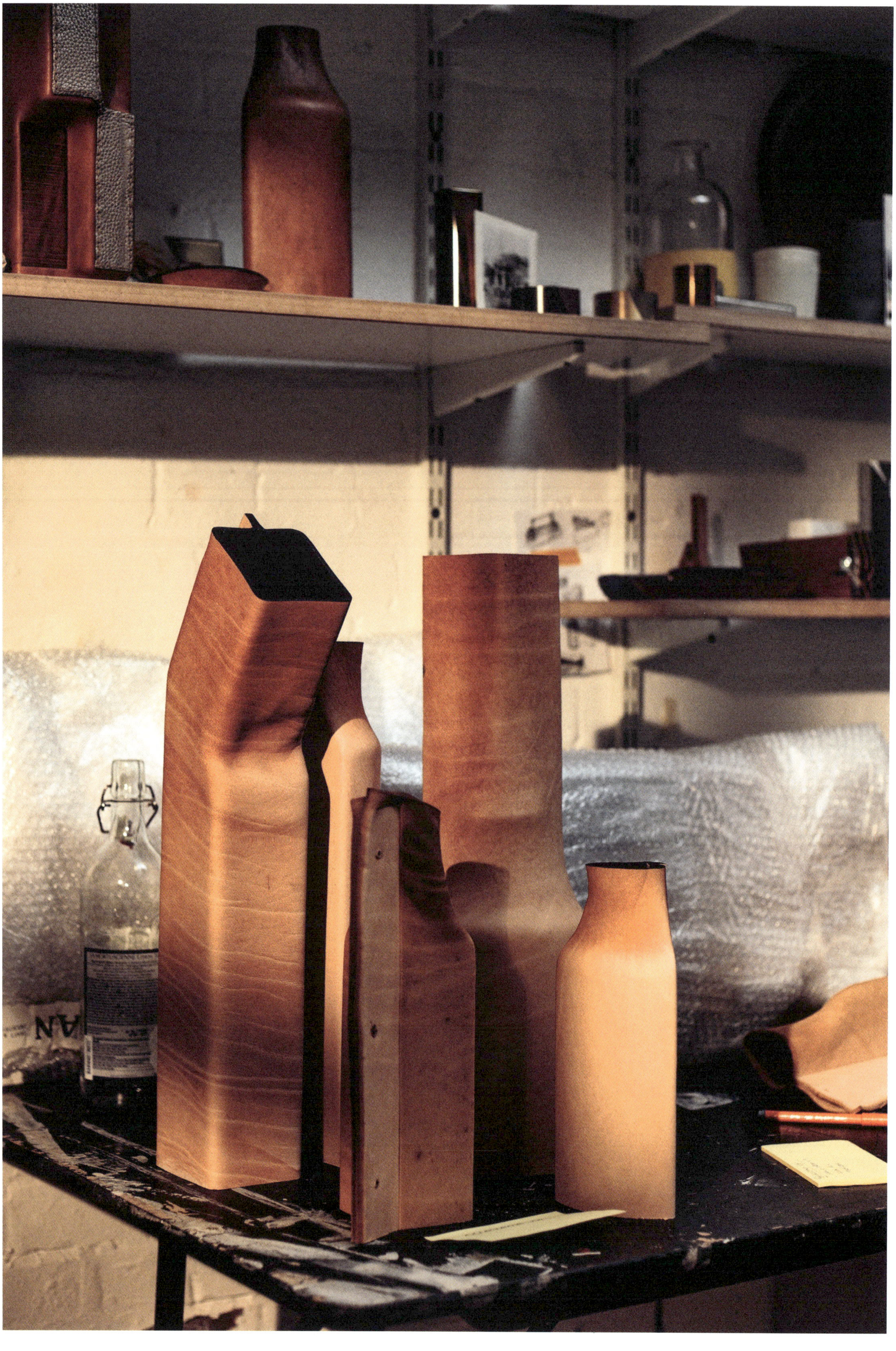

Simon Hasan

Leather craftsman and designer

London,
United Kingdom

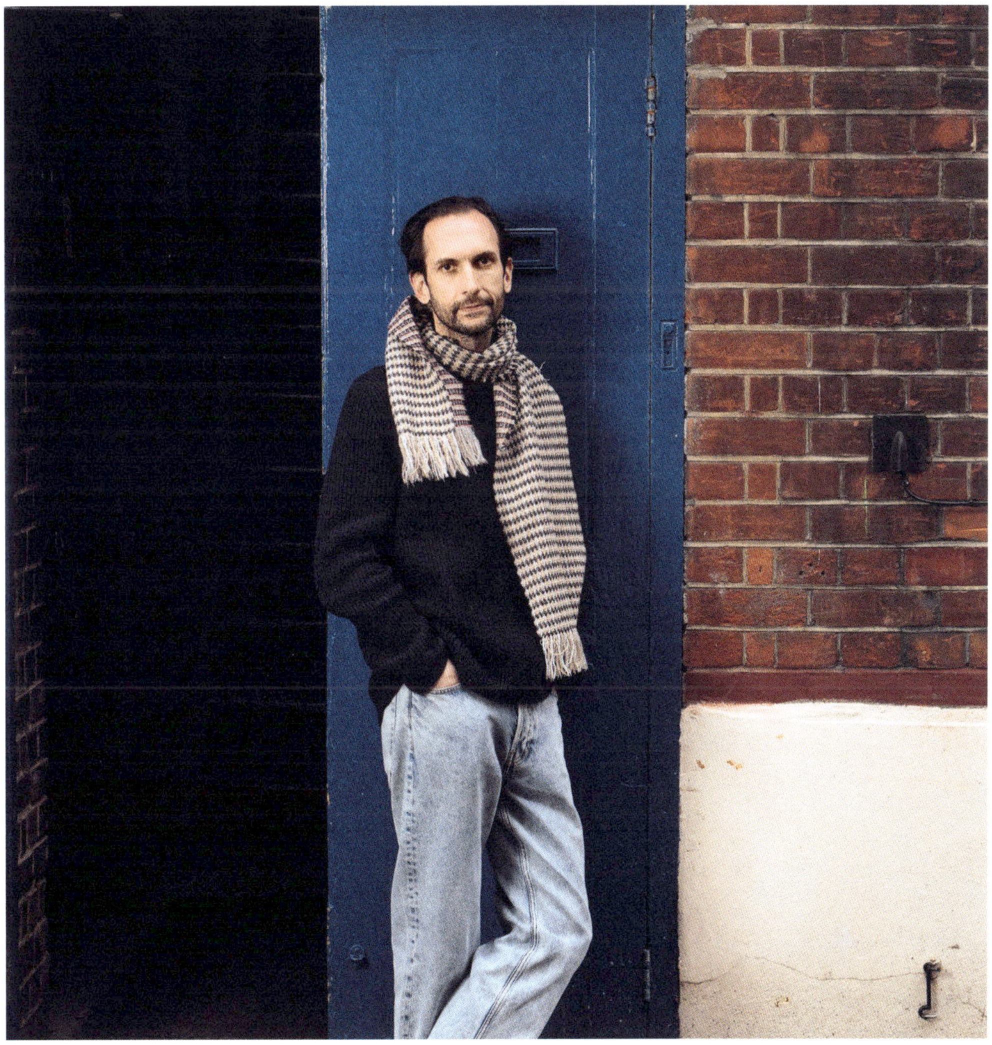

My name is Simon Hasan, and I am a designer with an interest in reinterpreting and recontextualizing tradition. I do this for global luxury brands as well as for my own studio-generated projects.

I have always been interested in history. My mother used to take me to archaeological excavation sites, where I would spend Sundays scraping away layers of soil to reveal pieces of pottery and bone. Craftsmanship and crafts necessarily contain histories and stories, and they have ethnographic value, which I find endlessly captivating.

I originally studied marketing and worked in advertising agencies, before deciding to retrain as a designer at the Royal College of Art in London. During my studies, I loved to spend time in the library. One day, I found a book that referred to an old armor-making technique that used *cuir bouilli*. This heated, vegetable-tanned leather was common in England around the thirteenth to fifteenth centuries and was used to make armor, buckets, helmets, jugs, tankards, and such. I was totally fascinated by the idea of heating leather, which today we think of as a luxury material, to make it hard. It was like alchemy; I had to try it for myself.

I work mostly with leather. I only use very lightly finished, vegetable-tanned hides from reputable tanneries in the United Kingdom, Belgium, and Spain. When I see a skin, I think about how it will respond to my process and the object I have in mind for it. Leather varies greatly depending on what part of the animal's body it comes from—the back, the shoulder, or the belly. Likewise, how the leather has been tanned has a great influence. A leather used for the sole of a shoe differs significantly from one intended for a horse saddle or harness.

Depending on what I'm designing or making, the leather is immersed in hot water, or placed in a hot oven, until it can be molded and shaped. Skins can be sculpted and shaped by hand, molded on wooden formers, or press-molded in two-part molds. I take techniques from different industries such as shoe making, sheet-metal forming, and plywood forming, and apply them to leather. I like the material's adaptability and enjoy subverting the rules to create something new. I'm not interested in just repeating what has been done before—I want to understand the rules so that I can break them.

My emotions vary depending on what I'm doing: sometimes I feel frustration, boredom, relief, or excitement. It is not a spiritual experience for me; I am driven by curiosity and a desire to tell a story. I use the material and the process as a vehicle to say things about the world around me.

Nobody can predict the future. During the pandemic, we were gifted time to think and reflect on what is really important and valuable in life. We've realized that simple pleasures are the most precious—family, friends, a hug, good food, home. I think it's a great time to be discussing what each industry, what each company should be doing better. There's a great opportunity for brands to rethink their values. I think people want authenticity, generosity, honesty, and transparency. The creative industries have a huge role to play in shaping culture. I'd love to work with more heritage brands, contributing to the country's collective imagination and identity to help them shape the future.

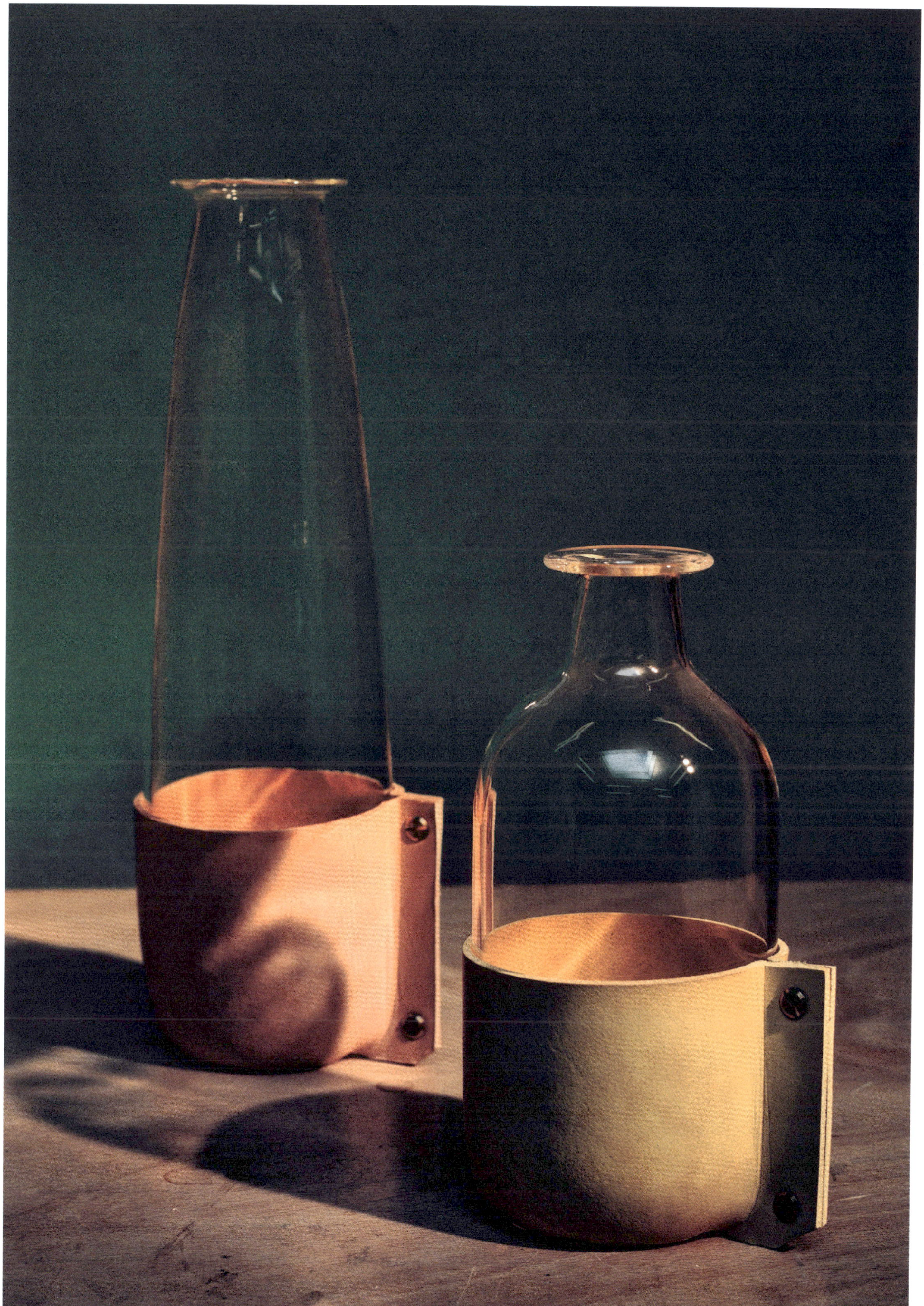

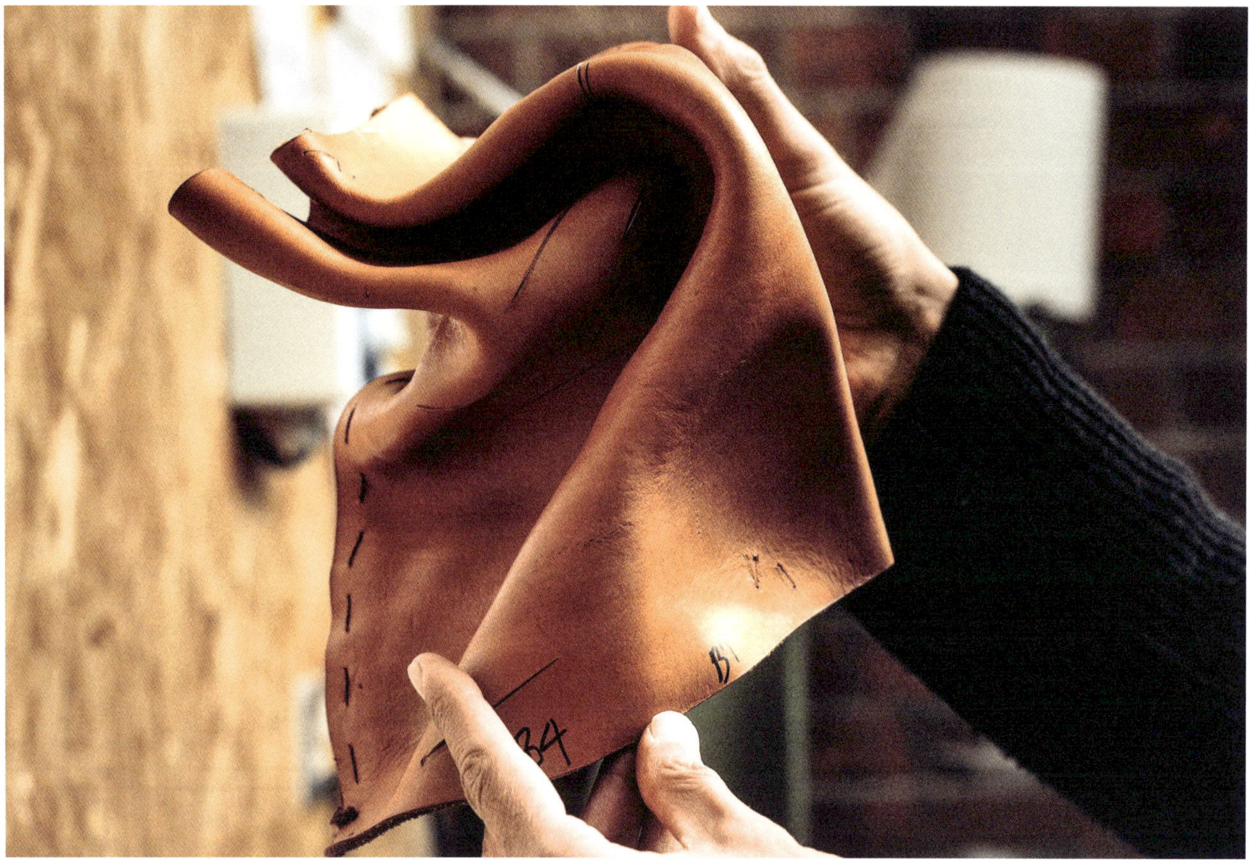
34

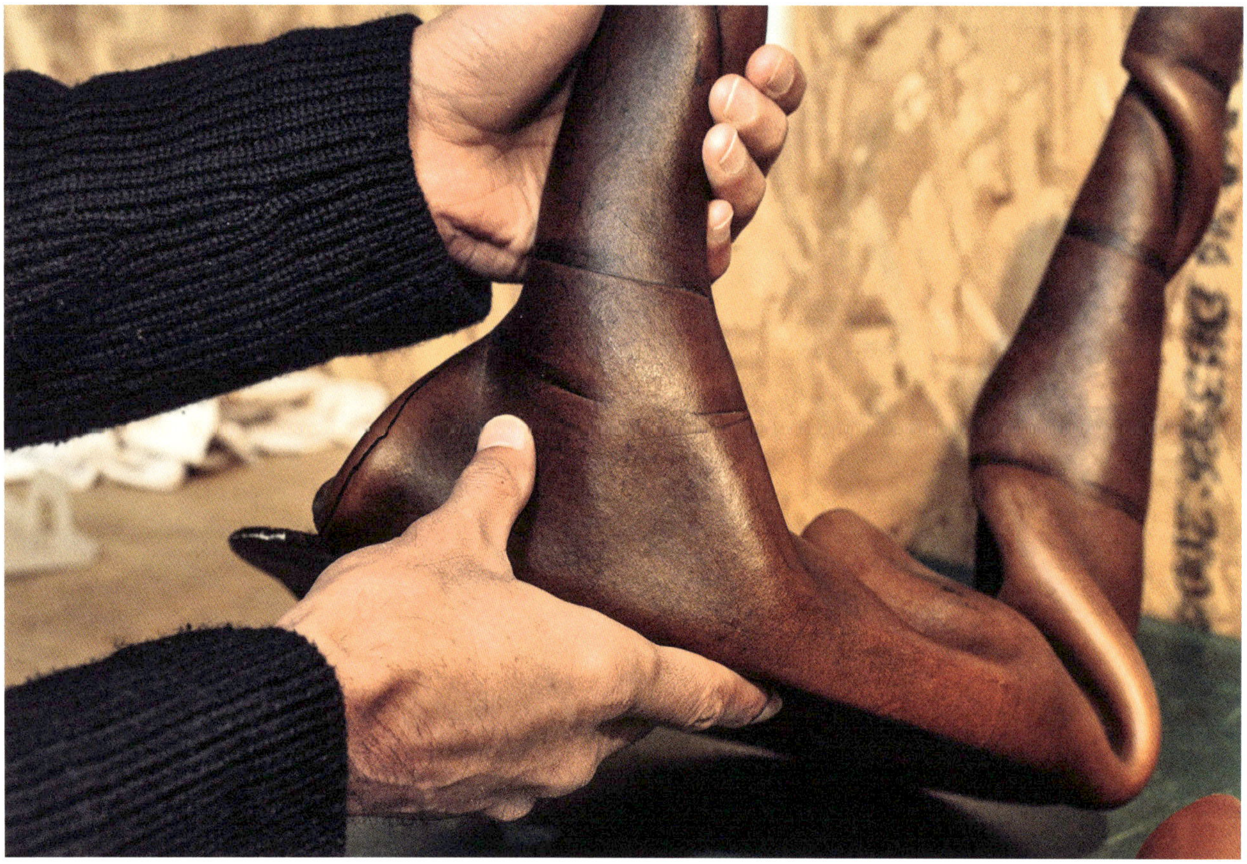

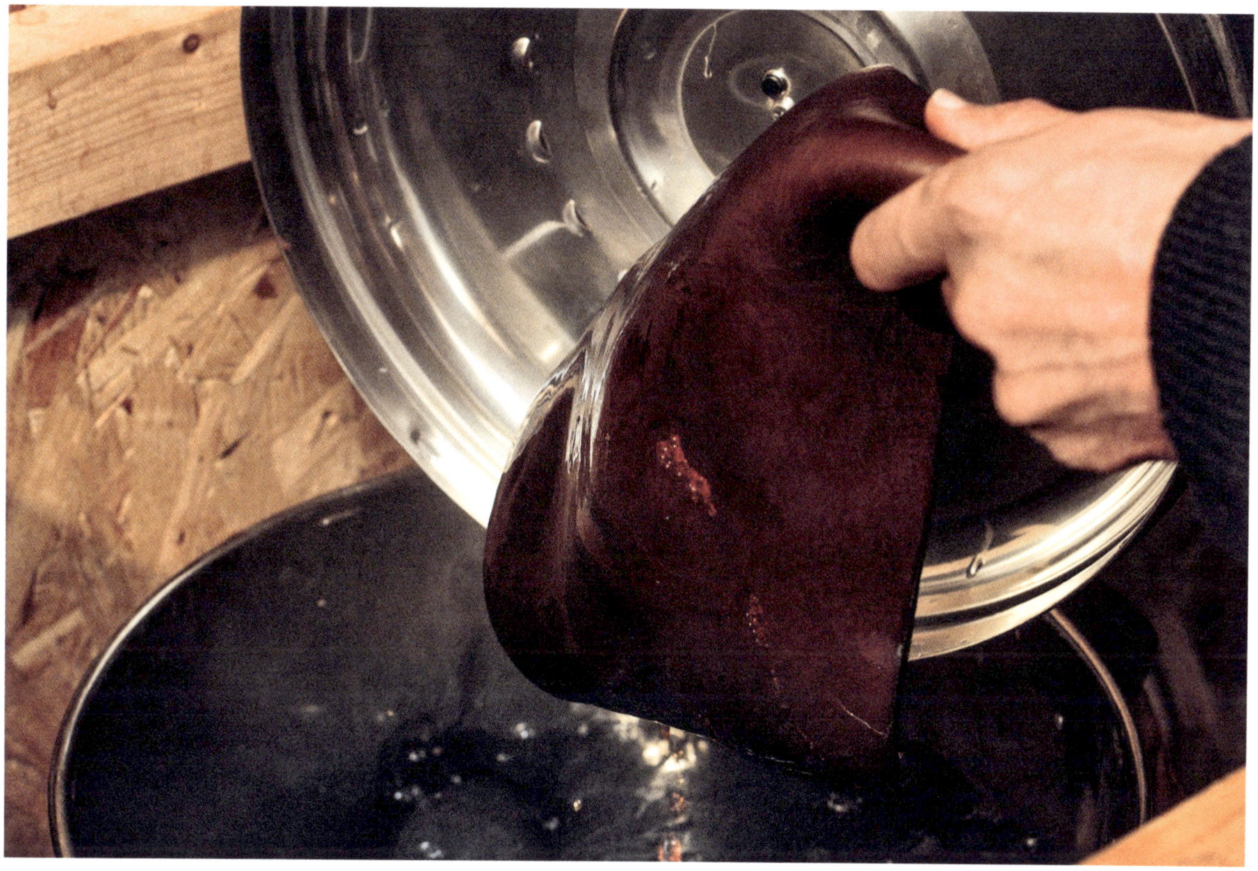

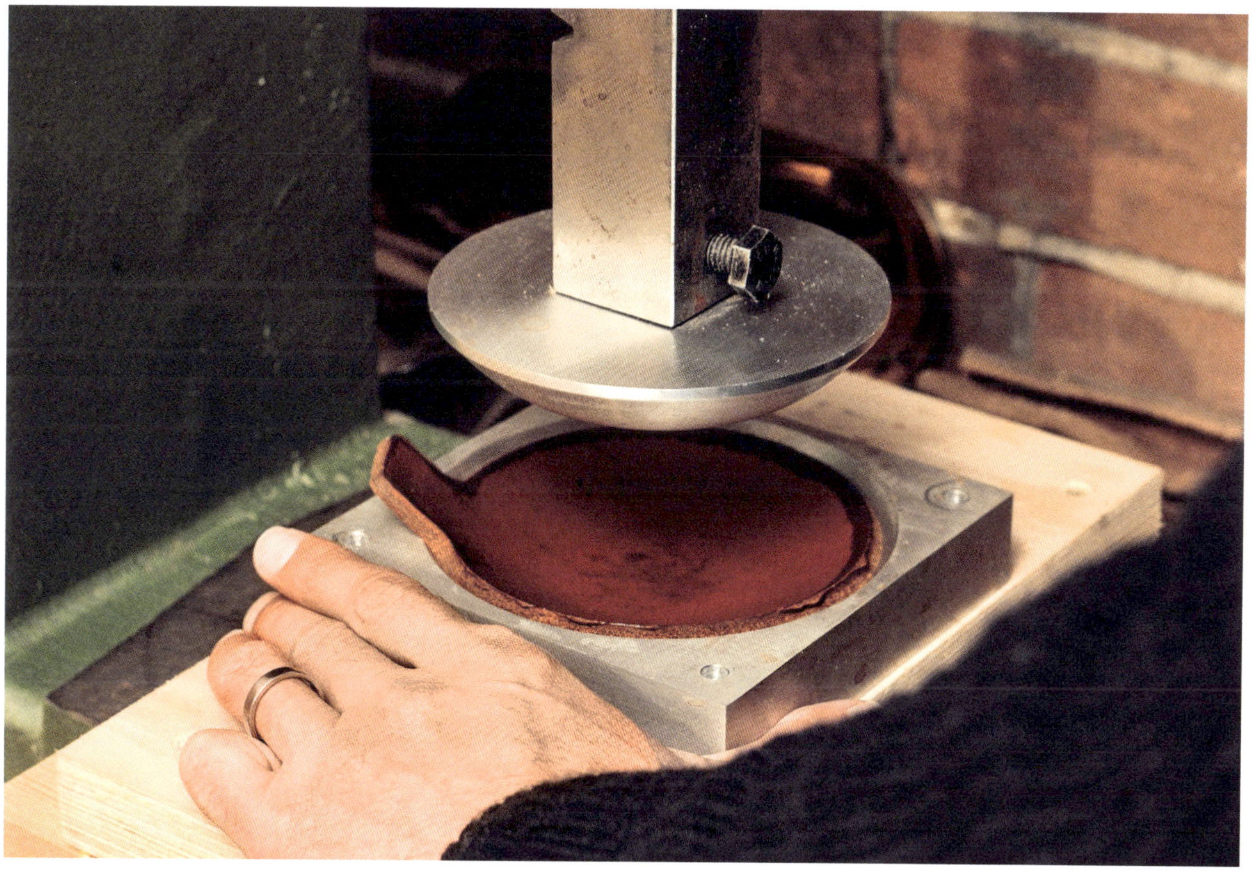

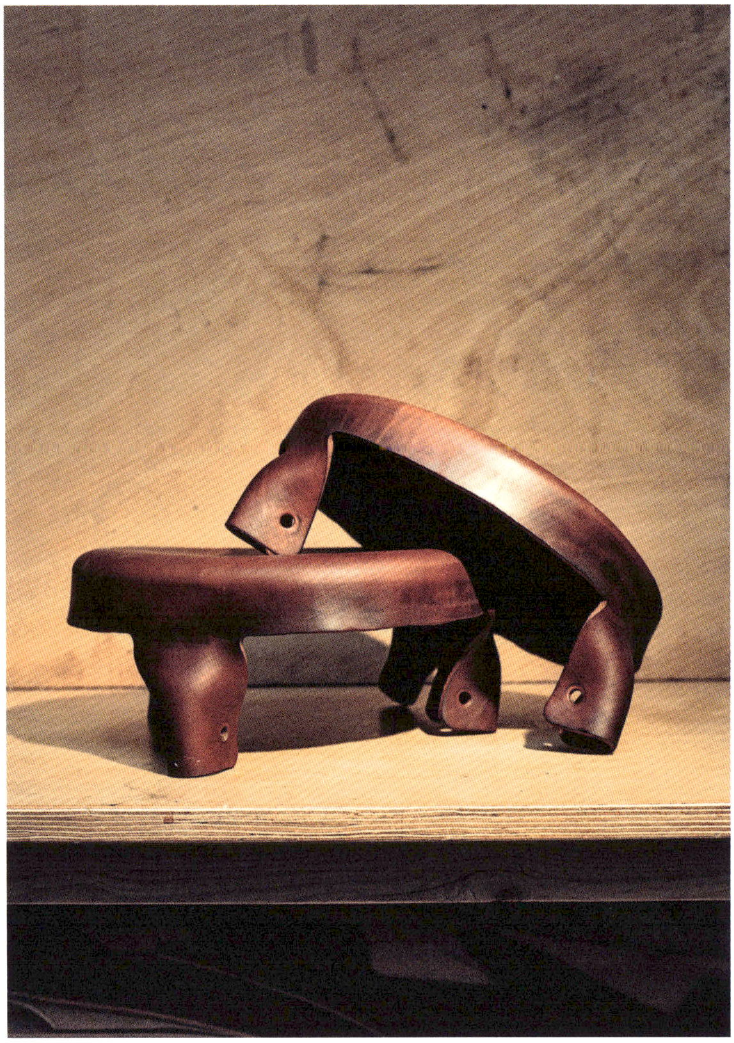

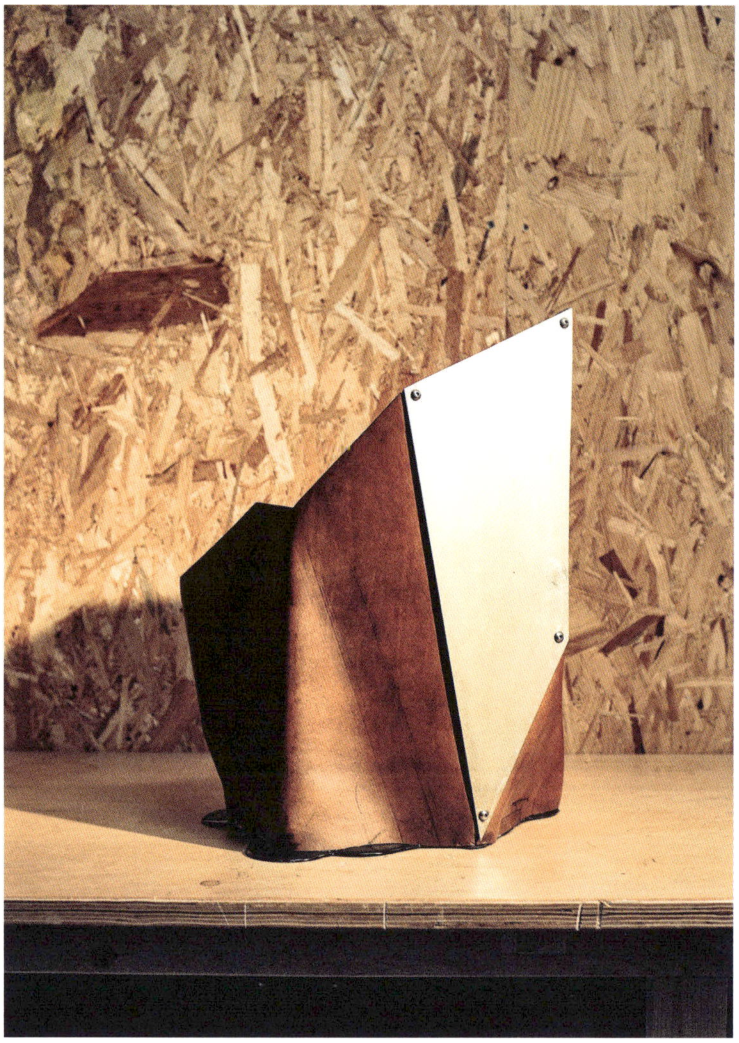

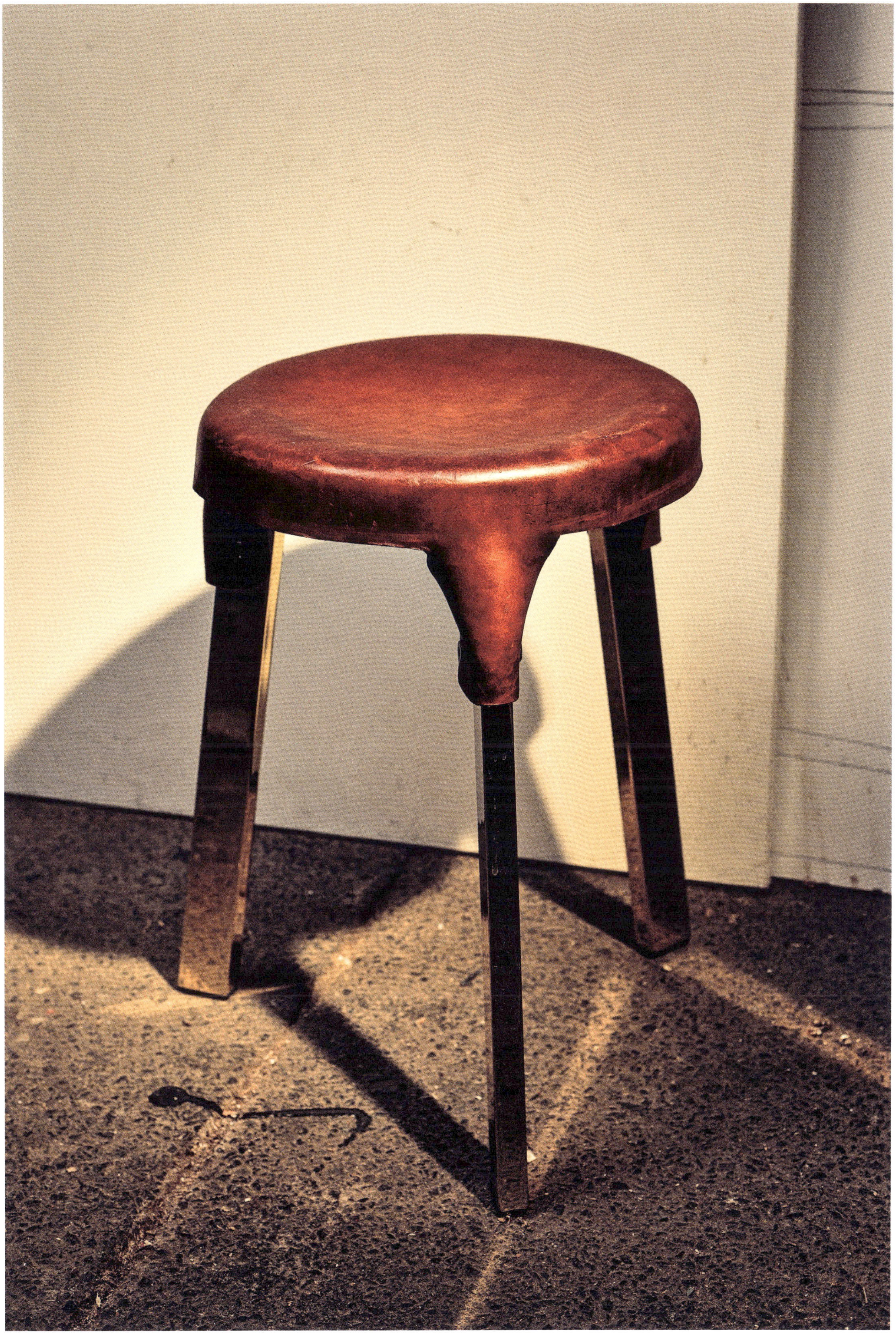

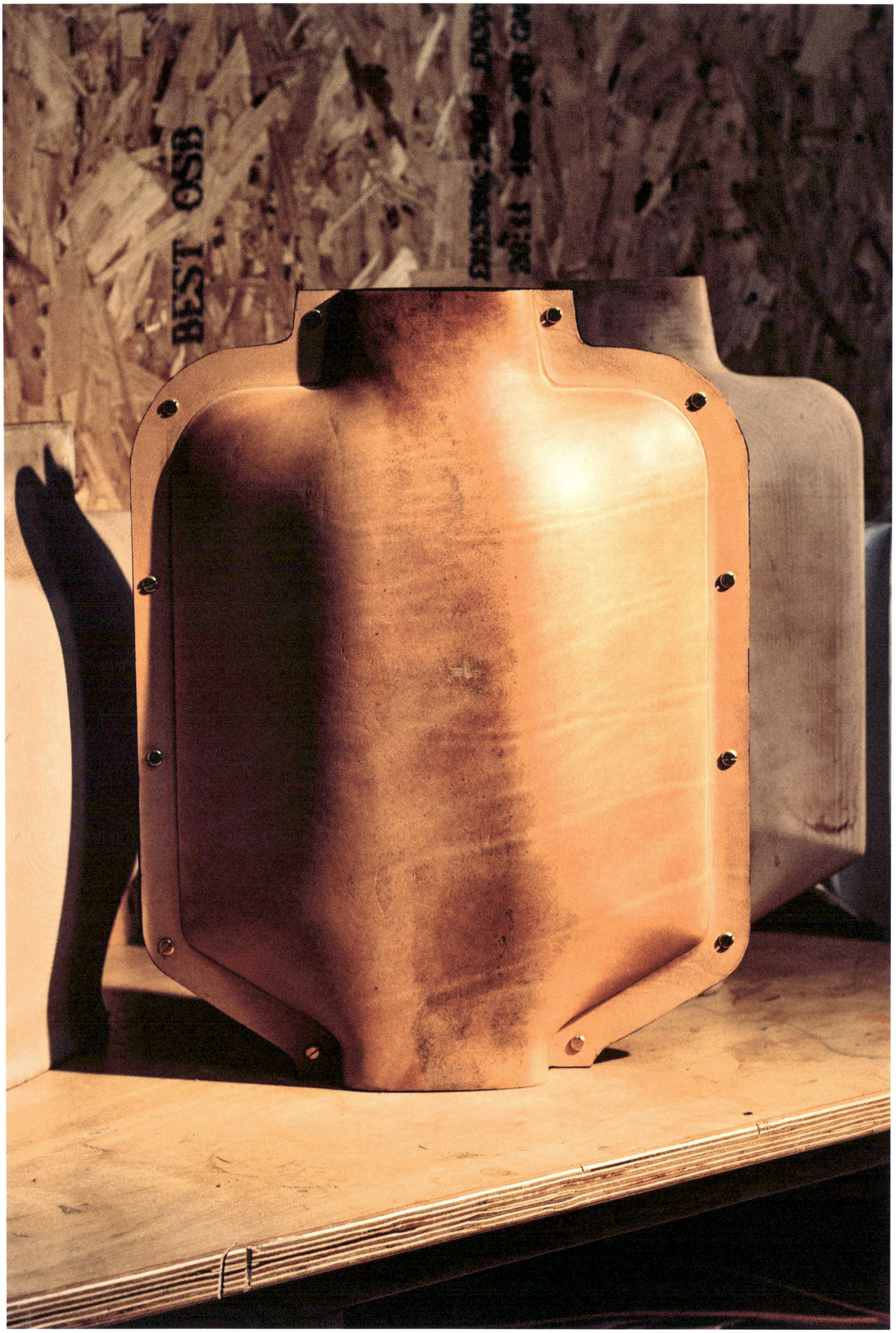
BEST OSB

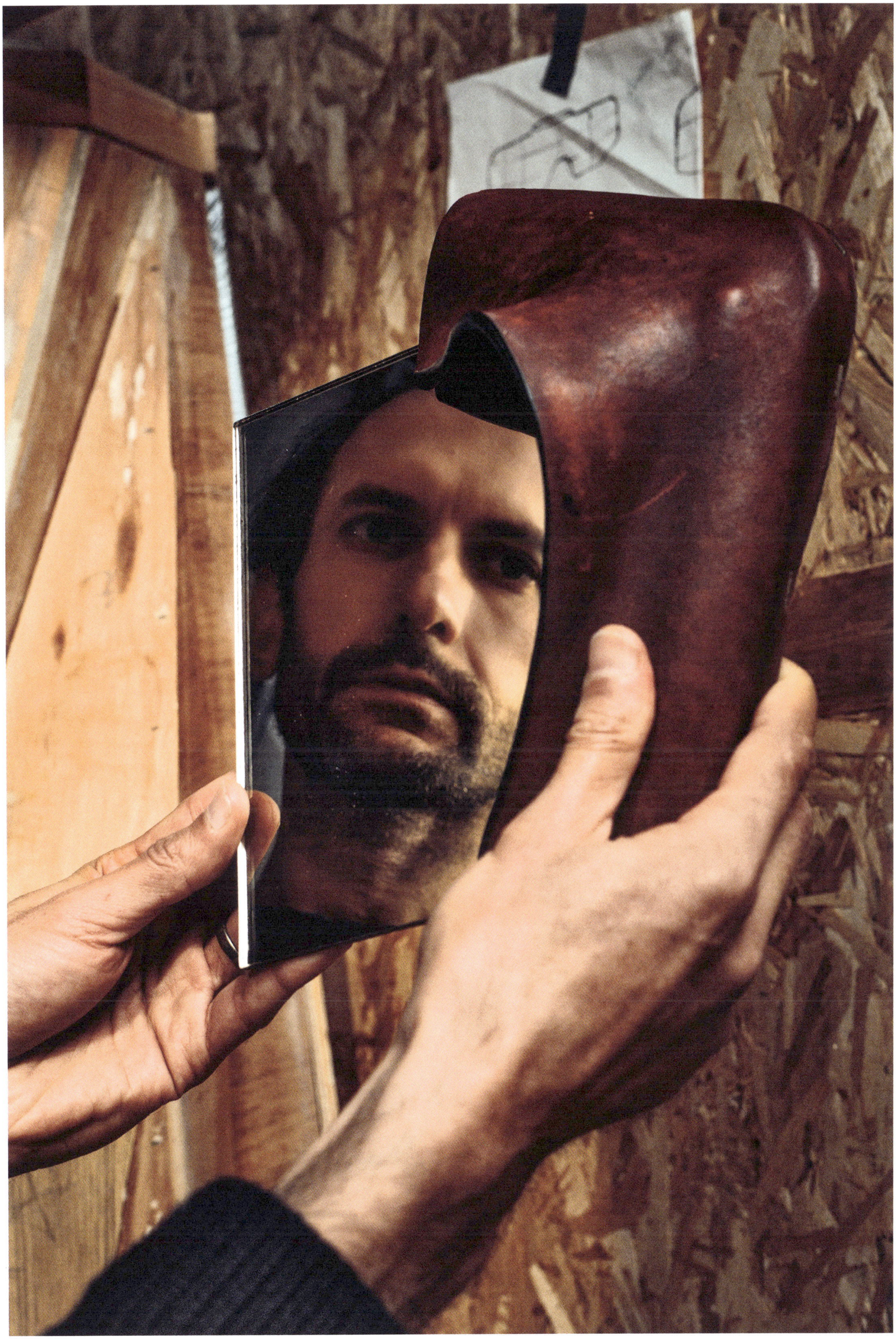

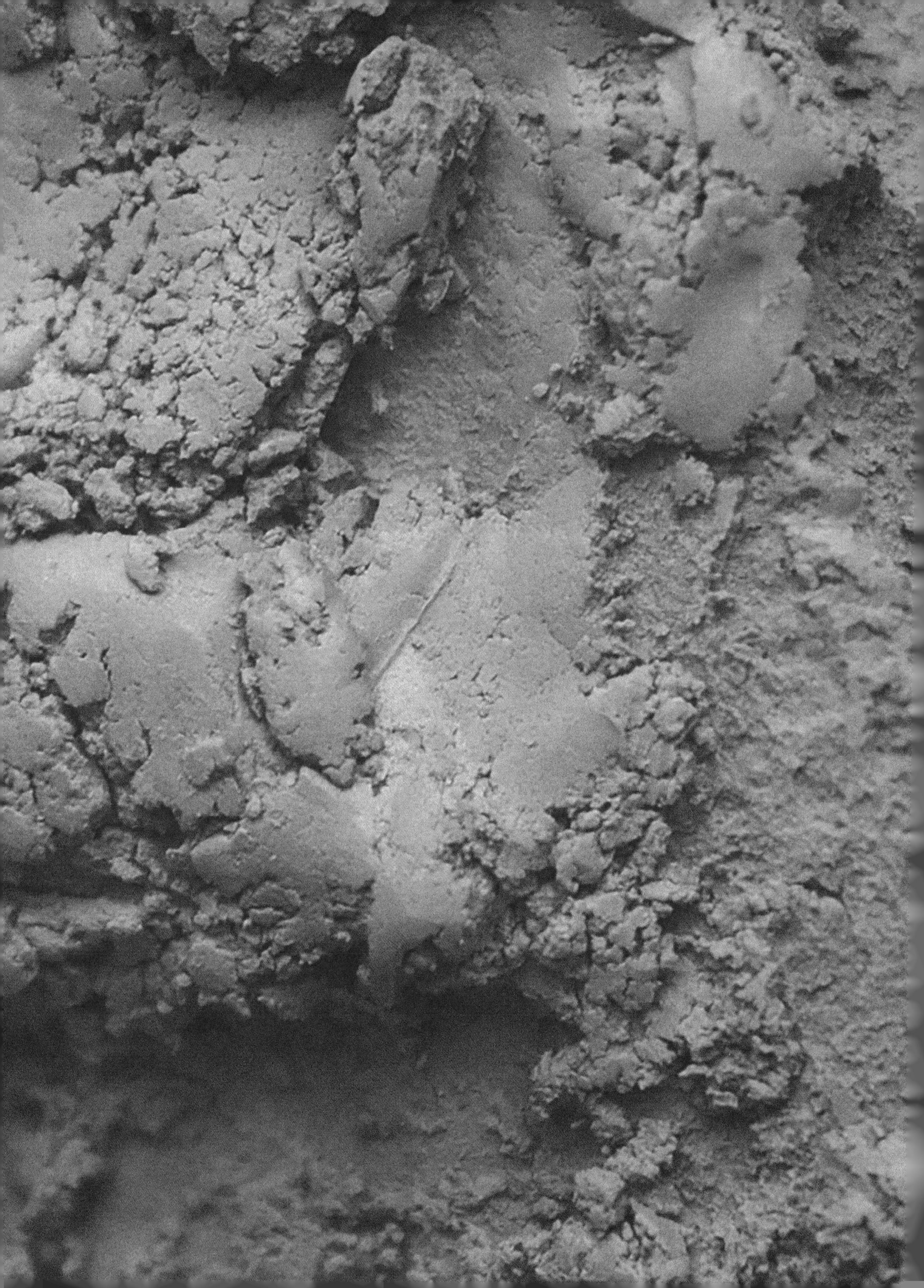

Stone

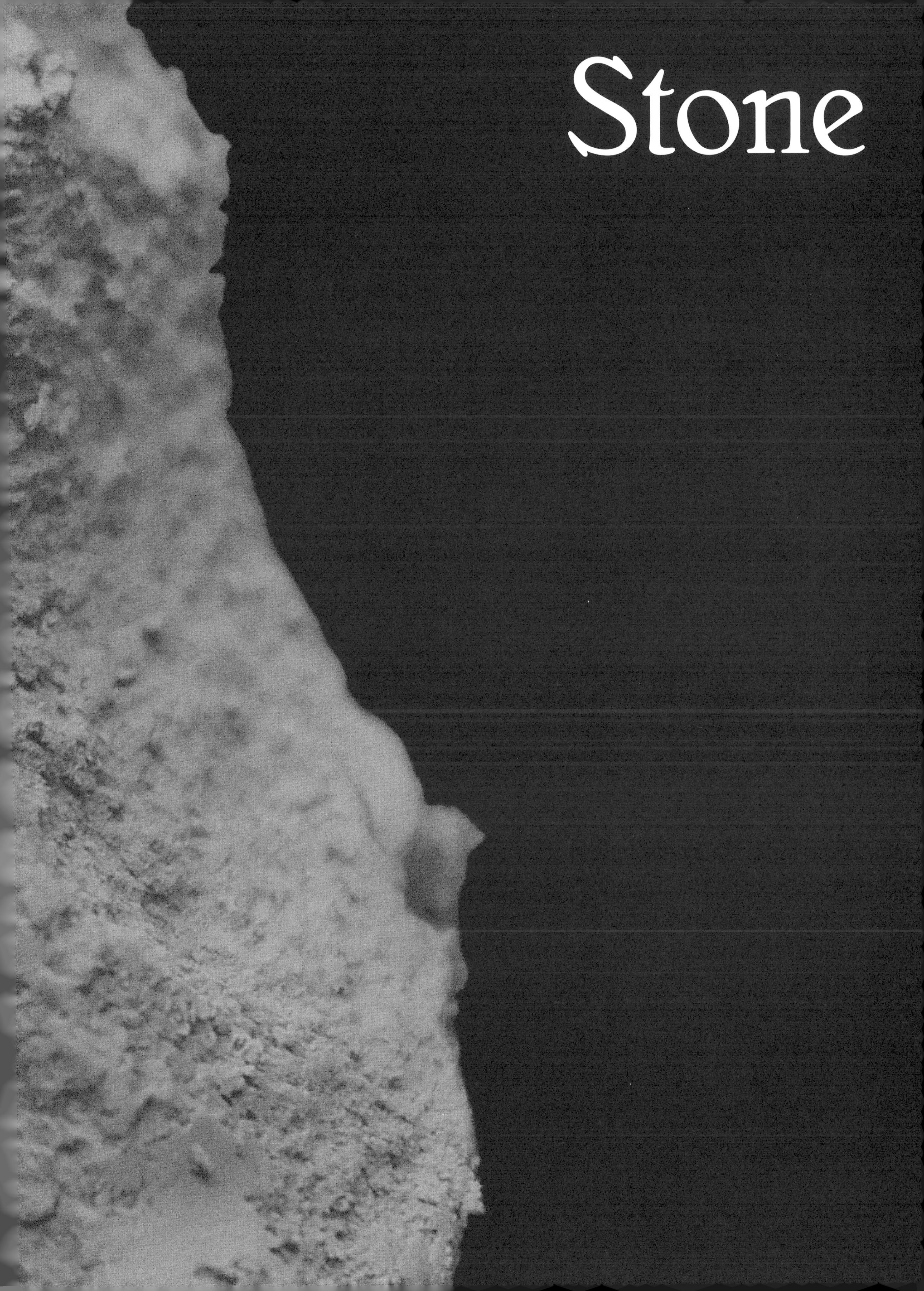

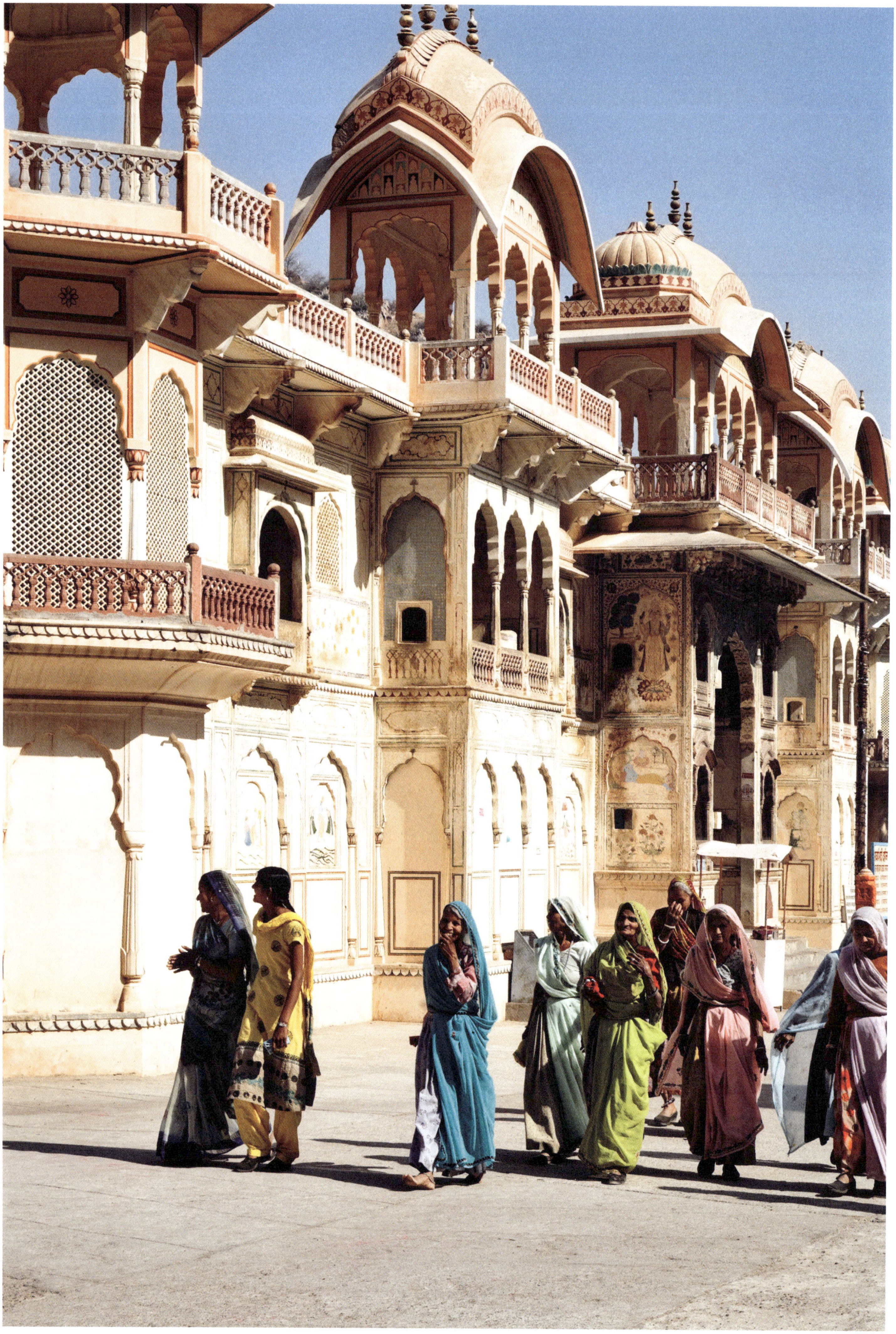

Varun Seth

Stonecutter

Jaipur, India

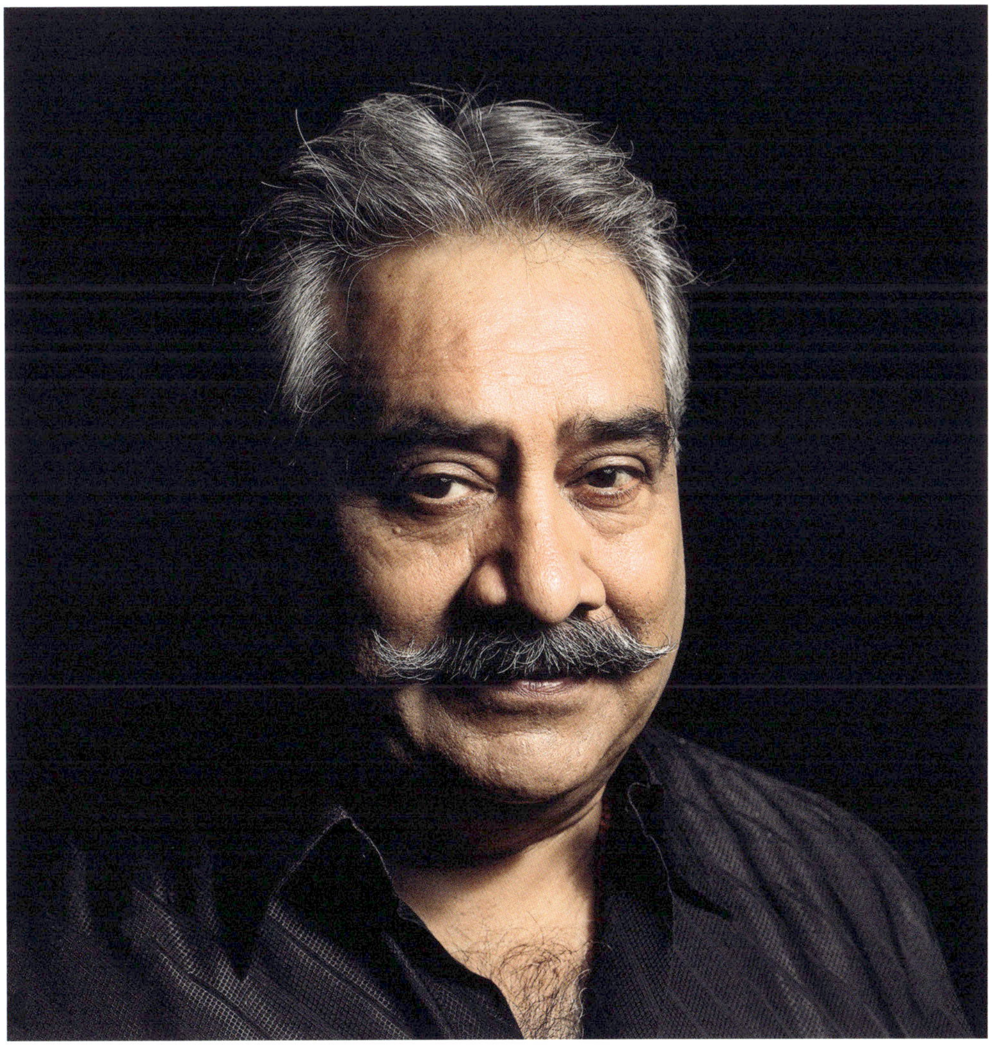

My name is Varun Seth, and I am a stonecutter who creates fine objects. For a stonecutter, stone is more than just a material. It contains something within it—a shape or a memory.

As a child, I admired beautiful things. When I was eighteen, I started working in a five-star hotel made of beautiful carved stone. On the hotel lawn there was a white marble fountain—simple yet so profound. It was inspired by the work of British architect Sir Edwin Lutyens, who, along with Sir Herbert Baker, played a key role in the construction of New Delhi's administrative buildings. I was fascinated by it. I began to study stone more closely, and in doing so I became confident in talking about it. I became a kind of expert.

One day, I was discussing the subject with an American gentleman and he entrusted me with the task of restoring a small, carved marble pedestal. It was incredible: I was over the moon! I could earn my living doing this.

When I encounter a stone, I am overcome with joy. Just as the full moon makes the tide rise, a piece of stone stirs something within me. I go into a trance, I can't control myself; I have to get it and keep it close to me. Over the last thirty years, I have gathered over fifty tons of the most beautiful stones: lapis lazuli from Afghanistan, agates from Brazil, bright malachite from Congo, perfect crystals from Madagascar, and jasper from the Indian subcontinent. Some stones are sophisticated; others are bright and colorful—so eye-catching that they almost have a therapeutic effect. Others still are plain and simple, with no adornment but a lot of character.

Stone is resistant and does not appreciate being handled by a novice. But in the hands of a master, it turns to putty; it purrs contentedly, as though in the hands of Michelangelo. When, for a particular project, I am asked to cut a stone into smaller parts, I try to resist. Sometimes I have to give in, but most of the time I win.

In my thirty-five-year career, I have seen some techniques fade away, despite my efforts to preserve them. When I started here, there were artisans who could slice hard stone to a thickness of $1/32$ of an inch (1 mm) using a simple steel wire. Now technology plays an important role. Everyone uses diamond blades, but they don't cut like wire. They are limited to thicknesses of at least $3/16$ of an inch (5 mm).

My master craftsman, Ramawtar, has two favorite tools: the hammer and the chisel. He often tells me that the brain controls the hand and the hand wields the hammer. Emotions flowing from the brain take shape through the hammer and chisel, which become extensions of the hand. As for me, the tool I always have with me is my heart: the greatest tool that God made.

The stonecutter's craft is timeless. Each generation leaves a mark reflective of its era. In India, the craft sector is turning over a new leaf; there are renewed interests, new demands, and new awareness. If all of that is properly channeled, I think that the twenty-first century could see a renaissance of craftsmanship in India. But if we forget our legacy in the arts, we have no future.

Today, I am very proud of my profession. I feel like a peacock dancing in the rain.

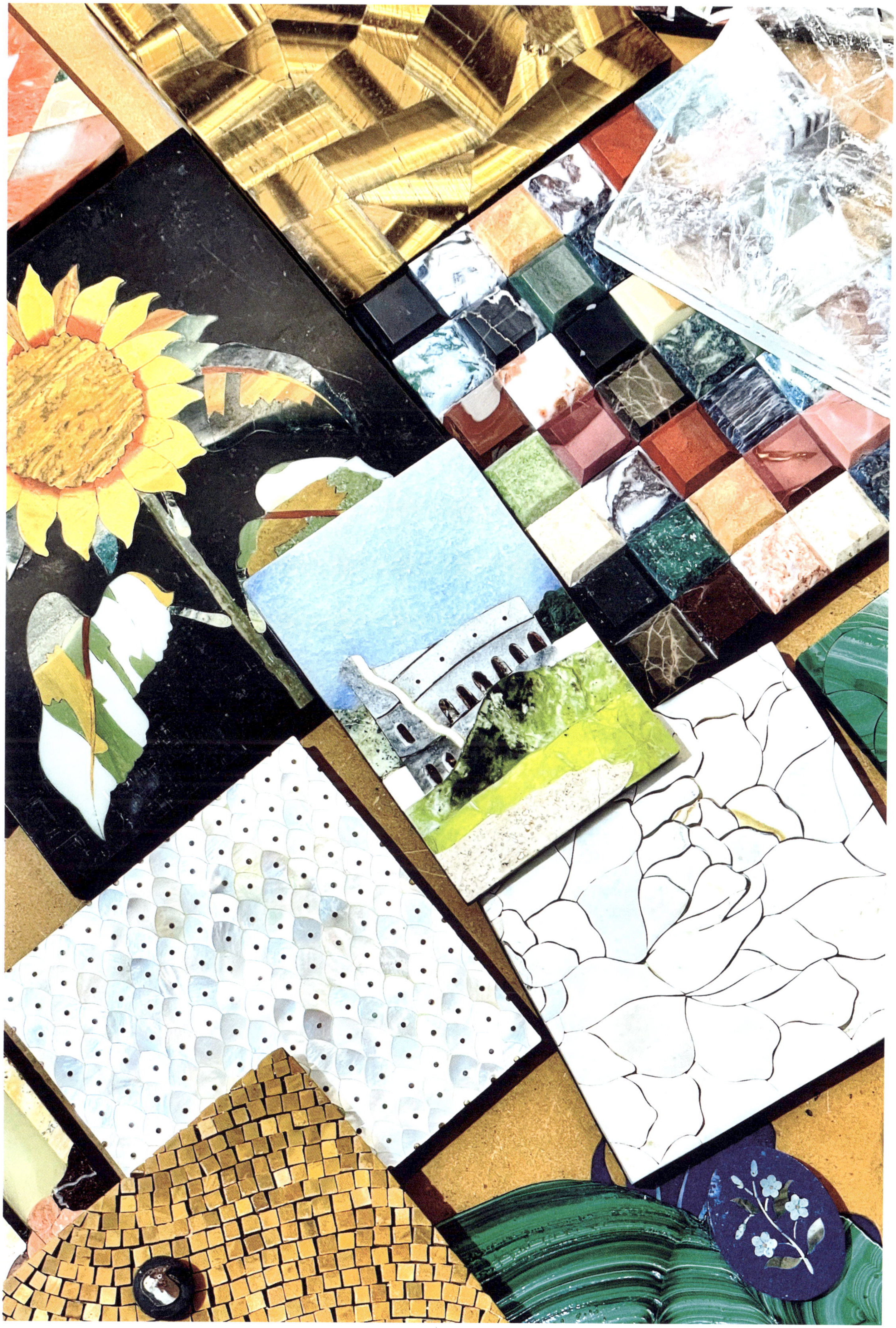

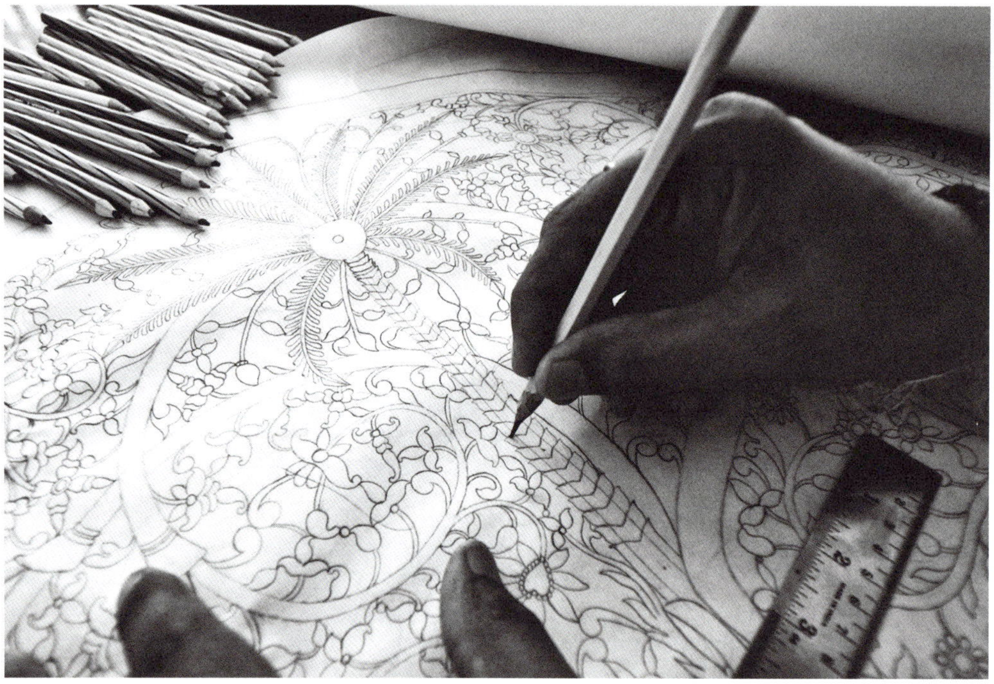

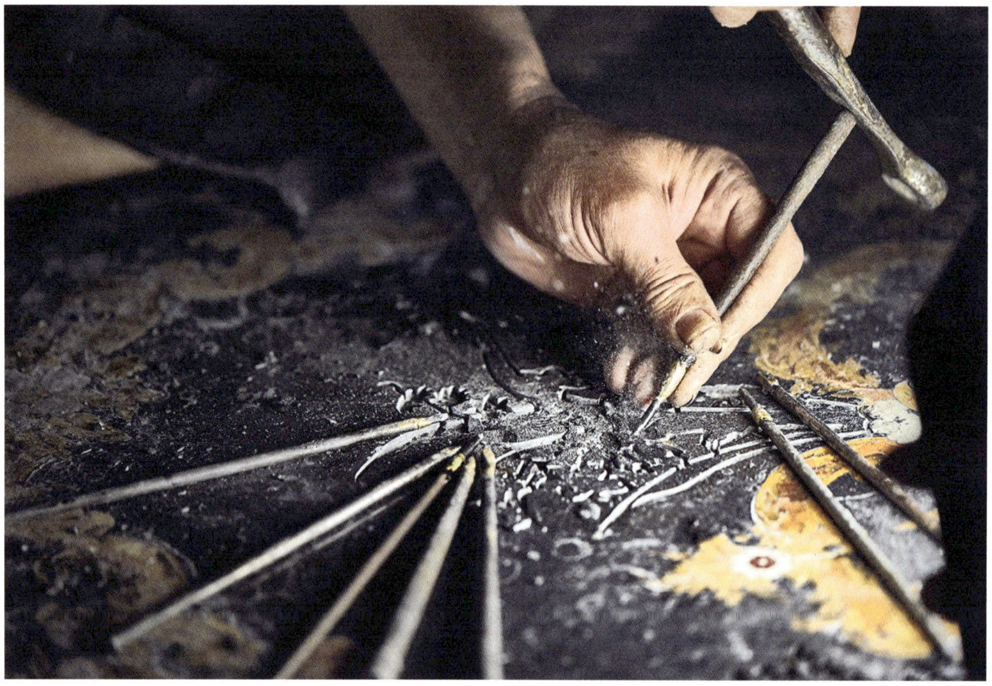

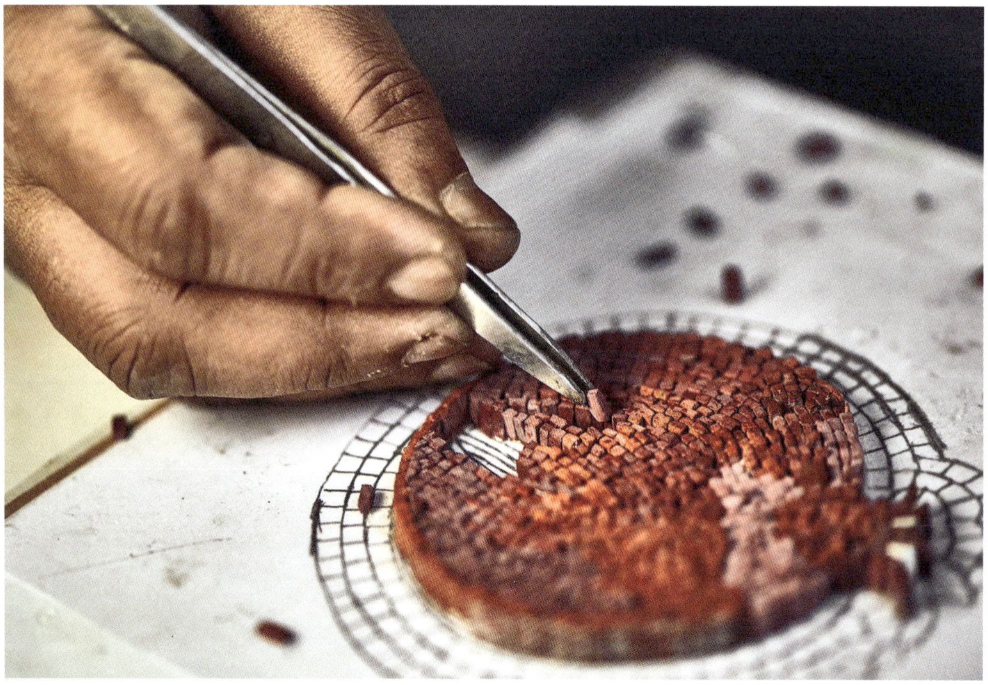

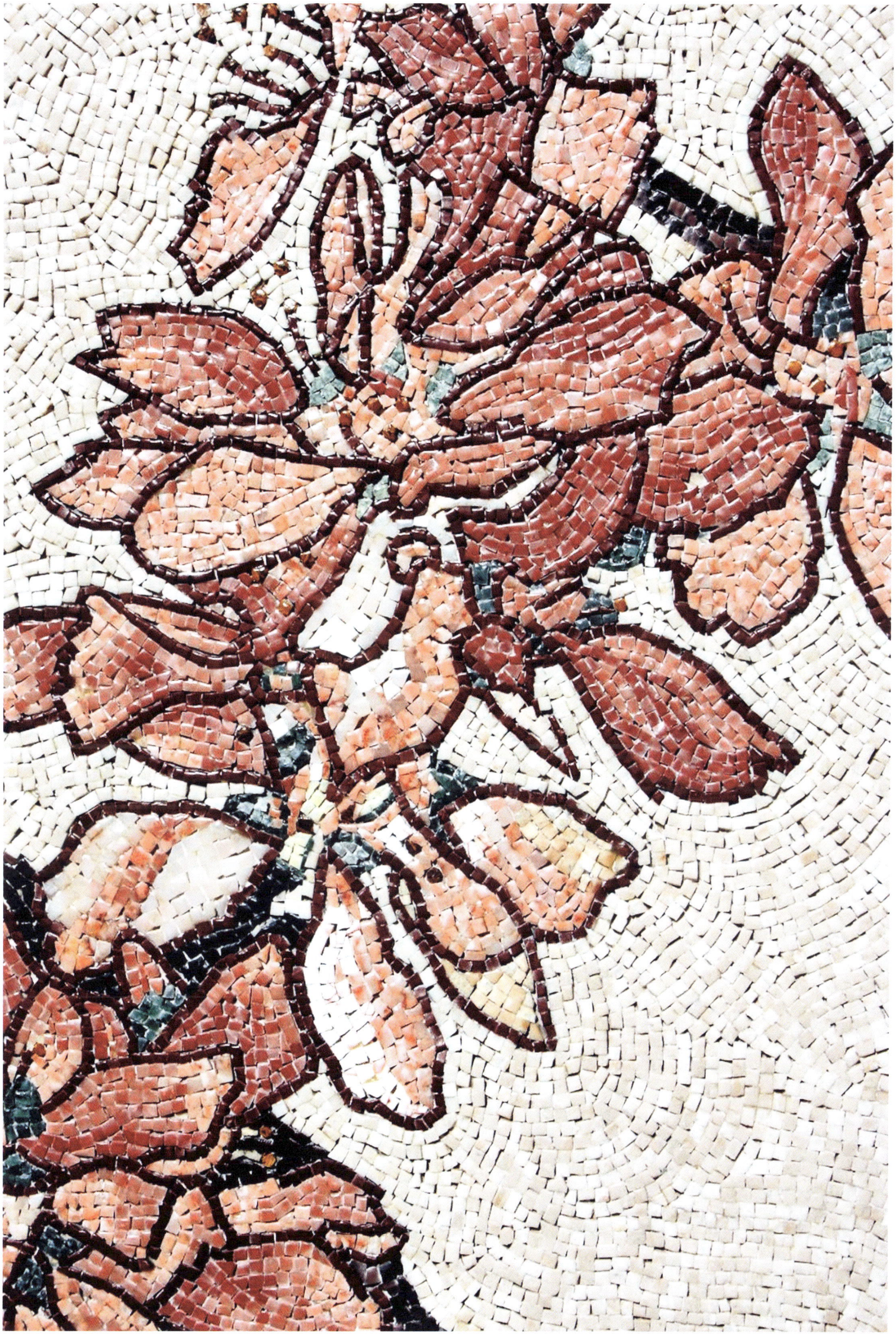

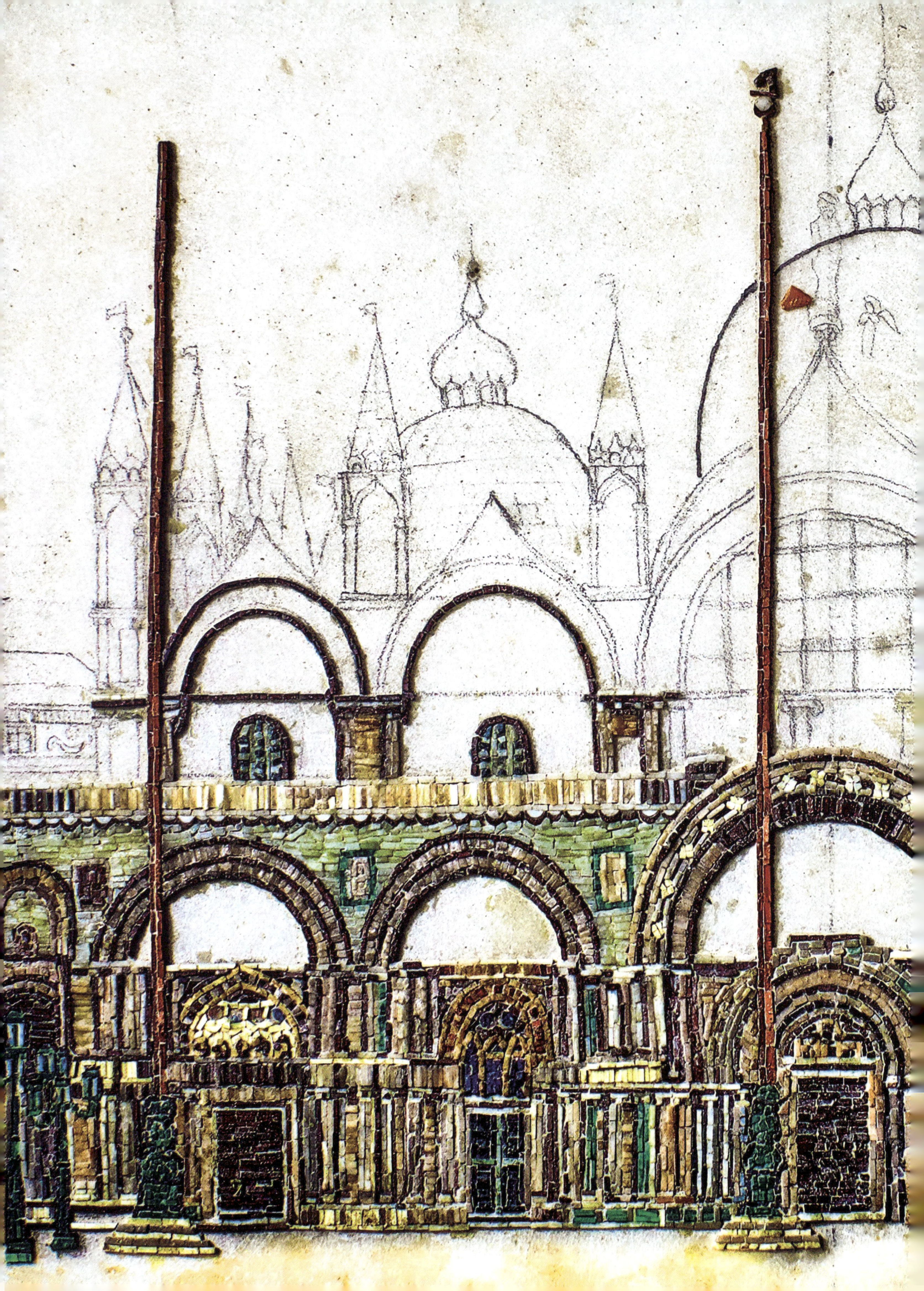

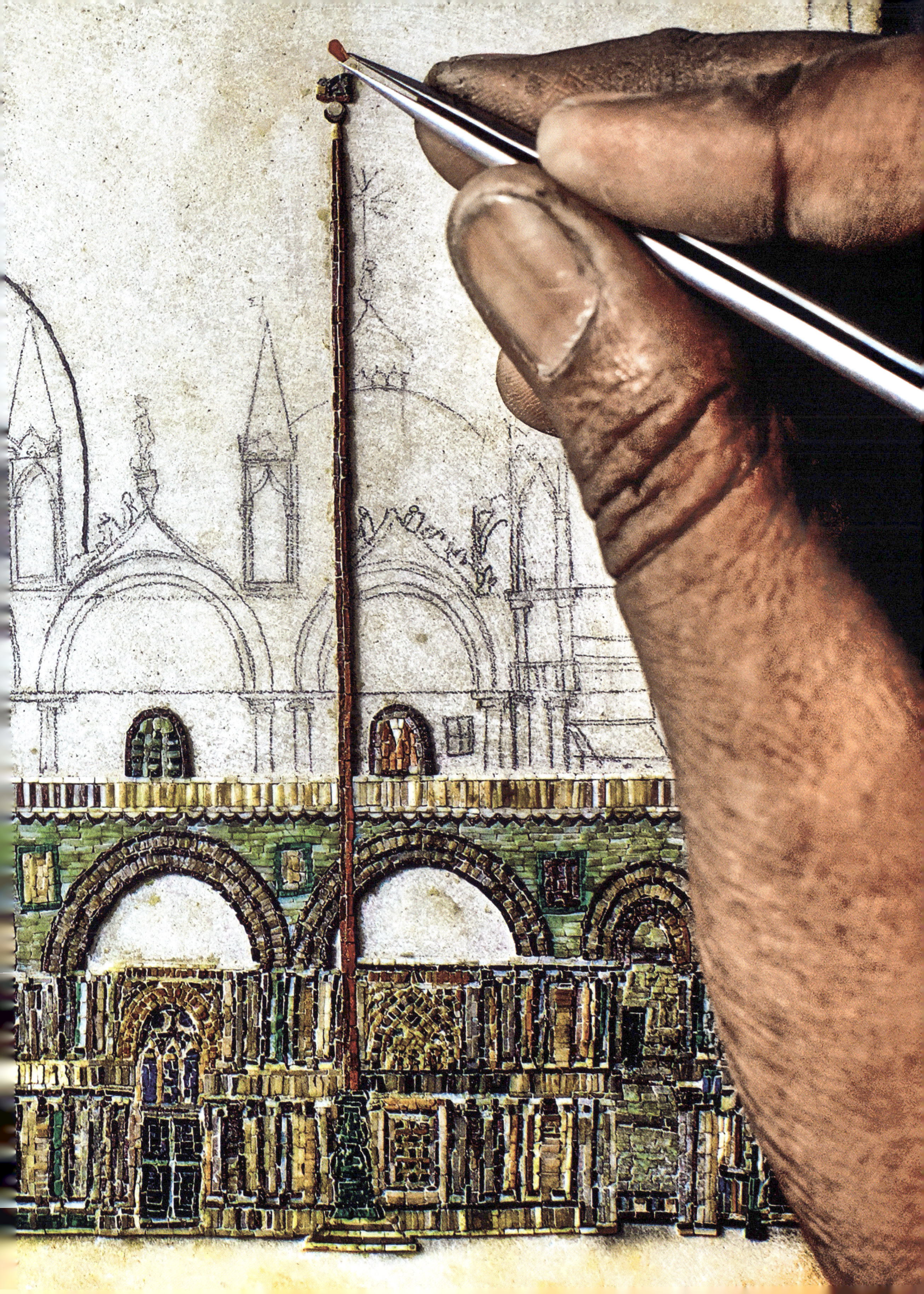

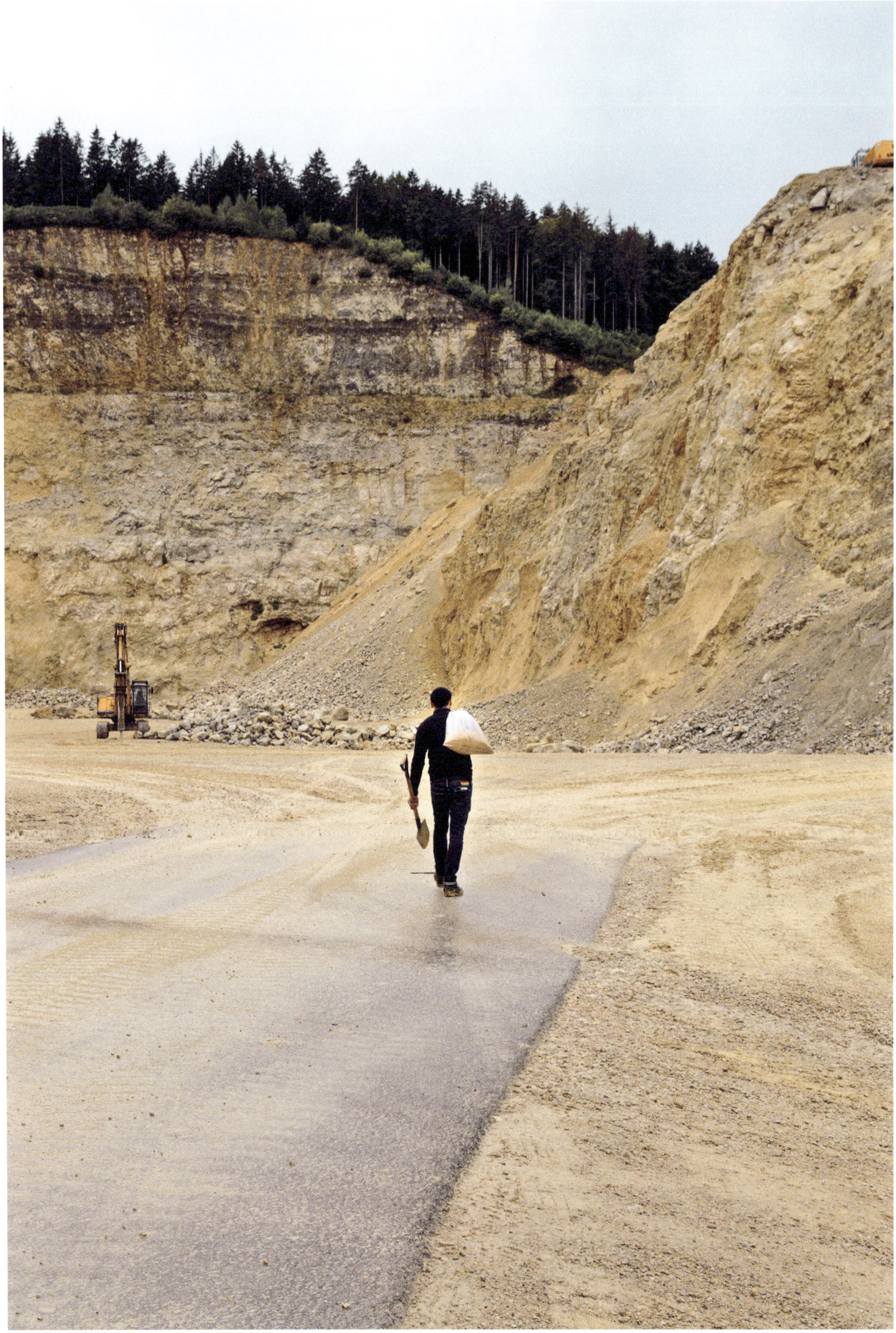

David Kremer

Pigment maker

Aichstetten,
Germany

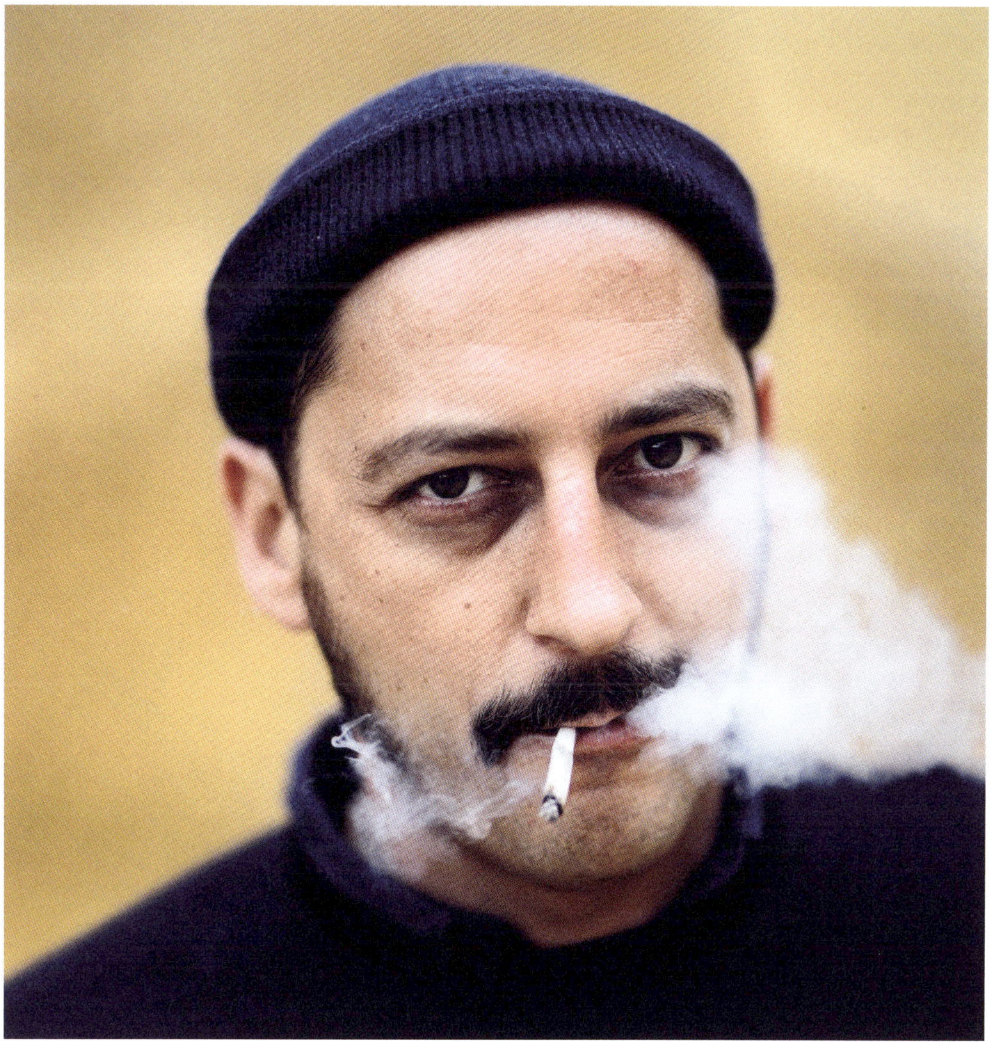

My name is David Kremer; some people also call me "Colorman." My profession entails making old and new pigments accessible, and encouraging their manufacture using raw materials. My family has been exploring this domain for over forty years and, in a way, I was born into a cauldron of colors.

Visits to workshops, museums, and galleries have always been part of our lives. Over lunch, we often discussed the difficulties associated with materials, art and restoration techniques, and historical and modern procedures. This enthusiasm has shaped our environment.

The workshop came into being almost by accident. A restorer wanted to use the original pigment found in a fresco: smalt, a cobalt-blue glass. The pigment had been abandoned years earlier, and the restorer wasn't satisfied with the industrial alternatives. My father—a chemist with a passion for art and history—found the formula in an old manual and made the pigment according to the traditional recipe. The workshop evolved over the next forty years, during which time we recovered many pigments, as well as varnishes, waxes, and other materials that had been replaced by cheaper, less labor-intensive alternatives.

When I see a stone, the first questions I ask myself focus on where it comes from, what it is made of, and how it was formed. Then, of course, I look into its color. The real journey begins there.

Pigments are insoluble particles: colored solids composed of various materials that alter the color of the light they reflect. They can be extracted or produced from all kinds of things and come from all over the world. Our catalog even includes meteorite brown from outer space. All solid, colored materials can be used as pigments or transformed as such. Mineral pigments—in other words, rocks such as lapis lazuli, malachite, or cinnabar—are the most common, as the stones are easily ground. Other materials—like plants or roots—require a more labor-intensive process; and still others—like old banknotes—present real challenges.

The "formulas," handed down for centuries, come from books of secret recipes that must be adapted to modern technology depending on how they will be used. Many pigments are simple to create: all that is required is to crush the stones, clean and filter them, and purify the coloring element. Many others, however, require historical research, testing, and experimentation. We have found some of them by chance, while traveling, reading a book, or even thanks to our customers—like the one who wanted to turn his iPhone into a pigment.

We are always open to new ideas and original projects. It is by learning, exploring, and experimenting that we have grown and continue to grow. We produce around three hundred pigments from a variety of materials, including plants, stones, and bones. But raw materials with limited availability will eventually disappear from the world and, consequently, from our product range.

Colors are not invented; they have always existed. What we have invented are new ways of processing them. Ultimately, my profession goes back to the Stone Age. Today, it is increasingly difficult to produce pigments with the same qualities as those from the past. We have become too perfectionist and no longer appreciate the impurities of bygone days.

Modern industrial pigments are, indeed, highly efficient, extremely standardized, and, in a way, flawless. By comparison, old-fashioned or hand-crafted pigments can be considered imperfect, even those of the highest quality. The artist or craftsperson has to grapple with them, to dialogue with the materials—but isn't this precisely what makes a painting, a work of art, or objects beautiful?

In this sense, I think my profession has an element of modernity: preserving the knowledge and techniques of past centuries and adapting them to modern needs. Every day, I discover new things, and I try to pass this attitude on to the next generation—to my children.

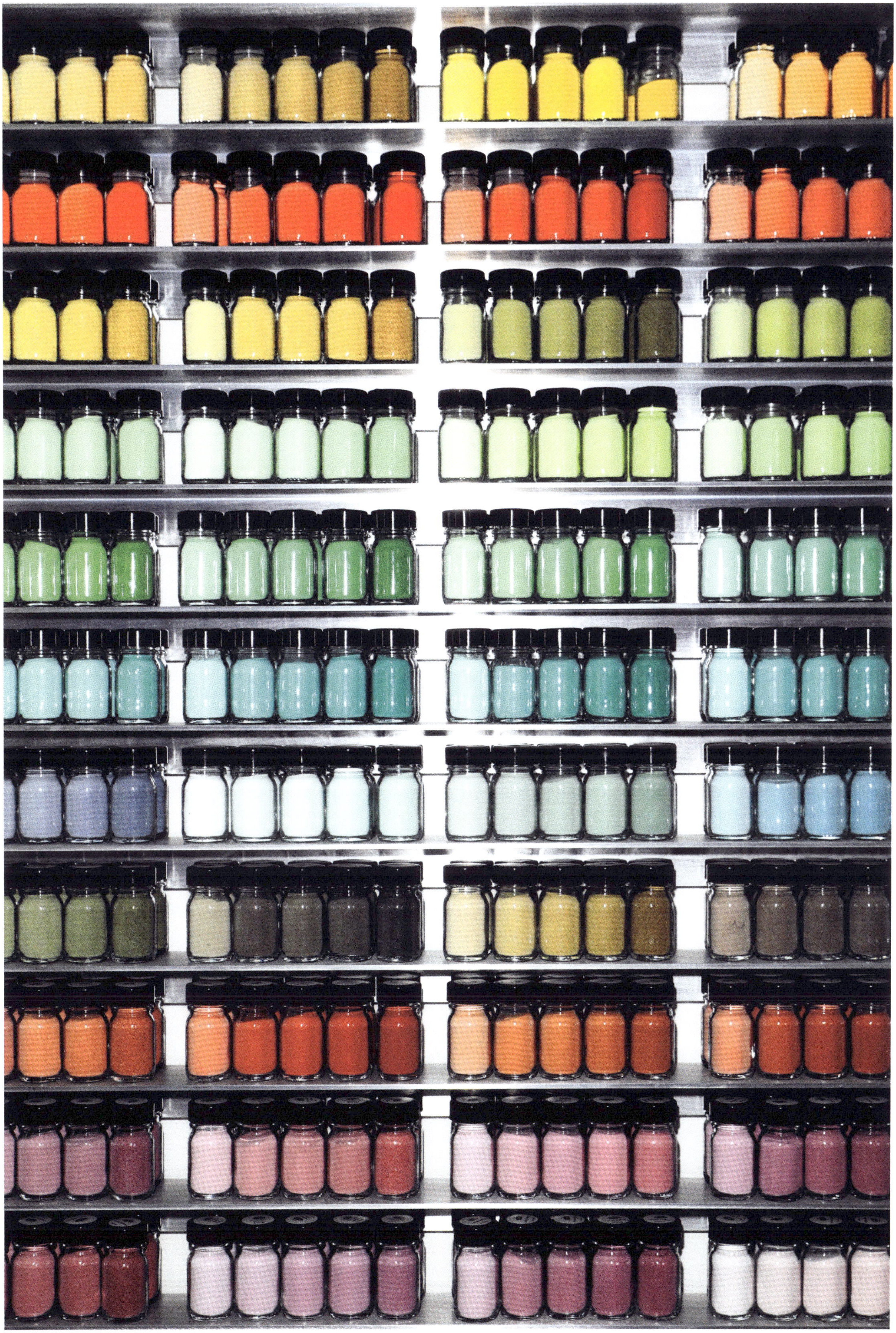

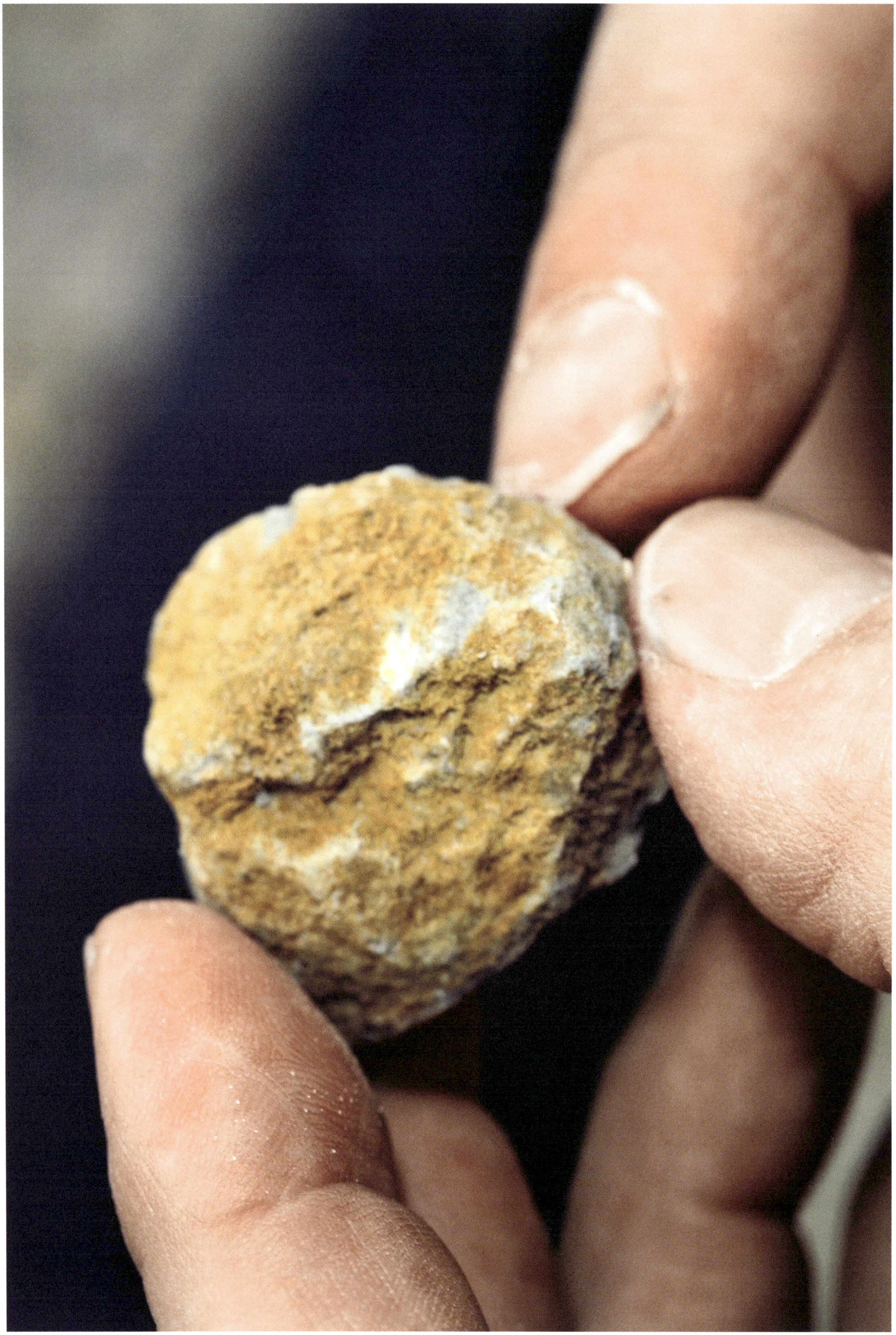

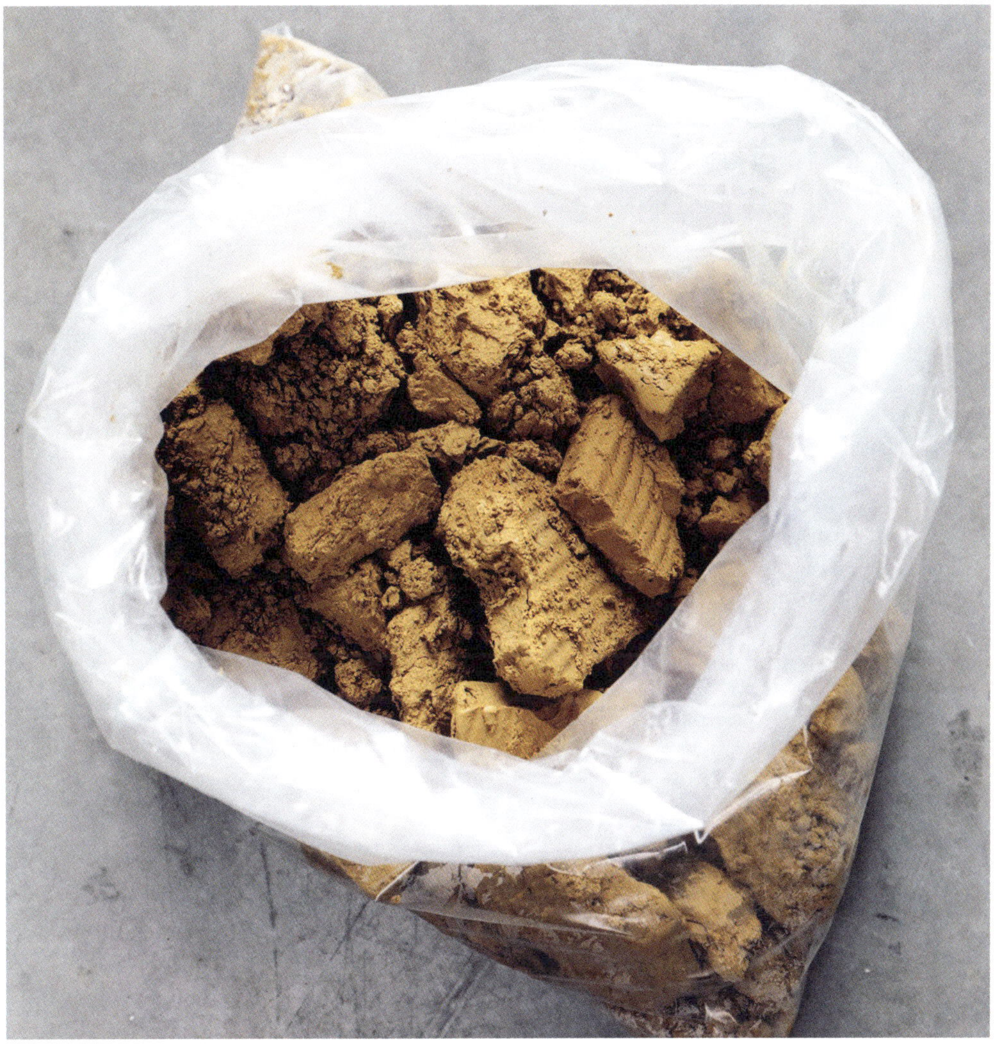

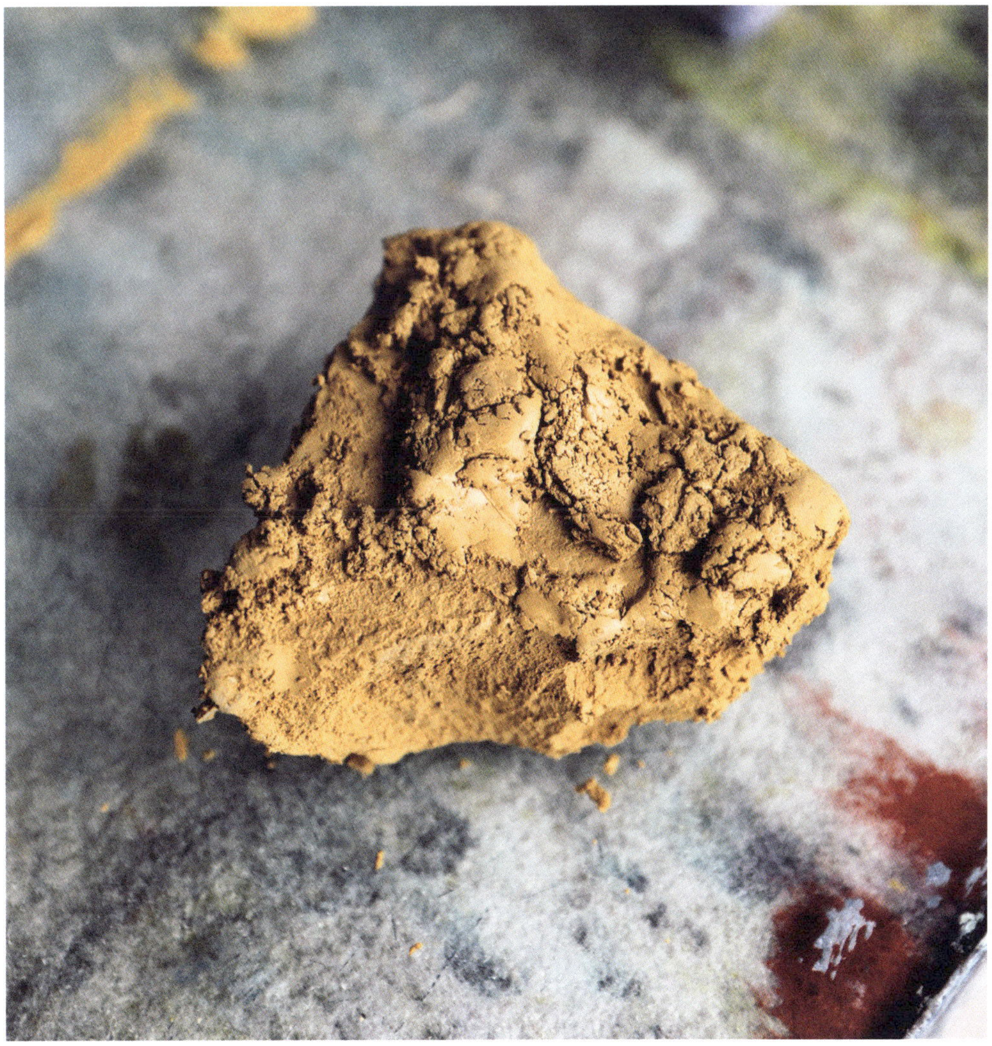

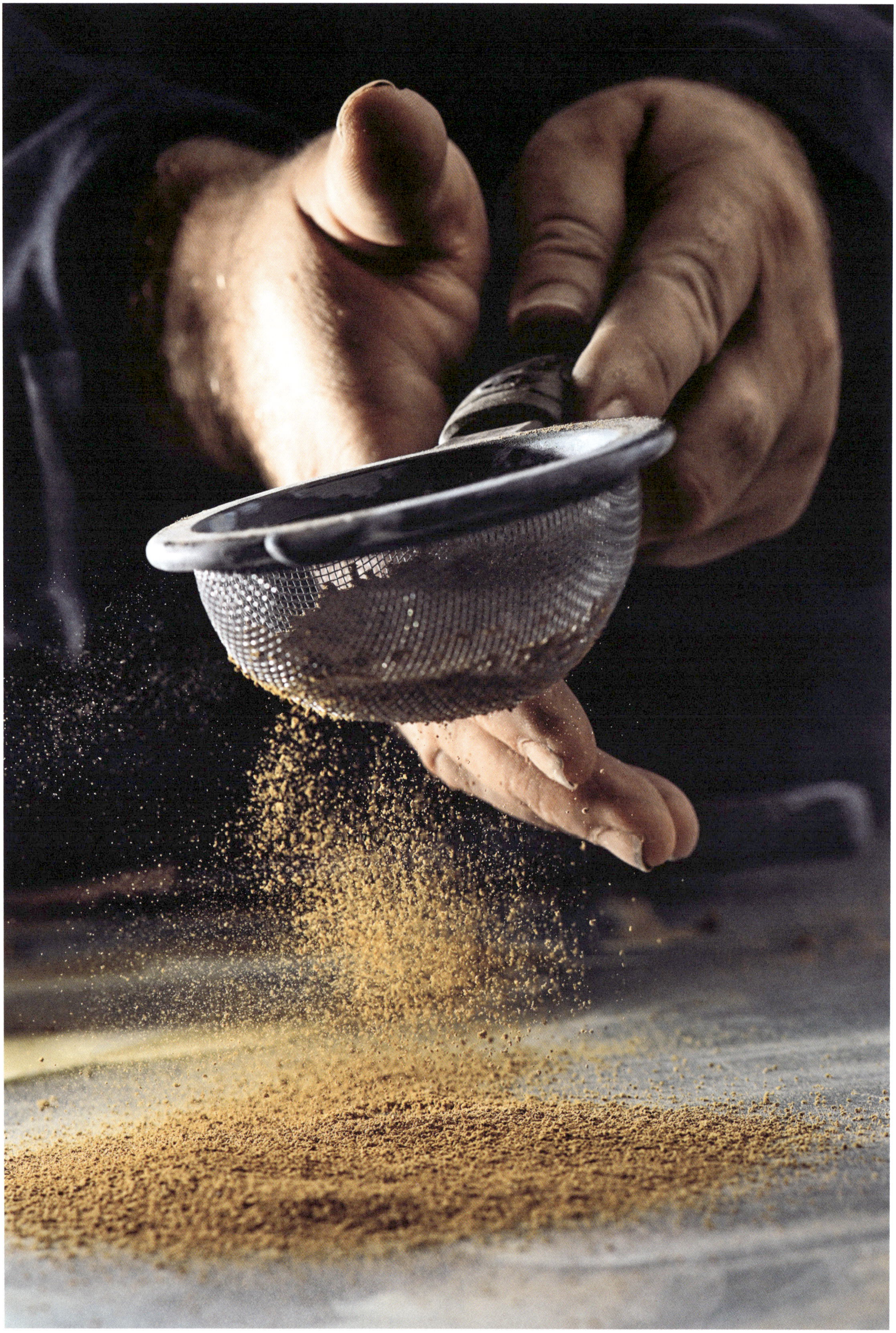

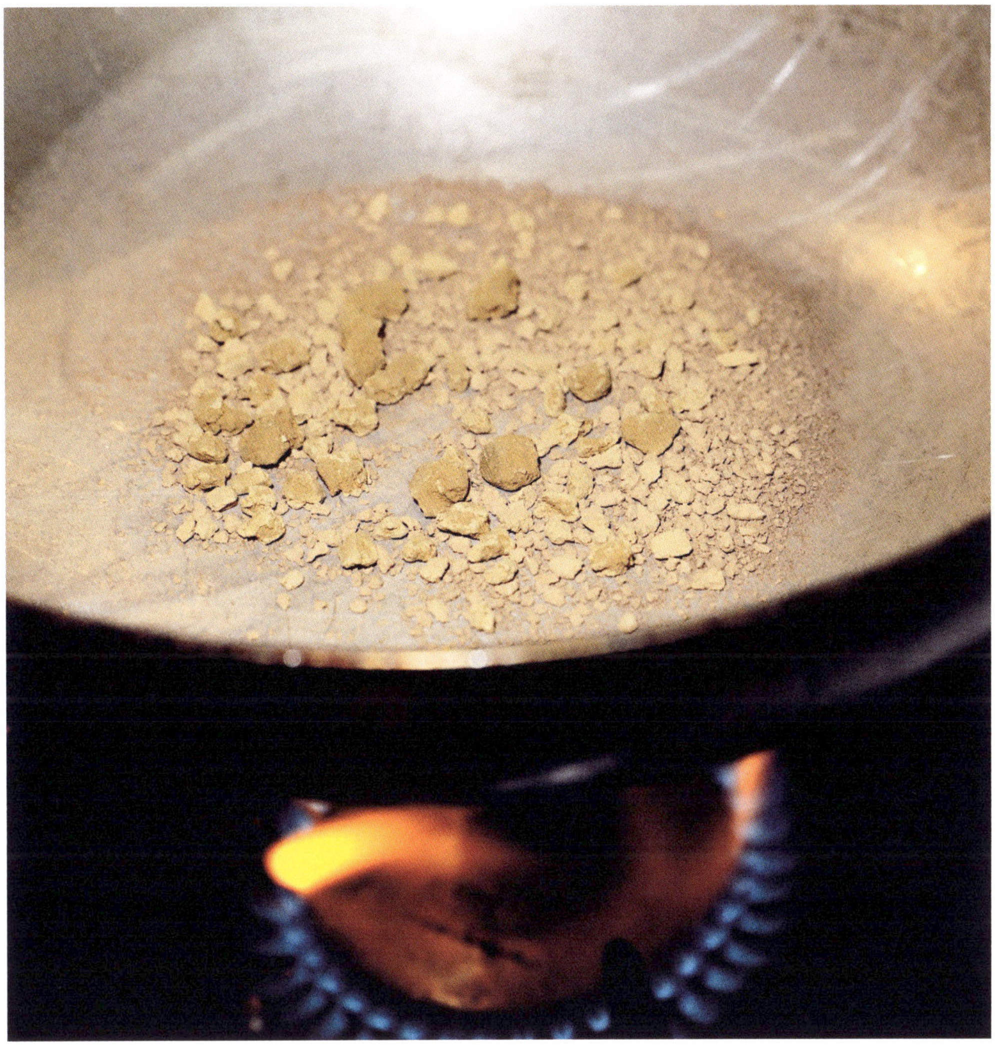

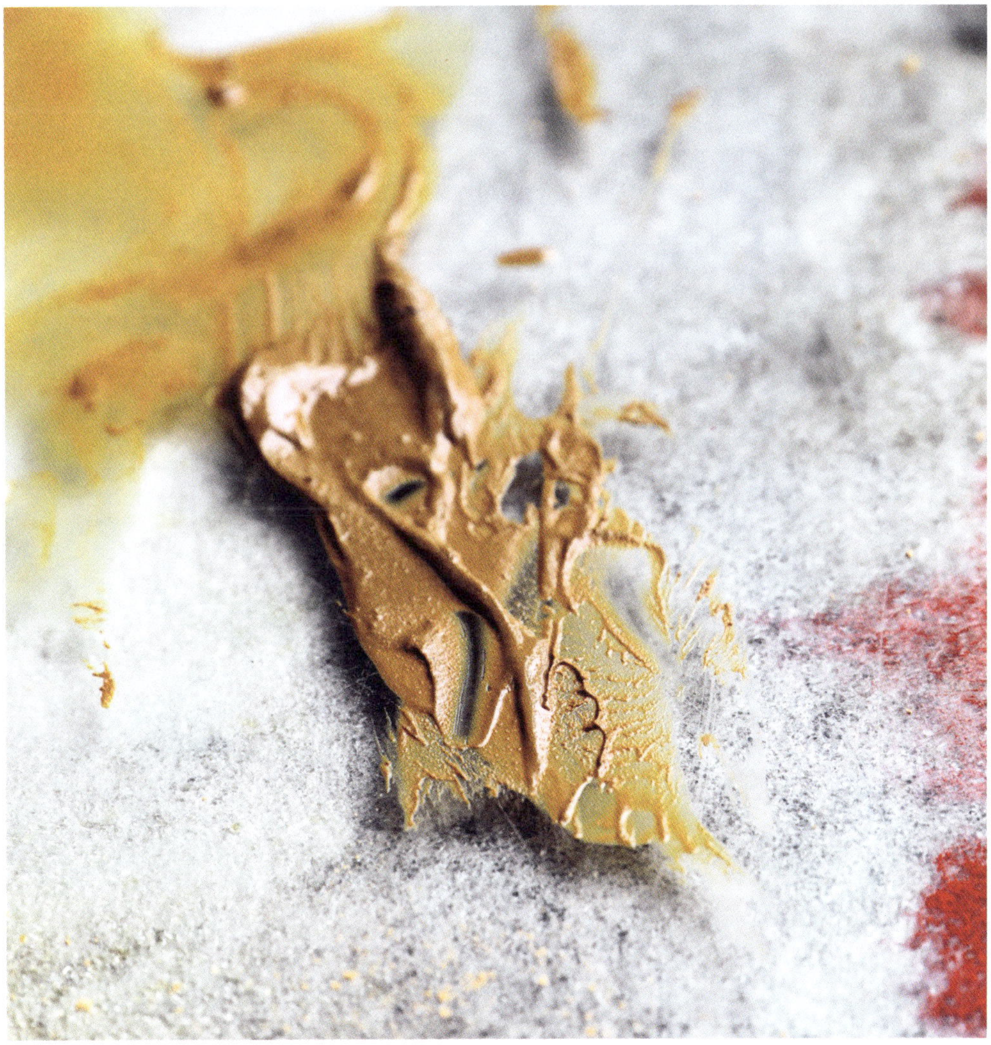

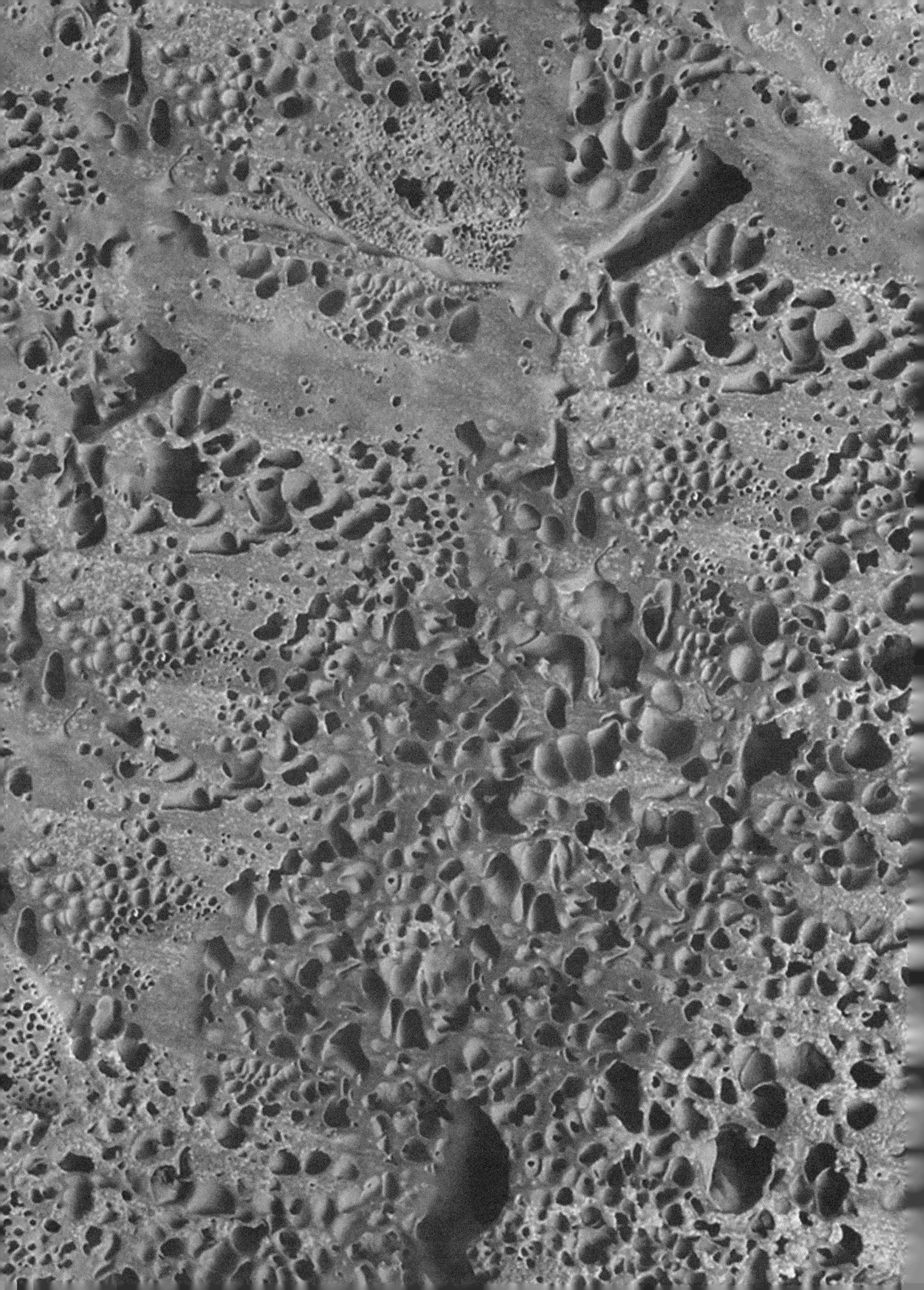

New Materials

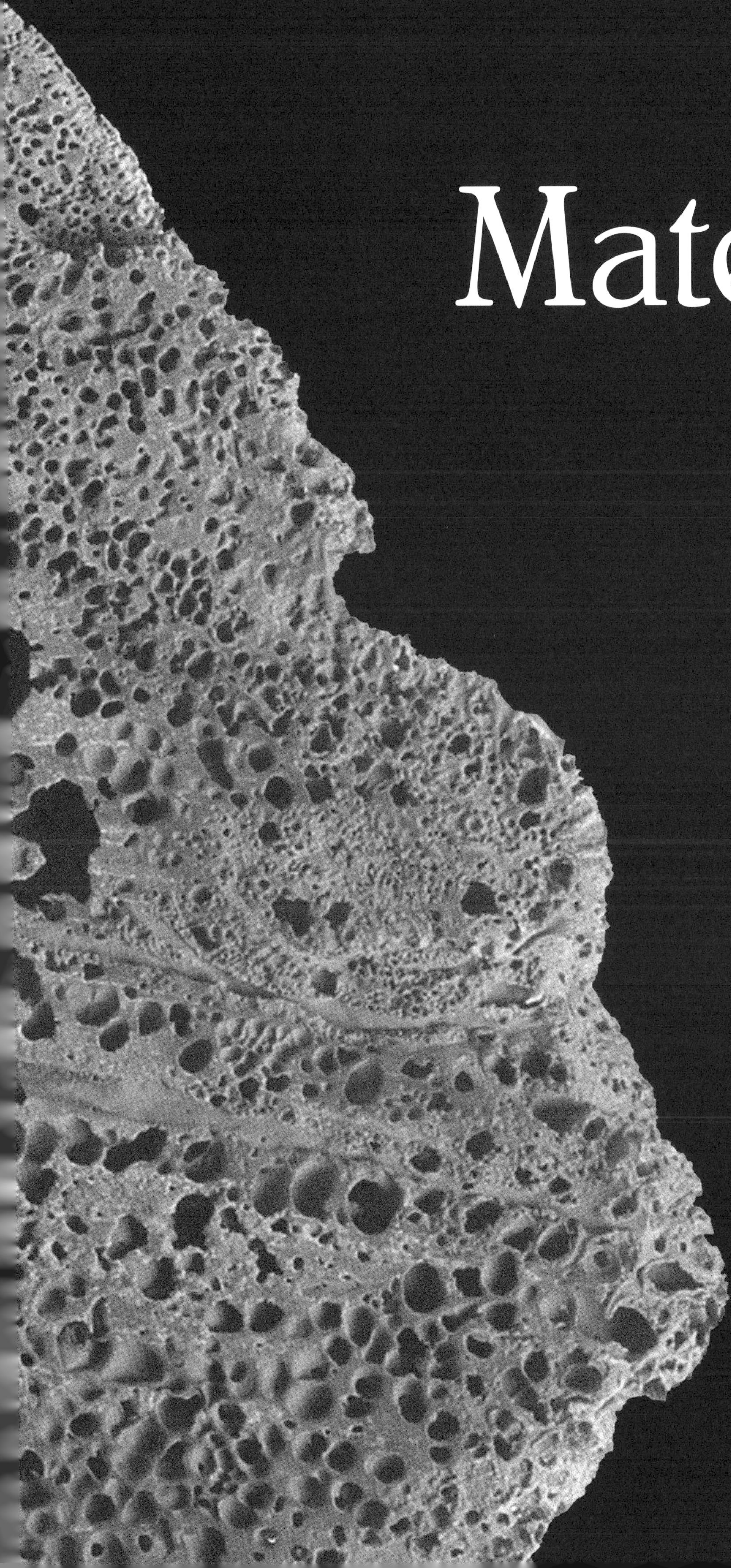

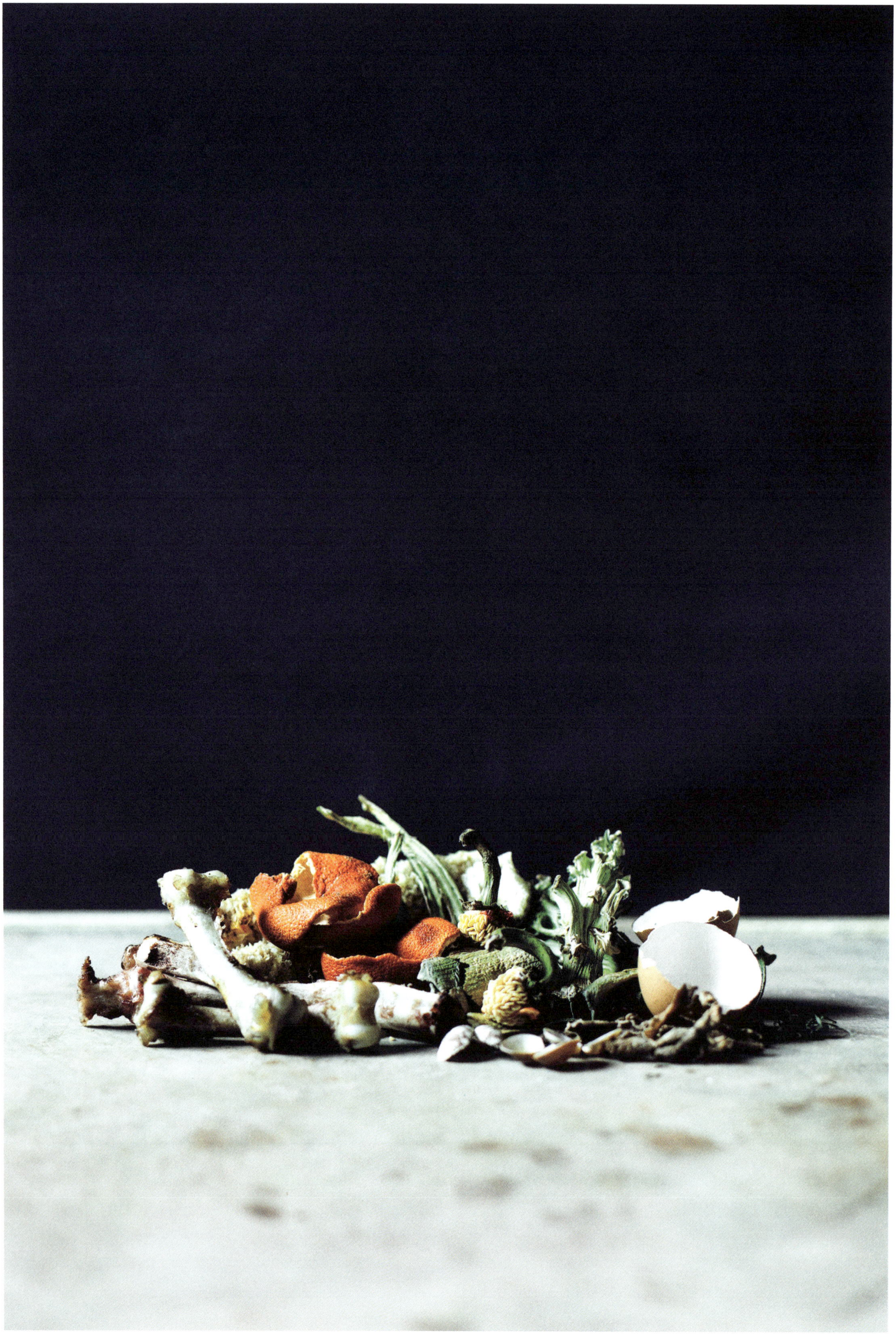

Kosuke Araki

Designer

Tokyo, Japan

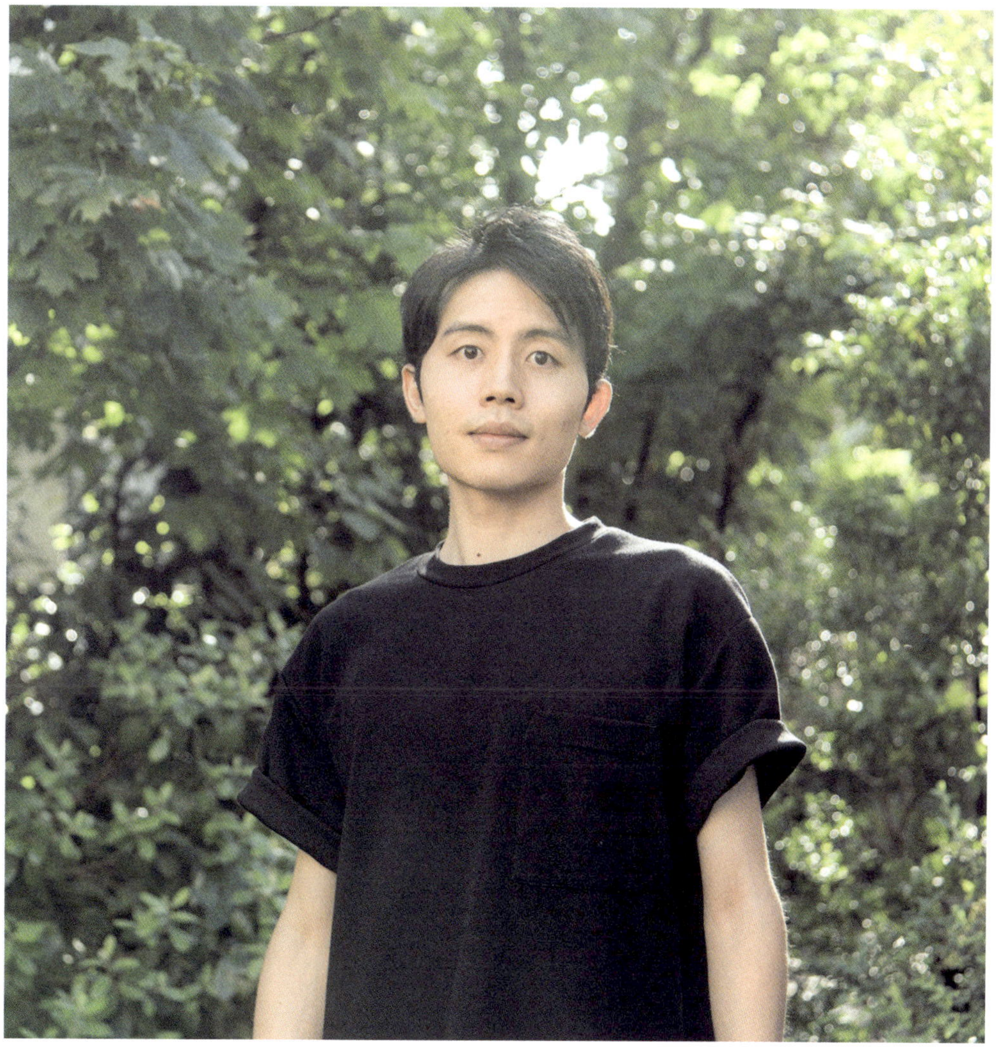

My name is Kosuke Araki, and I am a designer. I believe that the place and country in which you live have a great influence on what you do. The structure of the things that you see and touch, materials and forms, are the same everywhere, but the language you use shapes your way of thinking. I realized this when I went abroad to study.

I was born in Geneva and grew up in Tokyo. I inherited from my mother a flair for drawing and an interest in making objects. I was sure that I wanted to create things using my hands, so I enrolled in art school to acquire the necessary skills, such as sketching and modeling. But at that time I had no idea what the word "design" really meant. Through my studies, I gradually began to grasp its meaning and value. I graduated from the product design course at Tama Art University in Tokyo in 2010.

In 2013, I went to London to study at the Royal College of Art. During my time there, I planted the seeds of a project called *Food Waste Ware:* the goal was to create dishware using food waste collected from London's markets and grocery stores. My intention was to put food waste front and center, and raise awareness about the problem among the general public. At the time, the objects I created were made from carbonized vegetables and glue rendered by boiling the meat and bones of animals—the project was more conceptual than practical. Upon my return to Japan, I wanted to develop this work in a more efficient and practical way: now I dry food waste in the sun, then crush it and mix it with lacquer to create a moldable putty or paste. After several days, the material hardens and can be removed from the mold, then sanded down with sandpaper.

I have always been attracted by the depth, mystery, and unique brilliance of black lacquer, so I was interested in creating pieces using traditional Japanese lacquer. Although this interest consequently led me to create this tableware, I deliberately chose not to use black lacquer [traditionally used for tableware in Japan], in order to highlight the texture of this composite material. I finish the outside of these pieces with a cloth and the inside with a brush, using relatively transparent lacquer to give them a deep sheen and durability.

Traditional black lacquer gets its color from a chemical reaction with iron. My pieces appear black (in reality, they are very dark brown), but this is not through the use of black lacquer. The color is derived from the oxidization of the unrefined sap of the *urushi* tree, which is lacquer in its raw state.

I would describe this material as "new" rather than as "innovative." This evolution in my creative process and methods prompted me to give the new project a new name: *Anima*. The essence of this project inherited from *Food Waste Ware* is reinforced by its name, encouraging us to rethink our relationship with nature.

Novelty arises when things that are usually difficult to connect come together. This requires an understanding of context. I think it is impossible to create and understand something without a physical connection. Esen if you create a 3D print, there are sensations and thoughts that only arise when you touch the objects. It is critical that these feelings are passed on, as well as the technology used to make the objects.

I'm currently reflecting on a lifestyle that is compatible with nature: ocean pollution is extremely serious, and massive forest fires are erupting around the world. I am extremely pessimistic. The cause of these problems is invisible and is exacerbated by overproduction. Do we still need such abundance? We must urgently examine our lifestyles, or we will not be able to resolve these problems. The consequences of the pandemic seem to have been beneficial for the planet. The state of fauna, flora, the atmosphere, and the oceans has visibly improved. Humans are suffering, but the Earth is regenerating. For this to continue, we must reconsider our lifestyles. Even though a vaccine has been developed, I don't think I will go back to the way I was. We must adapt our lifestyles to a new world. Modesty and respect will be very important for future production. We are entering a very difficult period during which we will have to improve on or resolve existing problems. How can we make humanity and the planet healthier? Each of us must ask ourselves if another world is possible.

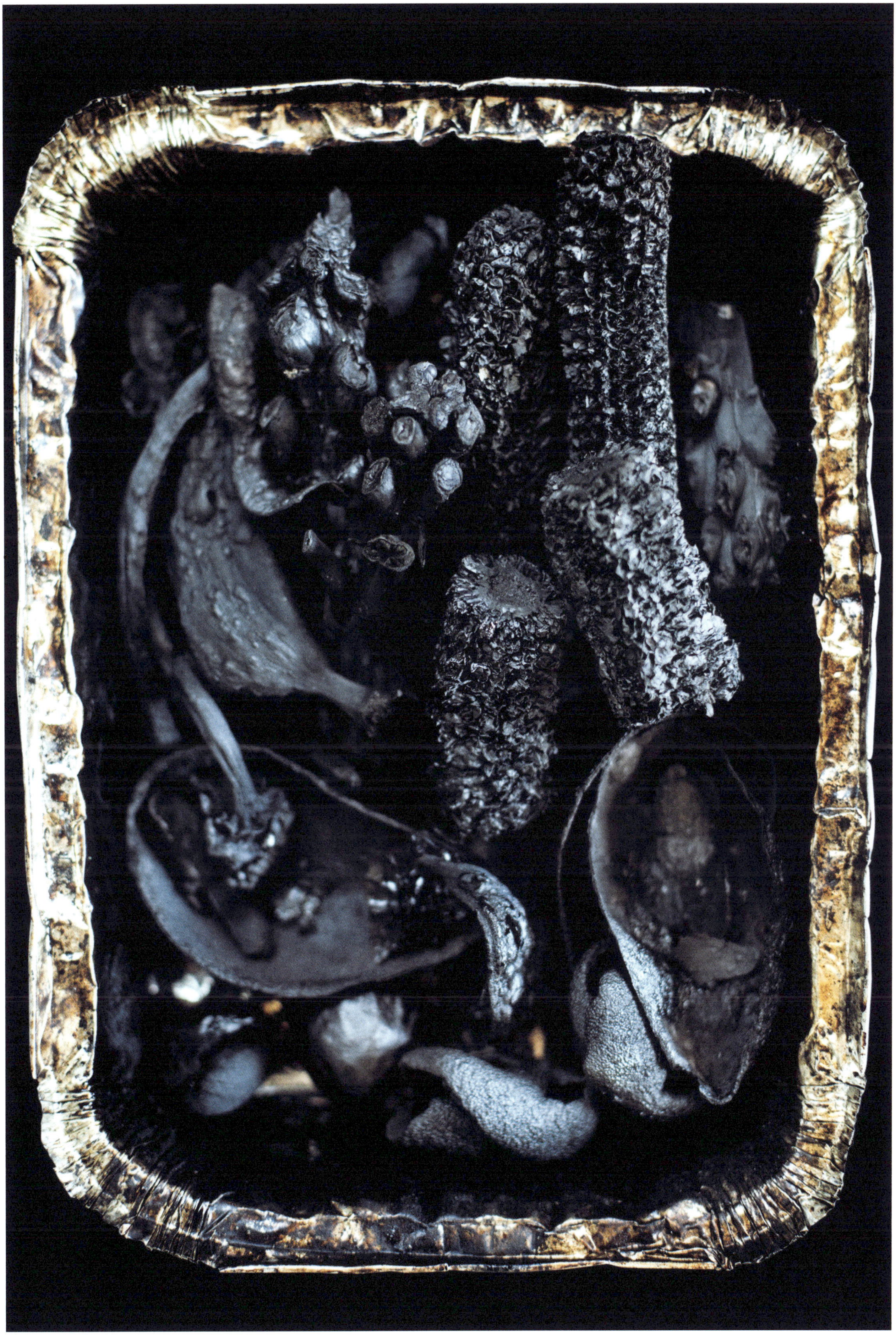

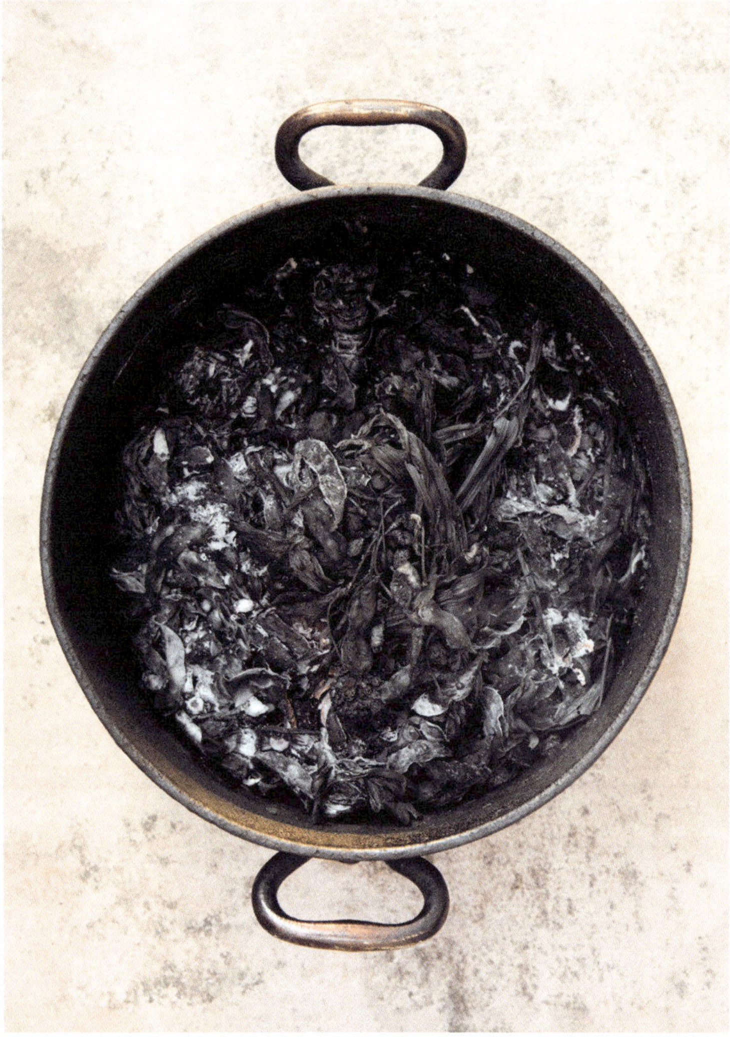

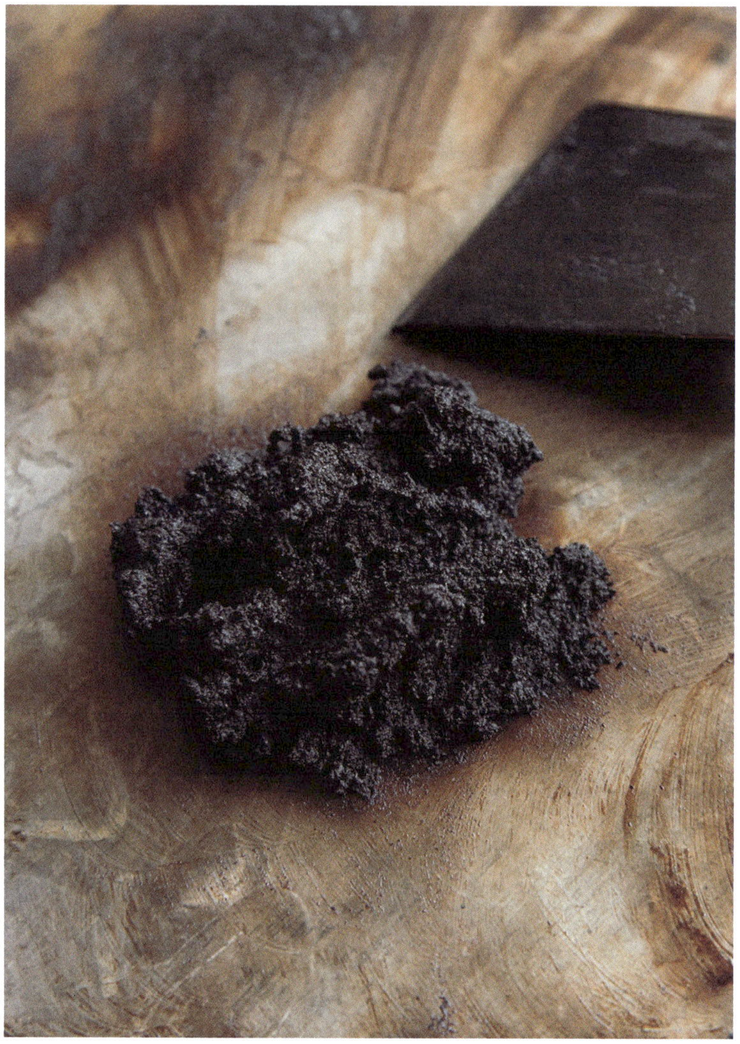

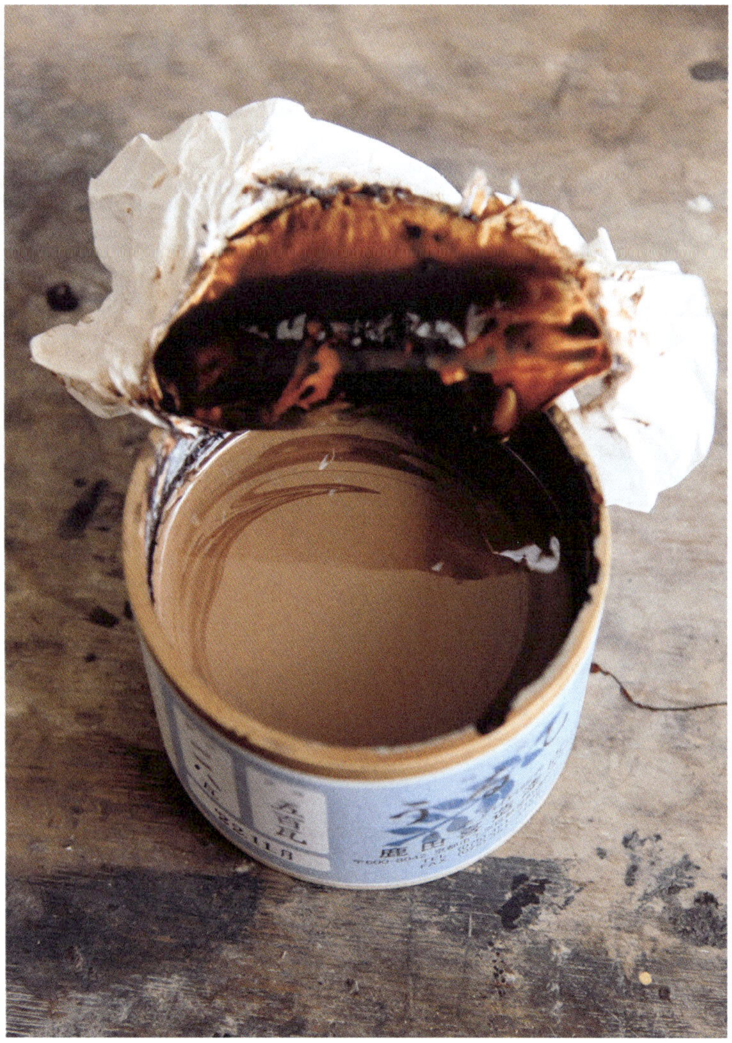

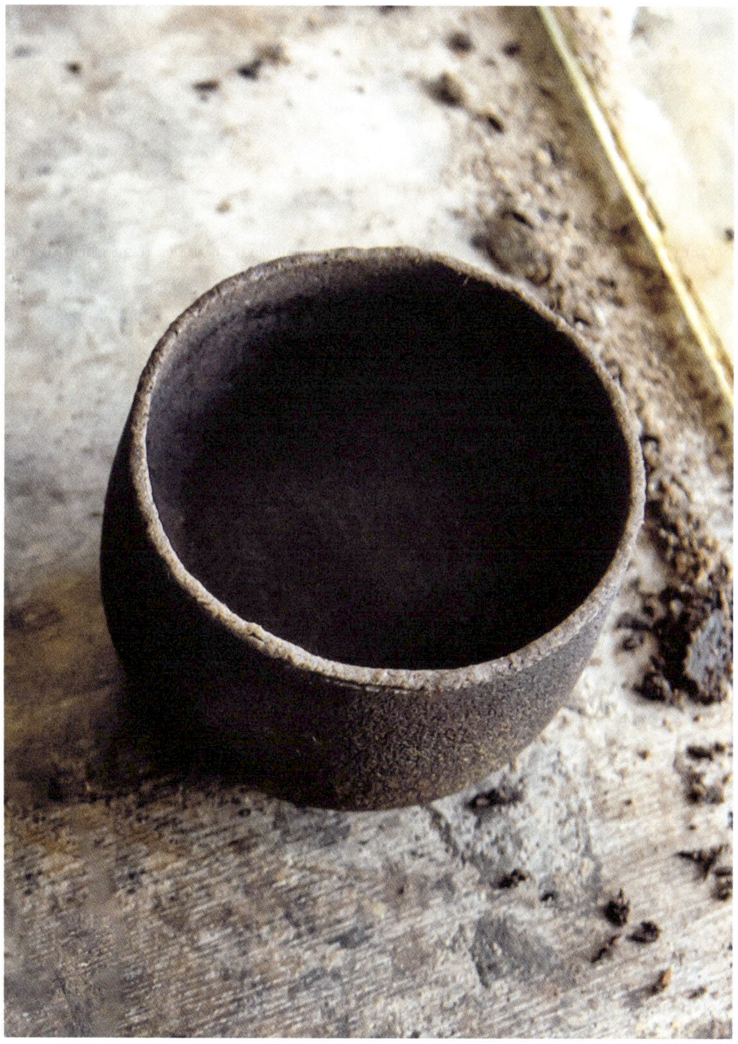

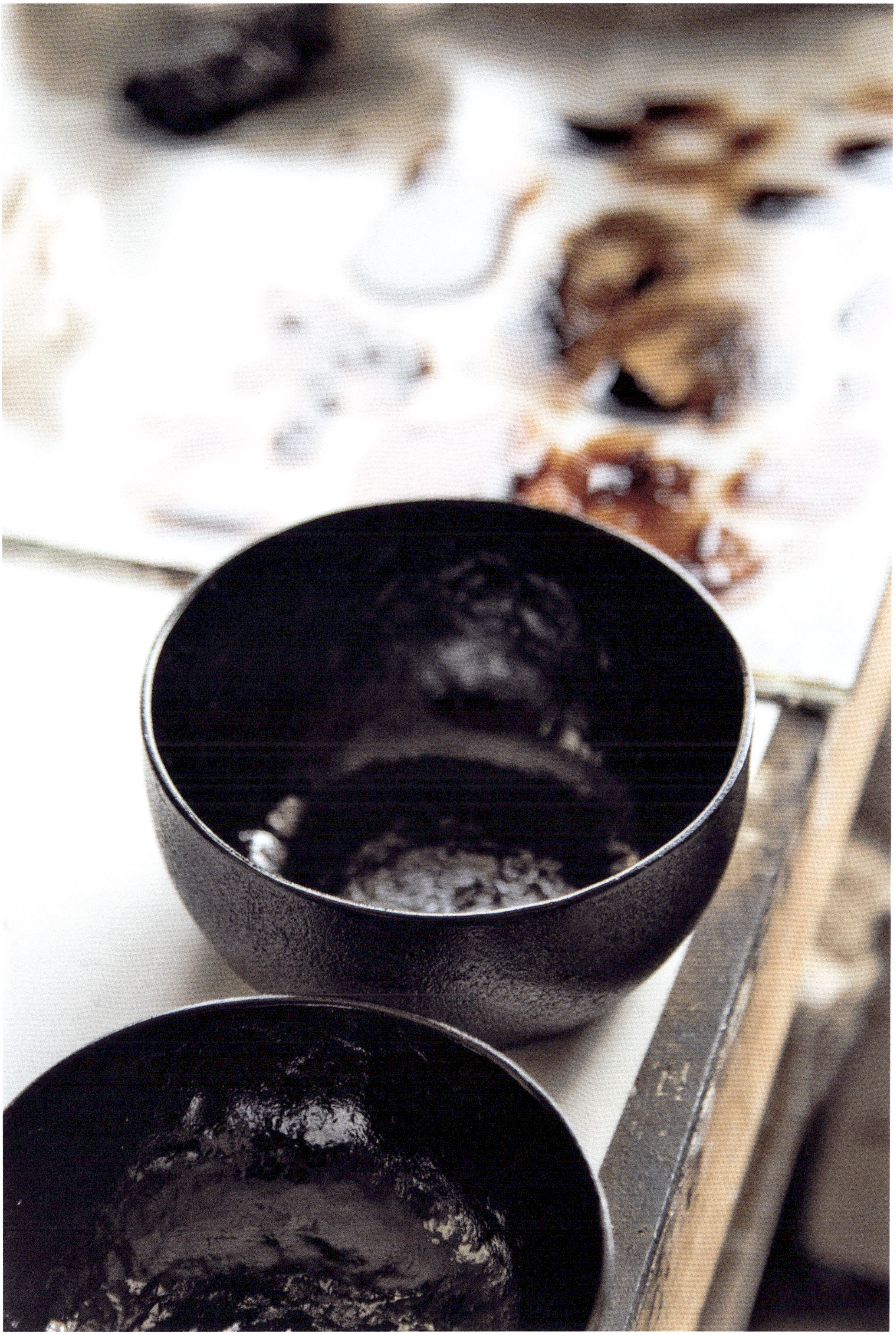

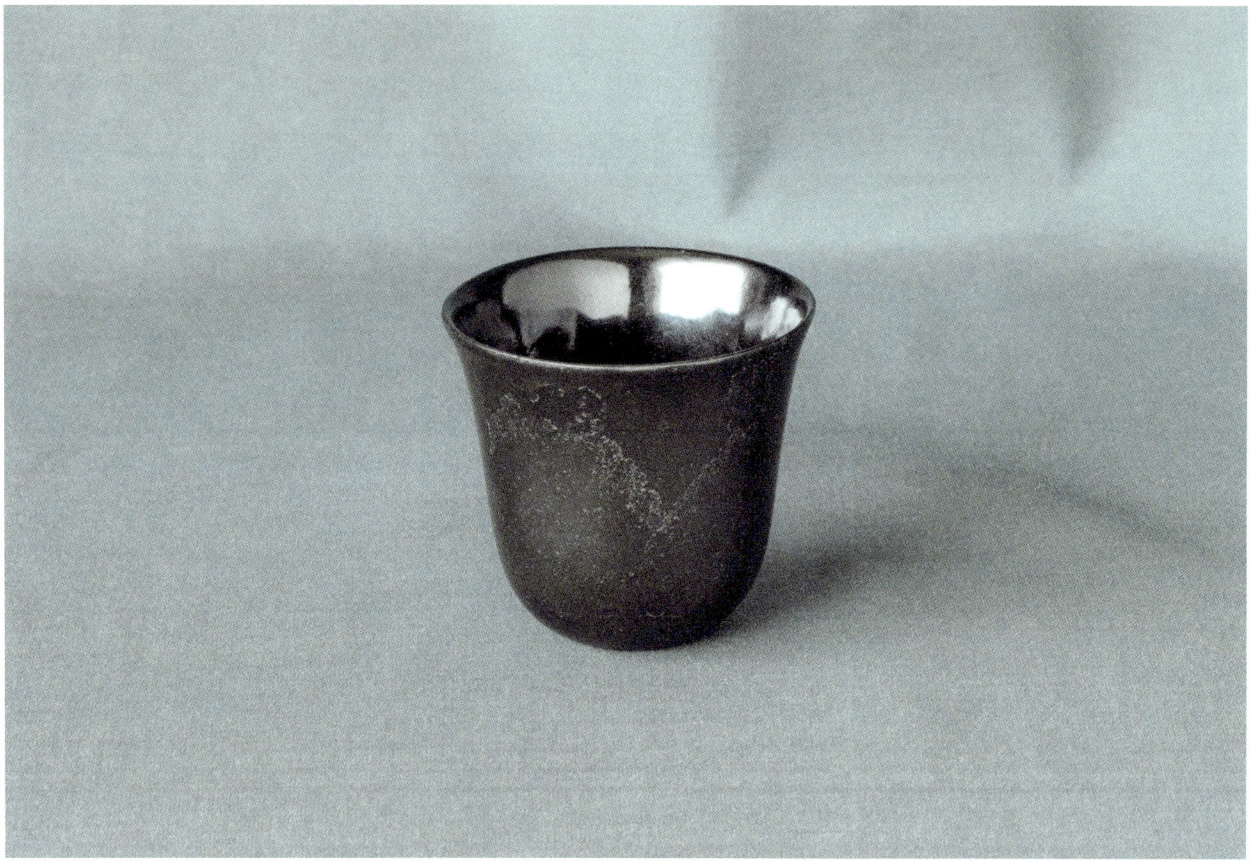

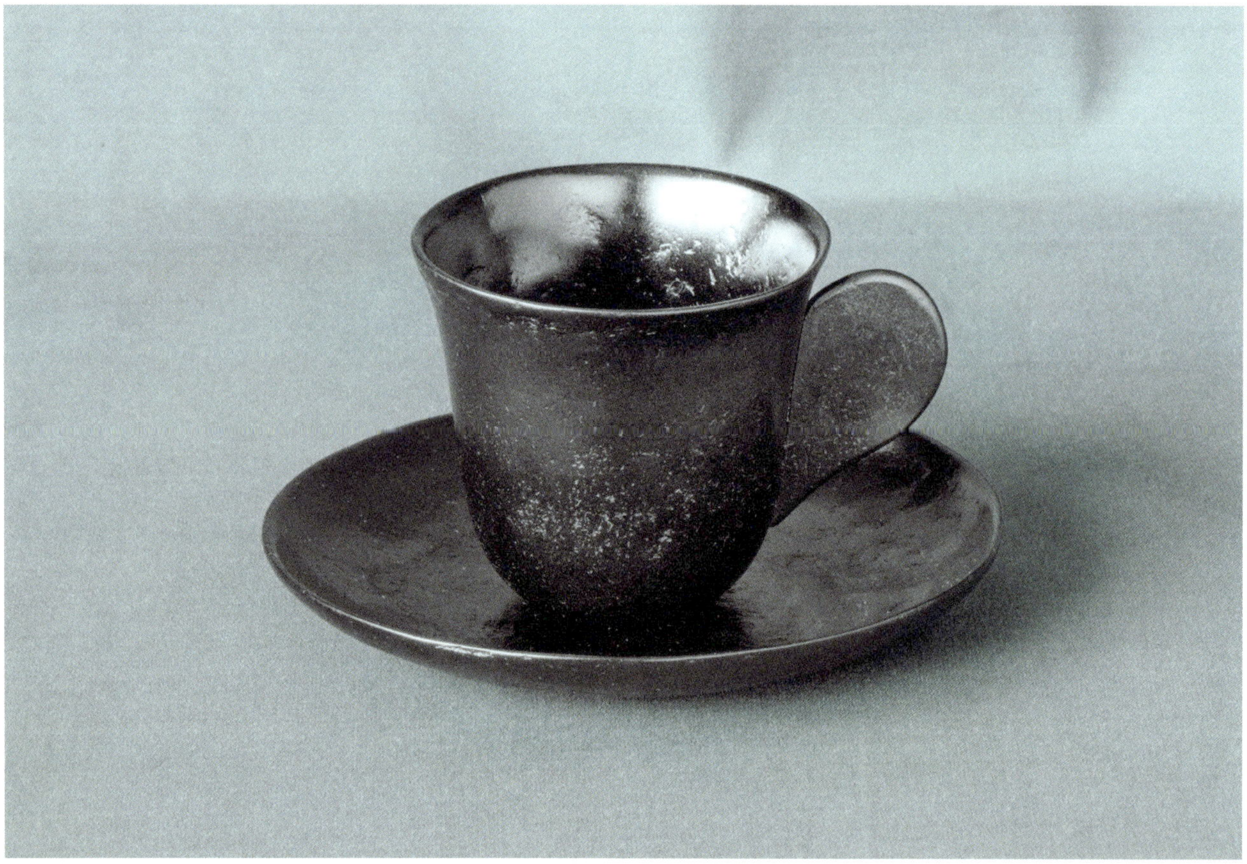

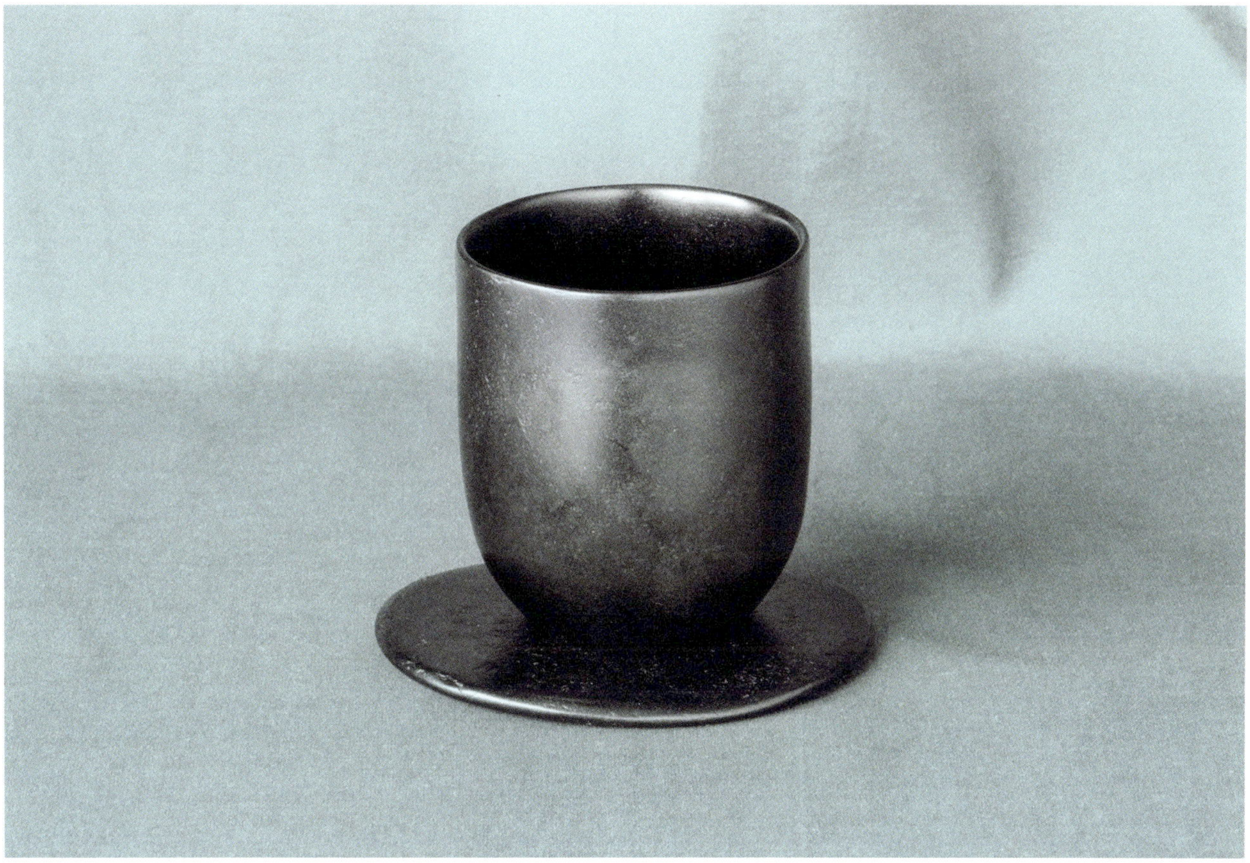

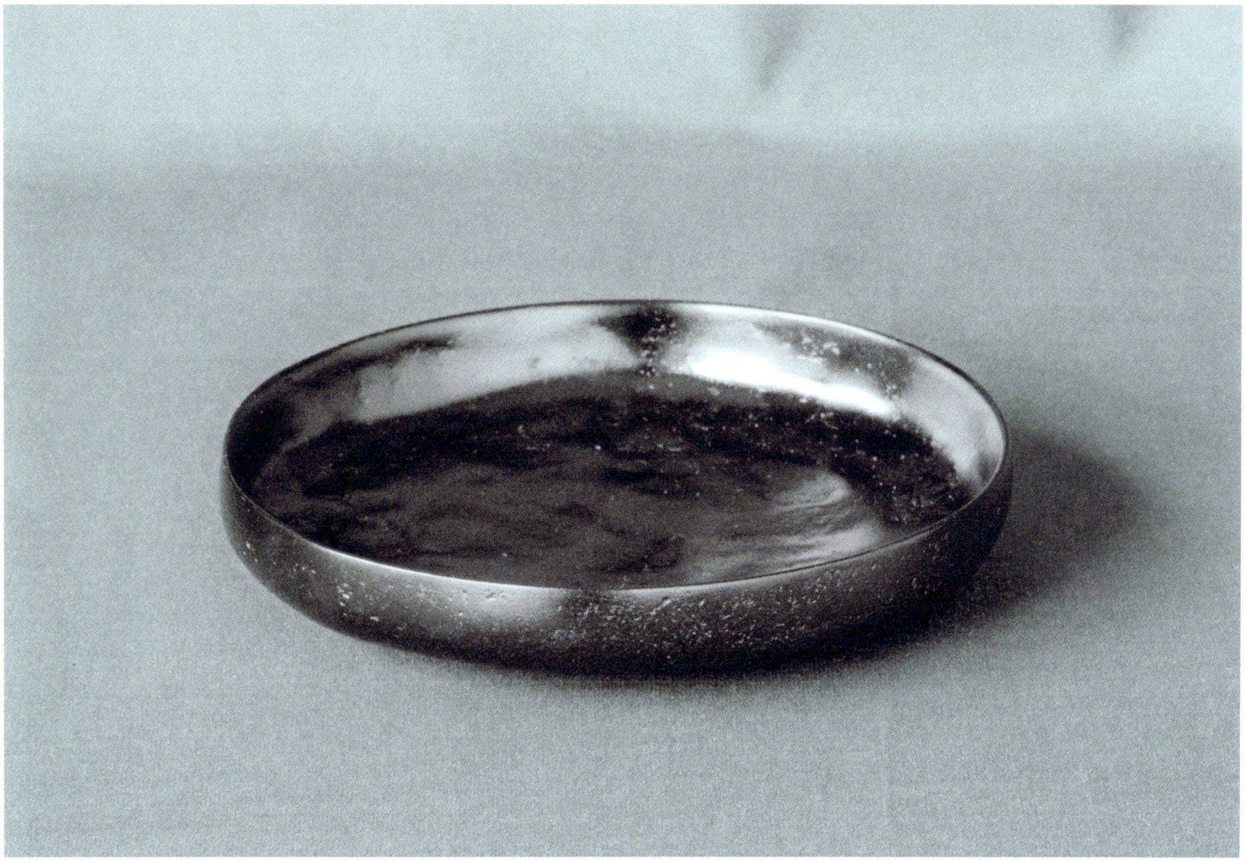

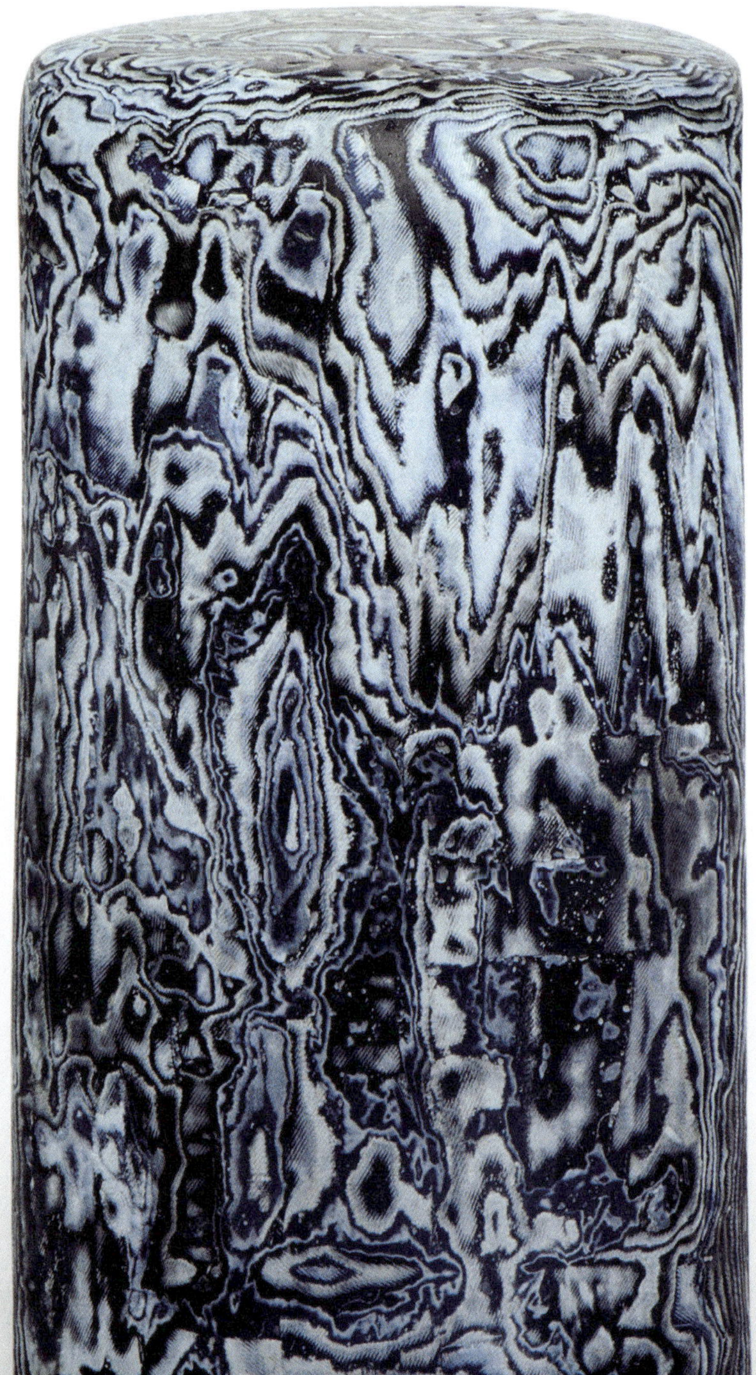

Sophie Rowley

Designer and experimental artisan

Berlin, Germany

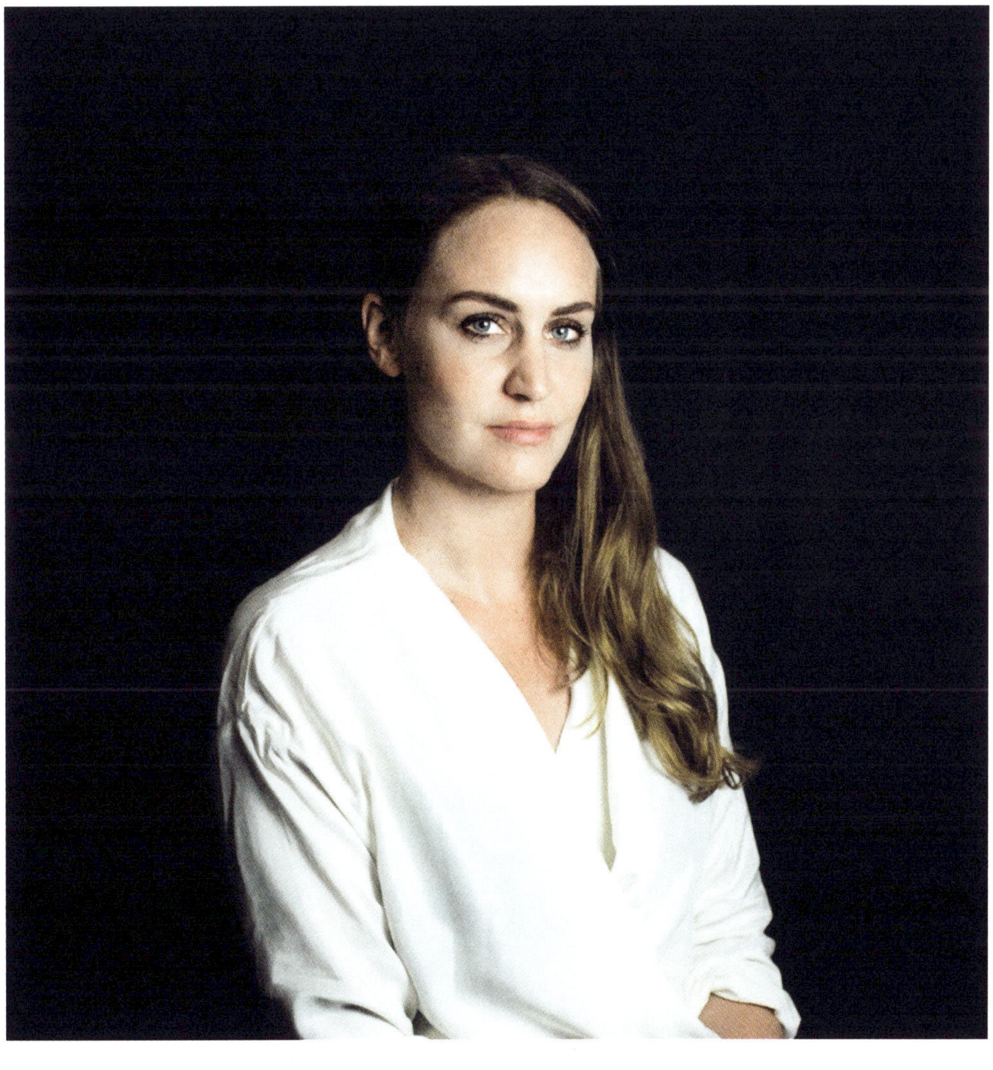

My name is Sophie Rowley, and I am a craftsperson who works with materials and textiles in experimental ways. I enjoy working with materials that are very universal. Denim, for example, is a fabric that is present everywhere on the planet; it is free from any cultural or social significance. Denim waste is abundant in every country, whether as a result of domestic production or post-consumer waste.

My childhood spanned two continents. I lived in Auckland, New Zealand, until I was eight years old, when my family moved to Tübingen, in southern Germany. In New Zealand, I had already been exposed to many different crafts by my mother, as well as my grandmother, who practiced textile crafts all her life. After high school, I pursued a degree in fashion design, and explored textiles and embroidery design in a more professional sense. Then I decided to focus on textile innovation and went on to complete an MA in Material Futures at Central Saint Martins in London.

My graduation project was a research study on waste. It resulted in a collection of new materials that I developed by recycling trash to create artifacts simulating natural materials: *Material Illusions*. My decision to work with waste arose from necessity in a way. During my studies, I had very few financial resources, and I had to work with what I had. My only assets were my time and my ability to transform materials using the processes I was learning.

First, I selected generic waste like glass, expanded polystyrene foam, textiles, and plastic. I experimented with these materials by applying a combination of craft and industrial processes until they took on a completely new aesthetic and began to resemble natural materials such as stone, wood, coral (from polystyrene foam), or marble (from denim).

The idea of creating something aesthetic from something common or worthless has always appealed to me. I want to prove that the source material is not necessarily what gives value to objects, but rather how we work with the materials themselves and the processes we apply to them. Usually I experiment a lot with a material to see where it takes me. I have to be connected with the material in order to come up with new ideas. There have been times when I thought I would fail—I still think that frequently. Scaling up successful samples and dealing with the inconsistencies of waste materials present a huge challenge.

Someone once told me that my work explores both the past and the future—they were right. I enjoy learning from traditional crafts in order to explore them in new ways. That's what you might call innovation, which, for me, arises when conventional ways of seeing things are called into question and reexamined. Innovation is an improvement or a new interpretation of something familiar. It occurs in small continuous steps, by learning, adapting, and improving.

I believe craft is grounding. Handmade objects carry more value and soul than their industrially produced counterparts. In our fast-paced lifestyles, it is essential that we surround ourselves with meaningful, long-lasting objects.

In the future, I see myself continuing to develop new ways of innovating materials suited to craftsmanship, in order to keep the "handmade" alive. I hope to have found a place as a textile artist and that my work remains in step with the times.

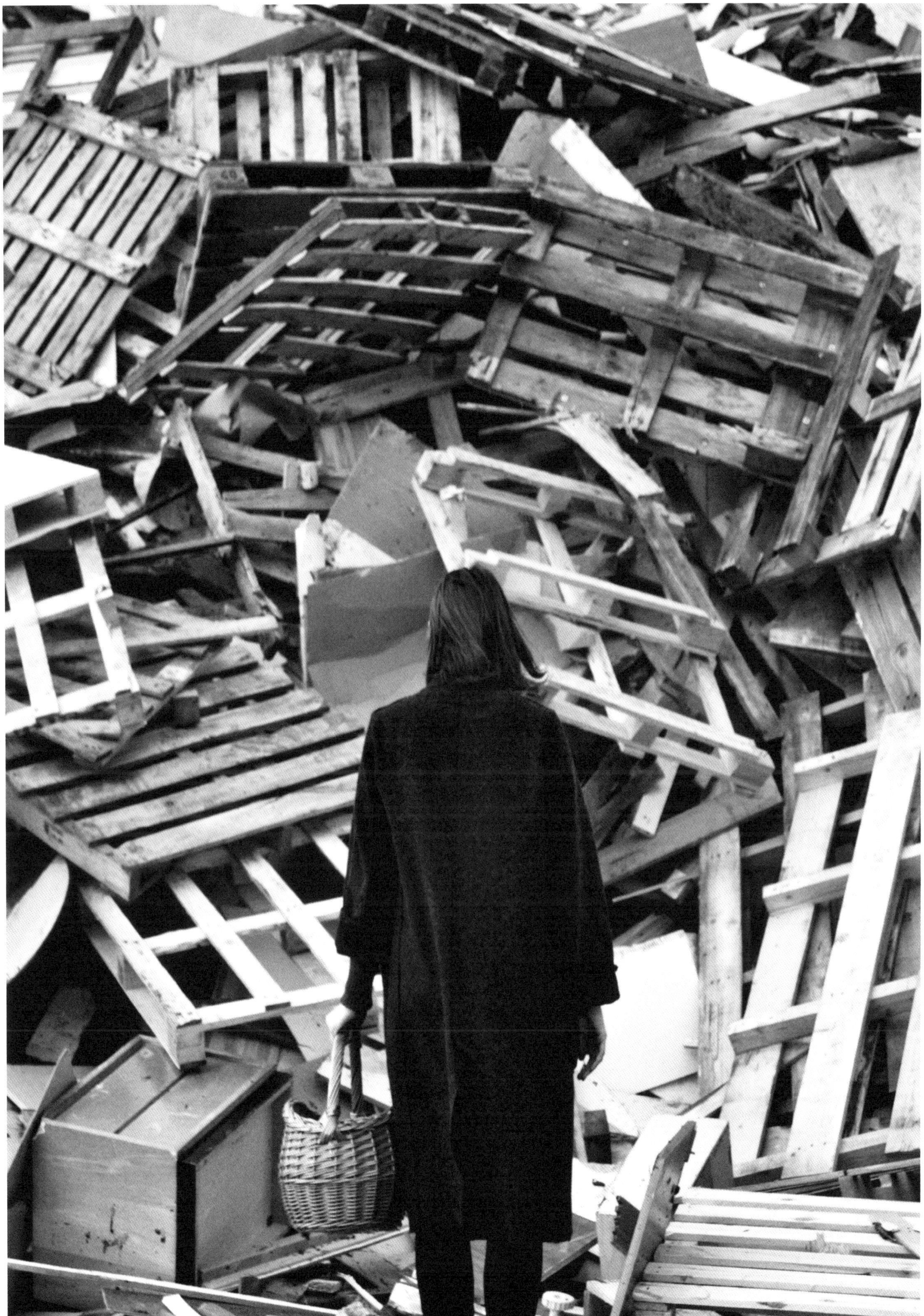

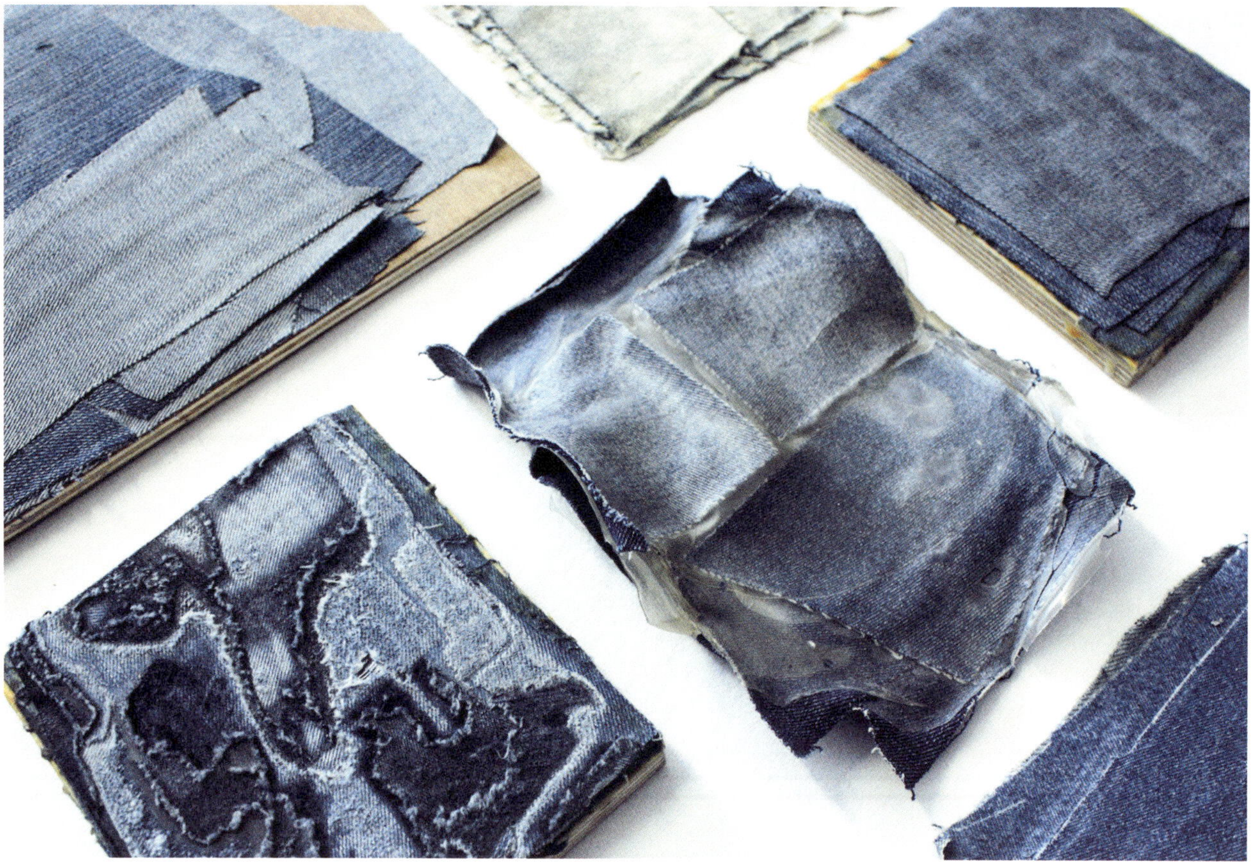

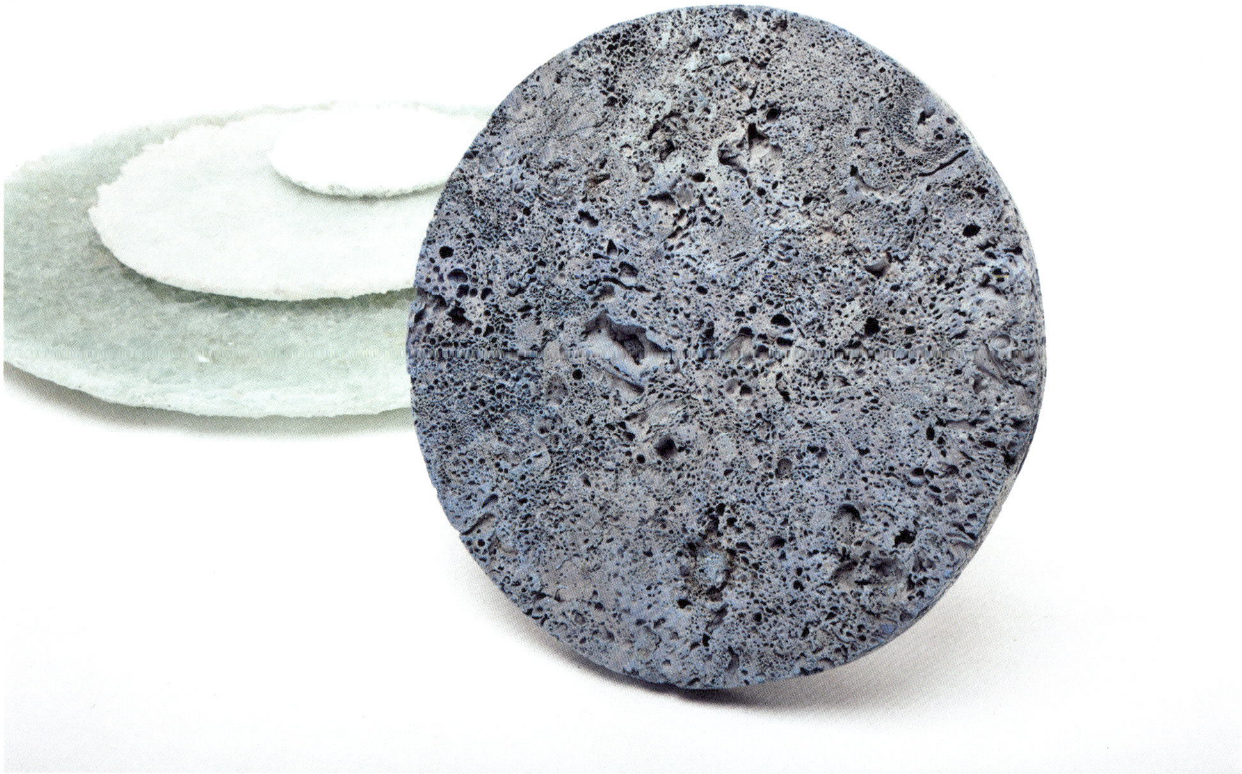

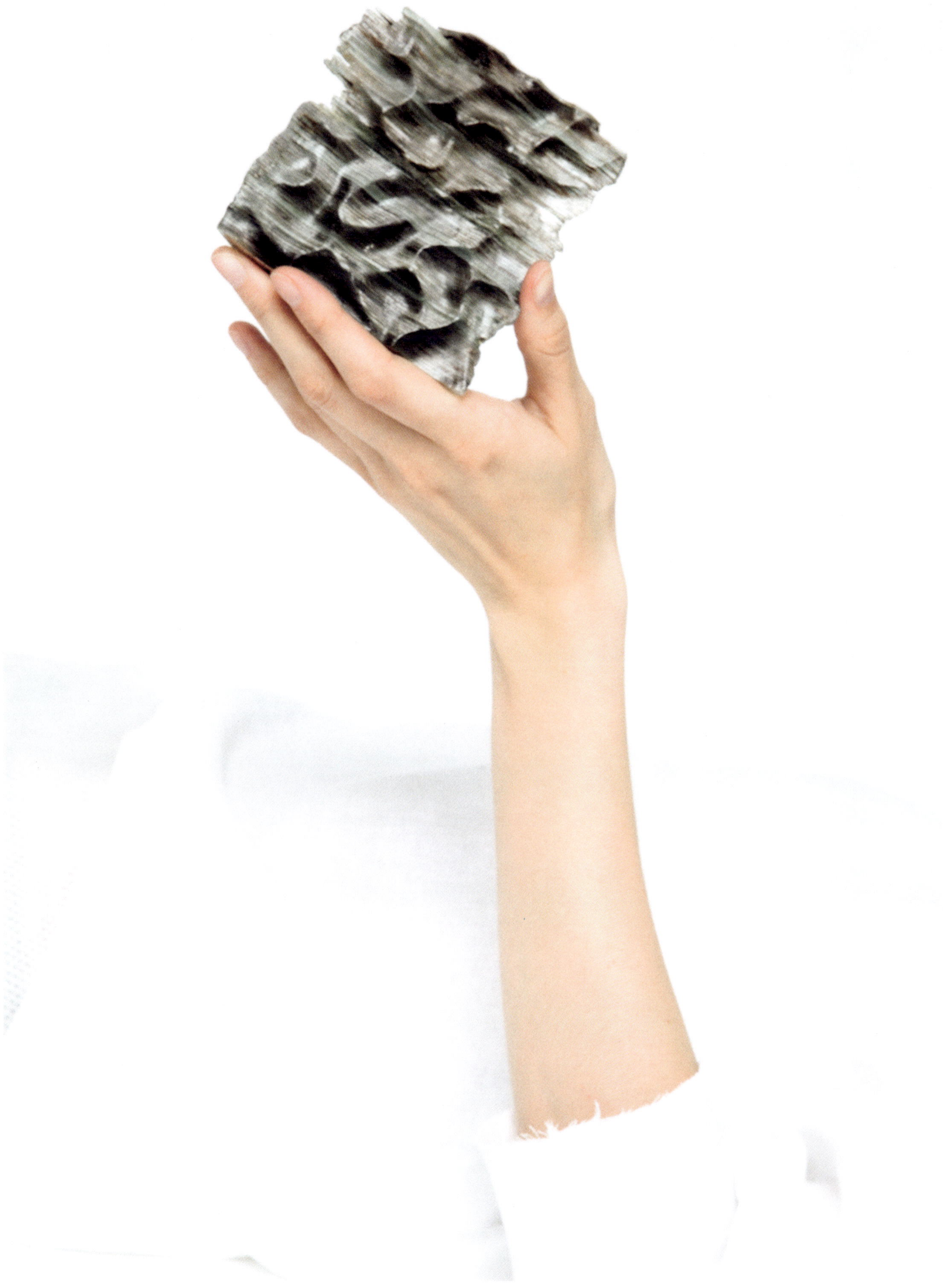

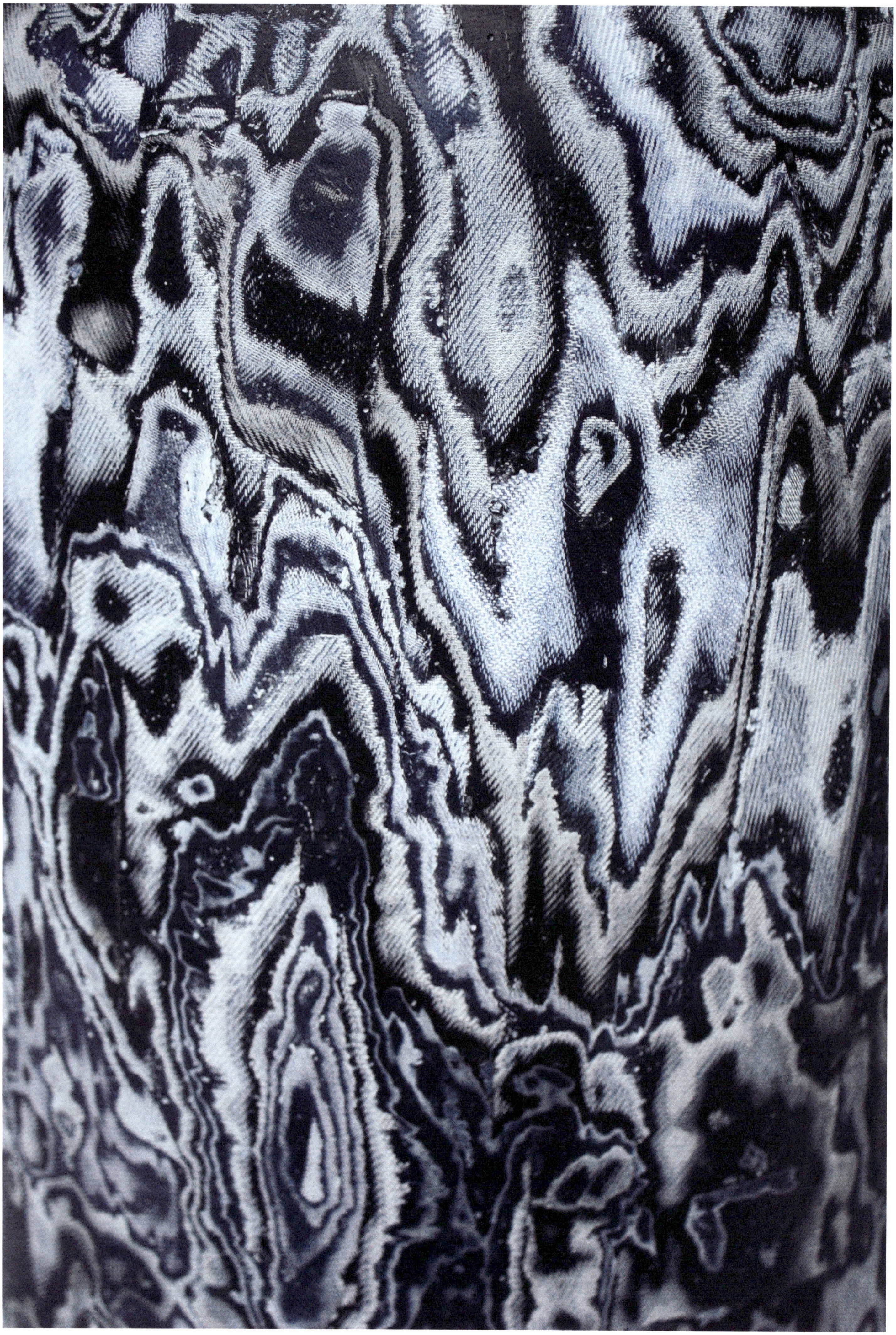

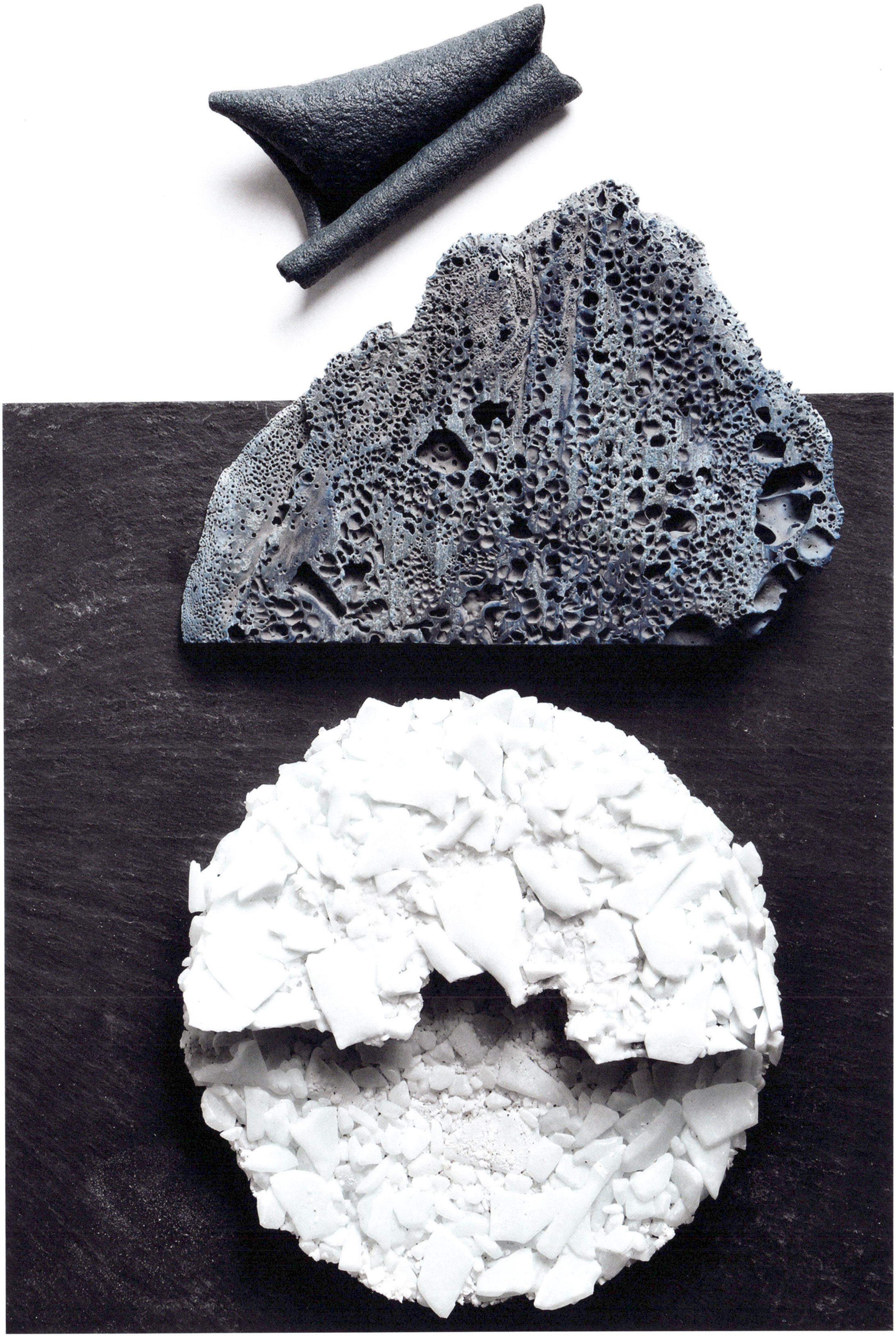

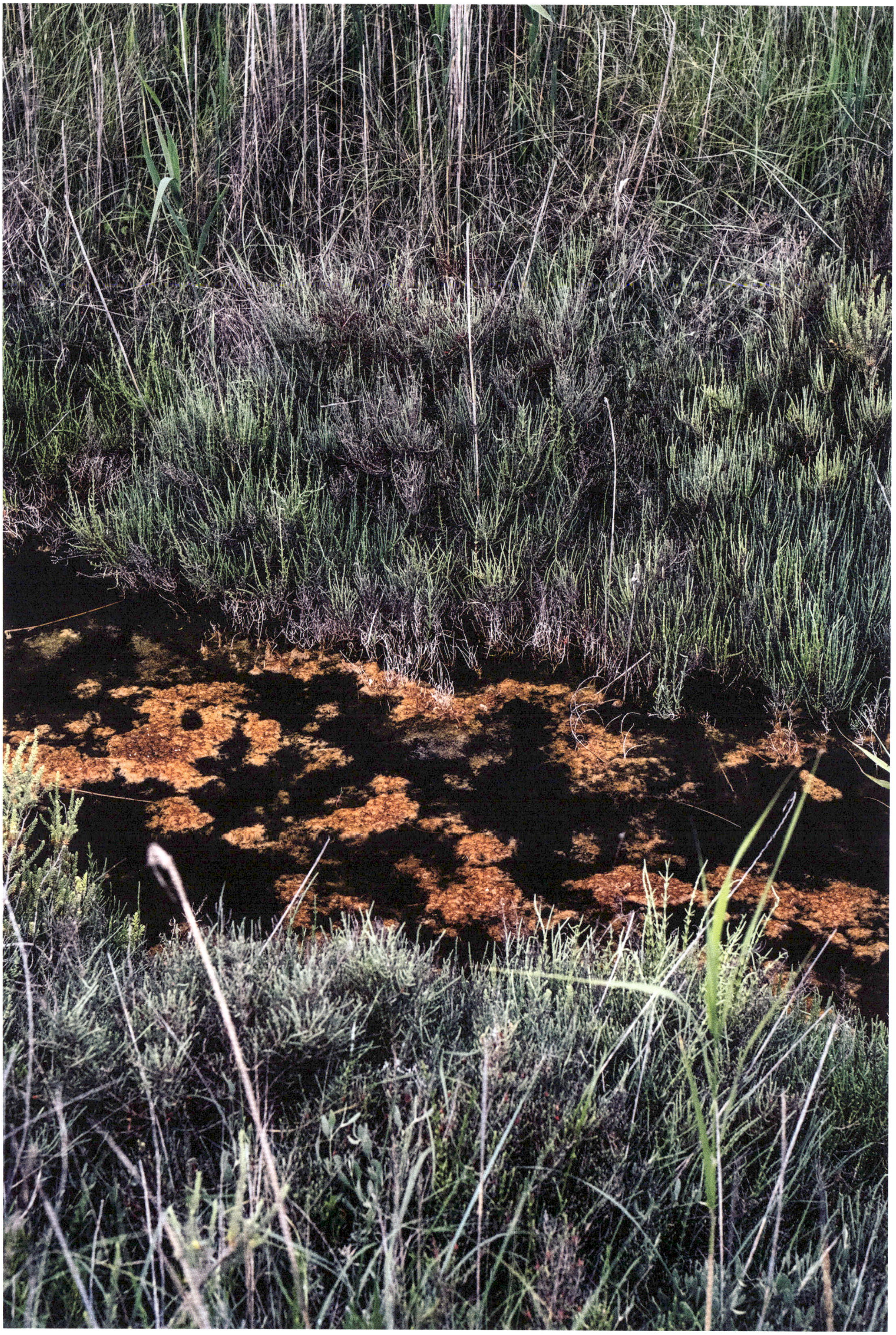

Henriette Waal

Social designer

Arles, France

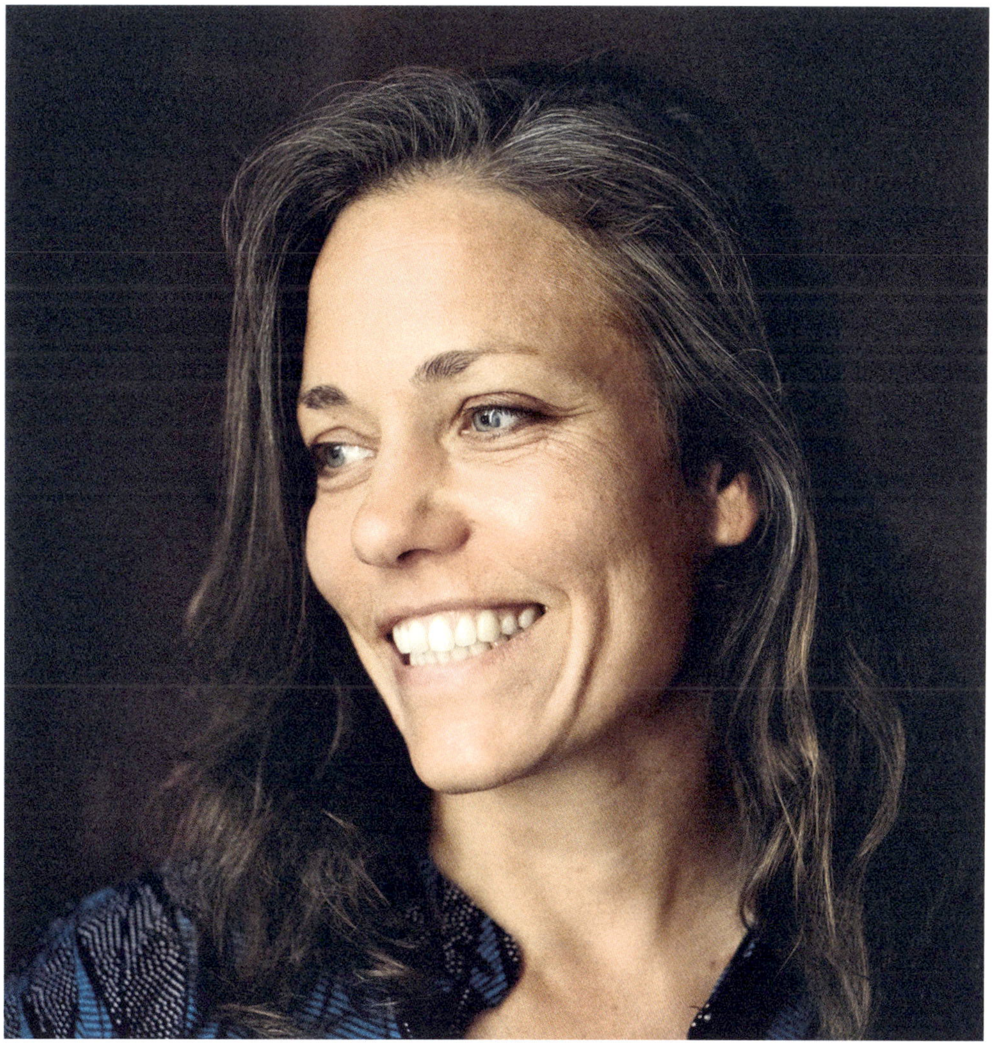

My name is Henriette Waal. In 2017, I was invited, along with Maartje Dros and Eric Klarenbeek from the design studio Klarenbeek & Dros, to set up Atelier Luma's Labo Algues, in Arles, on the site of the city's former SNCF rail workshops. The Atelier Luma program was launched in 2016 by the Luma Foundation, to realize founder Maja Hoffmann's project of creating an interdisciplinary center that would draw on resources, materials, expertise, and talent from the region and beyond. The goal of the project is to find new ways of living, consuming, building, and evolving, using design as a tool for transition.

Dros and Klarenbeek are interested in bio-based design and had already worked on projects using algae and macroalgae in the Netherlands. Their idea was to capitalize on the potential of these living organisms to replace non-biodegradable plastics and develop a biopolymer (a fiber) that could be used to create innovative products. This material is made from dried algae that are pulverized and mixed with organic polymer powder, PLA, or potato starch, then placed in an extruder, which feeds a thread of the material into a 3D printer. We scanned some Roman glassware found in the Rhône River that belonged to the collection of the Musée Départemental Arles Antique, and then reproduced it using this new material made from locally grown algae.

For more than ten years, Eric, Maartje, and I have been interested in combining social design, ecology, and technology. Today, I am a "social designer" and research director at Atelier Luma. For as long as I can remember, I have always been interested in forms of creation and interacting with others through the creative act. My training, which began in childhood, was based on observation. My parents were anthropologists. My mother, a volunteer guide, raised public awareness about the natural environment surrounding our village. She observed the materials around our house. This direct, concrete observation gives us a better understanding of our environment; it should be a mandatory part of the design process, because to design something, you have to understand it.

Seaweed also has immense advantages in terms of color. The pink hue of *Dunaliella salina* seen under the Camargue sun in June is an emotive sight. Understanding this color, in other words, understanding the algae that make up this living pigment, allows us to work with it. Color is an essential and ubiquitous part of our environment and ourselves, and it shapes the atmosphere, forms, and feelings. Color is not innocent; it is a powerful cultural, political, and economic force.

I have taken the Labo Algues project from its experimental phase to the development of a platform that embraces the Mediterranean. I have set up workshops in Cairo, Istanbul, Sardinia, and elsewhere to pass on our knowledge and manufacturing processes to designers, so they, in turn, can apply this methodology to their own regions and develop an innovative economic model.

Finding creative ways to export the models that we have developed in Arles, at Atelier Luma, to other regions of the Mediterranean and promoting knowledge exchange will directly influence the learning opportunities available to students and practitioners.

Today, I see craft as the wealth of the Earth. Through my field tests at Atelier Luma, I am already trying to change the mentality of artisans and find effective links between the market and production. The new activities I am developing have yet to be named, but they are all craft-digital hybrids tied to renewable resources.

We need to go much further than simply preserving craftsmanship; we must develop scenarios for its evolution that are in line with technological advances, and geographic and socio-economic factors. The concept of "local" has changed considerably. Much of what is considered to be typical local craft is often a banal and outdated representation of that culture. We must make a shift from national craftsmanship to transnational craftsmanship.

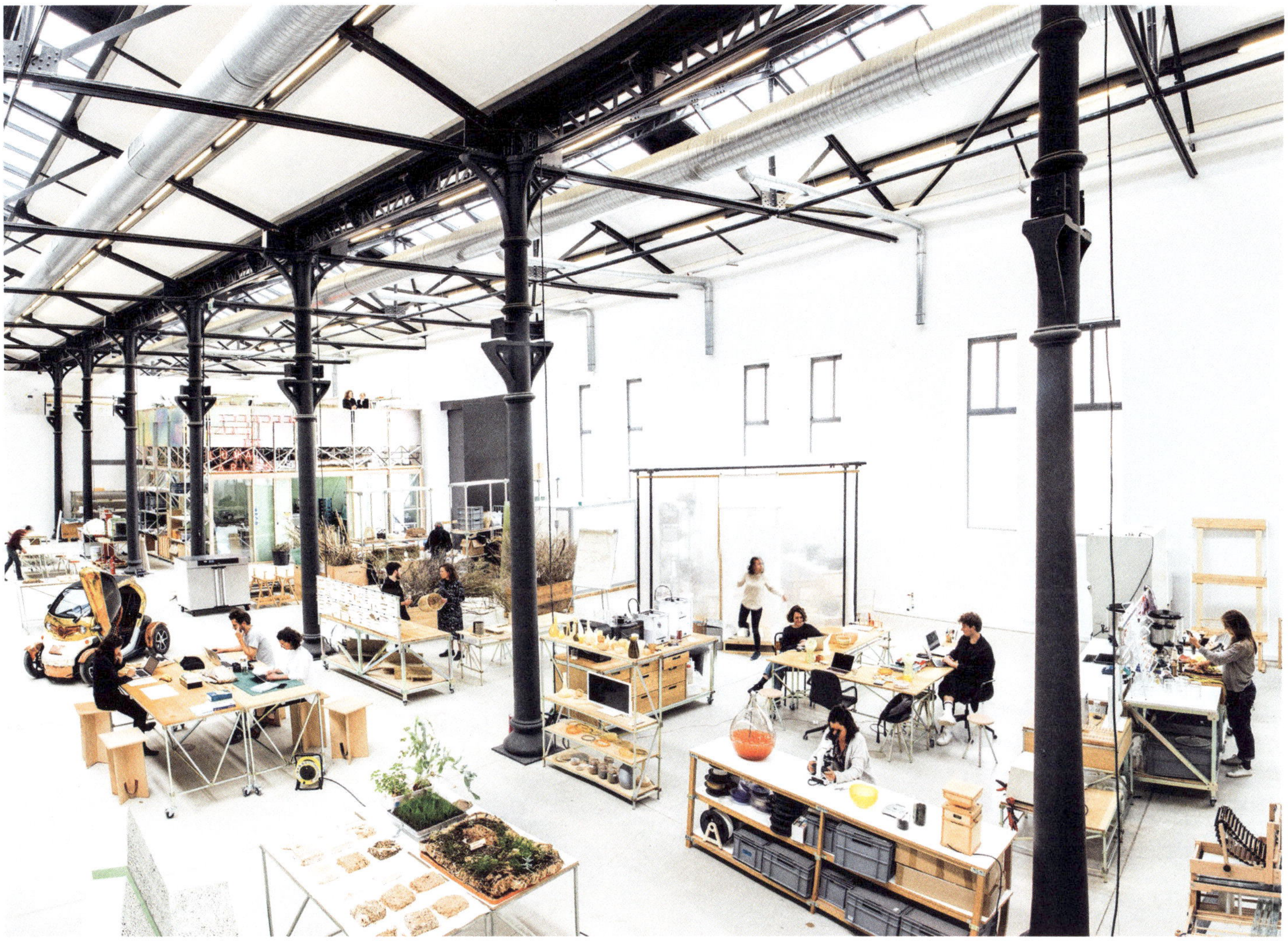

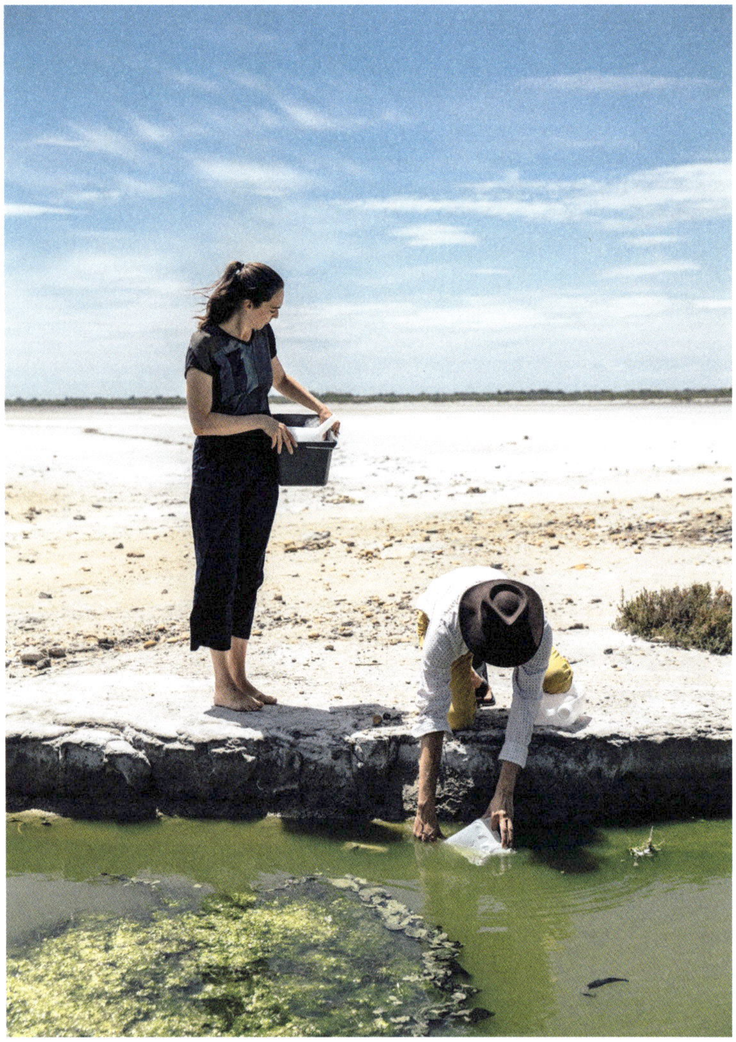

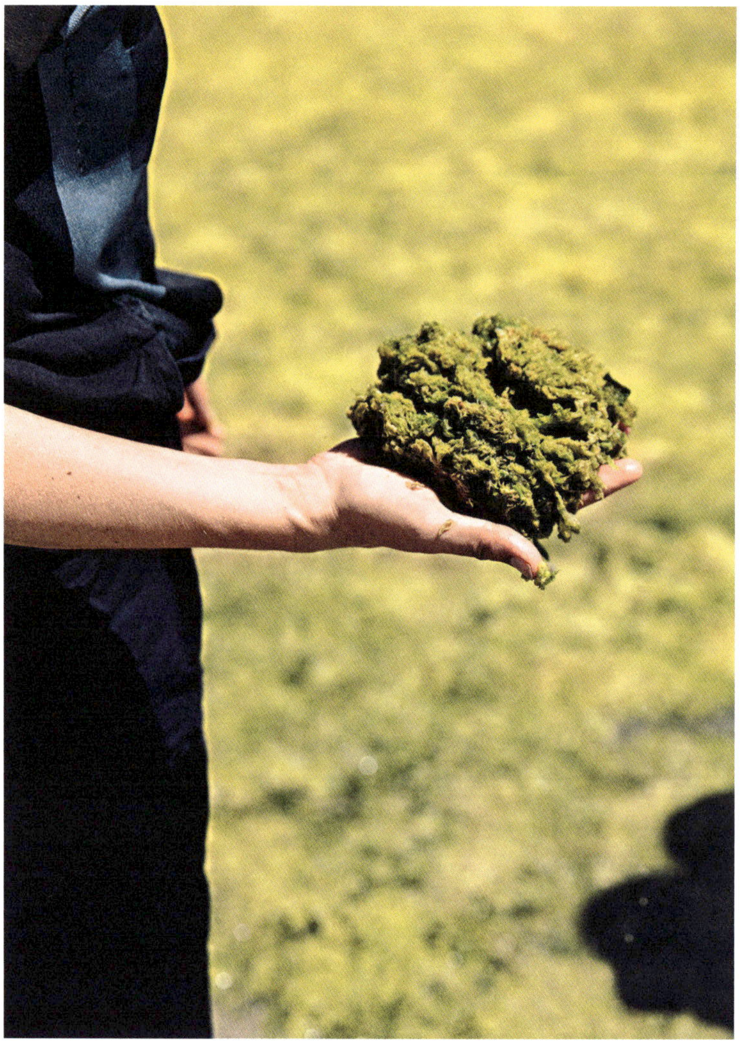

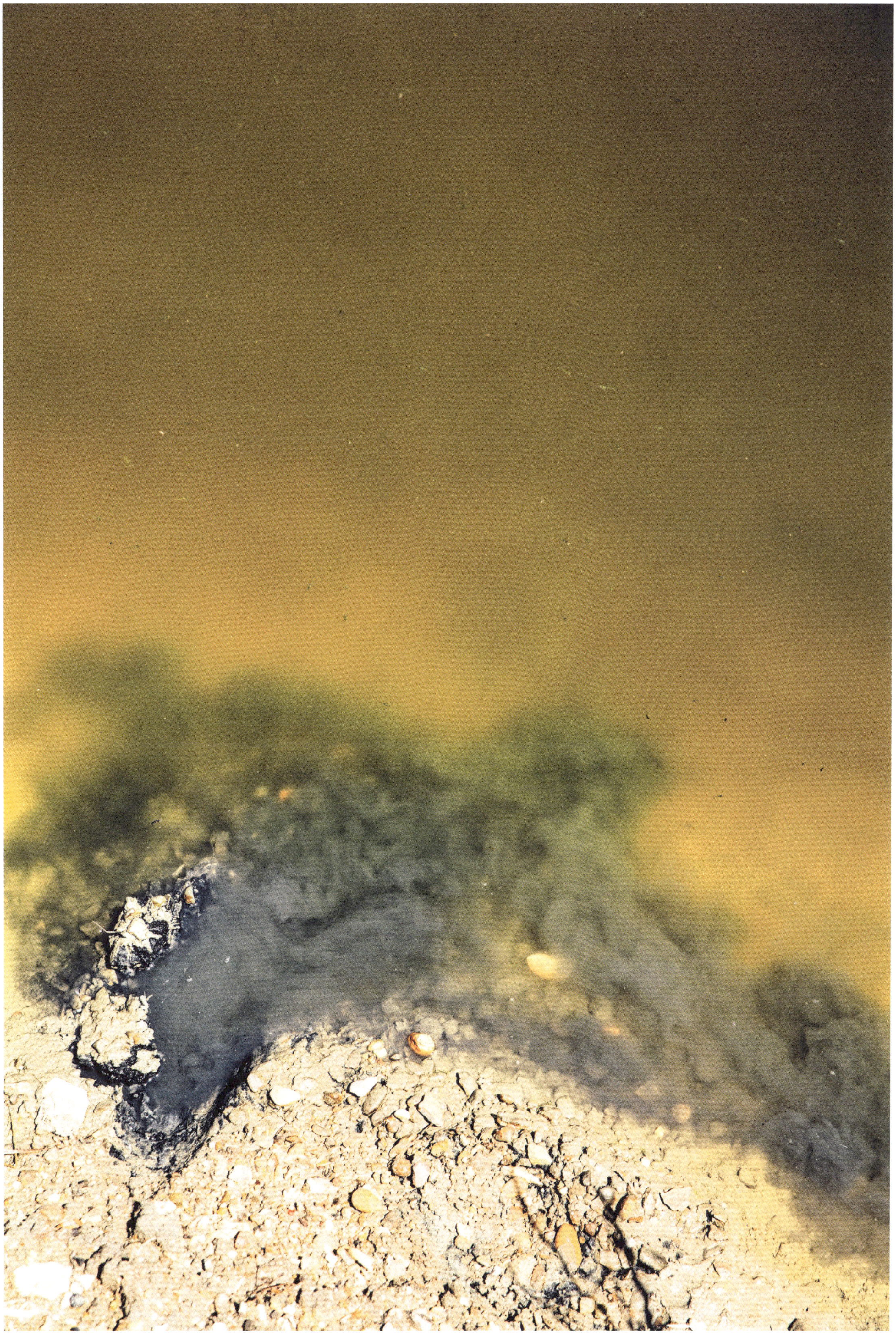

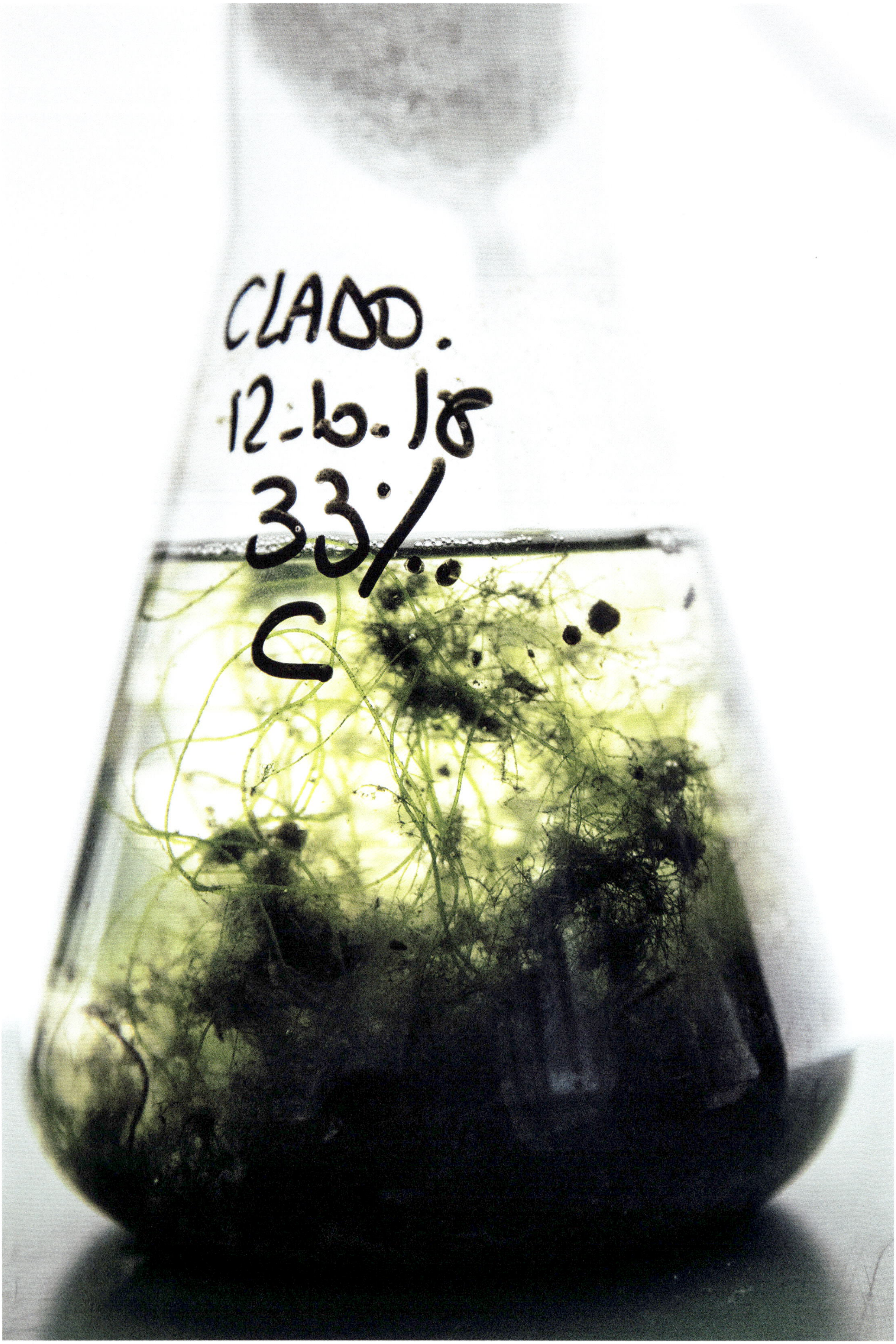
CLADO.
12-6-18
33%
C

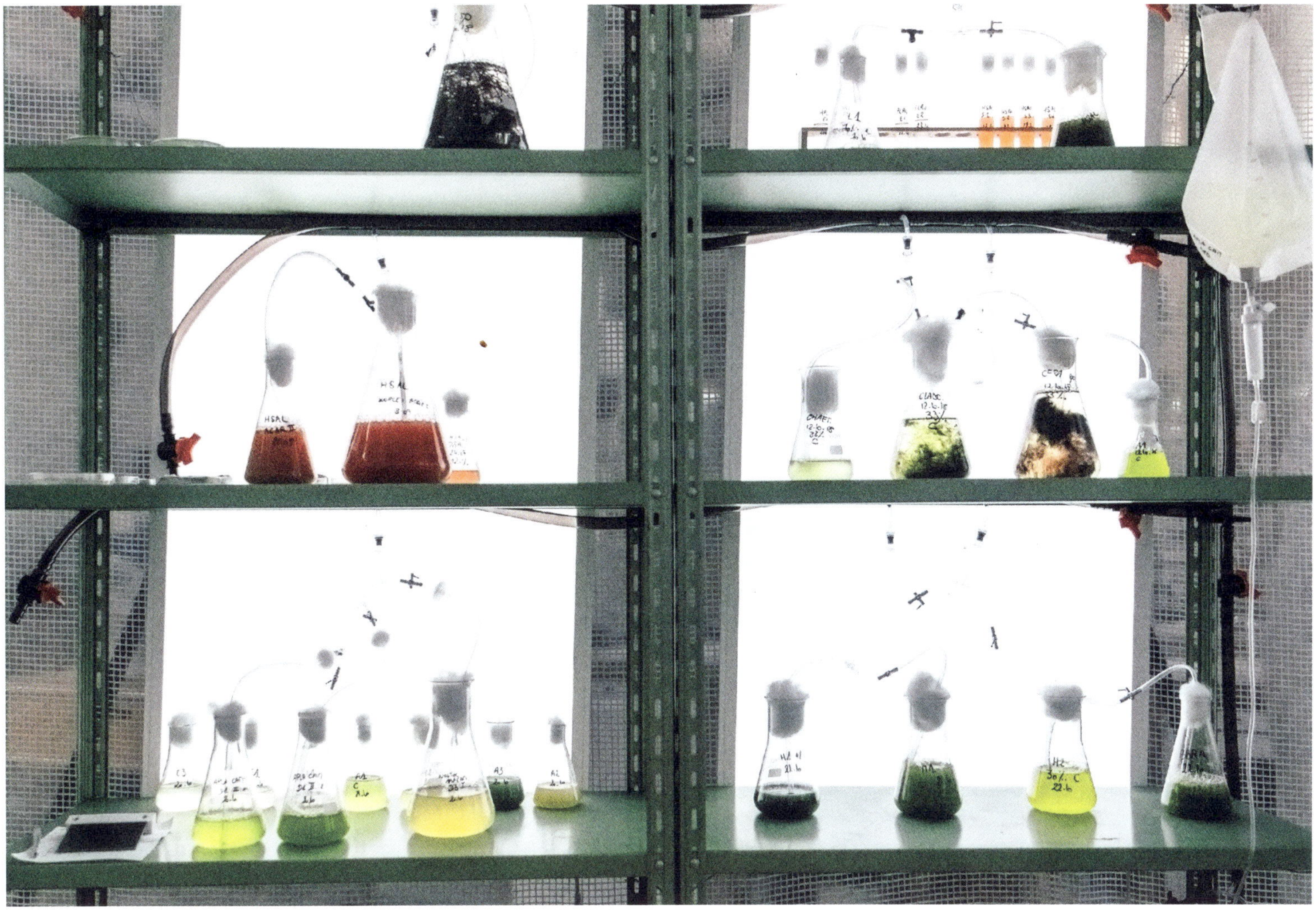

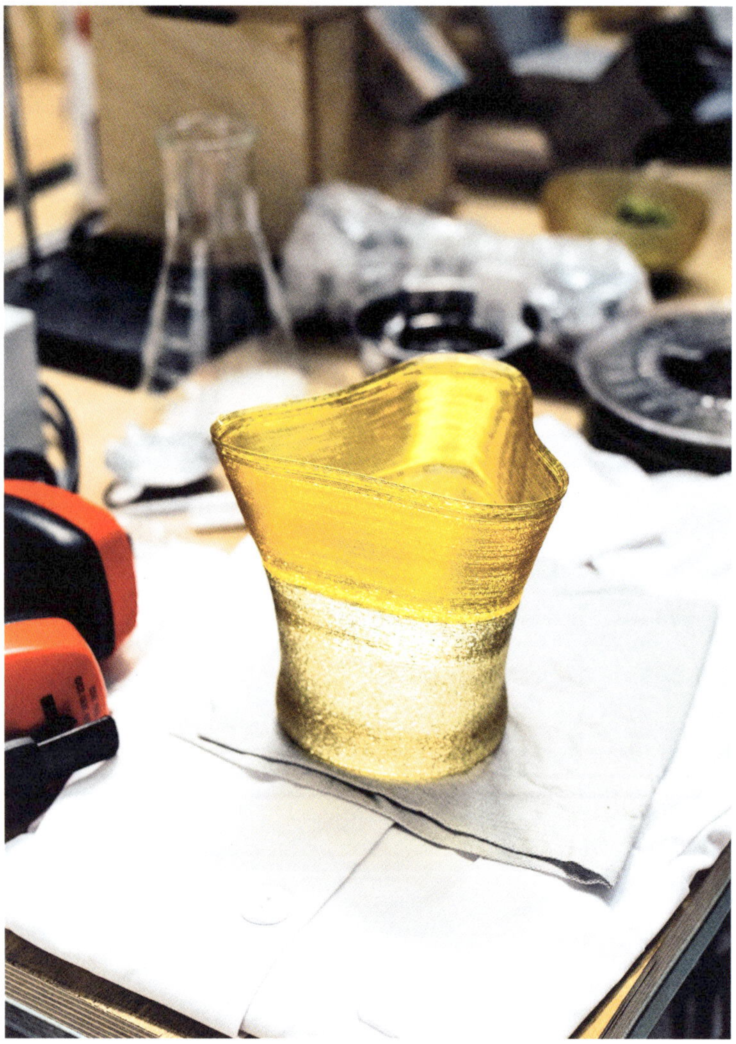

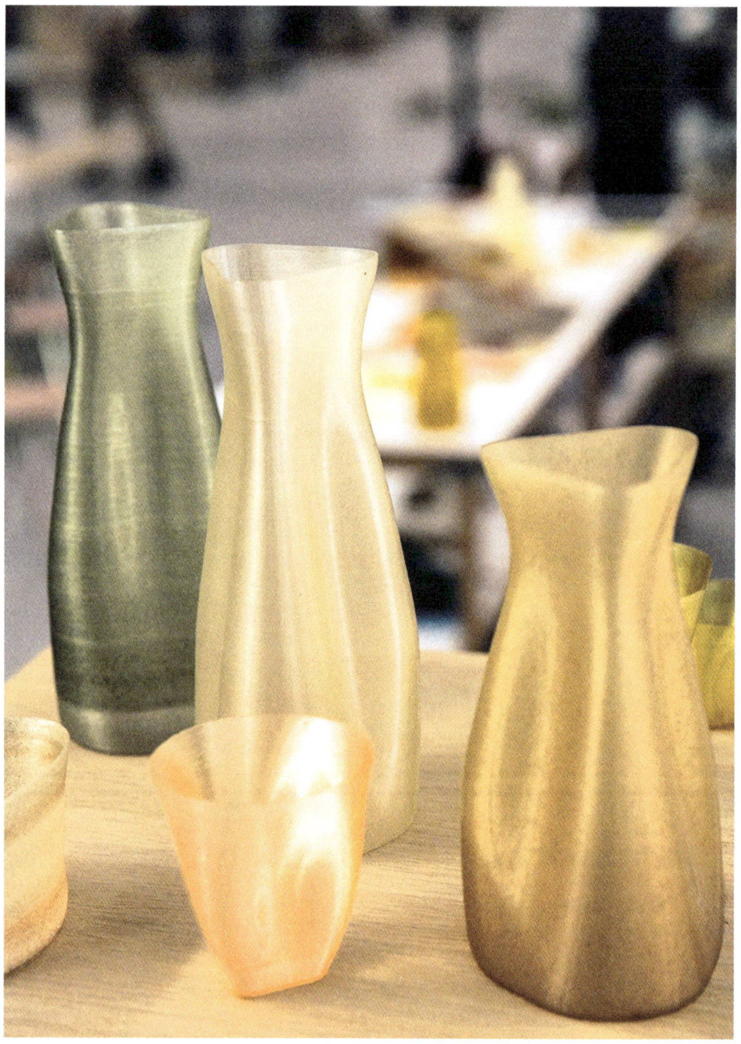

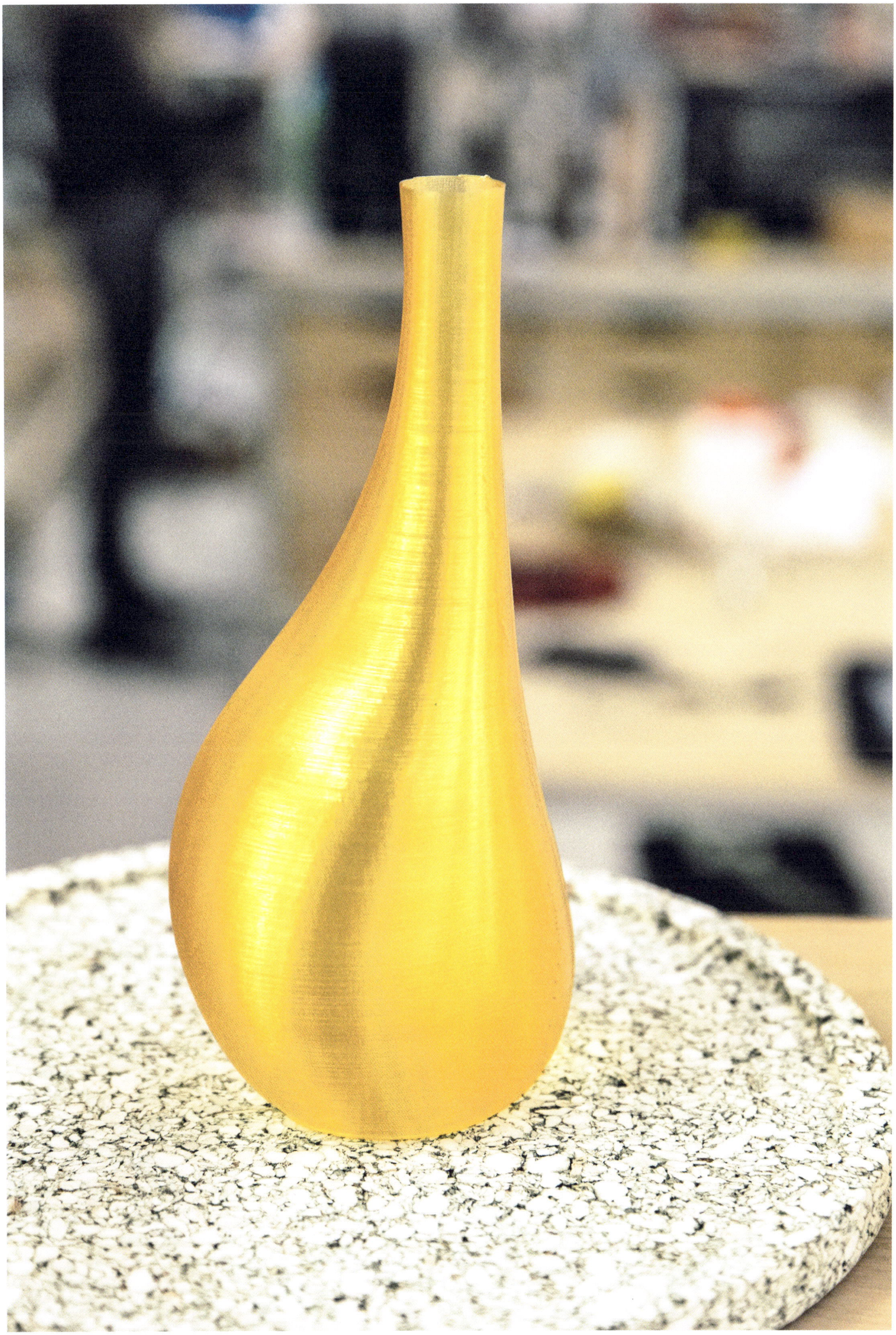

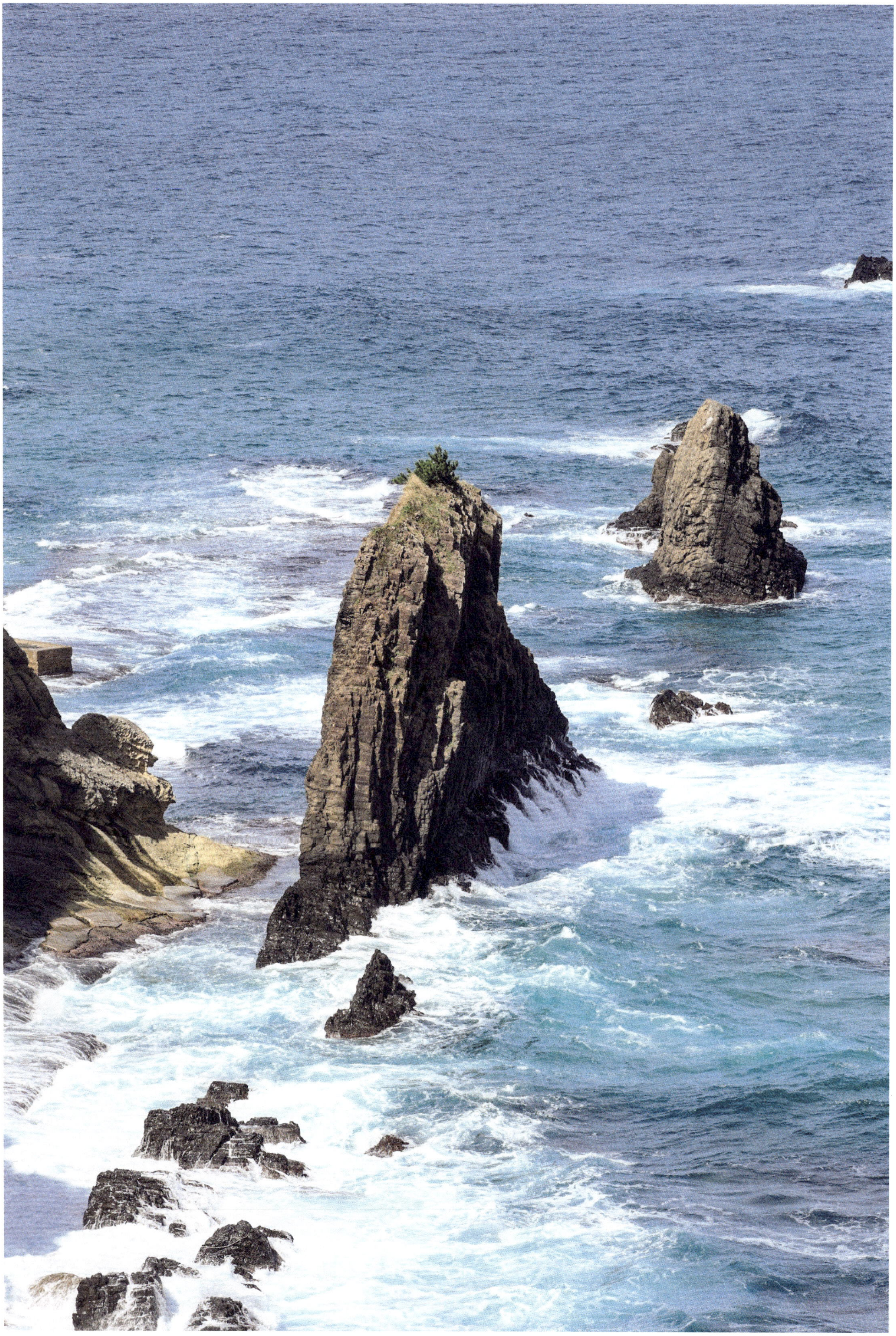

Kyoji Tamiya

Shell weaver

Kyōtango, Japan

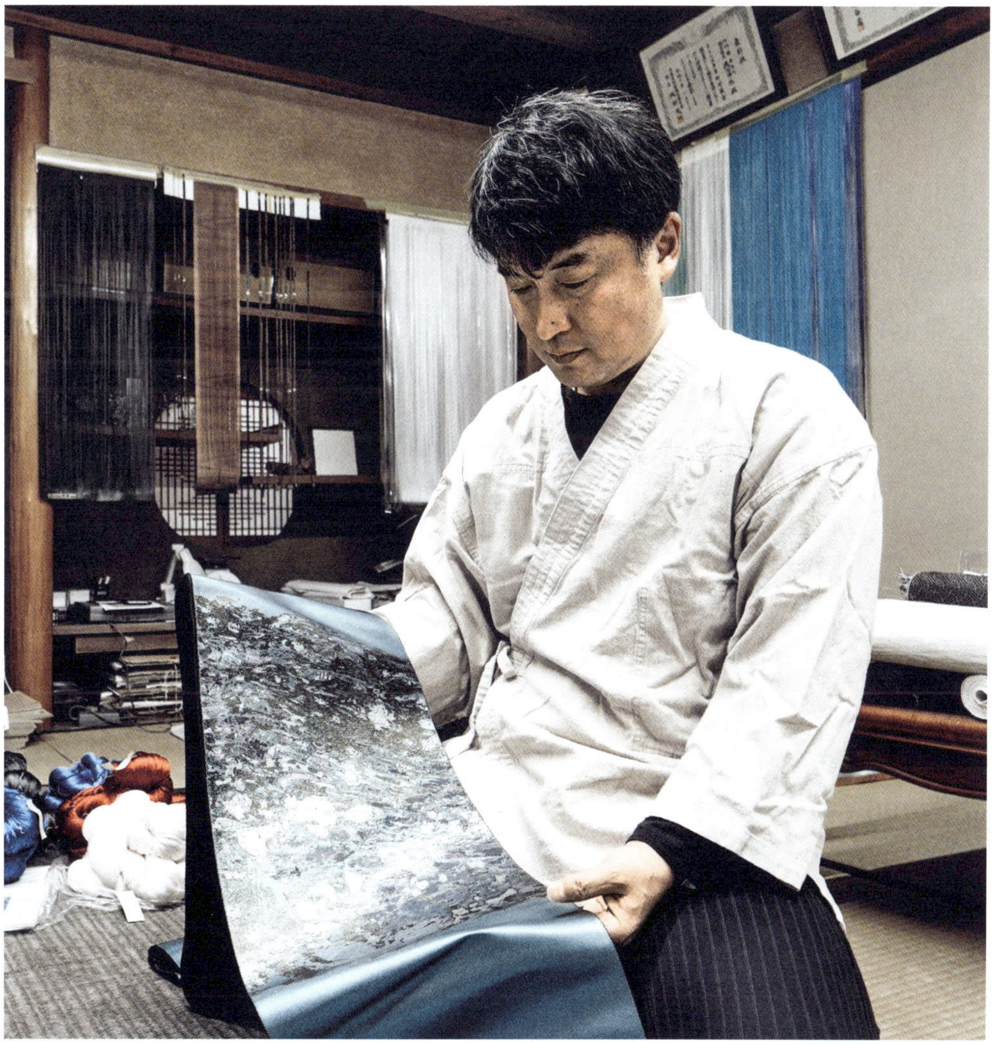

My name is Kyoji Tamiya, and I mainly make kimono belts (*obi*) using mother-of-pearl inlays woven from seashells. I live on the Tango Peninsula, where silk weaving has been a flourishing industry for more than thirteen hundred years. My grandmother, father, and mother were all involved in making *obi*—a kind of broad sash—working until midnight every day. I grew up in this studious atmosphere.

Raden is a decorative mother-of-pearl inlay technique that was originally developed for lacquer, which was inlaid with rhythmically placed seashell fragments and carved according to a pattern. In the eighth century, during the Tang dynasty, treasures made in Persia were brought to the Shoso-in temple in Nara via the Silk Road.

In the ninth century, *raden* was introduced to the European aristocracy. The technique was used to decorate altars in Christian churches and small cabinets. At the end of the Heian period (794–1185), the Japanese aristocracy enriched temple decorations with objects made using the technique, in order to ensure their access to heaven, known as the "Pure Land." By the end of the Edo period (1603–1868), it was used on luxury accessories for samurai.

Visually, *raden* weaving resembles the original *raden* technique, but uses completely different skills: the shells are cut finely and flat according to the pattern, then glued to sheets of *washi* paper. These sheets are then cut into thin strips and used as weft threads. Each thread is woven in the same order as the original. Most of the work is done by hand and requires a great deal of time and patience.

I was originally interested in the visual effect of this unusual material, which possesses a unique light that is at once profound, uplifting, and soothing. In addition to its implications for the creative process, *raden*'s essence is linked to prayer, wealth, and authority. It shifts the light in complex and profound ways, unlike any other material. I feel as if an oyster's nacre concentrates and traps the light inherent in the source of life—the sea. Color is also one of the most important ways of influencing the viewer's emotions, as a symbol of hope and pleasure. Shadows, on the other hand, summon despair and pain, and the relationship between light and shadow influences the human spirit. We cannot experience the happiness of light alone, nor can we live solely in shadow. The pearly layer of an oyster shell, like the light of the sea, contains both these states. I think it appeals to people's hearts in a sensual way.

I view *raden* weaving as a utilitarian beauty through which we can connect with the spiritual element in our daily lives. The original *raden* technique was inflexible until the creation of *raden* weaving, but since that technical development, the range of creative possibilities for its use has expanded considerably. Similarly, in the near future, as artificial intelligence is expected to be deployed for mundane tasks, people will be able to concentrate on creative work, and to produce objects and services that will contribute to the happiness of the general population—making and delivering the product to the "right" people who need it at the "right" price. If AI technology is fully utilized in this cycle, it will be possible to identify with greater precision what is "right," and the flow from production to the end consumer will be streamlined. I believe this will open up more options for living a life that suits everyone's idea of happiness.

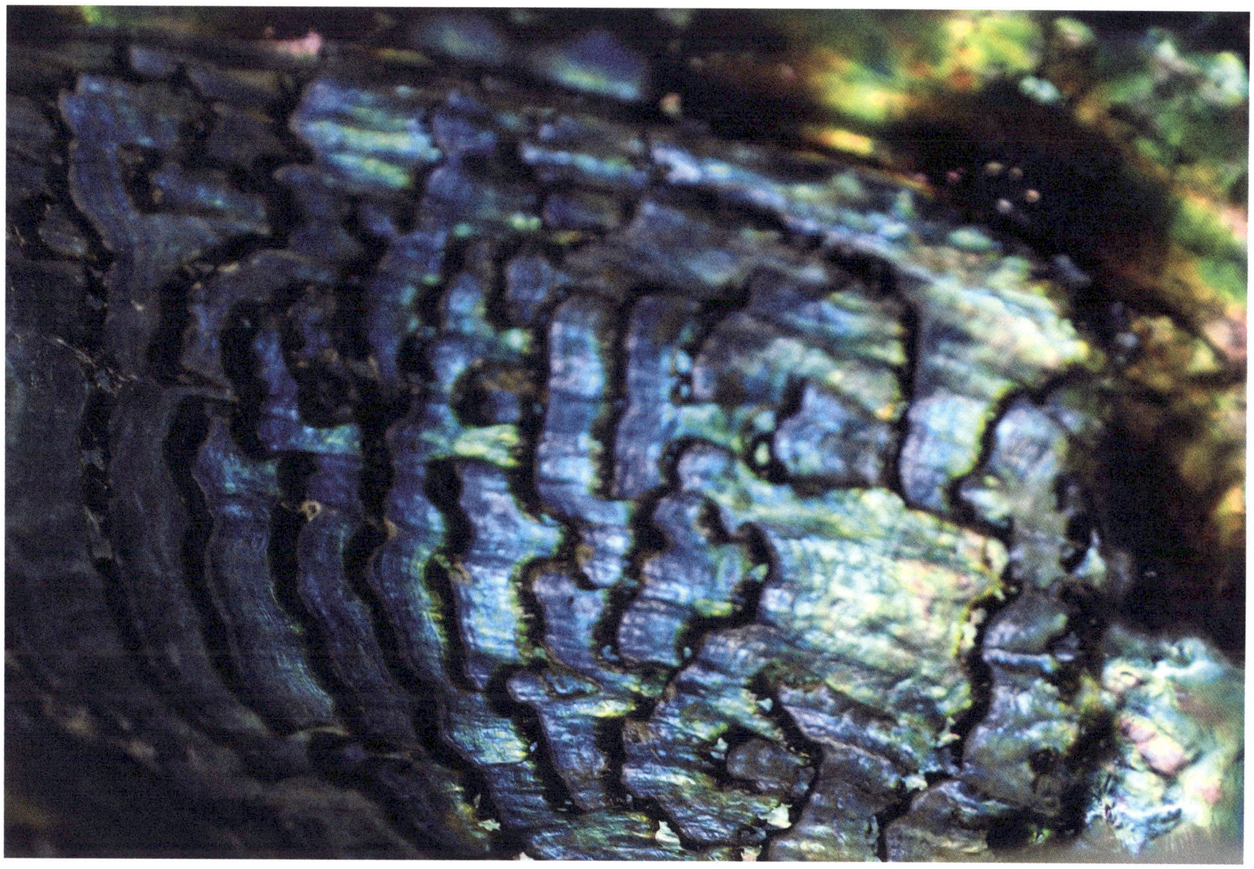

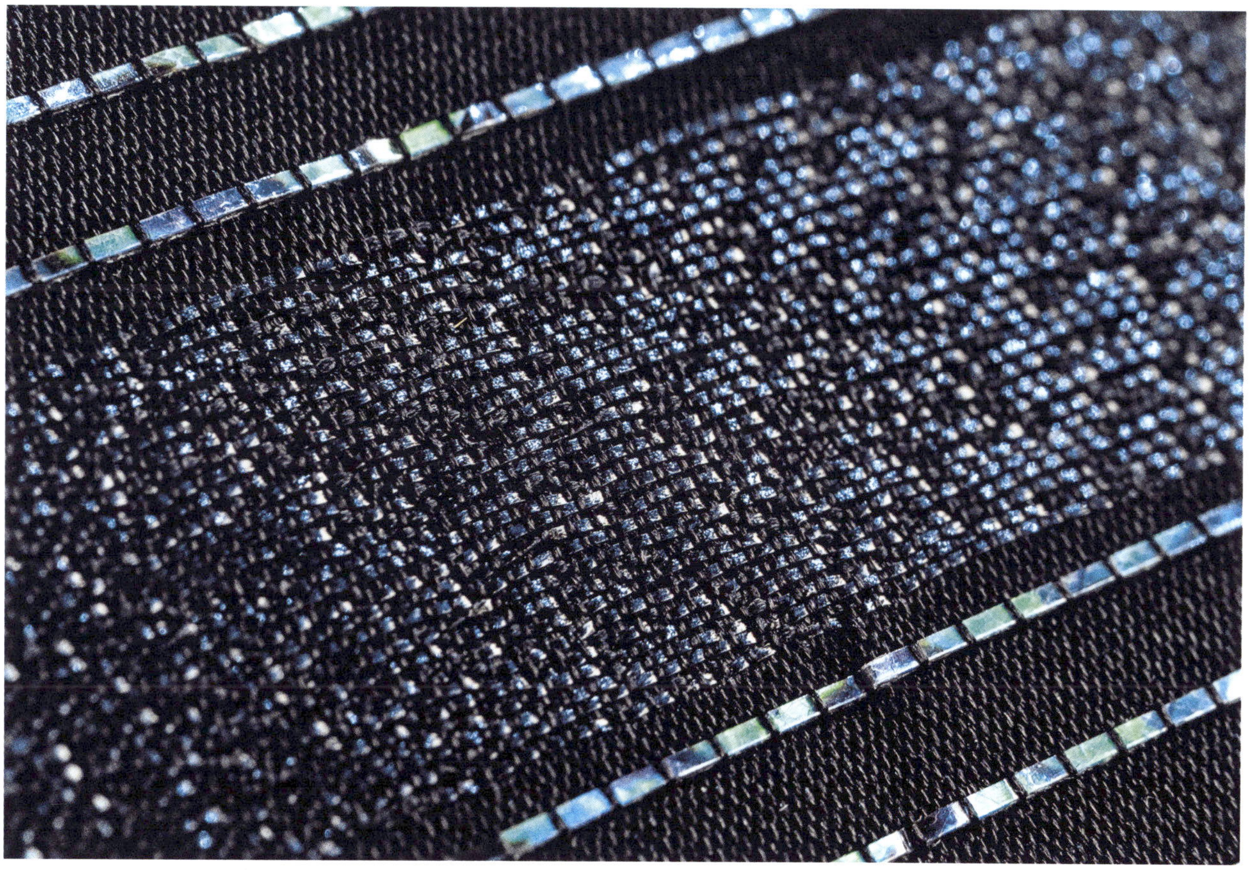

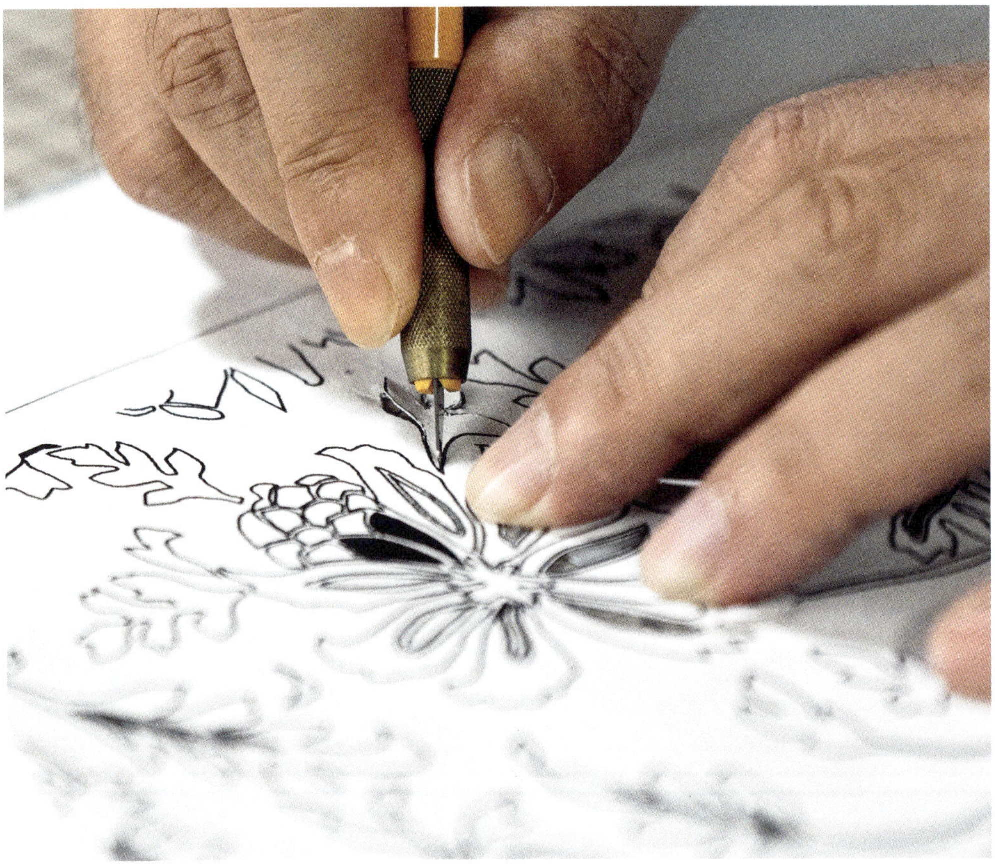

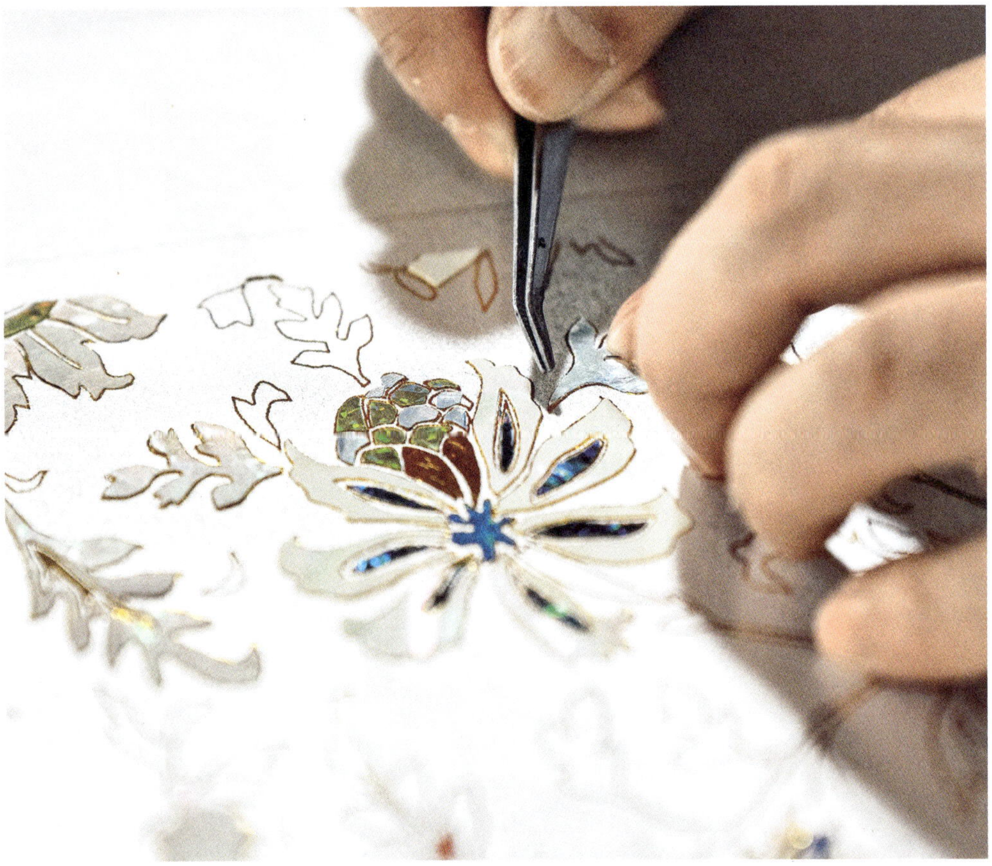

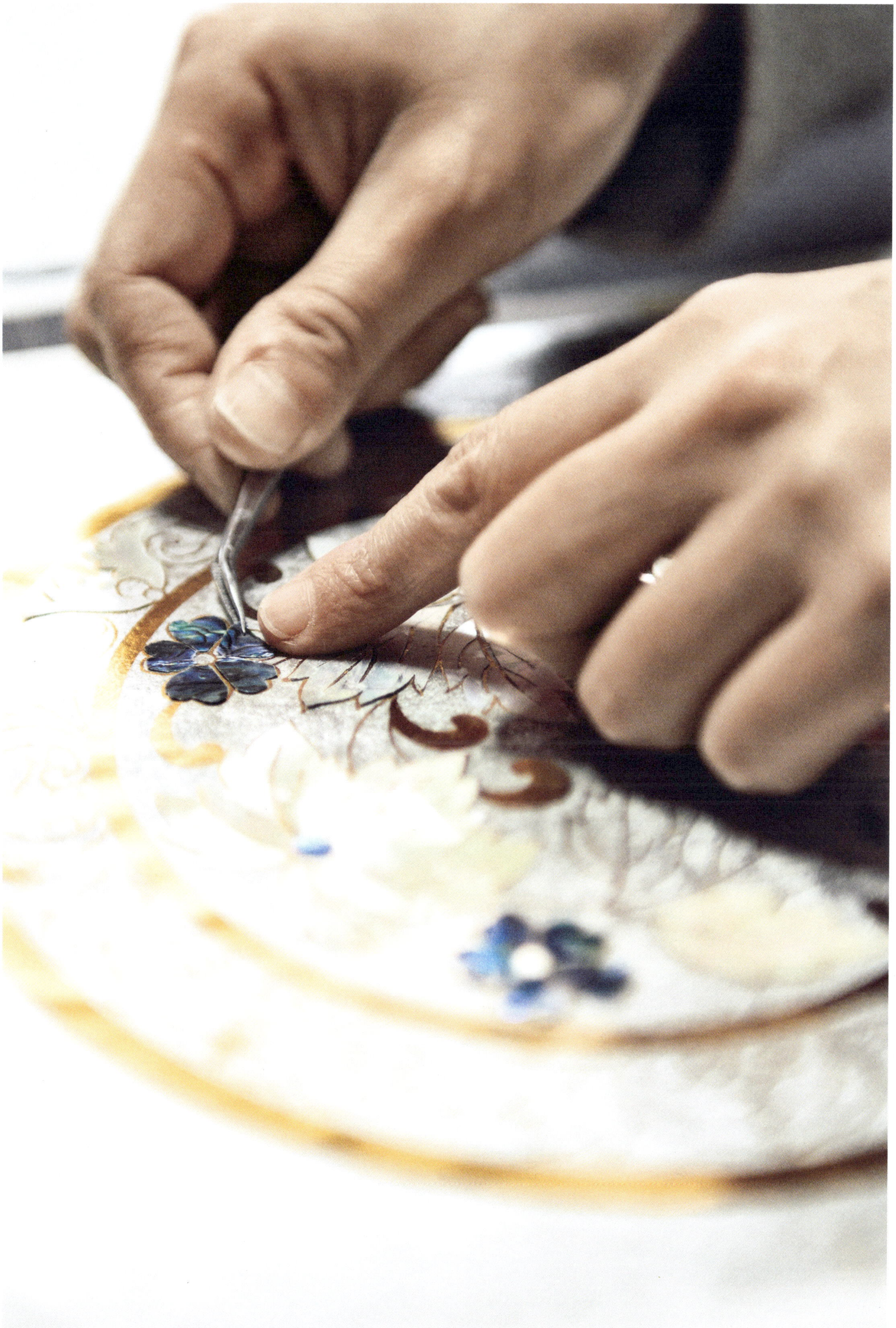

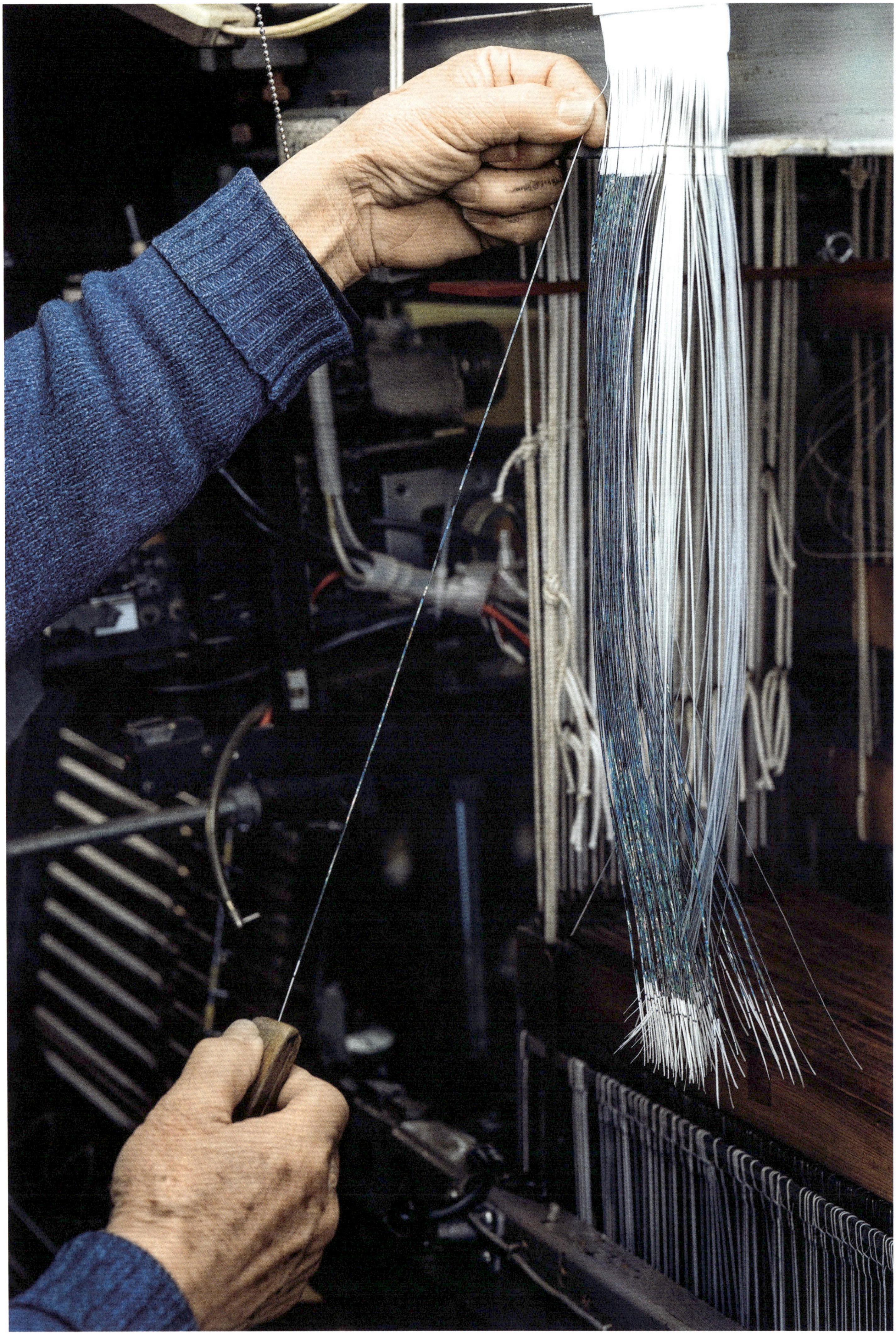

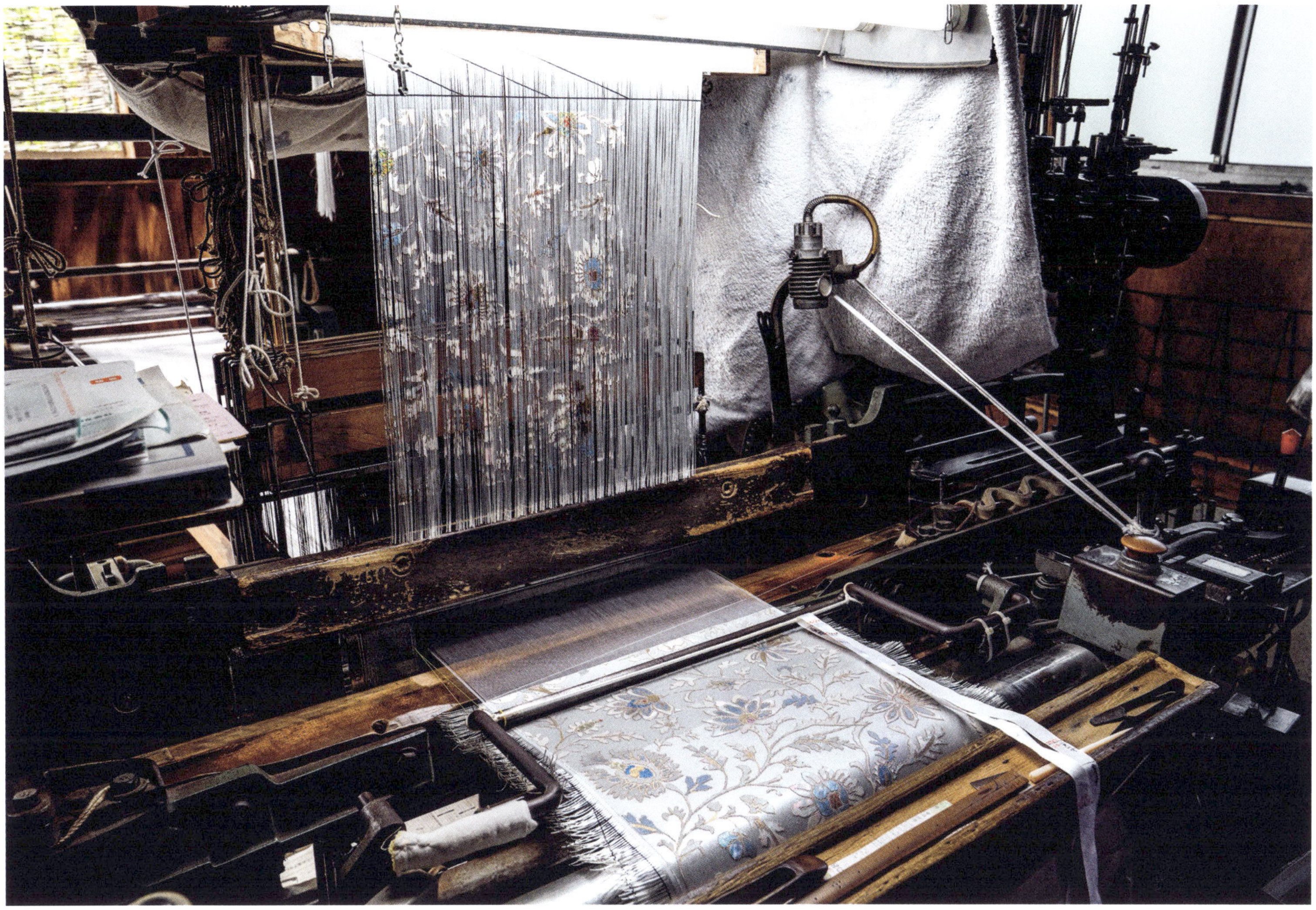

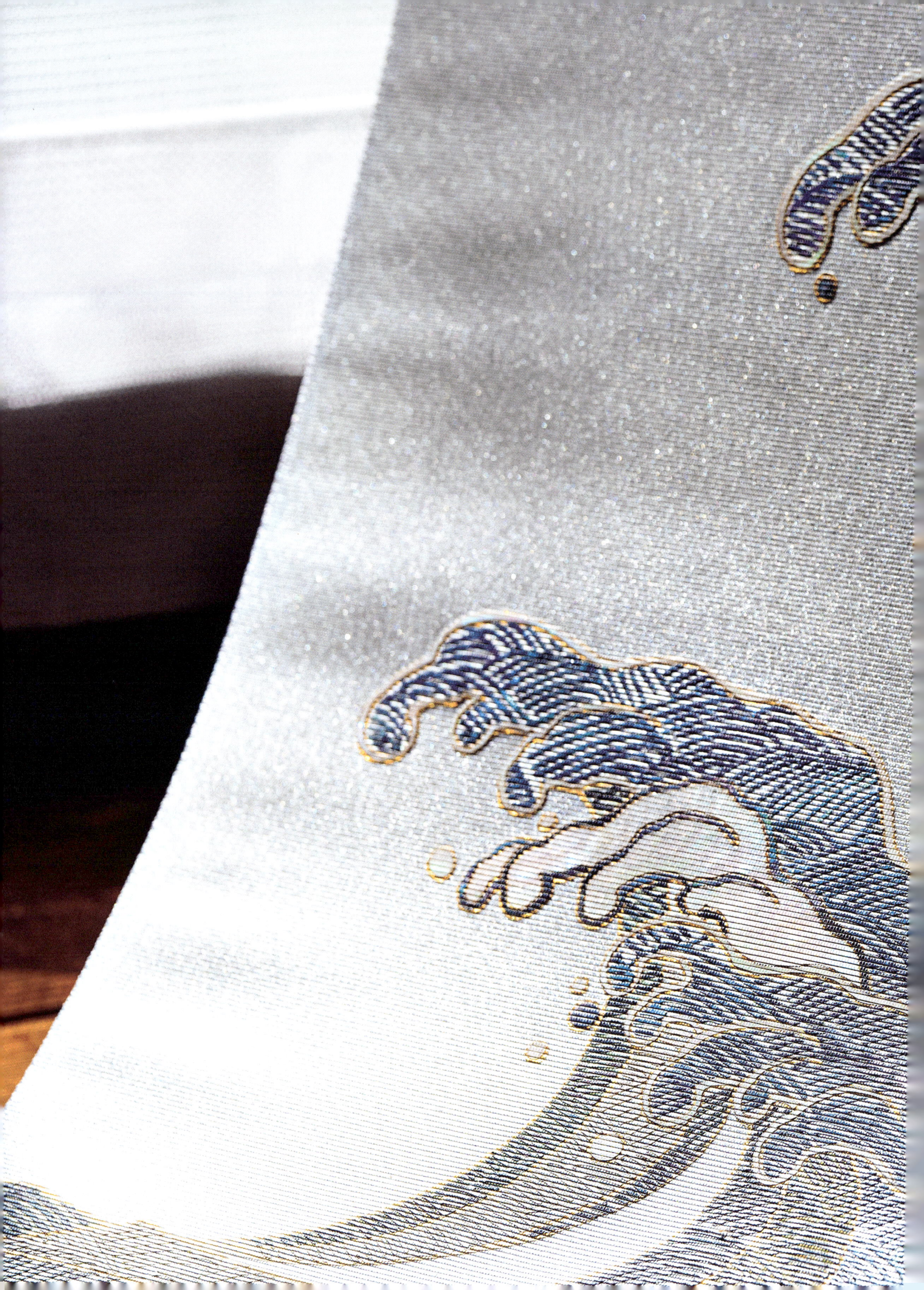

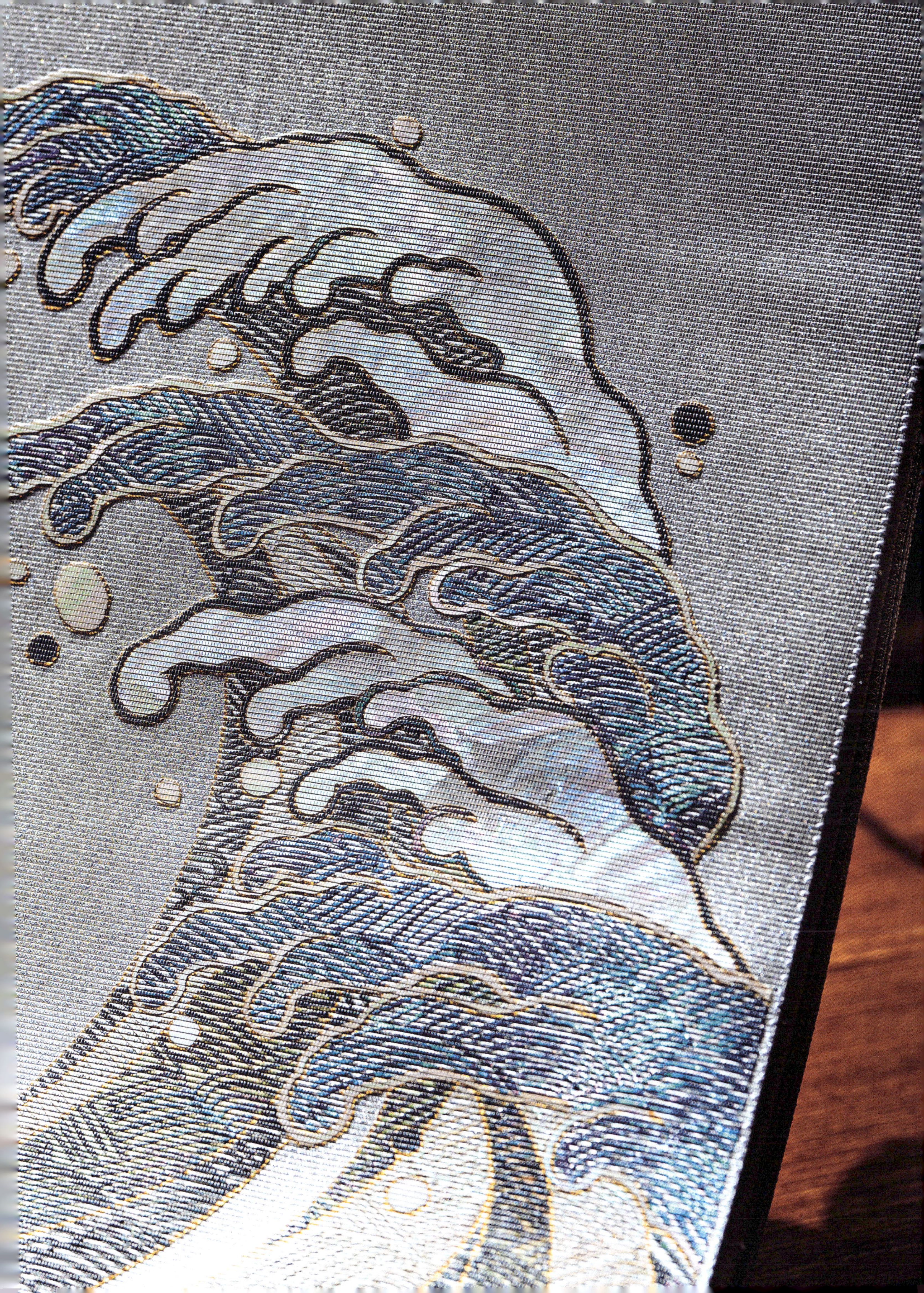

Addresses

Wood

• Museum for Wood Culture
kinodendo.jp
Wachi-951, Muraoka-ku, Kami-cho, Mikata-gun, Hyogo 667-1347, Japan

Paper

• Basler Papiermühle: Schweizerisches Museum für Papier, Schrift und Druck (Basel Paper Mill: Swiss Museum of Paper, Writing, and Printing)
baslerpapiermuehle.ch
St. Alban-Tal 37, 4052 Basel, Switzerland

• Musée du Papier Peint (Wallpaper Museum)
museepapierpeint.org
La Commanderie (right wing), 28 Rue Zuber, 68170 Rixheim, France

Clay

• The Centre of Ceramic Art
centreofceramicart.org.uk
York Art Gallery, Exhibition Square, York YO1 7EW, UK

• Museo Internazionale delle Ceramiche (International Museum of Ceramics)
micfaenza.org
Viale Alfredo Baccarini 19, 48018 Faenza, Italy

• Museu del Càntir (Museum of the Water Jug)
museucantir.org
Plaça Església 9, 08310 Argentona, Barcelona, Spain

• Museu Nacional do Azulejo (National Tile Museum)
museudoazulejo.gov.pt
R. Me. Deus 4, 1900-312 Lisbon, Portugal

• Sèvres – Manufacture et Musée Nationaux (National Sèvres Museum and Manufactory)
sevresciteceramique.fr
2 Place de la Manufacture Nationale, 92310 Sèvres, France

Glass

• La Grande Place – Musée du Cristal Saint-Louis (Saint-Louis Crystal Museum)
saint-louis.com
Rue Coëtlosquet, 57620 Saint-Louis-lès-Bitche, France

• Museo del Vetro di Murano (Murano Glass Museum)
museovetro.visitmuve.it
Fondamenta Giustinian 8, 30141 Murano, Italy

Textiles

• The Calico Museum of Textiles
calicomuseum.org
opp. Underbridge, Jain Colony, Shahibag, Ahmedabad, Gujarat 380004, India

• Cité Internationale de la Tapisserie (International City of Tapestry)
cite-tapisserie.fr
Rue des Arts, 23200 Aubusson, France

• Musée des Tissus et des Arts Décoratifs (Museum of Fabric and Decorative Arts)
museedestissus.fr
34 Rue de la Charité, 69002 Lyon, France

• Museo del Merletto (Lace Museum)
museomerletto.visitmuve.it
Piazza Baldassarre Galuppi 187, 30142 Burano, Italy

• Museo Textil de Oaxaca (Textile Museum of Oaxaca)
museotextildeoaxaca.org
Miguel Hidalgo 917, Centro Histórico, 68000 Oaxaca de Juárez, Mexico

• Museum Tuch + Technik (Museum of Cloth and Technology)
tuchundtechnik.de
Kleinflecken 1, 24534 Neumünster, Germany

• The State Hermitage Museum, Costume Gallery
hermitagemuseum.org
2 Palace Square, Saint Petersburg 190000, Russia

• Textilmuseum (Texile Museum)
textilmuseum.ch
Vadianstrasse 2, CH-9000 St. Gallen, Switzerland

Leather

• Walsall Leather Museum
go.walsall.gov.uk/museums-libraries-and-galleries/walsall-leather-museum
Littleton St West, Walsall WS2 8EW, UK

Stone

• Associazione Laboratorio del Marmo Artificiale (Artificial Marble Laboratory Association)
marmoartificiale.com
Località Rima 44, 13020 Rima San Giuseppe, Italy

• Diamond Museum
diamondmuseum.com
Paulus Potterstraat 8, 1071 CZ Amsterdam, Netherlands

• Museo di Palazzo Grimani (Grimani Palace Museum)
polomusealeveneto.beniculturali.it/musei/museo-di-palazzo-grimani
Castello Ramo Grimani 4858, 30122 Venice, Italy

New Materials

• MOA Museum of Art
moaart.or.jp
26-2 Momoyama-cho, Atami, Shizuoka 413-8511, Japan

Decorative Arts Museums

• Craft Contemporary
craftcontemporary.org
5814 Wilshire Boulevard, Los Angeles, CA 90036, USA

• The Japan Folk Crafts Museum
mingeikan.or.jp
4-3-33 Komaba, Meguro-ku, Tokyo 153-0041, Japan

• Kyoto Museum of Crafts and Design
kmtc.jp
B1F Miyakomesse, 9-1, Okazaki Seishoji-cho, Sakyo-ku, Kyoto 606-8343, Japan

• Musée des Arts Décoratifs (Museum of the Decorative Arts)
madparis.fr
107 Rue de Rivoli, 75001 Paris, France

• Musée des Beaux-Arts de Nancy (Nancy Museum of Fine Arts)
musee-des-beaux-arts.nancy.fr
3 Place Stanislas, 54000 Nancy, France

• Smithsonian American Art Museum, Renwick Gallery
si.edu/museums/renwick-gallery
Pennsylvania Avenue at 17th Street, NW, Washington, DC 20006, USA

• Victoria and Albert Museum
vam.ac.uk
Cromwell Road, London SW7 2RL, UK

Institutions and Foundations Providing Support for Artisans

• Le 19M
le19m.fr
2 Place Skanderbeg, 75019 Paris, France

• L'Atelier Luma
atelier-luma.org
53 Parc des Ateliers, Chemin des Minimes, 13200 Arles, France

• Baba Tree
babatree.com

• Craft Revival Trust
craftrevivaltrust.org
S-4 Khirki Extension, New Delhi – 110 017, India

• Crafts Council Nederland
craftscouncil.nl
Hoogt 10, 3512 GW Utrecht, Netherlands

• Centre de l'Innovation et du Design
cid-grand-hornu.be
Site du Grand-Hornu, 82 Rue Sainte-Louise, 7301 Hornu, Belgium

• Centre International de Recherche sur le Verre et les Arts Plastiques (CIRVA) (International Glass and Visual Arts Research Center)
cirva.fr
62 Rue de la Joliette, 13002 Marseille, France

• Fayoum Pottery School
Qaroun, Youssef Al Seddik, Al Fayyum Governorate 2822651, Egypt

• Fondation Bettencourt Schueller
fondationbs.org
27–29 Rue des Poissonniers, 92522 Neuilly-sur-Seine, France

• Fondation Bruckner
ceramique-bruckner.ch
Chemin de Grange-Collomb 38, 1227 Carouge, Switzerland

• Fondation d'Entreprise d'Hermès
fondationdentreprisehermes.org
24 Rue du Faubourg Saint-Honoré, 75008 Paris, France

• Fondation Olorun
africine.org/structure/fondation-olorun/445

• Fondazione Cologni dei Mestieri d'Arte
fondazionecologni.it
Via Lovanio 5, 20121 Milan, Italy

• JSW Foundation
jsw.in/foundation
Bandra Kurla Complex, Near MMRDA Grounds, Bandra East, Mumbai 400 051, India

• Korea Craft & Design Foundation
kcdf.or.kr
53, Yulgok-ro, Jongno-gu, Seoul, South Korea & 8, Insadong 11-gil, Jongno-gu, Seoul, South Korea (gallery office)

• Loewe Foundation
loewe.com

• Métiers d'Art Suisse
metiersdart.ch
Case Postale 1028, 1260 Nyon, Switzerland

• Michelangelo Foundation
michelangelofoundation.org
Pont de la Machine 1, 1204 Geneva, Switzerland

• Norbulingka Institute of Tibetan Culture
norbulingka.org
P.O. Sidhpur, Dharamsala 176057, India

• Somaiya Kala Vidya
somaiya-kalavidya.org
Somaiya Kala Vidya, SDB 41/42, Opposite Hari Om Trust Hospital, Adipur, Kutch 370 205, Gujarat, India

• Timendotes Association
timendotes.com

• Women Weave Charitable Trust
womenweave.org
9/350 Lalita Park, Laxmi Nagar, Delhi 110092, India

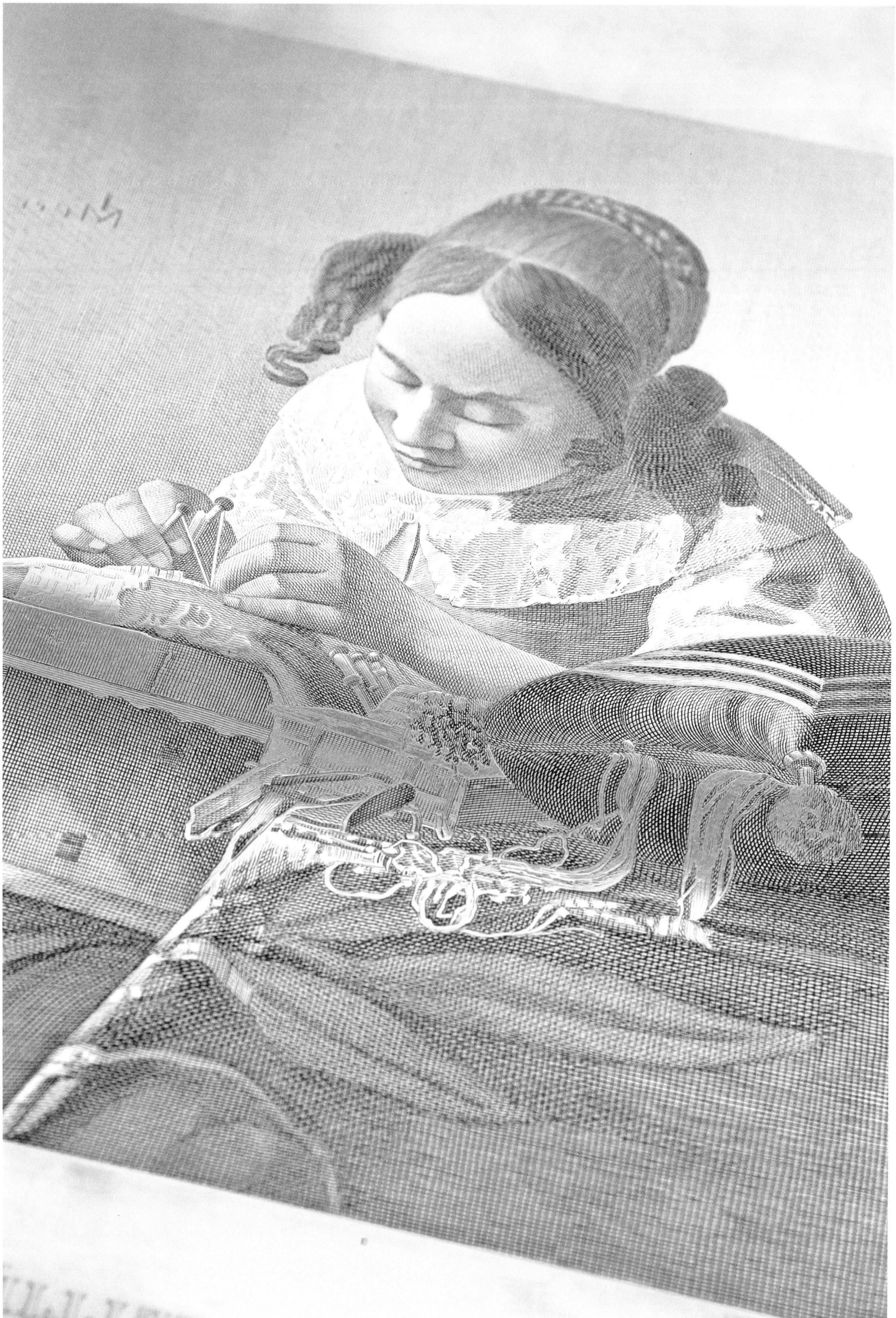

Acknowledgments

I would like to thank everyone who made this book possible:

First, Julie Rouart, for her support, energy, and commitment to making this book a reality.

Marion Doublet, who entrusted me with writing this book, which was so important to her.

The women and men at the heart of the story: the artisans who fill these pages and play such a decisive role.

My daughter, Joséphine Dupuy Chavanat, who helped me put my ideas in order.

Those who translated some of the stories: Hélène Bergaz, Aimée Moribayashi, Michel and Angelo Pastore, Susanna Pozzoli, Yutaka Yamamoto, and Kim and Dechen Yeshi.

Kate Mascaro and Helen Adedotun, for their work on the English edition.

All those who offered me their advice and suggestions, particularly Francesco Balzano, Miquel Barceló, Valérie Barkowski, Alexandra Bernard, Rose Chalalai Singh, Jill Coulon, Mélanie Courbet / Les Ateliers Courbet, Nicole Ghali, Christopher Giercke, Luciano Giubbilei, Nelly Guyot, Lauren Hadler, Couli Jobert, Mona Kim, Joël Laiter, India Mahdavi, Clara Murray, Pascale Mussard, Yusuke Nakanishi, Fanny Pellegrin, Cécile Pesce, Lucille Reyboz, Gaëlle Riout, Nelson Sepulveda, and Marie-Hélène de Taillac.

The photographers around the world, who so elegantly and sensitively translated into images the creations of the artisans and captured their studios or workplaces, in particular Anne-Laure Camilleri, François Halard, Victor Picon, and Susanna Pozzoli.

Those who accompanied me on this adventure: Marie Audet, who used every trick in the book to reach artisans on the other side of the world, as well as Sarah Martinon and Marie-Lou Étienne, who brought these stories to life on the page.

Those who offered their assistance from the very beginning, especially Alberto Cavalli and Corinne Paget-Blanc from the Michelangelo Foundation. I thank them for their patience.

So many people helped and supported me throughout this journey that I am bound to have overlooked someone, so I especially wish to express my gratitude to anyone I may have forgotten.

Last but not least, I would like to extend my warmest thanks to François Halard, who once again provided me with his guidance and support. His assistance and attentive eye are so precious to me.

Credits

t: top; b: bottom; l: left; r: right; c: center

© Abhay Maskara: p. 245; © Adagp, Paris 2023. Photo © Frigesch Lampelmayer: pp. 82–83, 100, 104 (t and b), 105, 106–107; © Adagp, Paris 2023. Photo © RMN-Grand Palais / image RMN – GP: p. 67 (c); © Addictive Creative / Shutterstock: p. 44; © Adriana Zehbrauskas: pp. 75 (t and b), 176–177, 178 (b), 182 (b); © aiyoshi597 / Shutterstock: p. 108; © Alana Wilson: pp. 109, 111, 112 (l and r), 113, 114, 115 (t and b), 116 (l and r), 117; © Alexis Frespuech: pp. 234, 235, 237 (t and b), 238 (all 4 images), 239, 241 (t and b), 242 (t and b); © Angelo Giampiccolo / Shutterstock: p. 300; © Anne-Laure Camilleri, SAIF, 2023: pp. 258, 259, 261, 262, 263, 264, 265, 266–267; © Annie O. Waterman: pp. 55, 58 (t and b), 59, 60–61; © Arturo Mio / Jill Coulon: pp. 156, 157, 159 (t, c, and b), 160 (all 6 images), 161 (t, c, and b), 162 (all 6 images), 163 (t, c, and b); © Camilla Blousson / Martin Rietti Studio: pp. 213, 215 (t and b); © Charlotte Mary Pack: p. 124 (all 9 images); Courtesy of the Michelangelo Foundation for Creativity & Craftsmanship. Susanna Pozzoli / © Michelangelo Foundation for Creativity & Craftsmanship, 2018: pp. 129, 131 (t and b), 132 (all 4 images), 133 (t and b), 134 (all 6 images), 135, 253, 255 (t and b), 256 (all 4 images), 257; Courtesy of The National Gallery of Victoria. Photo © Alexandra Kehayoglou Studio: pp. 220, 222–223; Courtesy of Villa Eugénie, Dries van Noten. Photo © Villa Eugénie: p. 216; Courtesy Yoshiaki Kojiro: p. 139 (t and b); © Daniel Ankarstrand: p. 287; © David Gutiérrez: p. 172; © David Horsman: p. 304 (t); © Dinis Santos: p. 54; © Emelie Flood: p. 331; © Francis Kokoroko / The Baba Tree: pp. 28–29, 45, 48, 52–53; © François Goudier: pp. 8, 184, 185, 187, 188, 189, 190 (all 4 images), 191 192–193; © François Halard: pp. 90, 91, 93, 94 (all 4 images), 95, 96, 97 (all 4 images), 98, 99, 205, 207, 208, 209 (t and b), 210–211; © Ganga Maki Textile Studio: pp. 164; 168 (all 4 images), 169 (all 4 images), 170, 171; © Gregory McCarthy / The Baba Tree: pp. 47, 49 (t and b), 50, 51; © Hidenori Suzuki: p. 30; © Isabelle Dupuy Chavanat: pp. 62–63, 72, 73, 75 (t and b), 76 (t and b), 77, 78, 79 (t and b), 80–81; © Iwan Baan: pp. 165, 167; © Javier Lazo Gutiérrez: pp. 178 (t), 183; © Joe Hogan: pp. 39 (t and b), 40 (t and b), 41; © Jon Mogard: pp. 280, 283, 286; © Jono Photography / Shutterstock: p. 144; © Joselito Tirados: p. 212; © Julien Paquin: pp. 270, 271, 273 (t and b), 274, 275 (b), 278–279; © Kalhath Institute Lucknow: pp. 244, 247 (t and b), 248, 249, 251; © Karlo Curis / Shutterstock: p. 36; © Kazuki Nagayama: pp. 85, 87 (t); © Kazunori Hamana: pp. 84, 87 (c and b), 88 (l and r), 89; © Kerry Murray Photography / Shutterstock: p. 128; © Kohei Yamamoto: p. 195; © Kosuke Araki: pp. 319, 322 (all 4 images), 323, 324 (t and b), 325 (t and b); © KPG-Payless / Shutterstock: p. 344; © Lukas Breuer: pp. 101, 103 (t, c, and b); © Lydia Rowley: p. 329; © Markus Burke: pp. 298–299, 308, 309, 311, 312, 313 (t and b), 314, 315 (t and b); © Masahiro Katano: p. 136; © Masami Naruo: pp. 318, 321 (t), 325 (t); © Mona KIM, for *Moowon* magazine, SAIF, 2023. "Man in Wood: John Alfredo Harris": pp. 14, 15, 17 (t, c, and b), 18, 19; © Naoyuki Ogino: p. 33 (t and b); © Nikhol Esteras: p. 179 (b); © Nuno Henriques: p. 57 (t and b); © Parth Seth: pp. 301, 303, 304 (c and b), 305, 306–307; © Paul Glendell: p. 276 (t, c, and b), 277 (t, c, and b); © Peter Pearson, courtesy of Design & Crafts Council Ireland: p. 37; © Petter Bäcklund: pp. 281, 284 (t and b), 285; Photo © Alexandra Kehayoglou Studio: pp. 154–155, 217, 218 (all 4 images), 219 (all 4 images), 221; Photo © RMN-Grand Palais / image RMN – GP: p. 356; Photo: Kin Coel © Norlha: pp. 224, 228, 229, 231 (all 4 images), 232, 233; Photo: Nikki McClarron © Norlha: pp. 225, 227, 230; © Raphaël Neal: pp. 118, 119, 121, 122 (l and r), 123, 125, 126–127, 145, 147 (t and b), 148 (t and b), 149, 150 (t and b), 268–269, 288, 289, 291, 292 (t and b), 293 (t and b), 294 (l and r), 295, 296, 297; © Robert Hall: pp. 151, 152 (all 4 images), 153 (all 4 images); © Roland Paschhoff, courtesy of RDS: pp. 42–43; © Ryohei Yanagihara: p. 137; © Saint-Denis [2009], Réunion des Musées Nationaux – Grand Palais: p. 64; © Saint-Denis [2016], Réunion des Musées Nationaux – Grand Palais: pp. 70–71; © Saint-Denis [2019], Réunion des Musées Nationaux – Grand Palais: pp. 65, 67 (t and b), 68 (all 6 images), 69; © Sophie Rowley: pp. 316–317, 326, 330 (t and b), 332, 333; © Soraya Matos: pp. 173, 179 (t), 180, 181, 182 (t); © Soumya Annapourna: p. 327; © Stefan Rotter / Shutterstock: p.252; © T. Venkanna / Gallery Maskara, Mumbai: p. 250; © Taiki Iai: pp. 194, 197 (all 4 images), 198, 199, 200, 201, 203; © Tamiya Raden: pp. 7, 345, 347 (t and b), 349, 350 (t and b), 351, 352–353; © Tiao Nithakhong Somsanith: pp. 240, 243; © Tolo Balaguer / AGE / Photo12: p. 204; © Tutumi Yano: p. 202 (all 4 images); © Victor Picon: pp. 334, 335, 337, 338 (l and r), 339, 340, 341, 342 (l and r), 343; © Yan Kallen: pp. 31, 34 (t and b), 35; © Yen-An Chen: pp. 12–13, 20, 23, 25, 26–27; © Yoshiaki Kojiro: pp. 140, 142 (t and b), 143 (t and b); © Yoshiaki Kojiro / Courtesy Keiko Art International, Japan: p. 141; © Yu-An Chen: pp. 21, 24 (t and b).

Excerpt p. 38, "For the Artist at the Start of Day" from *To Bless the Space Between Us: A Book of Blessings* by John O'Donohue, copyright © 2008 by John O'Donohue. Used by permission of Doubleday, an imprint of the Knopf Doubleday Publishing Group, a division of Penguin Random House LLC. All rights reserved.